www.wadsworth.com

www.wadsworth.com is the World Wide Web site for Wadsworth and is your direct source to dozens of online resources.

At *www.wadsworth.com* you can find out about supplements, demonstration software, and student resources. You can also send email to many of our authors and preview new publications and exciting new technologies.

www.wadsworth.com
Changing the way the world learns®

Controversies in American Public Policy

Third Edition

John A. Hird

University of Massachusetts Amherst

Michael A. Reese

University of Massachusetts Amherst

Matthew Shilvock

University of Massachusetts Amherst

THOMSON

™

WADSWORTH

Australia • Canada • Mexico • Singapore • Spain
United Kingdom • United States

THOMSON
WADSWORTH

Publisher: Clark Baxter
Executive Editor: David Tatom
Editorial Assistant: Dianna Long
Technology Project Manager: Melinda Newfarmer
Marketing Manager: Janise Fry
Marketing Assistant: Mary Ho
Advertising Project Manager: Nathaniel Bergson-Michelson
Project Manager, Editorial Production: Matt Ballantyne
Print/Media Buyer: Jessica Reed
Permissions Editor: Elizabeth Zuber

Production Service: Carlisle Communications, Ltd.
Copy Editor: Judy Duguid
Illustrator: Carlisle Communications, Ltd.
Cover Designer: Sue Hart
Cover Image: Copyright © Jim Arbogast/Getty Images, Ltd.
Compositor: Carlisle Communications, Ltd.
Text and Cover Printer: Webcom Limited

For more information about our products, contact us at:
Thomson Learning Academic Resource Center
1-800-423-0563
For permission to use material from this text, contact us by:
Phone: 1-800-730-2214 **Fax:** 1-800-730-2215
Web: http://www.thomsonrights.com

Library of Congress Control Number: 2003103833

ISBN 0-534-61848-0

Wadsworth/Thomson Learning
10 Davis Drive
Belmont, CA 94002-3098
USA

Asia
Thomson Learning
5 Shenton Way #01-01
UIC Building
Singapore 068808

Australia/New Zealand
Thomson Learning
102 Dodds Street
Southbank, Victoria 3006
Australia

Canada
Nelson
1120 Birchmount Road
Toronto, Ontario M1K 5G4
Canada

Europe/Middle East/Africa
Thomson Learning
High Holborn House
50/51 Bedford Row
London WC1R 4LR
United Kingdom

Latin America
Thomson Learning
Seneca, 53
Colonia Polanco
11560 Mexico D.F.
Mexico

Spain/Portugal
Paraninfo
Calle/Magallanes, 25
28015 Madrid, Spain

ABOUT THE AUTHORS

John A. Hird is Director of the Center for Public Policy and Administration at the University of Massachusetts Amherst. He received his Ph.D. in Public Policy from the University of California at Berkeley, and has served as Research Fellow at The Brookings Institution and Economist with the President's Council of Economic Advisers. He is the author of *Superfund: The Political Economy of Environmental Risk*, and he has published articles in the *American Political Science Review*, *Journal of Policy Analysis and Management*, *Yale Journal on Regulation*, *Social Science Quarterly*, and other professional journals. He serves on the editorial board of the *Journal of Policy Analysis and Management*, and has consulted on issues ranging from regulatory reform to state agency research. He is the first recipient of the Mills Award from the Policy Studies Organization for an outstanding contributor to policy studies under age 35, and is currently writing a book on environmental policy and another on the use of public policy expertise in democratic institutions.

Michael A. Reese is a Ph.D. candidate in the Department of Political Science at the University of Massachusetts Amherst. He received his B.S. in Political Science from Willamette University and his M.A. in Political Science from the University of Massachusetts Amherst. He has taught a variety of courses in American politics and political theory, and has served as a researcher at the Massachusetts Institute for Social and Economic Research and the Oregon Health Sciences University. He is interested in the normative dimensions of public policy, with a particular focus on the ways in which democratic theory can inform public policy choice.

Matthew Shilvock has just completed a Master's in Public Policy and Administration at the University of Massachusetts Amherst. His principal interests are in arts policy of the U.S. government and organizational theory of nonprofit institutions. He holds a B.A. in music from Christ Church, University of Oxford, and is currently a fellow with OPERA America, developing skills in the general management of North American opera.

For Sharon, Kelly, Will, and Sam
J.A.H.

For Linda and Ethan
M.A.R.

For Katie
M.S.

CONTENTS

Preface   xiii

Introduction   **1**

Chapter 1. **Growth Management:** *"Should Governments
Adopt 'Smart Growth' Policies to Curb
Suburban Sprawl?"*   **8**

    YES   *Bruce Katz and Jennifer Bradley* "Divided We
            Sprawl" *The Atlantic Monthly*   14

    NO   *Peter Gordon and Harry W. Richardson* "Prove It:
          The Costs and Benefits of Sprawl" *Brookings Review*   24

    Discussion Questions   27
    Web References   28
    Further Reading   28

Chapter 2. **Education Policy:** *"Will Uniform Standards
and Testing Improve Public Education?"*   **30**

    YES   *Abigail Thernstrom* "Testing and Its Enemies: At
            the Schoolhouse Barricades" *National Review*   37

    NO   *Deborah Meier* "Educating a Democracy: Standards
          and the Future of Public Education" *Boston Review*   41

    Discussion Questions   55
    Web References   55
    Further Reading   56

Chapter 3. **Entitlements:** *"Should Social Security
Be Privatized?"*   **57**

    YES   *Michael Tanner* "'Saving' Social Security
            Is Not Enough" The Cato Institute   63

    NO   *Brooke Harrington* "Investor Beware: Can Small
          Investors Survive Social Security Privatization?"
          The American Prospect   78

    Discussion Questions   84
    Web References   84
    Further Reading   84

Chapter 4. Globalization: *"Does Globalization Promote Economic Equality?"*   **86**

YES   ***David Dollar and Aart Kraay*** "Spreading the Wealth" *Foreign Affairs*   94

NO   ***James K. Galbraith*** "The Crisis of Globalization" *Dissent*   106

Discussion Questions   110
Web References   111
Further Reading   111

Chapter 5. Climate Change and Environmental Policy: *"Should the United States Make the Reduction of Greenhouse Gas Emissions an Immediate Policy Priority?"*   **113**

YES   ***Thomas C. Schelling*** "What Makes Greenhouse Sense? Time to Rethink the Kyoto Protocol" *Foreign Affairs*   120

NO   ***Daniel Sarewitz and Roger Pielke, Jr.*** "Breaking the Global Warming Gridlock" *The Atlantic Monthly*   128

Discussion Questions   143
Web References   144
Further Reading   144

Chapter 6. Immigration Policy: *"Should the United States Admit Fewer Immigrants?"*   **146**

YES   ***Roy Beck*** "Roy Beck's Numbers" in *Blueprints for an Ideal Immigration Policy*, Center for Immigration Studies   151

NO   ***Stephen Moore*** "A Strategic U.S. Immigration Policy for the New Economy" in *Blueprints for an Ideal Immigration Policy*, Center for Immigration Studies   160

Discussion Questions   165
Web References   166
Further Reading   166

Chapter 7. Campaign Finance Reform: *"Should Elections Be Publicly Funded?"*   **168**

YES   ***David Donnelly, Janice Fine, and Ellen S. Miller*** "Going Public" *Boston Review*   176

NO   *John Samples* "Government Financing of
       Campaigns: A Public Choice Perspective"
       The Cato Institute   188

Discussion Questions   204
Web References   205
Further Reading   205

Chapter 8. Abortion Policy: *"Should Minors Be Required
            to Obtain Parental Consent Prior to Receiving
            an Abortion?"*   **207**

YES   *Anne Marie Morgan* "Alone among Strangers:
       Abortion and Parental Consent" *Chronicles*   213

NO   *National Organization of Women* "The Tragedy
       of Parental Involvement Laws" *The National
       NOW Times*   218

Discussion Questions   222
Web References   223
Further Reading   223

Chapter 9. Welfare Policy: *"Has Welfare Reform Been a Success?"* **225**

YES   *Ron Haskins* "Giving Is Not Enough: Work
       and Work Supports are Reducing Poverty"
       Brookings Review   234

NO   *Peter Edelman* "Reforming Welfare—Take Two"
       The Nation   239

Discussion Questions   244
Web References   245
Further Reading   246

Chapter 10. Health Policy: *"Should the United States Adopt
             a Universal, Single-Payer Health Plan?"*   **248**

YES   *Physicians' Working Group on Single-Payer
       National Health Insurance* "Proposal for Health
       Care Reform"   256

NO   *Merrill Matthews, Jr., and Robert J. Cihak*
       "Health Care Quality: Would It Survive a
       Single-Payer System?" Washington Policy Center   273

Discussion Questions   289
Web References   290
Further Reading   290

Chapter 11. Affirmative Action/Equal Opportunity: *"Should Affirmative Action Policies Be Continued?"* **292**

    YES   *Stanley Fish* "Reverse Racism or How the Pot Got to Call the Kettle Black" *The Atlantic Monthly* 299

    NO   *Shelby Steele* "A Negative Vote on Affirmative Action" *New York Times Magazine* 307

    Discussion Questions 312
    Web References 313
    Further Reading 313

Chapter 12. Drug Policy: *"Should Drugs Be Legalized?"* **316**

    YES   *Ethan A. Nadelmann* "The Case for Legalization" *The Public Interest* 323

    NO   *James Q. Wilson* "Against the Legalization of Drugs" *Commentary* 347

    Discussion Questions 366
    Web References 367
    Further Reading 367

Chapter 13. Gun Control: *"Should the Sale of Handguns Be Strictly Controlled?"* **369**

    YES   *Steven Riczo* "Guns, America, and the 21st Century" *USA Today Magazine* 375

    NO   *Daniel D. Polsby* "The False Promise of Gun Control" *The Atlantic Monthly* 382

    Discussion Questions 395
    Web References 395
    Further Reading 396

Chapter 14. Energy Policy: *"Should Increasing the Supply of Fossil Fuels Be the Focus of National Energy Policy?"* **398**

    YES   *Secretary of Energy Spencer Abraham,* speech delivered to the National Petroleum Council 407

    NO   *Senator John F. Kerry* "Energy Security Is American Security," speech delivered to the Center for National Policy 416

    Discussion Questions 427
    Web References 427
    Further Reading 428

Credits **429**

PREFACE

As the title of this book and the articles it contains indicate, public policy questions generate significant disagreement and controversy. This should not be surprising, given that they require arriving at a collective decision about the appropriate course of government action, and therefore must reconcile competing interests, viewpoints, and values. If the history of public policy debates in the United States is any indication, such controversy is unlikely to end; public policy questions—whether they deal with immigration, the environment, or welfare policy—have always generated significant debate in this country, and seem likely to do so for quite some time. Indeed, it would be more surprising—and perhaps disturbing—if such controversy did not exist. Rather than representing a problematic feature of American politics, disagreement and debate about the appropriate goals of government action and the best means to achieve those goals are an essential part of a healthy deliberative democracy. Examining such controversies offers us the opportunity to develop a better understanding of American public policy and politics. The challenge for students and practitioners of public policy is not to eliminate controversy but rather to find ways to reach policy decisions in the midst of considerable disagreement.

However, if opinion polls and anecdotal evidence are to be believed, public policy controversies and the political context in which they arise have contributed to considerable public disenchantment with American political institutions. One cause of this disenchantment has been the seemingly widespread belief that policy disagreement results solely from a competition among "special interests" seeking to advance an agenda with narrow appeal. But as the essays in this book demonstrate, public policy disagreements do not stem simply from interest-group influence, pork-barrel politics, or political corruption. To be sure, some interest groups have disproportionate influence in the policymaking process, but it is important to recognize that "special interests" include groups whose missions have broad public support, such as the American Association of Retired Persons (among senior citizens), Greenpeace (among environmentalists), the National Rifle Association (among gun owners), Common Cause (among campaign finance reform supporters), and many others. Furthermore, many citizens underestimate the degree to which legislators take their cues from voter opinion rather than from lobbyists; indeed politicians often rely heavily on public opinion polls to interpret quickly the attitudes of their constituents toward political issues and policies, sometimes excessively so.

Along with the belief that policy disagreements can be reduced to competing interests is the notion that they stem from insufficient knowledge and could be easily resolved if only we would listen to the advice of "experts" in particular issue areas. The perception that simple solutions to complex public policy problems are attainable if only experts would hash out the issues—health care one week, education the next—has a long tradition in American politics, most evident during the Progressive Era of the early twentieth century. But as the positions on the important issues in this book show, experts can and do disagree vehemently over the proper course of public policy. Policy "solutions" are not simple, and go beyond reconciling technical issues for which experts' advice is especially valuable. In fact, while expert knowledge may offer the possibility of improved public policy, it often does little to reduce controversy and frequently increases debate over policy decisions.

Certainly, competing interests and insufficient knowledge play a significant role in shaping the terrain upon which policy controversies take place. But in many cases, such controversy results from fundamental disagreements over strongly held values; indeed, the diversity of these values frequently generates significant debate about the appropriate goals and methods of governmental action. Furthermore, there is often considerable disagreement about what criteria should be used to judge public policies. Some argue that justice should be the primary criterion, others efficiency, and still others personal liberty. In many cases, it is difficult to reconcile competing criteria, and policy disagreements emerge over which criterion should predominate in a particular policy area. This controversy is compounded by the inevitable uncertainty surrounding attempts to predict the effects of particular policies. Finally, the policy process itself involves divergent interests and agendas, complicated technical issues, confusing (and not always public) forms of communication, and political actors with varied motivations, not to mention different views of what constitutes the public interest. Taken together, these factors help to make controversy an essential characteristic of public policy discussions, complicating efforts to "do the right thing," or even to identify what the "right thing" is.

CHAPTER LAYOUTS

Each chapter contains an introductory section designed to familiarize readers with the history and context of the public policy issue; however, these should not be taken as comprehensive summaries, and readers are encouraged to consult the supplemental readings to learn more about each issue. In addition, students should keep in mind that much of the information that is relevant to making public policy decisions, such as government statistics and budget figures, changes often—so often, in fact, that some of the data supplied in the introductions will be outdated by the time this book goes to press. Fortunately, a veritable wealth of information is now available on the Internet, which should allow students to check relevant data in a matter of minutes. Most government agencies now maintain comprehensive sites that contain up-to-date statistics and other relevant information (such as www.fedstats.gov and www.census. gov), many intellectual magazines maintain websites (www.theatlantic.com and www.economist.com), various policy forums have emerged in recent years (www.publicagenda.org), and websites maintained by nonprofit and issue advocacy groups often contain timely and useful information. Further, we have included debate-specific web links at the end of each chapter for students looking for more detailed information. Of course, this is intended to supplement, not substitute for, material found in books and journals not accessible on the Internet. Suggested books and articles for additional reading are also listed at the end of each chapter.

A few caveats are in order. First, there are (obviously) more than two sides to these debates; we have attempted only to supply major arguments that represent significant viewpoints in each policy area, and we encourage instructors and students to explore and devise alternative ways of viewing each issue. Second, the policy areas included here are not exhaustive; there are many other issues we could have included in this book. However, a thorough examination of this material should provide students with the intellectual tools they will need to identify opposing viewpoints in other policy areas. Clearly, the organization of the text into issue-specific chapters does not mean that any of these policy areas are self-contained or unrelated to other policy questions; there is clearly some overlap between some of these debate topics, as there is between most public policy issues. Instructors are encouraged to point out linkages among these debate topics. In fact, a useful discussion point is to ask students to identify some important connections, such as between immigration and affirmative action or between welfare and health care policy.

USING THIS BOOK

Structured as it is around substantive debates, this book demonstrates the character and prevalence of controversy in a wide variety of policy areas. The format is particularly useful for teaching courses in public policy and American politics because it provides an introduction to the dimensions of debate within each area as well as an example of the diversity of viewpoints that contribute to public policy discussions in the United States. While surely not comprehensive, the articles here are sufficient to introduce students to competing perspectives, and students interested in a particular area can then explore it in more detail using the bibliographies provided.

There are several ways for instructors to use this book in class. First, the readings can serve as the basis for in-class debates, in which two teams of students present arguments on each side of the question in front of the rest of the class, followed by a class discussion. These discussions can serve several purposes: to allow the entire class to become involved in the debate and to question and challenge the debaters, to clarify ambiguous or confusing points, to sharpen the discussion on key subjects, to convey the complexity of policy issues, to show that there are more than two sides to each issue, and to make connections to other public policy issues and perspectives. Second, the readings can be used to illustrate different policy perspectives or to provide a foundation for class discussions of substantive policy issues. Third, the book can be used to complement large lectures in American government or public policy, with smaller discussion sections focusing on particular policy issues.

ACKNOWLEDGMENTS

We would like to acknowledge the significant contributions of several people whose comments and assistance were of considerable help in formulating the third edition of *Controversies in American Public Policy*. They made a variety of substantive comments that improved the quality of this book. These people are B. Dan Wood of Texas A&M University, Kathleen Murphy of Gateway Community College, Mark Rushefsky of Southwest Missouri State University, Janet Campbell of Mt. Hood Community College, Patricia Caperton Parent of Southwest Texas State University, Daniel J. Tichenor of Rutgers University, Ross Cheit of Brown University, and Edward P. Weber of Washington State University. Finally, we would like to thank the many wonderful undergraduate students at the University of Massachusetts Amherst whose comments on earlier editions have greatly improved this one.

John A. Hird
Michael A. Reese
Matthew Shilvock

Center for Public Policy and Administration
University of Massachusetts
Amherst, Massachusetts

INTRODUCTION

Public policy is a subject of study, not a discipline. As such, numerous disciplines, from the social sciences to the humanities and natural and biological sciences, all contribute to our understanding of public policy and how changes in policy can improve society. Not only is public policy best understood from the vantage point of different disciplines, the subject of inquiry is broad, including the process of policymaking, the social determinants of policy evolution, the historical trajectories of policymaking, the ethical basis of public policy, the economic impacts of public policy, the impacts of new technologies on public policy (and vice versa), and a long list of others. In order to provide our readers—many of whom may be studying public policy for the first time—with an overview of the field, we divide our discussion into four major areas: studying public policy, making public policy, choosing public policy, and the role of the policy analyst.

STUDYING PUBLIC POLICY

We can think of policy research generally in three broad categories: research that treats public policy as an *explanation* of social/economic/political factors (in which we might say that policy research is seen as an independent variable), research that treats public policy as something to be *explained* (public policy as a dependent variable), and research that develops *information* that provides substantive input into public policymaking.

Public policy research that focuses on policy as an explanation of different outcomes is generally conducted by social scientists (economists, anthropologists, sociologists, political scientists, and so forth). For example, economists study the impact of changes in the minimum wage on unemployment rates and household income, and sociologists study the impact of welfare reform on family structure, crime, and other social variables. Political scientists study the impact that public policy has on the formation of interest groups and the politics surrounding an issue, such as crime or banking deregulation.

Political scientists and political sociologists are principally involved in the study of public policy as a dependent variable, where they seek to discover why public policies emerge in the patterns we observe. For example, political scientists study why major deregulatory initiatives happened in the late 1970s and early 1980s, why environmental laws are generally federal but involve states in significant ways, how social insurance programs have evolved over time, and more generally how policy decisions are made. Political sociologists study the role of money in politics, or how, in comparative terms, we can explain the emergence of one type of health care system in the United States and quite another in most other industrialized nations.

The broadest range of disciplines is involved with providing information for public policy decisions. While the first two categories are reserved mostly for the social sciences, when it comes to providing information for policy-making, the natural and biological sciences are heavily involved (e.g., witness the membership and emphasis of the National Research Council), as are the humanities (e.g., ethical issues surrounding cloning). Besides making claims on the federal budget, scientists and humanists contribute significantly to policymaking, such as economists testifying on the impact of deregulation on electricity markets, biologists forecasting species losses from changes in development policies, philosophers and bioethicists studying the ethical issues involved in the use of genetic information, doctors assessing the impacts of changes in Medicaid on health care delivery, and geoscientists predicting vulnerability to natural hazards. In this regard, many individuals identify themselves and their disciplines as involved in public policy.

MAKING PUBLIC POLICY

There are two different strands of inquiry related to making public policy. The first focuses on the policy process, or how public policies are made procedurally. The second focuses on developing theories of policymaking that try to explain the determinants of policymaking.

The Policy Process

The process of making public policy has both theoretical and empirical dimensions. Theoretically, the policy process is generally conceptualized as a series of stages through which policies pass, namely (1) problem identification, (2) development of policy alternatives, (3) policy selection, (4) implementation, and (5) evaluation. While this model divides the process into a series of somewhat manageable steps, it does not explain well policymaking in practice, nor does it explain how a policy might move from one stage to another. And if viewed too simply, it may obscure the important political, cultural, and sociohistorical dimensions that shape each step.

A variety of other explanations has been developed to explain the policymaking process, from policy ideas that emerge from the "policy primeval soup,"[1] to an "advocacy coalition,"[2] to the importance of symbols in policymaking,[3] to the "issue attention cycle."[4] While none explains the full complexity of policymaking in reality, nor is any model intended to, taken together they provide a far more sophisticated understanding of policymaking than the policy stages that typify many discussions. Many excellent case studies point to the complexity of actual policymaking, such as Martha

Derthick's examination of tobacco politics in *Up in Smoke*. The serious student of public policy will understand both the theoretical explanations and the complexity of political reality.

Theories of Policymaking

How policies emerge in the way they do (e.g., Why does the United States have the current system of old-age pensions?) is the subject of intense inquiry and debate, and seemingly people will each give their own version of why things are the way they are (e.g., "All politicians are crooked"). Even among academics there are various unique explanations of how policies emerge in the shape they do. Many of these different strands of thought can be organized into a set of reasonably coherent possible explanations for the pattern of public policymaking. These include the rational actor model, elite theory, and interest group pluralism.

The rational actor model presents an image of individualistic, self-interested behavior as a way of understanding public policy. In one interpretation, based originally on Adam Smith's *The Wealth of Nations*, individuals pursuing their own self-interest lead to collectively desirable outcomes, namely greater social wealth. While their efforts are self-interested, it is argued that market mechanisms produce outcomes that benefit society as a whole. However, important exceptions to this argument include a group of goods referred to as "common pool resources." The "tragedy of the commons" is that individual self-interest can lead to collectively ruinous outcomes, as evidenced in Garrett Hardin's example of the overgrazing of commonly owned land that is ultimately destroyed by individual self-interest. Variations of the rational actor model include tools of economic decision making, such as benefit-cost analysis, which seek to assess the advantages and disadvantages of public policy changes, convert them into common currency, and recommend a course of action based on whether benefits exceed costs. Another variation on the rational actor model is what is known as "public choice," the application of self-interest as an explanation of individual and political decisions, such as voting and the behavior of congressional committees.

Elite theory views the actions of public organizations as instruments of the policy elite to further their own goals through public means. While government actions may appear to be serving the public interest, in fact they serve to advance the goals of wealthy, powerful individuals who are elites. In the chapter on globalization (Chapter 4), for example, elite theory suggests that while multinational assistance to developing nations may serve to improve living standards marginally among the world's poor, the larger goal is to enrich powerful individuals and corporations in the developed world.

Interest group pluralism suggests that public policy is the result of the interplay between sometimes strong and sometimes weak interest groups. In its most benign interpretation, interest groups can be seen to represent the underlying preferences of individuals; the AARP, for example, should be powerful because its members include millions of retired seniors, while the National Model Railroad Association, with a relatively small membership, should have less influence over public policy. Therefore, this interpretation of pluralism suggests that the power of the organization appropriately represents social interests, and that policy outcomes represent an appropriate mix of these interests as represented by groups.

The more common interpretation of interest group theory challenges the notion that interest groups accurately reflect social values, and instead argues that particular, "special" interests often trump broad social interests in policy formulation. For example, if farmers are the only group to lobby for agricultural price supports, and no one is inclined to lobby against farm price supports because the benefits are too diffused to make it worthwhile for any person to do so, then special interests such as farmers will win particularized benefits at the expense of the broad public interest. In many chapters in this volume, one can see the influence of special interest groups on the formation or implementation of public policy; just a few examples include education policy (Chapter 2), environmental policy (Chapter 5), and health care (Chapter 10).

CHOOSING PUBLIC POLICY

The formation and expression of individual policy preference, while often informed by empirical evidence, is fundamentally a normative exercise. Policy choice involves developing a preference for what society can and should collectively try to accomplish and how to go about it (usually through government action, but potentially using some other means). Such preferences spring less from scientific or empirical analysis than from already existing individual values, norms, world views, and beliefs that together form the analytical framework within which policy choices are analyzed and preferences formed. The identification of problems that policies are supposed to alleviate also proceeds from these different perspectives, so that something that may seem a problem within one framework is not seen as such from another. While such frameworks may overlap in some ways, in many cases they represent fundamentally different ways of viewing the world, and thus cannot be synthesized into a single, shared framework. Often, these perspectives cannot be compared along a single continuum. What's more, individual decisions over various policy options rarely follow the simple and logical chain of argument characteristic of philosophical debate (for example).

So what must be kept in mind when reading debates over policy issues like those presented here is that there are multiple perspectives on any given policy issue, that such perspectives spring from different and often irreconcilable premises, and that understanding policy debates requires not only an analysis of conclusions or even *stated* preferences but also an attempt to understand the often unstated premises from which each argument starts. Such premises/perspectives are almost infinite, but it is possible to identify several basic viewpoints that, with some modification, reemerge in debates over a variety of policy issues.

For example, there is considerable disagreement over both the scope and goal of government action. Should government be held responsible for providing a basic safety net for all citizens with social welfare and health care programs, or should that be left to private forces? Should government go beyond ensuring basic rights? These are questions with no simple answers, and yet sometimes through reflection and conversation/debate, people begin to realize other sides of the issue, some of the impacts on groups they may not have considered, and may begin to adjust their positions accordingly. Therefore, while individuals bring to debates preconceived notions of appropriate responses to policy problems, debate is as much about listening as it is talking, and it is our hope that greater understanding will emerge from both forming a coherent argument and listening to those of others.

If we examine education policy, we can see how different orientations to public policy produce different sets of preferred policy outcomes. Those with a limited government or free market approach would tend to favor vouchers or other market mechanisms to support free choice in choosing schools. Egalitarians, who support a more equal distribution of resources, may favor policies that improve equality, such as raising per-pupil expenditures in poorer school districts or even redistributing funds from wealthier to poorer districts. Communitarians may view school choice as desirable in some respects but as working to erode the social cohesion formed by the communities that develop around neighborhood schools. Social conservatives may focus not on funding or testing but instead on an issue such as school prayer. Finally, those who believe in policies that promote economic efficiency may rely more on studies that track achievement levels of students graduating from schools with different institutional forms (e.g., some with school choice, some without) to determine the appropriate ways to commit resources. In short, the old political adage that "where you stand depends on where you sit" in many cases holds for preconceived political views as well.

THE ROLE OF THE POLICY ANALYST

Some of you may choose to enter the policy arena professionally, either directly as an elected official or more indirectly (and commonly) as a journalist or activist seeking to understand or influence policy outcomes. Broadly conceived, these are all roles of a "policy analyst," a professional who spends at least part of the time thinking about improving public policy and management for the public's good. (In contrast, a lobbyist may seek to influence public policy for the benefit of a special interest group.)

The role of the policy analyst has changed considerably over time. Once policy analysts were conceived of purely as "number crunchers" for the federal government, focusing on technocratic solutions to public problems. Over time, however, the role of the policy analyst has broadened considerably, as has training in graduate schools, to include a wide range of career options, from running local governments, to being activists with international nonprofit organizations, to working at private consulting firms conducting work for federal government clients.

There are numerous graduate programs in public policy, public affairs, public administration, and public management that provide professional training for careers in public service. Some are more oriented to economics and analytical methods, others to management and administration, and still others to specific policy areas such as environmental or family policy. Most provide broad professional education, generally leading to a master's degree in public policy and/or administration, and can lead to exciting careers in public service in the public, nonprofit, and private sectors. National organizations, such as the Association for Public Policy Analysis and Management (APPAM, at www.appam.org), can provide listings of graduate programs in public policy and management.

Endnotes

1. John Kingdon, *Agendas, Alternatives, and Public Policies* (Boston: Little, Brown, 1984).
2. Paul Sabatier, *Policy Change and Learning: An Advocacy Coalition Approach* (Boulder, Colo.: Westview Press, 1993).
3. Murray Edelman, *Symbolic Uses of Politics* (Champaign-Urbana, Ill.: University of Illinois Press, 1985).
4. Anthony Downs, *Up and Down with Ecology: The 'Issue-Attention Cycle' The Public Interest* (Summer 1972).

FURTHER READING

Bardach, Eugene. *A Practical Guide for Policy Analysis.* New York: Chatham House, 2000.

Bardach, Eugene. *The Implementation Game: What Happens after a Bill Becomes Law.* Cambridge, Mass.: MIT Press, 1977.

Bobrow, Davis B. and John S. Dryzek. *Policy Analysis by Design.* Pittsburgh: University of Pittsburgh Press, 1987.

deLeon, Peter. *Advice and Consent: The Development of the Policy Sciences.* New York: Russell Sage, 1988.

Derthick, Martha A. *Up in Smoke: From Legislation to Litigation in Tobacco Politics.* Washington, D.C.: Congressional Quarterly Press, 2001.

Edelman, Murray. *Symbolic Uses of Politics.* Champaign-Urbana, Ill.: University of Illinois Press, 1985.

Ingram, Helen and Steven Rathgeb Smith. *Public Policy for Democracy.* Washington, D.C.: Brookings Institution, 1993.

Kingdon, John. *Agendas, Alternatives, and Public Policies*. Boston: Little, Brown, 1984.

Light, Paul. *The New Public Service*. Washington, D.C.: Brookings Institution, 1999.

Lowi, Theodore. *The End of Liberalism*, 2d ed. New York: Norton, 1979.

MacRae, Duncan and Dale Whittington. *Expert Advice for Policy Choice*. Washington, D.C.: Georgetown University Press, 1997.

Majone, Giandomenico. *Evidence, Argument, and Persuasion in the Policy Process*. New Haven, Conn.: Yale University Press, 1989.

Neustadt, Richard and Ernest May. *Thinking in Time*. New York: Free Press, 1986.

Olson, Mancur. *The Logic of Collective Action*. Cambridge, Mass.: Harvard University Press, 1965.

Ostrom, Elinor. *Governing the Commons*. New York: Cambridge University Press, 1990.

Pressman, Jeffrey L. and Aaron Wildavsky. *Implementation*, 3d ed. Berkeley, Calif.: University of California Press, 1984.

Radin, Beryl. *Beyond Machiavelli: Policy Analysis Comes of Age*. Washington, D.C.: Georgetown University Press, 2000.

Riccucci, Norma M. *Unsung Heroes: Federal Execucrats Making a Difference*. Washington, D.C.: Georgetown University Press, 1995.

Rivlin, Alice. *Systematic Thinking for Social Action*. Washington, D.C.: Brookings Institution, 1971.

Schneider, Anne Larason and Helen Ingram. *Policy Design for Democracy*. Lawrence, Kans.: University of Kansas Press, 1997.

Schultze, Charles. *The Public Use of Private Interest*. Washington, D.C.: Brookings Institution, 1977.

Stone, Deborah. *Policy Paradox and Political Reason*. New York: Norton, 2001.

Weimer, David L. and Aidan R. Vining. *Policy Analysis: Concepts and Practice*, 3d ed. Englewood Cliffs, N.J.: Prentice Hall, 1999.

Wildavsky, Aaron. *Speaking Truth to Power: The Art and Craft of Policy Analysis*. Boston: Little, Brown, 1979.

Chapter 1

GROWTH MANAGEMENT

"Should Governments Adopt 'Smart Growth' Policies to Curb Suburban Sprawl?"

YES: Bruce Katz and Jennifer Bradley "Divided
We Sprawl" *The Atlantic Monthly*

NO: Peter Gordon and Harry W. Richardson "Prove It:
The Costs and Benefits of Sprawl" *Brookings Review*

Managing the effects of population growth and development in metropolitan areas has become one of the most pressing and visible policy issues at the state and local levels. In fact, when citizens were asked to name the "most important problem" facing their local community, the most popular answer—mentioned by 18 percent of all respondents and by 26 percent of those living in suburban areas—was the group of issues related to growth and development; only crime was mentioned as often.[1] The importance of the issue should come as no surprise. Anyone who has lived in or traveled through almost any major city in the country has experienced some of the characteristics of fast-growing urban areas: increased traffic congestion, dying urban centers, seemingly endless suburban development, the loss of open space, and an environment of increased air and water pollution.

As cities and states have become aware of the difficulties of directing growth in desirable ways, many have turned to the policies endorsed by a movement usually referred to as "smart growth." Accepting that population growth is inevitable, and that "no growth" policies are impractical, smart growth proponents focus on ways to manage growth to reduce its undesirable effects. Smart growth strategies—ranging from urban growth boundaries to tax incentives encouraging dense development—are premised on the notion that unplanned, market-driven growth will not produce desirable outcomes, and that public intervention is in some way needed to guide growth toward improved quality of life for citizens.

From the smart growth perspective, at the roots of nearly every problem growing metropolitan areas face is the low-density, sprawling development characteristic of most suburbs. Sprawl has caused a set of concrete and measurable problems: from deterioration of the urban core, loss of open space, traffic congestion, and increased and inefficient public spending on services, such as sewer and water, to increasingly distant housing developments and environmental degradation. Other problems are a bit more abstract: deterioration of vibrant urban life, loss of sense of community, and social isolation, to name a few. Examples of these phenomena are not hard to find: Cities like Los Angeles and Atlanta, argue smart growth proponents, experience nearly all the problems of unplanned or minimally planned growth. Due to past inadequate land-use planning, both cities have become examples of the type of development no city would want to emulate: unchecked suburban growth, traffic congestion, pollution, loss of open space, and the disappearance of traditional and vibrant neighborhoods.

The data supporting some of these claims can be compelling. According to the Agriculture Department, for example, between 1992 and 1997 roughly 16 million acres of open space—an area the size of West Virginia—were developed.[2] It need not be so, argue smart growth proponents. If cities and states enact policies aimed at increasing density—that is, fitting more people on the same amount of land—they would find that many of the problems associated with urban growth disappear. The amount of open space and wilderness areas would stay roughly the same; abandoned inner-city neighborhoods could be rejuvenated; and public transportation could more efficiently serve all areas in the metropolitan area, thereby reducing traffic congestion. The centerpiece of the smart growth strategy, then, is to increase urban density by eliminating, or at least reducing, sprawl.

But the underlying causes of sprawl are complex. While it is often thought to be an unavoidable result of population growth, research suggests that population increases do not entirely explain the pattern and magnitude of sprawl. Between 1960 and 1990, for example, population in 213 urbanized areas in the United States increased 47 percent while the amount of urbanized land increased at more than twice that rate, by 107 percent.[3] A more recent study shows that between 1982 and 1997 the amount of urbanized land in the United States increased 47 percent while population grew by only 17 percent.[4] Urban flight—large numbers of people abandoning central cities in favor of suburban development—has played an important role in many cities. The decisions of large employers in metropolitan areas to move to the suburbs, where land is plentiful and relatively inexpensive, has provided employees the opportunity to live in large suburban houses on large lots with only a short commute to work. The crux of the debate about sprawl stems from the apparent fact that many people *like* the benefits that low-density development provides: Housing on the fringes of, or outside, metropolitan areas is often far less costly; the houses and yards are bigger; crime rates are lower; amenities like grocery stores, shopping malls, and moderately priced restaurants are nearby; and parking at any of these places is never difficult. Therefore, what some view as a problem, others view as a desirable lifestyle.

Some argue that suburban sprawl, past and present, is at least partly a result of planning decisions made at the local, state, and federal levels. Many of the policies resulting from those decisions have, at best, allowed suburban sprawl and, at worst, encouraged it. When a government spends money on roads, schools, sewer and water lines, and other public services at its fringes, it provides the infrastructure that makes sprawl possible and profitable. In fact, critics argue, without this subsidy it rarely would make economic sense to build housing developments, shopping malls, and movie theaters on the outer fringes of, and beyond, cities. Of course, government subsidies provide incentives for other kinds of growth as well: Rural development has been encouraged by rural electrification, the public highway system, agricultural subsidies, and subsidized mail service, while urban development has received help from state and federal aid to cities in the form of money for mass transit, education, and enterprise zones, to name a few.

What is needed to discourage low-density growth, say smart growth proponents, is a new and more holistic approach to long-range urban planning, one that is committed to preserving or increasing urban density. Of course, planning laws and regulations are themselves nothing new. Cities, counties, and states have established and enforced local building codes and zoning laws for more than a hundred years. But this sort of planning has traditionally played a very narrow role, ensuring, for example, that residential zones were kept separate from industrial zones and that buildings met relevant construction codes. What this sort of planning usually has not done is to set density goals for an entire metropolitan area and then take the steps needed to achieve those goals, such as setting maximum allowable lot sizes for single-family homes. Traditionally, in most cities if a person owned several acres of land and wanted to build a single home, she or he need only be sure the lot is in a residential area and meets necessary building codes. Of course, increasing land prices would raise the opportunity costs of maintaining large open spaces in densely populated areas, thereby increasing pressure to subdivide and develop the land.

The smart growth movement advocates a far different and far more powerful role for urban planning, and so far the movement has had significant success in affecting growth planning and legislation throughout the country. In fact, one-fourth of states are implementing smart-growth-type legislation, and another one-third of states are considering such policies.[5] While the policies themselves differ widely from state to state, the goal of more compact urban growth—and the resulting preservation of open space, environmental benefits, and efficient use of public funds—is shared.

Oregon is the most commonly cited example of smart growth in action, and it is also a pioneer in using the methods favored by smart growth proponents. Oregon's current system of land-use planning began in the mid-1970s with a state law requiring each of the 241 cities in the state to prepare a comprehensive future land-use plan based on projected population growth, including establishing and maintaining an "urban growth boundary"—that is, a line around the city within which growth can occur and outside of which it cannot. In the early 1990s, voters in the city of Portland and the cities that surround it—which collectively make up the largest metropolitan area in the state—established a regional government, "Metro," to plan and manage growth across the entire metropolitan area. Responsibilities include developing, enforcing, and if necessary modifying a single shared urban growth boundary for the city and all of its suburbs to replace the existing fragmented structure of growth boundaries around each city. As the only directly elected regional government in the country, Metro has quickly become the most important long-range planning body in the state, responsible for all issues of "metropolitan concern" across the 3 counties and 24 cities that share the urban growth boundary. So rather than responding to the fragmented policies of individual cities and towns, growth in the area is guided according to the comprehensive regional plan that Metro develops along with citizens and stakeholders in the area. By unifying planning power across the region, Metro is able to define areas of dense growth, connect them with public transportation, locate retail space nearby, and establish parks and green spaces near them. Largely because of these policies, downtown Portland's neighborhoods have been revitalized to such an extent that they are now some of the most attractive places to live and work in the metro area. As a result, between 1990 and 2000 the urban growth boundary expanded by only 2 percent despite the fact that population in the region increased by nearly 20 percent.[6]

Of course, this increased density has not come without costs. The average lot size within the urban growth boundary is less than half what it was in the 1980s. Transportation spending has emphasized public transportation rather than road building, to the disappointment of commuters in outlying areas. Existing neighborhoods have had to absorb dense building patterns that have often changed the character of the communities, with row houses, townhouses, and duplexes being squeezed into every vacant area in neighborhoods of single-family homes. And while every attempt has been made to include affordable housing in all new development, housing prices inside the urban growth boundary have more than doubled in some inner-city neighborhoods, where primarily white, upper-middle-class families have replaced the predominantly African-American moderate- and low-income families that had lived in these neighborhoods for decades.

While Oregon's approach to managing growth may be unique, the goal itself is shared by a variety of communities across the nation. In Maryland, for example, the approach used to increase urban density and preserve open space relies upon incentives for compact growth and disincentives to sprawling growth. The Smart Growth program, established by the state in 1997, directs most state spending on infrastructure like roads, bridges, and sewer and water lines to "priority funding areas" designated for growth by local governments.[7] By directing these funds to projects designed to revitalize inner cities and preserve the density of urban areas, the state provides an incentive for developers and local governments to avoid sprawl. At the same time, by not subsidizing suburban development—that is, by not extending infrastructure like roads, sewer lines, etc.—the state provides a disincentive for developers to build in such areas. When the state subsidy is removed and builders are faced with the cost of providing the infrastructure that extended suburban development requires, such development is rarely worth the cost. While Oregon manages growth by preventing its cities from growing spatially and Maryland by a carrot-and-stick approach, voters in New Jersey have taken a different, more direct approach by passing a law in 1998 to spend $1 billion over the course of 10 years to buy half of the remaining open space in the state.

Despite the apparent popularity of these smart growth policies, there are certainly critics of such approaches. Few people would argue that urban areas should grow in "stupid," as opposed to "smart," ways, but there are plenty of critics who question whether the development patterns that the smart growth movement encourages are all that smart after all. Arguments in favor of smart growth are often accompanied by what critics contend is a romantic view of city life and an unfairly harsh view of suburban life. What's more, critics contend, is that the free market, if left alone, will produce precisely the growth patterns that most citizens prefer. If people truly want to live in a densely populated urban center, the demand for that type of housing will increase and homebuilders will inevitably decide to supply that type of housing. In fact, some argue, while many people may frown upon the characteristics of suburban sprawl in the aggregate, when it comes to choosing a place to live those same people will often choose a large house with a big backyard in a suburban community. In addition, critics contend, by limiting the supply of developable land, these policies are artificially increasing home values to such an extent that middle- and low-income families are effectively priced out of the market. Perhaps the most important criticism of these policies is that there is little or no evidence (so far) that they increase the efficiency of public spending.

Many smart growth policies are far too recent to determine their long-term effects, and so many discussions of these policies take place without the sort of empirical evidence characteristic of most policy debates. In this chapter, Peter Gordon and Harry Richardson make precisely that point, arguing that there is as yet little or no empirical evidence to support arguments about the benefits of density over sprawl. What's more, they argue, the available empirical evidence tends to cast doubt on many of the predicted benefits of density over sprawl. Bruce Katz and Jennifer Bradley, after criticizing current planning policies for subtly supporting sprawl and its added cost, propose a new and different way of thinking about cities and suburbs. "Metropolitanism" views cities and their suburbs as interconnected parts of a whole metropolitan area such that useful growth management will require a new metrowide set of policies directed at increasing density by reducing sprawl, preserving open spaces, revitalizing the urban core, and connecting core areas with outlying suburbs through a new and more rational transportation scheme.

Endnotes

1. *Straight Talk from Americans—2000*, a National Survey for the Pew Center for Civic Journalism conducted by Princeton Survey Research Associates (2000), http://www.pewcenter.org/doingcj/research/r_ST2000.html.
2. Marlow Vesterby and Kenneth S. Krupa, "Major Uses of Land in the United States, 1997," *ERS Statistical Bulletin*, no. 973 (Washington, D.C.: U.S. Department of Agriculture, September 2001).
3. "Debate on Theories of David Rusk," *The Regionalist*, vol. 2, no. 3 (Fall 1997).
4. William Fulton, Rolf Pendall, Mai Nguyen, and Alicia Harrison, "Who Sprawls Most? How Growth Patterns Differ across the U.S.," The Brookings Institution, Survey Series (July 2001).
5. American Planning Association, "Planning for Smart Growth: 2002 State of the States," http://www.planning.org/growingsmart/states2002.htm.
6. Metro (Portland, Oregon), http://www.metro.dst.or.us/metro/.
7. Department of Planning, State of Maryland, http://www.op.state.md.us/.

YES

Divided We Sprawl

Bruce Katz and Jennifer Bradley

BY many accounts *Baltimore* is a comeback city. It has a beautiful piece of calculated nostalgia in the Camden Yards baseball stadium, which draws tens of thousands of visitors throughout the spring and summer. It has a lively waterfront district, the *Inner Harbor*, with charming shops and hot snacks for sale every hundred yards or so. But although it may function well as a kind of urban theme park (and there are plenty of cities that would love to achieve that distinction), as a city it is struggling. For twenty years Baltimore has hemorrhaged residents: more than 140,000 have left since 1980. Meanwhile, the surrounding suburbs have steadily grown. The population of Howard County, a thirty-minute drive from the city, has doubled since 1980, from 118,600 to 236,000. The people who have stayed in Baltimore are some of the neediest in the area. The city has 13 percent of Maryland's population but 56 percent of its welfare caseload. Only about a quarter of the students who enroll in a public high school in the city graduate in four years.

And Baltimore is not unique. The image of America's cities has improved greatly over the past few years, thanks to shiny new downtowns dotted with vast convention centers, luxury hotels, and impressive office towers, but these acres of concrete and faux marble hide a reality that is in many cases grim. St. Louis, Cleveland, Philadelphia, and Washington, D.C., lost population throughout the 1990s. These cities are also losing their status as the most powerful economies in their regions. Washington started the 1990s with a respectable 33 percent of the area's jobs. Seven years later it had only 24 percent. The rate of population growth in the nation's suburbs was more than twice that in central cities—9.6 percent versus 4.2 percent—from 1990 to 1997. In just one year—1996—2.7 million people left a central city for a suburb. A paltry 800,000 made the opposite move. In the major urbanized areas of Ohio 90 percent of the new jobs created from 1994 to 1997 were in the suburbs. Ohio's seven largest cities had a net gain of only 19,510 jobs from 1994 to 1997; their suburbs gained 186,000. The 1990s have been the decade of decentralization for people and jobs in the United States.

Not even cities that are growing—southern and western boom cities—are keeping pace with their suburbs. Denver has gained about 31,000 people in the 1990s (after having lost residents during the 1980s), but the counties that make up the Denver metropolitan area have gained 284,000 people—about nine times as many. In Atlanta and Houston central-city growth is far outmatched by growth in outlying counties. And these cities, too, are losing their share of the jobs in their respective regions. In 1980, 40 percent of the jobs in the Atlanta region were in the city itself; by 1996 only 24 percent were.

Meanwhile, the poor have been left behind in the cities. Urban poverty rates are twice as high as suburban poverty rates, and the implementation of welfare reform appears to be a special problem for cities. Although welfare caseloads are shrinking in most cities, in general they are not shrinking as quickly as they are in the states and in the nation as a whole. Often cities have a disproportionate share of their states' welfare recipients. Philadelphia County, for example, is home to 12 percent of all Pennsylvanians but 47 percent of all Pennsylvanians on welfare. Orleans Parish, in which the city of New Orleans is located, has 11 percent of Louisiana's population but 29 percent of its welfare recipients. This hardly adds up to an urban renaissance.

Cities—both the lucky, booming ones and the disfavored, depleted ones—are losing ground for two reasons. First, they push out people who have choices. Urban crime rates have fallen, but they are still generally higher than suburban rates. Some urban school systems are improving, but in most of the nation's twenty biggest urban school districts fewer than half of high school freshmen graduate after four years. City mayors have cut taxes, but urban tax rates (and insurance rates, too) are often higher than suburban ones. Second, suburbs pull people in. This is not a secret. What is less well known—in fact, is just beginning to be understood—is how federal, state, and local policies on spending, taxes, and regulation boost the allure of the suburbs and put the cities at a systematic, relentless disadvantage. People are not exactly duped into living in detached houses amid lush lawns, peaceful streets, and good schools. Still, it is undeniable that government policies make suburbs somewhat more attractive and affordable than they might otherwise be, and make cities less so.

Federal mortgage-interest and property-tax deductions give people a subtle incentive to buy bigger houses on bigger lots, which almost by definition are found in the suburbs. States also spend more money building new roads—which make new housing developments and strip malls not only accessible but financially feasible—than they do repairing existing roads. Environmental regulations make building offices and factories on abandoned urban industrial sites complicated and time-consuming, and thus render untouched suburban land particularly appealing.

Together these policies have set the rules of the development game. They send a clear signal to employers, householders, builders, and political leaders: build out on open, un-urbanized, in some cases untouched land, and bypass older areas. These policies were never imagined as a coherent whole. No individual or committee or agency wrote the rules of development as such. No one stopped to consider how these rules, taken together, would affect the places where people live and work. The rules are simply the implacable results of seemingly disparate policies, each with unintended consequences.

When the policies that made it easier for people to flee the cities and move to the suburbs hurt only urban neighborhoods, the people who chose or had to stay behind suffered. Now, however, these policies, together with the problems of decay and decline in the cities and rapid suburban development, are causing problems for suburbanites, too—most notoriously the problem known as sprawl.

Thus much of the unhappiness of the cities is also the unhappiness of the suburbs. The familiar image of a beleaguered urban core surrounded by suburban prosperity is giving way to something more realistic and powerful: metropolitan areas in which urban and suburban communities lose out as a result of voracious growth in undeveloped areas and slower growth or absolute decline in older places. The idea that cities and suburbs are related, rather than antithetical, and make up a single social and economic reality, is called metropolitanism.

Metropolitanism describes not only where but also in some sense how Americans live—and it does this in a way that the city-suburb dichotomy does not. People work in one municipality, live in another, go to church or the doctor's office or the movies in yet another, and all these different places are somehow interdependent. Newspaper city desks have been replaced by the staffs of metro sections. Labor and housing markets are area-wide. Morning traffic reports describe pileups and traffic jams that stretch across a metropolitan area. Opera companies and baseball teams pull people from throughout a region. Air or water pollution affects an entire region, because pollutants, carbon monoxide, and runoff recognize no city or suburban or county boundaries. The way people talk about where they live reflects a subconscious recognition of metropolitan realities. Strangers on airplanes say to each other, "I'm from the Washington [or Houston or Los Angeles or Chicago or Detroit] area." They know that where they live makes sense only in relation to other places nearby, and to the big city in the middle. Metropolitanism is a way of talking and thinking about all these connections.

The old city-versus-suburb view is outdated and untenable. We can no longer talk about "the suburbs" as an undifferentiated band of prosperous, safe, and white communities. There are two kinds of suburbs: those that are declining and those that are growing. Declining suburbs, which are usually older and frequently either adjacent to the city or clustered in one unfortunate corner of the metropolitan area, are starting to look more and more like central cities: they have crumbling tax bases, increasing numbers of poor children in their schools, deserted commercial districts, and fewer and fewer jobs. For such suburbs to distance themselves from cities makes about as much sense as two drowning people trying to strangle each other.

Growing suburbs are gaining, sort of. They are choking on development, and in many cases local governments cannot keep providing the services that residents need or demand. Loudoun County, a boom suburb in northern Virginia, epitomizes this kind of place. The county school board predicts that it will have to build twenty-three new schools by 2005 to accommodate new students. In February of this year the board proposed that the next six new schools be basic boxes for learning, with low ceilings, small classrooms, and few windows. "We cannot ask the voters to keep voting for these enormous bonds," a county official told *The Washington Post* earlier this year, referring to a $47.7 million bond issue in 1998 for the construction of three new schools. "Nor can we continue to raise taxes every single year to pay for school construction." Predictably, parents complained about the cutbacks in amenities—after all, they had moved there for the schools. "I just think they have to maintain their standards," a disgruntled parent told *The Washington Post*. But these suburbs cannot maintain their standards. There are simply too many new people who need too much new, expensive infrastructure yesterday—not just schools but also sewer and water lines, libraries, fire stations, and roads.

Whether they moved to these places for rural tranquillity, lovely views, and open space, or for good schools, or for the chance to buy a nice house, or just because they wanted to get away from urban hassles, residents of growing suburbs sense that frantic, unchecked growth is undermining what they value and want to keep. The old paradigm of cities and suburbs as opposites, or partisans in a pitched battle, doesn't explain the relationship between these gaining suburbs and their declining older cousins a few exits back on the highway.

Suburbs are not the enemies of cities, and cities are not the enemies of suburbs. That is the first principle of metropolitanism. Cities and suburbs have a common enemy—namely, sprawl. The cycle described above, of draining the center while flooding the edges, is familiar to almost anyone who has driven from one edge of a metropolitan area to another. It is endlessly repeatable, at least potentially: the center just gets bigger, and the edges move out. Metropolitanism is a way of thinking that might break this cycle.

Alas, the city-suburb dichotomy is alive and well in law and in policy. The result is a tangle of regulations and programs that are excellent at throwing growth out to the edges of metropolitan areas and ineffectual at bringing it back to or sustaining it in the metropolitan core. One reason the problem of growth has not been solved is that the city-versus-suburb analysis doesn't properly describe it. The metropolitan reality requires different kinds of policies—ones that take connections and the varying impact of growth into account.

The metropolitanist policy agenda has four basic elements: changing the rules of the development game, pooling resources, giving people access to all parts of a metropolitan area, and reforming governance. These are interlocking aspects of how to create good places to live; they are closely related and can be hard to distinguish. To understand the cascade of consequences that policies can have, consider the policy chain reaction that would begin if the rules of the development game were changed to fit the metropolitanist paradigm. Those rules are mainly the policies that guide transportation investments, land use, and governance decisions, all of which are themselves entangled. Start at one end of the knot: transportation. Major highways, built by federal and state dollars, act as magnets for new development. This has been clear ever since the 1950s, when the interstate-highway system made the suburbs widely accessible and hugely popular. A metropolitanist viewpoint recognizes that these highways will probably pull lots of investment and resources away from the metropolitan core. New development, spawned by highways, will necessitate expensive state-funded infrastructure, such as sewer systems, water pipes, and new side roads. Meanwhile, existing roads, pipes, and sewers, which already cost taxpayers plenty of money, are either not used to the fullest or starved of funds for repair.

A metropolitanist transportation policy might eschew a new beltway and instead direct federal transportation dollars to public transit, which draws development toward rail stations rather than smearing it along a highway, or to repairing existing roads rather than building new ones. That is what Governor Parris Glendening, of Maryland, and Governor Christine Todd Whitman, of New Jersey, have proposed for their states, and what elected officials are working on or have accomplished in the metropolitan areas of Boston, Chattanooga, and Portland, Oregon. New businesses and housing developments will be steered toward where people already live and public investments have already been made.

At this point land use comes into play. "Land-use planning" may sound a little soporific, but it is simply a brake on chaos. It allows communities to prepare for growth in a way that avoids gridlock and preserves public resources. It connects the basic places of life: where people work, where they live, where they play, drop off their dry cleaning, check out a library book, buy a box of cereal. A metropolitanist land-use scheme would preserve open spaces and create parks and other public areas, thereby taking big parcels of suburban land off the development market. Where, then, would all the new development go? An enormous amount of vacant land already exists inside the boundaries of metropolitan areas, which generally have developed in leapfrog fashion, with big gaps between one subdivision or strip mall and the next. Parks and open spaces will not fill all those gaps, which could support development—as could the abandoned urban properties known as *brownfields.*

Land-use decisions can affect how as well as where things are built. Zoning policies can call for transit-oriented development—clusters of shops, apartment buildings, and offices around bus or rail stops, so that people will drive a little less. They can require or at least encourage varied housing near office buildings and supermalls, so that everyone who works there, from the receptionist to the escalator repairer to the middle manager to the chief financial officer, can live near his or her workplace.

Pooling resources is the second element of a metropolitanist agenda. In most metropolitan areas a new office complex or amusement park or shopping mall tends to confer benefits on a single jurisdiction by adding to its property-tax coffers. Meanwhile, neighboring communities are stuck with some of the burdens of development, such as additional traffic and pollution and the loss of open space. Pooling resources—specifically, a portion of the extra tax revenue from development—means that development's benefits, like its burdens, are spread around. The Twin Cities area has a tax-base-sharing scheme whereby 40 percent of the increase in commercial and industrial property-tax revenues since 1971 is pooled and then distributed so that communities without substantial business development are not overwhelmed by needs and starved of resources. In other parts of the country regional jurisdictions have agreed to tax themselves to support cultural and sports facilities; this makes sense, because the entire region benefits from those facilities.

The third element of a metropolitanist agenda is giving everyone in the metropolitan area access to all its opportunities. Access is easy for people with decent incomes and decent cars. They can live where they wish, and they can get from their houses to their jobs without enduring extraordinary hassles. Poor people do not have this kind of mobility.

There are three ways to solve the access problem: make it easier for urban workers to get to suburban jobs; provide affordable housing (through new construction or vouchers) throughout a metropolitan region; or generate jobs in the metropolitan core or at least near public-transportation routes. State and federal governments are now implementing programs that help people to overcome core-to-edge transportation problems, and through housing vouchers are giving low-income people more choices in the metropolitan housing market. Across the country churches and nonprofit organizations are running jitney services and private bus lines to get people to work. A group of Chicago business leaders has called on major employers to weigh affordable-housing options and access to public transit in their business location and expansion decisions. Businesses and nonprofit groups are also trying to bring jobs and people closer together. Housing vouchers administered by nonprofit organizations with a metropolitan scope allow low-income families to move into job-rich municipalities. The nonprofits counsel families about their options and develop relationships with landlords. In the Atlanta region BellSouth will soon consolidate seventy-five dispersed offices, where 13,000 people have worked, into three centers within the Atlanta beltway, all of which are easily accessible by mass transit. After studying where employees lived, the company picked locations that would be of roughly equal convenience for commuters from the fast-growing northern suburbs and from the less-affluent southern suburbs.

The final element of the metropolitanist agenda has to do with governance. Whereas markets and—more important—lives operate in a metropolitan context, our governmental structures clearly do not. They hew to boundaries more suited to an eighteenth-century township than to a twenty-first-century metropolis. Chicago's metropolitan area, for example, encompasses 113 townships and 270 municipalities. This fragmentation works against sustainable metropolitan areas and facilitates segregation by race, class, and ethnicity. Welfare-to-work programs are hindered when public transportation stops at the city-suburban border, for example. Issues that cross jurisdictional borders—transportation, air quality, affordable housing—need cross-jurisdictional solutions and entities that bring together representatives from all the places, small and large, within a metropolitan area to design and implement these solutions. Some such entities already exist: In every urban region in the country a metropolitan planning organization coordinates the local distribution of a chunk of federal transportation funds. Oregon and Minnesota have established metropolitan governments for their largest urban areas, Portland and the Twin Cities. But informal metropolitan governance, in which local governments coordinate their policies and actions, is possible and efficacious. Also, it's necessary.

Metropolitanism is a genuinely different view of the American landscape, and politicians from both parties are beginning to think that a majority of voters might find something to like in it. Like Governor Glendening and Governor Whitman, Governor Thomas Ridge, of Pennsylvania, has laid out land-use objectives for his state that include linking new development to existing infrastructure and encouraging metropolitan cooperation. Governor Roy Barnes, of Georgia, has proposed a strong metropolitanist transportation authority for Atlanta, and in March the state legislature approved it. Governors and state legislators are central to the metropolitanist agenda, because states control an important array of tax, land-use, governance, transportation, work-force, and welfare issues.

Vice President Al Gore clearly recognizes the political potential of this issue and is trying to establish it as one of his signature issues. "We're starting to see that the lives of suburbs and cities are not at odds with one another but closely intertwined," he said in a speech last year. "No one in a suburb wants to live on the margins of a dying city. No one in the city wants to be trapped by surrounding rings of parking lots instead of thriving, livable suburban communities. And no one wants to do away with the open spaces and farm-land that give food, beauty, and balance to our post-industrial, speeded-up lives." For more than a year Gore has been talking about America's growing "according to its values," and has even implied that development is not always welcome.

Of course, the idea of cities and suburbs coming together to solve common problems has been around for decades. No one ever before thought of using it to propel a presidential campaign, because the idea of metropolitanism had yet to prove its appeal, in referenda or in elections or in state legislatures. This is no longer the case.

These ideas are only just beginning to penetrate a recalcitrant real-estate-development industry, however. Christopher Leinberger is a managing director of one of the nation's largest real-estate advisory and valuation firms and a partner in a new urbanist consulting company. He has thought a lot about how the industry works, and he has concluded that sprawl is extremely attractive to the industry, because the kind of development it involves is simple and standardized—so standardized that it is sometimes hard to tell from the highway whether one is in Minneapolis or Dallas or Charlotte. These cookie-cutter projects are easy to finance, easy to build, and easy to manage. Builders like the predictability of sprawl. They know how much a big parking lot is worth, but they aren't sure how to value amenities in older communities, such as density, walkability, and an interesting streetscape. More or less the same can be said of big retail chains. For example, they often overlook the fact that although people in core neighborhoods may have low incomes, they are densely concentrated, which works out to a significant amount of purchasing power. Developers and retailers will have to be willing to think differently if development is to come back to the core. There are encouraging signs. Magic Johnson Theaters, Rite Aid pharmacies, and Pathmark supermarkets are all recognizing that the people left in core communities need places to earn money and to spend it; each of these companies has opened outlets in central cities in recent years. The National Association of Homebuilders has joined with Gore, the U.S. Conference of Mayors, and the U.S. Department of Housing and Urban Development to encourage the development of a million new owner-occupied homes.

Of course, for the politicians' plans to work and the developers' projects to take off, urban core communities will have to win people over. Unless these places have good schools, safe streets, and efficient governments, people will not move from the edge back toward the center. Some mayors have realized this and are trying to make their cities better places to live. Richard Daley, of Chicago, and Stephen Goldsmith, of Indianapolis, are finding innovative ways to address issues that have bedeviled cities for decades: schools, crime, public services, and taxes. It is hard and often unpleasant work; it means privatizing some services, eliminating others, and ending wasteful patronage. But cities must be ready to take advantage of the opportunities that metropolitanist policies offer them.

Academics, architects, and bohemians may decry the soullessness of sprawl, but people seem to like it. Why put up such a fight to save dying places, whether they are called cities or older suburbs or metropolitan cores? After all, as people who see no harm in sprawl like to point out, Americans are living on a scant five percent of the land in this country. Why not just keep sprawling?

There are several reasons to defend not cities against suburbs but centeredness against decentralization, metropolitanism against sprawl. One reason to encourage development in metropolitan cores is a familiar one: the people who live there are among the poorest in their regions—indeed, in the country—and they need these opportunities and this investment. It is not fashionable to talk about having a moral obligation to poor people, but that doesn't mean that the obligation has disappeared. John Norquist, the mayor of Milwaukee, is fond of saying "You can't build a city on pity"; but disinvestment and the resulting lack of good schools, good jobs, and good transportation options is also impractical. The U.S. economy needs workers, and there are people in the metropolitan cores who are not getting into the work force. The need for workers will only increase as the average age of the population rises. By 2021 almost 20 percent of the American people will be over sixty-five, as compared with about 12.7 percent today. Whatever Social Security and Medicare reforms are enacted, these elderly people will need an abundance of payroll-tax-paying workers to support them.

The aging of the U.S. population will soon make it clear that sprawl is of no benefit to people who cannot drive. For a seventy-five-year-old without a car, sprawl can be uncomfortably close to house arrest. But metropolitan core communities where public transportation is available and distances are shorter between homes, pharmacies, doctors' offices, and libraries are navigable for older people in a way that settlements on the metropolitan fringe are not.

Apartment buildings for the elderly are being built in the suburbs, with a variety of services under one roof, and vans to get people from here to there. But there should be choices for elderly men and women who do not want to be segregated from neighborhoods where babies and teenagers and middle-aged people also live.

Unlimited suburban development does not satisfy everyone. Metropolitanism will probably provide a greater range of choices, for the elderly and for everyone else. Policies that strengthen the metropolitan core lead to safer, more viable urban neighborhoods for people who prize the density and diversity of city life. These policies can reinvigorate older suburbs, with their advantages of sidewalks and public transit and a functioning Main Street. And, of course, they allow for brand-new, sizable single-family houses with yards.

It is also possible to argue against sprawl because of a commitment to community. Throughout this essay we have used the word "community" interchangeably with "township," "suburb," "municipality," "jurisdiction," "city," and "place." But "community" also designates a feeling, an ideal—as in "a sense of community," which many people worry that they have lost and would like to re-create. And they are trying to re-create it. Newspaper dispatches from the suburbs of Detroit and Washington, D.C., report that developers are trying to build what people left behind in older places: town centers, with wide sidewalks and big storefronts, where a person can perhaps run into a friend or an interesting stranger and have a place to hang out in public. In a 1998 essay titled "The City as a Site for Free Association," the political philosopher Alan Ryan writes, "If people are to be self-governing, they must associate with each other in natural and unforced ways from which their political association can spring." By "political association" Ryan means involvement in public life and public decision-making. The underlying assumption of a democracy is that this involvement is a wonderful thing. Yet it is unclear whether the new town centers can generate the unforced inter-actions that make municipalities feel like communities. For all the good intentions of the developers who build them and the government officials who support them, they are not natural centers. They are places where people are invited to go and be social or civic-minded, but, as Ryan says, "Telling people to go to such and such a café in order to promote political cohesion and political activity is like telling people to be happy; there are many things they can do that will make them happy, but aiming directly at being happy is not one of them."

These town centers are actually some of the few places where suburban people might mingle with crowds and see people who are not like themselves. They are, along with shopping malls, the public spaces of sprawl. Free association, in the sense of unexpected, unplanned encounters that draw us out of ourselves, is hard to come by in decentralized environments. Driving alone or with family members or close friends from one destination to another leaves little opportunity for spontaneity. Sprawl can create a kind of cultural agoraphobia that depletes public life.

Certainly, the outer edges of metropolitan areas are not the only places that are finding public life difficult to sustain. The most depleted neighborhoods of metropolitan cores, with their forlorn "community centers," dingy streets, and empty sidewalks, are not fertile ground for free association either. And yet the architecture and layout of these places are at least supposed to facilitate inter-action. Moreover, Ryan writes, there are still "galleries and concert halls, city parks, monuments, and other such places" in our urban cores for communities to come together, group by group and interest by interest. . . . To the degree that this is irreplaceable by seeing and hearing it all on television or on the stereo system, it encourages people to understand themselves as members of one society, engaged in a multitude of competing but also cooperative projects. A society that does not understand this about the basis of its cultural resources is a society in danger of losing them. At present, we seem to be such a society. Suburbs are not new. They have been in existence in the United States since the nineteenth century. But hypersuburbanization, decentralization, and sprawl are new—less than two generations old. Americans are now discovering how hard it is to live without a center. In a typical attempt to move simultane-ously in opposite directions, they are moving out but also trying to come back. This is not merely nostalgia for some dimly remembered era of civility and good cheer. People are honestly trying to balance the frantic privacy of the suburbs with some kind of spontaneous public life. By now it seems clear that continued sprawl will make this public life very hard to achieve—at the edges of metropolitan areas, where there are no places to gather, and at the cores of metropolitan areas, where the gathering places are unsafe or abandoned. Is this really a good trade for a big back yard?

NO

Prove It:
The Costs and Benefits of Sprawl

Peter Gordon and Harry W. Richardson

Cities have been generating suburbs for as long as records have existed. Most of the world's large cities are growing outward now, and very likely the pace will accelerate in the new age of information networking. Unpopular as the word is in some quarters, it is hard to avoid concluding that "sprawl" is most people's preferred life-style. Because no one wants to appear to contradict popular choices and interfere with the principle of consumer sovereignty, the critics of sprawl instead blame distorted prices, such as automobile subsidies and mortgage interest deductions, and claimed but unregistered costs of sprawl, such as unpaid-for infrastructure, lost agricultural output, congestion, and dirty air.

The cost position, however, is encumbered with at least two problems. First, most of us are not cost minimizers. Rather, we trade off costs for perceived benefits. And second, the costs argument is empirically shaky. Traffic "doomsday" forecasts, for example, have gone the way of most other dire predictions. Why? Because suburbanization has turned out to be the traffic safety valve. Increasingly footloose industry has followed workers into the suburbs and exurban areas, and most commuting now takes place suburb-to-suburb on faster, less crowded roads. The last three surveys by the Nationwide Personal Transportation Survey (NPTS) show increasing average work trip speeds—28 mph in 1983, 32.3 mph in 1990, and 33.6 mph in 1995.

The alleged loss of prime farmlands is, in the words of the late Julian Simon, "the most conclusively discredited environmental-political fraud of recent times." U.S. cropland use peaked in 1930. Each year American farmers grow *more* crops using *less* land and labor.

As for the "compactness equals efficiency" argument, technological change takes us in the direction of efficient small-scale provision, weakening the old idea that scale economies of utility generation are there to be exploited by more compact urban forms. Large retail establishments, for example, can now keep low-kilowatt natural gas turbines on the premises.

U.S. public policies do not have a singular spatial thrust. Some policies, such as subsidized downtown renewal, subsidized and downtown-focused transit, subsidized downtown convention centers, sports stadia, and similar facilities,

Peter Gordon and Harry W. Richardson are professors in the University of Southern California's School of Policy, Planning, and Development, as well as the USC Department of Economics.

favor centralized settlement. Others, including inflexible zoning codes and the deductibility of mortgage interest and real estate property tax, favor dispersal.

The much vaunted subsidies to the auto-highway system consist mainly of decisions by government policymakers not to tax drivers to recover the cost of such externalities as congestion and environmental damage. And that issue recedes in importance as highway speeds increase and internal combustion engines become cleaner. The mortgage interest tax deduction raises land values throughout the metropolitan region. It has contributed much less to central-city decline than have suburban minimum lot size restrictions and poorer central-city amenities. In any event, reducing subsidies makes more sense than equalizing them, as, for example, through trying to equate automobile and transit subsidies.

The evidence that has been assembled on the difficult issue of infrastructure services costs is, at best, mixed. Even if it could be conclusively demonstrated that suburban and exurban infrastructure costs are higher than central-city costs, the solution is not to ban suburbanization and low-density development or introduce strict growth management controls. A better approach is to use developer impact fees (fees per residential unit imposed on new development) to recoup any difference between the fiscal costs and revenues from residential development.

THE NEED FOR CLARITY

The sprawl discussion is distorted by a high degree of misinformation. To take one example, state and local growth management, "smart growth," and anti-sprawl protagonists frequently cite Los Angeles as the sprawl capital of the United States, with a land use pattern to be avoided at all costs. In fact, the urbanized area of the Los Angeles metropolitan region has the highest residential densities in the United States—higher even than the New York urbanized region—largely the result of its high land prices.

Casual observers have been deceived by looking at only the gross densities based on all the land area, much of which consists of vast unbuildable areas such as mountains and peripheral deserts. Another false conception is that suburban areas are dominated by single-family homes on large lots. In fact, the suburban and exurban "attached house" share of the metropolitan housing stock is about 50 percent. Of the nation's presumably higher-density attached housing, then, half is located outside central cities.

Increasingly, the attack on sprawl is being justified by the need to achieve the goal of "sustainable urbanization." But no one has defined the term satisfactorily. Rather, the talk is of recycling, increasing densities, and promoting transit as instruments for preserving resources for future use. The concern for future generations that sustainability implies gives insufficient weight to today's problems of poverty and inequality. In the words of Nobel Prize–winning economist

Robert Solow, "There is at least as strong a case for reducing contemporary inequality (and probably stronger) as for worrying about the uncertain status of future generations." In our view, these problems cannot be alleviated significantly via the social engineering of urban space.

Some observers see compact and high-rise development as an accommodation to inferior forms of transportation that have been eclipsed by the automobile. The universal choice is for the freedom and flexibility that come only with personal transportation. Collective transportation loses in any head-to-head contest, as the widespread operations of large numbers of clandestine "gypsy" cabs and vans above one of the world's premier subway systems in New York City make clear. Even in New York, many origins and destinations are too dispersed to be serviced by fixed-route systems. The record of conventional transit throughout the United States is the same theme writ large. After hundreds of billions of dollars of public subsidy, transit use per capita is now at a historic low. The evolution of American cities and life-styles has outgrown 19th-century-style urban transit. Ironically, the mass transit favored by anti-sprawl activists—street cars, subways, and urban rail systems of earlier days—was the prime instrument of suburbanization. The automobile merely diversified its radial pattern.

And though mass transit supporters argue for higher densities to reduce congestion and improve air quality, in fact the relationship between density and traffic congestion is positive rather than negative, and the link between congestion and air quality is very complex and highly technical.

In the end, the goals of the anti-sprawl position are unattainable. Opportunities for infill development in central cities exist, but they are limited. There is a small, if growing, scattering of compact new developments in the suburban and, more often, exurban environments, but their impact on anti-sprawl goals is minimal. There is, for example, no evidence that they reduce off-site trips. Any reasonable assumptions about the extent of future compact developments must yield the conclusion that their influence on tomorrow's urban landscape is minuscule.

Proponents of the New Urbanism claim the ability to design community-friendly neighborhoods, thus joining the movement to revive communitarianism. While there is a lively debate over the current state of civil society . . . the case of the New Urbanists is much less clear. Residential developments and whole neighborhoods are being supplied by market-savvy builders attentive to the trade-offs that their customers are eager to make. People in compact communities live as privately as those in low-density suburbs. Were people to demand cozier spatial arrangements, they would soon get them. Moreover, the public's demand for "community" is being met in other ways, facilitated by the auto and even Internet access. In terms of transportation, we know that the overwhelming amount of travel is nonwork travel. About one-fifth of person-trips are for work-related purposes, one-fifth are for shopping, and three-fifths are for "social" reasons (including the NPTS categories "other family and personal business," "school/church," "visit friends or relatives," and "other social or recreational" purposes).

DEALING WITH THE COSTS OF SPRAWL

We are not advocating a "laissez-faire" approach to the development of our cities. Cities are, almost by definition, the cause of myriad unintended costs. Many problems (not all) can, and should, be resolved by low-cost negotiation between the affected parties (for example, developers and environmentalists) or by the exchange of expanded property rights (using such measures as emission fees, congestion prices, and development credits). The more radical measures proposed by critics of American cities—maximum densities, restrictions on automobile use, and mandatory fees and taxes to pay for transit—are grounded in misconceptions and are unlikely to achieve their stated goals.

The principle of consumer sovereignty has played a powerful role in the increase in America's wealth and in the welfare of its citizens. Producers (including developers) have responded rapidly to households' demands. It is a giant step backward to interfere with this effective process unless the benefits of intervention substantially exceed its costs. Bans on the amount of land that individuals can consume, or even worse, on driving, are extremely difficult to justify. In fact, when households purchase a single-family home in the suburbs, they are not consuming land per se. Rather, they are buying a number of attributes—good public schools, relative safety from crime, easy access to recreation and shopping opportunities, low taxes, responsive public services. Lot size is rarely crucial to the decision. In any event, lot sizes are becoming smaller as a result of rising land prices, and there may be opportunities for developers through creative design to reduce lot sizes still further while preserving privacy. But smaller lots are not going to revive the central city or alter significantly the consequences of suburban and exurban development.

Paradoxically, as the U.S. political system increasingly emphasizes deregulation and market processes at the federal, and sometimes the state, level, command-and-control restrictions and interest-group impositions at the local level are growing and are frequently being reinforced by actions in the courts. Much of this shift, exemplified by the expansion of land use regulations, reflects a retargeting of regulatory activity from economic sectors to such social concerns as education, health, and the environment. But for the cost-benefit calculus advocated by the anti-sprawl protagonists to prevail, the quality of their empirical evidence must be improved.

DISCUSSION QUESTIONS

1. Despite the widespread use of the term "sprawl," it often means different things to different people. How do you define sprawl? Can you name some regions in your state that are poorly developed or "sprawling"? Do you live in such an area?

2. How do you feel about extended low-density development? If you could choose a place to live, would it be in such an area? Why or why not?
3. What incentives do governments provide that encourage sprawl? Are there any that discourage it, or encourage urban growth? If the government did not provide any such subsidies—for either cities or suburbs—how would growth patterns change? What would be the effect on people in urban areas?
4. Should land development be dictated by market decisions (e.g., land prices, consumer preference)? Are markets "free" in this case? Can you describe some ways in which markets are heavily influenced by local, state, or federal government policies with respect to land use? Is this influence mostly positive or negative?
5. What type of growth management is more likely to meet the goal of reducing sprawl while preserving or improving quality of life, the Portland approach or the Maryland approach? Are programs that purchase open space to preserve it likely to be as effective?
6. Should the federal government become involved in growth management issues, or are they primarily local issues that should be solved by local and state governments with mostly local and state funding?

WEB REFERENCES

Brookings Institution Center on Urban and Metropolitan Policy, http://www.brookings.edu/dybdocroot/es/urban/urban.htm.

Congress for the New Urbanism, http://www.cnu.org/.

Metro (Portland, Oregon), http://www.metro.dst.or.us/metro/.

Smart Growth Network, http://www.smartgrowth.org/.

Sprawl Watch, http://www.sprawlwatch.org/.

U.S. Bureau of Census Data on Urbanized Land, http://www.sprawlcity.org/.

FURTHER READING

Aspen Institute. *Suburbs and Cities: Changing Patterns of Metropolitan Living.* Washington, D.C.: The Aspen Institute Domestic Strategy Group, 1995.

Benfield, Kaid, Matthew Raimi, and Donald Chen. *Once There Were Greenfields; How Urban Sprawl Is Undermining America's Environment, Economy, and Social Fabric.* New York: Natural Resources Defense Council, 1999.

Bullard, Robert D. *Sprawl: City—Race, Politics, and Planning in Atlanta.* Washington, D.C.: Island Press, 2000.

Bullard, Robert D. and Glenn S. Johnson. *Just Transportation—Dismantling Race and Class Barriers to Mobility.* Stony Creek, Conn.: New Society Publishers, 1997.

Diamond, Henry L. and Patrick F. Noonan. *Land Use in America: The Report of the Sustainable Use of Land Project.* Washington, D.C.: Island Press, 1996.

Downs, Anthony. *New Visions for Metropolitan America.* Washington, D.C.: The Brookings Institution, and Cambridge, Mass.: Lincoln Institute of Land Policy, 1994.

Duany, Andres, et al. *Suburban Nation: The Rise of Sprawl and the Decline of the American Dream.* New York: North Point Press, 2000.

Freeman, Lance. "The Effects of Sprawl on Neighborhood Social Ties." *Journal of the American Planning Association,* vol. 67, no. 1 (2001), pp. 69–77.

Gordon, Peter and Harry W. Richardson, "Are Compact Cities a Desirable Planning Goal?" *Journal of the American Planning Association,* vol. 63, no. 1 (Winter 1997), pp. 95–106.

Gratz, Roberta Brandies and Norman Mintz. *Cities Back from the Edge—New Life for Downtown.* New York: Preservation Press, 1998.

Hiss, Tony. *The Experience of Place.* New York: Knopf, 1990.

Jackson, Kenneth T. *Crabgrass Frontier: The Suburbanization of the United States.* New York: Oxford University Press, 1985.

Kahn, Matthew. "Does Sprawl Reduce the Black/White Housing Consumption Gap?" *Housing Policy Debate,* vol. 12, no.1 (2001), pp. 77–86.

Kennedy, Maureen and Paul Leonard. "Dealing with Neighborhood Change: A Primer on Gentrification and Policy Choices." A Discussion Paper Prepared for the Brookings Institution Center on Urban and Metropolitan Policy and PolicyLink, April 2001.

Kunstler, James Howard. *The Geography of Nowhere: The Rise and Decline of America's Man-Made Landscape.* New York: Simon & Schuster, 1993.

Langdon, Philip. *A Better Place to Live: Reshaping the American Suburb.* New York: HarperPerennial, 1994.

Lewis, Paul G. "Looking Outward or Turning Inward? Motivations for Development Decisions in California Central Cities and Suburbs." *Urban Affairs Review,* vol. 36, no. 5 (May 2001), pp. 696–720.

Moe, Richard and Carter Wilkie. *Changing Places: Rebuilding Community in the Age of Sprawl.* New York: Henry Holt & Co., 1997.

Pastor, Manuel, Jr., Jim Sadd, and John Hipp. "Which Came First? Toxic Facilities, Minority Move-in, and Environmental Justice." *Journal of Urban Affairs,* vol. 23, no.1 (2001), pp. 1–21.

Sigelman, Lee and Jeffrey R. Henig. "Crossing the Great Divide: Race and Preferences for Living in the City versus the Suburbs." *Urban Affairs Review,* vol. 37, no. 1 (2001), pp. 3–18.

Southworth, Michael. "Walkable Suburbs? An Evaluation of Neotraditional Communities at the Urban Edge." *Journal of the American Planning Association,* vol. 63, no. 1 (Winter 1997), pp. 28–44.

Squires, Gregory D., ed. *Urban Sprawl: Causes, Consequences & Policy Responses.* Washington, D.C.: Urban Institute Press, 2002.

Suarez, Ray. *The Old Neighborhood—What We Lost in the Great Suburban Migration: 1966–1999.* New York: Free Press, 1999.

Chapter 2

EDUCATION POLICY

"Will Uniform Standards and Testing Improve Public Education?"

YES: Abigail Thernstrom "Testing and Its Enemies: At the Schoolhouse Barricades" *National Review*

NO: Deborah Meier "Educating a Democracy: Standards and the Future of Public Education" *Boston Review*

Despite occasional controversy over its character and content, education has been accepted throughout American history as a primary public responsibility and remains one of the most important government functions in the United States. This is particularly true with respect to elementary and secondary education, where a free public education available to all students has traditionally formed the cornerstone of American educational policy. American schools educate nearly 55 million students in grades K through 12; 89 percent of those students attend public schools and 93 percent of the $338 billion spent on K–12 education in the United States comes from public sources.[1] Perhaps because of its prominence as a public responsibility, as well as the central role it plays in American society, the public education system has been closely scrutinized throughout history and has rarely enjoyed a period without criticism and calls for reform.

Criticism of public schools has often focused on issues of pedagogy and curriculum, and has also been a reflection of larger cultural controversies as in debates over the role of religion in schools and the desegregation of schools during the civil rights era. Recently, however, critics have begun to question the ability of America's schools to properly prepare all—or even most—students to graduate with the skills and knowledge needed to lead successful lives. For decades, there has been widespread concern that, even with adequate funding, schools are not achieving what they should. In the early 1980s, after scores on standardized tests had been declining for more than a decade and had begun to lag scores from many other industrialized nations, fears about the impact of a failing educational system became widespread, and a federal report issued in 1982 warned of "a nation at risk." Since that time, talk of "our failing schools" and of students and entire communities "left behind" by the education system has become almost dogma. In 1973, for example, 58 percent of the public had a "great deal" or "quite a lot" of confidence in public schools, 27 percent "some confidence," and only 11 percent "very little" or "none." By 1999, 36 percent had a "great deal" or "quite a lot" of confidence, 37 percent "some confidence," and 26 percent "very little" or "none."[2]

While such criticisms have been motivated by a variety of factors, critics have often relied upon test scores to show that schools are becoming less effective. However, such scores present a decidedly ambiguous picture. It is true that results of the often-cited Scholastic Aptitude Test (SAT) indicate declines in both verbal and mathematical aptitude over the past several decades, with average combined SAT scores falling from 1159 in 1967 to 1020 in 2001. But such declines have recently been reversed. The SAT is particularly suspect as a measure of educational achievement because it is neither designed nor used for that purpose, and because the pool of test takers has expanded to include students who may not have considered applying to college in the past (and so who might be expected to lower the average). In fact, scores on proficiency tests designed to measure knowledge in a variety of subjects improved for all age groups in math and science between 1977 and 1998, and reading scores among 17-year-olds increased during the same period.[3] However, there remains concern with how well students compare with students in other industrialized nations. Recent data showing that U.S. students routinely score low in geography, science, and mathematics compared with students from other wealthy nations have fueled fears for the economic as well as educational health of the nation. But parents are far fonder of the schools their children attend than they are of the quality of public education in general, with 78 percent reporting that they are "completely" or "somewhat" satisfied with the quality of their oldest child's education, while only 36 percent say the same of the U.S. educational system in general.[4]

Elementary and secondary education policy in the United States is unusual among major public functions in that it is dominated by local interests and funding. In 1997–98, for example, states provided 48 percent, local sources 45 percent, and the federal government only 7 percent of the $344.9 billion spent on elementary and secondary schools.[5] Most of the local financial contribution—78 percent in 1997–98—is derived from local property taxes, while the state contribution usually comes from each state's general fund.[6] In most cases, primarily local governments and school boards in more than 15,000 school districts exercise control of the schools. In addition, over half of state and local government employment throughout the United States is devoted to education (including higher education). In contrast, the federal government generally plays a relatively minor financial role, providing approximately $43.8 billion in the 2000 fiscal year to elementary and secondary schools and students. More than half of federal government spending on local schools is directed toward education support programs; $8.9 billion, for example, funds child nutrition programs, and $8.5 billion provides grants and assistance to disadvantaged children.[7]

In contrast to elementary and secondary education, there is no tradition of free higher education in the United States, and a mixture of state, federal, and private sources has provided funding for higher education. The United States spends a larger portion of its gross domestic product on public and private higher education than any other industrialized country, educating roughly 14.5 million students in colleges and universities.[8] While most spending at the K–12 levels is provided from public sources, a much smaller percentage of higher education funding derives from public sources. In 1997, 28 percent of funding for higher education institutions was provided by tuition and fee payments, 23 percent by state governments, 12 percent by the federal government, and the remainder from a variety of other, mostly private, sources.[9] Not only does the federal government play a more prominent role in funding higher education than it does in elementary and secondary education, providing loans and grants to students as well as funding research, but private sources contribute significantly to spending on higher education as well.

Judging from a variety of statistical measures, the U.S. education system has produced some impressive achievements over the past several decades: The percentage of individuals (age 25 and older) with 4 or more years of college education increased sharply from 10.7 percent in 1970 to 25.6 percent by 2000; the portion of individuals with more than 12 years of schooling has increased from 52 percent to 84 percent over the same period; the percentage of high school dropouts has fallen slightly from 12.2 percent to 10.9 percent; 33 percent of adults ages 25 to 29 held bachelor's degrees in 2000; and the system of higher education in the United States continues to attract hundreds of thousands of foreign students from around the world.[10] In addition, education has provided a variety of benefits that cannot be easily measured, such as promoting a shared civic culture and responsibility, integrating immigrants into American customs and culture, and improving employment skills.

The perception that American schools are failing to educate students adequately has resulted in a variety of reform proposals directed at the elementary and secondary educational system in the United States, although there is little agreement over the nature or cause of the problems facing American education. Some have criticized regional differences in educational preparation that result from the fact that school spending and achievement vary widely across states and communities. New Jersey, with the nation's highest per-pupil expenditures ($10,787) in 2001, spent roughly 2½ times per student compared with Utah, which spent the least ($4,372).[11] This disparity partly reflects differences in purchasing power (a dollar buys more in Utah than in New Jersey), partly the relative incomes of different states, and partly the emphasis voters place on educational spending. While there is not necessarily a correlation between spending and achievement, states vary in educational achievement as well. For example, the high school graduation rate in West Virginia (75.1 percent) in 1999 trailed the national average of 83.4 percent as well as national leaders Alaska (92.8 percent), Washington (91.2 percent), and Minnesota (91.1 percent).[12]

Another concern among policymakers and educators is the vast disparity in funding levels between wealthy school districts and very poor districts even within the same state. Because school spending is strongly tied to a community's property tax receipts, and because wealthy districts enjoy significantly more property tax revenue than poor districts which lack the property values or income levels to provide such revenues, spending on education in wealthy districts far outpaces that in poor districts. As a result, conditions in many schools located in poor districts are dismal, a situation described eloquently by Jonathan Kozol in *Savage Inequalities*. Some have argued that this vicious circle—where poor districts lead to poor schools, leading to reduced economic opportunities for the residents, in turn fueling further economic decline—unfairly disadvantages some, especially the poor and minorities. Such inequality does not appear to be a significant concern among many voters, however. In fact, efforts to decouple property taxes and school spending are sure to meet substantial political resistance. For mobile or affluent families, school quality is an important criterion for deciding where to live, and families pay a premium in terms of housing prices for living in a town with excellent schools. Therefore, decoupling school spending and property taxes would mean substantial wealth transfers from areas with high per-pupil spending to those with lower educational spending. The inability of state legislatures to reconcile these political differences has led courts in many states to order changes in state school financing, generally in ways that attempt to equalize school funding throughout the state either by providing additional state funding for poor districts or by decoupling property taxes and school funding levels. As a result, a more common state response to inequality has been to raise funding levels in poor districts through state aid, not to redistribute funds from rich to poor districts.

While criticisms are legion, systematic reform proposals, such as creating magnet schools, raising teacher salaries, and extending the school year, often require funds that many localities cannot afford or do not want to spend. In addition, such criticisms often reveal fundamental disagreements over what public schools can and should hope to achieve, and thus disagreements over how they should be reformed. One of the most controversial reform proposals, for example, calls for allowing students and their parents to choose which schools the students will attend. Such "educational choice" or "school voucher" programs stem from the underlying principle that applying a consumer-oriented market model to education effectively will force schools to improve or risk "going out of business." And, supporters argue, rather than relying on policymakers to figure out how best to serve students and bureaucracies to execute these policies, such improvement will rely upon the so-called invisible hand of the market to guide efficient competition, experimentation, and innovation toward school success. Some school districts have used limited school choice programs among a relatively small number of public schools. But the inclusion of private schools in such programs has been limited—partly because voters tend not to support such a move and partly because there is concern that, given that many private schools are also religious schools, such a policy is unconstitutional. However, on June 27, 2002, the Supreme Court ruled (in a 5-4 vote) that a pilot program in Cleveland, Ohio, that awarded vouchers for use in either public or private/religious schools did not violate the establishment clause of the Constitution prohibiting the government from establishing religion. Experimentation with school choice policies has begun too recently to provide evidence of success or failure, but there will undoubtedly be additional pilot programs over the next several years.

Discussion of school choice has occupied a significant role in the political arena, but the reform movement that has exerted the most powerful influence on American education in recent years—and the subject of this chapter's debate—is the standards-based reform movement. On this view, schools face two problems: First, students are not being taught (or at least are not learning) the proper content in core academic subjects like math, history, and science. Second, there are few, if any, measures in place to hold students, teachers, and schools accountable for success or failure; students are rarely held back or denied graduation, teachers are rarely punished if their students fail or rewarded if they succeed, and schools themselves are not penalized (or, for that matter, provided assistance to improve) if their students underperform.

One possible solution to the first problem, and the first step toward "raising educational standards," is for states (or the federal government) to establish a state or nationwide curriculum for key subjects in each grade, to orient teacher training around the curriculum, and to make requirements for each grade clear to students and their parents. For these standards to have any effect, the second problem must be solved, and the proposed solution is to test students in all schools on a regular basis in these subject areas. Then, based on the results, hold students accountable (in some proposals, by denying high school graduation), hold teachers accountable (by denying promotion or tenure), and hold schools accountable (by intervening at failing schools). If these policies are followed, it is argued, all students will receive a better education, and disparities created by wealth, location, or poor teaching will be reduced.

Proposals for reforming educational standards enjoy significant support across the political spectrum (in contrast to support for school choice proposals, for example, which often comes from conservative voters and politicians). Such policies have been enacted by legislatures and governors in nearly every state, and have been supported by Presidents Bill Clinton and George W. Bush. Public support for the general idea of establishing educational standards has also been high: More than half of Americans (59 percent) say low academic standards are a "very serious concern," and 69 percent of Americans support required tests for high school graduation. However, when their own schools or children are concerned, 57 percent of people feel that standards are "about right" locally, and 62 percent of parents with children in grades K–12 strongly agree that "it is wrong to use the results of just one test to decide whether a student gets promoted or graduates."[13]

Critics of so-called high-stakes testing argue that the sort of problem-solving abilities, creativity, and critical-thinking skills that are most important for students to develop cannot be standardized or tested. Extensive use of testing will force teachers to "teach to the test" rather than developing such abilities and skills, and students will emerge from high school able to recite the 50 state capitols but unable to solve simple real-world problems. Tests have begun to attract increasing and passionate criticism from parents at the local level (especially in wealthy suburban districts) as the tests are implemented and parents realize that their children are at risk of not graduating. In Massachusetts, one of the first states to adopt widespread tests, there has been heated protest from parents and children, and a number of parents have encouraged their children to boycott the tests.

Because such standards are generally phased in over time, followed by a phase-in of tests, it is far too early to determine the effects of such policies. A preliminary report published by Fairtest (an educational advocacy organization critical of high-stakes testing) shows that students in states with graduation tests were less likely than students in states that do not require such tests to score at a "proficient" level on national math and reading tests. What's more, contrary to the argument that high-stakes tests will improve the performance of the worst students, the proportion of students scoring below "basic" on national tests was consistently above average.[14] However, until more data are available, it is difficult to say what, if any, effect such tests will have on the quality of American education.

In this chapter's discussion, Abigail Thernstrom, a member of the Massachusetts State Board of Education, argues that improved educational standards and high-stakes tests are needed to bring educational equality as well as overall improvements in all student learning. Deborah Meier, a longtime teacher and principal at successful schools in New York and Boston, argues that the imposition of standards and tests will undermine the very purpose that schools serve: to teach students how to think critically while at the same time instilling democratic character. High-stakes testing threatens both goals and consequently is a threat not only to the quality of American education, but also to American democracy itself.

Endnotes

1. *Digest of Education Statistics, 2001*, February 2002, National Center for Education Statistics.
2. Poll by Gallup Organization, August 2000. Much of the data in this section are provided by the National Center for Education Statistics, and updated figures can be found at http://www.nces.ed.gov.
3. U.S. Bureau of the Census, *Statistical Abstract of the United States: 2000* (Washington, D.C.: U.S. Government Printing Office, 2001).
4. Poll by Gallup Organization, op. cit.

 5. U.S. Department of Education, National Center for Education Statistics, Common Core of Data, "National Public Education Financial Survey," School Year 1997–1998; http://www.nces.gov/.
 6. U.S. Department of Education, op. cit.
 7. *Digest of Education Statistics, 2001*, op. cit.
 8. Ibid.
 9. U.S. Bureau of the Census, op. cit.
10. *Digest of Education Statistics, 2001*, op. cit.
11. U.S. Department of Education, op. cit., "Early Estimates of Public Elementary/Secondary Education Survey," 2000–01; "National Public Education Financial Survey" and "State Nonfiscal Survey of Public Elementary/Secondary Education," 1996–97 through 1999–2000.
12. U.S. Bureau of the Census, op. cit.
13. Poll by Public Agenda, September 2000.
14. Monty Neill, "High Stakes Do Not Improve Student Learning," *A FairTest Report* (1998).

YES

Testing and Its Enemies: At the Schoolhouse Barricades

Abigail Thernstrom

In her recently published autobiography, Brenda Webster describes going to New York's pricey and progressive Dalton School. "To learn grammar," she writes, "we sat in a circle and imagined what part of speech we would have invented first if we were cavemen…. This was fun, but when I graduated from high school [in 1954] I still had no idea where to place a comma."

No wonder educational backlash has finally set in. The ideas that animated progressive education spread far and wide, and they are far from dead; many teachers still seem to think that learning grammar stifles creativity. But across the nation, states are now insisting that students know where to place that comma.

Every state except Iowa has established academic standards in at least some subjects, and 44 have standards in the core academic disciplines (English, math, history, and science). Forty-eight have statewide testing programs, and most have aligned the tests to the standards in at least one subject. By 2003, according to current plans, students in 26 states will not graduate without passing a statewide test. Thirteen states and a number of school districts have also gotten tough about grade promotion.

Seemingly great news, but, alas, the Fordham Foundation estimates that only eight states and the District of Columbia have acceptable standards in all four subjects. The rest have "mediocre to miserable expectations for their students"—perhaps worse than no standards at all. And while 40 states are issuing report cards on schools, very few are actually rewarding those that do well. In fact, in many districts, it pays to be a lousy school, since poor performance earns extra money.

Nevertheless, the states are stumbling in the right direction—over the loud objections of some of the nation's leading educational lights. Deborah Meier—recipient of a MacArthur "genius" award, and the much-celebrated founder of schools in New York and Boston—has plenty of company in wanting "life scores based on living." Theodore Sizer, former dean of the Harvard Graduate School of Education, views "the myriad, detailed and mandatory state 'curriculum frameworks,' of whatever scholarly brilliance" as "attacks on intellectual freedom." High-stakes tests just "compound the felony." Jonathan Kozol, a man with many fans in the world of education and beyond, is positively apoplectic on the subject. Statewide tests, he says, force "scripted journeys, where there is no room for whimsical discoveries and unexpected learnings." They evoke memories of "another social order not so long ago that regimented all its children . . . to march with pedagogic uniformity, efficiency, and every competence one can conceive—except for independent will—right into Poland, Austria, and France, and World War II." (Mysteriously, France—with its own "pedagogic uniformity"—managed to avoid having such a pernicious social order.)

The views of Meier, Sizer, and Kozol are echoed by many teachers, parents, and students, whose voices the press seems eager to record. Their complaints seldom vary. "Standardize tests, standardize class, then standardize my mind!" Tests "do not measure creativity, music and artistic ability, ethics, human relationships, or independent thinking." "The fact that a child's future should be determined by knowing or not knowing certain dates or formulas is ridiculous and unfair."

Columnists and op-ed writers, too, are often part of the chorus of critics. Richard Rothstein, who writes on education for the *New York Times*, acknowledges that test scores are rising, but cautions: "More teenagers have fatty diets ... adolescent obesity has soared. Neither children nor our economy will prosper if graduates have higher scores, but are overweight, with poor exercise habits or irresponsible sexual behavior."

Maybe the readers of the *Times* lap up such material, but in general the public isn't buying. Eighty-three percent of parents (according to Public Agenda's nonpartisan polling) want standards, and 78 percent agree that children who don't know their stuff should not be promoted to the next grade. Roughly the same percentage favor high-stakes tests, and 63 percent believe inner-city youngsters should be held to the same standards as those in well-to-do suburbs.

But here's the rub: Standards (parents assume) mean minimum basic skills. Nothing fancy. And while they want high-stakes testing, fully half oppose using one test to decide promotion or graduation. The states that have a high-school exit exam thus have their work cut out for them. They all provide multiple opportunities to retake the test, but 50 percent of parents seem to want something more: alternative ways of assessing the students who don't pass, standards with exceptions. And that spells trouble ahead. Parental doubts will only increase as the high-stakes tests kick in. "When parents start to realize their [child] ... may not get a high-school diploma, more and more people will start raising their voices," a Massachusetts history teacher predicted in June. He is probably right. Failure rates have been high in his state. Last year, half the tenth-graders did not pass the statewide math test, while a third flunked English. These will become exit exams in 2001, although students will have numerous chances to retake the test before the end of twelfth grade.

The overall numbers are bad; those for black and Hispanic students are tragic. Across Massachusetts, 80 percent of non-Asian minority students failed the tenth-grade math assessment. Fifty-seven percent flunked English. And Massachusetts is not unique: The National Assessment for Educational Progress (NAEP) data describe a nationwide catastrophe. On average, black

17-year-olds are performing at the same level as (or below) white 13-year-olds. The Hispanic picture is the same or only slightly better, depending on the subject tested.

Civil-rights activists frequently charge that high-stakes tests are discriminatory and punitive. They "have a very large cost for people who are politically powerless," argues Gary Orfield of Harvard's Graduate School of Education. "If we take kids who are getting a bad education and coming from a situation of social crisis and then make them unemployable in the process, we are not helping them or their communities." The Mexican American Legal Defense and Education Fund has already been in court trying (unsuccessfully) to stop Texas from using its statewide test to determine high-school graduation. Hugh Price, president of the National Urban League, wants to halt all high-stakes testing until "school systems have introduced all of the ingredients for quality education."

In the absence of standards over many decades, however, those "ingredients" were never introduced. Disadvantaged students have never gotten the education they need. Kati Haycock heads the Education Trust, a Washington, D.C., organization devoted to promoting academic achievement among blacks, Hispanics, and poor children. "Traditionally, of course, most advocates for such children have shied away from high standards and high stakes," she notes. She is unequivocal, however, in her demand for no-nonsense standards with uncompromising consequences for those who fail to meet them. "Backing off from testing would just kick the problem of low student achievement under the rug again," she says.

Hugh Price wonders why future "deliverymen" and "short-order cooks" need to pass academic tests when they aren't college-bound. But if expectations for both students and teachers are raised, many kids who now seem headed for blue-collar work would acquire the skills that college-level courses and well-paid jobs require. And of course, youngsters do not become less employable (as Orfield suggests) when they fail to receive a meaningless diploma. Denying a student a fake credential does not keep him from getting a job; a worthless piece of paper does not impress an employer looking for workers who can read, write, and calculate.

The opponents of standards and accountability do have some legitimate arguments. It is the rare state that has superb tests like those in Massachusetts. Moreover, the least skilled students may get discouraged and drop out at a higher rate than they do today, economists Julian R. Betts and Robert M. Costrell say in a forthcoming Brookings Institution paper. On the other hand, by tenth grade, those at the bottom are already virtual dropouts. Their scores reflect poor attendance at school, Massachusetts data indicate. And anecdotal evidence suggests that even when they come, they are hardly present. They wander in and out of classes, pay little attention to instruction, and do no homework.

The disconnected are among the many students who need much better schooling at an earlier age. A lucky few are getting it in first-rate schools like the KIPP Academies in New York and Houston, recently showcased at the

Republican national convention. All the students at KIPP's South Bronx school are from very poor black or Hispanic families. As the school's literature acknowledges, "Illiteracy, drug abuse, broken homes, gangs, and juvenile crime" are rampant in the neighborhood in which these youngsters live. But KIPP has the highest reading and math scores of any middle school in the Bronx. KIPP's secret is a combination of inspired leadership and dedicated staff, a demanding curriculum, a strict behavioral code, long days—and continuous testing. "The more you test, the better students do," says David Levin, KIPP's director. "Regardless of what teaching style you use, there has to be a constant assessment in place that demonstrates real mastery of what you are teaching."

David Grissmer and three of his colleagues recently analyzed NAEP data for the RAND Corporation and found that "well-designed standards linked to assessments and some forms of accountability may change the incentives and productivity within public schools." This suggestion squares with much anecdotal information in Massachusetts: Kim Marshall, for example, is a fine principal in an inner-city elementary school in Boston. His students did poorly on the statewide tests, and he mobilized the school to respond. "We had a curriculum and test we could focus on," he says. Many districts across the state have responded to the new pressure by running summer programs for both students and teachers, placing new emphasis on intervention in the early grades, adding more reading and writing to the curriculum, and making other essential changes.

But will such efforts suffice? It's unlikely. More sweeping change is needed. Only a minority of public-school teachers, Public Agenda reports, have changed their teaching as a result of new state demands. That's not surprising, given the poor quality of leadership that principals often provide, and the general resistance to change. In addition, in too many schools, principals don't control their budgets, and have limited say over whom they hire. The market does not determine salaries. The school day and year are both too short, an astonishing amount of time is wasted, and homework is seldom assigned. Schools need the gifted graduates of the nation's best colleges, but the requirements for certification are often mind-numbing, and the work conditions a disaster. Rude and disorderly behavior is rampant, and the rewards for doing a bang-up job nonexistent. In fact, idealistic young teachers who give their all to their students frequently find themselves resented and isolated, they report.

Schools like KIPP are the face of success. But without further radical change, how many schools will come to look like KIPP in the foreseeable future? We're taking the right steps, but many more are needed. Time is short. The window of opportunity will quickly close if our urban students don't make impressive gains—if the racial gap in academic achievement doesn't narrow significantly. Either we move fast, or failing kids and public alarm will kill the long-overdue drive for rigorous standards and real accountability.

NO

Educating a Democracy: Standards and the Future of Public Education

Deborah Meier

In the past two years, the number of students expelled from elementary and secondary schools in Chicago has nearly doubled. Expelled kids get sent to something called "safe schools," run by for-profit organizations. When a reporter asked Chicago officials why the number of spaces in the for-profit academies was far smaller than the number of expelled students, the reporter was reassured. Not to worry. They don't all show up. Meanwhile, the city is writing new categories and new zero-tolerance policies to push reform along. Chicago is the home of get-tough reform, and all these changes have been made in the name of upgrading "standards." The results? Test scores over the past three years have risen, we are told, by 3.4 percent in Chicago. That's a few more right answers on a standardized test, maybe.

Back in my home state, Massachusetts, the town of Lynnfield announced that it was time to end METCO, a program that for twenty years brought minority children into nearly all-white, middle-class, suburban communities. The Board members explained to the press that the program wasn't helping the Lynnfield schools raise their "standards"—that is, their scores on the new tough state tests. Sometimes equity and excellence just don't mix well. So sorry.*

The stories of Chicago and Lynnfield capture a dark side of the "standards-based reform" movement in American education: the politically popular movement to devise national or state-mandated standards for what all kids should know, and high-stakes tests and sanctions to make sure they all know it. The stories show how the appeal to standards can mask and make way for other agendas: punishing kids, privatizing public education, giving up on equity.

I know how advocates of the movement to standardize standards will respond: "Good reform ideas can always be misused. Our proposals are designed to help kids, save public education, and ensure equity."

I disagree. Even in the hands of sincere allies of children, equity, and public education, the current push for far greater standardization than we've ever previously attempted is fundamentally misguided. It will not help to develop young minds, contribute to a robust democratic life, or aid the most vulnerable

---

* Eventually, Lynnfield backed off and decided to keep METCO but impose more stringent standards on METCO students than others—a decision that prompted METCO to cut off its relationship with Lynnfield.

of our fellow citizens. By shifting the locus of authority to outside bodies, it undermines the capacity of schools to instruct by example in the qualities of mind that schools in a democracy should be fostering in kids—responsibility for one's own ideas, tolerance for the ideas of others, and a capacity to negotiate differences. Standardization instead turns teachers and parents into the local instruments of externally imposed expert judgment. It thus decreases the chances that young people will grow up in the midst of adults who are making hard decisions and exercising mature judgment in the face of disagreements. And it squeezes out those schools and educators that seek to show alternate possibilities, to explore other paths.

The standardization movement is not based on a simple mistake. It rests on deep assumptions about the goals of education and the proper exercise of authority in the making of decisions—assumptions we ought to reject in favor of a different vision of a healthy democratic society. Drawing on my experience in schools in New York City and Boston, I show that this alternative vision isn't utopian, even if it might be messy—as democracy is always messy.

STANDARDS-BASED REFORM

Standards-based reform systems vary enormously in their details. But they are generally organized around a set of four interconnected mechanisms: first, an official document (sometimes called a framework) designed by experts in various fields that describes what kids should know and be able to do at given grade levels in different subjects; second, classroom curricula—commercial textbooks and scripted programs—that are expected to convey that agreed-upon knowledge; third, a set of assessment tools (tests) to measure whether children have achieved the goals specified in the framework; and fourth, a scheme of rewards and penalties directed at schools and school systems, but ultimately at individual kids, who fail to meet the standards as measured by the tests. Cut-off points are set at various politically feasible points—in some states they are pegged so that nearly 90 percent of the students fail whereas others fail less than 10 percent. School administrators (and possibly teachers) are fired if schools fail to reach particular goals after a given period of time, and kids are held back in grade, sent to summer school, and finally refused diplomas if they don't meet the cut-off scores.

Massachusetts, for instance, has recently devised tests in English, mathematics, history, and science (to be followed by other subjects over time) covering the state's mandated frameworks. The tests are given in grades four, eight, and ten. Beginning in 2003, students will need to pass the grade-ten tests to get a Massachusetts high school diploma; moreover, the tests are intended to serve as the sole criteria for rating schools, for admission to public colleges, and for as many other rewards and sanctions as busy state officials can devise.

The Massachusetts tests are not typical, but then each state has its own variant. The Massachusetts tests are unusually long (fifteen to twenty hours), and cover a startling amount of material. For fourth graders the history and social studies portions allow the test makers to ask questions about anything that happened between prehistoric times and 500 AD in "the world," and in the United States until 1865. While world history expands in the upper grades, you can get a high school diploma without ever studying US history after 1865. The science and math portions are equally an inch deep and a mile wide. And the selections and questions on the reading tests were initially designed with full knowledge (and intent) that, if scores do not immediately improve, eighty percent of all fourth graders would fail—even though Massachusetts fourth graders rank near the top in most national reading assessments.

But the specifics of the tests are not the central issue. Even if they were replaced by saner instruments, they would still embody a fundamentally misguided approach to school reform. To see just how they are misguided, we need first to ask about their rationale. Why are these tests being imposed?

Why Standards?

Six basic assumptions underlie the current state and national standard setting and testing programs now off the ground in 49 of 50 states (all but Iowa):

1. *Goals:* It is possible and desirable to agree on a single definition of what constitutes a well-educated 18-year-old and demand that every school be held to the same definition. We have, it is argued, gotten by without such an agreement at a great cost—witness the decline of public education—in comparison to other nations with tight national systems.
2. *Authority:* The task of defining "well-educated" is best left to experts—educators, political officials, leaders from industry and the major academic disciplines—operating within a system of political checks and balances. That each state's definition at the present time varies so widely suggests the eventual need for a single national standard.
3. *Assessment:* With a single definition in place, it will be possible to measure and compare individuals and schools across communities—local, state, national, international. To this end, curricular norms for specific ages and grades should be translated into objective tests that provide a system of uniform scores for all public, and if possible private, schools and districts. Such scores should permit public comparisons between and among students, schools, districts, and states at any point in time.
4. *Enforcement:* Sanctions, too, need to be standardized, thus removed from local self-interested parties—including parents, teachers, and local boards. Only a more centralized and distant system can resist the pressures from people closest to the child—the very people who have become accustomed to low standards.

5. *Equity:* Expert-designed standards, imposed through tests, are the best way to achieve educational equity. While a uniform national system would work best if all students had relatively equal resources, equity requires introducing such a system as rapidly as possible regardless of disparities. It is especially important for schools with scarcer resources to focus their work, concentrating on the essentials. Standardization with remotely controlled sanctions thus offers the best chance precisely for underfunded communities and schools, and for less well-educated and less powerful families.

6. *Effective Learning:* Clear-cut expectations, accompanied by automatic rewards and punishments, will produce greater effort, and effort—whether induced by the desire for rewards, fear of punishment, or shame—is the key to learning. When teachers as well as students know what constitutes failure, and also know the consequences of failure, a rational system of rewards and punishments becomes an effective tool. Automatic penalties work for schooling much as they do for crime and punishment: consistency and certainty are the keys. For that reason compassion requires us to stand firm, even in the face of pain and failure in the early years.

A Crisis?

The current standards-based reform movement took off in 1983 in response to the widely held view that America was at extreme economic risk, largely because of bad schools. The battle cry—called out first in *A Nation at Risk*—launched an attack on dumb teachers, uncaring mothers, social promotion, and general academic permissiveness. Teachers and a new group labeled "educationists" were declared the main enemy, thus undermining their credibility, and setting the stage for cutting them and their concerns out of the cure. According to critics, American education needed to be reimagined, made more rigorous, and, above all, brought under the control of experts who—unlike educators and parents—understood the new demands of our economy and culture. The cure might curtail the work of some star teachers and star schools, and it might lead, as the education chief of Massachusetts recently noted, to a lot of crying fourth graders. But the gravity of the long-range risks to the nation demanded strong medicine.

Two claims were thus made: that our once-great public system was no longer performing well, and that its weaknesses were undermining America's economy. Most critics have long agreed that the data in support of the claim about school decline are at best weak (see Richard Rothstein's 1998 book, *The Way We Were?*). As a result, the debate shifted—although the average media story hardly noticed—to an acknowledgement that even if there wasn't a decline in school achievement, the demands of the new international economy required reinventing our schools anyway. Whether the crisis was real or imagined, change was required. But efforts to induce changes in teaching and learning met with widespread resistance from many different quarters—from citizens, parents, teachers, and local officials. Some schools changed dramatically, and some changed bits and pieces, but the timetable was far too slow for the reformers. The constituents who originally coalesced around *A Nation at Risk* began to argue that the fault lay either in the nature of public schooling itself or in the excesses of local empowerment. The cure would have to combine more competition from the private or semi-private sector and more rigorous control by external experts who understood the demands of our economy and had the clout to impose change. This latter viewpoint has dominated the standards-based reform movement.

Unfortunately, a sense of reality has been lost in these shifting terms of debate. Now, fifteen years after analysts discovered the great crisis of American education, the American economy is soaring, the productivity of our workforce is probably tops in the world, and our system of advanced education is the envy of the world. In elementary school literacy (where critics claim that sentimental pedagogues have for decades failed to teach children how to read), the United States still ranks second or third, topped only by one or another of the Scandinavian countries. While we rank lower in math and science tests, we continue to lead the world in technology and inventiveness. If the earlier argument was right and economic prowess requires good schooling, then teachers in America ought to be congratulated, and someone should be embarrassed by the false alarm. Instead, the idea that schools are a disaster, and that fixing them fast is vital to our economy, has become something of a truism. It remains the excuse for all reform efforts, and for carrying them out on the scale and pace proposed.

Educators from the Progressive tradition are often accused of "experimenting" on kids. But never in the history of the nation have Progressives proposed an experiment so drastic, vast, and potentially serious in its real-life impact on millions of young people. If the consequences are other than those its supporters hope for, the harm to the nation's educational system and the youngsters involved—maybe even to our economy—will be large and hard to undo.

The Real Crisis

The coalition of experts which produced *A Nation at Risk* were wrong when they announced the failure of American public education and its critical role in our economic decline. Constructive debate about reform should begin by acknowledging this misjudgment. But it should then also acknowledge the even bigger crisis that schools have played a major part in deepening, if not actually creating, and could play a big part in curing. This crisis requires quite a different set of responses, often in direct conflict with standardization.

An understanding of this other crisis begins by noting that we have the lowest voter turnout by far of any modern industrial country; we are exceptional for the absence of responsible care for our most vulnerable citizens (we spend less on child welfare—baby care, medical care, family leave—than almost every competitor); we don't come close to our competitors in income equity; and our high rate of (and investment in) incarceration places us in a class by ourselves. All of these, of course, affect some citizens far more than others: and the heaviest burdens fall on the poor, the young, and people of color.

These social and political indicators are suggestive of a crisis in human relationships. Virtually all discussions—right or left—about what's wrong in our otherwise successful society acknowledge the absence of a sense of responsibility for one's community and of decency in personal relationships. An important cause of this subtler crisis, I submit, is that the closer our youth come to adulthood the less they belong to communities that include responsible adults, and the more stuck they are in peer-only subcultures. We've created two parallel cultures, and it's no wonder the ones on the grown-up side are feeling angry at the way the ones on the other side live and act: apparently foot-loose and fancy-free but in truth often lost, confused, and knit-together for temporary self-protection. The consequences are critical for all our youngsters, but obviously more severe—often disastrous—for those less identified with the larger culture of success.

Many changes in our society aided and abetted the shifts that have produced this alienation. But one important change has been in the nature of schooling. Our schools have grown too distant, too big, too standardized, too uniform, too divorced from their communities, too alienating of young from old and old from young. Few youngsters and few teachers have an opportunity to know each other by more than name (if that); and schools are organized so as to make "knowing each other" nearly impossible. In such settings it's hard to teach young people how to be responsible to others, or to concern themselves with their community. At best they develop loyalties to the members of their immediate circle of friends (and perhaps their own nuclear family). Even when they take on teen jobs their fellow workers and their customers are likely to be peers. Apprenticeship as a way to learn to be an adult is disappearing. The public and its schools, the "real" world and the schoolhouse, young people and adults have become disconnected, and until they are reconnected no list of particular bits of knowledge will be of much use.

In my youth there were over 200,000 School Boards. Today there are fewer than 20,000, and the average school, which in my youth had only a few hundred students, now holds thousands. As I write, Miami and Los Angeles are in the process of building the two largest high schools ever. The largest districts and the largest and most anonymous schools are again those that serve our least advantaged children.

Because of the disconnection between the public and its schools, the power to protect or support them now lies increasingly in the hands of public or private bodies that have no immediate stake in the daily life of the students. CEOs, federal and state legislators, university experts, presidential think tanks make more and more of the daily decisions about schools. For example, the details of the school day and year are determined by state legislators—often down to minutes per day for each subject taught, and whether to promote Johnny from third to fourth grade. The school's budget depends on it. Site-based school councils are increasingly the "in" thing, just as the scope of their responsibility narrows.

Public schools, after a romance with local power—beginning in the late 1960s and ending in the early '90s—are increasingly organized as interchangeable units of a larger state organism, each expected to conform to the intelligence of some central agency or expert authority. The locus of authority in young people's lives has shifted away from the adults kids know well and who know the kids well—at a cost. Home schooling or private schooling seem more and more the natural next step for those with the means to do so and the desire to remain in authority.

Our school troubles are not primarily due to too-easy coursework or too much tolerance for violence. The big trouble lies instead in the company our children keep—or, more precisely, don't keep. They no longer keep company with us—the grown-ups they are about to become. And the adults they do encounter seem less and less worthy of their respect. What kid, after all, wants to be seen emulating people he's been told are too dumb to exercise power, and are simply implementing the commands of the real experts?

ALTERNATIVE ASSUMPTIONS

Just as the conventional policy assumptions emerge naturally from a falsely diagnosed crisis, so does the crisis I have sketched suggest an alternative set of assumptions.

1. *Goals:* In a democracy, there are multiple, legitimate definitions of "a good education" and "well-educated," and it is desirable to acknowledge that plurality. Openly differing viewpoints constitute a healthy tension in a democratic, pluralistic society. Even where a mainstream view exists, alternate views that challenge the consensus are critical to the society's health. Young people need to be exposed to competing views, and to adults debating choices about what's most important. As John Stuart Mill said, "It is not the mind of heretics that are deteriorated most, by the ban placed on all inquiry which does not end in the orthodox conclusions. The greatest harm is done to those who are not heretics, and whose whole mental development is cramped, and their reason cowed, by the fear of heresy."

2. *Authority:* In fundamental questions of education, experts should be subservient to citizens. Experts and laymen alike have an essential role in shaping both ends and means, the what and the how. While it is wise to involve experts from both business and the academy, they provide only one set of opinions, and are themselves rarely of a single mind. Moreover, it is educationally important for young people to be in the company of adults—teachers, family members, and other adults in their own communities—powerful enough to decide important things. They need to witness the exercise of judgment, the weighing of means and ends by people they can imagine becoming; and they need to see how responsible adults handle disagreement. If we think the adults in children's lives are, in Jefferson's

words, "not enlightened enough to exercise their control with a whole-some discretion, the remedy is not to take it from them, but to inform their discretion by education."

3. *Assessment*: Standardized tests are too simple and simple-minded for high-stakes assessment of children and schools. Important decisions regarding kids and teachers should always be based on multiple sources of evidence that seem appropriate and credible to those most concerned. These are old testing truisms, backed even by the testing industry, which has never claimed the level of omniscience many standards advocates assume of it. The state should only require that forms of assessment be public, consti-tutionally sound, and subject to a variety of "second opinions" by experts representing other interested parties. Where states feel obliged to set norms—for example, in granting state diplomas or access to state universities—these should be flexible, allowing schools maximum autonomy to demon-strate the ways they have reached such norms through other forms of as-sessment.

4. *Enforcement*: Sanctions should remain in the hands of the local com-munity, to be determined by people who know the particulars of each child and each situation. The power of both business and the academy are already substantial; their access to the means of persuasion (televi-sion, the press, etc.) and their power to determine access to jobs and higher education already impinge on the freedom of local communities. Children, their families, and their communities should not be required to make decisions about their own students and their own work based on such external measures. It is sufficient that they are obliged to take them into account in their deliberations about their children's future options.

5. *Equity*: A more fair distribution of resources is the principal means for achieving educational equity. The primary national responsibility is to narrow the resource gap between the most and least advantaged, both between 9 a.m. and 3 p.m. and during the other five-sixths of their waking lives, when rich and poor students are also learning—but very different things. To this end publicly accessible comparisons of educational achieve-ment should always include information regarding the relative resources that the families of students, schools, and communities bring to the school-ing enterprise.

6. *Effective Learning*: Improved learning is best achieved by improving teach-ing and learning relationships, by enlisting the energies of both teachers and learners. The kinds of learning required of citizens cannot be accomplished by standardized and centrally imposed systems of learning, even if we desired it for other reasons. Human learning, to be efficient, effective, and long-lasting, requires the engagement of learners on their own behalf, and rests on the relationships that develop between schools and their commu-nities, between teachers and their students, and between the individual learner and what is to be learned.

No "scientific" argument can conclusively determine whether this set of assumptions or the set sketched earlier is true. Although some research suggests that human learning is less efficient when motivated by rewards and punishments, and that fear is a poor motivator, I doubt that further research will settle the issue. But because of the crisis of human relationships, I urge that we consider the contrary claims more seriously than we have. We may even find that in the absence of strong human relationships rigorous intellectual training in the most fundamental academic subjects can't flourish. In a world shaped by centralized media, restoring a greater balance of power between local communities and central authorities, between institutions subject to democratic control and those beyond their control, may be vastly more important than educational reformers bent on increased centralization acknowledge.

An Alternative Model

Suppose, then, that we think about school reform in light of these alternative assumptions. What practical model of schools and learning do they support? In brief, our hope lies in schools that are more personal, compelling, and attractive than the internet or TV, where youngsters can keep company with interesting and powerful adults, who are in turn in alliance with the students' families and local institutions. We need to surround kids with adults who know and care for our children, who have opinions and are accustomed to expressing them publicly, and who know how to reach reasonable collective decisions in the face of disagreement. That means increasing local decision-making, and simultaneously decreasing the size and bureaucratic complexity of schools. Correspondingly, the worst thing we can do is to turn teachers and schools into the vehicles for implementing externally-imposed standards.

Is such an alternative practical? Are the assumptions behind it mere sentiment?

At the Mission Hill in Boston, one of ten new Boston public schools initiated by the Boston Public Schools and the Boston Teachers Union, we designed a school to support such alternative practices. The families that came to Mission Hill were chosen by lottery and represent a cross-section of Boston's population. We intentionally kept the school small—less than 200 students ages five to thirteen—so that the adults could meet regularly, take responsibility for each others' work, and argue over how best to get things right. Parents join the staff not only for formal governance meetings, but for monthly informal suppers, conversations, good times. Our oldest kids—the eighth graders—will graduate only when they can show us all that they meet our graduation standards, which are the result of lots of parent, staff, and community dialogue over several years.

All our students study—once when they are little, once when they are older—a school-wide interdisciplinary curriculum. Last fall they all became experts on Boston and Mission Hill, learning its history (and their own), geography, architecture, distinct neighborhoods, and figures of importance.

Last winter they all recreated ancient Egypt at 67 Allegheny Street. This coming winter they will recreate ancient China. Each spring they dig into a science-focused curriculum theme. The common curriculum allowed us, for example, to afford professional and amateur Egyptologists who joined us from time to time as lively witnesses to a life-long passion. We have a big central corridor which serves as our public mall, where kids paint murals, mix together to read, and talk across ages. High school students, who share the building with us, read with little ones, take them on trips, and generally model what it can mean to be a more responsible and well-educated person.

We invented our own standards—not out of whole cloth but with an eye to what the world out there expects and what we deem valuable and important. And we assessed them through the work the kids do and the commentary of others about that work. Our standards are intended to deepen and broaden young people's habits of mind, their craftsmanship, and their work habits. Other schools may select quite a different way of describing and exhibiting their standards. But they too need to consciously construct their standards in ways that give schooling purpose and coherence, and then commit themselves to achieving them. And the kids need to understand the standards and their rationale. They must see school as not just a place to get a certificate, but a place that lives by the same standards it sets for them. Thus the Mission Hill school not only sets standards but has considerable freedom and flexibility with regard to how it spends its public funds and organizes its time to attain them. All ten pilot schools offer examples of different ways this might play out, ways that could be replicated in all Boston schools.

Standards of assessment are not once-for-all issues. We reexamine our school constantly to see that it remains a place that engages all of us in tough but interesting learning tasks, nourishes and encourages the development of reasonable and judicious trust, and nurtures a passion for making sense of things and the skills needed to do so. We expect disagreements—sometimes painful ones. We know that even well-intentioned, reasonable people cross swords over deeply held beliefs. But we know, too, that these differences can be sources of valuable education when the school itself can negotiate the needed compromises.

What is impressive at Mission Hill, in the other Pilot schools, at the Central Park East Schools in New York's East Harlem (where I worked for 25 years), and the thousands of other small schools like them, is that over time the kids buy in. These schools receive the same per capita public funding as other schools, are subject to city and state testing, and must obey the same basic health, safety, and civil rights regulations. But because these schools are small, the families and faculties are together by choice, and all concerned can exercise substantial power over staffing, scheduling, curriculum, and assessment, the schools' cultural norms and expectations are very different than most other public schools.

The evidence suggests that most youngsters have a sufficiently deep hunger for the relationships these schools offer them—among kids and between adults and kids—that they choose it over the alternative cultures on the Net, tube, and street. Over ninety percent of Central Park East's very typical students stuck it out, graduated, and went on to college. And most persevered through higher education. Did they ever rebel, get mad at us, reassert their contrary values and adolescent preferences? Of course. Did we fail with some? Yes. But it turns out that the hunger for grown-up connections is strong enough to make a difference, if we give it a chance. Studies conducted on the other similar schools launched in New York between 1975 and 1995 showed the same pattern of success.

Standards, yes. Absolutely. But as Ted Sizer, who put the idea of standards on the map in the early 1980s, also told us then: we need standards held by real people who matter in the lives of our young. School, family, and community must forge their own, in dialogue with and in response to the larger world of which they are a part. There will always be tensions, but if the decisive, authoritative voice always comes from anonymous outsiders, then kids cannot learn what it takes to develop their own voice.

I know this "can be" because I've been there. The flowering of so many new public schools of choice over the past two decades proves that under widely different circumstances, very different kinds of leadership and different auspices, a powerful alternative to externally-imposed standards is available.

But I also know the powerful reasons why it "can't be"—because I've witnessed first-hand the resistance to allowing others to follow suit, much less encouraging or mandating them to do so. The resistance comes not simply from bad bureaucrats or fearful unions (the usual bogeymen), but legislators and mayors and voters, from citizens who think that anything public must be all things to all constituents (characterless and mediocre by definition), and from various elites who see teachers and private citizens as too dumb to engage in making important decisions. That's a heady list of resisters.

But small self-governing schools of choice—operating with considerable flexibility and freedom—also resonate with large numbers of people, including many of those who are gathering around charter schools, and even some supporters of privatization and home schooling. They too come from a wide political spectrum and could be mobilized.

Accountability

And yet doubts about accountability will linger. In a world of smaller, more autonomous schools not responsible to centralized standards, how will we know who is doing a good job and who isn't? How can we prevent schools from claiming they're doing just fine (and being believed), when it may not be true? Are we simply forced to trust them, with no independent evidence?

What lies behind these worries? For those who accept the conventional assumptions, anything but top-down standardization seems pointless. But for those whose concern is more practical there are some straightforward answers to the issue of accountability that do not require standardization.

To begin with, I am not advocating the elimination of all systems for taking account of how schools and students are doing. In any case, that is hardly a danger. Americans invented the modern, standardized, norm-referenced test. Our students have been taking more tests, more often, than any nation on the face of the earth, and schools and districts have been going public with test scores starting almost from the moment children enter school. By third or fourth grade (long before any of our international competitors bother to test children) we have test data for virtually all schools—by race, class, and gender. We know exactly how many kids did better or worse in each and every subcategory. We have test data for almost every grade thereafter in reading and math, and to some degree in all other subjects. This has been the case for nearly half a century. Large numbers of our eighteen-year-olds now take standardized college entry tests (SATs and ACTs). In addition, the national government now offers us its own tests—the NAEP—which are given to an uncontaminated sample of students from across the United States and now reported by grade and state. And all of the above is very public.

In addition, public schools have been required to produce statements attesting to their financial integrity—how they spend their money—at least as rigorously as any business enterprise. They are held accountable for regularly reporting who works for them and what their salaries are. In most systems there are tightly prescribed rules and regulations; schools are obliged to fill out innumerable forms regarding almost every aspect of their work—how many kids are receiving special education, how many incidents of violence, how many suspensions, how many graduates, what grades students have received, how many hours and minutes they study each and every subject, and the credentials of their faculties. This information, and much more, is public. And the hiring and firing of superintendents has become a very common phenomenon.

In a nation in which textbooks are the primary vehicle for distributing school knowledge, a few major textbook publishers, based on a few major state textbook laws, dominate the field, offering most teachers, schools, and students very standardized accounts of what is to be learned, and when and how to deliver this knowledge. Moreover, most textbooks have always come armed with their own end-of-chapter tests, increasingly designed to look like the real thing; indeed, test makers also are the publishers of many of the major standardized tests.

In short, we have been awash in accountability and standardization for a very long time. What we are missing is precisely the qualities that the last big wave of reform was intended to respond to: teachers, kids, and families who don't know each other or each other's work and don't take responsibility for it. We are missing communities built around their own articulated and public standards and ready to show them off to others.

The schools I have worked in and support have shown how much more powerful accountability becomes when one takes this latter path. The work produced by Central Park East students, for example, is collected regularly in portfolios; it is examined (and in the case of high school students, judged) by tough internal and external reviewers, in a process that closely resembles a doctoral dissertation oral exam. The standards by which a student is judged are easily accessible to families, clear to kids, and capable of being judged by other parties. In addition such schools undergo school-wide external assessments which take into account the quality of their curriculum, instruction, staff development, and culture as well as the impact of the school on student's future success (in college, work, etc.).

Are the approaches designed by Central Park East or Mission Hill the best way? That's probably the wrong question. We never intended to suggest that everyone should follow our system. It would be nice if it were easier for others to adopt our approach, but it would be even better if it were easier—in fact required—that others adopt alternatives to it, including the use of standardized tests if they so choose. My argument is for more local control, not for one true way.

I opt for more local control not because I think the larger society has no common interests at stake in how we educate all children, nor because local people are smarter or intrinsically more honorable. Of course not. The interests of wider publics are important in my way of thinking. I know that pressure exists at Mission Hill not to accept or push out students who are difficult to educate, who will make us look worse on any test, or whose families are a nuisance. It's a good thing that others are watching us to prevent such exclusion.

But in 1999, the United States is hardly in danger of too much localized power in education. (The only local powers we seem to be interested in expanding are those that allow us to re-segregate our schools by race or gender.) What is missing is balance—some power in the hands of those whose agenda is first and foremost the feelings of particular kids, their particular families, their perceived local values and needs. Without such balance my knowledge that holding David over in third grade will not produce the desired effects is useless knowledge. Neither is my knowledge of different ways to reach him through literature or history. This absence of local power is bad for David's education and bad for democracy. A back-seat driver may know more than the actual driver, but there are limits to what can be accomplished from the rear seat.

In short, the argument is not about the need for standards or accountability, but about what kind serves us best. I believe standardization will make it harder to hold people accountable and harder to develop sound and useful standards. The intellectual demands of the 21st century, as well as the demands of democratic life, are best met by preserving plural definitions of a good education, local decision-making, and respect for ordinary human judgments.

EDUCATION AND DEMOCRACY

If we are to make use of what we knew in Dewey's day (and know even better today) about how the human species best learns, we will have to start by throwing away the dystopia of the ant colony, the smoothly functioning (and quietly humming) factory where everything goes according to plan, and replace it with a messy, often rambunctious, community, with its multiple demands and complicated trade-offs. The new schools that might better serve democracy and the economy will have to be capable of constantly remaking themselves and still provide for sufficient stability, routine, ritual, and shared ethos. Impossible? Of course. So such schools will veer too far one way or the other at different times in their history, will learn from each other, shift focus, and find a new balance. There will always be a party of order and a party of messiness.

But if schools are not all required to follow all the same fads, maybe they will learn something from their separate experiments. And that will help to nurture the two indispensable traits of a democratic society: a high degree of tolerance for others, indeed genuine empathy for them, and a high degree of tolerance for uncertainty, ambiguity, and puzzlement, indeed enjoyment of them.

A vibrant and nurturing community, with clear and regular guideposts—its own set of understandings, and a commitment to each other that feels something rather like love and affection—can sustain such rapid change without losing its humanity. Such a community must relish its disagreements, its oddballs, its misfits. Not quite families, but closer to our definition of family than factory, such schools will make high demands on their members, have a sustaining and relentless sense of purpose and coherence, but be ready also to always (at least sometimes) even reconsider their own core beliefs. We will come home exhausted, but not burned out.

Everything that moves us toward these qualities will be good for the ideal of democracy. A democracy in which less than half its members see themselves as "making enough difference" to bother to vote in any election is surely endangered—far more endangered, at risk, than our economy. It's for the loss of belief in the capacity to influence the world, not our economic ups and downs, that we educators should accept some responsibility. What I have learned from thirty years in small powerful schools is that it is here above all that schools can make a difference, that they can alter the odds.

We can't beat the statistical advantage on the next round of tests that being advantaged has over being disadvantaged; we can, however, substantially affect the gap between rich and poor where it will count, in the long haul of life. Even there it's hard to see how schools by themselves can eliminate the gap, but we can stop enlarging it. The factory-like schools we invented a century ago to handle the masses were bound to enlarge the gap. But trained mindlessness at least fit the world of work so many young people were destined for. We seem now to be reinventing a 21st century version of the factory-like school—for the mindworkers of tomorrow.

It is a matter of choice—such a future does not roll in on the wheels of inevitability. We have the resources, the knowledge, and plenty of living examples of the many different kinds of schools that might serve our needs better. All we need is a little more patient confidence in the good sense of "the people"—in short, a little more commitment to democracy.

DISCUSSION QUESTIONS

1. Many Americans seem to feel that school quality is declining. Do you agree? Do you think that schools are effectively educating students? Are graduates of public schools able to compete successfully in the world economy?
2. Will accountability measures improve student learning? Are students who are not learning likely to improve their performances in response to a change in the incentive structure (such as a test for graduation)? Or do these students face more fundamental challenges to learning?
3. Proponents like Thernstrom argue that standards and accountability measures will help students at failing schools most of all. Why do they think this is the case, and do you agree with this argument? What about students at the best schools—will they benefit?
4. One of the controversies over shared standards is that they define a single set of things to be learned, and that that set often excludes some of the more marginal voices and issues in American culture. Since such issues and voices often tend to be the most critical of American culture and history, there is the danger that such standards will lead to an uncritical mass of conformists graduating from our schools. Is such a concern justified? Are there ways to avoid this danger? How would you go about selecting a list of standards in a field such as history, for example?
5. Each of these articles contains an implicit notion of what goals we should set and what results we should ask of a system of public education. What are these competing notions? In what ways do you see them as adequate or inadequate?
6. What role do you think public education should play in a democracy? Do the arguments in either of the articles provide a policy proposal that would help the school system play the role that you think it should?
7. What role should the federal government have in formulating and enacting an education policy? Should the federal government be more actively involved in elementary and secondary education policy, or should that role be largely retained by states and localities?

WEB REFERENCES

Brown Center on Education Policy, Brookings Institution, http://www.brookings.edu/dybdocroot/gs/brown/brown_hp.htm.

CRESST Homepage, http://cresst96.cse.ucla.edu/index.htm.

Education Next: A Journal of Opinion and Research, http://www.educationnext.org/.

National Center for Education Statistics, http://nces.ed.gov/.

National Center for Fair and Open Testing, http://www.fairtest.org.

National Council on Measurement in Education, http://www.ncme.org.

National Library of Education, http://www.ed.gov/NLE/.

FURTHER READING

Berliner, David C. and Bruce J. Biddle. *The Manufactured Crisis: Myths, Fraud, and the Attack on America's Public Schools.* New York: Addison-Wesley, 1995.

Hanushek, Eric A. and Dale W. Jorgenson, eds. *Improving America's Schools: The Role of Incentives.* Washington, D.C.: National Academy Press, 1996.

Hill, Paul T. and Robin J. Lake. *Charter Schools and Accountability in Public Education.* Washington, D.C.: Brookings Institution, 2002.

Hirsch, E. D. *The Schools We Need: And Why We Don't Have Them.* New York: Anchor Books, 1999.

Hirsch, E. D. and Mulcahy, Pat, eds. *Cultural Literacy: What Every American Needs to Know.* Boston: Houghton Mifflin, 1987.

Jennings, John F. *Why National Standards and Tests? Politics and the Quest for Better Schools.* Thousand Oaks, Calif.: Sage Publications, 1998.

Kearns, David T. and James Harvey, eds. *A Legacy of Learning: Your Stake in Standards and New Kinds of Public Schools.* Washington, D.C.: Brookings Institution, 2000.

Klein, Stephen P. and Laura Hamilton. *Large Scale Testing: Current Practices and New Directions.* Santa Monica, Calif.: RAND Education, 1999.

Kohn, Alfie. *The Case against Standardized Testing: Raising the Scores, Ruining the Schools.* Portsmouth, N.H.: Heinemann, 1999.

Kozol, Jonathan. *Savage Inequalities: Children in America's Schools.* New York: Crown Publishers, 1991.

Lemann, Nicholas. *The Big Test: The Secret History of the American Meritocracy.* New York: Farrar, Straus and Giroux, 1999.

Lieberman, Myron. *Public Education: An Autopsy.* Cambridge, Mass.: Harvard University Press, 1993.

Loveless, Tom, ed. *The Great Curriculum Debate: How Should We Teach Reading and Math?* Washington, D.C.: Brookings Institution, 2001.

National Endowment for the Humanities, Lynne V. Cheney, chairman. *National Tests: What Other Countries Expect Their Students to Know.* National Endowment for the Humanities, 1991.

Ohanian, Susan. *One Size Fits Few: The Folly of Educational Standards.* Portsmouth, N.H.: Heinemann, 1999.

Peterson, Paul E. "A Report Card on School Choice." *Commentary,* vol. 104 (October 1997).

Ravitch, Diane. *Left Back: A Century of Failed School Reforms.* New York: Simon & Schuster, 2000.

Ravitch, Diane, ed. *Brookings Papers on Education Policy: Accountability and Its Consequences for Students: Are Children Hurt or Helped by Standards-Based Reforms?* Washington, D.C.: Brookings Institution, 2002.

Rothstein, Richard. *The Way We Were? Debunking the Myth of America's Declining Schools.* New York: Century Foundation Press. 1998.

Sacks, Peter. *Standardized Minds: The High Price of America's Testing Culture and What We Can Do to Change It.* Cambridge, Mass.: Perseus Books, 2000.

Smith, Kevin B. and Kenneth J. Meier. *The Case against School Choice: Politics, Markets, and Fools.* New York: M. E. Sharpe, 1995.

Strickland, Kathleen and James Strickland. *Reflections on Assessment: Its Purposes, Methods, and Effects on Learning.* Portsmouth, N.H.: Boynton/Cook Publishers, 1998.

Chapter 3

ENTITLEMENTS

"Should Social Security Be Privatized?"

YES: Michael Tanner "'Saving' Social Security Is Not Enough" The Cato Institute

NO: Brooke Harrington "Investor Beware: Can Small Investors Survive Social Security Privatization?" *The American Prospect*

Since its inception more than half a century ago, Social Security has enjoyed widespread public support. It continues to be one of the most politically popular federal programs—so popular, in fact, that it is often referred to as the untouchable "third rail" of American politics because tampering with Social Security has been considered tantamount to political suicide for elected officials. But in recent years the third rail of American politics appears to be losing some voltage. Amid growing concern that Social Security as it is currently structured will be unable to meet the demand for benefits likely to arise with the retirement of the baby boom generation, calls for overhauling the system have become more frequent, and there appears to be widespread support for some type of reform. Politicians, including former President Clinton in his 1998 State of the Union speech, have openly called for making Social Security a priority; before spending projected budget surpluses on other programs, President Clinton implored legislators to "save Social Security first." More recently, the Bush administration has proposed the use of voluntary personal retirement accounts that would purportedly provide higher pension incomes and streamline the efficiency of the Social Security system. The President's Commission on Social Security argues that "by allowing investment choice, individuals would be free to pursue higher expected rates of return on their Social Security contributions," and concludes that "Social Security will be strengthened if modernized to include a system of voluntary personal accounts."[1]

Social Security is perhaps the most visible of a range of entitlement programs that have been the subject of reform efforts in recent years. Such programs—which include Medicare, Medicaid, farm price supports, unemployment insurance, and food stamps as well as Social Security—are referred to as entitlements because all who meet legally established requirements are entitled to receive benefits. Unlike nonentitlement programs, for which total spending is determined by the legislature, spending on such programs is determined entirely by the number of eligible recipients. The result, of course, is that as the number of eligible recipients increases, the budgets of such programs grow accordingly without explicit political decisions to increase spending. The impetus for reforming these programs comes not only from their current size and rapid growth, but from the expectation that future growth may produce budgetary shortfalls.

Social Security was initiated in 1935 when President Roosevelt signed the Social Security Act into law. At the time, the program was designed to protect the elderly from a life of poverty; indeed, much of the political support for Social Security derives from its function as a retirement program. But Social Security is more than that: In addition to retirement benefits, Social Security provides disability benefits to workers unable to work, and benefits to survivors (including children) of workers who die before they retire. Taken together, these benefits are significant and widespread: Almost 45 million Americans received more than $385 billion in old-age benefits, survivor benefits, or disability insurance benefits in 1999 as a result of Social Security.[2] Less than 66 percent of Social Security recipients are retired workers; 12 percent are survivors of deceased workers, 16 percent are spouses and children, and 11 percent are disabled workers. The value of survivor and disability benefits provided by Social Security is significant, particularly when compared with the cost of comparable policies in the private sector. For example, it is estimated that Social Security benefits for an individual amount to a $203,000 disability policy in the private sector, and that the life insurance that Social Security provides for a young person with two children nearly equals a $295,000 policy.

To receive Social Security benefits, workers must contribute for at least 10 years, and they must reach the minimum retirement age of 65 (reduced benefits are available from the age of 62, and special credit is given for those who delay retirement until 70). The retirement age is gradually being adjusted upward, to the age of 67 for those born in 1960 or later.[3] Contributions take the form of a payroll tax, which initially was just 1 percent of income—reflecting its more modest beginnings—but has grown considerably since that time. The current payroll tax rate is 15.3 percent, with half that percentage supplied by employees and the other half by employers. Fully 96 percent of American workers currently contribute to the Social Security program. The tax is applied to all income below a legally defined income level adjusted annually for inflation, which was $84,900 in 2001;[4] earnings in excess of that level are not subject to the payroll tax.[5] As a result, Social Security contributions tend to be regressive, with low- and middle-income workers paying a larger percentage of their total earnings than high-income workers. Benefit levels are based on earnings over 35 years, and because the program is wholly operated by the federal government, there are no differences across states or cities for individuals with similar work histories (e.g., cost-of-living differences are not accounted for). Though contributions are regressive, the benefit formula is progressive. The percentage of income replaced for high-income earners is lower than for low-income earners; so while high-income earners receive a larger benefit, the percentage of income replaced is lower. For example, average low-wage earners receive approximately 78 percent of their preretirement income, whereas high-wage earners receive approximately 35.5 percent.[6] Further, a guaranteed minimum monthly benefit protects the lowest-wage earners.

While Social Security taxes are paid into a trust fund, the program is truly a pay-as-you-go system, with current workers paying for existing retirees. Politically, this type of system is easy to initiate and difficult to terminate. Initially, social insurance programs funded in this way benefit from large receipts paid by existing workers contributing to a program on which relatively few retirees draw; therefore, initial tax rates can be modest. However, once the program is fully developed, with current workers' contributions actuarially equivalent to benefit payments, such programs are exceedingly difficult to terminate because future liabilities—commitments to existing workers to pay their future retirement benefits—continue while contributions would evaporate. Therefore, terminating a pay-as-you-go program requires paying for these unfunded liabilities, which in the case of Social Security would amount to trillions of dollars. In addition to the economic difficulties, attempts to end such a system would face significant political resistance from current and future beneficiaries as well as from the interest groups organized to protect such programs.

The aging U.S. population, coupled with existing entitlement commitments, leads to future scenarios where an increasing share of national income is devoted to Social Security and subsidized medical care. In 1995, the United States spent about 4.1 percent of gross domestic product (GDP) on pension support, while some European countries spent over 10 percent.[7] According to 1999 budget projections, Social Security expenditures as a percentage of GDP are projected to rise from 4.5 percent in 1997 to 6.5 percent in 2050, while Medicaid and Medicare expenditures are projected to rise from 3.6 percent of GDP in 1997 to 12.8 percent in 2050.[8] The projected growth in this spending is even more striking when viewed as a percentage of the federal budget. In 1962, Social Security expenditures were $14.0 billion, or 13 percent of total federal government outlays of $106.8 billion. By 2000, total annual Social Security outlays were $407 billion, and in 2003 it is estimated that they will reach $470 billion, or 24 percent of total federal outlays. More prominently in budget terms, Social Security outlays were approximately equal to domestic federal discretionary spending in 1962, while today they are nearly twice as large.[9]

Projected demographic changes play an important role in assessing the financial viability and future of Social Security. In 1965, just 9 percent of the U.S. population was over age 65; by 2020 it is projected that 20 percent of the population will be over 65.[10] Consequently, current estimates suggest that by 2016 the Social Security trust fund will have to use interest on the trust fund to meet obligations, and by 2025 it will have to draw upon principal to pay benefits (i.e., receipts will not cover benefit payments); by 2038 it is estimated that the fund will be exhausted.[11] To give a sense of the magnitude of this issue, benefit payments are estimated to be $2.5 trillion per year by 2029, and receipts will finance only three-quarters of the bill. Social Security's projected insolvency is what current reform efforts seek to address.

Social Security has enormous political appeal, not only because of the large number of current recipients and the fact that they vote in greater proportion than other age groups, but also because the baby boom generation plans to retire over the next few decades. There is ample skepticism that the program's trust fund will be adequate to provide retirement benefits for that large bulge of workers, and that prospect—particularly after a lifetime of contributions by those workers to the trust fund—concerns policymakers. While polls differ in their specifics, significant majorities believe that Social Security should be continued, and most would be willing to pay higher taxes to maintain benefits (less than one-tenth believe that too much is spent on Social Security).[12]

Though support for the program remains quite high, there is also widespread acceptance that Social Security will require reform in the next few decades, and several solutions have been offered. The first is to curtail Social Security benefits so that future benefit payments do not outstrip contributions. This can be achieved in a number of ways, including extending the retirement age, limiting cost-of-living adjustments, and changing the benefit formula. A second solution is to increase contributions to the trust fund by raising payroll tax rates, lengthening required working years, and/or raising the cap on income subjected to the payroll tax.

A third, more radical, solution is to "privatize" Social Security. While this can be achieved in different ways, the idea is to allow workers to control the investment of some or all of their required insurance contributions and reap the rewards (or liabilities) of good (or poor) investments as individuals rather than as a group. Part of the initial appeal of privatization stemmed from the enormous growth in the stock market in the 1990s and the increase in the number of individual investors in stocks, bonds, and mutual funds. Jubilant over double-digit annual returns, many investors were willing to bet that their investment stream would outstrip any benefits provided by Social Security. However, many of these investors were new and did not experience directly the dramatic fluctuations in share prices of earlier generations until 2001 and 2002. Subsequent stock market declines have dampened the enthusiasm for relying solely on stock market returns to finance retirement.

Social Security is sometimes perceived as a program conferring excessive benefits to senior citizens, derisively referred to as "greedy geezers," because the benefits for current (and, particularly, older) retirees are often far in excess of their contributions, even factoring in accumulated interest. For example, an average wage earner retiring in 1996 would have, by 2002, exhausted all of his or her contributions, with interest. (Low-wage earners would do so in just over 4 years, and high-wage earners in almost 9 years.)[13] Since beneficiaries live on average far beyond 4 to 9 years of retirement, the system provides substantial subsidies to current retirees paid for by current workers. But the importance of the program as a source of retirement income should not be overlooked. Approximately one-third of Social Security recipients rely on the program for more than 90 percent of their total income, and for 18 percent of all recipients it is their only source of income. Forty percent of beneficiaries rely on the program to keep their incomes above the poverty level.[14] Elderly women are particularly dependent upon Social Security; more than a third of elderly women living alone derive more than 90 percent of their income from Social Security, despite the fact that the average retired woman's benefit was $665 a month in 1999 compared with $884 for the average retired man.[15]

For all of the concern over Social Security reform, the system's overall achievements are generally underappreciated. First and foremost, Social Security has been a dramatic success in reducing old-age poverty; poverty rates among the elderly today are one-third of the rate in 1959. Second, despite polls showing that Americans believe the costs of administering Social Security to be more than 50 percent, administrative costs are only 1 percent of benefits, compared with administrative costs for private insurance of 12 to 14 percent. Third, Social Security has been self-financing to date: Receipts have always been sufficient to finance benefit payments, and the trust fund currently has a balance of hundreds of billions of dollars. (The balance is held mostly in the form of U.S. government securities; in effect the federal government borrows from the Social Security surpluses to finance its current operations.)

Whatever the future of Social Security, there is little question that reform efforts are likely to be more successful and less painful if taken early—when changes need not be so dramatic to maintain benefit payments or tax rates—rather than later when the options are more limited and far less palatable. In the articles that follow, Michael Tanner argues that private retirement accounts not only would provide higher rates of return, but would also correct current inequities in the system and depoliticize Social Security. Brooke Harrington believes that private investment plans would add a "lottery" element to the system, especially for those not comfortable investing in the stock market. Harrington argues that those most able to realize large returns on invested pension plans are those who do not rely on Social Security as a primary retirement income.

Endnotes

1. President's Commission on Social Security, "Strengthening Social Security and Creating Personal Wealth for All Americans" (December 2001), http://www.csss. gov/reports/Final_report.pdf, 11.
2. U.S. Social Security Administration, http://www.ssa.gov/statistics/Supplement/ 2000/oasdi.pdf.
3. Ibid.

4. The Century Foundation, http://www.tcf.org/Publications/Basics/2002_Social_Security/full_pamphlet.pdf.
5. Social Security Administration, http://www.ssa.gov.
6. The Century Foundation, op. cit.
7. Ibid.
8. These data are drawn from the Budget of the United States Government, Fiscal Year 1998, Historical Tables.
9. Ibid.
10. The Century Foundation, op. cit.
11. Ibid.
12. Ibid.
13. Ibid.
14. Social Security Administration, http://www.ssa.gov/statistics/Supplement/2000/oasdi.pdf.
15. The Century Foundation, op. cit.

YES

"Saving" Social Security
Is Not Enough

Michael Tanner

EXECUTIVE SUMMARY

It seems that no politician discusses Social Security these days without a call to "save" the program. Certainly, it is possible to see why the program needs saving. It is facing financial insolvency: it is more than $20 trillion in debt and will be running a deficit in just 15 years.

But to focus on "saving" Social Security is to miss the larger point. Merely finding sufficient funding to preserve Social Security fails to address the serious shortcomings of the current system. The question should be, not whether we can provide the best possible retirement system for American workers. Social Security fails both as an anti-poverty program and as a retirement program. It contains numerous inequities and leaves future retirement benefits to the whims of politicians. Why should the goal of public policy be to save such a program?

Instead of saving Social Security, we should begin the transition to a new and better retirement system based on individually owned, privately invested accounts. The new system would allow workers to accumulate real wealth that would prevent their retiring to poverty. Because a privatized system would provide a far higher rate of return, it would yield much higher retirement benefits. Because workers would own their accounts, money in them could be passed on to future generations as an inheritance. That would particularly benefit the poor and minorities. Finally, workers would no longer be dependent on politicians for their retirement incomes.

Michael Tanner is director of the Cato Institute Project on Social Security Privatization and coauthor of *A New Deal for Social Security* (1998).

INTRODUCTION

We need to *save Social Security.*

President Bill Clinton[1]

I'm fighting *to save Social Security* the right way.

Vice President Al Gore[2]

My economic agenda sets aside $2 trillion of the $4 trillion unified budget surplus to *save Social Security.*

Gov. George W. Bush[3]

We should work on a real plan that *saves Social Security.*

Rep. Bill Archer (R-Tex.)[4]

The corridors of Washington are ringing with calls to "save" Social Security. And it is certainly easy to understand why the program needs "saving." Social Security is rapidly heading for financial insolvency. By 2015 the program will begin running a deficit, paying out more in benefits than it takes in through taxes. The resulting shortfall will necessitate at least a 50 percent increase in payroll taxes, a one-third reduction in benefits, or some combination of benefit cuts and tax increases. Overall, Social Security faces a long-term funding shortfall of more than $20 trillion.[5]

As a result, there have been numerous proposals designed to shore up the program's shaky finances. Those proposals generally take one of two tracks: setting aside current Social Security surpluses in some form of "lock box" or injecting general revenue financing into the system.

There are serious flaws in both of those approaches. The lock-box proposals do not, in fact, do anything to change Social Security's financing. Currently, surplus Social Security taxes are used to purchase government bonds, which are held by the Social Security trust fund. Those bonds will eventually have to be repaid. To do so, the government will have to raise revenue. Thus the bonds represent nothing more than a claim against future tax revenues, in essence a form of IOU.[6] Revenue from the purchases of those bonds is credited to the unified federal budget and used to pay the general operating expenses of the federal government. Under lock-box proposals, the revenue from the purchase of the bonds could be used only to pay down the national debt. Paying down the national debt may or may not be a good thing, and it may make it easier for the federal government to borrow money in the future, but it does nothing to change the date at which Social Security will begin to run a deficit. As the *Washington Post* has pointed out, "The same IOUs are put in the trust fund whether the surplus is used to finance other programs or pay down debt."[7]

Some proposals go beyond setting aside Social Security surpluses and would inject all or part of the current general revenue budget surpluses into the Social Security system. Aside from the fact that Social Security's liabilities far outstrip the amount of surplus available, it is impossible to prefund Social Security under the program's current structure. Any additional funds put into the system today would simply purchase more government bonds, which would have to be paid in the future from whatever tax monies were available then.

However, setting aside the important point that none of the current proposals to save Social Security actually does so, the current focus on "saving" Social Security is itself misguided. Merely finding sufficient funding to preserve Social Security fails to address the serious shortcomings of the current system. The question should be, not whether we can save Social Security, but whether we can provide the best possible retirement system for American workers. Such a system should keep seniors out of poverty as well as improve prospects for future generations. It should provide an adequate retirement income and the best possible return on an individual's money. It should be fair, treating similarly situated people equally. Certainly, it should not penalize the disadvantaged in society such as the poor and minorities. And it should allow people to own their benefits, freeing seniors from dependence on politicians and politics for retirement benefits.

On all those scores, Social Security is an abysmal failure. It fails both as an anti-poverty program and as a retirement program. It contains numerous inequities and leaves future retirement benefits to the whims of politicians. Why should the goal of public policy be to save such a program?

Instead of saving Social Security, we should begin the transition to a new and better retirement system based on individually owned, privately invested accounts. A privatized system would allow workers to accumulate real wealth that would prevent their retiring to poverty. Because a privatized system would provide a far higher rate of return, it would yield much higher retirement benefits. Because workers would own their accounts, money in them could be passed on to future generations. That would particularly benefit the poor and minorities. Finally, again because workers would own their retirement accounts, they would no longer be dependent on politicians for their retirement incomes.

SOCIAL SECURITY AS AN ANTI-POVERTY PROGRAM

Social Security has elements of both an insurance and a welfare program. It is, in effect, both a retirement and an anti-poverty program.[8] Although people most often think of the retirement component of the program, the system's defenders often focus on its anti-poverty elements. For example, Rep. Bill Archer (R-Tex.), chairman of the House Ways and Means Committee and author of a proposal to save Social Security, calls the program "the country's greatest anti-poverty program."[9] But is it really?

There is no question that the poverty rate among the elderly has declined dramatically in the last half century. As recently as 1959, the poverty rate for seniors was 35.2 percent, more than double the 17 percent poverty rate for the general adult population.[10] Today, it has declined to approximately 11.9 percent.[11]

Clearly, Social Security has had a significant impact on that trend. A 1999 study by the Center on Budget and Policy Priorities found that in the absence of Social Security benefits approximately 47.6 percent of seniors would have incomes below the poverty level.[12] That suggests that receipt of Social Security benefits lifted more than 35 percent of seniors, approximately 11.4 million people, out of poverty. CBPP also points out that the percentage of elderly who would have been in poverty in the absence of Social Security has remained relatively constant over the last several decades, while the percentage of elderly in poverty after receiving Social Security benefits has been steadily declining, indicating the increased importance of Social Security as an anti-poverty remedy.[13]

The primary problem with this line of analysis is that it assumes that any loss of Social Security benefits would not be offset by income from other sources. In other words, it simply takes a retiree's current income and subtracts Social Security benefits to discover, no surprise, that total income is now lower and, indeed, frequently low enough to throw the retiree into poverty.

Social Security benefits are a substantial component of most retirees' income. Those benefits constitute more than 90 percent of retirement income for one-quarter of the elderly. Nearly half of retirees receive at least half of their income from Social Security.[14] The question, therefore, is not whether the sudden elimination of Social Security income would leave retirees worse off—clearly it would—but whether in the absence of Social Security (or an alternative mandatory savings program) retirees would have changed their behavior to provide other sources of income for their own retirement.

For example, we could ask how many seniors, in the absence of Social Security, would still be working. If they were, they would have a source of income not considered by the CBPP study. Clearly, not all seniors are able to continue working. However, many can and would. Indeed, Congress recently repealed the Social Security earnings test precisely because there are many seniors who *want* to continue working.

A more important question is whether workers, without Social Security to depend on, would have changed their behavior and saved more for their retirement. The evidence is strong that Social Security discourages individual savings. For example, Martin Feldstein of Harvard University and Anthony Pellechio of the National Bureau for Economic Research have found that households reduce their private savings by nearly one dollar for every dollar of the present value of expected future Social Security benefits.[15] Other studies have put the amount of substitution somewhat lower but still indicate a substantial offset. Even two researchers for the Social Security Administration, Dean Leimer and David Richardson, have conceded that "a dollar of Social Security wealth substitutes for about three-fifths of a dollar of fungible assets."[16]

Therefore, given that many seniors would have replaced Social Security income with income from other sources, the impact of Social Security on reducing poverty among the elderly may be overstated.

However, even taking the arguments of Social Security's defenders on their own terms, the evidence suggests that Social Security fails as an anti-poverty tool. After all, despite receiving Social Security benefits, nearly one of eight seniors still lives in poverty. In fact, the poverty rate for seniors remains slightly higher than that for the adult population as a whole.[17]

For some subgroups, the problem is far worse. For example, although the poverty rate for elderly married women is relatively low (6.4 percent), the poverty rate is far higher for elderly women who never married (21.1 percent), widowed women (21.5 percent), and divorced or separated women (29.1 percent).[18] African American seniors are also disproportionately left in poverty. Nearly 30 percent of African Americans over the age of 65 have incomes below the poverty level.[19]

Social Security's failure as an anti-poverty program is not surprising since Social Security benefits are actually quite low. A worker earning the minimum wage over his entire working life would receive only $6,301 per year in Social Security benefits, well below the poverty level of $7,990. As mentioned above, poor seniors receive nearly 80 percent of their retirement income from Social Security. Many have no other income at all. Social Security is insufficient to raise those seniors out of poverty.

This can be contrasted with what those people would have received had they been able to invest their payroll taxes in real capital assets. For example, if the minimum wage worker described above had been able to invest his payroll taxes, he would be receiving retirement benefits of $20,728 per year, nearly three times the poverty level.[20] Clearly, by forcing workers to invest in the current pay-as-you-go system, rather than in real capital assets, Social Security is actually contributing to poverty among the elderly.

Not only does Social Security contribute to poverty among current seniors, it also helps perpetuate poverty for future generations. Social Security benefits are not inheritable. A worker can pay Social Security taxes for 30 or 40 years, but, if that worker dies without children under the age of 18 or a spouse over the age of 65, none of the money paid into the system is passed on to his heirs.[21] As Jagadeesh Gokhale, an economist at the Federal Reserve Bank of Cleveland, and others have noted, Social Security essentially forces low-income workers to annuitize their wealth, preventing them from making a bequest of that wealth to their heirs.[22]

Moreover, because this forced annuitization applies to a larger portion of the wealth of low-income workers than of high-income workers, it turns inheritance into a "disequalizing force," leading to greater inequality of wealth in America. The wealthy are able to bequeath their wealth to their heirs, while the poor cannot. Indeed, Gokhale and Boston University economist Laurence Kotlikoff estimate that Social Security doubles the share of wealth owned by the richest 1 percent of Americans.[23]

Feldstein reaches a similar conclusion. He suggests that low-income workers substitute "Social Security wealth" in the form of promised future Social Security benefits for other forms of savings. As a result, a greater proportion of a high-income worker's wealth is in fungible assets. Since fungible wealth is inheritable, whereas Social Security wealth is not, a small proportion of the population holds a stable concentration of fungible wealth.[24] Feldstein's work suggests that the concentration of wealth in the United States would be reduced by as much as half if low-income workers were able to substitute real wealth for Social Security wealth. Individual accounts would allow them to do so.

Thus, far from being "the country's greatest anti-poverty program," Social Security appears to do a poor job of lifting seniors out of poverty and may in fact perpetuate their poverty while increasing inequality in this country.

SOCIAL SECURITY AS A RETIREMENT PROGRAM

If Social Security is an inadequate anti-poverty program, does it at least meet its second goal as a retirement program? When Franklin Roosevelt proposed Social Security, he promised a program that would provide retirement benefits "at least as good as any American could buy from a private insurance company."[25] While that may have been true at one time, it certainly is no longer the case.

Social Security's rate of return has been steadily declining since the program's inception and is now far lower than the return from private capital investment. According to the Social Security Administration, workers born after 1973 will receive rates of return ranging from 3.7 percent for a low-wage, single-income couple to just 0.4 percent for a high-wage-earning single male.[26] The overall rate of return for all workers born in a given year was estimated at slightly below 3 percent for those born in 1940, 2 percent for those born in 1960, and below 1 percent for those who will be born this century.[27] Numerous private studies predict future rates of return for an average-wage earner ranging from 2 percent to a negative 3 percent.[28]

To make matters worse, the studies generally assume that Social Security will be able to pay all its promised benefits without increasing payroll taxes. However, the Social Security system is facing a long-term financial shortfall of more than $20 trillion. According to the system's own Board of Trustees, either taxes will have to be raised by at least 50 percent or benefits reduced by 25 percent. As a result, the rate of return will be even lower than the rates cited above. In many cases the return will actually be negative.[29]

By comparison, the average rate of return to the stock market since 1926 has been 7.7 percent.[30] That return has held despite a major depression, several recessions, World War II, two smaller wars, and the turbulent inflation-recession years of the 1970s. Of course, there have been ups and downs in the market, but there has been no 20-year period since 1926 during which the market was a net loser. Indeed, there has never been a 20-year period in which the market performed worse than projected future returns from Social Security.[31]

Even corporate bonds have consistently outperformed Social Security. Discounting the period 1941–51, when government price controls artificially reduced the return, corporate bonds have paid an average real annual return of more than 4 percent.[32]

Thus, because it deprives American workers of the ability to invest in private capital markets, the current Social Security system is costing American retirees hundreds of thousands of dollars. A single-earner couple, whose wage earner is 30 years old in 2000 and earning $24,000 per year, can expect to pay more than $134,000 in Social Security taxes over their lifetimes and receive $292,320 in lifetime Social Security benefits (including spousal benefits), assuming that both husband and wife live to normally expected ages.[33] However, had they been able to invest privately, they would have received $875,280.[34] That means the current Social Security system is depriving them of more than half a million dollars.

A second way to consider Social Security's adequacy as a retirement program is to look at the replacement rate, that portion of preretirement income replaced by Social Security benefits. Most financial planners say that a person will need retirement benefits equal to between 60 and 85 percent of preretirement wages in order to maintain his or her standard of living.[35]

However, Social Security provides only 42.4 percent of preretirement income for average-income workers. Because Social Security has a progressive benefit formula, low-income workers do better with a replacement rate of 57.1 percent, still below what is needed. That is especially true since low-income workers lack other forms of retirement income. The replacement rate for high-income workers is only 25.6 percent. In the future, the situation will grow even worse. Even under current law, replacement rates are scheduled to decline significantly. By 2030 Social Security will replace only 36.7 percent of an average-wage earner's preretirement income. However, because Social Security cannot pay all promised future benefits, the Congressional Research Service estimates that the replacement rate for an average worker will decline to as low as 26 percent, a 40 percent decline from the current already inadequate levels.[36] Clearly, Social Security, both now and in the future, leaves many seniors without the income necessary to maintain their standard of living.

Again, compare this with the replacement rates provided under a system of private investment. Assuming that the worker described previously were able to invest the full nondisability portion of his Social Security taxes (10.6 percent of wages), his replacement rate would be an astounding 260 percent of preretirement income! If he invested just 4 percent of wages, he would still have a replacement rate equal to 100 percent of his preretirement income.

SOCIAL SECURITY IS UNFAIR

As if it were not bad enough that Social Security fails in its stated mission as an anti-poverty and retirement program, the program also contains very serious inequities that make it fundamentally unfair.

The program's most obvious unfairness is *intergenerational.* Retirees currently receiving benefits paid a relatively low payroll tax over their working lifetimes and receive a fairly high rate of return. That high return is subsidized by much higher payroll taxes on today's young workers who, in turn, can expect much lower future benefits. As Daniel Shapiro, professor of philosophy at West Virginia University, has pointed out, one of the basic precepts of social justice is the minimization of *unchosen* inequalities.[37] However, the future generations forced to bear the burden of Social Security's unfunded liabilities must do so entirely because of the time of their birth and not through any fault or choice of their own.

The program's *intragenerational* inequities are less visible but just as unfair. As we have already noted, Social Security benefits are not inheritable. Therefore, lifetime Social Security benefits depend, in part, on longevity. As a result, people with identical earnings histories will receive different levels of benefits depending on how long they live. Individuals who live to be 100 receive far more in benefits than individuals who die at 66. Therefore, those groups in our society with shorter life expectancies, such as the poor and African Americans, are put at a severe disadvantage.

Of course, Social Security does have a progressive benefit formula, whereby low-income individuals receive proportionately higher benefits per dollar paid into the system than do high-income workers.[38] The question, therefore, is to what degree shorter life expectancies offset this progressivity.

The findings of studies that use income as the sole criterion are mixed. Some studies, such as those by Eugene Steuerle and Jan Bakja of the Urban Institute and Dean Leimer of the Social Security Administration, conclude that shorter life expectancies diminish but do not completely offset Social Security's progressivity.[39] However, there is a growing body of literature—including studies by Daniel Garrett of Stanford University, the RAND Corporation, and others—that shows that the progressive benefit formula is completely offset, resulting in redistribution of wealth from poor people to the already wealthy.[40]

The question of Social Security's unfairness to ethnic minorities appears more straightforward, particularly in the case of African Americans. African Americans of all income levels have shorter life expectancies than do whites. As a result, a black man or woman, earning exactly the same lifetime wages and paying exactly the same lifetime Social Security taxes as his or her white counterpart, will likely receive far less in lifetime Social Security benefits. For example, assume that a 30-year-old black man and a 30-year-old white man both earn $30,000 per year over their working lifetimes. By the time they retire, they will each have paid $136,740 in Social Security taxes over their lifetimes[41] and will be entitled to monthly Social Security benefits of $1,162.

However, the white man can expect to live until age 81.[42] If he does, he will receive $189,389 in total Social Security benefits. The black man, in contrast, can expect to live only to age 79.[43] He can expect to receive only $161,750, almost $27,000 less than his white counterpart. This may actually understate the unfairness of the current system, since it is based on life expectancies at age 65. However, if both men are age 30 today, the life expectancy for the white man is 78; for the black man it is only 69.[44] If those projections are accurate, the black man can expect to receive nearly $100,000 less in lifetime Social Security benefits than his white counterpart and, indeed, will receive less than half what he actually paid into the program.

It seems amazing that this disparate impact, which would not be tolerated in any other government program, is so easily accepted within the current Social Security system.[45]

The current program is also unfair to women who work outside the home. Under the current system, a woman is automatically entitled to 50 percent of her husband's benefits, whether or not she has worked outside the home or paid Social Security taxes.[46] However, if a woman is able to claim benefits both as a spouse and in her own right, she may receive only the larger of the two. Because many women work only part-time, take years off from work to raise children, or earn lower wages than their husbands, 50 percent of the husband's benefits is frequently larger than the benefits a woman would be entitled to as a result of her own earnings. She will, therefore, receive only the benefits based on her husband's earnings. She will receive no additional benefits even though she may have worked and paid thousands of dollars in payroll taxes. Indeed, she would receive exactly the same benefits as if she had never worked a day outside the home or paid a dime in Social Security taxes. The taxes she paid earn her exactly *nothing*.[47]

Anyone concerned with fairness and equity in government programs must acknowledge that our current Social Security system falls far short of meeting those goals.

SOCIAL SECURITY AND THE DIGNITY OF OLDER AMERICANS

Finally, it should be noted that the current Social Security system makes American seniors dependent on government and the political process for their retirement income. In essence, it reduces American seniors to supplicants, robbing them of their dignity and control over their own lives.

Americans, of course, do not get back the money that they individually paid into Social Security. Under our pay-as-you-go Social Security system, the money that workers pay in Social Security taxes is not saved or invested for their own retirement; it is instead used to pay for benefits for current retirees. Any over-payment is used by the federal government to pay its general operating expenses or, under various lock-box proposals, to pay down the national debt.

In exchange, workers receive a promise that the government will tax future workers in order to provide benefits to today's workers when they retire. However, that promise is not any sort of legally enforceable contract. It has long been settled law that there is no legal right to Social Security. In two important cases, *Helvering v. Davis* and *Flemming v. Nestor*, the U.S. Supreme Court has ruled that Social Security taxes are simply taxes and convey no property or contractual rights to Social Security benefits.[48]

As a result, a worker's retirement security is entirely dependent on political decisions made by the president and Congress. Benefits may be reduced or even eliminated at any time and are not directly related to Social Security taxes paid into the system.

Therefore, retirees are left totally dependent on the whims of politicians for their retirement income. A person can work hard, play by the rules, and pay thousands of dollars in Social Security taxes but at retirement his benefits depend entirely on the decisions of the president and Congress. Despite their best intentions, seniors have been turned into little more than wards of the state.

CONCLUSION

If Social Security didn't exist today, would we invent it? The current Social Security system is a failure by almost every criterion. It fails to lift many seniors out of poverty or to improve prospects for future generations. Indeed, it may actually redistribute money from the poor to the wealthy. Because it forces the poor to annuitize their savings, it prevents the accumulation of real wealth and prevents the poor from passing that wealth on to future generations. Social Security also fails as a retirement program. It does not provide an adequate retirement income or yield the best possible return on an individual's money. Nor is the program fair. It includes numerous inequities that unfairly discriminate against minorities, the poor, and working women. And, finally, because people do not have any legal ownership of their benefits, it leaves seniors dependent on politicians and politics for their retirement benefits.

Surely this cannot be what we seek from Social Security, especially when there are alternatives available. Workers should be allowed to take the money they are currently paying in Social Security taxes and redirect it to individually owned, privately invested accounts, similar to individual retirement accounts or 401(k) plans. The funds that accumulated in those accounts would be invested in real assets such as stocks and bonds, with safeguards against highly risky or speculative investments. The funds would be the account holders' personal property. At retirement, workers could convert all or part of their accumulated funds into an annuity or take a series of programmed withdrawals from the principal. If they choose the latter option, any funds remaining at their death would become part of their estate, fully inheritable by their heirs.

A retirement program based on individually owned, privately invested accounts would provide higher retirement benefits and a better rate of return than does Social Security. It would lift more seniors out of poverty, and, because funds are inheritable, accumulated wealth could be passed on to future generations. It would not penalize groups with shorter life expectancies and would eliminate the penalty on working women. And workers would own their benefits and thus be free from political risk and dependence.[49]

When it comes to Social Security, policy-makers should consider whether it is more important to save a system or to provide a better retirement for American seniors.

Endnotes

1. "Remarks by the President at Reception for the DCCC," White House, Office of the Press Secretary, M2 Presswire, April 4, 2000. Emphasis added.
2. "Gore Touts 'Fairer' Social Security," *Arizona Republic* April 5, 2000. Emphasis added.
3. Quoted in "Election 2000 on the Issues: National Debt," *Allentown (Pa.) Morning Call*, March 22, 2000. Emphasis added.
4. Quoted in Robert A. Rosenblatt and Alissa J. Rubin, "Economy Boosts Social Security Medicare Life; Benefits: Higher Tax Revenues Will Support Each for Longer Than Previously Thought. The New Solvency Changes the Political Debate for Both Parties," *Los Angeles Times* March 31, 2000. Emphasis added.
5. Board of Trustees, Federal Old-Age and Survivors Insurance and Disability Insurance Trust Funds, *2000 Annual Report* (Washington, D.C.: Government Printing Office, 2000).
6. As President Clinton's own budget notes: "[Trust fund] balances are available to finance future benefit payments and other trust fund expenditures—but only in a book-keeping sense. These funds are not set up to be pension funds like the funds of private pension plans. They do not consist of real economic assets that can be drawn down in the future to fund benefits. Instead, they are claims on the Treasury that, when redeemed, will have to be financed by raising taxes, borrowing from the public, or reducing benefits or other expenditures. The existence of large trust fund balances, therefore, does not, by itself, have any impact on the government's ability to pay benefits." Executive Office of the President of the United States, *Analytical Perspectives: Budget of the United States Government, Fiscal Year 2000* (Washington, D.C.: Government Printing Office, 1999), p. 337.
7. "Ploys Will Be Ploys," Editorial, *Washington Post*, October 28, 1999.
8. W. Andrew Achenbaum, *Social Security: Visions and Revisions* (Cambridge: Cambridge University Press, 1986), pp. 54–55. See also Peter Ferrara, *Social Security: The Inherent Contradiction* (Washington, D.C.: Cato Institute, 1980).
9. Bill Archer, Comments at Hearing on Social Security before the House Committee on Ways and Means, 106th Cong., 1st sess., June 9, 1999, transcript, p. 48, Federal News Service.
10. Daryl Jackson et al., "Understanding Social Security: The Issues and Alternatives," American Institute of Certified Public Accountants, Washington, D.C., November 1998, p. 17.
11. Bureau of the Census, Current Population Reports, Series P60, 1998.
12. Kathryn Porter, Kathy Larin, and Wendell Primus, "Social Security and Poverty among the Elderly: A National and State Perspective," Center on Budget and Policy Priorities, Washington, D.C., April 1999.

13. Ibid., p. 16.
14. Neil Gilbert and Neung-Hoo Park, "Privatization, Provision, and Targeting: Trends and Policy Implications for Social Security in the United States," *International Social Security Review* 49 (January 1996): 22.
15. Martin Feldstein and Anthony Pellechio, "Social Security and Household Wealth Accumulation: New Microeconomic Evidence," *Review of Economics and Statistics* 61 (August 1979): 361–68.
16. Dean Leimer and David Richardson, "Social Security, Uncertainty, Adjustments, and the Consumption Decision," *Economica* 59 (August 1992): 29.
17. Bureau of the Census, Current Population Reports, Series P60.
18. Seven Sandell, "Adequacy and Equity of Social Security," *Report of the 1994–1995 Advisory Council on Social Security* (Washington, D.C.: Government Printing Office, 1997), vol. 2 pp. 321–27.
19. Bureau of the Census, Population Report P60–175, 1996, Table 6, p. 18.
20. Assumes investment in stocks earning actual returns and that the individual was born in 1935, earned the minimum wage his entire working life, and retires in 2000.
21. Survivors' benefits may be extended to age 21 if the child is enrolled in college.
22. Jagadeesh Gokhale et al., "Simulating the Transmission of Wealth Inequality via Bequests," *Journal of Public Economics* (forthcoming, 2000).
23. Jagadeesh Gokhale and Laurence Kotlikoff, "The Impact of Social Security and Other Factors on the Distribution of Wealth," National Bureau of Economic Research, Cambridge, Mass., October 1999.
24. Martin Feldstein, "Social Security and the Distribution of Wealth," *Journal of the American Statistical Association* 71 (December 1976): 800–807.
25. Quoted in Warren Shore, *Social Security: The Fraud in Your Future* (New York: Macmillan, 1975), p. 2.
26. Barbara Bovbjerg, "Social Security: Issues in Comparing Rates of Return with Market Investments," U.S. General Accounting Office Report HEHS-99–110, August 1999.
27. Dean Leimer, "Cohort-Specific Measures of Lifetime Net Social Security Transfers," Social Security Administration, Office of Research and Statistics, Working Paper no. 59, February 1994.
28. For example, in our 1998 book, *A New Deal for Social Security*, Peter Ferrara and I updated a study that Ferrara conducted for the National Chamber Foundation in 1986. Using economic and demographic assumptions taken from the Social Security trustees' intermediate assumptions, adjusting for survivors' and disability benefits, and assuming that, somehow, Social Security would pay all promised benefits, we found that most workers who entered the workforce after 1985 would receive rates of return of 1.0 to 1.5 percent or less. Peter J. Ferrara and Michael Tanner, *A New Deal for Social Security* (Washington, D.C.: Cato Institute, 1998), p. 69. Those results closely matched the results of a study that Ferrara conducted in 1985 with Professor John Lott, then at the Wharton School and now at Yale Law School. The 1985 study, which looked at workers entering the workforce in 1983, also showed rates of return from Social Security for most workers in the range of 1.0 to 1.5 percent. Peter J. Ferrara and John Lott, "Social Security's Rates of Return for Young Workers," in *Social Security: Prospects for Real Reform*, ed. Peter Ferrara (Washington, D.C.: Cato Institute, 1985), pp. 13–36. The Heritage Foundation concluded in 1998 that the rate of return to an average two-earner

family (both 30 years old) was just 1.23 percent, while the return to African American men was actually negative. William Beach and Gareth Davis, "Social Security's Rate of Return," Report no. 98–01 of the Heritage Center for Data Analysis, Washington, D.C., January 15, 1998. In a 1988 study for the National Bureau of Economic Research, John Geanakopolis, Olivia Mitchell, and Stephen Zeldes concluded that workers born after 1970 could expect a rate of return of less than 2 percent. John Geanakopolis, Olivia Mitchell, and Stephen Zeldes, "Social Security's Money Worth," National Bureau of Economic Research Working Paper no. 6722, Washington, D.C., September 1988. The U.S. General Accounting Office reports that a two-earner couple born in 1973 and making average wages would receive a rate of return from Social Security of approximately 2.1 percent. Bovbjerg, p. 13. The nonpartisan Tax Foundation suggests future rates of return as low as a negative 3 percent. Arthur Hall, "Forcing a Bad Investment on Retiring Americans," Tax Foundation Special Report no. 55, November 1995.

29. See, for example, Jagadeesh Gokhale and Laurence Kotlikoff, "Social Security's Treatment of Postwar Americans: How Bad Can It Get?" National Bureau of Economic Research Working Paper no. 7362, Cambridge, Mass., September 1999. See also Hall; Beach and Davis; and Geanakopolis, Mitchell, and Zeldes.

30. Gokhale and Kotlikoff, "Social Security's Treatment of Postwar Americans," p. 15.

31. Jeremy J. Siegel, *Stocks for the Long Run* (New York: McGraw-Hill, 1998), p. 26. Of course, critics of privatization point out, correctly, that the past is no guarantee of future performance. But the critics' contention that the future performance of private capital markets will be significantly lower than past averages is unpersuasive. See, for example, Peter Ferrara, "Social Security Is Still a Hopelessly Bad Deal for Today's Workers," Cato Institute Social Security Paper no. 18, November 29, 1999.

The critics generally argue that, using the Social Security trustees' projections for future economic growth, economic growth will be too slow to sustain continued stock market gains. Dean Baker and Mark Weisbrot, for example, suggest that future returns will be below 3.5 percent. Dean Baker and Mark Weisbrot, *Social Security: The Phony Crisis* (Chicago: University of Chicago Press, 1999), pp. 88–104. However, the critics fail to acknowledge that the issue is not simply the return to capital markets but the spread between the return to capital markets and the return to Social Security. As Gokhale and Kotlikoff point out, Social Security tax payments and benefit receipts are closely linked to overall labor productivity growth, which is highly correlated with economic performance, which, in turn, is correlated with stock market performance. It is entirely reasonable to compare the real rate of return from stocks with the return from Social Security. Gokhale and Kotlikoff, "Social Security's Treatment of Postwar Americans," p. 15. In other words, if economic growth is so slow as to reduce the returns from private capital investment, it will also reduce the taxes collected by the Social Security system, exacerbating its fiscal imbalance, leading to lower benefits or higher taxes and a reduced Social Security rate of return. Thus, both Social Security's return and the return on capital could go up or they could go down, but private capital markets will always outperform Social Security. It is even possible to envision a scenario in which capital returns increase while Social Security tax receipts do not, for example, if wage growth takes place largely above the cap, or if economic growth translates to nonwage compensation rather than increased real wages. However, it is difficult to foresee a scenario under which real wages (and therefore Social Security revenues) rise while private capital markets do not.

Critics of privatization also suggest that the return to private capital markets should be reduced to reflect administrative costs and the costs associated with the transition to a privatized system. Both arguments have been refuted extensively elsewhere. However, it is worth noting that the U.S. General Accounting Office suggests that administrative costs would range from a low of 10 basis points to a high of 300 basis points, with most estimates closer to the low end of the range. U.S. General Accounting Office, "Social Security Reform: Administrative Costs for Individual Accounts Depends on System Design," GAO/HEHS-99–131, June 1999. A study for the Cato Institute concluded that administrative costs would range between 30 and 65 basis points. Robert Genetski, "Administrative Costs and the Relative Efficiency of Public and Private Social Security Systems," Cato Institute Social Security Paper no. 15, March 9, 1999.

The question of transition costs is also highly misleading. First, it has been clearly demonstrated that it is possible to pay for the transition without additional taxes. See, for example, Ferrara and Tanner, pp. 175–204. Even more important, however, Milton Friedman and others have shown that, when Social Security's current unfunded liabilities are considered, there are no new costs associated with the transition. Milton Friedman, "Speaking the Truth about Social Security Reform," Cato Institute Briefing Paper no. 46, April 12, 1999. Indeed, as William Shipman has demonstrated, the cost of paying for the transition, regardless of the financing mechanism chosen, will always be less than the cost of preserving the current system. William Shipman, "Facts and Fantasies about Transition Costs," Cato Institute Social Security Paper no. 13, October 13, 1998.

32. Calculated from Moody's Investor Service, *Moody's Industrial Manual* and *Moody's Bond Survey*, 1920–96.

33. Assumes husband retires at age 67, husband collects full Social Security benefit, and wife collects spousal benefit until husband dies at age 75. Wife then collects widow's benefit until she dies at age 81.

34. Assuming historical rates of return.

35. A. Haeworth Robertson, *Social Security: What Every Taxpayer Should Know* (Washington, D.C.: Retirement Policy Institute, 1992), p. 218.

36. David Koitz, "Social Security Reform: Assessing Changes to Future Retirement Benefits," Congressional Research Service Report for Congress RL-30380, December 14, 1999.

37. Daniel Shapiro, "The Moral Case for Social Security Privatization," Cato Institute Social Security Paper no. 14, October 29, 1998.

38. Social Security benefits are based on a formula that provides benefits equal to 90 percent of the first $495 of monthly income (adjusted according to a formula that takes into account the growth in wages), 32 percent of the next $2,286, and 15 percent of remaining income up to the wage cap.

39. See C. Eugene Steuerle and John Bakija, *Retooling Social Security for the 21st Century: Right and Wrong Approaches to Reform* (Washington, D.C.: Urban Institute, 1994), pp. 91–132; and Dean Leimer, "Lifetime Redistribution under the Social Security Program: A Literature Synopsis," *Social Security Bulletin* 62 (1999): 43–51.

40. Daniel Garrett, "The Effects of Differential Mortality Rates on the Progressivity of Social Security," *Economic Inquiry* 33 (July 1995): 457–75; W. Constantijn,

A. Panis, and Lee Lillard, "Socioeconomic Differentials in the Return to Social Security," RAND Corporation Working Paper no. 96–05, February 1996; and Beach and Davis.

41. Counting only the OASI portion of the payroll tax. This figure does not include the disability portion.

42. Bureau of the Census, *Statistical Abstract of the United States, 1995* (Washington, D.C.: Government Printing Office, 1996), Table B-1.

43. Ibid.

44. Projected life expectancy at age 30. Centers for Disease Control, "United States Abridged Life Tables, 1996," *National Vital Statistics Report*, no. 13 (December 24, 1998): Table 3.

45. Supporters of the current system maintain that, overall, African Americans benefit from the current Social Security system because they earn lower incomes than whites and are more likely to have periods of unemployment. Therefore, they are more likely to benefit from the program's progressive benefit formula. However, as we have seen, the lifetime progressivity of Social Security is questionable. Supporters of the status quo also suggest that African Americans benefit disproportionately from the program's disability and survivors' benefits. However, there are no empirical studies to support that contention. Indeed, the Social Security Administration rejected a request from the 1996–98 Social Security Advisory Council to conduct such a study. Sylvester Schieber and John Shoven, *The Real Deal: The History and Future of Social Security* (New Haven, Conn.: Yale University Press, 1999), p. 227.

46. The provision is gender neutral, applying to both men and women. However, because of earning patterns in the United States, it affects women almost exclusively.

47. For a full discussion of the impact of the current Social Security system on women and the benefits of privatization for women, see Darcy Ann Olsen, "Greater Financial Security for Women with Personal Retirement Accounts," Cato Institute Briefing Paper no. 38, July 20, 1998; and Ekaterina Shirley and Peter Spiegler, "The Benefits of Social Security Privatization for Women," Cato Institute Social Security Paper no. 12, July 20, 1998.

48. For a thorough discussion of this issue, see Charles Rounds, "Property Rights: The Hidden Issue of Social Security Reform," Cato Institute Social Security Paper no. 19, April 19, 2000.

49. For a full discussion of how a privatized Social Security system would work, see Ferrara and Tanner.

NO

Investor Beware:
Can Small Investors Survive Social
Security Privatization?

Brooke Harrington

It has become nearly axiomatic in this country to argue that everything would be better if it were run like a business. In response, government has shifted its mission: If it used to operate like Super Glue, bonding Americans to one another, it is now working more like WD-40, minimizing friction in the pursuit of individual (and corporate) profit. Social Security is not only the largest government program but the embodiment of the Super Glue approach to politics: the ultimate test case for privatization. The Bush administration proposes to allow contributors to invest a portion of their public Social Security pensions in the stock market. What a coup that would be for the WD-40 contingent.

Privatization proponents rest their proposal on three claims: Social Security funds are comparable to private investments, like IRAs; since most Americans manage their own IRAs, there is no reason they shouldn't manage their public pensions as well; and given the average returns on American stocks, we'd all have much more money at retirement if we could take some of our Social Security fund out of government bonds and put it into the stock market.

This shift could be interpreted as the financial equivalent of "bowling alone," Robert Putnam's much-quoted phrase about the decline of community life in the United States. Or you could think of it as the 401(k)-ification of America: The defined-contribution plan has shifted our view of retirement into something that is purely an individual matter, rather than a collective one.

A *New York Times* poll conducted earlier this year indicates that many Americans are increasingly persuaded by these ideas. Despite the market downturn, there has been a marked increase in the percentage of Americans who expect to rely only on their own savings—rather than private pension plans or Social Security—in retirement. Only 15 percent now believe that Social Security will be a primary source of their retirement funds. As one survey participant put it, "These decades to come are going to be more about what you do for yourself, as opposed to what you allow other people to do for you. It's not pro-government, not anti-government, just me, myself, and I." But while Americans may think they are well prepared to give up a piece of their social safety net, the evidence from recent economic studies suggests otherwise.

The prospect of higher returns is the main attraction of privatization, despite the seemingly insurmountable problems of logistics, costs, and implementation it poses. Belief in this claim seems to be curiously robust, even in the face of the recent stock-market decline and attempts to explain the costs, risks, and problems associated with privatization. People have dollar signs in their eyes, and nothing seems able to dislodge them.

In part, this can be attributed to the increasing displacement of belief in the public good by belief in the marketplace. The movements to bring market forces to the management of public schools, Medicare, and electrical-power transmission are among the most visible recent examples.

The central problem facing these hybrid public-private organizations is "information asymmetry": Market forces can't bring efficiency if there are large information differences among sellers and buyers. The classic example is the purchase of a used car. The seller has more information than the buyer and has no incentive to tell the buyer the truth. Therefore, the buyer may end up (1) buying a lemon or (2) spending a lot of time and money on research, both of which offset the savings from getting a "bargain" on the price.

When you introduce market forces into a formerly public service, you run into all of these problems of information asymmetry and opportunism. Thus, the key question for success in any hybrid is: Are citizens prepared to act as informed consumers?

In the case of Social Security, support for a privatized system rests entirely (and often implicitly) on assumptions about public knowledge and competency with regard to stock investing. But recent studies by economists and finance scholars suggest that Americans really don't understand the risks associated with stock investments and stand a good chance of doing worse financially under a hybrid system than under the current one.

RISK, RETURN, AND TRANSACTION COSTS

In the language of finance, the benefits of a privatized Social Security system depend upon the "equity premium." This is the increased return that investors can get for investing in risky securities such as stocks as opposed to risk-free securities such as Treasury bonds. Investors are compensated for assuming risk; the higher the risk, the greater the compensation.

During the century that just ended, the return on U.S. stock investments has averaged about 11 percent per year. The U.S. Treasury bonds in which Social Security funds are invested returned much less—averaging more like 5 percent per year. Offered a choice between the two investments, the answer seems obvious: Take the higher return. But of course there is a catch—two catches, in fact. The equity premium is not guaranteed (if it were, there would be no risk). It is just an average return, and some individual investors will actually lose money on stock investments. Not only are the risks of any individual stock unpredictable, but the historical-average return of U.S. stocks may not apply in a given time period. A grinding bear market or high inflation around the time you retire could mean that you have to cash out your portfolio when it's under water. In any case, the historical-average returns involve periods much longer than the relevant individual time frame, which is basically the 40-odd years between the start of one's working life and retirement. That means many of us will not be able to capitalize on long-range returns; as Keynes put it, "in the long run, we are all dead."

A second, related catch is that once investors capture the equity premium, they have to be careful not to give it away to their brokers. Trading stocks incurs transaction costs: Each buy or sell order means paying a commission. These costs can easily eat up all the gains from a profitable investment. Unless the government wants to become the world's first no-commission broker, transaction costs are going to be a serious issue in a privatized Social Security system.

The entire proposition that Social Security participants will come out ahead financially in a privatized system depends on their knowledge of and ability to manage investment risk and transaction costs. The evidence on this subject is not encouraging. For example, polls conducted to examine Americans' attitudes toward Social Security privatization have shown that it is alarmingly easy to reverse support for the proposal by simply mentioning risk. When questions about privatization are phrased so that they don't mention risk, about 58 percent of Americans support the proposal. But if the questions are rephrased so that they mention risk in any way, the results are reversed: 59 percent of respondents *oppose* privatization.

Studies of actual investor behavior support the polls. Ordinary individuals seem to have a polarized response to risk; they become either very conservative or very risk-seeking. Unfortunately, neither strategy is profitable. Though on *average* risk is compensated by *return* in the stock market, some risks don't pay off. Rather than being a linear relationship, in which more risk always pays off with higher returns, the risk-return relationship is more like an inverted U-shaped curve: Risks pay off up to a certain point, after which they become a waste of money. As with gambling, most of the fun in investing consists of locating that fine line between risks that pay off and those that don't.

Unfortunately, the vast majority of people guess wrong. Finance professor Terrance Odean has found that the portfolios of average American households and of investment clubs underperform the stock market by about 4 percent annually. In addition, Odean found that Americans trade their accounts excessively, creating high transaction costs. Apparently unaware that they were giving away their profits in the form of commissions, American households turned over their portfolios—that is, sold existing stocks and bought new ones—at the astronomical rate of 75 percent per year. Investment clubs weren't far behind, with a 65 percent annual turnover rate. At the end of the day, they mostly made money for their brokers. There is no reason to expect that Americans would fare any better or trade any less in a privatized system.

Of course, an ultraconservative approach to investing doesn't provide much of an alternative. Several economic studies indicate that the populations most likely to need Social Security in old age—people of color and women—are also the least likely to benefit from a privatized system. For example, a study by economists Nancy Jianokoplos and Alexandra Bernasek indicates that women invest too conservatively, putting only 40 percent of their investment dollars into stocks, compared with 46 percent for men. This conservatism doesn't pay off: If a man and a woman start with equal amounts of investment capital (which is of course a highly stylized assumption in itself) and invest it according to the averages over a 20-year period, that 6 percent difference in allocation results in the woman having 47 percent less money in her retirement fund than the man has. Thus, conservative behavior in a privatized system may not result in more retirement dollars for everyone. For the people who need a nest egg most, privatization may be no better, and perhaps worse, than the current public system.

This difference doesn't have anything to do with innate characteristics of men and women—or of blacks and whites—but rather with lack of exposure to investment opportunities, such as working the kind of job where you get a 401(k) plan that forces you to learn something about investing. That's how most Americans got into investing in the first place. But the investing bandwagon that swept the country during the 1990s left behind large numbers of women, people of color, and the poor. To correct this problem, the government would have to create a national investor-education program—an undertaking so costly that the Social Security trustees warned against it in 1999, saying that the expenses incurred would almost certainly outweigh the gains from privatization.

PRIVATIZATION: READY OR NOT?

Historically, Social Security has served multiple purposes, providing savings, insurance, and income redistribution in a single program. Privatization would shift the program away from redistribution and toward individual savings. This is part of the larger trend toward distrust of government and detachment from notions of the common good. In this sense, after years of erosion of public-sector institutions and faith in their mission, Americans *are* well prepared for a hybridized Social Security. More than 20 years of retreat from the notion of entitlement has changed our expectations and led many of us to accept the notion that we should individually bear most of the risk and responsibility for funding our retirements.

But all of us are vulnerable to the possibility of bad luck. Privatization would introduce a lottery-like element into the system that undercuts security for everyone. There is no guaranteed profit in the stock market: Neither risk seeking nor conservatism reliably pays off, and neither investment professionals nor ordinary Americans have been successful at guessing where stock prices would go. Americans may think that they know something about investing—remember when everyone agreed that you couldn't go wrong in dot-com stocks?—but their confidence, and the confidence of policy makers, is not supported by the evidence.

The evidence suggests that the people who would be most likely to see financial benefit from privatization in the Social Security system are white, male, affluent, and young. Unfortunately, recent polls indicate that these are also the people most likely to say they don't need Social Security and would like to drop out of the program entirely. The end of Social Security in its purely public form would mean losses for Americans that are not just economic but social. In abandoning the largest and most popular public program that binds us together through its benefits, we would lose an institutional and economic linchpin of our political community. When stacked up against the uncertain financial gains from privatization, the benefits of a public Social Security system look increasingly priceless.

Money and Moral Hazard

Those who favor an end to Social Security as we know it might want to take another look at the repeal of the estate tax. The two policy initiatives are linked by their conservative supporters as well as by timing: The President's Commission to Strengthen Social Security, charged with developing a privatization plan, met on June 11, just four days after President George W. Bush signed legislation that will phase out the inheritance tax. The substantive link between the two initiatives is less often noted: Both address the issues of financial redistribution and personal responsibility.

Yet despite all that the two initiatives have in common, policy makers seem to be heading toward diametrically opposed conclusions about them. Apparently, it is wrong to get money from the government but good to get it from relatives.

A major argument for the privatization of Social Security is that the current system creates "moral hazard"—harming recipients by giving them a perverse incentive to avoid responsibility for themselves in retirement. By this logic, the money that Social Security provides encourages workers to spend their earnings rather than save for old age. Such programs, privatization proponents argue, breed social pathology by rewarding laziness, incompetence, and an entitlement mentality.

Students of wealth in America will find this list of character defects eerily familiar: They practically constitute a job description for the heirs to large fortunes, known colloquially as "trust babies" or (among twenty-somethings) "trustafarians." Surely the moral threat posed by Social Security and other government programs is rivaled only by the threat of trust funds.

Numerous writers on the subject of inherited wealth have noted the devastating psychological consequences of inheritance, which seems to

breed the kinds of social pathologies among the very rich that
conservatives worry about among the poor and the middle class: lack of
initiative or ambition, a sense of being "owed" by others, and an
inability to plan for the future or set goals. Nelson Aldrich, Jr., heir to
one of this country's fabled fortunes, has noted that the beneficiaries of
inherited wealth are often justly accused of being "weak" in character,
"degenerate," and "doomed . . . to futility."

"Beneficiaries of Old Money," Aldrich writes, "never feel the bite of
costs and consequences. . . . Their money enables them to be saved
from many of the consequences of their actions, and relatively speaking,
from risk itself." Substitute the words *Social Security* for *money* and you
have the core arguments of the Cato Institute and other hard-line
proponents of Social Security privatization.

People who are worried about the moral hazards of Social Security
and other forms of government help should be trying to clamp down on
inherited wealth as well. They should be instituting the kind of
confiscatory policies toward inheritance that have been established in
Europe, to reduce the social pathologies associated with great wealth.
The "help" provided by inheritance is surely less defensible than that
offered by Social Security: at least Social Security retirement benefits are
pegged to some sort of contribution to the workforce, as well as a
working lifetime of payroll taxes. Inheritance is just an accident of birth.

This is a pressing issue, because concentrated wealth has increased
so dramatically that large inheritances today are no longer the province
of a stratospheric elite but of increasingly large segments of the
population. Whatever limitations the estate tax may have put on the
moral hazards of inheritance are now being eroded by President Bush's
decision to start repealing the tax. It was in recognition of this danger
that 100 of the country's wealthiest citizens—Warren Buffett, Steven
Rockefeller, and William Gates, Sr., among them—spoke out publicly
and vehemently against ending the estate tax. In testimony before
Congress earlier this year, Gates warned that repeal of the tax would
create "an aristocracy of wealth that has nothing to do with merit."

Conservatives were apparently unworried about the danger of
inherited wealth to our nation's moral fiber. So why are they worried
about the "moral hazard" of giving a few hundred dollars a month to
retired workers? Personal responsibility, in the Bush administration,
seems to lie in finding an opportunity to inherit. When Barry Goldwater
ran for president and proposed repealing Social Security, he was
lampooned by the cartoonist Herblock, who showed Goldwater, heir to
a dry-goods fortune, lecturing two urchins: "If you had any initiative,
you'd go out and inherit a department store." At the time, Goldwater's
views were widely considered ridiculous. Today they are national policy.

DISCUSSION QUESTIONS

1. Do you believe that Social Security benefits will be available to you when you retire?
2. What should be the goals of the Social Security program? Should the program provide an income floor for the elderly? Should Social Security operate as a pension plan that pays identical benefits to all contributing Americans? To individuals proportionate to their individual contributions? Should the goals be something other than those noted here?
3. Do you believe it is inappropriate for current workers to subsidize retirees?
4. What should be done now to avoid the future imbalance between Social Security receipts and projected benefit payments? Raise taxes? Reduce benefits? Something else?
5. Social Security was designed originally, in part, to be a social insurance program against old-age poverty. How does the prospect of privatizing the program affect this?
6. Would you be willing to invest your own retirement funds, rather than letting the government do it for you?
7. Economists use the term "moral hazard" to characterize insurance programs that might encourage contributors to take advantage of program benefits (e.g., arsonists who burn their own buildings to receive fire insurance benefits). How might this apply to Social Security, if at all?

WEB REFERENCES

Cato Institute Project on Social Security Privatization, http://www.socialsecurity.org/.

Institute for America's Future, http://socialsecurity.ourfuture.org/.

The Century Foundation, Social Security Network, http://www.socsec.org/.

National Center for Policy Analysis, http://www.mysocialsecurity.org/.

President's Commission to Strengthen Social Security, http://www.csss.gov/.

Social Security Reform Center (Heritage Foundation), http://www.socialsecurity reform.org/index.cfm.

Urban Institute Reports on Social Security, http://www.urban.org/content/IssuesInFocus/SocialSecurity/Reports/Reports.htm.

U.S. Social Security Administration, http://www.ssa.gov/.

FURTHER READING

Aaron, Henry, et al. *Should the United States Privatize Social Security?* Cambridge, Mass.: MIT Press, 1999.

Baker, Dean. "The Privateers' Free Lunch." *American Prospect,* vol. 32 (May–June 1997), pp. 81–84.

Berkowitz, Edward D. *Mr. Social Security: The Life of Wilbur J. Cohen.* Lawrence: University of Kansas Press, 1995.

Coll, Blanche D. *Safety Net: Welfare and Social Security 1929–1979.* New Brunswick, N.J.: Rutgers University Press, 1995.

Derthick, Martha. *Agency under Stress: The Social Security Administration in American Government.* Washington, D.C.: Brookings Institution, 1990.

Diamond, Peter A., David C. Lindeman, and Howard Young, eds. *Social Security: What Role for the Future?* Washington, D.C. : Brookings Institution, 1996.

Kingson, Eric R. and James H. Schulz, eds. *Social Security in the 21st Century.* New York: Oxford University Press, 1997.

Leone, Richard C. "Why Boomers Don't Spell Bust." *American Prospect,* vol. 30 (January–February 1997), pp. 68–72.

Marmor, Theodore R. and Jerry L. Mashaw, eds. *Social Security: Beyond the Rhetoric of Crisis.* Princeton, N.J.: Princeton University Press, 1988.

Marmor, Theodore R., Timothy M. Smeeding, and Vernon L. Greene, eds. *Economic Security and Intergenerational Justice: A Look at North America.* Washington, D.C.: Urban Institute Press, 1994.

Mashaw, Jerry L. and Theodore R. Marmor. "The Great Social Security Scare." *American Prospect,* vol. 29 (November–December 1996), pp. 30–37.

Panis, Constantijn W. A. *Social Security: Equity, Adequacy, Reforms.* Santa Monica, Calif.: Rand, 1996.

Peterson, Peter G. *Will America Grow Up before It Grows Old? How the Coming Social Security Crisis Threatens You, Your Family, and Your Country.* New York: Random House, 1996.

Peterson, Peter G. "Will America Grow Up before It Grows Old?" *Atlantic Monthly,* vol. 277 (May 1996), pp. 55–86.

Rauch, Jonathan. *Demosclerosis: The Silent Killer of American Government.* New York: Times Books, 1994.

Research and Policy Committee of the Committee for Economic Development. *Fixing Social Security: A Statement.* New York: Committee for Economic Development, 1997.

Samuelson, Robert J. *The Good Life and Its Discontents: The American Dream in the Age of Entitlement, 1945–1995.* New York: Times Books, 1995.

Sass, Steven A. and Robert K. Triest, eds. *Social Security Reform: Conference Proceedings.* Boston: Federal Reserve Bank of Boston, June 1997.

Seidman, Laurence S. *Funding Social Security: A Strategic Alternative.* Cambridge: University Press, 1999.

Tynes, Sheryl R. *Turning Points in Social Security: From "Cruel Hoax" to "Sacred Entitlement."* Palo Alto, Calif.: Stanford University Press, 1996.

Weisbrot, Mark and Dean Baker. *Social Security: The Phony Crisis.* Chicago: University of Chicago Press, 1999.

White, Joseph. *False Alarm : Why the Greatest Threat to Social Security and Medicare Is the Campaign to "Save" Them* (Century Foundation Book). Baltimore: Johns Hopkins University Press, 2001.

Chapter 4

GLOBALIZATION

"Does Globalization Promote Economic Equality?"

YES: David Dollar and Aart Kraay "Spreading the
Wealth" *Foreign Affairs*

NO: James K. Galbraith "The Crisis of Globalization"
Dissent

The protests of the World Trade Organization meetings in Seattle in 1999 drew international media attention to the ill effects of globalization. The protesters disrupted the meetings and local businesses, caused significant property damage, and catalyzed a growing movement of labor, environmental, women's, and other groups in opposition to the negative effects of the sort of large multinational institutions that have followed meetings of the WTO, World Bank, and other international organizations around the world. While this was hardly the first time debate had occurred regarding globalization, it visually depicted the animus between policy elites who support greater economic integration of national economies and activists who passionately oppose many forms of globalization.

The term "globalization" is heard almost everywhere, from town meetings and television to protesters and pundits. Yet because the term is so expansive, those who celebrate or renounce globalization often refer to only a few of its quite different dimensions, which include economic, commercial, political, cultural, and social factors. Thus, the meaning of globalization is itself something of an open question. Does it mean the growing dominance of English among spoken languages worldwide? Or the effects of the multi-billion dollar American and European agricultural subsidies on farmers in developing nations? Or the export of popular western culture, through films, television, and celebrities such as Michael Jackson, Kobe Bryant, and Julia Roberts, to traditional and nonwestern societies? Or the fact that commercial markets have opened to such an extent that a citizen of Germany, for example, is likely to be exposed to the same television shows, soft drinks, fast-food restaurants, and coffee shop chains as a resident of Muncie, Indiana? Or the fact that a car purchased in Montana may contain parts from more than

10 different nations, was partially assembled in two or more countries, and was sold by a dealership with investors from Canada, Mexico, and the United States? Or the reduction of tariffs affecting the export/import of goods and services from one country to another? Or the influence of multinational corporations—wherever they may be based—on workers and their working conditions around the world? Or the international transmission of infectious diseases? Or the flow of information worldwide through the Internet? Or apparel sweat-shops in Indonesia? Or the globalization of crime and terrorism through multinational networks? Or a long list of other possibilities? All of these can constitute one's understanding of globalization, and therefore its meaning is ambiguous.

While the particulars can vary, globalization generally refers to an expansion of linkages around the world that tend to break down national borders (in a nongeographical sense) and bring people into closer contact with other people, products, or information in sometimes distant places. Globalization is certainly nothing new: Ancient trade routes united peoples from distant lands long before the advent of "modern" technologies like refrigeration, railroads, shipping, the telephone, jet aircraft, and the Internet. What is relatively new is the rapid and sometimes instantaneous transmission of people, goods, and information around the world, and the perception that groups of people and institutions, who have never been linked, now are or can be through modern technologies. Some of these linkages are viewed favorably, such as fast and inexpensive communication or burgeoning democracy; others, however, reveal globalization's negative effects, such as international terrorism or the trafficking of women.

Even the economic integration of nations has been happening for centuries. Nevertheless, the development of new and efficient transportation systems, especially through shipping and rail, coupled with dynamic indus-trial development in the last half of the nineteenth century, propelled a new era of economic integration among nations. Technological improvements have dramatically reduced transportation and communications costs. Freight charges in 1990 were just one-third that of 1920, while the cost of a telephone call from London to New York City fell from $244 in 1930 to $3.32 by 1990.[1] This has been accelerated with the integration of financial markets in recent decades, and the Internet in some cases reduces the marginal transmission costs to zero. More recently, coupled with technological improvements have been public-sector changes that have reduced trade barriers through economic liberalization policies, such as reduced tariffs or other barriers to trade, in many countries that have facilitated trade. The share of U.S. exports as a proportion of the economy has doubled from 1900 to 2000, to approxi-mately 12 percent today. However, the world was in many ways substantially integrated economically more than a hundred years ago. Britain was far more integrated into the world economy in 1900 than today, and one scholar notes generally that "the world even by the turn of the millennium was no more integrated than that of the preceding turn of the century."[2]

After a retreat from globalization during the First and Second World Wars, the biggest push toward economic integration occurred after the Second World War. The conference among representatives of 45 nations at Bretton Woods, New Hampshire, in 1944 established the two key global financial institutions that continue to be involved with international finance and poverty alleviation in the world today: the International Monetary Fund (IMF) and the International Bank for Reconstruction and Development (the World Bank). The IMF comprises 184 member nations and is charged with promoting international monetary cooperation and expanding international trade. The World Bank consists of 180 member countries and works in developing nations to improve living standards and eliminate poverty, largely through billions of dollars annually in loan and direct-aid programs to governments. The Bretton Woods institutions now include the IMF, World Bank, World Trade Organization, and regional development banks, such as the Inter-American Development Bank and Asian Development Bank, among others. In addition, there are periodic meetings of G-5, G-7, and G-8 nations to discuss international economic affairs.[3]

These organizations were criticized long before the term "globalization" was popularized. The World Bank has suffered criticism that its support for projects in developing nations does more to promote domestic political and commercial interests than to alleviate poverty and suffering among citizens. The IMF, through its support of "structural adjustment," has been criticized for forcing (by withholding loans) poorer nations to undertake fiscal austerity programs that require cutting essential public-sector health and educational services that serve the poor in order to achieve the fiscal discipline that the IMF requires. The World Trade Organization, the subject of the Seattle protests, has been criticized for promoting free trade despite the possible deleterious implications for local industries and workers, particularly those in developing nations. And all of these institutions have been subject to the common criticism that they are promoting westernization rather than globalization and are really serving the interests of the developed world (i.e., the United States, Europe, and Japan) at the expense of their poorer neighbors. Further, critics charge them with hypocrisy when they require the reduction or elimination of barriers to free trade while wealthy nations continue to provide subsidies or trade barriers to agriculture, apparel, transportation, and other industries.

Recognizing the many facets of and dilemmas posed by globalization, this chapter focuses attention on one of the most important dimensions of the debate: whether globalization promotes greater equality among the world's people or, as detractors argue, whether economic integration empowers capitalists at the expense of low-skilled and unskilled workers and other marginalized groups. The debate, however, is extremely complicated, in large part due to the inherent ambiguity of the debate's two central terms: "globalization" and "equality."

As discussed above, different people conceive of globalization in different ways, and the same is true of equality. While equality or fairness is generally thought to be a desirable characteristic of any public policy, disagreements arise over the specifics. Does equality mean equality of material outcomes (e.g., all people have the same levels of health care)? Equality of opportunities? Equality of political representation to decide on policies and outcomes? Deborah Stone's book *Policy Paradox* contains a memorable section in which she describes the seemingly simple decision of fairly distributing a chocolate cake among a classroom of students. Should each person get the same size piece of cake? (But does that make sense if some people are hungrier than others, or some don't like chocolate cake?) Should the class vote on who gets cake? (But suppose a coalition forms to exclude 45 percent of the class from getting any cake?) Should there be a free-for-all? (But what about those who are physically weaker or less aggressive?) No matter how you cut it (excuse the pun), there are different views on what might be considered "equal" and, therefore, the appropriate way to divide the cake. The same holds with the inherently political decisions of what equality means within and across societies, although the stakes for many of the world's citizens are far less trivial than how much cake they deserve.

In addition to the conceptual difficulties of deciding what is meant by equality are the significant measurement difficulties involved in assessing equality. For example, suppose one decides that a nation's citizens should have relatively equal distributions of material resources, itself a controversial proposition. (Suppose some people are more skilled or work harder?) What measure of material well-being is appropriate? Should wealth or income be considered? (For example, is the senior citizen with a $15,000 annual income but ownership of a $300,000 home better off than the 24-year-old with no assets but a $40,000 income?) Should the purchasing power of money in different regions be considered? Should we consider income in absolute or relative terms? (For example, would you rather live in a society where your annual income was $45,000 compared with an average of $35,000 nationwide, or where your annual income was $60,000 income with the average income in that society of $90,000? In the first case, you are relatively rich but poorer in absolute terms compared with the second.) Equality is therefore difficult both to conceptualize and to measure.

In absolute terms, the level of material deprivation among many of the world's people is staggering, particularly among those in sub-Saharan Africa and parts of Asia and South America. Poverty rates in the entire continent of Africa are at 46 percent, and sub-Saharan Africa has the highest poverty rate in the world. Nearly one in three Asians is poor, with that continent containing three-fourths of the world's poor.[4] According to the *Global Poverty Report* prepared for the G-8 nations meeting in Okinawa, an estimated 1.2 billion people worldwide live on less than $1 per day, and more than twice that many on less than $2 per day. Fully 110 million of the world's children at the primary school level are out of school, with 60 percent of them girls. Many millions live without clean water, health care, and sufficient food, and an estimated 31 million people are infected with HIV/AIDS.[5] Worldwide, $1\frac{1}{2}$ billion people do not have access to clean drinking water, and an estimated 3 million children die each year from diseases that could be prevented with vaccines. Among the World Bank's regions classified as "developing," sub-Saharan Africa and South Asia face the greatest difficulties. Life expectancy at birth is 62 in South Asia and just 47 in sub-Saharan Africa; the under-5 mortality rate is 96 and 162 (respectively) per 1,000 people; and youth illiteracy rates are at 23 percent for males and 40 percent for females in South Asia, and 17 percent for males and 27 percent for females in sub-Saharan Africa. Clearly, the challenges facing these nations are multidimensional and overwhelm the current support capacities of poor nations.[6]

In comparative terms, there is little doubt that inequality both within countries and across countries has worsened in recent decades. The development economist Nancy Birdsall notes that "the ratio of income of the richest to the poorest country in the world has risen from about 9 to 1 at the end of the nineteenth century to 60 to 1 today."[7] There is some debate about whether inequality has increased among *people* worldwide as opposed to nations; they are not the same. Because China is far larger than Panama, it makes more sense to measure inequality among individuals rather than nations, which is where most current statistics are derived. And because large, relatively poor nations like China and India have increased living standards considerably in recent years, some have argued that per capita inequality has not worsened, even while it has using nations as the unit of measurement. While there is some disagreement about the nature of the differences (for example, the level of inequality is less pronounced when measured in purchasing power rather than at market exchange rates since the cost of living is lower in poorer nations), the chief debate remains why inequality has increased (at least among nations, if not people) and what role, if any, globalization has played in increasing inequalities.

To begin to understand these differences, it is important to understand why an overwhelming majority of economists as well as globalization advocates favor free trade. The advantages of free trade were first explicated by the economist David Ricardo describing the (somewhat counterintuitive) benefits to all countries of "comparative advantage." Suppose, for example, that there exist just two countries, and one can produce every commodity more cheaply than the other. Ricardo argued that even in this case, it made sense for the productive country to specialize in producing what it made most efficiently, while the unproductive country produces those goods that it makes efficiently relative to its other productive capacity and that of the other nation. In short, although one country may enjoy an absolute advantage in producing goods, the relevant consideration is the comparative advantage relative to other nations' capabilities. Why? Because total output will be greater if both nations specialize rather than one country producing both goods. As a commonly used example illustrates, a corporate CEO may be a faster typist than her secretary, but it still makes sense for her to focus on leading the company and for the secretary to do the typing. In other words, the total output of the CEO and her secretary would drop if the CEO performed both tasks, even though she is better at both. Economists therefore argue that tariffs or other restraints of trade—in this example, reducing or prohibiting the "trade" between the CEO and her secretary—reduces total output and therefore the wealth of both nations. There is little sense in growing bananas in the United States and apples in Panama, economists argue, when each country is better off specializing in production and then trading. Even where free traders acknowledge that trade barriers such as tariffs save U.S. jobs, they contend that they do so at great cost. For example, an earlier study by Gary Hufbauer and Kim Elliott of the Institute for International Economics found that protectionism in 21 of the most protected U.S. industries resulted in saving 191,000 jobs, but at an annual cost of $170,000 each (compared with the average hourly pay in those industries of $7.76). Economists therefore argue that everyone would be better off if protectionist tariffs were eliminated, thereby lowering prices to consumers, and workers who lost jobs compensated accordingly. (At $170,000 annually per job, there is plenty of room for mutual benefit to consumers and workers.)

Free trade advocates also argue that the benefits of trade have ripple effects in noneconomic areas such as health and the environment, and that it may encourage social and political equality. The wealthier a country becomes, they argue, the more the nation is able to provide health care and improve environmental conditions. Once people are able to provide for themselves clean drinking water, adequate food and shelter, and other necessities, all of which free traders argue are enhanced by liberal trade policies, they will be in the position to demand public-sector provision of better schools, roads, and other requirements for a more educated and developed society. Therefore, free traders argue, the benefits of trade extend well beyond simple economic necessities like food and shelter to health, education, and environmental improvements that citizens in many wealthy nations take for granted. Thus, once-poor nations like China and India have grown dramatically in recent decades and have been able to provide greater material resources for their citizens. Further, globalization supporters contend that the most effective way to reduce inequality is to support wealth-generating activities in poorer nations.

The power of free trade as a political as well as economic principle was evidenced by the support for NAFTA in the United States in the mid-1990s. NAFTA created the world's largest free trade area by forming an agreement to eliminate tariffs and encourage trade among the Mexican, Canadian, and U.S. economies. Signed into law in 1994 under a Democratic administration (some of whose constituencies, such as organized labor, strongly opposed such agreements), NAFTA pitted arguments for free trade against concerns of environmental degradation, job losses, and reduced labor standards voiced by many labor leaders and activists. The final agreement included provisions in the United States for compensating workers who lost their jobs due to NAFTA as well as side agreements on labor and environmental protection. Aside from the debate over economic integration, which continues today, NAFTA underscores the point that not all globalization efforts are driven by large multinational institutions like the IMF and World Bank, but are motivated in large part by the *idea* that free trade is desirable.

In recent years, one policy debate that has brought these issues to the fore involves so-called sweatshops in developing nations, where western companies have hired local workers to produce sneakers, clothing, and other goods in low-paying and poor-quality working conditions, at least by western standards. Firms such as Nike, the Gap, and many others have been subject to intense criticism that although they may be adhering to local workplace and compensation policies, they are exploiting individuals in developing nations who are paid pennies a day for producing soccer and basketball shoes that cost more than $100 per pair in wealthy nations like Germany and the United States. The maquiladoras in northern Mexico, where mostly U.S. assembly firms hire Mexican workers who work in areas with open sewers and atrocious environmental conditions, have been the subject of criticism by globalization opponents who see evidence of exploitation just across the U.S. border. For opponents of globalization, the image of wealthy western teenagers walking around in expensive sports shoes produced by impoverished children and adults working under grueling labor conditions in developing nations is symbolic of the economic and personal exploitation of the poor by rich companies and nations. For them, free trade simply encourages companies to move production to "less expensive" countries where environmental and labor standards either do not exist or are minimal; what inevitably results, it is argued, is a "race to the bottom" in which developing nations desperate for work and money further relax their standards in order to compete with one another to attract companies from developed nations (where environmental and labor standards are relatively strong, and relatively expensive). The result is lower prices for goods sold mostly in rich developed nations, but also the loss of jobs in those countries and the further exploitation of low- and middle-class workers and their environment in developing nations.

Globalization supporters acknowledge the terrible working and living conditions of the world's poor, but contend that life would be worse without even the low-paying jobs that multinational corporations bring to developing nations. Although Mexican workers, for example, are living far below western standards in the maquiladoras, the jobs are better than otherwise available in Mexico; as evidence, supporters point to the significant labor supply for jobs that are reasonably well paid by Mexican standards. Free traders argue that placing stringent environmental, health, and labor standards on developing nations will discourage firms from locating plants there and will actually raise international inequality by denying jobs to those who most need them, even if the working conditions are well below western standards.

In the articles that follow, World Bank economists David Dollar and Aart Kraay argue that globalization, especially that since 1980, has reduced poverty and economic inequality, and they support continued trade liberalization and international investment both to raise material living standards and to improve international equality. Economist James Galbraith, on the other hand, argues that economic trade liberalization, including privatization and deregulation efforts, has been a failure that has caused greater inequality worldwide, and he urges better development policies targeted to the poor who "need to eat every day."

Endnotes

1. Jeffrey Frankel, "Globalization of the Economy," in Joseph S. Nye and John D. Donahue, eds., *Governance in the Globalizing World* (Washington, D.C.: Brookings Institution), 2000, p. 46.
2. Ibid., p. 48.
3. The G-5 nations are France, Germany, Japan, the United Kingdom, and the United States. For the G-7 members, add Canada and Italy. The G-8 includes the above plus Russia.
4. *Global Poverty Report* (July 2000) (World Bank website, http://www.worldbank.org/html/extdr/extme/G8_poverty2000.pdf).
5. Ibid.
6. World Development Indicators database, World Bank, April 20, 2002, http://www.worldbank.org/data/databytopic/reg_wdi.pdf.
7. www.ceip.org/people/birdspeech121898.htm.

YES

Spreading the Wealth

David Dollar and Aart Kraay

A RISING TIDE

ONE OF THE MAIN CLAIMS of the antiglobalization movement is that globalization is widening the gap between the haves and the have-nots. It benefits the rich and does little for the poor, perhaps even making their lot harder. As union leader Jay Mazur put it these pages "globalization has dramatically increased inequality between and within nations" ("Labor's New Internationalism," *Foreign Affairs*, January/February 2000). The problem with this new conventional wisdom is that the best evidence available shows the exact opposite to be true. So far, the current wave of globalization, which started around 1980, has actually promoted economic equality and reduced poverty.

Global economic integration has complex effects on income, culture, society, and the environment. But in the debate over globalization's merits, its impact on poverty is particularly important. If international trade and investment primarily benefit the rich, many people will feel that restricting trade to protect jobs, culture, or the environment is worth the costs. But if restricting trade imposes further hardship on poor people in the developing world, many of the same people will think otherwise.

Three facts bear on this question. First, a long-term global trend toward greater inequality prevailed for at least 200 years; it peaked around 1975. But since then, it has stabilized and possibly even reversed. The chief reason for the change has been the accelerated growth of two large and initially poor countries: China and India.

Second, a strong correlation links increased participation in international trade and investment on the one hand and faster growth on the other. The developing world can be divided into a "globalizing" group of countries that have seen rapid increases in trade and foreign investment over the last two decades—well above the rates for rich countries—and a "nonglobalizing" group that trades even less of its income today than it did 20 years ago. The aggregate annual per capita growth rate of the globalizing group accelerated steadily from one percent in the 1960s to five percent in the 1990s. During that latter decade, in contrast, rich countries grew at two percent and nonglobaliz-

DAVID DOLLAR and AART KRAAY are economists at the World Bank's Development Research Group. The views expressed here are their own.

ers at only one percent. Economists are cautious about drawing conclusions concerning causality, but they largely agree that openness to foreign trade and investment (along with complementary reforms) explains the faster growth of the globalizers.

Third, and contrary to popular perception, globalization has not resulted in higher inequality within economies. Inequality has indeed gone up in some countries (such as China) and down in others (such as the Philippines). But those changes are not systematically linked to globalization measures such as trade and investment flows, tariff rates, and the presence of capital controls. Instead, shifts in inequality stem more from domestic education, taxes, and social policies. In general, higher growth rates in globalizing developing countries have translated into higher incomes for the poor. Even with its increased inequality, for example, China has seen the most spectacular reduction of poverty in world history—which was supported by opening its economy to foreign trade and investment.

Although globalization can be a powerful force for poverty reduction, its beneficial results are not inevitable. If policymakers hope to tap the full potential of economic integration and sustain its benefits, they must address three critical challenges. A growing protectionist movement in rich countries that aims to limit integration with poor ones must be stopped in its tracks. Developing countries need to acquire the kinds of institutions and policies that will allow them to prosper under globalization, both of which may be different from place to place. And more migration, both domestic and international, must be permitted when geography limits the potential for development.

THE GREAT DIVIDE

OVER the past 200 years, different local economies around the world have become more integrated while the growth rate of the global economy has accelerated dramatically. Although it is impossible to prove causal linkage between the two developments—since there are no other world economies to be tested against—evidence suggests the arrows run in both directions. As Adam Smith argued, a larger market permits a finer division of labor, which in turn facilitates innovation and learning by doing. Some of that innovation involves transportation and communications technologies that lower costs and increase integration. So it is easy to see how integration and innovation can be mutually supportive.

Different locations have become more integrated because of increased flows of goods, capital, and knowledge. From 1820 to 1914, international trade increased faster than the global economy. Trade rose from about 2 percent of world income in 1820 to 18 percent in 1914. The globalization of trade took a step backward during the protectionist period of the Great Depression and World War II, and by 1950 trade (in relation to income) was lower than it had been in 1914. But thanks to a series of multilateral trade liberalizations under the General Agreement on Tariffs and Trade (GATT), trade dramatically expanded among industrialized countries between 1960 and 1980. Most developing countries remained largely isolated from this trade because of their own inward-focused policies, but the success of such notable exceptions as Taiwan and South Korea eventually helped encourage other developing economies to open themselves up to foreign trade and investment.

International capital flows, measured as foreign ownership of assets relative to world income, also grew during the first wave of globalization and declined during the Great Depression and World War II; they did not return to 1914 levels until 1980. But since then, such flows have increased markedly and changed their nature as well. One hundred years ago, foreign capital typically financed public infrastructure projects (such as canals and railroads) or direct investment related to natural resources. Today, in contrast, the bulk of capital flows to developing countries is direct investments tied to manufacturing and services.

The change in the nature of capital flows is clearly related to concurrent advances in economic integration, such as cheaper and faster transportation and revolutionary changes in telecommunications. Since 1920, seagoing freight charges have declined by about two-thirds and air travel costs by 84 percent; the cost of a three-minute call from New York City to London has dropped by 99 percent. Today, production in widely differing locations can be integrated in ways that simply were not possible before.

Another aspect of integration has been the movement of people. Yet here the trend is reversed: there is much more international travel than in the past but much less permanent migration. Between 1870 and 1910, about ten percent of the world's population relocated permanently from one country to another; over the past 25 years, only one to two percent have done so.

As economic integration has progressed, the annual growth rate of the world economy has accelerated, from 1 percent in the mid-nineteenth century to 3.5 percent in 1960–2000. Sustained over many years, such a jump in growth makes a huge difference in real living standards. It now takes only two to three years, for example, for the world economy to produce the same amount of goods and services that it did during the entire nineteenth century. Such a comparison is arguably a serious understatement of the true difference, since most of what is consumed today—airline travel, cars, televisions, synthetic fibers, life-extending drugs—did not exist 200 years ago. For any of these goods or services, therefore, the growth rate of output since 1820 is infinite. Human productivity has increased almost unimaginably.

All this tremendous growth in wealth was distributed very unequally up to about 1975, but since then growing equality has taken hold. One good measure of inequality among individuals worldwide is the mean log deviation—a measure of the gap between the income of any randomly selected person and a general average. It takes into account the fact that income distributions everywhere are skewed in favor of the rich, so that the typical person is poorer than the group average; the more skewed the distribution, the larger the gap. Per capital income

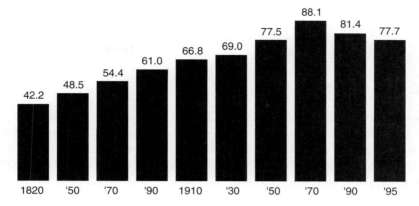

FIGURE 1   **Worldwide Income Inequality, 1820–1995, in percent**

Note: Figures represent the mean log deviation between a typical individual income and the average per capita income.

Sources: F. Bourguignon and C. Morrisson, "Inequality Among World Citizens, 1820–1992," working paper 2001–25 (Paris: Department and Laboratory of Applied and Theoretical Economics, 2001); and David Dollar, "Globalization, Inequality, and Poverty Since 1980," World Bank background paper, available at http://www.worldbank.org/research/global.

in the world today, for example, is around $5,000, whereas a randomly selected person would most likely be living on close to $1,000—80 percent less. That gap translates into a mean log deviation of 0.8.

Taking this approach, an estimate of the world distribution of income among individuals shows rising inequality between 1820 and 1975. In that period, the gap between the typical person and world per capita income increased from about 40 percent to about 80 percent. Since changes in income inequality within countries were small, the increase in inequality was driven mostly by differences in growth rates across countries. Areas that were already relatively rich in 1820 (notably, Europe and the United States) grew faster than poor areas (notably, China and India). Global inequality peaked sometime in the 1970s, but it then stabilized and even began to decline, largely because growth in China and India began to accelerate.

Another way of looking at global inequality is to examine what is happening to the extreme poor—those people living on less than $1 per day. Although the percentage of the world's population living in poverty has declined over time, the absolute number rose fairly steadily until 1980. During the Great Depression and World War II, the number of poor increased particularly sharply, and it declined somewhat immediately thereafter. The world economy grew strongly between 1960 and 1980, but the number of poor rose because growth did not occur in the places where the worst-off live. But since then, the most rapid growth has occurred in poor locations. Consequently the number of poor has declined by 200 million since 1980. Again, this trend is explained primarily by the rapid income growth in China and India, which together in 1980 accounted for about one-third of the world's population and more than 60 percent of the world's extreme poor.

UPWARD BOUND

THE SHIFT in the trend in global inequality coincides with the shift in the economic strategies of several large developing countries. Following World War II, most developing regions chose strategies that focused inward and discouraged integration with the global economy. But these approaches were not particularly successful, and throughout the 1960s and 1970s developing countries on the whole grew less rapidly than industrialized ones. The oil shocks and U.S. inflation of the 1970s created severe problems for them, contributing to negative growth, high inflation, and debt crises over the next several years. Faced with these disappointing results, several developing countries began to alter their strategies starting in the 1980s.

For example, China had an extremely closed economy until the mid-1970s. Although Beijing's initial economic reform focused on agriculture, a key part of its approach since the 1980s has involved opening up foreign trade and investment, including a drop in its tariff rates by two-thirds and its nontariff barriers by even more. These reforms have led to unprecedented economic growth in the country's coastal provinces and more moderate growth in the interior. From 1978 to 1994 the Chinese economy grew annually by 9 percent, while exports grew by 14 percent and imports by 13 percent. Of course, China and other globalizing developing countries have pursued a wide range of reforms, not just economic openness. Beijing has strengthened property rights through land reform and moved from a planned economy toward a market-oriented one, and these measures have contributed to its integration as well as to its growth.

Other developing countries have also opened up as a part of broader reform programs. During the 1990s, India liberalized foreign trade and investment with good results; its annual per capita income growth now tops four percent. It too has pursued a broad agenda of reform and has moved away from a highly regulated, planned system. Meanwhile, Uganda and Vietnam are the best examples of very low-income countries that have increased their participation in trade and investment and prospered as a result. And in the western hemisphere, Mexico is noteworthy both for signing its free-trade agreement with the United States and Canada in 1993 and for its rapid growth since then, especially in the northern regions near the U.S. border.

These cases illustrate how openness to foreign trade and investment, coupled with complementary reforms, typically leads to faster growth. India, China, Vietnam, Uganda, and Mexico are not isolated examples; in general, countries that have become more open have grown faster. The best way to illustrate this trend is to rank developing countries in order of their increases in trade relative to national income over the past 20 years. The top third of this list can be thought of as the "globalizing" camp, and the bottom two-thirds as the "nonglobalizing" camp. The globalizers have increased their trade relative to income by 104 percent over the past two decades, compared to 71 percent for rich countries. The nonglobalizers, meanwhile, actually trade less today than they did 20 years ago. The globalizers have also cut their import tariffs by 22 percentage points on average, compared to only 11 percentage points for the nonglobalizers.

How have the globalizers fared in terms of growth? Their average annual growth rates accelerated from 1 percent in the 1960s to 3 percent in the 1970s, 4 percent in the 1980s, and 5 percent in the 1990s. Rich countries' annual growth rates, by comparison, slowed to about 2 percent in the 1990s, and the nonglobalizers saw their growth rates decline from 3 percent in the 1970s to 1 percent in the 1980s and 1990s.

The same pattern can be observed on a local level. Within both China and India, the locations that are integrating with the global economy are growing much more rapidly than the disconnected regions. Indian states, for example, vary significantly in the quality of their investment climates as measured by government efficiency, corruption, and infrastructure. Those states with better investment climates have integrated themselves more closely with outside markets and have experienced more investment (domestic and foreign) than their less-integrated counterparts. Moreover, states that were initially poor and then created good investment climates had stronger poverty reduction in the 1990s than those not integrating with the global economy. Such internal comparisons are important because, by holding national trade and macroeconomic policies constant, they reveal how important it is to complement trade liberalization with institutional reform so that integration can actually occur.

The accelerated growth rates of globalizing countries such as China, India, and Vietnam are consistent with cross-country comparisons that find openness going hand in hand with faster growth. The most that these studies can establish is that more trade and investment is highly correlated with higher growth, so one needs to be careful about drawing conclusions about causality. Still, the overall evidence from individual cases and cross-country correlation is persuasive. As economists Peter Lindert and Jeffrey Williamson have written, "even though no one study can establish that openness to trade has unambiguously helped the representative Third World economy, the preponderance of evidence supports this conclusion." They go on to note that "there are no antiglobal victories to report for the postwar Third World."

Contrary to the claims of the antiglobalization movement, therefore, greater openness to international trade and investment has in fact helped

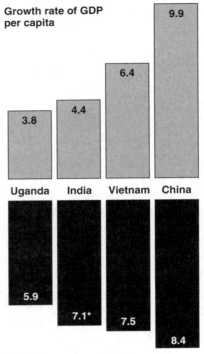

FIGURE 2   GDP Growth and Poverty Reduction in Uganda, India, Vietnam, and China, 1992–98, in percent per year

*India poverty reduction figure is for 1993–99.

Source: David Dollar, "Globalization, Inequality, and Poverty Since 1980," World Bank background paper, available at http://www.worldbank.org/research/global.

narrow the gap between rich and poor countries rather than widen it. During the 1990s, the economies of the globalizers, with a combined population of about 3 billion, grew more than twice as fast as the rich countries. The nonglobalizers, in contrast, grew only half as fast and nowadays lag further and further behind. Much of the discussion of global inequality assumes that there is growing divergence between the developing world and the rich world, but this is simply not true. The most important development in global inequality in recent decades is the growing divergence within the developing world, and it is directly related to whether countries take advantage of the economic benefits that globalization can offer.

THE PATH OUT OF POVERTY

The antiglobalization movement also claims that economic integration is worsening inequality within countries as well as between them. Until the mid-1980s, there was insufficient evidence to support strong conclusions on this important topic. But now more and more developing countries have begun to conduct household income and consumption surveys of reasonable quality. (In low-income countries, these surveys typically track what households actually consume because so much of their real income is self-produced and not part of the money economy.) Good surveys now exist for 137 countries, and many go back far enough to measure changes in inequality over time.

One way of looking at inequality within countries is to focus on what happens to the bottom 20 percent of households as globalization and growth proceed apace. Across all countries, incomes of the poor grow at around the same rate as GDP. Of course, there is a great deal of variation around that average relationship. In some countries, income distribution has shifted in favor of the poor; in others, against them. But these shifts cannot be explained by any globalization-related variable. So it simply cannot be said that inequality necessarily rises with more trade, more foreign investment, and lower tariffs. For many globalizers, the overall change in distribution was small, and in some cases (such as the Philippines and Malaysia) it was even in favor of the poor. What changes in inequality do reflect are country-specific policies on education, taxes, and social protection.

It is important not to misunderstand this finding. China is an important example of a country that has had a large increase in inequality in the past decade, when the income of the bottom 20 percent has risen much less rapidly than per capita income. This trend may be related to greater openness, although domestic liberalization is a more likely cause. China started out in the 1970s with a highly equal distribution of income, and part of its reform has deliberately aimed at increasing the returns on education, which financially reward the better schooled. But the Chinese case is not typical; inequality has not increased in most of the developing countries that have opened up to foreign trade and investment. Furthermore, income distribution in China may have become more unequal, but the income of the poor in China has still risen rapidly. In fact, the country's progress in reducing poverty has been one of the most dramatic successes in history.

Because increased trade usually accompanies more rapid growth and does not systematically change household-income distribution, it generally is associated with improved well-being of the poor. Vietnam nicely illustrates this finding. As the nation has opened up, it has experienced a large increase in per capita income and no significant change in inequality. Thus the income of the poor has risen dramatically, and the number of Vietnamese living in absolute poverty dropped sharply from 75 percent of the population in

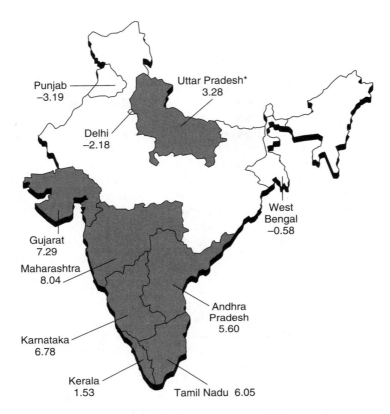

FIGURE 3   **Net Investment Rates in India, 1999, in percent**

*In September 2000, a new state. Uttaranchal, was created out of the northwestern section of Uttar Pradesh.

Note: Net investment rates represent the annual rate of growth of the capital stock of domestic and international firms. A negative rate implies that firms are pulling out.

Source: O. Goswami et al., "Competitiveness of Indian Manufacturing: Results of a Firm-Level Survey" (New Delhi: Confederation of Indian Industry, 2001).

1988 to 37 percent in 1998. Of the poorest 5 percent of households in 1992, 98 percent were better off six years later. And the improved well-being is not just a matter of income. Child labor has declined, and school enrollment has increased. It should be no surprise that the vast majority of poor households in Vietnam benefited immediately from a more liberalized trading system, since the country's opening has resulted in exports of rice (produced by most of the poor farmers) and labor-intensive products such as footwear. But the experience of China and Vietnam is not unique. India and Uganda also enjoyed rapid poverty reduction as they grew along with their integration into the global economy.

THE OPEN SOCIETIES

THESE FINDINGS have important implications for developing countries, for rich countries such as the United States, and for those who care about global poverty. All parties should recognize that the most recent wave of globalization has been a powerful force for equality and poverty reduction, and they should commit themselves to seeing that it continues despite the obstacles lying ahead.

It is not inevitable that globalization will proceed. In 1910, many believed globalization was unstoppable; they soon received a rude shock. History is not likely to repeat itself in the same way, but it is worth noting that antiglobalization sentiments are on the rise. A growing number of political leaders in the developing world realize that an open trading system is very much in their countries' interest. They would do well to heed Mexican President Vicente Fox, who said recently,

> We are convinced that globalization is good and it's good when you do your homework, . . . keep your fundamentals in line on the economy, build up high levels of education, respect the rule of law. . . . When you do your part, we are convinced that you get the benefit.

But today the narrow interests opposed to further integration—especially those in the rich countries—appear to be much more energetic than their opponents. In Québec City last spring and in Genoa last summer, a group of democratically elected leaders gathered to discuss how to pursue economic integration and improve the lives of their peoples. Antiglobalization demonstrators were quite effective in disrupting the meetings and drawing media attention to themselves. Leaders in developed and developing countries alike must make the proglobalization case more directly and effectively or risk having their opponents dominate the discussion and stall the process.

In addition, industrialized countries still raise protectionist measures against agricultural and labor-intensive products. Reducing those barriers would help developing countries significantly. The poorer areas of the world would benefit from further openings of their own markets as well, since 70 percent of the tariff barriers that developing countries face are from other developing countries.

If globalization proceeds, its potential to be an equalizing force will depend on whether poor countries manage to integrate themselves into the global economic system. True integration requires not just trade liberalization but wide-ranging institutional reform. Many of the nonglobalizing developing countries, such as Myanmar, Nigeria, Ukraine, and Pakistan, offer an unattractive investment climate. Even if they decide to open themselves up to trade, not much is likely to happen unless other reforms are also pursued. It is not easy to predict the reform paths of these countries; some of the relative successes in recent years, such as China, India, Uganda, and Vietnam, have come as quite a surprise. But as long as a location has weak institutions and policies, people living there are going to fall further behind the rest of the world.

Through their trade policies, rich countries can make it easier for those developing countries that do choose to open up and join the global trading club. But in recent years, the rich countries have been doing just the opposite. GATT was originally build around agreements concerning trade practices. Now, institutional harmonization, such as agreement on policies toward intellectual property rights, is a requirement for joining the WTO. Any sort of regulation of labor and environmental standards made under the threat of WTO sanctions would take this requirement for harmonization much further. Such measures would be neoprotectionist in effect, because they would thwart the integration of developing countries into the world economy and discourage trade between poor countries and rich ones.

The WTO meeting in Doha was an important step forward on trade integration. More forcefully than in Seattle, leaders of industrial countries were willing to make the case for further integration and put on the table issues of central concern to developing nations: access to pharmaceutical patents, use of antidumping measures against developing countries, and agricultural subsidies. The new round of trade negotiations launched at Doha has the potential to reverse the current trend, which makes it more difficult for poor countries to integrate with the world economy.

A final potential obstacle to successful and equitable globalization relates to geography. There is no inherent reason why coastal China should be poor; the same goes for southern India, northern Mexico, and Vietnam. All of these locations are near important markets or trade routes but were long held back by misguided policies. Now, with appropriate reforms, they are starting to grow rapidly and take their natural place in the world. But the same cannot be said for Mali, Chad, or other countries or regions cursed with "poor geography"— i.e., distance from markets, inherently high transport costs, and challenging health and agricultural problems. It would be naive to think that trade and investment alone can alleviate poverty in all locations. In fact, for those locations with poor geography, trade liberalization is less important than developing proper health care systems or providing basic infrastructure—or letting people move elsewhere.

Migration from poor locations is the missing factor in the current wave of globalization that could make a large contribution to reducing poverty. Each year, 83 million people are added to the world's population, 82 million of them in the developing world. In Europe and Japan, moreover, the population is aging and the labor force is set to shrink. Migration of relatively unskilled workers from South to North would thus offer clear economic benefits to both. Most migration from South to North is economically motivated, and it raises the living standard of the migrant while benefiting the sending country in three ways. First, it reduces the South's labor force and thus raises wages for those who remain behind. Second, migrants send remittances of hard currency back home. Finally, migration bolsters transnational trade and investment networks. In the case of Mexico, for example, ten percent of its citizens live and work in the United States, taking pressure off its own labor market and raising wages there. India gets six times as much in remittances from its workers overseas as it gets in foreign aid.

Unlike trade, however, migration remains highly restricted and controversial. Some critics perceive a disruptive impact on society and culture and fear downward pressure on wages and rising unemployment in the richer countries. Yet anti-immigration lobbies ignore the fact that geographical economic disparities are so strong that illegal immigration is growing rapidly anyway, despite restrictive policies. In a perverse irony, some of the worst abuses of globalization occur because there is not enough of it in key economic areas such as labor flows. Human traffic, for example, has become a highly lucrative, unregulated business in which illegal migrants are easy prey for exploitation.

Realistically, none of the industrialized countries is going to adopt open migration. But they should reconsider their migration policies. Some, for example, have a strong bias in their immigration rules toward highly skilled workers, which in fact spurs a "brain drain" from the developing world. Such policies do little to stop the flow of unskilled workers and instead push many of these people into the illegal category. If rich countries would legally accept more unskilled workers, they could address their own looming labor shortages, improve living standards in developing countries, and reduce illegal human traffic and its abuses.

In sum, the integration of poor economies with richer ones over the past two decades has provided many opportunities for poor people to improve their lives. Examples of the beneficiaries of globalization can be found among Mexican migrants, Chinese factory workers, Vietnamese peasants, and Ugandan farmers. Many of the better-off in developing and rich countries alike also benefit. After all the rhetoric about globalization is stripped away, many of the policy questions come down to whether the rich world will make integrating with the world economy easy for those poor communities that want to do so. The world's poor have a large stake in how the rich countries answer.

NO

The Crisis of Globalization

James K. Galbraith

The doctrine known as the Washington Consensus was, after its fashion, the Apostle's Creed of globalization. It was an expression of faith, that markets are efficient, that states are unnecessary, that the poor and the rich have no conflicting interests, that things turn out for the best when left alone. It held that privatization and deregulation and open capital markets promote economic development, that governments should balance budgets and fight inflation and do almost nothing else.

But none of this is actually true.

The truth is that poor people—vast majorities in most countries of the world—need to eat every day. Policies that guarantee that they can do so, and with steadily improving diets and housing and health and other material conditions of life over long time spans, are good policies. Policies that foster instability directly or indirectly, that prevent poor people from eating in the name of efficiency or liberalism or even in the name of freedom, are not good policies. And it is possible to distinguish policies that meet this minimum standard from policies that do not.

The push for competition, deregulation, privatization and open capital markets has actually undermined economic prospects for many millions of the world's poorest people. It is therefore not merely a naive and misguided crusade. To the extent that it undermines the stable provision of daily bread, it is actively dangerous to the safety and stability of the world, including to ourselves. The greatest single danger right now is in Russia, a catastrophic example of the failure of free market doctrine. But serious dangers have also emerged in Asia and Latin America and they are not going to go away soon. There is, in short, a crisis of the Washington Consensus.

The crisis of the Washington Consensus is visible to everybody. But not everybody is willing to admit it. Indeed, as bad policies produced policy failures, those committed to the policies developed a defense mechanism. This is the argument that treats every unwelcome case as an unfortunate exception. Mexico was an exception—there was a revolt in Chiapas, an assassination in Tijuana. Then Korea, Thailand, Indonesia became exceptions: corruption, crony capitalism on an unimaginably massive scale, was discovered, but after the crisis hit. And then there came the Russian exception. In Russia, we are told, Dostoyevskian criminality welled up from the corpse of Soviet communism to overcome the efficiencies and incentives of free markets.

But when the exceptions outnumber the examples, there must be trouble with the rules. Where are the continuing success stories of liberalization, privatization, deregulation, sound money and balanced budgets? Where are the emerging markets that have emerged, the developing countries that have developed, the transition economies that have truly completed a successful and happy transition? Look closely. Look hard. They do not exist.

In each of the supposed exceptions Russia, Korea, Mexico, and also Brazil state-directed development programs have been liberalized, privatized, deregulated. But then, capital inflows led to currency overvaluation, making imports cheap but exports uncompetitive. As early promises of "transformation" proved unrealistic, the investor mood soured. A flight to quality began, usually following moves to raise interest rates in the "quality" countries—notably the United States in 1994 and in early 1997. A very small move in U.S. interest rates in March 1997 precipitated the outflows of capital from Asia that led to the Thai crisis. I have elsewhere called this the "Butterfly Effect," with Alan Greenspan in the role of the butterfly.

The Russian case is especially sad and dramatic. In 1917 the Bolshevik revolution promised a war-weary Russian people liberation and deliverance from oppression. It took them seventy years to forget the essential lesson of that experience, which is that there are no easy, sudden, miraculous transitions. In 1992, the advocates of shock therapy followed the Bolshevik path, against the good sense of much of the Russian political order, by Bolshevik means. This was the true meaning of Yeltsin's 1993 military assault on the Russian parliament, an act of violence which we in the West tolerated, to our shame, in the name "economic reform."

Privatization and deregulation in Russia did not create efficient and competitive markets, but instead large and pernicious private monopolists, the oligarchs and the mafiosi, with control over competing industrial empires and the news media. And these empires sponsored their own banks, which were not banks at all but rather simply speculative pools, serving none of the essential functions of commercial banks. Meanwhile, the state followed a rigid policy of limiting expenditures, so that even wages and pension obligations duly incurred were not paid—as if the United States government were to refuse to pay Social Security checks because of a budget deficit! The private sector literally ran out of money. The payments system ceased to function; tax collection became impossible because there was nothing to tax. The state financed itself through a pyramid scheme of short-term debts, the GKO market, which collapsed as pyramids must on August 17th, 1998. This was the end of free-market radicalism in Russia—and still, the Washington Consensus holds that Russia must "stay the course" on "economic reform."

Throughout Asia in the 1990s, stable industrial growth gave way to go-go expansions based heavily on real-estate speculation and commercial office development. Many more office towers went up, in Bangkok, Djakarta, Hong Kong and Kuala Lumpur, than could reasonably be put to use. Once finished, these towers do not go away; they stay empty but available, and so remain a drag on the market, inhibiting new construction. Recovery from the crash of such bubbles is a slow process. It took five years or longer in Texas of the mid-1980s.

As for Brazil, through the early fall of 1998 it was said that the IMF would restore confidence and keep the Brazilian real afloat. But the real has since devalued and Brazil is heading for a deep recession. The problem here does not originate with Brazil, and cannot be resolved by any actions the Brazilians alone might take. It lies, rather, in the international capital markets. Investors with exposure in Asia, and with losses in Russia, must reduce their lending to other large borrowers, irrespective of conditions in those countries. It is this imperative that is Brazil's problem today.

Are there alternatives? Yes. The grim history I've just outlined is not uniform. Over the past half-century, successful and prolonged periods of strong global development have always occurred in countries with strong governments, mixed economic structures and weakly developed capital markets. This was the case of Europe and Japan following World War II, of Korea and Taiwan in the 80s and 90s, of China after 1979. These cases, and not the free market liberal examples—such as, say, Argentina after the mid-1970s or Mexico after 1986 or the Philippines or Bolivia—are the success stories of global economic development in our time.

If one examines Korea, for instance, one finds that the great period of economic development was, indeed, a time of repressive crony capitalism. After 1975, the Korean government took note of the fate of South Vietnam, drew its own conclusions about the depth of American commitment, and embarked on a program of heavy and chemical industrialization that emphasized dual use technologies: the first major product of Hyundai Heavy Industries, for example, was a knock-off of the M-60 tank.

The Korean industrialization policy was not, in any static sense, efficient. No market would have chosen this course of action. The major players in the Korean economy—the state, the banks, the conglomerates known as chaebols— were yoked together in pursuit of their goals. Workers and their wage demands were repressed. And the initial search for markets was by no means entirely successful. There wasn't a big demand for those tanks, and so Hyundai decided to try building passenger cars, instead.

And yet, when one adds up the balance sheet of the Korean model, can anyone seriously argue that the country would be richer today if it had done nothing in 1975? That it would be more middle class, or more democratic?

It is true that Korea experienced the first harsh blows of the Asian financial crisis. But why? By 1997, the industrial policy was a thing of the distant past. Korean banks had become deregulated in 1992. What they did was to diversify—supporting vast expansion and industrial diversification schemes of the chaebol—*Samsung*'s adventure into motor cars, for example—and lending to such places as Indonesia, where the Koreans evidently bought paper recommended to them by their American counterparts.. The crash of Indonesia spread to Korea by these financial channels. It was not a crisis of crony capitalism, but of crony banking—deregulated and globalized. One can multiply cases, but let us look at just one other, that of China.

China is a country with a fifty-year tradition of one-party government. For thirty of those years, it was a case study in regimentation, ideology, and economic failure. At one point, there occurred an entirely avoidable, catastrophic famine during which twenty or thirty million people perished. In the first years of the Great Proletarian Cultural Revolution, village rations amounted to a pound of rice per day.

Beginning in 1979, however, China embarked on reforms that changed the face of the country. These began with the most massive agricultural reform in human history, reforms which effectively ended food poverty in China in five years. After that, policies that welcomed long-term direct investment, that fostered township and village enterprises, joint ventures and private enterprises, put into place a vast and continuing improvement in human living standards. Over twenty years, average living standards more than quadrupled; indeed growth has been so rapid that many people can perceive the improvement in their standard of living from month to month.

China's case demonstrates the potential effectiveness of sustained development policies—of policies that emphasize the priority of steady improvement over long periods of time. Unlike Russia, China made the mistake of the Great Leap Forward only once. And it never liberalized its capital markets or its capital account, for fear that such actions would prove a fatal lure, unleashing a cycle of boom and bust that a poor nation cannot tolerate for long.

China is today no democracy. It is not politically free. But one must also acknowledge that the Chinese government has delivered on the essential economic demands of the Chinese people, namely food and housing, and that an alternative regime which did not deliver on these needs would not have been able to deliver internal peace, democracy, or human rights either.

So, what can the United States do now? To begin with we can, recognize that globalized finance makes the Federal Reserve central banker to much of the developing world. Interest rate cuts last fall had an important stabilizing effect on global markets. But this effect is temporary; and the Fed's powers are limited. After a cut, another one is eventually required; and the cut from one to one-half percent lacks the force of the reduction from six percent to four. There is a strong case for lower interest rates, but we must also remember that the long term arrives when such short term policies run out of steam.

Then there is fiscal policy. If it is a good idea for Japan to run a deficit to fight the global recession, why is it wise for the United States to be running a surplus that vastly offsets the deficit in Japan? It isn't wise. The United States should frankly expand its own economy using all the tools available for this purpose.

Then there is the matter of what we preach to the world and the policies we support. If it is a good idea for the government of the United States to grow in line with our economy, then it is also a good idea for the governments of other countries to grow as their economies do. Global development policy should be geared toward strengthening that capacity, not crippling it.

Every functional private economy has, and needs, a core of state, regional, and municipal enterprises and distribution channels to assure food and basic necessities to low-income populations. Such systems stabilize the market institutions, which work better for people with higher incomes. They help prevent criminal monopolization of critical distribution networks by setting up an accountable alternative. International assistance should seek to strengthen these public networks where they exist, and to build them where they do not. Efforts to do just this in Russia today, under the present government, should be supported and not opposed.

There is an obvious conflict between pro-growth policies and "investor confidence." Investors like to be repaid in the short run. But given that conflict, it is a fool's bargain to place investor confidence above the pursuit of development. Strong national governments have a sovereign right to regulate capital flows and banks operating on their soil—as much right as any nation has to control the flow of people across its national frontiers, and to regulate their activities at home. A Tobin Tax on foreign exchange should be enacted here, not only to slow speculation in the United States, but also to signal our acceptance of this principle for other countries, for whom different mechanisms of capital control may be more suitable in different cases.

Beyond this, a major reconstruction of world financial practices, aimed at restoring stability and strengthening the regulatory and planning capacities of national governments, is in order. The IMF needs new leadership, not tied to recent dogmas. But the IMF is also too small, and too thinly spread, to be useful in helping countries with the design and implementation of effective national development schemes. Regional financial institutions, such as suggested for Asia by Japanese Finance Minister Eisuke Sakakibara, are therefore also needed and U.S. opposition to them should be dropped.

Most of all, and in summary, we must give up illusions. The neoliberal experiment is a failure. And it is a failure not because of unforeseeable events, but because it was and is systematically and fundamentally flawed. We need many changes from this naive and doomed vision of an ungoverned world order. We need large changes, and the need is great while time, I believe, is short. We must bring the Reagan era to a final end. We must return to development policies for the people whose needs matter most in the large scheme of things, namely the millions of hard-working people in poor countries who need to eat every day.

DISCUSSION QUESTIONS

1. When you hear the term "globalization," what first comes to mind? Sweatshops? Imported cars? Increased travel opportunities? Terrorism?
2. Does an increasingly "global" world concern you? In what ways? Is economic globalization your biggest concern, or are other forms of globalization more troubling?

3. Is there anything that can be done about either promoting or restricting globalization? What? Is economic globalization easier to "manage" than other forms of globalization, such as cultural globalization?

4. "Equity" is a complex term, with many meanings for different people. Are there ways in which inequalities in income can be justifiable (e.g., if one person works harder than another)? How about inequality among nations? Which types of inequalities are not morally or ethically justifiable?

5. There is no doubt that extreme inequities exist in living standards around the world. What can be done to reduce these disparities?

6. Do you think free trade will improve or diminish environmental quality in developing nations over the long run? Why? What will the likely impact be on the environmental quality of developed nations?

7. Economists tend to focus on the overall impacts of free trade. Who do you think is helped by free trade? What individuals are harmed?

8. As a result of cultural, commercial, and communication globalization, some people are now proud to proclaim themselves "citizens of the world" rather than citizens of a particular nation or city. Is such a change exciting or troublesome? Is anything lost in such a change? Why do you suppose that citizens in many cultures fear such a change?

WEB REFERENCES

Berkeley Roundtable on the International Economy, brie.berkeley.edu/~briewww/.

Economist magazine, www.economist.com.

50 Years Is Enough: U.S. Network for Global Economic Justice, http://www.50years.org/.

The Globalization Website, www.emory.edu/SOC/globalization/index.html.

International Forum on Globalization, www.ifg.org.

International Monetary Fund, www.imf.org.

United Nations Conference on Trade and Development, www.unctad.org.

United Nations Development Program, www.undp.org.

World Bank, www.worldbank.org.

World Trade Organization, www.wto.org.

FURTHER READING

Bhagwati, Jagdish N. *Free Trade Today*. Princeton, N.J.: Princeton University Press, 2002.

Bhagwati, Jagdish N. *The Wind of the Hundred Days: How Washington Mismanaged Globalization*. Cambridge, Mass.: MIT Press, 2000.

Blustein, Paul. *The Chastening: Inside the Crisis That Rocked the Global Financial System and Humbled the IMF*. New York: Public Affairs, 2001.

Cornwell, Grant H. and Eve Walsh Stoddard, eds. *Global Multiculturalism: Comparative Perspectives on Ethnicity, Race, and Nation*. Lanham, Md.: Rowman & Littlefield Publishing, 2000.

Daly, Herman E. "The Perils of Free Trade." *Scientific American* (November 1993).

Danaher, Kevin and Roger Burbach, eds. *Globalize This! The Battle against the World Trade Organization and Corporate Rule*. Monroe, ME: Common Courage Press, 2000.

DeSoto, Hernando. *The Mystery of Capital: Why Capitalism Triumphs in the West and Fails Everywhere Else*. New York: Basic Books, 2000.

Falk, Richard. *Predatory Globalization: A Critique*. Oxford: Blackwell Publishers, 1999.

Findlay, Mark. *The Globalisation of Crime: Understanding Transnational Relationship in Context*, Cambridge: Cambridge University Press, 2000.

Friedman, Thomas L. *The Lexus and the Olive Tree: Understanding Globalization*. New York: Farrar, Straus & Giroux, 2000.

Gray, John. *False Dawn: The Delusions of Global Capitalism*. New York: New Press, 2000.

Hardt, Michael and Antonio Negri. *Empire*. Cambridge, Mass.: Harvard University Press, 2001.

Krugman, Paul. *The Age of Diminished Expectations*. Cambridge, Mass.: MIT Press, 1990.

Krugman, Paul. *Geography and Trade*. Cambridge, Mass.: MIT Press, 1991.

Krugman, Paul, ed. *Currency Crises*. National Bureau of Economic Research Conference Report. Chicago: University of Chicago Press, 2000.

Kuttner, Robert. *The End of Laissez-Faire: National Purpose and the Global Economy after the Cold War*. New York: Knopf, 1991.

Micklethwait, John and Adrian Wooldridge. *A Future Perfect: The Challenge and Hidden Promise of Globalization*. New York: Random House, 2000.

Mittelman, James H. *The Globalization Syndrome: Transformation and Resistance*. Princeton, N.J.: Princeton University Press, 2000.

Morris, Robert. "An Open Trade Alternative for the Next President." *The Brookings Review* (Summer 1988).

Nye, Joseph S. and John D. Donahue, eds. *Governance in a Globalizing World*. Washington, D.C.: Brookings Institution, 2000.

Reich, Robert B. *The Work of Nations: Preparing Ourselves for 21st-Century Capitalism*. New York: Knopf, 1991.

Scholte, Jan Aart. *Globalization: A Critical Introduction*. England: Macmillan, 2000.

Stiglitz, Joseph E. *Globalization and Its Discontents*. New York: Norton, 2002.

Stone, Deborah. *Policy Paradox: The Art of Political Decision Making*. New York: Norton, 2001.

Tomlinson, John. *Globalization and Culture*. Chicago: University of Chicago Press, 1999.

United Nations Conference on Trade and Development. *World Investment Report* (various years).

United Nations Development Program. *Human Development Report* (various years).

Yergin, Daniel and Joseph Stanislaw. *The Commanding Heights: The Battle for the World Economy*, revised and updated. Touchstone, 2002.

Chapter 5

CLIMATE CHANGE
AND ENVIRONMENTAL POLICY

"Should the United States Make the Reduction of Greenhouse Gas Emissions an Immediate Policy Priority?"

YES: Thomas C. Schelling "What Makes Greenhouse Sense? Time to Rethink the Kyoto Protocol" *Foreign Affairs*

NO: Daniel Sarewitz and Roger Pielke, Jr. "Breaking the Global Warming Gridlock" *The Atlantic Monthly*

Scientists increasingly believe that the effects of environmental pollutants can have global consequences with profound ecological, economic, and political ramifications. In a report issued by the U.S. Environmental Protection Agency to the United Nations in May 2002, the United States government formally acknowledged for the first time that human industrial actions such as oil refining, power generation, and automobile emissions have been a direct cause of global warming and that resulting climatic changes will have potentially detrimental effects on the population.[1] This public recognition echoes the concern of many scientists who, over the past half century, have monitored the rise in emissions of so-called greenhouse gases and predicted damaging effects on the global environment. President George W. Bush, however, failed to endorse openly this report. Although the Bush administration has committed to reducing greenhouse gas intensity by 18 percent over the next decade,[2] reductions are often framed in terms of gross domestic product, allowing absolute rises in greenhouse gases as the economy grows.

Although the United States is the largest emitter of greenhouse gases, the greenhouse effect is a problem caused by, and affecting, all nations of the world. As a result, there have been several attempts to address climate change through global agreements and treaties. One of the earliest was the 1987

Montreal Protocol on Substances That Deplete the Ozone Layer, with the aim of preserving the stratospheric ozone layer that absorbs harmful radiation from the sun. In 1992, signatory nations to the United Nations Conference on Environment and Development (UNCED) in Brazil agreed to reduce green-house gas emissions (like methane, CFCs, nitrous oxides, ozone, and other trace gases) to 1990 levels. Former President Clinton committed the United States to the reductions outlined in this agreement. The most important global agreement to date has been the Kyoto Protocol, signed by 150 nations in 1997. The protocol allows countries to trade carbon emission permits, based on the efficiency argument that some nations can more easily clean up their indus-tries than others. A nation that values continuing current emission levels over the cost of a permit will trade with a nation that is willing to sell a permit and reduce its emissions. Although the protocol was intended to cut greenhouse gases 5 percent by 2010, the widespread failure of signatory nations to ratify the agreement means that reductions are unlikely to be more than 1.5 per-cent.[3] President George W. Bush has signaled that he is unwilling to move ahead with ratification, believing that the levels set at Kyoto are unrealistic and disproportionately weighted against industrialized nations.[4] It is unclear what future the Kyoto Protocol has, although in March 2002 the 15 member-states of the European Union adopted the European Commission's proposal to ratify the protocol, irrespective of U.S. inclusion.

Finding a solution to the problem of climate change is hampered not only by the complexity of coordinating a global agreement, but also by the existence of substantial scientific uncertainty over both the nature and causes of climate change. There is no dispute that a "greenhouse effect" exists; indeed, without this phenomenon the earth would be cold and lifeless due to its inability to trap heat radiating from the sun. (It is seldom recognized that the major contributor to the greenhouse effect is not a man-made pollutant but rather water vapor.) Scientists for the most part agree that carbon emis-sions and airborne concentrations have been rising, that global temperatures probably increased over the past 150 years, and that there is a natural green-house effect. What remains disputed is how much future temperatures will rise, whether human activity is to blame for the increase in temperatures, and what the impacts will be. The global climate has been in constant flux since the birth of the planet, and it is possible that we are simply in another period of natural warming. Carbon dioxide levels and local temperatures exceeded current levels some 130,000 years ago—long before industrialization could be implicated.[5]

Complicating the ability to determine whether the earth's temperature is increasing or not is the fact that there is no single measure of the earth's temperature. Not only does the earth's temperature vary significantly from one region to the next, but it varies widely due to differences in the time of day, cloud cover, volcanic activity, and other natural changes as well. Indeed, two reputable scientific sources disagree over whether the oceans warmed or cooled during the 1980s.[6] Despite these natural regional and transient variations in climate conditions, some believe that all models are beginning to agree on the degree of change in particular aspects of global warming. Scientific reports combine historical data and sophisticated computer projections to assess the results of expected increases in the concentration of greenhouse gases. Over the course of the twenty-first century, the earth's temperature is expected to rise by some 3 to 9°F, with an increase in extreme wet and dry conditions. This would exacerbate the effects of changes in climate and increases in precipitation conditioned by a 1°F increase in temperatures in the United States over the past century.[7] Warming oceans would expand, irrespective of the melting of polar ice sheets, and recent estimates put the expected rise as high as 20 to 46 centimeters over the next 100 years. A 30-centimeter rise in ocean levels would typically lead to a 30-meter-span depletion of land.[8] It is estimated that a 1-meter rise in sea levels would destroy 1 percent of Egypt, 6 percent of the Netherlands, and 17.5 percent of Bangladesh.[9] Some scientists, while accepting the surface warming data, point out that parts of the troposphere have actually cooled, calling into question the causes of climate change and, therefore, the accuracy of predictions for the future.[10] Scientists have yet to determine whether the ice sheets of Greenland or Antarctica would melt (causing a large rise in sea level), what the ecological effects would be (e.g., most plants grow more vigorously in the heat, but there may also be reduced soil moisture, which reduces growth), whether cloud cover would increase (which could mitigate the greenhouse effect), and whether other feedback mechanisms in the earth's climate would worsen or dampen the predicted warming.

Regardless of the degree or exact future of global warming, it is clear that industrialized nations whose economies are relatively unaffected by climate change (agriculture, which is most affected, plays a relatively minor role in the economy) will suffer less than developing nations, where a large portion of economic output is driven by agriculture. Furthermore, coastal areas will presumably be hardest hit by predicted rising sea levels (due to melting ice), but the impacts have yet to be carefully assessed.[11]

One public policy problem is that individual nations are reluctant to act unilaterally to reduce greenhouse gas emissions because of a "free-rider" problem. If one nation reduces carbon emissions, it bears the full cost—in terms of outright financial costs, economic competitiveness, and lifestyle changes—of doing so and yet reaps only a small portion of the worldwide benefits of reduced global warming. Therefore, for each nation, the costs of reducing carbon emissions most likely outweigh the benefits that accrue to its citizens.

The actual cost to the U.S. economy of implementing the Kyoto Protocol is reported differently, depending on the source. A 1998 report by the consulting firm WEFA, posted on the website of the American Petroleum Institute, argues that meeting Kyoto would almost double energy prices, including a rise of 65 cents per gallon in gasoline prices. As a result of energy price rises, the report extrapolates a loss to real GDP of $300 billion and a reduction of 2.4 million jobs. WEFA's analysis stems from a belief that emission reductions would have to be achieved by constricting demand through higher prices; the report rejects the possibility of significant reduction through market-based tradable permits.[12]

A paper from the same year by the Union of Concerned Scientists and the Tellus Institute uses a variety of governmental research to conclude that Kyoto targets could be met at a possible cost *saving* to the economy by adopting improved technologies to both generate and use energy. One study cited in the paper, *Energy Innovations* from the Alliance to Save Energy, indicates that policies to meet Kyoto targets could yield a 0.4 percent increase in the number of jobs, a 0.27 percent increase in aggregate annual income, and a 0.03 percent increase in GDP by 2010.[13] Estimates of the national costs or benefits of meeting the Kyoto Protocol therefore depend on the methodologies and economic projections used to achieve emission targets.

The international costs or benefits of addressing global warming depend on how many countries commit to reducing emissions. Because of the global benefits of reducing greenhouse gas emissions, it is in the interest of all nations to cooperate to jointly attack the problem. It is because of this "prisoner's dilemma" that international agreements to address global problems such as the Kyoto Protocol are necessary. However, international cooperation is complicated by the disparity in wealth between the largest carbon emitters. The United States is one of the largest emitters of carbon dioxide, on both an absolute and per capita basis, largely due to heavy reliance on burning coal for electricity.[14] In 1999, 82 percent of U.S. greenhouse gas emissions were carbon dioxide, of which 98 percent resulted from fossil fuel combustion.[15] Fossil fuel combustion in 1999 was primarily the result of industrial uses (33 percent), transportation (31 percent), residential uses (20 percent), and commercial uses (16 percent).[16] Other causes of carbon emissions include cement manufacture, waste combustion, and lime manufacture. Changes in land use and forestry in 1999 did, however, result in an 18 percent decrease in carbon dioxide emissions.[17]

The United States is the largest absolute emitter of carbon dioxide, producing 1.5 billion metric tons of carbon in 1998. Other high-ranking emitters include China (0.8 billion metric tons), Russia (0.4 billion metric tons), and Japan (0.3 billion metric tons).[18] On a per capita basis, high-emitting countries are predominantly small island communities like the U.S. Virgin Islands (33.99 metric tons per person in 1998), Guam (6.97 metric tons), and Singapore (6.46 metric tons), and Middle Eastern nations including Qatar (22.05 metric tons), United Arab Emirates (10.23 metric tons), Bahrain (8.57 metric tons), and Kuwait (7.40 metric tons). The United States is ranked tenth on a per capita basis, emitting 5.43 metric tons of carbon per person in 1998.[19]

China and developing nations were responsible for 38 percent of carbon emissions in 1996, a figure that is projected to rise to 50 percent by 2020.[20] Therefore, substantially reducing total emissions will require sacrifices from developing nations, necessitating technology transfers and perhaps direct compensation from industrialized countries. Many argue that it is ethically questionable for already industrialized countries to expect developing countries to cut back on their burgeoning industrialization efforts. If the climate change of the last century was conditioned by western industry, why should Asian countries forfeit their own chance at economic development? Although developing countries are not signatories to the Kyoto Protocol, the United States has, in the past, demanded that developing countries establish their own emission standards to monitor and control greenhouse gas output.[21]

At the heart of the global warming controversy is the complexity of making public policy decisions when there is substantial scientific uncertainty and where the costs—of both action and inaction—are considerable. A further political complication in the United States is that no single government agency is devoted to climate change issues. Instead, an interagency coordinating committee brings together work from the Departments of Agriculture, Commerce, Defense, Energy, Justice, State, Transportation, and Treasury, along with the Environmental Protection Agency and USAID.[22]

Advocates of reducing greenhouse gas emissions have argued that because of the underlying uncertainty, prudence dictates that governments act now to avoid irreversible and possibly catastrophic future consequences. In other words, they argue it is better to be safe than sorry. Many people are already concerned about possible life-threatening effects of climate change. Researchers at the National Center for Atmospheric Research in Boulder, Colorado, believe that by the middle of the twenty-first century, melting snow and saturated ground will dramatically increase the risk of severe flooding.[23] Others urge waiting until more data are available with which to make more sound policy decisions. They argue that spending resources now either may be unnecessarily expensive or may attack the wrong problems, and urge additional study of the problems and the ways humans can cope with future climate changes. Basically, proponents of the two sides of the issue argue that society avoid what are called Type I and Type II errors. In this case, a Type I error is one that ignores the problem when it actually exists; if nations do not act, there is the chance that global warming will have catastrophic consequences for life on earth. A Type II error arises when society acts to avoid a problem that does not really exist; if nations do act and global warming is later found to have been a false concern, then resources would have been wasted that could have been used for programs to improve health, education, or economic well-being, for example. Therefore, neither option is truly "playing it safe" because there are costs to being wrong in either direction. The issue is whether the consequences (of both acting and not acting) warrant immediate action to address possible global warming.

Thomas Schelling argues that reductions in greenhouse gas emissions will come from both developed and developing countries, in the short term from the former and in the longer term from developing nations through financing and other assistance from wealthier, industrialized nations. He believes that emissions trading is impractical, and while he notes the difficulty of international institutions imposing penalties on individual nations, he points to some historical precedents for common commitments that may be encouraging for global cooperation. Daniel Sarewitz and Roger Pielke, Jr., argue that the huge political and economic resources currently expended on the global warming problem create conditions of political gridlock in which little can be achieved. They contend that global warming has been incorrectly framed in terms of emissions, and that a more constructive approach would be to target the social and political conditions that lead people to disrupt the environment. Land use, the development of democratic political systems, and recognition of human vulnerability to the forces of weather and climate are all proffered as alternatives.

Endnotes

1. U.S. Climate Action Report, 2002, http://www.epa.gov/globalwarming/publications/car/uscar.pdf.
2. Ibid., p. 3.
3. "The Politics of Climate Change," *New Scientist*, http://www.newscientist.com/hottopics/climate/climatepoliticsfaq.jsp.
4. See, for example, CNN (June 11, 2001), http://www.cnn.com/2001/ALLPOLITICS/06/11/bush.global.warming/.
5. Environmental Health Center, *Reporting on Change: Understanding the Science*, 2d ed. (2000), http://www.nsc.org/public/ehc/climate/chaptr2.pdf, p. 10.
6. They are the U.S. National Oceanographic and Atmospheric Administration's Comprehensive Ocean Atmosphere Data Set and the U.K. Meteorological Office's Global Ocean Surface Temperature Atlas. Boyce Rensberger, "Blowing Hot and Cold on Global Warming," *Washington Post National Weekly Edition* (August 2–8, 1993), p. 38.
7. U.S. Climate Action Report, op. cit., p. 85.
8. Damian Carrington, "Predicted Global Sea Level Rise Swells," *New Scientist* (February 19, 2002), http://www.newscientist.com/hottopics/climate/climate.jsp?id=ns99991951.
9. "Global Climate Trends," *New Scientist*, http://www.newscientist.com/hottopics/climate/climatetrends.jsp.
10. "All You Ever Wanted to Know about Climate Change," *New Scientist*, http://www.newscientist.com/hottopics/climate/climatefaq.jsp.
11. See William D. Nordhaus, "Reflections on the Economics of Climate Change," *Journal of Economic Perspectives* (Fall 1993).
12. WEFA, "Global Warming: The High Cost of the Kyoto Protocol," Executive Study, http://www.api.org/globalclimate/wefa/exec.pdf.
13. Union of Concerned Scientists, "A Small Price to Pay: U.S. Action to Curb Global Warming Is Feasible and Affordable," http://www.ucsusa.org/publications/smallprice.pdf, p. 5.
14. Carbon Dioxide Information Analysis Center, "A Compendium of Data on Global Change," http://cdiac.esd.ornl.gov/trends/emis/em_cont.htm.
15. U.S. Climate Action Report, op. cit., p. 38.

16. Ibid., p. 41.
17. Ibid., p. 38.
18. Carbon Dioxide Information Analysis Center, op. cit., http://cdiac.esd.ornl.gov/trends/emis/top98.tot.
19. Ibid., http://cdiac.esd.ornl.gov/trends/emis/top98.cap.
20. Environmental Protection Agency, http://yosemite.epa.gov/oar/globalwarming.nsf/content/EmissionsInternational/Projections.html.
21. "The Politics of Climate Change," op. cit. http://www.newscientist.com/hottopics/climate/climatepoliticsfaq2.jsp.
22. U.S. Climate Action Report, op. cit., p. 12.
23. Robert Adler, "Here Comes the Rain," *New Scientist* (December 22, 2001), http://www.newscientist.com/hottopics/climate/climate.jsp?id=23221300.

YES

What Makes Greenhouse Sense?
Time to Rethink the Kyoto Protocol

Thomas C. Schelling

The Kyoto Protocol should not be a partisan issue. The percentage reduction of greenhouse-gas emissions to which the United States committed itself by signing the 1997 Protocol to the 1992 UN Framework Convention on Climate Change was probably unachievable when the protocol was adopted. The protocol then languished in Washington for the final three years of the Clinton administration, which chose not to present it to the Senate for ratification. In accordance with a Senate resolution calling for the full participation of the main developing countries in the protocol's emissions-cutting requirements, that pause was supposed to allow time for negotiation to bring those countries on board. But nobody thought any such negotiation could produce results, and no negotiation was ever attempted. George W. Bush, succeeding to the presidency three years after the protocol's signing, had some choices and may not have made the best choice when he rejected the plan outright last year. But the one option he did not have was to submit the protocol to the Senate for ratification.

The U.S. "commitment" to the protocol meant cutting emissions significantly below their 1990 level by 2010—which required a 25 or 30 percent reduction in projected emissions levels. Such a cut was almost certainly infeasible when the Clinton administration signed the protocol in 1997. Three years later, with no action toward reducing emissions, no evidence of any planning on how to reduce emissions, and no attempt to inform the public or Congress about what might be required to meet that commitment, what might barely have been possible to achieve over 15 years—1997 to 2012—had become unreasonable. The Senate will not confirm a treaty unless it knows what actions the "commitment" entails, and no president could answer that question without a year's preparation. No such preparation appears to have been done in the Clinton administration. Bush, in stating that he would not submit the treaty to the Senate, at least avoided hypocrisy.

In declining to support the Kyoto Protocol, Bush outlined three concerns regarding any future greenhouse-gas agreement. First, the main developing countries need to adhere as full participants, as the Senate had earlier resolved; so far, developing countries have made clear they have no intention of doing

THOMAS C. SCHELLING is Distinguished University Professor of Economics and Public Affairs at the University of Maryland.

so. Second, he cited the immense uncertainty about the likely extent of climate change and its impact on society. Third, he expressed a preference for "voluntarism" over enforceable regulation, even though he did not make clear whether his "voluntarism" referred to domestic or international commitments.

A FAIR DEAL?

There is no likelihood that China, India, Indonesia, Brazil, or Nigeria will fully participate in any greenhouse-gas regime for the next few decades. They have done their best to make that point clear, and it serves no purpose to disbelieve them. Although their spokespersons regularly allege that rich countries are the most worried about climate change, developing nations have the most to lose from climate change. They are much more dependent on agriculture and will therefore suffer much more from global warming. Constrained by poverty and technological backwardness, their ability to adapt to climate change is limited. The best way for developing countries to mitigate global warming, therefore, is through economic growth.

There are undoubtedly opportunities in those countries for improved energy efficiencies that may simultaneously cut carbon dioxide emissions and improve public health; China, for example, could easily reduce its dependence on coal. But any major reductions in worldwide carbon dioxide emissions over the next few decades will have to be at the expense of the rich countries. Calling for the immediate participation of the big developing nations is futile. Once the developed countries have demonstrated that they can cooperate in reducing greenhouse gases, they can undertake arrangements to include developing countries in a greenhouse-gas regime, aiding them with economic incentives.

THE UNCERTAINTY PRINCIPLE

As Bush has emphasized, there are many uncertainties in the greenhouse-gas debate. But what is least uncertain is that climate change is real and likely to be serious. In any case, residual ambiguity about this question should not delay essential research and development in nonfossil energy sources, energy conservation, and policies to exploit the most cost-effective ways to reduce emissions.

A huge uncertainty that will make any lasting regime impossible for many decades to come, however, is how much carbon dioxide can safely be emitted over the coming century. A reading of the evidence—including climate sensitivity, regional climate changes, likely severity of impact, and the effectiveness of adaptation—suggests that the highest ceiling for carbon dioxide concentration, beyond which damage would be unacceptable, is probably between 600 and 1,200 parts per million. (It is currently about 370 ppm.) Further uncertainty exists about how much carbon dioxide can be absorbed into various natural sinks—oceans and forests—or sequestered underground or deep in the ocean. Thus any estimate of the level at which total carbon dioxide emissions worldwide over the coming hundred years should be capped is wide-ranging, falling between 500 billion tons and 2 trillion tons. (Worldwide emissions are currently approaching 7 billion tons, half of which stays in the atmosphere.) In any event, what is ultimately unacceptable depends on the costs of moderating emissions, and these costs are also uncertain.

As a result, any "rationing scheme" would necessarily be subject to repeated revision and renegotiation. It is noteworthy that the Intergovernmental Panel on Climate Change—the international body, comprising more than a thousand scientists from scores of countries, that is the acknowledged (if controversial) authority on the subject—has never proposed what concentration of green-house gases would constitute unacceptable damage. Nor has any other representative body yet dared to hazard an estimate.

IN THE LONG RUN

The Kyoto Protocol had a short-term focus. It assumed correctly that developed countries could achieve significant reductions in emissions fairly promptly. As the National Academy of Sciences emphasized ten years ago, there are a number of opportunities to reduce emissions at little or no cost. They are mostly one-time measures that are not indefinitely exploitable. Had they been promptly attempted, they might have made the Kyoto approach feasible. Postponing these steps merely loses time.

But the protocol was embedded in the 1992 Convention on Climate Change, which was oriented toward the long term. So it has been interpreted as heralding the beginning (for developed countries) of a long-term decline in carbon dioxide emissions. But any reasonable trajectory of emissions in the future ought to show a rise for some decades and a rapid decline later in the century.

There are several reasons for such a trajectory. First, the technologies needed to drastically reduce fossil-fuel consumption through alternative energy sources, greater energy efficiency, and sequestration of carbon dioxide or its removal from fuel are not developed. Decades of investment are needed. The necessary investments will not happen by themselves; government action and support, especially in arranging market incentives, will be essential.

Second, it is economical to use durable equipment until it is due for replacement; early scrapping is wasteful. Much capital, such as electric power plants, is very long-lived. Auto fleets can turn over in 15 or 20 years, but most industrial plants cannot. Furthermore, deferring expenses saves interest on loans for capital investment. Finally, the richer countries will almost certainly have higher incomes in the future and be better able to afford drastic changes in energy use.

The economical trajectory for emissions over the coming century will differ substantially among the developed countries. Thus any reasonable rationing scheme should contemplate a timeline of at least a century, not a few decades. But no possible consensus exists on how much total emissions should be allowed for the coming century. That confusion makes any scheme of fixed quotas, including "emissions trading," out of the question.

In short, the Kyoto Protocol's exclusive focus on the short term neglected the crucial importance of expanding worldwide research and development of technologies to make severe reductions feasible later in the century. It also adopted a format incompatible with the most economical trajectory of emissions over time: a rise for some decades followed by a sharp decline.

FREE TO CHOOSE?

The Bush administration has favored "voluntary" measures over "mandatory" ones. But it is not clear whether these terms referred mainly to domestic or to international measures. Domestically, a voluntary approach would make the greenhouse question unique among issues of environment and health, which fall under government jurisdiction. The research of the National Institutes of Health, for example, is universally acknowledged to be essential; leaving such research to the market or to voluntary industrial altruism would not appeal to anyone. The same approach should apply to research on new low-carbon or non-carbon energies or carbon sequestration. Major replacement of fossil fuels or reductions in energy demand, carbon dioxide "containment" efforts, or investment in new technologies to bring them about will not occur without serious market incentives. Domestically, "voluntarism" is an ineffectual approach that would put blame only on firms that have no market support for what they may be asked to do.

An international regime, in contrast, can be only voluntary. Commitments will not be "enforceable." At best they may be honored, because respectable governments prefer to keep commitments. The U.S. government has a strong aversion to any commitments it does not think it will keep. And neither the United States not the other major developed countries will likely accept serious sanctions for missing emissions targets. There is talk of "binding commitments," as if "commitment" itself was not binding, but there is no expectation of penalties for shortfall.

HOT AIR

Emissions trading is popular, especially with economists. Trading means that any nation that underuses its emissions quota (commitment) may transfer its unused quota (the excess of its allowed emissions over actual emissions) to any country that offers financial compensation. The "purchasing" nation then uses its bought allotment to increase its own emissions quota. The idea is to permit emissions to be reduced wherever their reduction is most economical. Countries that have the greatest difficulty (highest costs) in reducing emissions can purchase relief from countries that are comparatively most able to effect emissions reductions.

When 2,000 economists, including some Nobel laureates, circulated a recommendation a few years ago that nations should adopt enforceable quotas for carbon dioxide emissions and allow the purchase and sale of unused quotas, the concept was aesthetically pleasing but politically unconvincing. Although emissions should be reduced in those countries where they can be cut most economically, the economists' proposed trading system was perfectionist and impractical. The problem with trading regimes is that initial quotas are negotiated to reflect what each nation can reasonably be expected to reduce. Any country that is tempted to sell part of an emissions quota will realize that the regime is continually subject to renegotiation, so selling any "excess" is tantamount to admitting it got a generous allotment the last time around. It then sets itself up for stiffer negotiation next time.

Still, the latest version of the Kyoto Protocol, negotiated in November 2001, does contemplate trading and even anticipates who the sellers will be. It conceded carbon dioxide emissions quotas to Russia and Ukraine—countries that, because of their depressed economies, will keep their emissions relatively low during the Kyoto time period. They will have what is called "hot air" to sell to any Kyoto participant willing to pay to remain within its own commitment. This arrangement may have been an essential inducement to get Russia to ratify the Kyoto Protocol, and countries that were not sure they would meet their commitments on their own saw it as a cheap safety valve.

It requires a sense of humor to appreciate this latest modification of the Kyoto Protocol: respectable governments being willing to pay money, or make their domestic industries pay money, to an ailing former enemy in the guise of a sophisticated emissions-trading scheme. The purpose is to bribe the recipient into ratifying a treaty and providing governments a cheap way to buy out of emissions commitments, with the pretense that it serves to reduce emissions in accordance with the principle of comparative advantage.

PAST AS PROLOGUE

There is remarkable consensus among economists that nations will not make sacrifices in the interest of global objectives unless they are bound by a regime that can impose penalties if they do not comply. Despite this consensus, however, there is no historical example of any regime that could impose effective penalties, at least with something of the magnitude of global warming. But there are historical precedents of regimes that lacked coercive authority but were still able to divide benefits and burdens of a magnitude perhaps comparable to the demands of a global-warming regime. (In this case, cutting emissions is the burden; allowing emissions is the benefit.) There are two interesting precedents outside wartime. Both hold promise.

One is the division of Marshall Plan aid, which began in 1948. The magnitude of the aid, as a percentage of the national income of the recipient countries, is not easy to determine today, because most European currencies were grossly over-valued after the war. But a reasonable estimate places the aid's value anywhere from 5 percent to 20 percent of national income, depending on the recipient country.

For the first two years of the Marshall Plan, the United States divided the money itself. For the third year, it insisted that the recipient countries divide the aid among themselves. Government representatives therefore went through a process of "reciprocal multilateral scrutiny." Each government prepared extensive documentation of all aspects of its economy: its projected private and public investments, consumption, imports, exports, what it was doing about railroads and livestock herds, how it was rationing gasoline or butter, and how its living standard compared to prewar conditions. Each government team was examined and cross-examined by other government teams; it then defended itself, revised its proposals, and cross-examined other teams. More aid for one country meant less for the rest.

There was no formula. Rather, each country developed "relevant criteria." The parties did not quite reach agreement, but they were close enough that two respected people—the secretary-general of the Organization for European Economic Cooperation and the representative of Belgium (which was not requesting any aid)—offered a proposed division that was promptly accepted. Of course, the United States was demanding the countries reach agreement on aid. Today, there is no such "angel" behind greenhouse negotiations. Still, the Marshall Plan represents something of a precedent.

NATO went through the same process a year later (1951–52) in its "burden-sharing exercise." This time, it involved U.S. aid and included targets for national military participation, conscription of soldiers, investments in equipment, contributions to military infrastructure and real estate, and so on. Again, the process was one of reciprocal scrutiny and cross-examination, with high-level officials spending months negotiating. Again, they did not quite reach final agreement. But this time, three officials fashioned a proposal that was accepted. After one more year, NATO proceeded without U.S. aid—except for the contribution of U.S. military forces to NATO itself.

With the possible exception of the reciprocal-trade negotiations that ultimately created the World Trade Organization (WTO), the Marshall Plan and NATO experiences are the only non-wartime precedents in which so many countries cooperated over such high economic stakes. They were not aesthetically satisfying processes: no formulae were developed, just a civilized procedure of argument. Those examples are a model for what might succeed the Kyoto Protocol if it fails or evolves into something else. Their procedure is one that the main developed nations might pursue prior to any attempt to include developing nations. NATO has been an enormous success; member nations made large contributions in money, troops, and real estate. They did it all voluntarily; there were no penalties for shortfalls in performance. And, without explicit trading, they practiced the theory of comparative advantage (in geographical location, for instance, or demographics, or industrial structure). It was an example of highly motivated partnership, involving resources on a scale commensurate with what a greenhouse regime might eventually require.

The WTO experience is also instructive. It involves a much broader array of nations than NATO does, and it has its own system of sanctions: the enforcement of commitments. Because it is essentially a system of detailed reciprocal undertakings, and because most infractions tend to be bilateral and specific as to commodities, offended parties can undertake retaliation and make the penalty fit the crime (thus exercising the principle of reciprocity). A judicial system can evaluate offenses on their merits to authorize or approve the retaliatory measure. Fulfilling or failing WTO commitments is piecemeal, not holistic. There is no overall "target" to which a WTO member is committed. In contrast, if a greenhouse-regime nation fails to meet its target, there is no particular offended partner to take the initiative and penalize the offender—and if there were, it might be difficult to identify an appropriate "reciprocal" retaliatory measure.

PROMISES, PROMISES

One striking contrast between NATO and the Kyoto Protocol deserves emphasis: the difference between "inputs" and "outputs," or actions and results. NATO nations argued about what they should do, and commitments were made to actions. What countries actually did—raise and train troops; procure equipment, ammunition, and supplies; and deploy these assets geographically— could be observed, estimated, and compared. But results—such as how much each NATO nation's actions contributed to deterring the Warsaw Pact—could not be remotely approximated.

Like NATO, commitments under the WTO's auspices are also made to what nations will do, or will abstain from doing; there are no commitments to specific consequences. No nation is committed to imports of any sort from anywhere; it is committed only to its actions—such as tariffs and other restrictions, subsidies, and tax preferences.

With the Kyoto Protocol, commitments were made not to actions but to results that were to be measured after a decade or more. This approach has disadvantages. An obvious one is that no one can tell, until close to the target date, which nations are on course to meet their goals. More important, nations undertaking result-based commitments are unlikely to have any reliable way of knowing what actions will be required—that is, what quantitative results will occur on what timetable for various policies. The Kyoto approach implied without evident justification that governments actually knew how to reach

10-or 15-year emissions goals. (The energy crisis of the 1970s did not last long enough to reveal, for example, the long-run elasticity of demand for motor fuel, electricity, industrial heat, and so on.) A government that commits to actions at least knows what it is committed to, and its partners also know and can observe compliance. In contrast, a government that commits to the consequences of various actions on emissions can only hope that its estimates, or guesses, are on target, and so can its partners.

SPREADING THE WEALTH

Eventually, to bring in the developing nations and achieve emissions reductions most economically, the proper approach is not a trading system but financial contributions from the rich countries to an institution that would help finance energy-efficient and decarbonized technologies in the developing world. Examples might be funding a pipeline to bring Siberian natural gas to northern China to help replace carbon-intensive coal, or financing the imported components of nuclear-power reactors, which emit no greenhouse gases.

Such a regime will suffer the appearance of "foreign aid." But that is the form it will necessarily take. The recipients will benefit and should be required to assume commitments to emissions-reducing actions. Meanwhile, the burden on the rich countries will undoubtedly be more political than economic. Large-scale aid for reducing carbon dioxide emissions in China is economically bearable but enormously difficult to justify to the American public, or to agree on with Japan and the European Union.

While European countries are lamenting the U.S. defection from the Kyoto Protocol, a major U.S. unilateral initiative in research and development oriented toward phasing out fossil fuels over the next century would both produce welcome returns and display American seriousness about global warming.

The greenhouse gas issue will persist through the entire century and beyond. Even though the developed nations have not succeeded in finding a collaborative way to approach the issue, it is still early. We have been at it for only a decade. But time should not be wasted getting started. Global climate change may become what nuclear arms control was for the past half century. It took more than a decade to develop a concept of arms control. It is not surprising that it is taking that long to find a way to come to consensus on an approach to the greenhouse problem.

NO

Breaking the Global Warming Gridlock

Daniel Sarewitz and Roger Pielke, Jr.*

In the last week of October, 1998, Hurricane Mitch stalled over Central America, dumping between three and six feet of rain within forty-eight hours, killing more than 10,000 people in landslides and floods, triggering a cholera epidemic, and virtually wiping out the economies of Honduras and Nicaragua. Several days later some 1,500 delegates, accompanied by thousands of advocates and media representatives, met in Buenos Aires at the fourth Conference of the Parties to the United Nations Framework Convention on Climate Change. Many at the conference pointed to Hurricane Mitch as a harbinger of the catastrophes that await us if we do not act immediately to reduce emissions of carbon dioxide and other so-called greenhouse gases. The delegates passed a resolution of "solidarity with Central America" in which they expressed concern "that global warming may be contributing to the worsening of weather" and urged "governments, . . . and society in general, to continue their efforts to find permanent solutions to the factors which cause or may cause climate events." Children wandering bereft in the streets of Tegucigalpa became unwitting symbols of global warming.

But if Hurricane Mitch was a public-relations gift to environmentalists, it was also a stark demonstration of the failure of our current approach to protecting the environment. Disasters like Mitch are a present and historical reality, and they will become more common and more deadly regardless of global warming. Underlying the havoc in Central America were poverty, poor land-use practices, a degraded local environment, and inadequate emergency preparedness—conditions that will not be alleviated by reducing greenhouse-gas emissions.

At the heart of this dispiriting state of affairs is a vitriolic debate between those who advocate action to reduce global warming and those who oppose it. The controversy is informed by strong scientific evidence that the earth's surface has warmed over the past century. But the controversy, and the science, focus on the wrong issues, and distract attention from what needs to be done. The enormous scientific, political, and financial resources now aimed at the problem of global warming create the perfect conditions for international and

*Editor's Note: In order to shorten this article for publication, the editors have removed several paragraphs. Every attempt was made to preserve the depth and content of the author's original article.

domestic political gridlock, but they can have little effect on the root causes of global environmental degradation, or on the human suffering that so often accompanies it. Our goal is to move beyond the gridlock and stake out some common ground for political dialogue and effective action.

FRAMING THE ISSUE

In politics everything depends on how an issue is framed: the terms of debate, the allocation of power and resources, the potential courses of action. The issue of global warming has been framed by a single question: Does the carbon dioxide emitted by industrialized societies threaten the earth's climate? On one side are the doomsayers, who foretell environmental disaster unless carbon-dioxide emissions are immediately reduced. On the other side are the cornucopians, who blindly insist that society can continue to pump billions of tons of greenhouse gases into the atmosphere with no ill effect, and that any effort to reduce emissions will stall the engines of industrialism that protect us from a Hobbesian wilderness. From our perspective, each group is operating within a frame that has little to do with the practical problem of how to protect the global environment in a world of six billion people (and counting). To understand why global-warming policy is a comprehensive and dangerous failure, therefore, we must begin with a look at how the issue came to be framed in this way. Two converging trends are implicated: the evolution of scientific research on the earth's climate, and the maturation of the modern environmental movement.

Since the beginning of the Industrial Revolution the combustion of fossil fuels—coal, oil, natural gas—has powered economic growth and also emitted great quantities of carbon dioxide and other greenhouse gases. More than a century ago the Swedish chemist Svante Arrhenius and the American geologist T. C. Chamberlin independently recognized that industrialization could lead to rising levels of carbon dioxide in the atmosphere, which might in turn raise the atmosphere's temperature by trapping solar radiation that would otherwise be reflected back into space—a "greenhouse effect" gone out of control. In the late 1950s the geophysicist Roger Revelle, arguing that the world was making itself the subject of a giant "geophysical experiment," worked to establish permanent stations for monitoring carbon-dioxide levels in the atmosphere. Monitoring documented what theory had predicted: atmospheric carbon dioxide was increasing.

In the United States the first high-level government mention of global warming was buried deep within a 1965 White House report on the nation's environmental problems. Throughout the 1960s and 1970s global warming—at that time typically referred to as "inadvertent modification of the atmosphere," and today embraced by the term "climate change"—remained an intriguing hypothesis that caught the attention of a few scientists but generated little concern among the public or environmentalists. Indeed, some climate researchers saw evidence for global cooling and a future ice age. In any case, the threat of nuclear war was sufficiently urgent, plausible, and horrific to crowd global warming off the catastrophe agenda.

Continued research, however, fortified the theory that fossil-fuel combustion could contribute to global warming. In 1977 the nonpartisan National Academy of Sciences issued a study called *Energy and Climate*, which carefully suggested that the possibility of global warming "should lead neither to panic nor to complacency." Rather, the study continued, it should "engender a lively sense of urgency in getting on with the work of illuminating the issues that have been identified and resolving the scientific uncertainties that remain." As is typical with National Academy studies, the primary recommendation was for more research.

In the early 1980s the carbon-dioxide problem received its first sustained attention in Congress, in the form of hearings organized by Representative Al Gore, who had become concerned about global warming when he took a college course with Roger Revelle, twelve years earlier. In 1983 the Environmental Protection Agency released a report detailing some of the possible threats posed by the anthropogenic, or human-caused, emission of carbon dioxide, but the Reagan Administration decisively downplayed the document. Two years later a prestigious international scientific conference in Villach, Austria, concluded that climate change deserved the attention of policymakers worldwide. The following year, at a Senate fact-finding hearing stimulated by the conference, Robert Watson, a climate scientist at NASA, testified, "Global warming is inevitable. It is only a question of the magnitude and the timing."

At that point global warming was only beginning to insinuate itself into the public consciousness. The defining event came in June of 1988, when another NASA climate scientist, James Hansen, told Congress with "ninety-nine percent confidence" that "the greenhouse effect has been detected, and it is changing our climate now." Hansen's proclamation made the front pages of major newspapers, ignited a firestorm of public debate, and elevated the carbon-dioxide problem to pre-eminence on the environmental agenda, where it remains to this day. Nothing had so galvanized the environmental community since the original Earth Day, eighteen years before.

Historically, the conservation and environmental movements have been rooted in values that celebrate the intrinsic worth of unspoiled landscape and propagate the idea that the human spirit is sustained through communion with nature. More than fifty years ago Aldo Leopold, perhaps the most important environmental voice of the twentieth century, wrote, "We face the question whether a still higher 'standard of living' is worth its cost in things natural, wild, and free. For us of the minority, . . . the chance to find a pasque-flower is a right as inalienable as free speech." But when global warming appeared, environmentalists thought they had found a justification better than inalienable rights—they had found facts and rationality, and they fell head over heels in love with science.

Of course, modern environmentalists were already in the habit of calling on science to help advance their agenda. In 1967, for example, the Environmental Defense Fund was founded with the aim of using science to support environmental protection through litigation. But global warming was, and is, different. It exists as an environmental issue only because of science. People can't directly sense global warming, the way they can see a clear-cut forest or feel the sting of urban smog in their throats. It is not a discrete event, like an oil spill or a nuclear accident. Global warming is so abstract that scientists argue over how they would know if they actually observed it. Scientists go to great lengths to measure and derive something called the "global average temperature" at the earth's surface, and the total rise in this temperature over the past century—an increase of about six tenths of a degree Celsius as of 1998—does suggest warming. But people and ecosystems experience local and regional temperatures, not the global average. Furthermore, most of the possible effects of global warming are not apparent in the present; rather, scientists predict that they will occur decades or even centuries hence. Nor is it likely that scientists will ever be able to attribute any isolated event—a hurricane, a heat wave—to global warming.

A central tenet of environmentalism is that less human interference in nature is better than more. The imagination of the environmental community was ignited not by the observation that greenhouse-gas concentrations were increasing but by the scientific conclusion that the increase was caused by human beings. The Environmental Defense Fund, perhaps because of its explicitly scientific bent, was one of the first advocacy groups to make this connection. As early as 1984 its senior scientist, Michael Oppenheimer, wrote on the op-ed page of *The New York Times*,

> With unusual unanimity, scientists testified at a recent Senate hearing that using the atmosphere as a garbage dump is about to catch up with us on a global scale. . . . Carbon dioxide emissions from fossil fuel combustion and other "greenhouse" gases are throwing a blanket over the Earth. . . . The sea level will rise as land ice melts and the ocean expands. Beaches will erode while wetlands will largely disappear....Imagine life in a sweltering, smoggy New York without Long Island's beaches and you have glimpsed the world left to future generations.

Preserving tropical jungles and wetlands, protecting air and water quality, slowing global population growth—goals that had all been justified for independent reasons, often by independent organizations—could now be linked to a single fact, anthropogenic carbon-dioxide emissions, and advanced along a single political front, the effort to reduce those emissions. Protecting forests, for example, could help fight global warming because forests act as "sinks" that absorb carbon dioxide. Air pollution could be addressed in part by promoting the same clean-energy sources that would reduce carbon-dioxide emissions. Population growth needed to be controlled in order to reduce demand for fossil-fuel combustion. And the environmental community could reinvigorate its energy-conservation agenda, which had flagged since the early 1980s, when the effects of the second Arab oil shock wore off. Senator Timothy Wirth, of Colorado, spelled out the strategy in 1988: "What we've got to do in energy conservation is try to ride the global warming issue. Even if the theory of global warming is wrong, to have approached global warming as if it is real means energy conservation, so we will be doing the right thing anyway in terms of economic policy and environmental policy." A broad array of environmental groups and think tanks, including the Environmental Defense Fund, the Sierra Club, Greenpeace, the World Resources Institute, and the Union of Concerned Scientists, made reductions in carbon-dioxide emissions central to their agendas.

The moral problem seemed clear: human beings were causing the increase of carbon dioxide in the atmosphere. But the moral problem existed only because of a scientific fact—a fact that not only provided justification for doing many of the things that environmentalists wanted to do anyway but also dictated the overriding course of action: reduce carbon-dioxide emissions. Thus science was used to rationalize the moral imperative, unify the environmental agenda, and determine the political solution.

RESEARCH AS POLICY

The summer of 1988 was stultifyingly hot even by Washington, D.C., standards, and the Mississippi River basin was suffering a catastrophic drought. Hansen's proclamation that the greenhouse effect was "changing our climate now" generated a level of public concern sufficient to catch the attention of many politicians. George Bush, who promised to be "the environmental President" and to counter "the greenhouse effect with the White House effect," was elected that November. Despite his campaign rhetoric, the new President was unprepared to offer policies that would curtail fossil-fuel production and consumption or impose economic costs for uncertain political gains. Bush's advisers recognized that support for scientific research offered the best solution politically, because it would give the appearance of action with minimal political risk.

With little debate the Republican Administration and the Democratic Congress in 1990 created the U.S. Global Change Research Program. The program's annual budget reached $1 billion in 1991 and $1.8 billion in 1995, making it one of the largest science initiatives ever undertaken by the U.S. government. Its goal, according to Bush Administration documents, was "to establish the scientific basis for national and international policymaking related to natural and human-induced changes in the global Earth system." A central scientific objective was to "support national and international policymaking by developing the ability to predict the nature and consequences of changes in the Earth system, particularly climate change." A decade and more than $16 billion later, scientific research remains the principal U.S. policy response to climate change.

Meanwhile, the marriage of environmentalism and science gave forth issue: diplomatic efforts to craft a global strategy to reduce carbon-dioxide emissions. Scientists, environmentalists, and government officials, in an attempt to replicate the apparently successful international response to stratospheric-ozone depletion that was mounted in the mid-1980s, created an institutional structure aimed at formalizing the connection between science and political action. The Intergovernmental Panel on Climate Change was established through the United Nations, to provide snapshots of the evolving state of scientific understanding. The IPCC issued major assessments in 1990 and 1996; a third is due early next year. These assessments provide the basis for action under a complementary mechanism, the United Nations Framework Convention on Climate Change. Signed by 154 nations at the 1992 "Earth Summit" in Rio de Janeiro, the convention calls for voluntary reductions in carbon-dioxide emissions. It came into force as an international treaty in March of 1994, and has been ratified by 181 nations. Signatories continue to meet in periodic Conferences of the Parties, of which the most significant to date occurred in Kyoto in 1997, when binding emissions reductions for industrialized countries were proposed under an agreement called the Kyoto Protocol.

The IPCC defines climate change as any sort of change in the earth's climate, no matter what the cause. But the Framework Convention restricts its definition to changes that result from the anthropogenic emission of greenhouse gases. This restriction has profound implications for the framing of the issue. It makes all action under the convention hostage to the ability of scientists not just to document global warming but to attribute it to human causes. An apparently simple question, Are we causing global warming or aren't we?, has become the obsessional focus of science—and of policy.

Finally, if the reduction of carbon-dioxide emissions is an organizing principle for environmentalists, scientists, and environmental-policy makers, it is also an organizing principle for all those whose interests might be threatened by such a reduction. It's easy to be glib about who they might be—greedy oil and coal companies, the rapacious logging industry, recalcitrant automobile manufacturers, corrupt foreign dictatorships—and easy as well to document the excesses and absurdities propagated by some representatives of these groups. Consider, for example, the Greening Earth Society, which "promotes the optimistic scientific view that CO_2 is beneficial to humankind and all of nature," and happens to be funded by a coalition of coal-burning utility companies. One of the society's 1999 press releases reported that "there will only be sufficient food for the world's projected population in 2050 if atmospheric concentrations of carbon dioxide are permitted to increase, unchecked." Of course, neither side of the debate has a lock on excess or distortion. The point is simply that the climate-change problem has been framed in a way that catalyzes a determined and powerful opposition.

THE PROBLEM WITH PREDICTIONS

When anthropogenic carbon-dioxide emissions became the defining fact for global environmentalism, scientific uncertainty about the causes and consequences of global warming emerged as the apparent central obstacle to action. As we have seen, the Bush Administration justified its huge climate-research initiative explicitly in terms of the need to reduce uncertainty before taking action. Al Gore, by then a senator, agreed, explaining that "more research and better research and better targeted research is absolutely essential if we are going to eliminate the remaining areas of uncertainty and build the broader and stronger political consensus necessary for the unprecedented actions required to address this problem." Thus did a Republican Administration and a Democratic Congress—one side looking for reasons to do nothing, the other seeking justification for action—converge on the need for more research.

How certain do we need to be before we take action? The answer depends, of course, on where our interests lie. Environmentalists can tolerate a good deal more uncertainty on this issue than can, say, the executives of utility or automobile companies. Science is unlikely to overcome such a divergence in interests. After all, science is not a fact or even a set of facts; rather, it is a process of inquiry that generates more questions than answers. The rise in anthropogenic greenhouse-gas emissions, once it was scientifically established, simply pointed to other questions. How rapidly might carbon-dioxide levels rise in the future? How might climate respond to this rise? What might be the effects of that response? Such questions are inestimably complex, their answers infinitely contestable and always uncertain, their implications for human action highly dependent on values and interests.

Having wedded themselves to science, environmentalists must now cleave to it through thick and thin. When research results do not support their cause, or are simply uncertain, they cannot resort to values-based arguments, because their political opponents can portray such arguments as an opportunistic abandonment of rationality. Environmentalists have tried to get out of this bind by invoking the "precautionary principle"—a dandified version of "better safe than sorry"—to advance the idea that action in the presence of uncertainty is justified if potential harm is great. Thus uncertainty itself becomes an argument for action. But nothing is gained by this tactic either, because just as attitudes toward uncertainty are rooted in individual values and interests, so are attitudes toward potential harm.

Charged by the Framework Convention to search for proof of harm, scientists have turned to computer models of the atmosphere and the oceans, called general circulation models, or GCMs. Carbon-dioxide levels and atmospheric temperatures are measures of the physical state of the atmosphere. GCMs, in contrast, are mathematical representations that scientists use to try to understand past climate conditions and predict future ones. With GCMs scientists seek to explore how climate might respond under different influences—for example, different rates of carbon-dioxide increase. GCMs have calculated global average temperatures for the past century that closely match actual surface-temperature records; this gives climate modelers some confidence that they understand how climate behaves.

Computer models are a bit like Aladdin's lamp—what comes out is very seductive, but few are privy to what goes on inside. Even the most complex models, however, have one crucial quality that non-experts can easily understand: their accuracy can be fully evaluated only after seeing what happens in the real world over time. In other words, predictions of how climate will behave in the future cannot be proved accurate today. There are other fundamental problems with relying on GCMs. The ability of many models to reproduce temperature records may in part reflect the fact that the scientists who designed them already "knew the answer." As John Firor, a former director of the National Center for Atmospheric Research, has observed, climate models "are made by humans who tend to shape or use their models in ways that mirror their own notion of what a desirable outcome would be." Although various models can reproduce past temperature records, and yield similar predictions of future temperatures, they are unable to replicate other observed aspects of climate, such as cloud behavior and atmospheric temperature, and they diverge widely in predicting specific regional climate phenomena, such as precipitation and the frequency of extreme weather events. Moreover, it is simply not possible to know far in advance if the models agree on future temperature because they are similarly right or similarly wrong.

In spite of such pitfalls, a fundamental assumption of both U.S. climate policy and the UN Framework Convention is that increasingly sophisticated models, run on faster computers and supported by more data, will yield predictions that can resolve political disputes and guide action. The promise of better predictions is irresistible to champions of carbon-dioxide reduction, who, after all, must base their advocacy on the claim that anthropogenic greenhouse-gas emissions will be harmful in the future. But regardless of the sophistication of such predictions, new findings will almost inevitably be accompanied by new uncertainties—that's the nature of science—and may therefore act to fuel, rather than to quench, political debate. Our own prediction is that increasingly complex mathematical models that delve ever more deeply into the intricacies and the uncertainties of climate will only hinder political action . . . [because more research will likely increase rather than decrease scientific and political uncertainty].

That's a problem with science—it can turn around and bite you. An even more surprising result has recently emerged from the study of Antarctic glaciers. A strong argument in favor of carbon-dioxide reduction has been the possibility that if temperatures rise owing to greenhouse-gas emissions, glaciers will melt, the sea level will rise, and populous coastal zones all over the world will be inundated. The West Antarctic Ice Sheet has been a subject of particular concern, both because of evidence that it is now retreating and because of geologic studies showing that it underwent catastrophic collapse at least once in the past million years or so. "Behind the reasoned scientific estimates," Greenpeace warns, "lies the possibility of . . . the potential catastrophe of a six metre rise in sea level." But recent research from Antarctica shows that this ice sheet has been melting for thousands of years. Sea-level rise is a problem, but anthropogenic global warming is not the only culprit, and reducing emissions cannot be the only solution.

To make matters more difficult, some phenomena, especially those involving human behavior, are intrinsically unpredictable. Any calculation of future anthropogenic global warming must include an estimate of rates of fossil-fuel combustion in the coming decades. This means that scientists must be able to predict not only the amounts of coal, oil, and natural gas that will be consumed but also changes in the mixture of fossil fuels and other energy sources, such as nuclear, hydro-electric, and solar. These predictions rest on interdependent factors that include energy policies and prices, rates of economic growth, patterns of industrialization and technological innovation, changes in population, and even wars and other geopolitical events. Scientists have no history of being able to predict any of these things. For example, their inability to issue accurate population projections is "one of the best-kept secrets of demography," according to Joel Cohen, the director of the Laboratory of Populations at Rockefeller University. "Most professional demographers no longer believe they can predict precisely the future growth rate, size, composition and spatial distribution of populations," Cohen has observed.

Predicting the human influence on climate also requires an understanding of how climate behaved "normally," before there was any such influence. But what are normal climate patterns? In the absence of human influence, how stationary is climate? To answer such questions, researchers must document and explain the behavior of the pre-industrial climate, and they must also determine how the climate would have behaved over the past two centuries had human beings not been changing the composition of the atmosphere. However, despite the billions spent so far on climate research, Kevin Trenberth, a senior scientist at the National Center for Atmospheric Research, told the *Chicago Tribune* last year, "This may be a shock to many people who assume that we do know adequately what's going on with the climate, but we don't." The National Academy of Sciences reported last year that "deficiencies in the accuracy, quality, and continuity of the [climate] records . . . place serious limitations on the confidence" of research results.

If the normal climate is non-stationary, then the task of identifying the human fingerprint in global climate change becomes immeasurably more difficult. And the idea of a naturally stationary climate may well be chimerical. Climate has changed often and dramatically in the recent past. In the 1940s and 1950s, for example, the East Coast was hammered by a spate of powerful hurricanes, whereas in the 1970s and 1980s hurricanes were much less common. What may appear to be "abnormal" hurricane activity in recent years is abnormal only in relation to this previous quiet period. As far as the ancient climate goes, paleoclimatologists have found evidence of rapid change, even over periods as short as several years. Numerous influences could account for these changes. Ash spewed high into the atmosphere by large volcanoes can reflect solar radiation back into space and result in short-term cooling, as occurred after the 1991 eruption of Mount Pinatubo. Variations in the energy emitted by the sun also affect climate, in ways that are not yet fully understood. Global ocean currents, which move huge volumes of warm and cold water around the world and have a profound influence on climate, can speed up, slow down, and maybe even die out over very short periods of time—perhaps less than a decade. Were the Gulf Stream to shut down, the climate of Great Britain could come to resemble that of Labrador.

Finally, human beings have been changing the surface of the earth for millennia. Scientists increasingly realize that deforestation, agriculture, irrigation, urbanization, and other human activities can lead to major changes in climate on a regional or perhaps even a global scale. Thomas Stohlgren, of the U.S. Geological Survey, has written, "The effects of land use practices on regional climate may overshadow larger-scale temperature changes commonly associated with observed increases in carbon dioxide." The idea that climate may constantly be changing for a variety of reasons does not itself undercut the possibility that anthropogenic carbon dioxide could seriously affect the global climate, but it does confound scientific efforts to predict the consequences of carbon-dioxide emissions.

THE OTHER 80 PERCENT

If predicting how climate will change is difficult and uncertain, predicting how society will be affected by a changing climate—especially at the local, regional, and national levels, where decision-making takes place—is immeasurably more so. And predicting the impact on climate of reducing carbon-dioxide emissions is so uncertain as to be meaningless. What we do know about climate change suggests that there will be winners and losers, with some areas and nations potentially benefiting from, say, longer growing seasons or more rain, and others suffering from more flooding or drought. But politicians have no way to accurately calibrate the effects—human and economic—of global warming, or the benefits of reducing carbon-dioxide emissions.

Imagine yourself a leading policymaker in a poor, overpopulated, undernourished nation with severe environmental problems. What would it take to get you worried about global warming? You would need to know not just that global warming would make the conditions in your country worse but also that any of the scarce resources you applied to reducing carbon-dioxide emissions would lead to more benefits than if they were applied in another area, such as industrial development or housing construction. Such knowledge is simply unavailable. But you do know that investing in industrial development or better housing would lead to concrete political, economic, and social benefits.

More specifically, suppose that many people in your country live in shacks on a river's floodplain. Floodplains are created and sustained by repeated

flooding, so floods are certain to occur in the future, regardless of global warming. Given a choice between building new houses away from the floodplain
and converting power plants from cheap local coal to costlier imported fuels,
what would you do? New houses would ensure that lives and homes would be
saved; a new power plant would reduce carbon-dioxide emissions but leave
people vulnerable to floods. In the developing world the carbon-dioxide problem pales alongside immediate environmental and developmental problems.
The China Daily reported during the 1997 Kyoto Conference:

> The United States . . . and other nations made the irresponsible demand . . .
> that the developing countries should make commitments to limiting green-
> house gas emissions. . . . As a developing country, China has 60 million
> poverty-stricken people and China's per capita gas emissions are only
> one-seventh of the average amount of more developed countries. Ending
> poverty and developing the economy must still top the agenda of [the]
> Chinese government.

For the most part, the perspectives of those in the developing world—about
80 percent of the planet's population—have been left outside the frame of the
climate-change discussion. This is hardly surprising, considering that the frame
was defined mainly by environmentalists and scientists in affluent nations.
Developing nations, meanwhile, have quite reasonably refused to agree to the
targets for carbon-dioxide reduction set under the Kyoto Protocol. The result
may feel like a moral victory to some environmentalists, who reason that industrialized countries, which caused the problem to begin with, should shoulder
the primary responsibility for solving it. But the victory is hollow, because most
future emissions increases will come from the developing world. In affluent
nations almost everyone already owns a full complement of energy-consuming
devices. Beyond a certain point increases in income do not result in proportional
increases in energy consumption; people simply trade in the old model for a new
and perhaps more efficient one. If present trends continue, emissions from the
developing world are likely to exceed those from the industrialized nations
within the next decade or so.

Twelve years after carbon dioxide became the central obsession of global
environmental science and politics, we face the following two realities:

First, atmospheric carbon-dioxide levels will continue to increase. The
Kyoto Protocol, which represents the world's best attempt to confront the
issue, calls for industrialized nations to reduce their emissions below 1990
levels by the end of this decade. Political and technical realities suggest that not
even this modest goal will be achieved. To date, although eighty-four nations
have signed the Kyoto Protocol, only twenty-two nations—half of them
islands, and none of them major carbon-dioxide emitters—have ratified it. The
United States Senate, by a vote of 95-0 in July of 1997, indicated that it would
not ratify any climate treaty that lacked provisions requiring developing nations
to reduce their emissions. The only nations likely to achieve the emissions

commitments set under Kyoto are those, like Russia and Ukraine, whose economies are in ruins. And even successful implementation of the treaty would not halt the progressive increase in global carbon-dioxide emissions.

Second, even if greenhouse-gas emissions could somehow be rolled back to pre-industrial levels, the impacts of climate on society and the environment would continue to increase. Climate affects the world not just through phenomena such as hurricanes and droughts but also because of societal and environmental vulnerability to such phenomena. The horrific toll of Hurricane Mitch reflected not an unprecedented climatic event but a level of exposure typical in developing countries where dense and rapidly increasing populations live in environmentally degraded conditions. Similar conditions underlay more-recent disasters in Venezuela and Mozambique.

If these observations are correct, and we believe they are essentially indisputable, then framing the problem of global warming in terms of carbon-dioxide reduction is a political, environmental, and social dead end. We are not suggesting that humanity can with impunity emit billions of tons of carbon dioxide into the atmosphere each year, or that reducing those emissions is not a good idea. Nor are we making the nihilistic point that since climate undergoes changes for a variety of reasons, there is no need to worry about additional changes imposed by human beings. Rather, we are arguing that environmentalists and scientists, in focusing their own, increasingly congruent interests on carbon-dioxide emissions, have framed the problem of global environmental protection in a way that can offer no realistic prospect of a solution.

REDRAWING THE FRAME

Local weather is the day-to-day manifestation of global climate. Weather is what we experience, and lately there has been plenty to experience. In recent decades human, economic, and environmental losses from disasters related to weather have increased dramatically. Insurance-industry data show that insured losses from weather have been rising steadily. A 1999 study by the German firm Munich Reinsurance Company compared the 1960s with the 1990s and concluded that "the number of great natural catastrophes increased by a factor of three, with economic losses—taking into account the effects of inflation—increasing by a factor of more than eight and insured losses by a factor of no less than sixteen." And yet scientists have been unable to observe a global increase in the number or the severity of extreme weather events. In 1996 the IPCC concluded, "There is no evidence that extreme weather events, or climate variability, has increased, in a global sense, through the 20th century, although data and analyses are poor and not comprehensive."

What has unequivocally increased is society's vulnerability to weather. At the beginning of the twentieth century the earth's population was about 1.6 billion people; today it is about six billion people. Almost four times as many people are exposed to weather today as were a century ago. And this increase has, of course, been accompanied by enormous increases in economic activity, development, infrastructure, and interdependence. In the past fifty years, for example, Florida's population rose fivefold; 80 percent of this burgeoning population lives within twenty miles of the coast. The great Miami hurricane of 1926 made landfall over a small, relatively poor community and caused about $76 million worth of damage (in inflation-adjusted dollars). Today a storm of similar magnitude would strike a sprawling, affluent metropolitan area of two million people, and could cause more than $80 billion worth of damage. The increase in vulnerability is far more dramatic in the developing world, where in an average year tens of thousands of people die in weather-related disasters. According to the *World Disasters Report 1999*, 80 million people were made homeless by weather-related disasters from 1988 to 1997. As the population and vulnerability of the developing world continue to rise, such numbers will continue to rise as well, with or without global warming.

Environmental vulnerability is also on the rise. The connections between weather impacts and environmental quality are immediate and obvious—much more so than the connections between global warming and environmental quality. Deforestation, the destruction of wetlands, and the development of fragile coastlines can greatly magnify flooding; floods, in turn, can mobilize toxic chemicals in soil and storage facilities and cause devastating pollution of water sources and harm to wildlife. Poor agricultural, forest-management, and grazing practices can exacerbate the effects of drought, amplify soil erosion, and promote the spread of wildfires. Damage to the environment due to deforestation directly contributed to the devastation wrought by Hurricane Mitch, as denuded hillsides washed away in catastrophic landslides, and excessive development along unmanaged floodplains put large numbers of people in harm's way.

Our view of climate and the environment draws on people's direct experience and speaks to widely shared values. It therefore has an emotional and moral impact that can translate into action. This view is framed by four precepts. First, the impacts of weather and climate are a serious threat to human welfare in the present and are likely to get worse in the future. Second, the only way to reduce these impacts is to reduce societal vulnerability to them. Third, reducing vulnerability can be achieved most effectively by encouraging democracy, raising standards of living, and improving environmental quality in the developing world. Fourth, such changes offer the best prospects not only for adapting to a capricious climate but also for reducing carbon-dioxide emissions.

The implicit moral imperative is not to prevent human disruption of the environment but to ameliorate the social and political conditions that lead people to behave in environmentally disruptive ways. This is a critical distinction—and one that environmentalists and scientists embroiled in the global-warming debate have so far failed to make.

To begin with, any global effort to reduce vulnerability to weather and climate must address the environmental conditions in developing nations. Poor land-use and natural-resource-management practices are, of course, a reflection of poverty, but they are also caused by government policies, particularly those that encourage unsustainable environmental activities. William Ascher, a political scientist at Duke University, has observed that such policies typically do not arise out of ignorance or lack of options but reflect conscious tradeoffs made by government officials faced with many competing priorities and political pressures. Nations, even poor ones, have choices. It was not inevitable, for example, that Indonesia would promote the disastrous exploitation of its forests by granting subsidized logging concessions to military and business leaders. This was the policy of an autocratic government seeking to manipulate powerful sectors of society. In the absence of open, democratically responsive institutions, Indonesian leaders were not accountable for the costs that the public might bear, such as increased vulnerability to floods, landslides, soil erosion, drought, and fire. Promoting democratic institutions in developing nations could be the most important item on an agenda aimed at protecting the global environment and reducing vulnerability to climate. Environmental groups concerned about the consequences of climate change ought to consider reorienting their priorities accordingly.

Such long-term efforts must be accompanied by activities with a shorter-term payoff. An obvious first step would be to correct some of the imbalances created by the obsession with carbon dioxide. For example, the U.S. Agency for International Development has allocated $1 billion over five years to help developing nations quantify, monitor, and reduce greenhouse-gas emissions, but is spending less than a tenth of that amount on programs to prepare for and prevent disasters. These priorities should be rearranged. Similarly, the United Nations' International Strategy for Disaster Reduction is a relatively low-level effort that should be elevated to a status comparable to that of the Framework Convention on Climate Change.

Intellectual and financial resources are also poorly allocated in the realm of science, with research focused disproportionately on understanding and predicting basic climatic processes. Such research has yielded much interesting information about the global climate system. But little priority is given to generating and disseminating knowledge that people and communities can use to reduce their vulnerability to climate and extreme weather events. For example, researchers have made impressive strides in anticipating the impacts of some relatively short-term climatic phenomena, notably El Niño and La Niña. If these advances were accompanied by progress in monitoring weather, identifying vulnerable regions and populations, and communicating useful information, we would begin to reduce the toll exacted by weather and climate all over the world.

A powerful international mechanism for moving forward already exists in the Framework Convention on Climate Change. The language of the treaty offers sufficient flexibility for new priorities. The text states that signatory nations have an obligation to "cooperate in preparing for adaptation to the impacts of climate change [and to] develop and elaborate appropriate and integrated plans for coastal zone management, water resources and agriculture, and for the protection and rehabilitation of areas . . . affected by drought and desertification, as well as floods."

The idea of improving our adaptation to weather and climate has been taboo in many circles, including the realms of international negotiation and political debate. "Do we have so much faith in our own adaptability that we will risk destroying the integrity of the entire global ecological system?" Vice President Gore asked in his book *Earth in the Balance* (1992). "Believing that we can adapt to just about anything is ultimately a kind of laziness, an arrogant faith in our ability to react in time to save our skin." For environmentalists, adaptation represents a capitulation to the momentum of human interference in nature. For their opponents, putting adaptation on the table would mean acknowledging the reality of global warming. And for scientists, focusing on adaptation would call into question the billions of tax dollars devoted to research and technology centered on climate processes, models, and predictions.

Yet there is a huge potential constituency for efforts focused on adaptation: everyone who is in any way subject to the effects of weather. Reframing the climate problem could mobilize this constituency and revitalize the Framework Convention. The revitalization could concentrate on coordinating disaster relief, debt relief, and development assistance, and on generating and providing information on climate that participating countries could use in order to reduce their vulnerability.

An opportunity to advance the cause of adaptation is on the horizon. The U.S. Global Change Research Program is now finishing its report on the National Assessment of the Potential Consequences of Climate Variability and Change. The draft includes examples from around the United States of why a greater focus on adaptation to climate makes sense. But it remains to be seen if the report will redefine the terms of the climate debate, or if it will simply become fodder in the battle over carbon-dioxide emissions.

Finally, efforts to reduce carbon-dioxide emissions need not be abandoned. The Framework Convention and its offshoots also offer a promising mechanism for promoting the diffusion of energy-efficient technologies that would reduce emissions. Both the convention and the Kyoto Protocol call on industrialized nations to share new energy technologies with the developing world. But because these provisions are coupled to carbon-dioxide-reduction mandates, they are trapped in the political gridlock. They should be liberated, promoted independently on the basis of their intrinsic environmental and economic benefits, and advanced through innovative funding mechanisms. For example, as the United Nations Development Programme has suggested, research into renewable-energy technologies for poor countries could be supported in part by a modest levy on patents registered under the World Intellectual Property Organization. Such ideas should be far less divisive than energy policies advanced on the back of the global-warming agenda.

As an organizing principle for political action, vulnerability to weather and climate offers everything that global warming does not: a clear, uncontroversial story rooted in concrete human experience, observable in the present, and definable in terms of unambiguous and widely shared human values, such as the fundamental rights to a secure shelter, a safe community, and a sustainable environment. In this light, efforts to blame global warming for extreme weather events seem maddeningly perverse—as if to say that those who died in Hurricane Mitch were symbols of the profligacy of industrialized society, rather than victims of poverty and the vulnerability it creates.

Such perversity shows just how morally and politically dangerous it can be to elevate science above human values. In the global-warming debate the logic behind public discourse and political action has been precisely backwards. Environmental prospects for the coming century depend far less on our strategies for reducing carbon-dioxide emissions than on our determination and ability to reduce human vulnerability to weather and climate.

DISCUSSION QUESTIONS

1. Is it possible to address global warming at a national policy level, or is international cooperation required?
2. Should companies in developing countries be allowed to meet greenhouse gas reduction goals through investment abroad (e.g., by preserving forests in other countries, modernizing or even closing aging industrial facilities, etc.)? Or should companies be forced to make greenhouse gas reductions in their home nations?
3. Is the reduction of greenhouse gas emissions an issue that is better solved by the government or by the market economy? Can the two strategies be successfully combined, or are they mutually exclusive?
4. How should social decisions be made in the face of scientific uncertainty? Does the greatest danger in cases like this always arise from "doing nothing," or are there also dangers involved in undertaking a major policy change?
5. Are there any benefits from global warming? Do the benefits outweigh the costs?
6. Climate changes will not affect all nations equally. How does this affect the domestic and international politics of climate change agreements? To explore this question, gather several classmates and conduct a role-playing exercise in which each person takes the identity of a single country involved in negotiating a global climate treaty. Does the adoption of such a single perspective change how you view the issue?
7. Should compensation be paid to developing nations to reduce carbon emissions? If so, what form should that compensation take (cash, technology transfers, etc.) and who should pay it?
8. What industries would be most harmed by a carbon tax (a tax based on the carbon content of the fuel)? What political interests in the United States do you think would support or oppose a carbon tax? Why?

9. Do you think there is greater uncertainty over the course of action with respect to global warming than with other major policy decisions (addressing crime, trade, AIDS, etc.)?
10. How can the United States and other nations prepare for the effects of global warming? How do you think it will affect *you*?
11. Psychologists have found that most individuals have a far greater fear of events with large negative consequences even when the probability of occurrence is low (e.g., nuclear power plant meltdown) and much less fear of everyday risks (e.g., driving). Why do you think that is the case? How, if at all, should this finding affect the debate over global warming? Should it affect public policy decisions generally?

WEB REFERENCES

Environmental Protection Agency Global Warming Site, http://www.epa.gov/globalwarming/.

Global Warming Central, http://www.pace.edu/lawschool/env/energy/globalwarming.html.

Global Warming Headlines, http://search.news.yahoo.com/search/news?p=%22global +warming%22.

Kyoto Protocol Full Text, http://unfccc.int/resource/docs/convkp/kpeng.html.

UN Intergovernmental Panel on Climate Change, http://www.ipcc.ch/.

World Meteorological Organization, http://www.wmo.ch/.

FURTHER READING

Abrahamson, Dean Edwin, ed. *The Challenge of Global Warming*. Washington, D.C.: Island Press, 1989.

Bohringer, Christoph, et al., eds. *Controlling Global Warming: Perspectives from Economics, Game Theory and Public Choice*. Northampton, Mass.: Edward Elgar Publishers, 2002.

Cline, William R. *The Economics of Global Warming*. Washington, D.C.: Institute for International Economics, 1992.

Gore, Al. *Earth in the Balance*. Boston: Houghton Mifflin, 1992.

Haas, Peter M., Robert O. Keohane, and Marc A. Levy, eds. *Institutions for the Earth*. Cambridge, Mass.: MIT Press, 1993.

Houghton, John. *Global Warming: The Complete Briefing*, 2d ed. Cambridge: Cambridge University Press, 1997.

Leggett, Jeremy K. *The Carbon War: Global Warming and the End of the Oil Era*. London: Routledge, 2001.

McKibben, Bill. *The End of Nature*. New York: Anchor Books, 1989.

Melillo, Jerry. "Warm, Warm on the Range." *Science* (January 8, 1999), pp. 183–84.

Michaels, Patrick J. *Sound and Fury: The Science and Politics of Global Warming.* Washington, D.C.: Cato Institute, 1992.

National Academy of Sciences. *Policy Implications of Greenhouse Warming.* Washington, D.C.: National Academy Press, 1991.

Nordhaus, William D. "Reflections on the Economics of Climate Change." *Journal of Economic Perspectives* (Fall 1993).

Oberthur, Sebastian, et al. *The Kyoto Protocol: International Climate Policy for the 21st Century.* Heidelberg: Springer Verlag, 2000.

Philander, George. *Is the Temperature Rising? The Uncertain Science of Global Warming.* Princeton, N.J.: Princeton University Press, 1998.

Speth, James Gustave. *Environmental Pollution: A Long-Term Perspective.* Washington, D.C.: World Resources Institute, 1989.

United Nations. *Combating Global Warming: Study on a Global System of Tradeable Carbon Emission Entitlements.* New York: United Nations, 1992.

U.S. Office of Technology Assessment. *Preparing for an Uncertain Climate.* Washington, D.C.: Office of Technology Assessment, 1993.

Weyant, John P. "Costs of Reducing Global Carbon Emissions." *Journal of Economic Perspectives* (Fall 1993).

Wittwer, Sylvan H. "Flower Power: Rising Carbon Dioxide Is Great for Plants." *Policy Review* (Fall 1992).

Chapter 6

IMMIGRATION POLICY

"Should the United States Admit Fewer Immigrants?"

YES: Roy Beck "Roy Beck's Numbers" in *Blueprints for an Ideal Immigration Policy*, Center for Immigration Studies

NO: Stephen Moore "A Strategic U.S. Immigration Policy for the New Economy" in *Blueprints for an Ideal Immigration Policy*, Center for Immigration Studies

Immigration policy has become an increasingly contentious issue in many countries throughout the world, mixing issues of race, class, economic security, culture, and xenophobia. This tension has only heightened since the terrorist attacks of September 11, 2001. Citizens and political leaders in a variety of countries have begun to voice concern over the economic, cultural, political, and security effects of immigration. Hundreds of thousands of illegal immigrants try each year to enter the countries of the European Union. At the same time, immigrants in some countries have been subjected to poor treatment and occasional violence.

In the United States, many citizens seem to be of two minds about the merits of immigration. While America is often considered a "nation of immigrants," and many Americans can proudly trace their heritage to ancestors who arrived in the United States as immigrants generations ago, the welcoming inscription on the Statue of Liberty—"Give me your tired, your poor, your huddled masses yearning to breathe free"—does not seem to convey accurately the feelings of some Americans who are increasingly concerned about the effects of immigration. While many citizens reflect approvingly on the economic and cultural contributions made by immigrants in the past, there is increasing concern that immigration no longer provides the benefits to the United States that it once did. As a result, the shape of contemporary immigration policy has become an important issue for both citizens and decision makers in the United States.

The number and the composition of immigrants to the United States have changed dramatically over the past century, affected by a variety of economic, political, and social forces.[1] Both in absolute numbers and as a percentage of the U.S. population, immigration was at its peak between 1901 and 1910, when 8.8 million immigrants entered the United States, more than 10 for every 100 natives. Immigration rates dropped precipitously during the Depression period between 1931 and 1940 and rose only slowly during the next decade; in both decades, fewer than one immigrant per thousand natives entered the United States. Rising in number by more than 1 million per decade thereafter, immigration exceeded 6 million in the 1980s and stood at 7.6 million between 1990 and 1998, an amount equal to roughly 3 percent of the entire U.S. population.[2]

Because of changes in immigration policy as well as in the political and economic conditions of other countries, the origins of immigrants to the United States have changed markedly as well. In 1907, when the single largest influx of immigrants (1.285 million) was admitted to the United States, over 93 percent (1.200 million) came from Europe (including Eastern Europe); nearly half of all immigrants were from Italy and Central Europe, while only 42,000 came from the Americas. By 1998, of the total number of immigrants to the United States, the top 10 list of countries of immigrant origin did not include any European countries. Instead, immigrants originated from, in descending order, Mexico, China, India, the Philippines, the Dominican Republic, Vietnam, Cuba, Jamaica, El Salvador, and Korea. European immigrants made up only 14 percent of the total compared with roughly 11 percent from the Caribbean and 5 percent from Central America. Outside the Americas, Asia provided most immigrants to the United States in 1998, amounting to 33 percent of the total.[3]

Much public and media attention in recent years has focused on illegal immigration. Immigrants generally enter illegally in one of two ways: crossing the border illegally or overstaying temporary work, student, or tourist visas. Many Americans think of the "immigration problem" as stemming from illegal immigrants from Mexico and Central America crossing surreptitiously into California or Texas, or of Haitians and Cubans in dangerously crowded boats pouring into southern Florida. Some commentators, however, have suggested that more significant issues stem from legal rather than illegal immigration. More than 7 million immigrants were admitted legally between 1991 and 1998 alone, compared with an estimated 5 million illegal immigrants living in the United States (estimates vary widely, however). As of 1998, the most recent available data, approximately 660,000 immigrants entered the United States legally each year, compared with an estimated 250,000 to 300,000 illegal entries.[4] Despite the emphasis on immigration policy in the past decade, the percentage of the population that is foreign-born has declined from 13 percent in 1920 to 10 percent in 2000. Some suggest that the focus on illegal immigration has diverted attention from the numerous legal immigrants to the United States, particularly their job skills and their effect on the American economy.

U.S. immigration policy has undergone significant changes that have propelled many of these shifts in immigrant composition. Early responses to immigration in the late nineteenth century reflected xenophobic impulses and attempts to exclude certain classes of individuals, such as prostitutes, convicts, those with communicable diseases like tuberculosis, political radicals, and for the most part Asians. The rising popularity of anti-immigrant organizations like the Know-Nothing Party and the Ku Klux Klan in the late nineteenth and early twentieth centuries corresponded to a widespread anti-immigrant sentiment. Some states even imposed head taxes on immigrants before the Supreme Court struck down their constitutionality.[5] Partly as a result of this sentiment, however, the United States enacted significant restrictions on immigration and instituted a national-origins quota system in the 1920s. Under this system, the national origins of new immigrants were to reflect the composition of the country's population; for example, if 5 percent of U.S. citizens were of Polish origin, then 5 percent of immigrants could be admitted from Poland. In addition to severely restricting the total number of immigrants, this system effectively gave preference to European immigrants, since the United States was composed primarily of former immigrants from Europe or their descendants.

The national-origins quota system lasted until 1965, when amendments to the Immigration and Nationality Act substituted a policy whereby 80 percent of numerically limited visas were dedicated to close relatives of U.S. citizens; the other 20 percent were to be allocated based on labor skills. Further, an unlimited number of people could enter the United States if they were spouses, parents, or minor children of United States citizens. This led to dramatic increases in the number of Asian and Central and Latin American immigrants. In addition, as economist George Borjas points out, "only 4 percent of legal immigrants admitted in 1987 actually entered the United States because of their skills."[6] (This is not to say, of course, that 96 percent of immigrants were unskilled, only that their basis of admission was a criterion other than skill.) The Immigration Act of 1990 expanded the number of immigrants who could enter the United States by approximately 40 percent, and focused greater attention on attracting those with greater skills, particularly through permitting more employer-sponsored entrants to the United States.

Some recent reforms to immigration policy have been directed primarily at slowing illegal immigration. The Immigration Reform and Control Act of 1986 was directed at problems with illegal immigration, granting amnesty to aliens in the United States since 1982 and to agricultural workers, and made hiring illegal aliens unlawful. The most visible public debate over this issue came in response to the 1994 passage of Proposition 187 in California, which denied a variety of public services, including health services and education, to illegal immigrants. The debate surrounding passage of this referendum motivated action at the national level as well, and in an attempt to reduce illegal immigration, legislation passed by Congress in 1996 increased funding for border controls, restricted access to public services, and expanded employee verification programs. The creation of the Office of Homeland Security following terrorist attacks on the United States in September 2001 has led to a tightening of immigration policy and a review of the processes by which immigration may be abused to harm the United States.[7] Many have challenged the new rules of detainment and surveillance, and question whether this portends diminished constitutional protections. However, President Bush has indicated that he is committed to ensuring free trade, especially with Mexico, and a balance must be struck between tightening border controls and retaining a vibrant trade policy and legal immigration with other nations.

Far from being an isolated policy issue, immigration leads to numerous related disputes; for example, the increasingly diverse language skills of immigrants and their children have led to debates over bilingual education, and some have argued that English should be the official language in schools. But perhaps the most contentious part of the immigration debate centers on the degree to which immigrants displace native workers, causing unemployment and declining wages. Because immigrants are not uniformly distributed across the United States—in 1998, 65 percent of all new immigrants were admitted to California, Florida, Illinois, New Jersey, New York, and Texas, with an even higher percentage when illegal immigrants are added—political debates often flare up in cities or states with large immigrant populations. Immigration opponents argue that with a fixed job base, new workers—particularly immigrants willing to work for lower wages—will push native workers out of jobs, or at a minimum force these workers to accept reduced wages to keep their jobs. Besides the wage-job drain, immigration opponents complain of the high costs of programs, such as public schools and health care, that drain native taxpayers, particularly in the large cities and border states where new immigrants congregate, and dilute the political willingness of taxpayers to finance increasingly expensive social support programs intended to benefit the native poor.

Immigration supporters counter that far from reducing jobs, immigrants create them. Supporters point to studies showing that not only are immigrants more likely than natives to start new businesses, and therefore to hire additional workers, but that immigrants also create jobs through spending on goods and services. A larger immigrant population means that more people need basics such as shoes, food, and housing, which translates into additional native jobs to provide for immigrants' demands. As it turns out, most studies show that immigration has little net impact either on the wages of native workers or on the unemployment rate. Even in the case of the Mariel boatlift from Cuba, when 125,000 largely unskilled Cuban exiles descended on the Miami labor market virtually overnight, researchers found that there was no discernible impact on the wages or the unemployment rate of even unskilled workers, either white or nonwhite. Further, supporters of increased immigration concede that immigrants may drain local resources in providing education and health care services, but note that overall immigrants pay more in taxes than they receive in public services. The problem is that federal taxes comprise the bulk of tax receipts from immigrants, forcing localities to bear the economic burden of providing for immigrants' needs with little federal support.

Views on immigration do not always fall neatly along an ideological spectrum. Prominent conservatives variously support and oppose greater immigration, and the same can be said of liberals. A third view focuses not on the absolute numbers of immigrants, but on their job skills and educational background. This group holds that by allowing immigrants to enter the United States based only on familial relations (and not, for example, based on job skills or educational achievement), the United States is losing out in the world-wide competition for skilled labor to foreign economic competitors like Australia and Canada, which award immigration on a merit-based point system. The focus of reform, these adherents argue, should be to improve the job-skill composition of immigrants rather than being excessively concerned with the number of immigrants per se. Supporters of current policy counter that immigration based on family connections provides immigrants with important social and economic connections in the United States that can speed their entrance into the labor market and social milieu. In the following articles, Roy Beck expresses concern over the impact of high immigration levels on urban sprawl and environmental sustainability, and sets these issues against the benefits of immigration to deduce a need for annual reductions in admitted immigrants. Stephen Moore discusses the economic and cultural benefits of immigrant populations and the ability of America to absorb larger numbers of immigrants than at present.

Endnotes

1. U.S. Bureau of the Census, *Historical Statistics of the United States: Colonial Times to 1970, and Statistical Abstract of the United States: 1997* (Washington, D.C.: U.S. Government Printing Office, 1998).
2. 1998 is the most recently available date for these data.
3. U.S. Bureau of the Census, http://www.census.gov/prod/2002pubs/01statab/pop.pdf
4. Ibid.
5. George J. Borjas, *Friends or Strangers* (New York: Basic Books, 1990).
6. Ibid., p. 32.
7. See, for example, U.S. State Department, http://usinfo.state.gov/topical/pol/terror/01102907.htm.

YES

Roy Beck's Numbers

Roy Beck

The most important public policy issue concerning immigration is the numbers.

This is true in terms of the way immigration affects housing, schools, streets and roads, public transportation, bridges, other infrastructure, wages, social services, taxes, urban sprawl, traffic, natural habitat, air and water quality.

For example, challenges in every one of those issues and the governmental response to them are tremendously different based on which of the following two scenarios from the U.S. Bureau of Census would occur:

Scenario 1

If illegal immigration is substantially stopped and our overall legal immigration level is reduced to near the old 1776–1976 annual average of 235,000, that would lead to our U.S. population growing by another 50 million or so by mid-century.

Scenario 2

If net annual illegal immigration remains around 225,000 and we average around 800,000 legal immigrants a year (a reduction from the million a year of the 1990s), we would add another 130 million or so to our population.

The difference in the scenarios is 80 million people. Anybody who thinks that is insignificant must not have noticed the post-WWII Baby Boom. That giant bulge of Boomers (I admit, I'm at the front of the class) has changed every aspect of American life. But the numbers added by Baby Boomers were barely a third those that would be added under Scenario 2 above.

Clearly, the overall numerical level of immigration makes all the difference in the world as to what kind of country is being created and as to what governmental entities need to do to prepare.

Yet, each Congress and President for decades has resolutely avoided even discussing what the overall immigration level should be and what differing levels would mean for demands on the government. The result of not discussing has been the inadvertent quadrupling of legal levels to the million a year mark of the 1990s. It would be difficult to identify a major lobby or political force that has specifically advocated that we should have a million immigrants a year or 800,000 a year or 600,000 a year. The overall numbers have been the result of lots of changes of sub-categories without regard to their overall numerical effect.

Thus, it is obvious that not everybody agrees with me that the most important issue concerning immigration is the numbers.

The avoidance of discussing numbers is due to the way the immigration debate occurs in two very different patterns. There is the "numbers debate" among those of us who focus on the overall level of immigration, and the "characteristics debate" among those who focus on the characteristics of the immigrants.

Most discussion of immigration in the news media, by politicians, and by advocacy groups ignores the overall numbers question. All of those are among the "characteristics debaters" who fall on both sides of the issue. One side wants to primarily reduce immigrants who have certain characteristics; the other side wants solely to increase immigrants who have certain characteristics. Both say the overall numbers really don't matter.

Those desiring *reductions* according to characteristics often say they are willing to have the same level of overall immigration—or even higher—if the immigrants getting the green cards have different characteristics than those now getting them. This form of reduction advocacy includes arguments for a lowering of numbers of certain kinds of immigrants based on their culture, race, religion, education, skills, or nationality. These participants in the immigration debate are willing for the overall numbers to come down, but they are also willing to replace the barred immigrants with others who match the cultural, racial, religious, educational, skills or nationality profile the advocate prefers. The overall numbers simply don't matter much.

Those desiring *increases* by characteristic almost never suggest a reduction of any existing flow of immigrants even if they don't particularly like the characteristics of a specific group. They merely want more of their favored immigrants. For some, the characteristic is a particular skill that will enable them to fill jobs more quickly or more cheaply. For others, the characteristic is a culture, race, religion or nationality that usually matches their own. Lobbies and interest groups in this category have been primarily responsible for the escalation of overall numbers as they pushed increases in one sub-category after another. Even though the "characteristics debaters" say they aren't interested in the numbers—or refuse to define their overall numerical goals—everything they do is an attempt to increase the numbers in sub-categories.

"Numbers debaters" also fall on both sides of the immigration issue. Those who desire to reduce the overall numbers do so primarily for reasons dealing with the environment, education, culture, wages, sprawl, congestion, social cohesiveness or national unity. They commonly state specific numerical goals.

On the other hand, those who wish to increase overall numbers are less likely to state numerical goals, but they make appeals for increasing overall numbers in general. The common reasons for favoring overall increases are to expand the economy, hold down wages, provide population growth for real estate and consumer industries, eliminate a cultural or racial majority in the country, move the United States into more equilibrium with other countries in terms of higher population density or lower standard of living, or meet humanitarian goals of bringing in as many poor people as possible.

Picking an actual numerical goal subjects a person or group to criticism both for the potential immigrants who would be excluded because the chosen number wasn't higher and for the Americans who potentially would have their needs less well served because the chosen number wasn't lower. No matter what number one picks—unless one completely closes the borders or completely opens them—there will be losers in both camps. The only question is how the losses are apportioned between the two groups.

Thus, people or groups who fail to tell the public their numerical goals seek an advantage in the debate by seeming to avoid forcing losses to either potential immigrants or to Americans. But whether or not an overall number is picked, advocacy for any part of immigration policy will result in a specific number—and thus will result in some apportionment of loss to both potential immigrants and to Americans. Refusing to talk about the numbers is intellectually dishonest and should not be honored as a legitimate part of the public policy debate over immigration.

Although simply stating a numerical goal is sufficient to qualify a person or group as serious about immigration policy, I believe it is important to note (1) the principles behind picking the number, (2) the desired optimum level, and (3) a practical level that one would set as an immediate policy goal. Following are my answers to each:

PRINCIPLES

The most important question for Washington is whether a continuing stream of foreign workers and dependents into the country over the next few years will make it more or less difficult to achieve the economic, social or environmental goals of the American people. In other words, for the first time in decades Washington should consider basing its immigration policy on how many immigrants the nation actually needs. Officials should start the process at the zero level and add only the numbers that actually will help the Americans reach their goals.

The idea of immigration actually having to serve the goals of the American people will be considered somehow selfish by some. But a first principle of democratic nations is that their governments set public policy based on the will of the people. A people can choose goals in all kinds of ways that affect their material prosperity, their social comfort and their humanitarian desires. The government's choices should reflect the needs and desires of the people of this nation.

OPTIMUM LEVELS

In examining the research on a number of major societal concerns, I have concluded the following about optimum annual immigration levels:

American Need: Educational Quality, Optimum Immigration: up to 5,000

The worst education results in the country tend to be found in the school districts where most immigrants settle. That isn't necessarily the fault of the immigrants; many of the school districts were in bad shape before Congress began filling them with foreign students. But none of them has anything to gain by receiving another immigrant child. Congressional immigration policies may be at their cruelest in the way they diminish the chance that the children of some of America's poorest families will gain at their schools the education, the imagination, and the motivation to work for their share of the American dream.

To the extent that the immigrant children in those districts might receive a significant boost from the work of an especially talented foreign educator, those needs should easily be met if we set aside 5,000 slots each year for foreign professionals with extraordinary skills.

Cutting off all other immigration flow would allow those over-challenged, over-crowded districts to concentrate on educating the native and immigrant students at hand, instead of expending so much energy and money each year trying to accommodate additional students in an ever-expanding array of languages and cultures.

Until urban school districts no longer complain of being over-crowded or of having high dropout rates, any additional immigration is likely to be harmful.

American Need: Meeting Humanitarian Goals, Optimum Immigration: 15,000 to 50,000

Americans are an exceptionally generous people, especially in their private gifts to assist citizens of the developing countries. This is driven by a combination of religious, moral, and ethical impulses. I believe most Americans have an emotional or spiritual need to do their share in helping the tens of millions of refugees around the world. The numbers are so huge that one can make a case that it is unethical to spend any money on expensive resettlement of refugees in the United States when the same money would bring so much relief to so many more people in the camps and in assisting refugees to return home.

Nonetheless, the international community has a system for designating refugees who for political reason have virtually no chance of returning to their homelands—or who are in danger if they remain in camps. America's generally recognized fair share of those special needs refugees generally runs between 15,000 and 35,000 per year. Resettling refugees who do not meet the special needs criteria not only needlessly squanders limited resources but can create incentives for people to recklessly leave their homes and recklessly resist homeland return efforts. Thoughtful and effective humanitarianism would limit refugee admissions to the fair share of internationally recognized special needs refugees.

Similar considerations should also apply to asylum requests. Permanent asylum should be granted only to those seekers who meet the international standard for fear of persecution and who prove that there is little likelihood they could ever return home. But there should be a second level of temporary asylum that allows the persecuted to stay in America while waiting out the troubles back home but which assures that the asylee will leave the United States once the war is over, the dictator is deposed, or some other needed change has occurred. The United States should not make it easy for regimes to push their dissidents out of the country, nor should it be a magnet that draws such change agents from being part of the solution for their own peoples.

Thoughtful humanitarianism would not extend beyond those two categories. It certainly would not extend to those who would come to increase their consumption of material goods, education or health care. With 4.6 billion people living in countries below the average income of Mexico, there can be no ethical justification for showering a tiny fraction of a percent of the world's needy with U.S. residency at the expense of vulnerable Americans instead of turning all such outward humanitarian attention to the billions of people left behind in the sending countries.

American Need: Taming Urban Sprawl and the Destruction of Open Spaces, Farmland, and Natural Habitat, Optimum Immigration: Zero

Americans are absolutely fed up with the sprawl, traffic, congestion, and disappearing open-space opportunities that are the result of adding 1 million people each year. While it theoretically is possible to create so much population growth without those negative societal trends, there are no examples in America of that having occurred. U.S. Census Bureau measurements of changes in urbanized areas indicate that around half of all sprawl is related to population growth. The Census Bureau also shows that most U.S. population growth is the result of recent federal immigration policies.

Until there is a national consensus that our cities no longer have a problem of sprawl, congestion, and disappearing open spaces, the optimum level of immigration would be zero until the U.S. population size is stabilized.

American Need: Meeting Environmental Goals, Optimum Immigration: Zero

In a country where nearly half the lakes and rivers do not meet clean water standards and where 40 percent of the citizens live in cities that can't meet clean air standards, anything that adds to the total number of Americans flushing toilets, riding in vehicles, and consuming electricity is anti-environment.

Under current American fertility which is just under replacement level, any immigration over zero during the next few decades will increase the size of the U.S. population and put the country further away from meeting its environmental goals.

It is possible that the current number of Americans could reduce their consumption enough to meet all environmental goals and still have room for more people. But until the American people elect a government to institute the regulations, the taxes, and the enforcement to ensure that consumption is sufficiently reduced, any federal policy that forces U.S. population growth is an anti-environmental policy.

The point here is not that immigrants cause environmental problems but that people cause environmental problems—and federal immigration policy adds millions of extra people each decade.

The optimum level of immigration would be zero until we have substantially met most of the environmental goals that have been set by elected representatives of the American people.

American Need: Right of U.S. Citizens to Marry or Adopt Overseas, Optimum Immigration: Currently around 200,000

The United States has a long tradition of allowing its citizens to adopt orphans from other countries and to marry people in other countries and immediately bring them to America. This is part of the fabric of generous individual liberties that Americans cherish. Before the federal government began its major increases in immigration numbers back in the 1960s, around 40,000 additional immigrants each year moved to the United States based on this right of marriage and adoption. But because of the explosion in immigration, America is filled with a huge pool of foreign-born citizens—and their children—who have a much higher proclivity toward marrying overseas. There has been no limit on how many foreign people can be married and adopted each year so that this category alone surpasses 200,000 a year, almost as large as the entire annual immigration flow in an average year during the country's first 200 years (1776–1976).

Although there should be increased efforts to reduce the thousands of immigrants each year who engage in marriage fraud, the optimum number for the sake of preserving this right of citizens should be the present number with the flexibility to go up or down depending on the demand.

Many people claim that this individual freedom to marry and adopt overseas extends to naturalized foreign-born citizens being allowed to send for their adult brothers, sisters and parents. This strains credulity. Except for the small fraction of the immigrant flow that is refugees, immigrants chose to separate from their families by coming here. Nobody forced them. If they have a passionate need to live near their relatives, they should move back. Americans commonly live 3,000 miles from their brothers, sisters and parents inside the United States. There is no legitimate American need for immigrants to nurture a never-ending chain of family migration by sending for close adult relatives who send for their close adult relatives until in-laws and distant cousins of the original immigrant are coming. That was the wise conclusion of the bi-partisan national Commission on Immigration Reform chaired by the late Barbara Jordan. Parents of immigrants are a somewhat more difficult question. But generous visitor visas could allow for extended visits that would afford more time together than is the case for large numbers of native-born American citizens and their parents. Also, an immigrant is free to move back home to care for a parent during a crisis.

A final family category to consider is the one containing the spouses and minor children of immigrants who have green cards but who have not yet become citizens. There is quite a backlog right now because Congress has extended three amnesties to illegal aliens beginning in 1986. If a person becomes an immigrant through normal channels, he or she automatically can bring a spouse and minor children. But if an immigrant marries in another country before becoming a U.S. citizen, the spouse and children must wait. Currently, that backlog is whittled down each year. The surest solution to the backlog is for the immigrant to become a citizen. Still there may be reason to study this more to see if the backlog reduction numbers should be increased a bit.

American Need: Protection of Workers from Wage Depression, Optimum Immigration: Up to 5,000

No American wage earner benefits from having his or her elected officials import workers who may compete for the same jobs or help to depress wages. That is true whether the American worker is an unskilled lettuce picker, a slightly skilled chicken slaughterer, a skilled construction tradesman, or a college-educated engineer.

The recent spectacle of high government officials and major newspaper editorialists calling for increased immigration in order to hold down wages makes a mockery of the egalitarian ideals of this nation. Until recently, the primary answer to tight labor markets in this country has always been to increase productivity through innovation, invention and capital investment. That traditional style allowed wages to rise so that the vast majority of full-time working Americans could enjoy middle class lives of dignity.

Mass importation of foreign labor also violates American-style egalitarianism by creating vast underclass populations cast semi-permanently into the role of servants. Rising income disparity has always been the result of surges in immigration in this country.

Denying industries the immigrant workers they desire should not be a punitive measure. It is in the best interest of all Americans that our industries succeed—and, for that matter, that entrepreneurs and the owners of capital earn generous profits as they create jobs for the rest of us. The government should provide the industries the means to meet real short-term labor emergencies, as long as they do not impede efforts to train Americans to fill the needs later. Foreign workers given only temporary work visas, not by immigrants allowed to enter the United States for permanent residence, should fill nearly all skilled-job vacancies for which an American cannot be found. And temporary workers should be allowed into the country only after they have signed agreements of understanding that they will return to their home country at the end of the short time it may take to train enough Americans to take the jobs.

An allowance for 5,000 brilliant professionals would more than handle the number of scientists, professors, computer whizzes, and so forth who possess extraordinary genius and whom U.S. industries and universities want to steal from other countries each year.

American Need: All of the Above, Overall Optimum Immigration: 100,000

The dilemma in setting the overall numbers is that the optimal numbers for various American needs clash with each other. The American needs to meet environmental goals and to combat sprawl are best met with zero immigration for awhile, but the American need to have the individual liberty to fall in love with anybody in the world and then bring that person to the United States as a bride or groom calls for at least 200,000 immigrants each year. The American need for economic justice in wages and for educational relief for kids in overcrowded, underfunded schools is best met with no more than 5,000 immigrants each year. But the American need to take up our fair share of helping special refugees calls for up to 50,000 a year.

If one left out the issue of overseas marriages and adoptions, one could argue for an optimum immigration level of 55,000 a year.

But in weighing all American needs together, one could make a claim for an immigration level of around 100,000. That represents a compromise between the marriage rights and all other matters affecting Americans' quality of life. Combined with government estimates that more than 200,000 illegal aliens permanently settle in the United States each year, an overall ceiling of 100,000 legal immigrants still would exceed out-migration each year and add significantly to U.S. population growth. And that would further aggravate efforts to improve education, environmental quality, wage fairness and quality of life issues like sprawl. But the level would be relatively mild compared with present conditions.

PRACTICAL LEVEL

Individual liberty often trumps all other needs in the American culture. The optimum immigration numbers noted above would require tens of thousands of citizens to get in a waiting line of perhaps years to marry overseas or to bring a spouse from overseas after marrying. I do not see any practical possibility for limiting the virtually unlimited right of citizens to marry anybody they choose, regardless of home country, and immediately bringing them to this country. I believe Americans will insist on that right even though only a tiny fraction of them—especially native-born ones—will ever even think about using that right. This is a democracy; if Americans are willing to subjugate many of their other needs and desires to this particular right that is their choice. It also is my reluctant preference.

Thus, my proposed numerical level of overall immigration would be 255,000. That is near the number in the Census Bureau's Scenario 1 noted at the beginning of this essay.

I picked the number based on 200,000 spouses and minor children of U.S. citizens, 5,000 world-class skilled workers and professionals and 50,000 refugees, asylees and nuclear family of permanent resident aliens. If the refugee and asylee admissions fall below 50,000 each year, the leftover green cards could go to reduce the backlog of spouses and minor children of immigrants who have not become citizens.

Since the citizens' spouses and minor children category would go up and down each year, my number really is not a rigid 255,000 but a formula that would currently produce a number like that. The formulas would be: 55,000 a year, plus an unlimited number of spouses and minor children of U.S. citizens.

Trends suggest that my number might rise fairly close to 300,000 before it began coming down strongly. But as the years progressed and we had fewer and fewer recent immigrants in the marrying pool, my overall number should in a decade or two move back to the traditional immigration average, and maybe eventually even toward the 100,000 optimum level.

I am not pleased with the number I have had to pick because it will lead—according to Census projections—to at least another 50 million Americans by mid-century and at current fertility rates won't stop pressuring urban sprawl, congestion and natural habitat destruction until the next century. If not for a federal government that has refused to look at the effect of overall immigration numbers while constantly making decisions that increased them for four decades, those of us who are Baby Boomers would have lived to see the fruits of a stable population. Now I have already lost the chance to live in a stable America, but I feel guilty about denying the opportunity to my great-grandchildren. I have picked an annual immigration number so high that it compromises their future, as well as every generation in between. But I have picked the best number that I believe is possible. All who pick higher numbers—or who refuse to pick a number at all—propose to only accelerate the future damage from massive additional population growth.

NO

A Strategic U.S. Immigration Policy for the New Economy

Stephen Moore

OVERVIEW

In the 21st century global economy, the resource that is in greatest scarcity is human capital. There is a pervasive global shortage of world-class minds and cutting-edge skills. The whole world is in a search for excellence. Through immigration policy the U.S. has an awesome opportunity to import many of the best and brightest talents from around the world.

We ought to take advantage of this opportunity. A strategic immigration policy designed to attract many of these world-class workers is in the national interest and will enhance U.S. economic competitiveness in incalculable ways.

We do some of this now, but we can and should do better. U.S. immigration policy should be redesigned so that it becomes an integral part of an overall pro-growth economic policy.

All of this is to say that when it comes to U.S. immigration policy, quality matters now more than ever. We must greatly expand skill-based immigration.

But quantity matters, too. As America's workforce ages, we need the infusion of young workers—yes, even unskilled workers fill vital niches in our workforce—to keep our economy prosperous and to avoid the kind of serious demographic crisis that may soon beset most other advanced developed nations. A policy of gradually bumping up quotas from the current level of about 800,000 per year to a range of 1–1.5 million would ensure that we have a steady stream of young workers to keep our economy prosperous when the baby boomers begin to retire.

Finally, it is essential for the social cohesion of the nation that when newcomers are accepted into the United States, they Americanize like the immigrants of old. We should establish a policy that says: "yes to immigration, but no to welfare." And we should also adopt a policy that says: "immigration yes, assimilation yes." Assimilation would be facilitated by de-emphasizing ethnic separatist policies and identity group politics. Bilingual education and racial quotas should be abolished, for example. Greater influence in our schools should be placed on American history, American government, and western civilization, rather than celebrating and teaching multiculturalism.

HOW MANY IMMIGRANTS SHOULD WE ADMIT?

Most Americans have come to believe that the United States is accepting unprecedented numbers of immigrants—that the nation is virtually "under siege" from foreigners. Many of our politicians, such as Pat Buchanan, have tried to reinforce this sense of an out-of-control border by resorting in some cases to frightening rhetoric. Buchanan, for example, speaks of the need to "build a sea wall around the United States" to keep out "the rising masses of foreigners."*

The truth is that the numbers today are not unusually high or unmanageable. It is indeed true that in the 1980s and 1990s the U.S. admitted about 15 million new immigrants. This was the most immigrants to come to the United States since the great wave that arrived through Ellis Island between 1900–1910. Roughly half of all immigrants settled in just four states: California, Florida, Texas, and Illinois.

Perhaps the best measure of America's ability to absorb immigrants into the social and physical infrastructure is the number of immigrants admitted as a share of the total population. The U.S. immigration rate has risen from about 2.0 per 1,000 residents in the 1950s and 1960s to about 3.5 per 1,000 residents by 2000. In earlier periods of our history the immigration rate has been as high as 16 per 1,000, or five times higher than today. The average immigration rate over the past 150 years has been about 5 per 1,000 residents.

Today, more than 25 million Americans—or about one in ten—is foreign born. This is somewhat lower than the historical average of about one in eight Americans being foreign born. Our historical experience thus suggests that increasing immigrant quotas would not cause unprecedented immigration.

The birth rate in the U.S. today is slightly below replacement levels. For many industrialized nations, low birth rates are a huge long-term demographic problem. Thanks to immigration, our demographic problems are less severe than in Japan, Germany, Spain, Italy, and France, to name a few. As the Baby Boomers begin to retire in 10 years, America will need young workers through immigration more than ever.

> Policy recommendation: Historical experience shows that the United States can easily sustain an immigration level of one million new entrants per year. For at least the next 20 to 30 years, because of America's changing demographic profile, more workers will be needed to sustain the U.S. economy and pay the retirements costs of current workers. This can be achieved in part by modestly raising immigration levels. Certainly, it would be contrary to the national interest to be reducing immigration levels at this time.

IMMIGRANTS AND THE NEW ECONOMY

The resiliency of the U.S. economy continues to confound almost all economists and government forecasters. This is an expansion like almost no other in American history, with trillions of dollars of new wealth having been created in just the past decade. What is new and different about this expansion is that it is being driven in large part by one sector of the economy: high tech. As economist Lawrence Kudlow of CNBC has noted, "This bull market economy is being pulled along by dramatic productivity gains in the high technology sector." Today, the U.S. is globally dominant in almost every important high-tech field—from computer software to pharmaceuticals to robotics to semiconductors.

U.S. policymakers should be doing everything possible to facilitate and foster the continuation of the remarkable productivity revolution in the computer and information technology industries. The good news is that in most cases, this simply means leaving industry alone, and allowing the survival of the fittest, like Microsoft, to flourish.

But U.S. firms also desperately need access to the kinds of technically trained workers that created the Silicon Valley prosperity in the first place. This means that over the long term they need better-trained U.S. workers. But it also means they need to be able to hire high-skilled immigrant workers. The immigration laws are pathetically inadequate in this regard. Until a few years ago, U.S. firms were permitted to recruit just 65,000 skill-based immigrants per year under a program called H-1B. In 1998 that cap was raised to approximately 100,000 per year.

That is still too few visas relative to the need and the economic opportunity. We should immediately double or even triple high-skilled immigration visas. These talented engineers, scientists, teachers, and business professionals will not take jobs from American workers—they will almost certainly create jobs by making our industries more profitable and productive. As T. J. Rodgers, president of Cypress Semiconductors, has noted, "Immigration is a leading factor behind the U.S.'s commanding competitive position in semiconductors, as it is in almost every 21st century industry." The combination of good old American ingenuity and the top talent from the rest of the world gives the U.S. an awesome comparative advantage against foreign rivals.

> Policy Recommendation: What is the best way to attract high-skilled immigrants? Clearly the employer-sponsored system works well and should be made more generous. But additionally, the U.S. should establish 100,000–200,000 visas that would be allocated through a point-based selection system. Points should be awarded on the basis of: education level, occupational skills, English language ability, special talents, and perhaps other characteristics. Visas should be awarded to the immigrants with the highest point totals each year. Under such a system, we would roughly double the number of immigrant visas awarded on the basis of skills. With this change, the immigrants who come to the U.S. in the next 20 years will be the most talented people ever to come. It wouldn't be long before we had a Silicon Valley in every state in the union. This would be an incredibly bullish policy for an already stampeding U.S. economy.

FAMILY-BASED IMMIGRATION

Throughout American history immigrants have tended to come to the U.S. with some or all of their immediate family. Others come to reunite with family members. The system generally works well, providing newcomers with a natural social network and safety net to fall into when they arrive. Because the family is the basic socializing structure in America, it makes sense that our immigration policy should continue to emphasize immediate family preservation.

Family immigration is also an imperative of our immigration policy because if immigrant workers cannot get their family members into the U.S., many will not wish to come. If we want skilled immigrants, we need to allow them to bring their families. Although opponents of the family system argue that it encourages "chain migration," reports by the U.S. General Accounting Office indicate that chain migration is not a major problem.

> Policy Recommendation: Preserve family-based immigration. Moving toward greater emphasis on skilled immigration should be done as an add-on to the current immigration preference system, not as a substitute for current family immigration policies. The one exception is that the category preference that allows adult immigrants to bring in their elderly parents should be discontinued. Elderly immigrants provide almost no benefit to the U.S. and, unlike young immigrants, impose net costs on U.S. taxpayers.

ENCOURAGING ETHNIC DIVERSITY

The 1965 immigration law ended the national origin system for allocating immigrant visas and replaced that system with the family-based system. The pre-1965 laws had been criticized rightly for becoming a de facto barrier against non-European immigrants. However, a strong case can be made that the laws have swung too far in the opposite direction—excluding many Europeans who lack the family connections to come to the U.S. In the 1950s about half of our immigrants came from Europe. Now less than 20 percent do.

The drop-off of European immigration is troubling. Immigration is beneficial at least in part because of the ethnic and genetic diversity it brings to the U.S. Moreover, Europeans, like Asians, have tended to be highly skilled and thus desirable for the substantial human capital they bring with them.

One major reason why the U.S. has seen a decline in European immigration has had little to do with U.S. immigration policy, but rather the inability, until recently, of immigrants from former communist nations—including Poland, Russia, Hungary, and Romania—from traveling here. In the 1980s, only about 3 percent of America's immigrants came from the Eastern bloc.

The number of immigrants who came to the U.S. from all East Europe in the 1980s was roughly the same number that arrived from the small island of Jamaica.

> Policy Recommendation: One goal of U.S. immigration policy should be to encourage ethnic diversity. The U.S. should allow increased immigration from Eastern and Western Europe. A point system as described above might give preference to those from nations where historical immigration levels have fallen substantially.

IMMIGRANTS AND WELFARE

America's welfare system should not be a magnet for immigrants. For the most part it is not. Moreover, the welfare reform laws of 1996 tightened eligibility requirements, thus making it more difficult for immigrants to receive public assistance. The preliminary statistics indicate an encouraging decline in welfare use among immigrants in the wake of that law.

Studies at the Cato Institute, confirmed by other scholars, suggest that immigrants use welfare and other social services at about the same rate that U.S.-born citizens do, despite that the foreign born have higher rates of poverty. The taxes paid by immigrants typically cover the cost of public services used. The rate of welfare use is higher among immigrants living in high-benefit states, indicating that if states would reduce the value of their welfare packages, dependency rates among immigrants would decline still further.

> Policy Recommendation: What is clear is that Americans do not want to be paying taxes for immigrants on welfare. The good news is that immigrants as a group are not welfare abusers—particularly now that the new tighter eligibility laws have been adopted. One long-standing condition for entry for immigrants is that they not become "a public charge." This policy should be more strictly enforced. For their first five years in the U.S. immigrants should not be eligible for most cash and non-cash welfare benefits, with emergency medical care being a notable exception. Immigrants who go on welfare during their first five years in the U.S. should be denied continued residency in the U.S. Efforts by some welfare advocacy groups to roll back the welfare restrictions for immigrants in the 1996 law should be vigorously opposed.

The explicit purpose of refugee assistance programs is to "help refugees achieve economic self-sufficiency within the shortest time possible following their arrival in the United States." In practice the programs have had precisely the opposite effect, contributing to a culture of dependency within refugee communities. Most special refugee assistance programs should be eliminated. Non-profit resettlement agencies and ethnic associations should privately provide refugee assistance.

MAKING SURE THE MELTING POT STILL WORKS

We as Americans should expect—even demand—that those who come voluntarily to these shores become part of the American community. This should be a central part of the citizenship pact. This requires basic steps toward assimilation: learning the language, learning about how the American system of government works, staying off welfare, avoiding criminal behavior, gaining employment rapidly so to start the climb up the economic ladder of success.

Assimilation is not a dirty word. It binds our society together. Too many institutions in America celebrate our separateness, not our shared identity and our shared values. Studies tell us that assimilation is also a virtual pre-condition for immigrant success in the U.S. English language ability is a huge predictor of economic advancement for immigrants. The immigrants want to assimilate—if only we as a society will encourage it.

> Policy Recommendations: Abolish bilingual education. The California experience proves that English immersion is far superior for teaching immigrant children our common language. Abolish the system of quotas and preferences in the job market, the universities, and in government. Race-based preferences are not just an inherent injustice—a contradiction of the idea of equal treatment under the law—but also encourage an unhealthy entitlement mentality among racial and ethnic groups.

Finally, if our goal is to see immigrants become American citizens, we must take steps to reduce citizenship backlogs, of more than 1 million and counting. Citizenship tests should not be dumbed down, as some have suggested, and the residency requirements should remain in place, but it should not require years of delay for those who are eligible to become full-fledged American citizens.

Note

*Patrick Buchanan, "The Immigration Bomb," *The Washington Times* (October 11, 1990).

DISCUSSION QUESTIONS

1. How do the events of September 11, 2001, affect your views of immigration policy?
2. What impact do you think emigration has on countries like Mexico, China, Ukraine, Greece, and others?
3. Should the United States emphasize job skills in deciding who is allowed to enter the United States legally?

4. What impact, if any, does increasing global trade have on immigration? What are the implications?
5. Should U.S. cities receive additional federal assistance because most immigrants live in cities?
6. What benefits do you think immigrants provide to the United States? What are the costs?
7. Are there differences in the challenges faced by today's immigrants compared with those faced by immigrants in the early twentieth century? If so, what are these differences? How should this affect public policy, if at all?
8. One option for dealing with illegal immigrants to the United States has been to increase border patrols. Another is to impose sanctions on employers hiring illegal immigrants. How should the United States deal with the problem of illegal immigrants? What other policy options are available?

WEB REFERENCES

American Immigration Resources on the Internet, http://www.wave.net/upg/immigration/resource.html.

Center for Immigration Studies, http://www.cis.org/.

US Immigration and Naturalization Service, http://www.ins.usdoj.gov/.

USA Immigration Services, http://www.usais.org/.

FURTHER READING

Borjas, George J. *Friends or Strangers: The Impact of Immigrants on the United States Economy.* New York: Basic Books, 1990.

Borjas, George. *Heaven's Door: Immigration Policy and the American Economy.* Princeton, N.J.: Princeton University Press, 2001.

Borjas, George. "The New Economics of Immigration." *Atlantic Monthly* (November 1996).

Briggs, Vernon M., Jr. *Immigration and American Unionism.* Ithaca, N.Y.: ILR Press, 2001.

Briggs, Vernon M., Jr. "Immigration Policy: Political or Economic?" *Challenge* (September–October 1991).

Briggs, Vernon M., Jr. *Mass Immigration and the National Interest.* Armonk, N.Y.: M. E. Sharpe, 1992.

Brimelow, Peter. *Alien Nation: Common Sense about America's Immigration Disaster.* New York: Random House, 1995.

Chavez, Linda. *Out of the Barrio: Toward a New Politics of Hispanic Assimilation.* New York: Basic Books, 1991.

Chiswick, Barry R. *The Employment of Immigrants in the United States.* Washington, D.C.: American Enterprise Institute, 1983.

Conner, Roger L. "Answering the Demo-Doomsayers." *Brookings Review* (Fall 1989).

Dalaet, Debra L. *US Immigration Policy in an Age of Rights.* New York: Praeger Publishing, 2000.

Eldredge, Dirk C. *Crowded Lands of Liberty: Solving America's Immigration Crisis.* Bridgehampton, N.Y.: Bridge Works Publishing, 2001.

Fix, Michael and Paul Hill. *Enforcing Employer Sanctions: Challenges and Strategies.* Washington, D.C.: RAND–Urban Institute, May 1990.

Geyer, Georgie Anne. *Americans No More: The Death of Citizenship.* Boston: Atlantic Monthly Press, 1996.

Glazer, Nathan. *Ethnic Dilemmas, 1964–1982.* Cambridge, Mass.: Harvard University Press, 1983.

Graham, Hugh D. *Collision Course: The Strange Convergence of Affirmative Action and Immigration Policy in America.* New York: Oxford University Press, 2002.

Harrison, Lawrence E. "America and Its Immigrants." *National Interest* (Summer 1992).

Holden, Constance. "Debate Warming Up on Legal Migration Policy," *Science* (July 15, 1988).

Hutchinson, E. P. *Legislative History of American Immigration Policy, 1798–1965.* Philadelphia: University of Pennsylvania Press, 1981.

Kennedy, David. "Can We Still Afford to Be a Nation of Immigrants?" *Atlantic Monthly* (November 1996).

Mahardige, Dale. *The Coming White Minority.* New York: Vintage Books, 1999.

Massey, Douglas S. "March of Folly: U.S. Immigration Policy after NAFTA." *American Prospect* (March 1998).

Moore, Stephen and Vernon M. Briggs, Jr. *Still an Open Door?* Lanham, Md.: University Press of America, 1994.

Morris, Milton D. *Immigration—The Beleaguered Bureaucracy.* Washington, D.C.: Brookings Institution, 1985.

Nevins, Joseph and Mike Davis. *Operation Gatekeeper: The Rise of the 'Illegal Alien' and the Remaking of the US–Mexico Boundary.* London: Routledge, 2001.

Perea, Juan F., ed. *Immigrants Out! The New Nativism and the Anti-Immigrant Impulse in the United States.* New York: New York University Press, 1997.

Schuck, Peter H. *Citizens, Strangers, and In-Betweens: Essays on Immigration and Citizenship.* Boulder, Colo.: Westview Press, 2000.

Simon, Julian L. "Why Control the Borders?" *National Review* (February 1, 1993).

Ungar, Sanford J. *Fresh Blood: The New American Immigrants.* New York: Simon & Schuster, 1995.

Wattenberg, Ben J. and Karl Zinsmeister. "The Case for More Immigration." *Commentary* (April 1990).

Chapter 7

CAMPAIGN FINANCE REFORM
"Should Elections Be Publicly Funded?"

YES: David Donnelly, Janice Fine, and Ellen S. Miller
"Going Public" *Boston Review*

NO: John Samples "Government Financing of Campaigns: A Public Choice Perspective" The Cato Institute

Few things are as fundamental to the American democratic ideal as a system of free and open elections guaranteeing all citizens an equal role in selecting a government. But in recent years Americans have become increasingly cynical about how well the American electoral system is achieving that ideal. Beyond the controversy over the 2000 presidential election returns in Florida, there have been far deeper concerns over the power and influence of organized and well-funded interests in politics, the perceived inability of "ordinary" people to influence public policy, and the inordinate pressure exercised over politicians by corporate and other special-interest lobbyists.

The central role played by money in modern American politics stems from a simple fact: Campaigning for election in the United States is a costly business. During the 2000 elections, almost $4 billion was spent on federal and state campaigns for executive, legislative, and judicial offices.[1] In the presidential election, it has been estimated that George W. Bush spent almost $186 million on his successful campaign for the White House, while Al Gore spent $120 million. Included in these amounts are federal contributions of $67.5 million for Bush and $83 million for Gore (Gore received more because Bush declined matching funding for the primary).[2] In the U.S. congressional races, over $1 billion was spent on the 2000 campaigns, with the notable inclusions of a combined $70 million in the New York Senate race between Rick Lazio and Hillary Clinton and $63 million (mostly of personal funds) spent by Jon Corzine's successful campaign in the New Jersey senatorial election.[3]

When money becomes influential in elections, individuals and organizations will seek influence over political outcomes through campaign donations. Public recognition of candidates and issues becomes heightened through media exposure, public and private rallies, the dissemination of promotional materials, and a variety of other strategies that all require sizable sums of money. As candidates seek to gain prominence in the public's perception, ever-greater amounts are spent on campaign advertising and publicity, and a candidate's need for funding grows. As the need for funding grows, so does the amount of time candidates need to devote to fund-raising, and so too does the potential for those with money to influence the success rate of political candidates. This process need not be legally or even ethically corrupt—there are many legal channels through which campaigns can be financed—but it does make doubtful the equality of political influence and opportunity so essential to a democratic political system.

As a result of concerns over rising election costs and imbalances in the electoral process, the twentieth century witnessed a progression of federal legislation aimed at controlling and curbing the influence of private money in political campaigns. The Tillman Act of 1907 made it unlawful for companies to make contributions to any aspect of federal elections. Three years later, the Federal Corrupt Practices Act (also known as the Publicity Act) required the disclosure of campaign finances for party committees active in more than one state. Although other legislation was evident during the first four decades of the twentieth century, it was not until 1939 that Congress enacted significant new legislation with the Hatch Act and its amendments a year later. In an attempt to restrain the influence of unionized government workers on election outcomes, the Hatch Act prohibited political activity by federal employees, including fund-raising for political candidates. Perhaps more significantly, the amendment to the act also restricted the amount of money individuals were permitted to donate to federal campaigns to $5,000. This restriction did not apply to state and local party committees, however, leading to large sums being diverted through these lower-level organizations. A similar situation occurred as a result of the Taft-Hartley Act of 1947 that prohibited the use of labor union funds for political donations; unions responded by setting up political action committees (PACs), independent organizations that collected donations for nonelection political advertising and promotion.

Despite the proliferation of campaign finance regulations, the use of such loopholes as PACs and state and local party committees ensured the contin- ued growth of election spending. As a result, further legislation was created in the early 1970s with the Federal Election Campaign Act (FECA). The principal provision of FECA was to limit the amount that candidates could spend from personal funds on their campaigns, in an effort to reduce the advantage that wealthy candidates could have from self-financing: The limits were set at $50,000 for presidential races, $35,000 for Senate campaigns, and $25,000 for House campaigns. The law also limited the amount of media spending allowable throughout a campaign to $50,000, a measure aimed at curbing the extraordinary increases in campaign funding, largely believed to be an effect of television and radio advertising.[4] In the 1956 elections, $9.8 million, or 6 percent of campaign spending, went to media advertising.[5] FECA addressed concerns over electoral corruption, introducing disclosure requirements that mandated the reporting of names, addresses, and occupations of donors contributing $100 or more. Despite the measures of the legislation, campaign spending continued to rise significantly, with the 1972 elections seeing a 42 percent increase in campaign spending from the elections of 1968.[6]

It was really with the set of amendments to FECA, beginning with those of 1974, that substantial restrictions were placed on campaign financing, aimed at candidates, political parties, and individual donors. Candidates were given spending limits for state, congressional, and presidential campaigns, with presidential hopefuls restricted to a sum of $30 million in total campaign spending. New limits dictated that no individual could spend more than $1,000 on any single federal candidate, with an absolute maximum of $25,000 for all federal contributions.[7] The 1974 amendments to FECA also began the trend toward what has now become colloquially known as "clean elections," or elections financed by public rather than private funds. The legislation made available $20 million to presidential candidates of the Democratic and Republican Parties, with the proviso that they not raise additional money from private sources. Candidates were also eligible for matching funds of up to $5 million if they raised at least $5,000 in contributions of no greater than $250 in 20 states. The intention was to level the electoral playing field on the basis of not only the wealth of the candidate but also that of the candidate's financial entourage. The federal coffers were open for use by those presidential candidates who stayed free of individual financial influence. Later amendments to FECA in 1976 placed restrictions on PAC donations, limiting the amount that individuals could give to a PAC to $5,000 a year and limiting the amount that a PAC could give to a national party committee to $15,000 a year.

FECA's limitations on campaign contributions and spending were not without controversy. The most notable objection to the legislation came from Senator James L. Buckley (New York), Eugene McCarthy, and others who filed suit against the Federal Election Commission and its ex officio member, Francis R. Valeo, in 1975. After FECA was upheld by a U.S. court of appeals, the case of *Buckley* v. *Valeo* went to the Supreme Court. Here the sensitive balance between freedom of speech, as evidenced through unrestricted campaign financing, and the notion of equality of voting, as evidenced by fair electoral financing, was realized through a complex Supreme Court decision in 1976. The Court maintained that the campaign donation restrictions in FECA were an appropriate means to curb financial influence and protect the integrity of a democratic system. However, the Court went on to reject FECA's limitations on campaign expenditures, arguing that the varying size of support for particular candidates necessitated flexible expenditure levels. The Court also rejected limits on personal spending by candidates, seeing this as a violation of an individual's right "to engage in the discussion of public issues and vigorously and tirelessly to advocate his own election."[8] This rejection effectively removed the limit on individual attempts to promote or reject particular candidates, severely curtailing the effectiveness of FECA.

Despite this history of attempts to limit the inequities introduced into the electoral system by private contributions, there remained several ways for individuals to use large donations to affect electoral campaigns. PACs grew rapidly after their inception in the mid-1940s—between 1974 and 1984, they grew in number to more than 3,000.[9] The number of PACs has been relatively stable since that time, although their donations to campaigns have risen continually, with 1998 seeing $220 million in PAC donations.[10] PACs are still dominated by labor unions and professional associations; in 2001–2002. the top 10 contributing PACs to federal candidates were all labor groups, giving predominantly to Democratic candidates. Top corporations donating to PACs included SBC Communications, United Parcel Service, and FedEx Corporation, while the National Rifle Association (NRA) headed interest-group PAC giving; 87 percent of NRA giving went to Republican candidates.[11] Grouped by sector, corporate PAC electoral donations are largest, with $91.5 million donated to all federal campaigns in 1999–2000. This accounts for 35 percent of all PAC giving, with the remainder coming from labor organizations (20 percent); trade, membership, and health organizations (28 percent); corporations without stock (2 percent); cooperatives (0.9 percent); and unconnected PACs (14 percent).[12]

PACs are not the only means by which individuals can expand their monetary contribution to the U.S. electoral process. In response to complaints from local parties that the 1974 legislation made raising money for routine "party-building" activities such as get-out-the vote efforts difficult, 1979 amendments created the so-called soft-money loophole, which allows unlimited contributions and expenditures for campaign materials and activities on behalf of federal candidates. Recent years have seen an explosion in the use of "soft money"—funds without any regulatory restriction, supposedly used for the financing of general party activities, as opposed to specific elections. Although soft money is principally directed toward party-building and voter-turnout strategies, individual candidates can benefit from issue ads that promote their election promises without explicitly framing the issue around winning or losing. The use of soft money has grown in the past decade, from a total of $86 million in 1991–1992[13] to $441 million in 1999–2000.[14] In the 1999–2000 election cycle, the division of PAC funds between Democrats and Republicans was very close, with 49 percent going to Democrats and 51 percent to Republicans.[15] As with PACs, soft money is an ideal loophole for corporations wishing to engage in campaign financing without contravening the restrictions of the Tillman Act of 1907. In 1998, for example, the financial sector gave over $45 million of soft money to political parties, the communications and electronics sector gave over $20 million, and energy companies gave some $15 million. Seven out of the top ten soft-money donors to the Democratic Party in 1998 were unions, whereas five out of the top ten companies making Republican donations were involved with tobacco and telecommunications.[16]

Private donors can also take advantage of unrestricted issue ads to influence elections. Since there are no restrictions on the amount of money nonprofit organizations can spend on advertising to promote their policy goals (as long as they do not specifically endorse a candidate), interest groups are able to use such ads to promote the agenda even if not the persona of political candidates. By supplying money to such organizations, private donors can have an enormous influence over the results of an election, especially at the congressional and state levels.

That corporations can make such significant financial contributions to elections (directly through PACs or indirectly through soft money) is troubling to some, given the supposed separation of companies from electioneering, and has motivated political reaction from some candidates. Former Vice President Al Gore's 2000 presidential campaign, for example, did not use direct PAC contributions. In Congress, important campaign finance reform legislation, eliminating soft-money contributions, finally passed both chambers and was signed into law by President Bush in March 2002. After failing through Senate filibusters on two occasions, the McCain-Feingold bill and its House counterpart, the Shays-Meehan bill, created legislation that bans the use of soft money and restricts the ability of outside groups to air issue ads on the tacit behalf of a candidate. As expected, the law is being contested by those organizations only too aware of the political clout they will lose with the demise of soft money. The National Rifle Association and Senator Mitch McConnell of Kentucky have filed suit against the law, on the basis of unconstitutional inhibition of the First Amendment's provision for free speech. Representative Ron Paul stated on the House floor, "Campaign reform legislation blows a huge hole in these First amendment protections by criminalizing criticism of elected officials. Thus, passage of this bill will import into American law the totalitarian concept that government officials should be able to use their power to silence their critics."[17] Such opposition to the campaign finance reform legislation stems from the libertarian view that each person in the polity should be allowed to express political affiliation and support through whatever means so desired, be that a protest march on Capitol Hill, the formation of an interest group to lobby on a particular issue, the decision to vote in an election, or the bolstering of political campaigns through financial donations. Thus, opposition to this particular legislation is endemic of a wider concern over regulation of the campaign process. The dialectic is one between freedom of speech and equality of participation, both key tenets of the democratic ideal.

As with many policy initiatives, the move toward clean elections at the federal level is a reflection of bolder and more substantial experiments at the state level. With a poll conducted in April 2000 showing that a majority of voters from all political affiliations—53 percent of Republicans, 62 percent of Democrats, and 64 percent of independents—believe change is needed in the financing of election campaigns, it is not surprising that several states have begun to implement campaign finance reform passed by voters through successful ballot initiatives.[18] The first state to enact reform was Maine in 1996 with the Clean Election Act; Arizona soon followed and was successful in overcoming legal suits against the legislation. Vermont passed clean election legislation in 1997, but the act has been subject to lawsuits by the Republican Party and the Progressive Party, in addition to threats from Vermont Governor Dean and the House Appropriations Committee.[19]

Another New England state battling for enactment of successful clean election legislation is Massachusetts. The "Question 2" referendum, passed by voters on the state ballot in November 1998, bans soft-money donations to political parties and provides public funding for gubernatorial, legislative, and other public races, providing that campaign spending limits, donation limits of $100 per donor, and certain disclosure requirements are met. Many legislators are opposed to the law, including House Speaker Thomas Finneran, believing that public expenditure on elections is a poor use of taxpayer's money. As a result, the state senate, in approving $9.6 million to fund the Clean Election Law, required that a nonbinding question be placed on the 2002 ballot, asking voters whether they approve of public money being used to fund candidates.[20] Although the Massachusetts legislature appropriated clean election funds for 2002 candidates, it is unclear how stable election reform is in the state, and how the reform efforts, already 4 years old, will fare politically or substantively.

Other states have measures in place that go someway toward "clean" elections: Florida, Kentucky, Maryland, Michigan, New Jersey, Rhode Island, and Wisconsin all provide some level of matching public funds for various public offices; Hawaii provides up to 30 percent of the spending limit in public funds and Minnesota provides up to 50 percent. Nebraska makes public funds available to candidates who agree to a voluntary spending limit and whose opponent exceeds the spending limit.[21] However, it is only in Maine and Arizona that full public funding has been available to candidates in past elections.

Clean election regulations in Maine and Arizona require candidates to raise an initial number of $5 donations in order to qualify for public funding. (In Maine, candidates are required to collect 150 such donations for senate seats and 50 for house seats, while the level in Arizona is set at 200 contributions.) During this initial period of qualification, candidates are allowed to raise nominal sums of "seed money" to create an initial campaign fund; the cap on seed money is significantly more stringent in Maine at only $500 for a house candidate, compared with $2,500 in Arizona.[22] Once qualified, legislative candidates in Maine are eligible for up to $4,393 in public funding for house races and $17,244 for senate seats; in Arizona, $10,000 is available for a primary election and $15,000 for a general election. These levels can be raised if publicly financed candidates face privately financed candidates who raise sums exceeding the base public allowance.

The National Institute on Money in State Politics analyzed the 2000 state elections in Maine and Arizona and found that private campaign donations declined by 49 percent in Maine, but only by 9 percent in Arizona, where total political spending in that year actually rose by almost 30 percent.[23] In both states, the number of candidates running for office increased in 2000, while the number of incumbents seeking to hold seats decreased slightly. However, not all candidates opted for public financing: In Maine, 31 percent of candidates took advantage of the government finances, while the number in Arizona was only 25 percent. What is maybe the most instructive finding from this study is the reduction in the differential between the campaign finances of winners and losers. In Maine, losers raised an average of 78 percent of winners' campaign funds in 2000, compared with just 53 percent 2 years before. In Arizona, losers raised 69 percent of winners' funds, a rise of 23 percent from 1998.[24] It is too early to assess the benefits or disadvantages of clean elections as realized in actual elections: Two sample cases over 1 year of campaigning is far too little information, and outcomes between Maine and Arizona are not always consistent.

The debate over the funding of elections is one that touches upon numerous fundamentals of a democratic political system. Is the United States truly a country of one person–one vote when that one vote can be reached by the electronic media only through substantial campaign expenditures? Is it unconstitutional to deny citizens the right of free exchange by limiting or forbidding certain kinds of political donations? The appearance on U.S. presidential ballots of self-financing candidates such as billionaire Ross Perot is indicative of the level of electoral participation that personal wealth can still buy. Clean election reforms aim to remove the inequitable factor of wealth, both from candidates and from those who support them, leveling the competition to one of issues and personalities, rather than financial clout.

Whether public funding of elections is advisable, constitutional, and pragmatic is the subject of the following articles. David Donnelly, Janice Fine, and Ellen S. Miller argue that money is an inherently decisive factor in federal and state elections, with large corporate contributors gaining valuable subsidies and favorable governmental decisions. They believe that campaigns should be competitive, publicly accountable, fair, responsible, and participatory and see full public financing, or "clean money," to be the only system that goes far enough to ensure these criteria are met. John Samples of the Cato Institute contends that public financing of political candidates is tantamount to subsidizing those who cannot generate enough support in the free market of private financing. He argues that existing efforts to curb campaign spending, such as placing limits on the size of contributions, actually weaken political competition and work against Republican and libertarian candidates who reject opportunities for public funding. He regards public financing to be not only unconstitutional, but also immoral in that it denies the individual the freedom to choose the recipient of political donations.

Endnotes

1. Candice J. Nelson, "Spending in the 2000 Elections," in David B. Magleby, ed., *Financing the 2000 Elections* (Washington, D.C.: The Brookings Institution, 2002), pp. 22–48.
2. 2000 Presidential Race: Total Raised and Spent, http://www.opensecrets.org/2000elect/index/AllCands.htm.
3. Nelson, op. cit., p. 30.
4. Anthony Corrado, "A History of Federal Campaign Finance Law," in Magleby, op. cit.
5. Ibid., p. 31.
6. Ibid., p. 32.
7. Ibid., p. 54.
8. Hoover Institution Public Policy Inquiry—Campaign Finance, *Buckley v. Valeo,* http://www.campaignfinancesite.org/court/buckley1.html.
9. PAC Contributions: The Role of PACs, http://www.opensecrets.org/pubs/ bigpicture 2000/pac/index.ihtml.
10. Ibid.
11. Open Secrets, Political Action Committees, http://www.opensecrets.org/pacs/index.asp.
12. Federal Election Commission, "PAC Financial Activity 1999–2000," http://www.fec.gov/press/053101pacfund/tables/pacsum00.htm.
13. Soft Money Contributions, http://www.opensecrets.org/pubs/bigpicture2000/soft_money/index.ihtml.
14. Common Cause, "The Soft Money Laundromat—Top Soft Money Donors," http://www.commoncause.org/laundromat/stat/topdonors99.htm.
15. Ibid.
16. Soft Money Contributions, op. cit.
17. Rep. Ron Paul, "Why 'Campaign Finance Reform' Is Unconstitutional" (February 13, 2002), http://www.house.gov/paul/congrec/congrec2002/cr021302.htm.
18. Clean Elections, http://www.stateaction.org/issues/governance/cleanelections/index.cfm.
19. VPIRG, http://www.vpirg.org/campaigns/financeReform/cfr_page111.html.
20. Editorial, "A Loaded Question," *Boston Globe* (June 19, 2002).
21. Common Cause, "Public Financing in the States," http://www.commoncause.org/states/cf_financing.htm.
22. Samantha Sanchez, "First Returns on a Campaign Finance Reform Experiment: Maine, Arizona and Full Public Funding" (March 2001), http://www.followthe money.org/database/MaineArizona%20full%20report.html.
23. Ibid.
24. Ibid.

YES

Going Public

David Donnelly, Janice Fine, and Ellen S. Miller

There are only two important things in politics. The first is money and I can't remember the second.

Mark Hanna

On November 7, 1995, more than a thousand volunteers in Maine collected 65,000 signatures to put the Maine Clean Elections Act on the 1996 ballot. It was the country's most sweeping campaign finance reform proposal, and promised to blunt the domination of special interest money in Maine politics by establishing a system of full public financing of state elections. One year later, by a 56–44 margin, Maine voters enacted this fundamental change. In crisp and decisive terms, they stated that private money would no longer dominate their political life.

The situation in other states, however, remains at least as bad as it was in Maine, and at the federal level matters are much worse. The American people realize that money is eating away at the core of our democracy, and voters seem willing to take decisive action to stop it. But they need a model for reform. Maine's full public financing solution, the Clean Money Option, provides that model—so we will argue. To appreciate the good sense in the Maine solution, we need first to understand the problem, and then to appreciate the limits of the alternative solutions.

THE PROBLEM

Americans can no longer pick up a newspaper without being confronted with the latest campaign finance excesses—stories about use of the White House and trade missions for fundraising purposes, or invitations of special interest lobbyists into legislative drafting sessions on Capitol Hill, or Republican legislators vacationing with the largest donors to their Party. These stories describe a system gone awry, in which private money is increasingly driving public policy on an ever-wider array of issues—taxation, environmental regulation, and health care policy, just to name the most obvious. And it is all perfectly legal . . . or at least, as the President says, 90 percent of it is. The remaining ten percent—contributions to the Democratic National Committee from well-heeled Asian donors, for example—may be of questionable legality, and may create titillating headlines, but it is largely a sideshow (an ugly, xenophobic sideshow). The real scandal is the legal stuff.

The precise nature of the scandal was obscured for years by contributors' ingenuity and reformers' lack of information. According to the conventional story, reform efforts in the early 1970s had unwittingly encouraged the formation of political action committees (PACs) that, by coordinating individual contributions, multiplied their effects and drove up the costs of campaigning. The big problem was to do something about the PACs.

Skeptical about this conventional wisdom, the Center for Responsive Politics pioneered a system for documenting the thousands of individual contributions to congressional campaigns. As a result of these efforts, we now have a far more accurate picture of the flows of money. The basic elements of this picture are crystal clear: the total amount of money in the system is exploding; the vast majority of this money comes from individuals, not PACs; most of the individual and PAC contributions come from wealthy special interests with a direct stake in government decisions; businesses and corporations are increasingly good at targeting those contributions at members of committees who deal with their issues (corporations dealing with health care issues target their dollars to members of the health care committees, those dealing with banking issues target their contributions to members of the banking committees); and these political investments have sizable payoffs, in electoral victories and favorable legislative outcomes.

Consider some basic numbers.

A record $2.2 billion (estimated) was spent in American politics in 1996. About $742.6 million was spent by candidates for Congress—not including the money that parties and other organizations spent on behalf of candidates. (Common Cause estimates that these "independent expenditures," and issue advocacy ads, reached $100 million.) Presidential spending for the 1996 election—including the $177 million spent on the primaries—reached $1 billion for the first time.

Overall fundraising for the Democratic and Republican parties through their federal and non-federal accounts reached $866.1 million through the end of November. The GOP outspent the Democrats $550 million to $315.9 million. The defensive claims from the Democrats about their need to keep up with the Joneses seem somewhat true, but it is hard to feel sorry for the party who also claims to champion the cause of the working class—they did keep up with the GOP in "soft money" contributions ($149.6 million for Republicans and a cool $117.3 million for the Dems). Soft money refers to the tens or hundreds of thousand dollar gifts to parties for so-called party-building activities which invariably come from corporate interests, not working families.

As to the sources of the money: most political contributions for federal, state, and local election campaigns come from a small number of wealthy individuals and powerful organizations that are subject to government regulation and taxation or have some other stake in government policy making. For example in the 1996 election cycle less than one-fourth of 1 percent of the American people gave contributions of $200 or more to a federal candidate. Only four percent make any contribution of any size to any candidate for office—federal, state, or local. On average, only 20 percent of the money came from individuals giving contributions less than $200 per candidate. That means an astonishing 80 percent of political money comes from the tiny group of donors who give $200 or more. (The residents of one New York City zip code give more to congressional candidates than the residents of each of 24 states.)

Funds are intelligently targeted: According to the Center for Responsive Politics's *Cashing In Report*, the timber industry convinced Congress to allow logging of dead and dying trees on public lands, over the objections of environmental groups. The 54 Senators who supported the timber industry received an average of $20,000; the 42 against the idea received an average of $2,500. In the House, the 211 members who supported the industry received $2,500 while the 209 who opposed them received an average of only $542.

The military industry also wrote big checks and got big returns. The 213 members of Congress who voted to spend an additional $493 million on Northrop Grumman's B-2 stealth bombers received an average of $2,100 from the contractor; the 210 who voted against only got $100 on average.

With the devolution of important issues to the states, like the implementation of the new welfare laws, maybe welfare moms should start a political action committee or bundle their dwindling benefits checks to the chairs of the human resource committees in our state capitals. But how many corporate executives need to choose between making a political contribution and buying food for their children?

What does this money buy? *The Nation* has catalogued the "return on investment" that corporate America received in direct corporate welfare from the Commerce Department. Between 1992 and 1994, AT&T contributed $90,000 to the Democrats and received $34.2 million in Commerce Department grants. Boeing gave $127,000 and received $50.9 million from Commerce. General Electric gave $153,000 and got $14.8 million; Shell Petroleum gave $65,000 and got $12 million; and Texaco gave $22,000, and got $8.1 million. Nice work if you can get it.

And the money didn't just determine policy debates; it decided races. According to the latest data, in 1996 congressional campaigns the biggest spender won House races 90 percent of the time and Senate races 80 percent of the time. The Center for Responsive Politics has also determined that in both House and Senate races with no incumbent, candidates who spent the most beat their opponents by a two-to-one ratio. Races in 1996 were not financially competitive—in nearly 40 percent of House races, the winner outspent the loser by a factor of ten-to-one or more. No candidate who was outspent more than five-to-one was victorious.

The trends are the same in the states. Maine politics, for example, has also been dominated by a few wealthy donors and interest groups. Comparable figures—an estimated one half of one percent of all voters giving $50 or more to a state candidate—describe the same unlevel playing field for citizens in Maine as there is in Washington. Mainers were persuaded to support reform by studies showing an explosion in the cost to run for governor (an increase of

1609 percent over 20 years), and targeted special-interest giving to influence policy decisions. When the trucking industry successfully watered down the "Tired Truckers" bill despite public opinion squarely behind strict enforcement, they did so in part with political contributions. When Blue Cross/Blue Shield sought a change in their tax status from not-for-profit to for-profit, a move which could have netted them millions, a study showing their contributions to the Banking and Insurance Committee (released at a 'Blues'-sponsored fund raiser for the committee chair) crystallized public opinion and editorial opposition to the plan, eventually leading to its demise. When the timber industry's favorite incumbent legislator was in trouble in a 1994 re-election fight, paper companies poured $5,000 into the campaign for a last-minute radio spot that proved critical for his six-vote victory. Public outrage about these events was successfully harnessed for a pro-reform effort, culminating in an Election Day victory for reformers.

SOLUTIONS?

So we have a problem: simply put, there is too much private money in our political system. Despite the best efforts of a few conservative scholars and columnists, this point is no longer a topic of serious debate. The large issue is now: What role should private money play, and how can we correct the current imbalance? The field is now crowded with competing answers to these questions. To explain the advantages of the Maine strategy over the leading alternatives, we will start by setting out some basic principles that should guide reform efforts, and then describe the deficiencies of the alternatives in light of these principles.

PRINCIPLES

Broad principles should inform the proposals for campaign finance reform. We suggest five:

Competition: Reform must enhance electoral competition. It must encourage qualified Americans of diverse backgrounds and points of view, regardless of their economic means, to seek public office.

Accountability: Reform must increase government accountability and restore public confidence in government. It must eliminate the conflicts of interest created by privately financing the campaigns of our public officials.

Fairness: Reform must guarantee fairer and more equal representation for all citizens. The views of all Americans must be taken into account in the public policy making process irrespective of the ability to make campaign contributions.

Responsibility: Reform must stop the perpetual money chase. Elected officials should be attending to the people's business—meeting with constituents, attending important meetings, researching current policy
options—not lounging with large donors.

Deliberation: Reform must begin the process of reinvigorating public
participation in our democracy. It must reinstate public elections and
legislative debate as forums for deliberation about how best to address
the most pressing issues of the day.

ALTERNATIVES

While it would be impossible to develop an exhaustive list of proposals to
address the money in politics problem, six models dominate public discussion: lowering contribution limits; raising the contribution limits and enhancing disclosure; making lots of modest changes around the edges (like the
McCain-Feingold legislation in the Senate); instituting partial public financing or matching funds; challenging the Supreme Court's 1976 *Buckley v.
Valeo* decision, which substantially limited the measures that government can
use to regulate campaign finance; and full public financing.

Lower contribution limits. A first strategy of reform is to cut into the
flow of money as it passes from contributors to candidates—to limit the size
of the checks written to candidates for elective office, while not regulating
the overall size of spending. Pursuing this strategy, voters in several states
have passed proposals to limit contributions to $100 (or some other level).
But these proposals have run into legal trouble. Although the Supreme
Court has permitted limits on contributions to candidate campaigns—both
because such contributions threaten corruption and because potential contributors remain free to spend their money to influence politics without
giving it to candidates—the Court confined its concerns to "large" contributions. And lower courts have recently struck down $100 limits in DC,
Missouri, and Oregon as too stringent and therefore incompatible with First
Amendment speech rights.

Because of these legal troubles, we do not have much experience with
more stringent contribution limits. Still, we can make some informed judgments about their effectiveness on the basis of evidence gathered in a few
election cycles. Thus, although it appears that the overall money given to
candidates went down, there was a corresponding increase in money spent outside the system through independent expenditures. Moreover, these measures
may have the perverse effect of encouraging candidates to spend even more
time courting contributors because a larger number of contributions are
needed to wage a serious campaign. Furthermore, it is easier for incumbents to
find the numbers of contributors needed to mount strong campaigns than it is
for challengers. If reduced contribution limits lead to increased independent

expenditures, more candidate time on fundraising, and a playing field tilted toward incumbents, then they do not fare well on grounds of fairness, responsibility, and competitiveness, even if they help on accountability.

Raising contribution limits/more disclosure. A second strategy of reform would put increased weight on full disclosure of support, while raising contribution limits or eliminating them entirely. Pursuing this strategy would, we believe, put the financing of our elections even more securely in the hands of wealthy economic interests and cause an even more dramatic skewing of public policy in favor of the big campaign contributors. Raising the limits would skew the current imbalance in contributions even more. Business interests already contribute seven times as much as labor and ten times as much as ideological groups. For example, in 1996, energy interests gave $21 million in congressional races, whereas environmental groups gave just $2 million. As the principles of accountability, fairness, and deliberation imply, the issue isn't simply how much money is being spent and how much time it takes to raise it, but where it comes from, who provides it and who doesn't, what obligations and conflicts of interest result, and how the political debate itself gets skewed.

At the same time, the remedy of full disclosure falls short. Mere documentation does not correct the problems just noted. We already know that economic interests influence, skew, and control the political process. As Representative Barney Frank (D-MA) has commented, "We are the only human beings in the world who are expected to take thousands of dollars from perfect strangers on important matters and not be affected by it." Assuming a reliable source of information, disclosure may inform the public of how skewed the process is, but it won't shield our elected officials, nor will it correct for the unfair influence that contributors have over the political process. Citizens are like battered women: they already know who is hurting them, and how much. They need a way out, not more information about the source and extent of the damage.

Modest changes around the edges. A third strategy aims to control the flow of money—rather than simply providing greater information about it—but differs from contribution limits in the target of the controls. The leading such proposal at the federal level is the McCain-Feingold bill, which includes voluntary spending limits for US Senate candidates, a ban on PAC contributions to federal candidates, and regulations of "soft money," and would require candidates to rely substantially on in-state contributions. Candidates who agree to the spending limits will receive free television time and reduced postage rates.

Though not without merit, these changes would only bring slight advantages on the reform principles. The voluntary spending limits in McCain-Feingold, for example, are only slightly lower than the current average. The House companion bill (Shays-Meehan) sets these voluntary spending limits at higher than the current average for House candidates. More fundamentally, though, we would achieve at best limited gains in fairness and accountability. That's because the current problems are not principally a result of PACs or out-of-state state contributions. PACs are now responsible for only 25 percent of funding for congressional campaigns. And because PACs are not the exclusive vehicle for wealthy donors, a PAC ban might further slant the playing field: it would disarm labor unions and other interest groups that raise their money from a large number of small contributions from their members. Business interests do not now rely on PACs for their political contributions. If PACs were banned tomorrow, business would simply channel all, rather than most, of its money through large individual contributions. A PAC ban, if constitutional, would take us back to the days when there were no PACs and most of the money came from wealthy business executives.

Furthermore, the great majority of funds for these races already comes from in-state: For Senators, 63 percent of their funds came from within their home states, and 78 percent of House candidates' funds were raised from within their home states. Big contributors will continue to have an insurmountable advantage when it comes to gaining access and influence with elected officials; they will just be closer to home.

Partial public financing. The fourth strategy adopts a different angle on reform: Instead of looking for the optimal restrictions on private money, it aims to increase the role of public money as a supplement to private resources, perhaps by using public funds to match small contributions. Although the Maine proposal embraces the principle of public financing, we think that schemes of partial public financing are worst-of-both-worlds hybrids: they couple the most troubling effect of private financing with the most problematic aspects of public financing.

Consider the best-known case of partial public financing: the system of financing our presidential elections. Candidates must first raise lots of special interest money; after they have become indebted to those private contributors, the candidates then receive their public money. So we are asked to pay twice. First, through public financing, we support presidential candidates who are already obligated to private economic interests. Then we finance the tax breaks, subsidies, and other forms of corporate welfare granted to corporate sponsors as payback. But even systems of matching funds that—unlike the presidential scheme—attempt to amplify small contributions by providing a high ratio of public money to private money don't change the fundamental calculus, because they don't outlaw very large private contributions from wealthy special interests that, matching funds or no matching funds, are enormously influential.

Challenging "money equals speech." A fifth line of approach is less a reform strategy in its own right than an effort to set the stage for substantial reform by challenging the Supreme Court's claim that money equals speech. In its 1976 decision in *Buckley v. Valeo*, the Court determined that political spending was protected by the First Amendment. Though the Court agreed, as we indicated earlier, that contribution limits are legal, it also held that governments cannot impose overall spending limits on campaigns, or regulate candidates' spending from their own pockets, or limit independent expenditures (money spent by a private group or individual without coordinating with a party or candidate). Because of *Buckley*, there can be no mandatory spending limits, and any system of public financing must be optional.

Thus some reformers argue that the first order of business is to challenge *Buckley*, perhaps through a constitutional amendment that would restrict First Amendment protections of campaign spending. But this cannot be the entire solution to the growing problem of private money in our political system. Even if we could limit spending, we would still have not dealt directly with the corrosive element—the private sources of money that produce a conflict of interest. Moreover, as advocates of the Equal Rights Amendment and the Balanced Budget Amendment would argue, a Constitutional amendment effort takes years and marshaling the forces to enact it in two-thirds of the states is daunting.

What role should private money play in our political system? As our brief sketch of the reform landscape indicates, an answer to this central question substantially guides an assessment of different campaign finance reform proposals. Is contributing money to campaigns an equally legitimate form of participation alongside voting and volunteering—even though not every American has the means to do it and most do not? Are large contributions just another form of participation (like going to lots of meetings) or something else altogether? If not all voters have an equal potential to make large campaign contributions (and we know they do not), how can we square the current system with our egalitarian ideal of "one person, one vote?"

Though Americans accept the legitimacy of the economic inequality that enables the rich to buy fancier cars and more homes, they do not generally accept the current role of private money in our system because they do not think that the rich are entitled to greater representation. But the current system establishes precisely that entitlement: it effectively allocates political power according to economic status, and treats participation in the political system just as it treats participation in the market. That is unfair, and the large problem with all the reform proposals we have considered thus far is that they do not do enough to correct it. To ensure a fair system, in which citizens have equal opportunities for political influence, we need to look elsewhere.

CLEAN MONEY

Our preferred alternative—what we call the Clean Money Option—is a system of voluntary full public financing that cuts the cord of dependency between candidates and their special interest contributors. While no solution closes off all channels of influence, the Clean Money Option blocks the path that creates most trouble for the reform principles: the donations of large sums of money by special interests to candidates who, should they win, may be able to influence policy in areas of interest to these donors. This is the proposal that Maine voters enacted and that legislatures and citizens in, for example, Vermont, Connecticut, North

Carolina, Illinois, Massachusetts, Missouri, Idaho, Washington, and Wisconsin, will consider in the coming months and years.

The law that Maine voters passed was based on model legislation drafted by the Working Group on Electoral Democracy in the late 1980s for federal elections. The model legislation called for full public financing of campaigns for candidates who agree to spending limits, no private money, and a shorter campaign season. Over several years, Maine activists rewrote this model to fit the political reality of running for office in Maine, and running a state-wide referendum campaign to pass the legislation.

The Maine Clean Elections Act was drafted to go as far as possible in the public financing direction while remaining within the confines of *Buckley*. The construction of the Act makes as many changes as possible on the private side and it creates a public financing option. The measure sets lower, but not restrictive, contribution limits for candidates who continue to exercise their right to privately finance their campaigns, and, at its center, the Act established the "Clean Elections Option" to publicly finance candidates who agree to spending limits and to neither seek nor spend any private money.

For the first time, office seekers will have the option of qualifying for and accepting only public money for their election campaigns. Here is how it works: Candidates who choose to enter into the Clean Elections Option must agree to limit spending to the amount provided in public money and to refuse all private contributions once the public money comes in. They must also agree to a shorter campaign season. These candidates don't get something for nothing. To qualify for public funds, they must collect a specified number of $5 qualifying contributions from voters in their district (or state-wide in the case of governor). A small amount of private money can be raised as start-up "seed money," but these contributions are limited to $100 and there is an overall cap. The key difference from matching funds schemes is that they can neither raise nor spend any private money once they receive public money. Moreover, this law covers primaries as well as general elections. "Clean Election" candidates would also receive supplementary public funds if they are outspent by privately-financed opponents, or independent expenditures, or a combination of the two. These funds would be capped at twice the original amount provided to the candidate.

Returning to our five principles, then, what are the advantages of the Clean Money Option? By providing an alternative to the special interest system for financing elections, the Clean Money Option will level the playing field for candidates, thus enhancing electoral competition. At the same time, public money will lower the economic barriers now faced by citizens who might consider running for office and, by reducing the role of private money, increase the importance of the political activities available to all citizens. In both ways, Clean Money should mean a more fair political system, with greater equality in opportunities for political influence. Unlike any other proposals, the Clean Money Option also strengthens accountability by eliminating political contributions as a way of impacting legislative deliberation and policy making. In addition, the Clean Money Option would establish greater responsibility by freeing our elected officials from the perpetual money chase, and allowing them to use their time to engage important issues of the day free of the undue influence of special interest money. Finally, while the implications for political deliberation are uncertain, the same can be said for any of the other proposals. And there is no reason to think that public financing will produce even greater distraction from important public issues than the current system provides.

POLITICS

When Maine reformers first raised the possibility of a public financing system, they were told they were dreaming—that voters would never go for public financing. And with politicians like President Clinton urging that we squeeze politics into bite-sized morsels—school uniforms as a centerpiece of educational reform—proposing a total overhaul of the way we pay for elections seemed quixotic. But Maine voters countered prevailing wisdom and passed the proposal by a convincing margin.

Why was this case different? For three reasons.

First, and most straightforwardly, partial measures and tinkering around the edges are ineffective and the American public knows it.

Second, people are so disgusted with the problem of money in politics that they are willing to entertain fundamental changes in the rules of the game. Polling results consistently show that campaign finances lie at the heart of citizen discontent with politics. Americans believe that Washington's failure to address their problems is the direct result of politicians accepting too much campaign money from special interests. They believe that money forces politicians to bow to the agendas of those who sign the checks.

Public opinion is way ahead of politicians on the public financing solution. Polling by the Mellman Group (for the Center for Responsive Politics) shows that Americans are more supportive of a public financing solution to the problems of money and politics than at any time since Watergate. Gallup polling done before the recent revelations about campaign finances in Washington equaled support for public financing in the mid-1970s. A national poll done for Citizen Action by Stanley Greenberg showed 61 percent support for "a new law where the federal government would provide a fixed amount of money for the campaigns for Congress and all private contributions would be prohibited."

Other recent studies and public opinion research corroborate these findings. The League of Women Voters and the Harwood Group conducted a series of longitudinal focus groups/discussions with citizens in six cities across the country. The participants concluded that a system that provides an option for keeping all special interest money out and replacing it with public money was needed as one step in restoring faith in the democratic process. Bannon Research conducted five different state-wide polls in 1994 indicating similar sentiments.

But as political junkies like to say, the only poll that matters is on Election Day. And—here we come to the third factor—elections are won by organizations, and the Maine campaign provides instructive lessons for other efforts elsewhere.

The campaign waged by Maine Voters for Clean Elections was a result of years of research, coalition-building, and grassroots organizing. With ongoing technical assistance from the Northeast Citizen Action Resource Center, a regional network of progressive organizations and elected leaders, the Maine reformers identified the problem, established a role for their analysis in the public dialogue, and became the arbiters of what was—and was not—serious reform. Building a reputation for fair and nonpartisan research, Maine reformers reached out to all ends of the political spectrum to build the coalition base necessary to move the issue forward. Coalition partners—including the state chapters of the League of Women Voters, American Association of Retired People, Common Cause, the Maine AFL-CIO, leading environmental and women's organizations, the Citizen Action–affiliate, and the Perot-led Reform Party—met for two and a half years to draft a solution that would withstand constitutional challenge, effectively address the problem, and be politically viable. The idea was to be principled and to win.

When the coalition could not move a principled reform through the Maine State Legislature—forty reform bills, some good, most bad, died in the State Legislature over ten years—the members, under the banner Maine Voters for Clean Elections, decided to bring the issue to the voters. With substantial grassroots organizing, the coalition collected 65,000 signatures in a single day, and placed a binding referendum question on the 1996 ballot. Demonstrating the breadth of its appeal, the campaign recruited business leaders and received the active endorsement of the former director of the state's Chamber of Commerce and a well-respected former CEO of Bath Iron Works, the largest private employer in the state.

An aggressive public education campaign—waged door-to-door, at forums, in the media, and on the airwaves—ensued with the aim of persuading Maine voters to adopt, in the language of the ballot question, "new campaign laws and give public funding for state candidates who agree to spending limits." By mid-summer, the campaign had the support of a plurality of voters, but not a majority. The large hurdle was the public financing strategy itself: though a substantial majority supported the results that public financing would produce—blunting the influence of special interests and leveling the playing field—many had trouble believing that the system could be cleaned up and were especially hesitant about public financing as a means for advancing those goals. By stressing that the solution would clean up politics, the campaign was able to introduce a concept that historically has been unpopular (public financing) and couple it with strongly desired results (spending limits, no private money, shorter campaign, etc.). The idea was to frame the argument in terms of problems and goals, not of means: "What will Question 3 do? It will lower campaign spending by providing a Clean Elections Option of public money for candidates who agree not to take any private special interest money." The public education efforts similarly struck a balance between problem and proposed solution: for example, in the last eight weeks of the campaign, 200 people were encouraged to submit letters to the editor each week, alternating between discussing the problem and explaining the solution.

In short, Maine Voters for Clean Elections organized a broad coalition, well beyond the "usual suspects"; spoke directly to citizens, in countless forums and meetings; and kept an emphasis on the goals of reform, not simply the means. There are no formulas for political success. But reformers elsewhere might treat these features of the Maine experience as an instructive benchmark.

CONCLUSION

Can the Maine proposal be generalized to the federal level? A Clean Money Option will certainly face rough sledding in Washington, but so will all other serious reforms. Moreover, tangible signs suggest that Maine's success story is not falling on deaf ears. A number of senators are poised to introduce a Clean Money Option bill, which would at once signify progress and provide the opportunity for those of us who care about this approach to enter the national debate.

But the most dramatic and immediate impact of Maine's success will be in other states. Nearly a dozen states have some kind of full public financing under legislative consideration or headed for the ballot. Editorial endorsements have come from all over, from national, regional, and local papers, including *USA Today*, the *Boston Globe, St. Louis Post-Dispatch, Hartford Courant, Rutland Herald* (Vermont), and *Portland Press Herald* (Maine). The *Boston Globe* wrote that the Maine plan ought to be considered a "blueprint" for national reform.

While the near-term focus for debate on campaign finance reform will be in Washington, the real debate about the appropriate role of private money in our public elections and public policy will take place in the states. Inside the Beltway, the dominant question is: What can be won today? We should be asking: What is worth winning? Keeping that question in focus is the goal of a new national education effort—spearheaded by a new national organization, Public Campaign. It is working to galvanize broad public support behind reforms that fully address the central and most egregious aspect of today's campaign finance system—the direct financing of our public officials by private interests. And, in due course, the old adage from Downeast may once again come alive, "As goes Maine, so goes the nation."

NO

Government Financing of Campaigns:
A Public Choice Perspective

John Samples

In early 2002 Congress passed and the President signed the most extensive new regulations of campaign finance in a generation. Advocates of this legislation believe these new restrictions on political spending address only the "most egregious of the current abuses of campaign finance law."[1] They hope to next impose government financing of political campaigns, taking as their models recent laws in Maine and Arizona. They expect to foment enough popular support to persuade Congress to force taxpayers to fund House and Senate campaigns. We all should hope their effort fails.

POLITICAL LANGUAGE

The reader will notice that the following pages stay clear of loaded terms like "public financing," "campaign finance reform" and "clean elections." Such terms beg important questions at the heart of the debates over campaign finance; they seek to settle disputed issues by definition rather than argument, by emotion rather than reason. "Public" financing, for example, suggests a proposal in the public interest. Maybe it does, maybe it does not; calling the proposal "public" financing should not settle the argument. Similarly, naming a proposal "reform" equates its adoption with improving American politics and campaigns. Merely using the term "clean elections" clinches an argument by precluding debate.

Each of these loaded terms exemplifies a political strategy, an example of "the art of political manipulation" defined as "structuring the world so you win."[2] The politician, Riker notes, "uses language to manipulate other people."[3] Each term subtly biases our public debates toward a preordained conclusion. After all, who wishes to argue against "the public interest" or "reform" or in favor of "dirty" campaigns. Such manipulation shapes most political struggles. However, the proponents of government financing of campaigns say they wish to broaden public discussions and to add more voices to the political arena. Yet they manipulate language to make it impossible to disagree with them.

I use more accurate language to discuss these issues. Because the proposals in question use tax money to fund and to protect favored candidates, I call them government financing of campaigns. These proposals do not involve the funding of elections; state and local governments already do that by purchasing equipment, registering voters, and staffing polls. As we shall see, the proposals that generally go under the rubric "public financing" involve transferring tax revenues to political candidates to fund their campaigns. The proposals should be accurately called "government financing of political campaigns." I also will not write about "clean money" but rather of subsidies and regulations. Instead of "reform" I will refer to proposals, laws, programs and schemes; I make no assumption that new regulations and subsidies will improve our political life. Finally, "public" financing is a misnomer. Government financing of campaigns uses tax money to advance certain private interests.

PUBLIC CHOICE

Many Americans adopt a romantic view of politics and government. They believe that politicians and bureaucrats seek to achieve the public interest through law and policy. In contrast, public choice analysts assume that individuals seek to advance their self-interest through politics and policymaking.[4] For example, the public choice theory of regulation assumes that "rational, self-interested individuals, groups, or industries seek regulation as a means of serving their own private interests."[5] The reality of politics and government undermines the romantic view of many Americans.

Private Uses of Government

How does politics work according to public choice? Start with the market. An economic market comprises a set of exchanges among individuals who seek to satisfy their preferences through trade. The process of exchange over time leads both to allocative efficiency in using social resources and to a particular distribution of wealth. Some people do not like those outcomes, especially if they have less wealth than they wish. These dissatisfied people urge government to intervene in the free market to improve their outcomes relative to what they would receive from open competition. Government may, for example, subsidize or directly transfer money from taxpayers to members of favored interest groups or industries. Governments may also regulate markets to reduce competition and thereby improve the prospects of individuals or groups who would do relatively worse under competition (i.e., if the regulation did not exist). To put some meat on these conceptual bones, let's look at some examples.

Government sometimes pays companies to produce goods or services that would not attract enough paying customers to survive in a competitive market. Ethanol is a motor fuel produced from corn. Since 1979, Americans have paid a tax subsidy of 54 cents per gallon of Ethanol produced, a sum that by 2000 totaled over $11 billion.[6] Direct subsidies to farmers to grow and to not grow crops recently totaled $20 billion annually.[7]

Government also helps favored groups by limiting competition. For example, regulations protecting domestic firms from international competition transfers wealth from consumers to producers. Economists estimate that the steel tariffs of 2002 will cost American consumers $8 billion.[8] Similarly, airline regulations prior to 1978 limited competition and thereby transferred wealth from consumers to the managers and workers in the airline industry.[9]

These special interests say the costs they impose on others serve the public interest. Those who take the Ethanol subsidy argue it contributes to American energy independence. Those who receive farm subsidies say the money will preserve the small family farm and America's heritage. Trade protection often appeals to nationalism: American producers should be favored over foreign workers and owners whatever the cost. In economic life, these claims of a larger purpose for government favors rarely have merit, a point to keep in mind as we look at government financing of political campaigns.

Direct Subsidies

Talk of purity and corruption aside, government financing proposals are typical special interest politics: they offer subsidies and regulatory protection to favored candidates. Political candidates require money to market themselves and their electoral program. Individuals and groups give money to candidates because they wish to advance their interests (the investment theory of contributions) or to express their political values (the consumption theory of contributions).[10] Candidates who seem likely to win (or compete well) or who espouse widely shared values attract sufficient funding to make their case to the public. The only candidates who seek or need government financing are those who lack appeal to donors. Such failure may be a personal setback. However, no one should care that a particular candidate or cause fails to attract enough support to run a campaign for office. No one loses sleep because investors do not capitalize buggy whip factories or projects to colonize Venus. Like a declining industry whose products have lost out in market competition, failed candidates seek government subsidies for their campaigns for office.

Who pays these subsidies? Advocates of government financing prefer that candidates be directly subsidized by the taxpayer. Richard Briffault, for example, defines government financing as a campaign finance system "in which candidates or political parties receive cash grants for campaign purposes from the public treasury."[11] Public Campaign, an advocacy group that drafted the leading government financing model legislation, notes "the cost of establishing and maintaining a Clean Money/Clean Elections system will be borne principally by the public, via government funds." They also warn that whatever revenue might be mustered for government financing "the money still has to come from the treasury, which means it's a public expense."[12]

In practice, government financing schemes rely heavily though not exclusively on taxes. The federal system relies on a checkoff whereby a taxpayer directs a small part of his or her tax obligation to the presidential fund. Most states with partial government financing use either a checkoff system or a tax "add on" whereby a citizen can increase his or her tax bill and direct the money to the government financing scheme.[13] The three states that have adopted full government financing rely on varied funding sources. Arizona both imposes an annual $100 tax on lobbyists representing for-profit or commercial entities and a surcharge of ten percent on all civil and criminal fines collected in the state.[14] Massachusetts relies on a checkoff and general tax revenues to fund its system; the law limits the whole appropriation to .1 percent of the state budget.[15] Maine funds its program through several sources; for the 2000 election, almost all the funding came from income taxes and a checkoff system.[16]

Clearly Public Campaign is correct. However artfully disguised, almost all funding for government financing schemes, especially for the full government financing model (the so-called "clean elections" model), comes from general tax revenues.

Even when states do not rely on general taxes, government financing subsidizes favored candidates. The tax checkoff and add on methods locate small contributors for a candidate. Normally, such search costs would greatly outweigh the one or two dollar contribution generated from the donor. By socializing such search costs, checkoff systems create contributions that would not exist otherwise. Such contributions should be considered in total as a subsidy to the candidates who receive them. Fines or fees devoted to a government financing scheme constitute a tax hike: if the fines or fees did not go to the candidates, they could be used to pay for other government costs, and citizens could receive a tax cut equal to the fines and fees. In other words, government financing means taxes are higher than they need be. The "fines and fee" option merely obscures the role of taxes in a government financing program.

Protection from Competition

Under the Constitution, government may not prohibit private contributions or spending in elections. Government financed candidates face the danger that privately financed opponents may outspend them in the campaign. To meet this "threat" government financing schemes protect favored candidates through regulations and additional subsidies.

Federal law prohibits candidates who accept government financing for a presidential bid from raising private funds thereby mandating exact equality of funding between the two major party candidates. Unless both candidates typically raised equal sums, government financing implied that at least one of the candidates (generally, the Democratic) would be protected from being outspent by the other.[17]

Full government financing of campaigns controls private money in two ways: contribution limits and matching funds. Such laws often lower limits on contributions to candidates outside the government subsidy system. Arizona's law reduced by 20 percent existing contribution limits on candidates refusing to take public money.[18] Lowering limits does not prohibit non-government candidates from raising money. It does, however, increase the cost of fundraising. Let's see how that would decrease electoral competition.

A candidate running for an office supported by private donors must raise enough money to be competitive. He must raise that minimal sum within contribution limits. Raising campaign funds incurs large fixed costs associated with identifying individuals willing to give up to the maximum allowed by law. Table 1 shows the effects of lowering contribution limits on a hypothetical candidate with fixed costs of $200 per contributor who needs to raise $1 million to be competitive. As limits are lowered, the need to find more contributors to give the maximum (compared to a system with higher contribution limits) drives total costs up and net revenue down.

By reducing net revenue across the range, lowered contribution limits make it harder to run for office outside the government financing system. All things being equal, higher costs for anything lowers the demand for it; hence, lowered contribution limits should reduce the number of privately financed candidates running against government financed candidates. The rising sums in the "total costs" column also serve as an entry barrier to competition from privately financed candidates. It is much easier to run for an office if you must raise $40,000 rather than $400,000.

Public Campaign's model legislation also provides that "If participating candidates are outspent by non-participating opponents or targeted by independent expenditures, they may receive additional, matching funds with which to respond."[19] In Arizona, privately financed candidates are not subject to the spending limits of the law. However, if their spending exceeds the government-financed candidate, the latter receives funds to match the campaign spending of the non-participating candidate up to three times the original limit.[20] The matching funds provision includes spending by independent groups that are not part of a privately-financed candidate's campaign and yet are deemed to be supporting his candidacy.[21] Taken together these regulations and subsidies mean that a government-financed candidate will avoid being outspent by a privately-financed opponent and by independent groups.

TABLE 1   Effects of Contribution Limits

Limit	Fixed Cost	No. of Contributors	Total Costs	Net Revenue
$5,000	$300	200	$60,000	$940,000
$2,000	$300	500	$150,000	$850,000
$1,000	$300	1,000	$300,000	$700,000
$500	$300	2,000	$600,000	$400,000
$300	$300	3,333	$1,000,000	$0

Recipients of the Subsidies

Who receives government financing subsidies? The laws in question set conditions to qualify to receive government funding. A typical condition would be that a candidate must raise 1,000 $5 contributions from a district to qualify for government support. This can add up to contributions from as few as one-quarter of one percent of the voting age population.[22] This hardly indicates broad, grassroots support for a candidate. It does, however, provide a pretext to extract significant funding from other citizens of a state or district.

Beyond the abstractions of the law, experience indicates which candidates have been favored by government financing. The political scientists Michael Malbin and Thomas Gais found sharp partisan differences in participation. They studied gubernatorial elections in eleven states from 1993 to 1996 and found that 82 percent of Democratic candidates took taxpayer funding while 55 percent of Republican candidates participated.[23] Their data on legislative elections in Minnesota and Wisconsin show a similar partisan divide.[24] Malbin and Gais attribute these partisan variations to the libertarianism of Republicans: candidates who philosophically oppose government subsidies often do not accept them. In other words, government financing in practice provides an advantage to non-libertarian candidates.

Full government financing of campaigns in Arizona and Maine tells a similar story. In the 2000 election in Arizona, 41 percent of Democratic candidates and 50 percent of Green party candidates received public subsidies for their campaigns; 8 percent of Republicans accepted government money in the general election while no candidates of the Libertarian party took the subsidy.[25] In Maine's 2000 election 43.4 percent of Democratic Party candidates chose government financing compared to 24 percent of Republicans.[26]

The Moral Dimension

What could possibly justify forcing people to support views they oppose? Advocates of government financing say their subsidies and protections serve the public interest, despite the coercion. Let's see if they do.

THREE ARGUMENTS FOR GOVERNMENT FINANCING

Proponents claim government financing of campaigns serves three general interests: the integrity of elections and lawmaking, political equality, and electoral competitiveness.

Corruption

The Supreme Court held in *Buckley v. Valeo* that the government has a compelling interest in preventing corruption or the appearance of corruption in campaigns and policymaking, an interest that may outweigh the First

Amendment rights implicated in contributing to a political campaign. Allegations of corruption thus increase the probability that a law regulating campaign finance will pass constitutional muster.

Advocates of government financing claim the current system of largely private financing of campaigns fosters corruption (or its appearance) in several ways. They say campaign contributions buy favors from elected officials, the quid-pro-quo corruption noted in *Buckley*. Others say contributors receive favorable action on policies that attract little public attention and debate. Advocates also say private money fosters more subtle forms of favoritism; for example, members of Congress may allocate their time and effort in committees to help contributors.[27] If private money corrupts, the advocates conclude, the private financing system should be abolished in favor of government financing.

Academic studies of Congress have found little evidence to support these allegations of corruption.[28] Having surveyed the field, a supporter of government financing concludes: "One obstacle is that various studies have failed to produce the sort of evidence of a strong correlation between campaign donations and a representative's public actions needed to back up suspicions of general quid pro quo understandings."[29] Should we not have strong evidence to uproot our current system of campaign finance, especially when money is tied to the exercise of free speech?

If corruption involves using public power for private ends, government financing itself provides an example of corruption; after all the program takes money from everyone and gives it to particular interests. One might counter with Richard Briffault's argument that government financing cannot be corrupt because tax revenue "comes from everyone, and thus, from no one in particular."[30] But that leaves out an important part of the story. Tax money used to finance campaigns may come from everyone, but it goes, and is designed to go, to particular interests and groups within the American polity. Government subsidies to Ethanol are no less corrupt because everyone pays for them. Neither is government financing of campaigns.

Equality

Some Americans contribute to political campaigns; most apparently do not.[31] For advocates of government financing, these differences create intolerable inequalities that are "in sharp tension with the one person–one vote principle enshrined in our civic culture and our constitutional law. Public funding is necessary to bring our campaign finance system more in line with our central value of political equality."[32] Similarly, Public Campaign argues private financing "violates the rights of all citizens to equal and meaningful participation in the democratic process."[33] The principle of one person–one vote means "one man's vote in a congressional election is to be worth as much as another's" because assigning different weights to different votes in various House districts would violate Art. I, sec. 2 of the Constitution.[34] The principle applies to state elections because of the equal protection clause of the 14th Amendment.[35] Is one person–one vote thus "our central value of political equality?" A look at American institutions suggests otherwise.

The representation of states in the U.S. Senate assigns different weights to different votes in different states. Because the Electoral College also recognizes state representation, the election of the President also accords greater weight to votes in small states compared to those in large states. Moreover, the Supreme Court has not subjected judicial elections to the principle of one person–one vote.[36]

One person–one vote applies only to voting. No American has a right to "equal and meaningful participation in the democratic process" if that means the whole of political life. In particular, the rights of association and speech set out in the First Amendment have been explicitly protected from government efforts to compel "equal participation." In *Buckley*, the Supreme Court noted that federal election law sought to equalize the influence of individuals and groups over the outcome of elections. The justices demurred:

> But the concept that government may restrict the speech of some elements of our society in order to enhance the relative voice of others is wholly foreign to the First Amendment, which was designed "to secure 'the widest possible dissemination of information from diverse and antagonistic sources,'" and "'to assure unfettered interchange of ideas for the bringing about of political and social changes desired by the people.'"[37]

Far from being "our central political value," equal participation remains "wholly foreign to the First Amendment."

Moreover, even if the government financed all campaigns, we would not have equal participation in elections. Proponents of government financing focus on one source of political inequality: money. They ignore all other sources of inequality such as a talent for speaking, the ability to write, good looks, media ownership and access, organizational ability and so on. The proponents do not propose to restrain the many non-monetary sources of influence perhaps because such talents are often found among the proponents of government financing of campaigns. The leveling impulse, they imply, should not restrict such political talents; only people with money should be excluded from political influence.[38] Sometimes in public policy what is not regulated tells you more about a piece of legislation than what is covered. So it is with government financing of campaigns.

Enforcing equal participation would have other disadvantages. Imagine for a moment that politics aims at maximizing the preferences of citizens. If each voter holds their preference with equal intensity, simple majority rule will maximize aggregate preferences.[39] Let's imagine, however, that a majority of voters are indifferent about imposing new restrictions on campaign finance; a minority, however, feel quite strongly that such restrictions violate the Constitution. In that case, simple majority rule may lead to less overall "satisfaction of preferences" because the intensity of preferences would be left out of voting.

Allowing freedom of speech and related spending helps take account of the intensity of preferences.[40] In Federalist no. 10, James Madison argued that majorities might override the intense preferences of religious minorities and wealthy individuals.[41] We might also see freedom of speech and related spending as a way to allow such minorities to register intense preferences about public policy and thereby gain some protection from majorities who would always rule if each vote counts the same everywhere, every time.

Advocates of government financing may object that the intense preferences of the poor have no place in this model since they lack enough money to give to candidates or causes. In fact, the poor do not lack money for political contributions; they simply choose not to spend it contributing to campaigns. The average two-person poor household (annual income under $10,000) in the United States spends a little more than $500 annually on lotteries.[42] In 2001, the United States had 9,540,000 households with an income of $10,000 or less annually.[43] Roughly stated these households spend in total about $5 billion annually on lotteries. Each poor household could, in other words, contribute to a candidate the maximum legal limit during every two-year election cycle. They choose instead to spend the $520 annually on gambling. The poor clearly get more satisfaction out of playing the lottery than out of contributing to campaigns. That is their choice. But they could spend the money on candidates and thus make known the intensity of their preferences.

Finally, we should be clear how extensive, intrusive and dangerous a government financing system would be. Keep in mind that the goal of equalizing financial resources in an election requires extensive control and oversight of all electoral spending. The election authority must immediately know about all spending by privately financed candidates and every dollar laid out by any group participating in an election. Public Campaign's model legislation states that government financed candidates must use a government-issued debit card that draws solely on funds in an account created by the government.[44] Those who believe government usually acts benevolently will not worry about such extensive oversight and control of political activity. Those who expect abuses when government takes total control over anything—and especially over campaigns—will worry.

Competition

Over the past fifty years the high re-election rates of incumbents in the House of Representatives have risen modestly as shown by the trend line in Figure 1. During that same era, the percentage of the vote a candidate receives simply for being an incumbent has risen from 2 percent to 6 or 7 percent.[45]

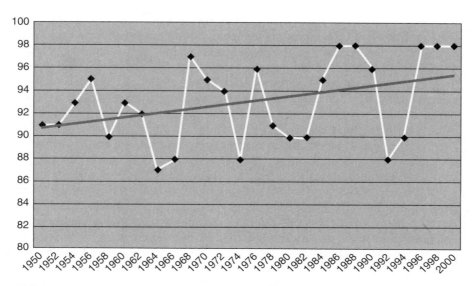

FIGURE 1   **House Re-election Rates 1950–2000**

Source: Data taken from Norman J. Ornstein, Thomas E. Mann, Michael J. Malbin, *Vital Statistics on Congress 1999–2000* (Washington, D.C.: The AEI Press, 2000), p. 57.

Advocates of government subsidies say the need to raise large sums to challenge an incumbent explains this dearth of competition. Government financing, they say, would overcome this barrier to entry by giving challengers tax money leading to a more competitive system.

We might note first how little variation exists in the re-election rates in Figure 1. The lowest re-election rate is 87 percent; all but four elections in those fifty years had re-election rates at 90 percent or higher. This suggests that other factors besides fundraising keep re-election rates up. In fact, the leading scholarly work on the topic fingers increased constituency service as the culprit for rising incumbency advantage.[46]

Government financing advocates say our system of largely private financing leads to a lack of competitiveness. Our system of campaign finance, though based on private contributions, is far from free. Since 1971, federal law has heavily regulated all campaigns and elections including House contests. The complaints about competition seem better directed at that regulated system. Advocates of government financing ask us to believe that ever more regulation and subsidies would bring more competition than the current system does or a deregulated system would. Would it?

Much depends on who designs the system of government financing. Spending levels strongly influence the competitiveness of challengers to incumbents; if a challenger can spend enough to make his name and causes known, a government financing scheme might foster more competition. If legislatures enact the system, of course, incumbents will design and pass the law. They will be tempted to set spending limits low to favor their own re-elections. For example, in 1997, Congress debated a government financing proposal that included spending caps: every challenger spending less than the proposed limits in Senate campaigns in 1994 and 1996 had lost; every incumbent spending less than the limits had won. Similarly, in the House, 3 percent of the challengers spending less than the proposed limits won in 1996 while 40 percent of the incumbents under the limits won.[47]

Such legislative design issues may explain why government financing of campaigns has not *in fact* increased the competitiveness of elections. The leading study of government financing in the states concluded: "There is no evidence to support the claim that programs combining public funding with spending limits have leveled the playing field, countered the effects of incumbency, and made elections more competitive."[48] Believing government financing will increase competitiveness seems to be a triumph of hope over experience.

Proponents of government financing may object that government financing laws passed by popular initiatives, not by incumbents, will enhance competition. Unfortunately these advocates also believe that Americans should spend less on elections which means the initiatives they write include low spending caps for government financed candidates.

Whatever the reason, the first two elections held under full government financing law did not lead to more competitive elections. My colleague Patrick Basham closely examined the outcomes of the 2000 election in Maine compared to the 1998 and earlier contests. He concludes:[49]

- The overall average margin of victory in both Senate and House races declined by an insignificant margin.
- Most Clean Money candidate victories came either against fellow Clean Money candidates or no opposition at all.
- Despite limits on campaign spending by incumbents, the advantages of holding office were almost impossible to overcome. Most victorious Clean Money candidates were incumbents and almost all incumbent Clean Money candidates retained their seats. The limits on House incumbent spending under public financing did not reduce their margins of victory.
- House seats that featured Clean Money candidates showed an insignificant decline in the average margin of victory compared with 1998.
- Government financing had little effect on competitiveness in the Senate. Those Senate seats that featured publicly funded candidates in 2000 experienced a very slight decline in the average margin of victory compared with 1998. Overall, in the 20 comparable seats, 10 were more competitive in 1998 than in 2000 while 10 were more competitive in 2000 than in 1998.
- The number of contested primaries rose only marginally from 1998 and remained well below the level of prior, privately funded elections.
- The lure of subsidized campaigning did not attract a significant number of independent and minor party candidates.

Arizona tells a similar story. Compared to the general election of 1996, 10 House races saw an increase in candidates while 8 saw a decrease. In the Senate, 8 races had more candidates while 7 had fewer. Yet, in Arizona as in Maine, term limits played a role in opening seats and fostering competition. Five of the 8 Senate races with more candidates than in 1996 involved seats opened up by term limits.[50]

Overall, the 2000 elections in Maine and Arizona produced mixed results at best. Of course, we cannot conclude from just one election cycle that government financing passed by an initiative will or will not lead to more competitive elections. We can say that the evidence so far does not support the proposition that government financing leads to more electoral competition.

PUBLIC SUPPORT

Proponents like to present government financing as a populist innovation which though resisted by the "powers that be" enjoys broad public support. The evidence suggests otherwise.

Public Opinion

Most polls shows significant support for changing campaign finance regulations though the public attaches little importance to such innovations.[51] At the same time, the polls suggest public disapproval of government financing of campaigns. In 1999, CBS News asked: "Public financing of political campaigns—that is, using tax money to pay for campaigns and prohibiting large donations from individuals and special interest groups—do you favor or oppose that?" 58 percent opposed government financing while 37 percent supported it. Similarly Rasmussen Research found in September, 1999 that 56 percent of Americans opposed public funding of Congressional campaigns. That same year a Wall Street Journal/NBC News poll indicated only 17 percent of respondents thought tax funding for Congressional candidates was the most important reform needed in campaign finance.[52] Some polls, especially one done at the behest of Public Campaign, show that the public supports government financing. It may well be that poll results in this area depend a great deal on wording.[53] Such mixed results hardly prove the public wants government financing. We turn now to other indicators of public preference.

Elections

The returns on ballot initiatives also paint a mixed picture. Maine passed its initiative in 1996 by a margin of 56 percent to 44 percent. Two years later, Massachusetts voters (by a 2-to-1 margin) approved an initiative modeled on the Maine legislation; meanwhile, Arizonans approved comparable campaign finance restructuring, in the form of Proposition 200, by a narrow 51 to

49 percent margin. In 2000, two government financing initiatives lost badly. In Missouri, the Clean Money Proposition B lost by 65 to 35 percent, while in Oregon the Clean Money Measure 6 was defeated by 59 to 41 percent. Since 1996, voters in five states have passed judgment on government financing initiatives. Three have been approved and two have been rejected. We should also keep in mind that turnout to vote on the Maine and Arizona initiative reached 57 percent and 46 percent respectively. That means the two initiatives passed with 32 percent and 21 percent of registered voters in Maine and Arizona respectively. We do not know if a majority of voters in either state supported full government financing of campaigns.[54] The recent electoral history of "clean money" initiatives hardly suggests Americans are clamoring for government financing of campaigns.

Contributions

Polling may not be the best measure of public views on this issue. If I ask you whether you would like to own a Rolls Royce, you might well say yes in the abstract. Faced with the actual concrete choice of whether to buy a Rolls Royce, you might elect to spend the money on other things. "Putting your money where your mouth is" better indicates a person's views than simply responding to a telephone call.[55]

Government financing schemes do allow citizens to "put their money where their mouth is" through tax add ons or checkoff systems. States with such programs have experienced steady declines over the years in both participation and revenues. The declines were such that Minnesota had to appropriate $1.5 million in 1993 to keep their program afloat.[56] Participation in the presidential checkoff system has also declined from about 28 percent in 1977 to 11.8 percent in 1999.[57] Americans who have the most experience with government financing of campaigns gradually withdraw their support. Their judgments should serve as a lesson for the rest of us.

CONCLUSION

Advocates of government financing of campaigns employ emotionally charged rhetoric at every turn. We are implored to "reform" the system to root out "corruption" and attain "clean elections." The reality of government financing belies this expansive rhetoric. Such proposals, especially the "clean elections" variant, simply transfer wealth from taxpayers to a preferred set of candidates and causes. That preferred set inevitably excludes candidates who believe forced transfers of wealth are immoral (viz. libertarians and Republican candidates with a libertarian outlook). Not surprisingly, government financing in the states has favored candidates of the left (viz. Democrats and third parties like the Greens). For that reason government financing of campaigns serves private goals through public means. Far from being a reform, government financing offers more "politics as usual" understood as the struggle to special favors from government.

Government financing of campaigns looks a lot like other political activity by individuals and groups that do not do well in private markets. Declining sectors of the economy—say, small farmers and large steel mill owners—want government help to overcome their own mistakes or unfavorable economic changes. Similarly, candidates who have little appeal to voters and campaign contributors seek public subsidies (like farmers) and regulatory protections from competition (like steel mill owners).

Government subsidies for candidates, however, are crucially different from funding for Ethanol. Government financing of campaigns takes money from taxpayers and gives it to a subset of all political candidates. For that reason, government financing seems either unnecessary or immoral. It is unnecessary if a taxpayer agrees with the candidate supported by the subsidy; the taxpayer may simply give the money directly to the candidate.

An example will make clear the immorality of the policy. Imagine I had the power to force Nick Nyhart, the Executive Director of Public Campaign, to contribute to the Cato Institute, thereby supporting the writing and marketing of the very arguments against government financing you are reading right now. Such compulsion would strike most Americans as wrong. We think individuals should not be forced to support ideas that contravene their deepest commitments, whether those commitments are religious, social, or political.[58]

Those who wish to support the candidates and causes favored by government financing may do so now; they need only send their check to the candidate or cause they favor. Government financing forces all taxpayers to financially support candidates they would not otherwise support, candidates whose views they may find repugnant. On the question of government financing of campaigns, Thomas Jefferson should have the last word: "To compel a man to furnish contributions of money for the propagation of opinions which he disbelieves, is sinful and tyrannical."[59]

Endnotes

1. See "211 and Counting," *Washington Post,* December 20, 2001, p. A42.
2. William H. Riker, *The Art of Political Manipulation* (New Haven, Conn.: Yale University Press, 1986), p. ix.
3. Ibid., p. x.
4. James M. Buchanan, "Politics without Romance: A Sketch of Positive Public Choice Theory and Its Normative Implications," in *The Collected Works of James M. Buchanan,* vol. 1 (Indianapolis: Liberty Fund, 1999), p. 46.
5. See Burton Abrams and Russell F. Settle, "The Economic Theory of Regulation and the Public Financing of Presidential Elections," *Journal of Political Economy* 86(April 1978):247.

6. See the General Accounting Office's report "Petroleum and Ethanol Fuels: Tax Incentives and Related GAO Work," RCED-00–301R, September 25, 2000, pp. 15–17.

7. See Chris Edwards and Tad DeHaven, "Farm Subsidies at Record Levels as Congress Considers New Farm Bill," Cato Briefing Paper no. 70, October 18, 2001 available at http://www.cato.org/pubs/briefs/bp70.pdf.

8. Steven Perlstein, "Bush Sets Tariffs on Steel Imports," *Washington Post,* March 2, 2002, p. E2.

9. Sam Peltzman, "The Economic Theory of Regulation after a Decade of Deregulation," Brookings Papers: Microeconomics, 1989.

10. Charles Stewart III, *Analyzing Congress* (New York: Norton, 2001), pp. 218–9.

11. Richard Briffault, "Public Funding and Democratic Elections," *University of Pennsylvania Law Review* 148(December 1999):566.

12. See Annotated Model Legislation for Clean Money/Clean Elections Reform at http://www.publicampaign.org/model_bill/index.html. Hereafter cited as PC Model. This website does not have pagination. However, the reader may easily confirm the quote by using the search function of his or her browser. I am using the version of the legislation posted in March 2002.

13. Michael J. Malbin and Thomas L. Gais, *The Day after Reform: Sobering Campaign Finance Lessons from the American States* (Albany, N.Y.: Rockefeller University Press, 1998), p. 54.

14. See John Fry, "The Citizens 'Clean' Elections Act: A Cure as Bad as the Disease," *Arizona State Law Journal* 31(Winter 1999):1377.

15. Kevin Deeley, "Recent Legislation: Campaign Finance Reform," *Harvard Journal on Legislation* 36(Summer 1999):556.

16. See the original Maine initiative at http://www.state.me.us/sos/cec/elec/intcon.htm#q3. The initiative provides $2 million in general taxes to fund the system.

17. When the presidential system was established, the Republicans enjoyed an advantage in fundraising. Equalizing expenditure may have cost Gerald Ford the presidency in 1976. See Bartlett and Steele, passim.

18. Robert J. Franciosi, "Is Cleanliness Political Godliness?: Arizona's Clean Elections Law after Its First Year," Arizona Issue Analysis 168, Goldwater Institute, November 2001, p. 5. Available at www.goldwaterinstitute.org.

19. PC Model.

20. See Fry, pp. 1377–8.

21. See PC Model.

22. PC Model states: "Based on discussions with expert signature gatherers and fund-raisers, and on the experience of the one locale in the U.S. that has been using a similar qualifying requirement (Tucson, AZ), the Working Group on Electoral Democracy set the requirement for a candidate running in a district with a population of approximately 500,000 (e.g., one congressional district) at 1,000 Qualifying Contributions. The Wellstone-Kerry bill sets the required number of Qualifying Contributions for U.S. Senate candidates at one-quarter of 1 percent of the voting age population of the state, or 1,000 such contributions, whichever is higher."

23. Malbin and Gais, p. 62.

24. Ibid., p. 71, Table 4–9. In recent years, Minnesota legislative elections indicate fewer differences in partisan participation rates.

25. Franciosi, p. 8.

26. See Patrick Basham, "Does Government Fund Lead to Competitive Elections?" Cato Policy Analysis, forthcoming, 2002. In the Maine House elections only five independent or minor party candidates received government assistance. This number seems too small to support any conclusions.

27. For a good review of the different allegations of corruption see Andrew C. Geddis, "Campaign Finance Reform after McCain-Feingold: The More Speech–More Competition Solution," *Journal of Law and Politics* 16(Summer 2000):585–90.

28. Bradley A. Smith, *Unfree Speech: The Folly of Campaign Finance Reform* (Princeton: Princeton University Press, 2001), pp. 127–8.

29. Geddis, p. 585.

30. Briffault, p. 579.

31. About 20 percent of individuals surveyed by the National Opinion Research Center in the mid-1980s reported having contributed "money to a political party or candidate or to any other political cause" in the past three or four years. See Codebook variable GAVPOL, question 352 at http://www.icpsr.umich.edu/GSS/index.html.

32. Briffault, pp. 577–8.

33. See PC Model; see also Molly Peterson, "Reexamining Compelling Interests and Radical State Campaign Finance Reforms: So Goes the Nation?" *Hastings Constitutional Law Quarterly* 25 (Spring 1998):445: "Equality of opportunity to influence the political process, sometimes characterized as 'leveling,' should be recognized as a constitutionally compelling governmental interest."

34. Justice Black in *Wesberry v. Sanders* 376 U.S.1 at 7–8.

35. *Reynolds v. Sims* 377 U.S. 577.

36. John E. Nowak and Ronald D. Rotunda, *Constitutional Law,* 6th ed. (St. Paul, Minn.: West Group, 2000), p. 969.

37. *Buckley v. Valeo* 424 U.S. 1, 49.

38. Bradley A. Smith, "Some Problems with Taxpayer-Funded Political Campaigns," *University of Pennsylvania Law Review* 148(December 1999):614.

39. James M. Buchanan and Gordon Tullock, "The Calculus of Consent: Logical Foundations of Constitutional Democracy," in *The Collected Works of James M. Buchanan,* vol. 3 (Indianapolis: Liberty Fund, 1992), p. 127.

40. This does not mean freedom of speech and related spending are identical to voting. It does mean they supplement voting in the political system.

41. James Madison, "Federalist no. 10," in *The Federalist,* Jacob E. Cooke, ed., (Middletown, Conn.: Wesleyan University Press, 1961), pp. 58–61.

42. Charles T. Clotfelter, Philip J. Cook, Julie A. Edell, and Marian Moore, "State Lotteries at the Turn of the Century: Report to the National Gambling Impact Study Commission," June 1, 1999, Table 11, at http://www.pubpol.duke.edu/people/faculty/clotfelter/lottrep.pdf.

43. See the Census Bureau table HINC-01. Selected Characteristics of Households, by Total Money Income in 2000 at http://ferret.bls.census.gov/macro/032001/hhinc/new01_001.htm.

44. PC Model.

45. Steven Ansolabehere, Charles Stewart III, and James M. Snyder, Jr. "Old Voters, New Voters, and the Personal Vote," *American Journal of Political Science* 44(Jan. 2000):17.

46. Morris P. Fiorina, *Congress: Keystone of the Washington Establishment,* 2nd ed. (New Haven, Conn.: Yale University Press, 1989), pp. 53–58.

47. Smith, *Unfree Elections,* p. 101

48. Malbin and Gais, p. 137.

49. Basham.

50. Franciosi, p. 9.

51. William G. Mayer, "Public Attitudes on Campaign Finance," in *A User's Guide to Campaign Finance Reform* Gerald C. Lubenow, ed., (Lanham, Md.: Rowman and Littlefield, 2001).

52. See the poll results at http://nationaljournal.com/members/polltrack/1999/issues/99campaignfinance.htm.

53. Richard Morin, "Who Supports Public Campaign Financing?" *Washington Post,* June 5, 2000.

54. For Maine, http://www.state.me.us/sos/cec/elec/ref96n1.htm. I am indebted to Robert Franciosi of the Goldwater Institute for the numbers on Arizona.

55. See Robert Weissberg, "Why Policymakers Should Ignore Public Opinion Polls," Cato Policy Analysis no. 402, May 29, 2001 available at http://www.cato.org/pubs/pas/pa-402es.html.

56. See Malbin and Gais, pp. 68–70, especially Tables 4–1,4–2,4–4.

57. See the chart at http://www.publicagenda.org/issues/factfilesdetail.cfm?issuetype= campaignfinance&list=20.

58. Of course, majorities do often compel minorities to financially support policies they find unwise. I have to pay taxes to build a road that I think endangers the environment. But compelling political speech through government financing is more like establishing a state church than like building a highway. Forcing me to contribute to an unwise highway project does not implicate my conscience and deepest convictions.

59. Thomas Jefferson, "A Bill for Establishing Religious Freedom," in *The Portable Thomas Jefferson* Merrill D. Peterson, ed., (New York: Viking Press, 1975), p. 252.

DISCUSSION QUESTIONS

1. Are elections in the United States significantly influenced by financial contributions? If yes, is it private money that makes them so? Can you think of any exceptions, such as where wealthy individuals and/or well-financed campaigns were defeated by poorly financed rivals?

2. Do you think the same applies to the formation of public policy?

3. Suppose you donated money to an interest group like the Sierra Club, which then decided that the best way to advance its (and your) policy goals was to run issue ads designed to defeat two congressional candidates in small midwestern states. In what ways is such a scenario an example of democracy in action? Is there anything problematic about it?

4. Does the First Amendment right to free speech apply to the ability of individuals to give money to whomever they choose? Are clean elections unconstitutional on this or any other basis?

5. Is $186 million too much to spend on campaigning for one of the most powerful jobs in the world?

6. Should corporations be allowed to donate directly to political candidates? Labor unions? Other organized interests?
7. Are there any other elements of election practice that you would like to see reformed—for example, length of campaigning time, voter turnout, voting procedure?
8. Who are the principal opponents to public financing of elections? Why?
9. What is the purpose of legislation that mandates the disclosure of campaign donations? Is such legislation likely to be effective?

WEB REFERENCES

Campaign Finance Information Center, http://www.campaignfinance.org/.

The Campaign Finance Institute, http://www.cfinst.org/.

Center for Responsive Politics, http://www.opensecrets.org.

Common Cause, http://www.commoncause.org.

Federal Election Commission, http://www.fec.gov.

Hoover Institution, Campaign Finance, http://www.cfinst.org/.

McCain-Feingold Campaign Reform Bill site, http://www.senate.gov/~mccain/cfrpage.htm.

The National Institute on Money in State Politics, http://www.followthemoney.org.

PBS, Campaign Finance Reform Debate, http://www.pbs.org/newshour/@thecapitol/cfr/.

Pew Charitable Trusts, Campaign Finance Reform Information, http://www.campaignfinanceinfo.org/.

Stanford Law School, Campaign Finance Resources, http://lawschool.stanford.edu/library/campaignfinance/.

FURTHER READING

Anderson, Annelise, ed. *Political Money: Deregulating American Politics, Selected Writings on Campaign Finance Reform*. Palo Alto, Calif.: Hoover Institution Press, 2000.

Ansolabehere, Stephen and James M. Snyder, Jr. "Soft Money, Hard Money, Strong Parties." *Columbia Law Review*, vol. 100, no. 3 (April 2000), pp. 598–619.

Corrado, Anthony. *Campaign Finance Reform: Beyond the Basics*. Washington, D.C.: Century Foundation Press, 2000.

Corrado, Anthony, et al., eds. *Campaign Finance Reform: A Sourcebook*. Washington, D.C.: The Brookings Institution, 2002.

Dwyre, Diana and Victoria A. Farrar-Myers. *Legislative Labyrinth: Congress and Campaign Finance Reform*. Washington, D.C.: Congressional Quarterly, 2000.

Gais, Thomas L. and Michael J. Malbin. *The Day after Reform: Sobering Campaign Finance Lessons from the American States.* Albany, N.Y.: Rockefeller Institute Press, 1998.

Green, Joshua. "Clean Money in Maine." *The American Prospect,* vol. 11, no. 21 (September 25, 2000), p. 36.

Karabell, Zachary. *The Last Campaign: How Harry Truman Won the 1948 Election.* New York: Vintage Books, 2001.

Lazarus, Theodore. "The Maine Clean Election Act: Cleansing Public Institutions of Private Money." *Columbia Journal of Law and Social Problems,* vol. 34, no. 1 (Fall 2000), pp. 79–132.

Magelby, David B., et al., eds. *Financing the 2000 Elections.* Washington, D.C.: The Brookings Institution, 2002.

McGehee, Meredith and Kenneth Forsberg. "Reforming Campaign Finance." *World and I,* vol. 17, no. 6 (June 2002), p. 40.

Nichols, John. "Campaign Finance: The Sequel." *The Nation,* vol. 274, no. 16 (April 29, 2002), p. 16.

Rosenkranz, Joshua. *Buckley Stops Here: Loosening the Judicial Stranglehold on Campaign Finance.* New York: Twentieth Century Fund, 1998.

Schneider, Deborah. "As Goes Maine? The 1996 Maine Clean Election Act: Innovations and Implications for Future Campaign Finance Reforms at the State and Federal Level." *Washington University Journal of Law and Policy,* vol. 2 (Winter 2000), pp. 627–664.

Schultz, David. *Money, Politics, and Campaign Finance Reform Law in the States.* Durham, N.C.: Carolina Academic Press, 2002.

Slabach, Frederick G. *The Constitution and Campaign Finance Reform: An Anthology.* Durham, N.C.: Carolina Academic Press, 1998.

Smith, Bradley A. *Unfree Speech: The Folly of Campaign Finance Reform.* Princeton, N.J.: Princeton University Press, 2001.

Chapter 8

ABORTION POLICY

"Should Minors Be Required to Obtain Parental Consent Prior to Receiving an Abortion?"

YES: Anne Marie Morgan "Alone among Strangers: Abortion and Parental Consent" *Chronicles*

NO: National Organization of Women "The Tragedy of Parental Involvement Laws" *The National NOW Times*

Few issues in American politics have been as divisive or polarizing as the question of what role the government should play in regulating abortion. This question, and the issue of abortion itself, has created a sharp division within American political life that seems unlikely to disappear. Those who support significant governmental restrictions on abortion argue that the unborn fetus represents a life with the same rights as the mother, and that the government has both the right and the duty to protect this life; not to do so, it is argued, is tantamount to sanctioning murder. Those who oppose governmental restrictions on abortion argue that, like other reproductive issues, the decision to have an abortion is intensely personal because it involves a woman's body, and that women have a fundamental right to make such decisions without the interference of government. Because the disagreement involves conflicting notions of liberty and life, it has generated intense passion on each side. Antiabortion activists have attempted to prevent access to abortion clinics, usually with blockades or pickets; in some cases, abortion clinics have been bombed, and in several instances doctors who performed abortions have been killed by protesters. Abortion rights supporters have been active as well, securing legal protections for access to abortion clinics, escorting patients into clinics, and seeking increased police protection for clinic workers.

While the intensity of the debate over abortion policy has been reflected in the political arena, most of the substantive decisions over what role the government can and should play in regulating abortion have been made in the judicial rather than the legislative arena. Indeed, it has been in the courts that abortion policy has seen some of its most rancorous debates. Although the liberalization of abortion law began in state legislatures in 1967, and many states permitted abortions with varying restrictions on availability, the origins of the modern abortion debate are most often traced to the *Roe* v. *Wade* decision of 1973. In *Roe*, the Court ruled as unconstitutional, and a violation of the right to privacy of a woman's reproductive choice implied in the Ninth Amendment, nearly all laws forbidding abortion in the first trimester. As Justice Blackmun wrote in the majority opinion, "The states are not free, under the guise of protecting maternal health or potential life, to intimidate women into continuing pregnancies." *Roe* did, however, permit restrictions in the second trimester, while still allowing abortions to protect the mother's health; and it expanded restrictions in the third trimester to protect the interests of the fetus, which was presumed viable outside the mother's womb. The companion case to the *Roe* decision, *Doe* v. *Bolton*, further prohibited state laws that created obstacles to obtaining abortions, such as residency restrictions, which were ruled as violations of a woman's rights.[1]

Because it effectively prohibited state governments from restricting abortion, the *Roe* v. *Wade* decision had the effect of shifting the debate over abortion policy from the state to the national level. Since it was now clear that the federal courts would play a prominent role in abortion policy, the appointment of federal judges—especially Supreme Court justices—became a significant political issue for voters and politicians, occupying an important position in the platform of each major political party and playing a prominent role in presidential campaigns. For the most part, the two major political parties took opposing positions on the government's role in regulating abortions, with Republican candidates generally supporting restrictions and Democratic candidates opposing them. Because of the success of Republican presidential candidates throughout the 1970s and 1980s, nominations to the Supreme Court and the lower courts were increasingly made by conservative Republican administrations (President Carter did not appoint a Supreme Court justice), leading to an ever-expanding conservative tilt to Court decisions. At the same time, abortion became an important issue in Congress, where antiabortion legislators have attempted to pass a constitutional amendment banning abortion and pro-choice legislators have attempted to pass laws designed to prevent additional governmental restrictions on abortion as well as guaranteeing access to abortion. While such legislation has been unsuccessful, it shows that the issue of abortion remains an important political topic.

The issue of abortion has been prominent not only in the United States, but throughout the world. In Europe, the availability of abortion varies greatly from country to country. Both Northern Ireland and the Republic of Ireland impose a total prohibition on abortions, although an estimated 18 women leave the Republic every day for abortions abroad.[2] In the Netherlands, abortion on demand is available through the first 24 weeks of pregnancy.[3] Belgium in 1990 partly relaxed its prohibition against abortion, and Spain in 1985 began allowing abortion up to 12 weeks of gestation in cases of rape,

22 weeks for genetic reasons, and with no limitation when the mother's life or health is threatened.[4] One of the more interesting cases has been that of Germany. Reunification brought together two nations with very different abortion laws. West Germany had a restrictive abortion law that allowed for abortion in the first 3 months only if a doctor has found a valid medical reason,[5] while East Germany allowed abortion on demand through the first trimester.[6] A compromise had to be reached between the two nations as part of the unification contract. It was agreed that each nation would retain its own abortion laws until the end of 1992 when a new abortion law was put into effect.[7]

While abortion policy has been debated in the United States for more than a quarter century, the practice of legal abortion has continued unabated since the early 1970s. The number of legal abortions in the United States increased drastically from 615,831 in 1973 to roughly 1.3 million in 1980; however, the increase throughout the 1980s was minimal, and the number of yearly abortions reached a high of 1.43 million in 1990. During the 1990s the number of legal abortions decreased (at least through 1997—the most recent year for which data are available), to an estimated 1.19 million in 1997. The abortion rate for women between the ages of 15 and 44 has been slowly decreasing, from a high of 25 per 1,000 women in 1980 to a rate of 20 abortions per 1,000 women in 1997. The vast majority of abortions—86 percent in 1997—take place in the first 12 weeks of pregnancy, with only a small percentage—1.4 percent in 1997—taking place after the twenty-first week of pregnancy.[8] While the number and the rate of abortions have remained steady over the past few decades, the age distribution of women having abortions has changed significantly; in 1980, 29.2 percent of abortions were performed on women 19 and younger, 35.5 percent on women between the ages of 20 and 24, and 35.3 percent on women age 25 and older; however, in 1997, only 20.1 percent of abortions were performed on those 19 and younger, 31.7 percent on women between 20 and 24, and 48.2 percent on women 25 and older.[9] The percentage of these abortions in women under 19 remained stable during the 1990s, but the same time period saw an increase in the percentage of abortions undertaken by women over the age of 25. While the vast majority of abortions are performed on mature adults, 161,416 abortions were performed on women 18 and younger in 1997; and the abortion rate among young women increases steadily as they reach 24, with a rate of 2 per 1,000 for women younger than 15, 7 per 1,000 for 15-year-olds, 13 per 1,000 for 16-year-olds, and 19 per 1,000 for 17-year-olds.[10] The most commonly cited reasons given by teenagers for seeking abortions include the belief that having a baby would change their lives, that they are not mature enough to have a child, and that they are experiencing financial problems.[11]

The fundamental legal right to an abortion in the United States has not been threatened in the 30 years since *Roe*, but restrictions on the availability of abortion have been successfully enacted at both the state and national level. The Hyde amendment banning federal funding for abortion (through

Medicaid), except in circumstances of rape or incest or where the life of the mother is threatened, was successfully attached to the fiscal year 1977 Labor—Health, Education and Welfare appropriation bill and was upheld by the Supreme Court as constitutional in *Harris* v. *McCrae* in 1980.[12] State restrictions on the availability of abortion, such as requiring the testing of fetal viability, banning public facilities and employees from being involved in abortions, and instituting mandatory abortion counseling and waiting periods, have been upheld in the recent decisions of *Webster* v. *Reproductive Health Services* and *Planned Parenthood* v. *Casey*.[13] The Bush administration has taken a firm position on abortion issues, with one of President G. W. Bush's first acts of office being to ban federal funding of international family planning groups that offer abortion or abortion planning.[14] The administration argues that embryos should be given the status of an "unborn child," but with the debate still clearly demarcated, it is unlikely that legislation to ban abortions in the United States will be possible. Another ongoing and contentious issue involves limits to protests at abortion clinics. Federal law has prevented protesters from blocking access to clinics where abortions are performed, from destroying property, or from intimidating women, doctors, and clinic staff. Legal battles continue over what levels of protest are permissible.

The current composition of the Supreme Court makes it unlikely that a judicial decision will substantially alter the fundamental legal right to an abortion outlined in *Roe*, and it seems unlikely that a substantial shift in policy will emerge from the political arena, especially if public opinion is any indication. Polling data for the years since the "legalizing" decision of *Roe* v. *Wade* in 1973 have shown consistently that a majority of Americans support the availability of abortion concurrent with some governmental regulation designed to discourage the number of abortions. A Gallup poll conducted in May 2001 showed that in a national sample, 58 percent favored legal abortion under certain circumstances, 26 percent thought that abortion should be legal in all cases, and 15 percent thought that abortion should never be legal. The opinions of males and females differed only slightly; 23 percent of men and 28 percent of women believed that abortion should be legal under any circumstance, while 16 percent of men and 15 percent of women believed that abortion should never be legal. There are many factors that lead to divergences in abortion beliefs, with the pollsters observing that "older Americans, Republicans, self-described conservatives, those with no college education, and low-income Americans tend more toward the pro-life positions than do their counterparts."[15] Despite a general unwillingness to eliminate the constitutional right to abortion outlined in *Roe*, there is evidence that a majority of citizens support various restrictions on abortion which would be allowed under current court rulings. For example, a 1998 CBS/New York Times poll indicated that more than 79 percent of people support a 24-hour waiting period; a 2000 *Los Angeles Times* poll found 82 percent favoring parental consent for women under 18; and a majority of Americans also support restriction of "partial birth" abortions and spousal notification laws.[16]

Thus, it is likely that the basic right to an abortion will be protected into the foreseeable future and the focus of debates over abortion policy will remain on the type of restrictions or regulations that may be applied to abortion. One of the most popular and widespread of such restrictions at the state level is parental notification, which requires that minors seeking abortions notify, or in some cases have the consent of, one or both of their parents before an abortion is performed. In 2002, 32 states had such laws in effect, and another 10 states had passed such laws but had not put them into effect because of legal challenges.[17] The Supreme Court has found that such laws do not violate the Constitution as long as they contain a provision, known as "judicial bypass," which allows a judge to determine either that the minor is mature enough to make an abortion decision or that the abortion would be in her best interests. Unlike the familiar arguments for and against abortion, the issue here is not simply whether or not abortion is appropriate, but whether or not young women should be able to make abortion decisions independently.

The following articles represent opposing views on the question of whether minors should be required to obtain parental consent prior to receiving an abortion. Anne Marie Morgan argues that parental involvement laws are necessary not only because minors are often incapable of making abortion decisions independently, but also because the absence of parental involvement in the decision to have an abortion may place minors at a significant health risk. The National Organization for Women disagrees, arguing that, in addition to infringing upon the rights of young women, parental consent laws force many young women to seek unsafe, illegal abortions because they are unwilling to obtain parental consent.

Endnotes

1. B. Packwood, "The Rise and Fall of the Right to Life Movement in Congress: Response to the Roe Decision," in J. D. Butler and D. F. Walbert, eds., *Abortion, Medicine, and the Law* (New York: Facts on File Publications, 1986), pp. 3–21.
2. BBC News, March 4, 2002, http://news.bbc.co.uk/hi/english/world/europe/newsid_1849000/1849395.stm.
3. R. H. Nicholson, "Abortion Remains a Live Issue," *Hastings Center Report* (September–October 1991), p. 5.
4. Ibid.
5. Annette Tuffs, "Germany: Abortion Ways and Means," cited in *Lancet* (November 23, 1991), p. 1323.
6. Nicholson, op. cit.
7. Ibid.
8. Lisa Koonin, Lilo Strauss, Camaryn E. Chrisman, and Wilda Y. Parker, "Abortion Surveillance—United States, 1997," Center for Disease Control, http://www.cdc.gov/mmwr/preview/mmwrhtml/ss4911a1.htm.
9. Ibid.
10. Ibid.

11. Alan Guttmacher Institute, *Sex and America's Teenagers* (New York: Alan Guttmacher Institute, 1994).
12. A. M. Pearson and P. M. Kurtz, "The Abortion Controversy: A Study in Law and Politics," in Butler and Walbert, eds., op. cit., pp. 107–135.
13. J. Rovner, "Abortion Ruling Slows Momentum of Freedom of Choice Act," *Congressional Quarterly Weekly Report* (July 4, 1992), pp. 1951–54.
14. See, for example, CNN, http://www.cnn.com/2002/US/01/31/unborn.child. coverage.
15. Data in this section from Lydia Saad, "Public Opinion about Abortion—An In-Depth Review," Gallup, http://www.gallup.com/poll/specialReports/pollSummaries/ sr020122 viii.asp.
16. Ibid.
17. Planned Parenthood, http://www.plannedparenthood.org/library/ABORTION/ StateLaws.html.

YES

Alone among Strangers:
Abortion and Parental Consent

Anne Marie Morgan

At the moment the U.S. Supreme Court upheld the right of states to enact parental consultation abortion statutes, the abortion-advocacy organizations went into high gear. The *Hodgson v. Minnesota* and *Ohio v. Akron Center for Reproductive Health* decisions "endangered teens," they claimed, and NOW President Molly Yard charged that the Court had "thrown down the gauntlet before the young women and girls of America." However, a rational—rather than emotive—analysis of the relevant issues reveals that the Court's decisions were very sensible ones. Notwithstanding the pained protests, the rulings should have a critical impact on whether young, frightened, pregnant minors will be the recipients of their parents' counsel or the abortionist's zeal, and whether the lucrative abortion-on-demand industry will continue virtually unrestrained.

Of the 1.5 million abortions performed in the U.S. annually, nearly one-third are on minors, many without parental consent or even *knowledge*. While state laws require parental *permission* for other surgery on minors, abortion has been the sancrosanct exception. Yet there is broad-based public support for parental involvement laws; for example, a 1989 *USA Today* poll reported that 75 percent believe parents should be notified before a female under 18 has an abortion. A nationwide *Los Angeles Times* survey of women *who have themselves undergone abortions* indicated that fully two-thirds agreed that "Minors should have to get their parents' permission before they can get an abortion."

Nonetheless, this is not the practice in most states. While 37 states have passed parental involvement statutes, until this Supreme Court decision most were temporarily or permanently enjoined. Other legislatures seeking passage became battlegrounds for bitter debates.

Why is there such intense opposition to laws that the public views as simply common sense? Privately, abortion advocates desperately fear that parental consultation laws mark the proverbial foot-in-the-door to overturning abortion-on-demand. Publicly, they offer an array of unsubstantiated objections.

Opponents' arguments can be examined in light of three compelling state interests for requiring parental consultation, as delineated in the High Court's 1976 *Bellotti v. Baird* decision: "The peculiar vulnerability of children; their inability to make critical decisions in an informed, mature manner; and the importance of the parental role in child rearing." In the past decade, substantial documentation has emerged to sustain the Court's position.

Critics contend that parents are extraneous, since minors will have abortions "in consultation with their doctors." This is an exaggeration. Many young girls never see a doctor until they undergo surgery. Most abortions are performed at free-standing abortion clinics, *not* in hospitals, and nearly all states have repealed clinic regulations or licensure. Pre- and post-abortion counseling and emergency equipment are not required, and any doctor (not solely obstetricians) may perform abortions. Justice Stevens's concurring statement in *Danforth* in 1976 is correct: "The majority of abortions now are performed by strangers in unfamiliar surroundings, where minors are alone, furtive and frightened visitors subjected to assembly line abortion techniques." Dr. Edward Allred, who owns an abortion clinic chain that performs 60,000 abortions annually, described clinic practices for the *San Diego Union* in an October 12, 1988, article:

> Very commonly we hear patients say they feel like they're on an assembly line. We tell them they're right. It is an assembly line . . . . We're trying to be as cost-effective as possible and speed is important . . . . [W]e try to use the physician for his technical skill and reduce the one-on-one relationship with the patient. We usually see the patient for the first time on the operating table and then not again.

The absence of clinic regulations to protect women's health and safety encourages slipshod operations, including "abortions" on women who were not pregnant. The lack of emergency equipment has resulted in tragedy. While Debra L. was undergoing her abortion, she swallowed her tongue and attendants were unable to restore her breathing to normal. The clinic's director called Debra's mother to convey that her daughter had had "minor surgery" and was having "respiratory problems." Hospitalized, Debra lay in a coma for two and a half months, then died. Her mother, an amicus in *Hodgson*, grieves that her daughter could have had an abortion without her knowledge.

Opponents of parental notification say abortions are so problem-free that parents are not necessary, but evidence suggests otherwise. Scores of medical journals report that women under 18 who obtain abortions are more susceptible to physical injury, and have some of the most catastrophic complications.

The *South Medical Journal* cited adolescent case studies of abortion-related complications, including uterine rupture or perforation, cervical lacerations, hemorrhaging, pelvic pain, endometritis, incomplete operations, infertility, and repeated miscarriage. A typical pattern emerges with a minor's complications: she will delay health care out of fear of parental discovery of the abortion, and then go to a hospital emergency room. "The teenager, frightened and mentally and physically traumatized by her abortion, will often not seek help until she is almost moribund. Her parents may be the last to know." Ironically, she must have parental consent for treatment.

Dr. James Anderson, a Virginia emergency room physician, shocked even committed abortion advocates at the Virginia General Assembly when he testified of his hospital experiences. Dr. Anderson frequently treats minors who have had abortions (without parental knowledge) for severe post-abortion complications. He also observes the perilous adolescent pattern of delaying treatment. One patient died last year after becoming so infected after an incomplete abortion that antibiotics could not save her. Furthermore, a doctor faces a life-threatening dilemma in diagnosing a problem when a patient denies having an abortion due to fear of parental discovery—because proper treatment relies on accurate diagnoses. The physician must guess at the truth. Dr. Anderson testified he is often forced to break the news to parents.

Hodgson amicus Rachel E. manifested this "vulnerability." After undergoing a clinic abortion at 17 on the advice of her high-school counselor, she developed flu-like symptoms. Without post-abortion instructions, she assumed that these were unrelated. Although she finally went to her family doctor, she did not inform him of her abortion. Bacterial endocarditis, a result of a post-abortion infection, caused a blood clot, stroke, and coma. Rachel regained consciousness, but remains a permanently wheelchair-bound hemiplegic.

Clearly, parental involvement alerts parents to potentially dangerous physical and emotional problems of which they otherwise would be unaware. Emotional vulnerabilities can be equally critical. More minors than older women suffer severe anxiety, acute depression, long-term guilt, consternation, and attempted suicide following abortion. The latter is particularly compelling. In *Pediatrics* (1981), Dr. Carl Tishler alerts physicians to adolescent suicidal tendencies from "anniversary reactions"—on the perceived birth date had the baby come to term. One wonders how many adolescent suicides were young, grief-stricken girls whose parents were unaware that abortion triggered their despondency.

Demographic evidence refutes the charge that parental involvement will cause teens to postpone care and undergo more dangerous late-term abortions. Missouri, whose parental-judicial consent statute was upheld by the High Court, provides excellent data to evaluate the law's effect. For young women under the age of 18, the number of abortions done in 1984 (the last full year before the statute took effect) was 2,564, with 361 done after 13 weeks. In 1987, those numbers were 1,859 and 286 respectively. In other words, the number of second-trimester abortions among Missouri minors dropped by 20 percent after the statute's enactment. The number of Missouri's total minor abortions also declined—by 27 percent.

The claim that births to teens will increase with parental involvement is patently false. Minnesota's parental notice law was in effect for four years before being enjoined. Its data exhibits an unexpected benefit: a drastic reduction in minor pregnancies, abortions, and births. The 1986 Report of the U.S. House of Representatives Select Committee on Children, Youth, and Families entitled *Teen Pregnancy: What Is Being Done? A State by State Look* related that from 1980 to 1983, following enactment of a 1981 parental notification law, births declined 23.4 percent, abortions decreased 40 percent, and pregnancies fell 32 percent among fifteen- to seventeen-year-olds.

The Minneapolis Star and Tribune (April 20, 1984) reported:

> The surprise finding raises new questions about the effect of a parental notification law that went into effect between those two years. It also raises the possibility of some changes in adolescent sexual patterns . . . ."It would appear that women under age 18 are reducing their risk of pregnancy," [Paul] Gunderson [the Health Department's chief of statistics] said.

Danforth noted the historical and necessary legal limitations of minors:

> Because he may not foresee the consequence of his decisions, a minor may not make an enforceable bargain. He may not lawfully work or travel where he pleases . . . . Persons below a certain age may not marry without parental consent and they may not vote . . . . But even if it is the most important kind of decision a young person may ever make, that assumption merely enhances the quality of the State's interest in maximizing the probability that the decision be made correctly and with full understanding of the consequences of either alternative.

Opponents say the decision to abort should be left to minors. But a 1989 *Los Angeles Times* poll of women who have undergone abortions indicates that one out of every four women (26 percent) "mostly regrets" her abortion. Such women subsequently experience profound grief.

Adolescents in particular manifest confusion about an abortion decision, changing their minds frequently. Abortion involves a severe double loss for some adolescents: fully 17 percent of minors who have abortions compensate for a first abortion by becoming pregnant again within one year.

Opponents of parental involvement laws wrongly argue that minors already notify parents. One study confirmed that 71 percent informed a best friend, while only 37 percent informed mothers and 26 percent informed fathers. In *Hodgson v. Minnesota* (1988), the Eighth Circuit noted the testimony of a clinic co-director: "Prior to the [parental notification] statute, approximately 25 percent of the pregnant women she counseled told one or both parents of their pregnancy and intended abortion."

In *Pierce v. Society of the Sisters*, the Court upheld the rights, authority, and responsibilities of parents over their minor children: "[T]he child is not the mere creature of the state; those who nurture him and direct his destiny have the right, coupled with the high duty, to recognize and prepare him for additional obligations." Other precedents concur, such as *Prince v. Massachusetts* in 1944: [P]arents . . . who have the primary responsibility for children's well-being are entitled to the support of law designed to aid discharge of that responsibility."

Opponents of parental consultation dismiss the significant issue of family integrity. Yet the parent-child relationship is a permanent bond, unlike that between an abortionist and his client, or between two teenage best friends. Research by Dr. Everett Worthington of Virginia Commonwealth University reveals that the anxiety and burden of secrecy in a teenager cause alienation, isolation, guilt, fear, depression, and an increase in family estrangement. In dissenting from invalidation of Minnesota's two-parent notice provision, Justice Anthony Kennedy agreed: "[T]o deny parents this knowledge is to risk, or perpetuate, estrangement or alienation from the child when she is in greatest need of parental guidance and support."

Critics also claim that parents will "beat, abuse, and even kill" their pregnant daughters, but there is no verifying evidence from states with such laws. Instead, there is substantial evidence that most parents support their daughter during an adolescent pregnancy. Worthington also found that after an initial period of disequilibrium, there emerges a more stable period of problem solving in which both mother and daughter take steps to resolve the pregnancy's difficulties.

In addition, a parental consultation statute usually contains a bypass permitting a doctor to proceed with abortion surgery *without* parental notice if the child is in an abusive home (including incest). Indeed, the abuse reporting requirement is an added safeguard for the minor to trigger remedial state intervention she otherwise may not have received in chronically abusive situations. As Justice Stevens wrote in 1981 in a concurring opinion for *H.L. v. Matheson*:

> A state legislature may rationally conclude that most parents will be primarily interested in the welfare of their children . . . . [A]n assumption that parental reaction will be hostile, disparaging or violent, no doubt persuades many children simply to bypass parental counsel which would in fact be loving, supportive and indeed, for some, indispensable.

Abortion tragedies rarely are reported honestly. Media attention instead focuses on the myth of abortion as the hallowed panacea for women. If the state legislatures explore the substantial evidence that has emerged, they will discover that the High Court's original concerns in *Bellotti* were right on target—and pass sensible laws restoring parental protection to pregnant minors in their time of critical need.

NO

The Tragedy of Parental Involvement Laws

National Organization of Women

Do parents want to know what is going on in their children's lives, especially if it involves serious problems? Sure they do.

In fact, this simple, and frankly simplistic, response is precisely the reason why parental consent and/or notification laws have taken hold in so many state legislative bodies across the country in the years since the *Roe v. Wade* Supreme Court decision legalizing abortion nationwide became the law of the land.

In the 17 years since the *Roe* decision was handed down some 35 states have enacted laws requiring some form of parental involvement of their minor daughters, albeit with mixed results.

While some of these laws are not enforced because of various legal challenges, enough are enforced to affect the lives of thousands of teenage girls and to put many of their lives at risk.

That, in a nutshell, is what's wrong with these laws. Girls dying from illegal or self-induced abortions—because they couldn't, or wouldn't, tell their parent(s) they were pregnant.

THE MYTH OF FAMILY PROTECTION

The most common argument heard in support of parental involvement in cases of minors' abortion is that parents have a "right" to know if a medical procedure is being performed on their children, since the parents are legally responsible for their children until they reach the age of majority at 18. Furthermore, the argument goes, parental consent is required by law for most medical procedures, such as appendectomies. So why should abortion be treated differently?

For the same reason that no one would argue that American society treats appendectomies and abortions the same way. The society, in fact, has treated matters of adolescent reproductive health differently for many years. For instance, the vast majority of states have laws that authorize minors to consent to treatment for venereal disease and even prenatal care without parental consent or notification. These laws were enacted in recognition of the fact that consent and notification laws hamper the willingness of minors to seek medical care for conditions affecting this area of their bodies and their lives.

Ironically, in many states these statutes rest side-by-side on the books with laws requiring parental consent and/or notification in matters of minors' abortions.

Even more ironic is that in a majority of states, once a minor has borne a child, she can consent to most, if not all, medical procedures for herself and her child. In other words, she must have her parents' consent or must notify them before obtaining an abortion. But once she's a mother herself, she gets control of her life in medical matters, and control of her child's life.

But legal rights and responsibilities aside, there are other compelling reasons why these laws are punitive and counterproductive and, instead of enhancing or protecting family relationships, in fact threaten just the opposite.

To begin with, there are the plain facts. Of the roughly 1.6 million legal abortions performed annually in this country, 12 percent or 192,000 are performed on minor girls. The majority of these girls, at least 55 percent, obtain abortions with their parents' knowledge—more often than not their parent(s) accompany them to the clinic or hospital. In the one percent of cases involving girls 15 or younger, the figure goes up to 75 percent of those who obtain abortions with their parents' knowledge.

All of which means that most teenager girls in America have the kind of family relationships that enable them to turn for help to those who care the most about them—their parents. And they don't need a law to compel them to do so.

At the same time, there are a full 25 percent of minor girls who have reported in repeated studies that they have not, and would not, tell their parents about a pregnancy, regardless of any law. The most common reasons they give are as recognizable as the headlines seen daily in any newspaper in America: the likelihood of an abusive response from the parents, ranging from verbal or physical abuse to throwing them out of the house; anti-abortion or "sex is dirty" views of the parents; illness or substance abuse of the parents; or, in the case of 30 percent of girls 15 to 17 years old, they live with only one parent and rarely see the other one, if at all.

In other words, many if not most of the teenagers who fall into this 25 percent come from dysfunctional family situations that no law passed anywhere by anybody can change, but which punitive laws can make worse by exposing young girls to abuse in order to punish them for being "bad." Not all of them, however, come from damaged family situations. There are some whose love and respect for their parents is so great, that they can't bear the thought of disappointing or hurting them. Such is the story of Becky Bell.

Becky Bell was a teenager in Indiana who died in 1988 at the age of 17. Because of that state's parental consent law, when she became pregnant Becky obviously could not receive a legal abortion in Indiana without first telling her parents and getting their permission. Unwilling to hurt the parents she loved with the news of her unintended pregnancy, according to her friends, she sought and obtained an illegal abortion. To this day Bill and Karen Bell don't know who performed the botched abortion on Becky, but they do know they lost her from a massive infection that set in as a result of the illegal abortion.

While their grief and their terrible sense of loss still hover over much of their daily lives, the Bells have dedicated themselves to speaking out against parental consent/notification laws because they "don't want to see happen to another girl what happened to Becky." As Karen Bell puts it, "you don't think it can happen to your family—until it does." Would Bill Bell trade his "parental right to consent" under Indiana law in order to have Becky back? Bill Bell will tell you he would trade anything to have Becky back.

THE HYPOCRISY OF JUDICIAL BYPASS

It should be noted that parental consent/notification laws dealing with minors' abortions have never been initiated from the medical, professional, social services, or advocacy groups who spend their time, talents, and energy trying to help women, teenagers, and their families.

These laws invariably have come from anti-abortion groups or legislators intent on making abortion illegal again in America. Period. These laws as well as others they have proposed or enacted, such as ending public funding for abortions for poor women, are seen as incremental gains in their agenda until they can stop legal abortions altogether.

The fact that much of the public has bought into the intended raw emotionalism of parental involvement in minors' abortion decisions is the result of a cynical, calculated campaign meant to distract the decidedly pro-abortion rights majority in this nation from the fundamental agenda of the anti-abortion camp which is an end to legalized abortion and, for many of them, most forms of birth control.

Unfortunately, the U.S. Supreme Court has upheld state parental consent/notification laws where these laws have provided an alternative to minors who are at risk if they involve their parents. The Court essentially has ruled that if an alternative is available for these teenagers to comply with consent/notification laws then their constitutional right to abortion guaranteed by the *Roe* decision is not violated.

The most common "alternative" found in these laws is called the judicial bypass. This provision allows a pregnant minor to petition the courts for an exemption to the law and, if a judge determines that the petitioner is mature enough to make an abortion decision independent of her parents or that an abortion is in her best interests, then the judge can give the consent.

The hypocrisy and ludicrous nature of this procedures is self-evident. If a teenager is not mature enough to make a decision to abort an unintended and unwanted pregnancy, how in the world could the same teenager be mature enough to bear and raise a child?

The anti-abortion camp's response to this, of course, is adoption. But in raising this so-called solution, they also conveniently ignore the fact that the public social services and foster care systems already are spilling over with children for whom adoptive homes can't be found.

Still, in fairness to the judges around the country who have been confronted with these cases, most have granted permission for most of the teenagers they have seen—even though some have behaved so bizarrely as to appoint an attorney to represent the fetus. The most common problem of this alternative is the thousands of teenagers the judges never do see.

The fact is, going to court for anything is an intimidating prospect for most people. Procedures for petitioning a court are beyond the knowledge of the average adult, much less a frightened, pregnant teenager. And finally getting to see a judge in light of the overload that jams most court dockets is an obstacle that can delay an abortion for weeks, not just days.

Given the fact that teenagers on average wait later into a pregnancy to seek an abortion than do older females, such delays can increase the medical risk of the abortion and, in too many cases, can result in the pregnancy being too advanced for a legal abortion unless there is a clear danger to the health or life of the teenager that mandates an affirmative decision.

The bottom line is that while the judicial bypass has been used successfully by a small number of pregnant minors, many more have fallen between the cracks of the system and have resorted to illegal options or have sacrificed their futures on the altar of compulsory motherhood.

THE PRICE OF TEENAGE MOTHERHOOD

Women who have abortions in America are predominantly young, single, and of modest financial means. More than half, some 58 percent, are under the age of 25 and, as noted above, 12 percent are under the age of 18.

It is also important to note that although teenagers tend to wait longer to get abortions than older adults, nonetheless more than half of the abortions performed in this nation occur in the first eight weeks of pregnancy and 91 percent within the first 12 weeks of pregnancy, the first trimester. Only one-half of one percent occur after 20 weeks (mostly at 21 or 22 weeks), and only .01 percent (or 100 to 200 out of 1.6 million) are performed after 26 weeks, which the medical and scientific communities cite as roughly the point of fetal viability. These latter abortions can be performed legally only if the life of the woman or girl is in danger from continuing the pregnancy.

But what happens to girls under 18 who give birth—coerced or voluntarily? For starters, girls under 18 who give birth are only half as likely to graduate high school as those 20 years old or older. One survey conducted in Minnesota, a state with a parental notification law that is one of two such laws currently being challenged before the Supreme Court, showed that a staggering 80 percent of mothers 17 years old or under never finish high school.

Studies of the effects of teenage pregnancy and childbirth also show that families headed by teenage mothers are seven times more likely than others to be poor and to need some form of public assistance.

By contrast, women who delay childbirth until their 20s are four to five times more likely to finish college. In general, it can be said that the younger the mother at childbirth, the lower her family income.

There is also the issue of the health of children of teenage mothers. These children are twice as likely to die in infancy as those born to women in their 20s and even have a greater infant mortality rate than children born to women in their 40s, a high-risk age group for pregnancy.

Much of this infant mortality is directly caused by low birth weight, a condition that also often leads to other problems, such as serious childhood illness and even birth injury and neurological defect, including mental retardation.

At the present time, Americans are awaiting Supreme Court decisions on two abortion rights cases—*Hodgson v. State of Minnesota* and *State of Ohio v. Akron Center for Reproductive Health*—both of which involve parental notification laws that include judicial bypass alternatives. The Minnesota law, however, also requires notarized proof that parents have been informed before an abortion occurs, and the Ohio law demands that a physician give notice to a parent or guardian in person before performing an abortion on a minor.

How the Court will rule on either or both of these cases is anybody's guess. But what is known is that more and more state legislatures are being pushed to enact parental consent/notification laws as a "compromise" on a highly volatile issue. And that they are responding to this pressure with little knowledge or concern for the consequences of their actions.

DISCUSSION QUESTIONS

1. Are teenagers mature enough to make abortion decisions independently? Should they be required to inform their parents of their decision? At what age should people be allowed to make such decisions without the help of a parent?
2. Why has the debate over abortion policy been decided primarily in courts rather than legislatures? Have courts been more successful than legislatures would have been at constructing an effective national policy on abortion?
3. Should decisions over abortion be treated differently by the government than decisions over other medical procedures? Why or why not?
4. Are the reproductive rights of women absolute? Do you think any restrictions should be placed on the availability of abortion?
5. Abortion in some countries is used to favor the birth of male children. Do you think the possibility exists that abortion could be used in the United States to select children with certain characteristics deemed advantageous by the parents? Is there any problem with this?
6. How have other nations dealt with the abortion issue? Has the issue been as divisive in other nations as in the United States? Why or why not?

7. What is the government's role in ensuring equity in the availability of abortion? Does it have a role at all? Why or why not?
8. What role should men play, if any, in deciding whether an abortion is appropriate?
9. Do you know anyone who has had an abortion? Describe her experience (as best you know it), and compare it with various stereotypical experiences of women who have had abortions. Are the experiences similar or different?
10. Do you think that subsidizing the cost of abortions would increase the number of abortions performed? Why or why not? How does this conclusion affect your argument for the debate question?

WEB REFERENCES

Abortion Laws, http://members.aol.com/abtrbng/index.htm.

National Abortion and Reproductive Rights Action League, http://www.massnaral.org/.

National Coalition of Abortion Providers, http://www.ncap.com/.

Planned Parenthood Federation of America, http://www.saveroe.com/.

Pro-Choice Public Education Project, http://www.protectchoice.org/.

Pro-Life Resource List, http://www.prolifeinfo.org/.

FURTHER READING

Bender, Daniel and Bruno Leone. *Abortion: Opposing Viewpoints.* St. Paul, Minn.: Greenhaven, 1997.

Bonavoglia, Angela, ed. *The Choices We Made: Twenty-Five Women Speak Out about Abortion.* New York: Random House, 1991.

Brodie, M. Janine, Shelley A. M. Gavigan, and Jane Jenson. *The Politics of Abortion.* Toronto: Oxford University Press, 1992.

Campbell, Dennis, ed. *Abortion Law and Public Policy.* Dordrecht, Netherlands: Martinus Nijhoff, 1984.

Craig, Barbara Hinkson and David M. O'Brien. *Abortion and American Politics.* Chatham, N.J.: Chatham House, 1993.

Dellinger, Walter. "Should We Compromise on Abortion?" *American Prospect* (Summer 1990).

Garrow, David J. *Liberty and Sexuality.* New York: Macmillan, 1994.

Glazer, Sarah. "Roe v. Wade at 25: Will the Landmark Abortion Ruling Stand?" *CQ Researcher,* vol. 7 (November 28, 1997).

Glendon, Mary Ann. *Rights Talk: The Impoverishment of Political Discourse.* New York: Free Press, 1991.

Grisez, Germain. *Abortion: The Myths, the Realities, and the Arguments.* New York: Corpus Books, 1970.

Halpern, Sue. "The Fight over Teenage Abortion." *New York Review of Books* (March 29, 1990).

Kaufmann, K. *The Abortion Resource Handbook*. New York: Simon & Schuster, 1997.

Korn, Peter. *Lovejoy: A Year in the Life of an Abortion Clinic*. New York: Atlantic Monthly Press, 1996.

Luker, Kristin. *Abortion and the Politics of Motherhood*. Berkeley: University of California Press, 1984.

McDonagh, Eileen L. *Breaking the Abortion Deadlock: From Choice to Consent*. New York: Oxford University Press, 1996.

McFarlane, Deborah R. and Kenneth J. Meier. *The Politics of Fertility Control: Family Planning and Abortion Policies in the American States*. Chatham, N.J.: Chatham House, 2000.

Mohr, James C. *Abortion in America: The Origins and Evolution of National Policy, 1800–1900*. New York: Oxford University Press, 1978.

Morowitz, Harold J. and James S. Trefil. *The Facts of Life: Science and the Abortion Controversy*. New York: Oxford University Press, 1992.

Noonan, John, ed. *The Morality of Abortion: Legal and Historical Perspectives*. Cambridge, Mass.: Harvard University Press, 1970.

Nossif, Rosemary. *Before Roe: Abortion Policy in the States*. Philadelphia: Temple University Press, 2002.

O'Connor, Karen. *No Neutral Ground? Abortion Politics in an Age of Absolutes*. Boulder, Colo.: Westview Press, 1996.

Rosenblatt, Roger. *Life Itself: Abortion in the American Mind*. New York: Random House, 1992.

Roth, Rachel. *Making Women Pay: The Hidden Costs of Fetal Rights*. Ithaca, N.Y.: Cornell University Press, 1999.

Tribe, Laurence H. *Abortion: The Clash of Absolutes*. New York: Norton, 1990.

Tushnet, Mark V. *Abortion*. New York: Facts on File, 1996.

Warnke, Georgia. *Legitimate Differences: Interpretation in the Abortion Controversy and Other Public Debates*. Berkeley: University of California Press, 1999.

Wills, Garry. *Under God: Religion and American Politics*. New York: Simon & Schuster, 1960.

Wishner, Jane B., ed. *Abortion and the States: Political Change and Future Regulation*. Chicago: American Bar Association, 1993.

Chapter 9

WELFARE POLICY

"Has Welfare Reform Been a Success?"

YES: Ron Haskins "Giving Is Not Enough: Work and Work Supports Are Reducing Poverty" *Brookings Review*

NO: Peter Edelman "Reforming Welfare—Take Two" *The Nation*

Since its inception, federal welfare policy has been a hot-button political issue receiving significant attention in nearly every presidential campaign since the early 1960s. But after decades of passionate and often vitriolic debate over the structure and goals of federal cash assistance programs, the effectiveness of the existing welfare program, the responsibility of the government to assist the poor, and the obligations the government can reasonably impose upon those receiving assistance, the late 1990s began a period of relative calm precipitated by the most noteworthy shift in federal welfare policy in nearly 30 years. On August 22, 1996, President Clinton signed welfare reform legislation that effectively fulfilled his 1992 campaign promise to "end welfare as we know it." The Personal Responsibility and Work Opportunity Reconciliation Act (PRWORA) replaced the 61-year-old federal guarantee of financial assistance to the poor with a system of grants to the states. States were given the flexibility to design their own poverty assistance programs as long as they imposed work requirements and a 5-year lifetime limit on welfare benefits, among other requirements. Of course, the legislation was not universally popular, and it met with considerable criticism. Given different background conditions, it might have generated even more controversy; however, the legislation took effect during a period in which economic conditions—in particular, low unemployment rates—may have ameliorated its potential flaws, and to most it appeared that the new program was likely better—and certainly no worse—than its predecessor. While members of the public and politicians may since have turned much of their attention elsewhere, the new legislation is unlikely to end the debate over welfare policy. Rather, it is likely to focus attention on components of the new program and the question of whether or not the new welfare reform law is an improvement over previous government attempts to assist the poor.

While much political and public attention has been paid to welfare programs that provide cash assistance to the poor, such programs represent only one component of a social welfare system in this country that includes not only need-based income assistance, but also medical assistance for the poor and elderly, housing and food for the poor, social insurance programs that provide retirement assistance, and unemployment benefits. The majority of such programs are neither targeted toward the poor nor administered as cash assistance programs; rather, the welfare system in the United States is oriented mostly as social insurance against old-age poverty, loss of employment, and the inability to finance medical costs. Social insurance expenditures—the largest programs being Social Security, Medicare, workers' compensation, and unemployment insurance—constitute the bulk of federal social welfare expenditures, more than $600 billion annually, and do not use income as a criterion to measure eligibility, i.e., are not considered to be "means tested." In addition to such broadly targeted social insurance programs are those social welfare programs targeted to the alleviation of poverty, most of which do use income as a criterion of eligibility. These programs include Medicaid; Temporary Assistance to Needy Families (TANF, formerly Aid to Families with Dependent Children); Supplemental Security Income (SSI) for the blind, disabled, and aged; food stamps; and public housing and education assistance. Such programs received $241.5 billion in federal spending in 2001. About three-fourths of spending on such antipoverty programs is not directed toward providing cash assistance to the poor, but rather toward providing food, housing, medical care, education, job training, energy assistance, and other in-kind benefits, the largest portion being Medicaid, which accounted for $129.4 billion in 2001.[1]

Means-tested welfare spending has never occupied a significant part of the federal budget. In 2001, for example, federal funding for family support assistance (the bulk of which was directed toward TANF) was $21.9 billion, representing less than 1 percent of the entire federal budget. When state and federal contributions are combined, annual spending on AFDC (the precursor to TANF) was roughly $25 billion throughout the 1990s. While it is true that social welfare spending broadly defined has increased, this increase has not been driven by increased cash assistance to the poor but rather by significant growth in spending for more inclusive "entitlement" programs such as Social Security (which more than tripled in real terms between 1970 and 2000), Medicare (which increased eightfold during the same period), and Medicaid (which grew ninefold).[2]

Despite the scope of the American welfare state and the relatively small portion of expenditures specifically targeted to the poor, most public perceptions of welfare policy focus on programs providing cash assistance to the poor. These programs have a long and complicated history in this country. While state-run antipoverty programs have existed since the late nineteenth century, especially those providing financial assistance to mothers, children, and soldiers, large-scale federal involvement did not emerge until 1935 when

Aid to Dependent Children (ADC) was created as part of the Social Security Act. Designed to assist states in providing aid to poor women and their children, ADC provided matching funds to expand existing aid programs and coincided with the passage of many of the programs making up the American welfare state, such as Social Security. While the program remained quite small in financial terms, it initiated a federal commitment to provide open-ended cash payments to the poor. Renamed Aid to Families with Dependent Children (AFDC) in 1962, the program was given additional funding so that welfare payments could be increased, and states were allowed to require recipients to participate in community work and attend training programs in order to receive benefits. The expansion of eligibility criteria, benefit levels, and outreach efforts beginning in the 1960s with the Johnson administration resulted in an increase in the number of people receiving AFDC benefits as well as increased expenditures. While only 3 million people, or 2 percent of the population, received benefits in 1960, by 1971 10.2 million people were receiving welfare, an amount equal to 5 percent of the population. Partly as a result of these increased caseloads, real (inflation-adjusted) AFDC expenditures doubled between 1962 and 1972.[3]

This increase in caseloads and expenditures motivated concern over the growth of AFDC, but there were also concerns over the effectiveness of the program. In particular, some lawmakers and citizens argued that cash assistance provided by AFDC did little to motivate or prepare recipients for work. As a result of such concerns, Congress passed the Work Incentive (WIN) Program in 1967 to require states to offer worker training programs and work incentives to AFDC recipients. While it was amended in 1971 and expanded in 1981 to give states greater flexibility to encourage work, the WIN Program did little to provide training or encourage work among large numbers of recipients, at least partly because it was given low funding levels and served only a small percentage of those receiving benefits.[4] Nevertheless, the attempt to reform welfare continued in the 1980s, and in 1988 the Family Support Act (FSA) was passed. FSA combined a strengthened emphasis on work requirements with the provision of job training and child care, but the states were given considerable flexibility in applying such requirements, and many exempted large numbers of welfare recipients; in fact, nationwide only 43 percent of welfare recipients participated.[5] Adding to the challenges faced by such reform efforts, the late 1980s and early 1990s brought a severe economic recession, decreasing the availability of jobs and increasing the number of AFDC recipients.

While AFDC remained a federal responsibility during this period, funded in large part by federal money and governed by federal requirements, in the late 1980s and early 1990s the federal government began to grant individual states freedom to experiment with welfare programs, waiving federal rules and requirements in some states and effectively providing those states with block grants to run their own welfare programs. The reforms adopted by these states varied widely: Some increased spending on support services such as training and child care and allowed welfare recipients to use welfare benefits to supplement income, while others imposed time limits on welfare benefits and financial penalties for women who had additional children while on welfare. In nearly every case, states focused on encouraging work, some by providing training and job search assistance, others by simply threatening to end welfare benefits for those who did not find work.

These policy changes emerged within the context of public debates over the effectiveness of existing welfare policy. Beginning in the late 1970s, George Wiley's statement to the Democratic platform committee in 1968 in Chicago—"the basic cure for poverty is money"—was no longer accepted as the truism it once appeared to be. The debate over welfare policy since that time has been dominated less by how much money should be provided to the poor, and more by if and how welfare policies cause "dependency," "cultures of poverty," and the "underclass," and how welfare reforms may attenuate or eliminate these alleged effects. Conservatives like the influential writer Charles Murray contended that far from reducing poverty and dependence, welfare programs like AFDC worsened the situation by, for example, providing financial incentives for single-parent families. Further, such critics contend, AFDC as administered in the 1980s did little to encourage welfare recipients to prepare for work, and provided them no incentive to seek work because it provided lifetime benefits without work requirements. Thus, it was argued, AFDC recipients became entirely dependent upon assistance and had little chance of becoming independent. This "cycle of dependency" was, from this view, the direct result of such cash assistance programs. Other conservatives complained of excessive waste in welfare programs, such as President Reagan's frequent references to "welfare queens" bilking the public coffers.

There is considerable disagreement over what the federal government's vast social welfare expenditures—most not targeted to the poor—have actually accomplished. Some argue that the welfare state has been much more successful in eliminating poverty than critics give it credit for, although paradoxically through programs that are not directed at the poor (such as Social Security, which has dramatically reduced old-age poverty). And there is little question that, regardless of the other effects it has had on the poor, the availability of cash, food, and housing assistance has at the very least improved the daily living conditions of many in poverty. While some gains have been made in reducing poverty in the United States, particularly among the elderly where poverty rates are substantially below those of the nation as a whole, stubborn problems remain, such as unemployment among African-American male youths, the number of children living in poverty, poor educational achievements, and the general inability of welfare programs to deal effectively with the "underclass."

Such criticisms in some cases resonated with a public increasingly concerned about the perceived ineffectiveness of welfare policy. Concern that welfare was not effectively ending poverty and that welfare recipients were staying on welfare too long was combined with a sense that both the number of people relying on welfare and the amount spent on welfare were increasing at a significant rate. However, despite such popular perceptions, the average number of welfare recipients remained fairly stable from 1978 to 1989 at between 10.5 and 11 million recipients per month, representing roughly 4.5 percent of the entire U.S. population. It was only during and after the recession of the early 1990s that the total number of welfare recipients increased significantly, reaching a high of 14.2 million in 1994.[6] When asked in 1995 if the welfare system needed change, 59 percent felt it should be "fundamentally overhauled," and another 34 percent thought it should be "adjusted somewhat"; only 3 percent felt it should be left alone.[7]

Whatever the successes or failures of welfare policy prior to 1996, it was in the context of these sorts of concerns, as well as a long and rancorous political battle between President Clinton and congressional Republicans, that significant reforms to the federal welfare program emerged. Experimentation on the state level in the late 1980s had represented a significant policy shift, but the most significant change in federal welfare policy came in 1996 with the passage of the PRWORA. This act replaced AFDC with the new TANF program under which the federal government ended its open-ended financial commitment to individuals who met eligibility criteria and replaced it with a system of block grants to states that then have the authority to design and administer welfare programs as well as set eligibility requirements. Rather than an entitlement that varies according to the demand for welfare as it did under AFDC, the contribution of the federal government was set at a lump sum equivalent to prior funding levels for AFDC, so that the total federal block grant was set at $16.8 billion annually until fiscal year 2002.[8]

TANF was passed as a work-oriented approach to ending poverty that required recipients to engage in work-related activity and set time limits for receipt of welfare benefits. While they were given considerable freedom under TANF, to receive federal funds states were required to maintain at least 80 percent of 1994 levels of welfare spending and to meet both work requirements and lifetime limits on welfare: 25 percent of welfare recipients in all states were required to be working or to be off welfare by 1997 and 50 percent by 2002. In addition, an individual lifetime limit of 5 years of welfare benefits was imposed. Failure to meet these goals was to result in severe reductions in federal funding. PRWORA also strengthened child support enforcement programs, contained "marriage promotion" provisions to encourage two-parent households, reduced spending on the food stamp program, eliminated aid to both legal and illegal immigrants, and slightly increased funding for some training and child care services.

At the time, the political significance of these changes to the federal welfare system, especially the elimination of the federal obligation to assist the poor and the imposition of time limits for the receipt of such benefits, was difficult to exaggerate. Since President Roosevelt's New Deal in the 1930s, the Democratic Party had historically been committed to a comprehensive federal safety net to include an almost unconditional financial obligation to the poor. That a Democratic president would accept, let alone push for, changes that ended such a commitment struck many from the traditionally liberal wing of the Democratic Party as scandalous. In fact, several senior staff members in the Clinton administration resigned in protest over the law, including prominent welfare experts Wendell Primus and Peter Edelman, the latter labeling acceptance of the new welfare law "the worst thing Bill Clinton has done."

Proponents of the new legislation contended that by giving the states the authority to design systems with work requirements and strict time limits, welfare reform under TANF would yield a variety of programs that effectively prepare and encourage welfare recipients for work. Critics, many of whom also supported changes to AFDC, contended that the new law would do little to expand work opportunities for the poor primarily because it lacked sufficient funding for support services like training and child care, and also because there simply would not be enough jobs available, particularly during an economic recession. Welfare programs that require work are much more expensive to administer successfully than are those that simply provide cash, because they may also provide child care, job training, and additional medical coverage. Taking advantage of the strong economy and declining welfare rolls, some states have used a portion of the federal block grant to support such programs.

Ever since the reforms introduced by PRWORA, an aura of success has surrounded the new federal approach to welfare policy. When asked, in 2001, if the new welfare law was working well, 61 percent answered yes compared with 23 percent who answered no.[9] Despite widespread public confidence that the reforms have been successful, however, the new law has not been in effect long enough to make sound judgments about its independent effects. But while definitive conclusions regarding the effects of the new welfare law will take years to emerge, early results do suggest significant changes. There is little question that state experimentation (an important goal for reformers) has increased and that there now is a diversity of state approaches to distributing welfare benefits to recipients. For example, some states—such as Wisconsin— have established comprehensive systems of work supports, incentives, and requirements; other states have developed plans that require adult recipients to complete parenting or money management courses, or that penalize adult recipients based on the attendance of their children at school; others have increased support for child care and expanded health benefits.

The change that has received the most attention is the remarkable decline in the number of welfare recipients in the years since TANF took effect. Average monthly recipients dropped by 56.4 percent—from 12.2 million to 5.3 million—between 1996 and 2001.[10] And in 2001 the number of welfare recipients as a percentage of the total U.S. population decreased to its lowest levels since the early 1960s—less than 2 percent compared with 4.8 percent in 1996 and a high of 5.5 percent in both 1993 and 1994.[11] The sharp decline in the number of recipients began to level off in late 2001, and nearly a dozen states reported slight increases in the number of people receiving assistance.[12] Together with the drastic decline in caseloads, the change pointed to most often by supporters of TANF is the number of recipients working. In the 1997 fiscal year, 30.7 percent of all families receiving TANF benefits were involved in work-related activities, and by the 2000 fiscal year, the rate had increased to 34 percent (49 percent among two-parent families).[13] Despite the TANF emphasis on encouraging marriage, only 18.4 percent of adult TANF recipients were married in 1999. As was the case with AFDC, the vast majority (72 percent) of TANF recipients are children.[14]

All sides of the debate seem to agree that the changes initiated by TANF are, at first glance, striking. Even liberal opponents of TANF concede that caseload reductions were much greater than they had anticipated. But critics are less sanguine about the apparent success of TANF. Welfare reform, these critics contend, was undertaken at a propitious time during which a variety of other policy changes and background events provided most of the impetus for declining caseloads and transitions to work. Most obvious among these was the strong economy of the mid-to-late 1990s, which brought with it consistently strong economic growth, rising wages, low unemployment, and an increased supply of new and transitional jobs. Some early research suggests that the "old" welfare system would have fared just as well against this backdrop: In 1996, 2,400 families in Connecticut were randomly assigned to receive benefits under pre-TANF rules, and during the 4-year study, 81 percent left welfare for jobs.[15]

Significant policy changes, particularly those designed to "make work pay," also proved important in moving people from welfare to work during this period. The earned income tax credit (EITC) program—a program that provides a refundable tax credit for eligible work by those meeting income requirements—was essential in helping encourage and then support the working poor. Laws passed in 1990 and 1993 increased the size and reach of the EITC program: Real expenditures (in 1999 dollars) increased from $7.5 billion in 1990 to $21.1 billion in 1994, and between 1986 and 1996 expenditures increased by nearly 1,200 percent.[16] At the same time, the federal minimum wage increased from $4.25 per hour to $5.15 per hour in September 1997.

Many policymakers and members of the public are concerned that, despite declining caseloads, poverty remains an important and seemingly intractable problem in America. The poverty rate for all ages and races declined steadily between 1993 and 2000, reaching a 27-year low of 11.3 percent. But despite declines, the poverty rate for children remained at 16.2 percent in 2000, and racial differences in poverty rates remained disturbing: In 2000, 22.1 percent of black residents and 21.2 percent of Hispanic residents were living below the poverty line compared with 9.4 percent of whites.[17] To be sure, there has been progress in eliminating much poverty, but even as they celebrate the successes of antipoverty policy, many Americans are becoming concerned that the easy work has been done and that the populations that remain in poverty or on welfare will prove far more difficult to help with current methods.

As attention turned to reauthorization of TANF in the fall of 2002, a variety of proposals were being floated for changes to the program. The Bush administration proposed, among other things, to increase the number of working hours required from 30 to 40 and to increase incentives for welfare recipients to marry. Others have proposed increasing federal support for work support programs like child care and health insurance. Whatever changes are enacted, they will depend in large part on how the first 5 years' experiences with TANF are judged.

The articles in this section attempt the beginnings of such a judgment. Ron Haskins, chief welfare adviser to congressional Republicans from 1986 to 2000 and currently a fellow at the Brookings Institution, celebrates the success of TANF at reducing poverty and argues that the work requirements, as well as work supports, were central to this success. Peter Edelman, formerly an assistant secretary at the Department of Health and Human Services (the federal agency responsible for AFDC and, now, TANF), who resigned to protest the PRWORA law, argues that TANF's flaws were covered up by the strong economy, but that, even so, it was not the unqualified success so many assume and that it will require a fundamental overhaul if it is to serve the interests of the poor—working or not.

Endnotes

1. Office of Management and Budget, *The Budget for Fiscal Year 2003*, Historical Tables (Washington, D.C.: U.S. Government Printing Office, 2002).
2. Ibid.
3. Ibid.
4. Mary Jo Bane and David Ellwood, *Welfare Realities: From Rhetoric to Reform* (Cambridge, Mass.: Harvard University Press, 1994).
5. Ibid.
6. U.S. Department of Health and Human Services, Administration for Children and Families, http://www.acf.dhhs.gov.
7. Poll conducted by Public Agenda, December 8–17, 1995.
8. U.S. Department of Health and Human Services, http://www.acf.dhhs.gov. Specifically, the program provides funding on a state-by-state basis at a level equivalent to whichever of the following is greatest: fiscal year 1994, fiscal year 1995, or the average of fiscal years 1992–1994 funding levels.
9. International Communications Research, Kaiser Family Foundation, and Harvard University poll conducted January 4 through February 27, 2001. Fifteen percent of respondents had no opinion.
10. U.S. Department of Health and Human Services, Administration for Children and Families, "Percent Change in AFDC/TANF Families and Recipients, August 1996—September 2001," http://www.acf.dhhs.gov.
11. U.S. Department of Health and Human Services, Administration for Children and Families, http://www.acf.dhhs.gov.
12. Laura Meckler, "Welfare Cases Rise in Some States," Associated Press (April 3, 2001).

13. U.S. Department of Health and Human Services, Administration for Children and Families, Office of Planning, Research, and Evaluation, "TANF Work Participation Rates, Fiscal Year 2000," http://www.acf.dhhs.gov.
14. U.S. Department of Health and Human Services, Administration for Children and Families, Office of Planning, Research, and Evaluation, "Characteristics and Financial Circumstances of TANF Recipients, Fiscal Year 1999," http://www.acf.dhhs.gov.
15. Nina Bernstein, "In Control Group, Most Welfare Recipients Left the Rolls Even without Reform," *The New York Times* (February 20, 2002).
16. Dennis J. Ventry, "The Collision of Tax and Welfare Politics: The Political History of the Earned Income Tax Credit, 1969–1999," *National Tax Journal*, vol. 53, no. 4 (part 2), pp. 983–1026.
17. U.S. Bureau of the Census, "Poverty in the United States, 2000."

YES

Giving Is Not Enough:
Work and Work Supports Are
Reducing Poverty

Ron Haskins

The essence of the 1996 welfare reform law was work. Under the new law, welfare recipients, previously subject to only loose requirements of any type, were to be strongly encouraged—even forced—to work. The legal entitlement to cash welfare was to be ended in favor of a system that required work and other signs of personal responsibility as a condition of receiving benefits. Previous welfare law had paid lip service to work but had imposed no work requirements for single mothers. For those few welfare recipients selected to meet a work participation standard, such as education, the law had exacted few consequences for failure. But in 1996, and even earlier as some states began to impose work requirements by obtaining waivers from federal law, the requirement to work became real. Recipients who refused to work or prepare for work had their benefits reduced; more than 30 states adopted a sanction policy that terminated benefits completely. States that did not place a specific percentage of their recipients in work or work preparation programs suffered financial penalties. Recipients were also subjected to a five-year limit on benefits, a strong signal that self-support is a must.

FROM WELFARE TO WORK

Coupled with a booming economy and public policies to help the working poor, these tough reforms have been associated with an historic decline in the welfare rolls—more than 50 percent from the peak welfare enrollment of 5.1 million families in the spring of 1994. So mothers are leaving welfare in record numbers. But are they finding work?

Brookings economist Gary Burtless has shown, using national employment data from the Census Bureau, that after a decade of stagnation at about 57–58 percent, the employment rate of single mothers increased slightly in 1994 and then shot up dramatically every year between 1995 and 1999 to 72 percent, an all-time high. More remarkable still, the employment rate of never-married mothers, who are the most likely to have little education or job experience and long stays on welfare, increased even more. Between 1992 and 1996, their employment rate rose gradually from around 43 percent to

49 percent. But in the three years after enactment of the 1996 legislation, the rate exploded. By 1999 it had risen to 65 percent, also an all-time high and an increase of 33 percent in just three years.

IS POVERTY FALLING?

Virtually everyone in the policy world agrees that since the 1996 reforms were enacted, welfare rolls have fallen dramatically and employment by female family heads, especially never-married heads, has risen impressively. But most observers are not satisfied with declines in welfare and increased work. They want to know if the mothers and children formerly on welfare are financially better off.

Of the many measures that could be picked to examine financial well-being, one of the most useful is the poverty measure used by the U.S. Census Bureau. Although not without its critics, the measure stands out as a reasonable means to trace changes in family material well-being for two reasons. First, it is widely used by social scientists, reporters, and politicians. Second, it has been computed in a standard manner that produces a continuous data series on poverty from 1959 to 1999.

Figure 1 compares the annual percentage change in the welfare caseload, the Census Bureau measure of child poverty, and the Census Bureau measure of black child poverty during 1995–99. All three measures fell every year. Even the smallest annual decline in the welfare rolls during those five years, around 7 percent in 1995, exceeds those of any year before 1995, highlighting the historic nature of the decline in cash welfare.

The declines in overall child poverty and black child poverty are also impressive. Not only did both rates decline every year, but the black child

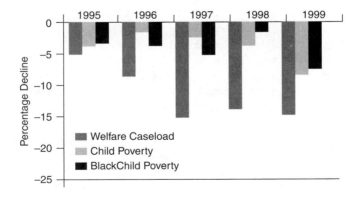

FIGURE 1   **Decline in Welfare Caseloads and Child Poverty, 1995–99**

Source: Caseload data from Congressional Research Services, poverty data from Census Bureau.

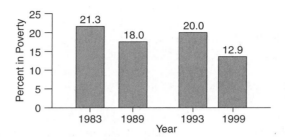

FIGURE 2   **Child Poverty, Including In-Kind Government Benefits and Tax Benefits, 1983–89 and 1993–99**

Source: Bureau of the Census.

poverty rate has been falling for seven straight years, the most sustained decline since the Census Bureau began measuring it in 1974. Further, the declines in black child poverty in 1997 and 1999, 6.8 percent and 9.8 percent respectively, are the largest ever recorded and the rate today is the lowest it has ever been. In fact, between 1974 and 1992, the general drift of black child poverty was up. Over this 17-year period, as Congress greatly increased spending on welfare programs, poverty among black children fell in nine years and grew in eight; overall the rate increased from 39.9 percent to 46.6 percent, well over 15 percent. Indeed, during the prolonged economic expansion of the 1980s, as the American economy added nearly 20 million jobs, black child poverty never fell below 43.1 percent, as compared with 33.1 percent in 1999.

Despite this historic progress against poverty, the Census Bureau's official poverty measure understates the progress the nation is now making against child poverty because it does not take into account in-kind federal benefits (such as food stamps) or tax benefits (such as the earned income tax credit) for which low-income working families generally qualify. Indeed, by not counting these two benefits alone, the official poverty measure ignores at least $35 billion in benefits enjoyed by low-income working families. Fortunately, the Census Bureau also publishes an experimental poverty measure that includes these and a few similar benefits like housing. Figure 2 uses this alternative measure to show the true progress the nation made in reducing children's poverty during the economic expansions of the 1980s and the 1990s. In both expansions, child poverty declined. But it fell more than twice as much during the 1990s as during the 1980s—35.5 percent as against 15.5 percent.

WAS IT THE ECONOMY?

Two developments explain the vast differences in poverty reduction during the two decades. But before examining them, I address one widely cited factor in explaining the difference—namely, the economy. During the boom of the

1980s, the American economy added a net of almost 20 million jobs. If, as many analysts and pundits claim, a hot economy plucks people off welfare, then we would expect the welfare rolls to have declined during the 1980s. But let's look at the data. When the economy first began adding jobs in the spring of 1983, the welfare rolls were growing. As the economy added a net of about 1 million jobs over the next year, they continued to climb. Between 1984 and the winter of 1988, as the economy added another 9 million jobs, the welfare rolls remained relatively flat, moving up and down in no apparent pattern. By 1988, they stood at about 3.7 million families, about the same as at the beginning of recovery in 1983 when a total of 16 million fewer Americans held jobs. Then over the next 18 months, as the economy added another 3 million jobs, the rolls shot up nearly 12 percent to more than 4 million families. During the entire 1980s expansion, the American economy added 20 million jobs and the welfare rolls grew by nearly half a million families. Those who want to attribute the recent remarkable decline in welfare rolls to the booming economy of the 1990s must account for why an economy that was almost as superb during the 1980s failed to reduce, and on the contrary, was associated with an actual increase in welfare rolls.

WHAT MADE THE 1990s DIFFERENT?

The 1990s have been a different story. For the first two-plus years of the recovery, between roughly December 1991 and March 1994, as the economy added about 6 million jobs, the welfare rolls grew by a surprising 700,000 families. But then, as more than half the states implemented work programs by 1994 and especially after enactment of the sweeping federal welfare reform legislation in 1996, the welfare rolls began a sustained decline that has yet to stop. Even more interesting, the nation is also in a sustained period during which poverty is declining more sharply than at any time since the 1950s.

Here's why. First, the mandatory work requirements outlined above spurred people to leave welfare and take jobs. Before the 1996 reforms, families accumulated on the welfare rolls and stayed for long spells. In fact, the average stay, counting repeat spells, for families on the rolls at any given moment was a shocking 12 years. Thus, even though the economy might expand rapidly, as it did during the 1980s, most families on welfare could not possibly benefit from the rising opportunity because they weren't even in the job market. And public policy did not encourage or, where necessary, force them into the job market. In the 1990s, by contrast, in large part because of the much more demanding welfare system, many families who would have been on welfare in previous years entered the job market and found jobs.

But the jobs they found generally paid low wages. So how did so many of them escape poverty? The answer brings us to the second cause for the great drop in poverty during the 1990s. Since roughly 1985, Congress has been quietly building a work support system that provides public benefits for low-income working families, especially those with children. This work support system includes housing, food stamps, the earned income tax credit, Medicaid, the Child Health Insurance Program, the child tax credit, child care, child support enforcement, and a variety of nutrition benefits for children such as school lunch, food subsidies for day care, and a major food program for mothers and infants. All have one feature in common: working families can receive benefits as long as their income is below a cutoff point that varies by program but is quite high. For example, the cutoff for food stamps is around $18,000; that for the EITC is more than $29,000. Thus, a mother with two children leaving welfare and earning $10,000 a year can supplement her income by $4,000 in cash from the EITC and by more than $2,000 in food stamps, bringing her total pretax income to $16,000 and lifting her and her children out of poverty.

BUILD ON SUCCESS

As the time approaches to reauthorize the 1996 welfare reform legislation, it is important that members of Congress, their staffs, and the public realize how successful the 1996 legislation has been in reducing poverty. Although Congress created scores of new programs and increased spending by billions of dollars in the decades leading up to welfare reform, no progress was made against children's poverty. Government action in simply giving away money, in-kind benefits, and social services—some on an entitlement basis—turned out to be a lousy way to reduce poverty. But the 1996 legislation marks a departure from providing guaranteed benefits to an approach demanding individual responsibility and then providing public subsidies for work. The result is historic declines in welfare, increases in work, and declines in poverty.

To continue and even expand this new approach, both liberals and conservatives must recognize that their favorite solutions to poverty are inadequate. Giving people benefits leaves them in poverty, reduces their propensity to work, and arguably impedes family formation. But pushing people to leave welfare for work does not ensure that they and their families will avoid poverty. Such are the work skills of millions of American parents that the value of their labor in the market is inadequate to support a family. In view of this stubborn reality, the best strategy is to require work and then provide public subsidies that lift working families out of poverty. As experience since the seminal 1996 reforms shows so clearly, only the combination of work and work subsidies will both promote personal responsibility and effectively fight poverty. At last, after three decades of failing to help families leave poverty by giving them lots of cash and in-kind welfare, we have found that both material and behavioral poverty are best attacked by the policy of mandatory work supplemented by government work supports.

NO

Reforming Welfare—Take Two

Peter Edelman

In a more progressive political world, the current recession would alter and even accelerate the debate over reauthorization of the 1996 welfare law, which expires this year. Far from a success in any case, the 1996 law was at best a policy designed for times when jobs are plentiful. Its drafters were heedless of what a recession would bring, perhaps thinking the business cycle, like history, was no longer operative.

Whatever they thought, the recession is here, and we entered it with a severely weakened safety net. Our unemployment compensation system has been deteriorating for decades. It will reach slightly more than a third of those who lose their jobs and replace only about a third, on average, of the wages of those who do qualify for help. Welfare, with its time limits and complete freedom for states to offer as little help as they like, will not fill the gap. People who go to the welfare office for cash help, food stamps and Medicaid will often be turned away, legally or illegally, because of restrictions on benefits for immigrants, a "work first" welfare office culture that will be slow to change even when there are no jobs available, and lawless practices that divert families away from the help they need.

It's possible the new year will bring a readiness to think a little more carefully—as governors contemplating declining revenues come to Washington with palms outstretched, but also as people mobilize to demand better policy. A wave of organizing in low-income communities over the past five years—now joined by labor, children's, women's, faith and civil rights organizations—has strengthened the constituency for action. Polls show a renewed trust in government, and there has been an outpouring of community concern for the victims of terror and its economic aftershocks. Even President Bush has suggested that legal immigrants should be entitled to food stamps.

Public opinion about welfare has changed, too. The 1996 law did at least end the debate over the decrepit system that no one—least of all low-income parents—liked. The resentment and anger that surrounded the old system have largely dissipated, and the public is surprisingly supportive of positive policy. A recent survey conducted by the (admittedly liberal) Washington pollster Diane Feldman found wide support for expanded education and training, assisting families who are working but still poor, focusing welfare policy on poverty reduction and reducing or eliminating work requirements for families with young children.

Of course, the issues go far beyond reauthorizing Temporary Assistance to Needy Families (TANF), the program created in 1996. The challenges include making up for a labor market that fails to provide millions of workers with a living wage, health insurance or the possibility of advancement; addressing the ever-increasing shortage and skyrocketing cost of rental housing; ameliorating the struggles that low-income parents go through to hold jobs and nurture their children at the same time; making sure that both women and men have full opportunities for job success; rectifying the exclusion of immigrants from access to supports that other Americans enjoy; and repairing unemployment insurance so that adequate benefits are available to a greater proportion of the jobless. But welfare reauthorization is coming, and it is important, both intrinsically and because the welfare system is in many ways the "canary in the coal mine" that signals the quality of our national commitment to low-income families.

The aim in TANF reauthorization should be to transform the program nationally into what it has become in a handful of places: a ladder of opportunity for all low-income families, and a safety net for children in families who have lost jobs or have other problems that keep them from success in the job market. Welfare should be one part of a set of policies that promote a living income, grounded in the realities and limitations of low-wage jobs in America today. Viewed in this way, welfare policy would build on ideas emerging from the grassroots that reflect a value base more broadly shared than previous visions of welfare and antipoverty policy. This in turn would, at least relatively, create more political space for advocacy efforts.

WELFARE REFORM AS WE KNOW IT

There is some good news, which has been trumpeted by politicians, and much bad news, about which we have heard far less. Welfare caseloads are still down dramatically, although with the recession they have begun to climb back up. Low-income single mothers are still in the labor market in unprecedented numbers. Poverty is down somewhat, at least through the year 2000. That's the good news.

For the poorest families life actually got worse even before the recession hit. From 1995 to 1999, roughly 2 million families, with average incomes of about $7,500, lost about 8 percent of their income. This happened because they lost more in benefits, both welfare and food stamps, than they gained in earnings from work.

Most of those who are working are far from out of the woods. Their median income is about $7 an hour, and their median hours of work are about forty a week. The earned-income tax credit and other benefits will lift a full-time minimum-wage worker with two children over the poverty line, but the large number of part-time workers and those with larger families don't even get that far (assuming a poverty line of $14,600 for a family of three has any meaning anyway).

Many families face hard choices between work and their children, but low-income families feel this tension most acutely. Obtaining safe and reliable childcare is a major struggle. And low-wage jobs aren't family friendly—you generally can't take time off to care for a sick child. An important new study by Jody Heymann and others at Harvard shows that mothers who receive welfare for more than two years have children with chronic health problems at twice the rate of mothers who have never been on welfare—41 percent versus 21 percent. But poor parents are far less likely than other parents to have benefits at their jobs that help to meet those greater needs. Thus, "work first," the mantra of TANF, often means that work trumps parental responsibilities.

One of the secrets to the "success" of declining welfare rolls, meanwhile, is shrinking eligibility. Immigrants make up about 20 percent of the low-wage work force today, and our economy gains heavily from their labor and the taxes they pay. But even legal immigrants are barred by TANF from receiving federally financed cash assistance for the first five years they are in the country, and eligibility after that is completely up to the states. More than 60 percent of poor children get no welfare help, and the number of ineligible families is going to rise as more people use up their lifetime eligibility with each passing year (in all but a handful of states the lifetime limit is five years, or even less).

Still, eligibility doesn't mean much. The red tape (multiple appointments, complicated forms, interminable waiting, worker rudeness and murky rules) discourages even the most desperate from seeking help. In many states, the official policy is "diversion"—if the applicant looks fit she is told to seek work.

Benefit levels have gone up a little in some states but are below the poverty line everywhere and below half the poverty line in many states. The price of assistance in some places—such as New York City—is to go to a "workfare" program that teaches no skills, provides no help in finding a job, pays no wage (and therefore allows no access to the earned-income tax credit), often denies necessary safety equipment and applies sanctions for the slightest infraction, real or alleged.

A LADDER OF OPPORTUNITY

It doesn't have to be this way. Welfare can be transformed from a punitive system cycling people in and out of the low-wage labor market into a ladder of opportunity for all low-income families—low-wage workers, unemployed parents, two-parent families and immigrants. If low-income people had access to the supports they need, most could lift and keep themselves out of poverty and take better care of their families.

Some states have adopted innovative policies that suggest a new vision for TANF nationally. Many of these changes have come about at least partly as a result of impressive organizing. Typically, low-income people develop an agenda and then work closely with others to advance it, including organized labor, faith-based groups and public-interest lawyers. Tactics have ranged from applying direct pressure at welfare centers, to exposing what is happening to families, to direct action and mobilization of large numbers of people. State legislatures have in the past been a tough sell for progressive antipoverty policies, but greater sophistication among grassroots groups and stronger alliances with other sectors have opened up more possibilities. Recent successes fall into three main areas:

- *Opening up access.* In a few states you can receive TANF services if you are poor whether you get cash assistance or not. Some provide support to both single and two-parent families. Others have used state funds to replace benefits that immigrants lost under the 1996 law. Still others apply no time limits to people unable to find a job or otherwise not in a position to work.
- *Increasing family incomes and providing opportunity.* The Minnesota Family Investment Program, among others, has shown that supplementing low wages pays off in family and child well-being. The Parents as Scholars program in Maine and equivalent efforts in Maryland and elsewhere have invested in the long-term prospects of low-income parents by allowing education and training to "count" as a work activity. Pennsylvania provides wage-paying jobs and training opportunities to unemployed parents. Some states and cities have adopted higher minimum wages and enacted living-wage ordinances. "Self-sufficiency standards" that measure the real cost of living for families of various sizes in different parts of states are now routinely used by some policy-makers.
- *Supporting family and child well-being.* Montana's at-home infant care program allows low-income parents to care for their own young children. A number of states have torn down barriers to enrollment in food stamps. Some states and cities have provided health insurance to both parents and children at levels well above the poverty line, expanded childcare availability and quality, and extended family leave and unemployment insurance coverage to low-wage workers. Michigan has no time limit for families that comply with program requirements, thereby rewarding families trying to get out of poverty.

We have learned from these experiences, but only the federal government can build on these examples with leverage and send positive signals about the goals of TANF to welfare offices across the country. With a souring economy and state retrenchment likely, the need for such signals is more urgent than ever.

To begin with, the federal government could draw attention to important precedents in health insurance and childcare policies embraced by some states. These changes accommodate the reality of low-income people's lives by making benefits more seamless, less tied to their immediate circumstances. Because of the nature of the low-wage job market and the fragility of childcare and transportation arrangements, low-income people move in and out of jobs with frequent bouts of unemployment. To take this into account, some states are basing health coverage solely on income—for example, giving coverage to all children or parents below some multiple of the poverty line. Similar (although less sweeping) changes have been made in childcare programs. Overall, this means these benefits are more widely accessible to low-income people, instead of being designated for either "welfare families" or "working families"—a distinction that makes little sense given the constantly shifting status of low-income families.

TANF programs have not yet followed suit. In most states, a family must still have virtually no income or resources to qualify for cash assistance or TANF-funded education and training. Families that have been receiving TANF payments do sometimes qualify for cash supplements and services once they find employment (although in nearly all states time clocks continue to tick). But working families that never received TANF are excluded from those benefits and services. Thus, while parents receiving welfare are given support when they work, those who have remained off the rolls are not accorded the same treatment.

FRAMING THE COMING DEBATE

As Congress revisits the welfare debate in 2002, three principles underlie a meaningful agenda for reform: Income support, education and training should be more widely available to low-income families; families and the government should both be responsible; and the well-being of families matters most.

The old system divided the welfare poor from the working poor, splitting the constituency for such programs. With the rolls now so small, the safety net of cash assistance has even fewer defenders. Emphasizing TANF's relevance to a broader segment of the working poor makes sense not only as policy but as political strategy. The recession accentuates the point. TANF is an integral part of the panoply of protections for the unemployed, distinguishable only in technical details from the rest of the antirecession toolbox (unemployment insurance, food stamps, energy and housing assistance, and so on). One crisis, one people, one safety net. The politics and the policy can go hand in hand.

Moreover, advocates will command moral authority by exposing how the current system consigns even rule-abiding TANF recipients to continuing poverty. Not applying time limits to families who "play by the rules" is a matter of fairness. So is making sure that two-parent families qualify for benefits, and assuring that child-support payments actually go to the children they are supposed to support instead of being kept by the state to offset past welfare payments. It is both better policy and better politics to offer TANF benefits to low-income workers—including cash supplements as well as education and training—regardless of whether a family received TANF before a member got a job.

Political force also inheres in the idea that families and the government should both be responsible. When people take responsibility for themselves but need support to achieve an income they can live on, they should get it. When the economy falters either nationally or locally, and when people with limited work experience and capacity cannot find work, time limits should be suspended and public jobs programs should offer work, training and placement assistance. Sufficient assistance should be guaranteed as the economy sours and joblessness continues to rise.

Family well-being is another idea that represents both policy truth and political saliency. Especially to protect children, an adequate cash safety net needs to be in place at all times. Requiring states to measure and report on the sufficiency of their cash grant levels against a fair standard is a minimum step to be taken. Requiring states and localities to follow their own rules is another. The federal government should penalize states that create a lawless culture in the welfare office, that inappropriately divert or arbitrarily sanction families, or that fail to screen and serve families in crisis, including domestic violence survivors. The meanest states need to be reined in—by, for example, requiring face-to-face interviews before anyone is cut off. Accommodating parents with sick, disabled or very young children, or infirm relatives, by reducing work requirements and suspending time limits would also promote family well-being, as would requiring employers to expand family-friendly policies and offering states incentives to establish paid family leave. At the end of the day, state performance should be measured against outcomes that matter, including the reduction of family and child poverty. States should be required to collect and publicly report data on their performance, broken down by race and ethnicity to insure that services are provided equitably.

A new vision for welfare will require many changes in perspective. Policymakers and political elites will have to acknowledge that TANF needs to accommodate the realities facing low-income families today. States and welfare administrators will have to change the orientation of the system from "beat them down" and "get them off" to "lift them up." Federal and state resources must be sufficient to meet the scale of the need.

Low-income people and their allies will have to articulate a bold new vision for poverty reduction and create the public will to realize it. This is a daunting task. Good antipoverty policy has never been a hallmark of the American social fabric.

But elements auguring positive movement are in play. People are in motion at the grassroots level. The public seems more receptive. The convergence of recession, time limits and brewing state fiscal crises creates an opening for change. In this context, a new vision for welfare may gain broader support than one might initially suppose. Certainly the price of inaction—for low-income people and for our society—is far too high.

DISCUSSION QUESTIONS

1. The welfare reform law passed in 1996 requires states to impose strict work requirements on able-bodied adult welfare recipients. Since most adult recipients are single mothers, what sort of support services are

needed to assist these women in finding and keeping jobs? Should the federal government provide additional funding for support services, such as day care?

2. Do Americans have an obligation—moral or otherwise—to provide assistance to the poor? What form should such assistance take (cash assistance, medical insurance, housing)?

3. In what ways might need-based welfare assistance be considered degrading to recipients? Do work requirements ameliorate these effects? Is the same true of Social Security benefits? Why or why not?

4. Do you agree with the premise of the 1996 welfare reforms, which suggests that financial assistance carries with it a responsibility on the part of recipients to seek work?

5. Should programs designed to help the working poor (such as the earned income tax credit program, which provides tax benefits to low-income workers that are gradually phased out as incomes rise) be expanded? If so, should these programs be funded at the expense of other social welfare programs?

6. How should we evaluate the effect of the 1996 welfare reforms? Which factors are relevant in analyzing the success or failure of TANF—poverty levels, employment levels, the number of TANF recipients, or other factors?

7. TANF will most likely continue to be reformed in the future. Some hope that reforms to the program will contain even more marriage and work incentives; others would prefer more funding for support programs that provide health care or child care. Which reforms do you prefer? Should these reforms be adopted by the federal government or by state governments? Should total spending by the federal government increase? Why or why not?

WEB REFERENCES

Administration for Children and Families, http://www.acf.dhhs.gov/news/welfare/index.htm.

Center for Law and Social Policy, http://www.clasp.org/pubs/TANF/tanffederal.htm.

Center on Budget and Policy Priorities, http://www.cbpp.org/.

Heritage Foundation: Welfare, http://www.heritage.org/library/welfare.html.

Institute for Research on Poverty, University of Wisconsin, http://www.ssc.wisc.edu/irp/.

Manpower Demonstration Research Corporation, http://www.mdrc.org/welfare_reform.htm.

Urban Institute, http://www.urban.org/.

Welfare Information Network, http://www.welfareinfo.org.

FURTHER READING

Abromivitz, Mimi. *Regulating the Lives of Women.* Boston: South End Press, 1988.

Albelda, Randy. *Lost Ground: Welfare Reform, Poverty, and Beyond.* Boston: South End Press, 2002.

Bane, Mary Jo and David T. Ellwood. *Welfare Realities: From Rhetoric to Reform.* Cambridge, Mass.: Harvard University Press, 1994.

Blank, Rebecca M. *It Takes a Nation: A New Agenda for Fighting Poverty.* Princeton, N.J.: Princeton University Press, 1997.

Burtless, Gary and Kent Weaver. "Reinventing Welfare—Again." *Brookings Review,* vol. 15 (Winter 1997).

Danziger, Sheldon and Peter Gottschalk. *America Unequal.* Cambridge, Mass.: Harvard University Press, 1995.

Duncan Greg J. and P. Lindsay Chase-Lansdale. *For Better and for Worse; Welfare Reform and the Well-Being of Children and Families.* New York: Russell Sage, 2002.

Friedlander, Daniel. *Five Years After: The Long-Term Effects of Welfare-to-Work Programs.* New York: Russell Sage, 1995.

Funiciello, Theresa. *Tyranny of Kindness: Dismantling the Welfare System to End Poverty in America.* New York: Atlantic Monthly Press, 1993.

Gans, Herbert J. *The War against the Poor: The Underclass and Antipoverty Policy.* New York: Basic Books, 1995.

Gueron, Judith M. "A Research Context for Welfare Reform." *Journal of Policy Analysis and Management,* vol. 15 (Fall 1996), pp. 547–61.

Jencks, Christopher. *Rethinking Social Policy.* Cambridge, Mass.: Harvard University Press, 1992.

Katz, Michael B. *The Undeserving Poor: From the War on Poverty to the War on Welfare.* New York: Pantheon Books, 1989.

Kelman, Steven. "A Case for In-Kind Transfers." *Economics and Philosophy,* vol. 2 (1986).

Loprest, Pamela. "Families Who Left Welfare: Who Are They and How Are They Doing?" Discussion Paper 99–02. Washington, D.C.: Urban Institute Press, 1999.

Marmor, Theodore R., Jerry L. Mashaw, and Philip L. Harvey. *America's Misunderstood Welfare State.* New York: Basic Books, 1990.

Mead, Lawrence M., ed. *The New Paternalism: Supervisory Approaches to Poverty.* Washington, D.C.: The Brookings Institution, 1997.

Murray, Charles. *Losing Ground: American Social Policy 1950–1980.* New York: Basic Books, 1984.

Murray, Michael. *And Economic Justice for All: Welfare Reform for the 21st Century.* New York: M. E. Sharpe, 1997.

Nightingale, Demetra Smith and Robert Havemann, eds. *The Work Alternative: Welfare Reform and the Realities of the Job Market.* Washington, D.C.: Urban Institute Press, 1995.

Olasky, Marvin N. *Renewing American Compassion.* New York: Free Press, 1996.

Piven, Frances Fox. *Work, Welfare and Politics: Confronting Poverty in the Wake of Welfare Reform.* Eugene: University of Oregon Books, 2002.

Piven, Frances Fox and Richard A. Cloward. *Regulating the Poor: The Functions of Public Welfare.* New York: Vintage Books, 1971.

Sawhill, Isabel. " From Welfare to Work: Making Welfare a Way Station, Not a Way of Life." *Brookings Review* (Summer 2001), pp. 4–7.

Schorr, Lisbeth B. *Common Purpose: Strengthening Families and Neighborhoods to Rebuild America.* New York: Anchor Books/Doubleday, 1997.

Schram, Sanford F. *Welfare Reform: A Race to the Bottom?* Washington, D.C.: Woodrow Wilson Press, 1999.

Seefeldt, Kristin S. *Welfare Reform.* Washington, D.C.: CQ Press, 2001.

Tanner, Michael. *The End of Welfare: Fighting Poverty in the Civil Society.* Washington, D.C.: Cato Institute, 1996.

Weil, Alan and Kenneth Finegold, eds. *Welfare Reform: The Next Act.* Washington, D.C.: Urban Institute Press, 2002.

Weir, Margaret. "Is Anybody Listening? The Uncertain Future of Welfare Reform in the Cities." *Brookings Review*, vol. 15 (Winter 1997).

Wilson, William Julius. *When Work Disappears: The World of the New Urban Poor.* New York: Knopf, 1996.

Chapter 10

HEALTH POLICY

"Should the United States Adopt a Universal, Single-Payer Health Plan?"

YES: Physicians' Working Group on Single-Payer National Health Insurance "Proposal for Health Care Reform"

NO: Merrill Matthews, Jr., and Robert J. Cihak "Health Care Quality: Would It Survive a Single-Payer System?" *Washington Policy Center*

Unlike many other western nations, the United States has no universal health care provision, made available irrespective of age, income, or need. Many European countries, along with Canada, Australia, and New Zealand, have some form of national health care, provided as an entitlement to all citizens. Because these systems provide health care through centralized administrative systems, they are often referred to as single-payer systems. A single-payer system does not, by definition, need to be provided by a national government; it merely refers to a system in which all people under a given jurisdiction pay into a common insurance pool (through taxation or otherwise) and receive similar benefits.

In general, working citizens in the United States must choose from a variety of private health care coverage options, largely health maintenance organizations (HMOs) or preferred provider plans (PPPs), with each offering different deductibles and coverage options. In 1999, over $400 billion worth of premiums were paid into private health insurance plans, with another $187 billion paid in out-of-pocket expenses.[1] In addition to private health insurance options, federal and state governments provide health care coverage to certain groups based on income and age through the Medicare and Medicaid programs, discussed below. There are numerous health care options in the United States, and they consume a vast proportion of the national income: 13 percent of GDP in 1998–1999. In 1999, U.S. spending on health care, including research and infrastructure, totaled $1,211 billion. When assessed on a per capita basis, this amounted to $4,270 in 1998–1999, compared with $1,675 in the United Kingdom, $2,288 in France, $1,939 in Canada, $1,163 in

New Zealand, and $2,145 in Sweden.[2] The average per capita spending on health care in developing countries is a mere $81.90.

Some argue that the administrative burden of so many forms of health insurance makes health expenditure in the United States excessive and inefficient. Each insurance plan must enforce checks and balances to ensure recipients are billed correctly; each must market its products, and each pays executive salaries to its leadership. Two studies commissioned by the Massachusetts Medical Society in 1998 found that a move to a single-payer health system in the state would save enough money to provide comprehensive health coverage to all residents.[3] Under most proposals, individual billing would be largely eliminated, with hospitals (possibly private) receiving payments directly from the government to cover services. Some estimate that a national single-payer system could reduce health costs by as much as $225 billion by 2004, although it is unclear to what extent those savings would be in the public realm and thus transferable to covering all citizens' health care needs.[4]

Cost savings are not enough to convince some of the necessity for a single-payer system in the United States. Arguments against a national insurance program range from the libertarian view that health care is outside the justifiable realm of government to the more pragmatic notion that a single-payer system, if poorly run, affects everybody adversely. Many critics focus on problems evident within the current single-payer systems of such countries as Britain, Canada, and New Zealand. Nina Owcharenko of the Heritage Institute cites a report by the Canadian Fraser Institute that found the average waiting time for surgery in Canada to be 4 months in 2000–2001. She also notes a recent study finding that reported 1 million people to be on waiting lists for Britain's National Health Service (NHS), with one in four cardiac patients dying while waiting.[5]

The fact that many Britons are now moving to private health care insurance may be indicative of the growing failure of its NHS: Data from the latter half of the 1990s show that 12.5 percent of Britons were covered by private health insurance. However, access to private health care in Britain is highly correlated with income and professional status, with around 40 percent of those in the highest-income decile having private coverage, while only 5 percent of the poorest decile having some form of nonpublic health provision.[6] Britain may thus become something of a two-tiered system, analogous to the U.S. Social Security system: The NHS provides a foundation of services available to all (as with Social Security pensions), but individuals are free to manage their own health care if they are able (as with private pensions). In Canada, however, private health care endeavors are strictly limited to those services not provided under the public national insurance, leading to an enforced single-payer system with no opt-out.[7]

Perhaps the most repeated argument in favor of a single-payer health care system is the disturbing level of uninsured citizens within the United States. In 1999, more than 42 million Americans were without health insurance, or around 15 percent of the population. A report issued by the Kaiser Foundation notes that this figure has been slowly growing; in 1998, the figure was 34 million.[8] These figures do not include those covered by Medicare or Medicaid. The report also points out that these numbers are only "snapshots" in time, and do not reflect the fact that many people are temporarily without health insurance for significant periods of time. In 1997, one-third of working-age adults reported that they had been without health insurance at some point in the past 2 years.[9] Because the poorest in the United States are covered by Medicaid, 73 percent of the uninsured are above the poverty level, with 27 percent earning incomes three times or more that of the federal poverty level. Most of the uninsured are in full-time working families; 57 percent are in families with children. Demographically, minorities are more likely to be uninsured, with 37 percent of Hispanics without insurance, 24 percent of Native Americans, 24 percent of blacks, 22 percent of Asians, and only 14 percent of whites.[10] People from southern states are disproportionately uninsured. Ten southern states have uninsured rates over 20 percent, while only one northern state (Montana) has this level. In New Mexico, over one-quarter of the population has no health coverage.[11]

Two-thirds of the uninsured do not have health insurance because it is prohibitively costly, even for those receiving employee benefits; workers paid more than three times as much for health care benefits in 1998 compared with 1977. Only 8 percent felt that they did not need insurance, and only 7 percent were without health insurance because of changes in employment.[12] Without insurance, many go without needed medical care, or wait until diseases have become serious and, therefore, more costly to treat, before seeking assistance. Preventive or diagnostic health care is not an option for many without insurance: Only 16 percent of uninsured women reported having a mammogram in 1999, compared with 42 percent of insured women, and as such, are 40 to 50 percent more likely to die from breast cancer.[13]

As already noted, the U.S. government does make some provision for those unable to afford private health coverage, notably the Medicare and Medicaid programs, launched as key ingredients of President Johnson's Great Society program. Medicare is a federally funded program that provides health care coverage to all who qualify for Social Security benefits, including the elderly and some disabled. Medicaid, in contrast, is designed to provide health care coverage primarily to low-income families, although it also provides coverage to the blind, elderly, and disabled who are covered by Supplemental Security Income. Medicaid costs are shared by the federal and state governments, with the federal government providing matching funds to states at a rate inversely related to a state's per capita income.[14] The Medicaid program is operated strictly at the state level, and states generally determine how the program will be administered, although the states are required to follow broad guidelines set by the federal government. As a result, eligibility, the coverage of medical procedures, levels of reimbursement for medical providers, and other fundamental program designs vary considerably from state to state.

Taken together, Medicaid and Medicare provide an important source of health care coverage for those who would be unable to obtain affordable health care elsewhere, funding health care services for 39 million people under Medicare and 40 million people under Medicaid in 1999.[15] Indeed, while employer-sponsored health insurance plans remain the most widespread source of health care funding, state and federal governments funded a projected 44 percent of all health care expenditures in the United States in 2002. This figure has gradually risen since the inception of the Medicaid and Medicare programs when government funding covered only about a third of health expenditures.[16]

Medicare is almost exclusively directed toward the elderly, with 87 percent of all enrollees in 1999 being persons over 65 and 13 percent disabled. Medicare comprises two elements: hospital insurance (HI) and supplemental medical insurance (SMI). HI is available to anybody over 65 who is eligible for Social Security retirement payments, and generally covers inpatient hospital fees. SMI is an optional addition that requires the payment of a monthly premium ($54 in 2002), covering outpatient services including doctors' appointments and physical therapy.[17] Fully 95 percent of Medicare enrollees in 1999 took advantage of SMI.[18] In 1999, 59 percent of Medicare disbursements went to HI ($130 billion), and 41 percent went to SMI ($89 billion).[19]

Medicaid is a particularly diverse program, with 52 percent of its enrollees in 1999 being under age 18 and 11 percent being over 65 in 1999.[20] Although Medicaid is targeted to the poor (47 percent of those covered by Medicaid in 1999 were below the poverty level),[21] a surprisingly small portion of total Medicaid expenditures winds up in the hands of persons receiving financial assistance from programs like Aid to Families with Dependent Children (AFDC) or, more recently, Temporary Assistance for Needy Families (TANF); 68 percent of Medicaid recipients were also receiving TANF benefits in 1998, but they received only 26 percent of expenditures.[22] Instead, most expenditures are devoted to the permanently and totally disabled (42 percent) and the elderly (persons over age 65 receive 29 percent of Medicaid expenditures).[23] Surely some or many of these individuals may be poor, but their basis of eligibility is not welfare assistance, and the notion that Medicaid expenditures are largely a medical handout to able-bodied working-age persons is unfounded (although this group comprises the majority of recipients). Indeed, it is not uncommon for elderly individuals who cannot afford costly long-term care to "spend down" their assets to qualify for Medicaid assistance; this of course has proved to be a costly drain on Medicaid resources as well.

Like other health care expenditures, Medicare and Medicaid costs have increased dramatically in the last several decades. Total Medicare costs increased by 510 percent between 1980 and 1998,[24] with Medicaid costs increasing 511 percent over the same time period.[25] Medicare costs are set to rise even higher if planned legislation passes to subsidize the cost of prescription drugs to the elderly. Medical payments make up 41.4 percent of all government transfers to individuals, including Social Security payments.[26] In terms of governmental assistance to those in need of income support, Medicaid payments are almost 11 times as large as family assistance programs including TANF.[27] This large differential has increased in recent years as family assistance payments have decreased between AFDC and TANF; in 1990 Medicaid expenditures were only four times as large as governmental family support. Medicaid thus occupies a significant role in the welfare state. In recent years, states have also suffered from increasing costs due to federal Medicaid coverage requirements, spiraling Medicaid costs, and growing numbers of eligible recipients. In response, many states have either restricted eligibility or cut back on payments to doctors and hospitals. As a result, doctors in some states refuse to treat Medicaid patients, and the poor are sometimes shifted to public or university-run hospitals, many of which are then forced to charge patients with private insurance higher rates to make up for low Medicaid reimbursements.

Throughout the course of the twentieth century, governments have made occasional moves toward a single-payer health care system, but none have yet been successful. The American Association of Labor Legislation (AALL) drafted a bill for a national health care system for low-income workers in 1915; although the American Medical Association supported the bill, staunch opposition from other labor organizations and private insurance companies halted its progress. During the 1920s, the most prominent proponent of a single-payer system was the Committee on the Cost of Medical Care (CCMC), which consisted of economists, physicians, health specialists, and interest groups. The CCMC believed that Americans in general needed more health care and believed that a voluntary, not mandatory, national health system was most appropriate.[28]

One of the most promising windows of opportunity for a single-payer health care system was the Great Depression: The heightened reliance of the citizenry on government and the concomitant expansion of government functions created a situation favorable to the creation of national health care. However, reforms toward a welfare state focused on more pressing issues of unemployment and retirement benefits, and President Roosevelt excluded a universal health system from his Social Security legislation, lest it threaten passage of the bill. Truman was the first president to unequivocally support a national health system and was committed to establishing health care for all, irrespective of social class and without the stigma of socialist welfare that had reappeared during World War II. With Congress in the hands of the Republicans, and the AMA spending $1.5 million in 1945 alone on lobbying efforts against national health care, Truman's plan did not make it out of congressional committees, and proponents of a single-payer system realized that a more modest alternative was the only option. Once the debate shifted to providing health care for the aged, opposition was far more difficult, and a compromise was reached with the bipartite structure of Medicare in 1965.[29]

A few fundamental changes have been made to the basic structure of Medicare and Medicaid since the 1960s. Former President Clinton, who campaigned in 1992 with a pledge to expand health care and constrain costs, made attempts at reform with his establishment of a Task Force on National Health Reform, headed by his spouse, Hillary Clinton. A confluence of factors led to the failure of reform efforts: the absence of a clear policy direction, the secrecy in which the task force operated, the diversion of attention toward events in Somalia, Haiti, and Russia, and the ever-present opposition to expanding the public health care system. Although Clinton pledged in his 1994 State of the Union Address to veto any legislation that failed to provide private health insurance for every American, the momentum for radical change had disappeared, and Clinton failed to gather the support that he saw subsequently with welfare reform in 1996.[30]

The most recent movement toward a single-payer system has not been at the federal level, but rather in California, where proposals for a statewide health care system were unveiled in April 2002. Concerned about soaring Medicaid costs, the Healthcare Options Project (approved by Governor Davis in 1999) proposed a universal health care system in which public funds would finance private hospitals, providing a comprehensive benefit package to all Californians. An elected health commissioner, a public state board, and regional boards would oversee the system and manage eligibility, reimbursement, and financial operations. The benefit package would cover medical procedures including dialysis, mental health services, prescription drugs, rehabilitation, prenatal care, hospice and long-term care, and dental and vision care. The plan would not subject users to co-payments, but would be financed through existing health care appropriations in addition to a special tobacco tax, a payroll tax of 8 percent levied on employers, and a personal income tax of 2.5 percent.[31] Proponents hope that employers, concerned over spiraling premiums, would back the plan, as would labor unions keen to see universal coverage for members. Some even believe that physicians are warming to the idea of a single-payer plan.[32] The proposal is clearly still in a policy formation stage and requires the kind of broad political support necessary to initiate such fundamental reform.

The United States is a nation wealthy enough to provide health care coverage to all of its citizens, and it currently spends far more than any other country when private health care funding is included. However, this massive per capita expenditure disguises the fact that health care is very much apportioned by ability to pay. While government programs do provide support to the elderly and to certain sectors of the poor, 15 percent of the population remains uninsured. The following articles debate the feasibility and the desirability of expanding U.S. health care policy to cover all citizens. The Physicians' Working Group on Single-Payer National Health Insurance argues that health care should be treated as a social service, not a mercantile commodity. The group believes that public funding of private hospitals and clinics would save some $150 billion annually through administrative streamlining—access would be increased and costs reduced. Merrill Matthews and Robert Cihak assess single-payer plans in terms of medical quality, defined by a complex mix of access, affordability, doctor-patient relationship, patient choice, medical outcomes, and patient satisfaction. They argue, with examples from countries already offering single-payer systems, that the benefits of universal coverage disguise serious shortcomings in quality. Using Washington State as their point of reference, Matthews and Cihak contend that free market policy options can increase the number of insured in America, without risking the reductions in service levels likely with a single-payer system.

Endnotes

1. U.S. Bureau of the Census, *Statistical Abstract of the United States*, http://www.census. gov/prod/2002pubs/01statab/health.pdf, Table 120.
2. The World Bank, http://devdata.worldbank.org/external/dgcomp.asp?rmdk= 110& smdk=473886&w=0.
3. The Massachusetts Campaign for Single Payer Healthcare, http://www.masscare. org/what.htm.
4. See Physicians for a National Health Program, http://usliberals.about.com/gi/ dynamic/offsite.htm?site=http%3A%2F%2Fwww.pnhp.org%2Fbasicinfo.html.
5. Nina Owcharenko, "Medicaid: A Grim Diagnosis," http://www.heritage.org/ views/ 2002/ed041502b.html.
6. Carl Emmerson, et al., *Pressures in UK Healthcare: Challenges for the NHS*, http://www.ifs.org.uk/health/nhsspending.pdf.
7. See, for example, Jeremiah Hurley, et al., *Parallel Private Health Insurance in Australia: A Cautionary Tale and Lessons for Canada*, http://cepr.anu.edu.au/ pdf/DP448.pdf.
8. Kaiser Foundation, *Uninsured in America*, http://www.kff.org/content/2000/ 3013/KeyFacts.PDF.
9. Ibid.
10. Ibid.
11. U.S. Bureau of the Census, op. cit., Table 145.
12. Kaiser Foundation, op. cit.
13. Ibid.
14. The principal federal agency overseeing and funding Medicaid is the Health Care Financing Administration (which controls Medicare as well) in the Department of Health and Human Services. The minimum matching rate, for the richest states, is one federal dollar for every state Medicaid dollar spent, an amount that rises for poorer states.
15. U.S. Bureau of the Census, op. cit., Tables 131 and 140.
16. Ibid., Table 119.
17. www.medicare.gov.
18. U.S. Bureau of the Census, op. cit., Table 131.
19. Ibid., Table 132.
20. Ibid., Table 137.
21. Ibid.
22. Ibid., Table 139.
23. Ibid.
24. Ibid., Table 132.

25. Ibid., Table 139, and http://www.census.gov/prod/1/gen/95statab/health.pdf, Table 166.

26. U.S. Bureau of the Census, *Statistical Abstract of the United States*, http://www.census.gov/prod/2002pubs/01statab/socinsur.pdf, Table 518.

27. Ibid.

28. Karen S. Palmer, *A Brief History: Universal Healthcare Efforts in the U.S.: Late 1880s to Medicare*, http://usliberals.about.com/gi/dynamic/offsite.htm?site=http%3A%2F%2Fwww.pnhp.org%2Fbasicinfo.html.

29. Ibid.

30. See PBS Online Newshour, http://www.pbs.org/newshour/forum/may96/background/health_debate_page1.html, for history.

31. California Healthcare Options Project, http://www.healthcareoptions.ca.gov/nov01/asp/UCSF_pg3.asp.

32. Healthcare for All, http://www.healthcareforall.org/.

YES

Proposal for Health Care Reform

Physicians' Working Group on Single-Payer
National Health Insurance

EXECUTIVE SUMMARY

The United States spends more than twice as much on health care as the average of other developed nations, all of which boast universal coverage. Yet over 42 million Americans have no health insurance whatsoever, and most others are underinsured, in the sense that they lack adequate coverage for all contingencies (e.g., long-term care and prescription drug costs).

Why is the U.S. so different? The short answer is that we alone treat health care as a commodity distributed according to the ability to pay, rather than as a social service to be distributed according to medical need. In our market-driven system, investor-owned firms compete not so much by increasing quality or lowering costs, but by avoiding unprofitable patients and shifting costs back to patients or to other payers. This creates the paradox of a health care system based on avoiding the sick. It generates huge administrative costs, which, along with profits, divert resources from clinical care to the demands of business. In addition, burgeoning satellite businesses, such as consulting firms and marketing companies, consume an increasing fraction of the health care dollar.

We endorse a fundamental change in America's health care—the creation of a comprehensive National Health Insurance (NHI) Program. Such a program—which in essence would be an expanded and improved version of Medicare—would cover every American for all necessary medical care. Most hospitals and clinics would remain privately owned and operated, receiving a budget from the NHI to cover all operating costs. Investor-owned facilities would be converted to not-for-profit status, and their former owners compensated for past investments. Physicians could continue to practice on a fee-for-service basis, or receive salaries from group practices, hospitals or clinics.

A National Health Insurance Program would save at least $150 billion annually by eliminating the high overhead and profits of the private, investor-owned insurance industry and reducing spending for marketing and other satellite services. Doctors and hospitals would be freed from the concomitant burdens and expenses of paperwork created by having to deal with multiple insurers with different rules—often rules designed to avoid payment. During the transition to an NHI, the savings on administration and profits would fully offset the costs of expanded and improved coverage. NHI would make it possible to set and enforce overall spending limits for the health care system, slowing cost growth over the long run.

A National Health Insurance Program is the only affordable option for universal, comprehensive coverage. Under the current system, expanding access to health care inevitably means increasing costs, and reducing costs inevitably means limiting access. But an NHI could both expand access and reduce costs. It would squeeze out bureaucratic waste and eliminate the perverse incentives that threaten the quality of care and the ethical foundations of medicine.

"Health care is an essential safeguard of human life and dignity, and there is an obligation for society to ensure that every person be able to realize this right."

Cardinal Joseph Bernardin

INTRODUCTION

U.S. health care is rich in resources. Hospitals and sophisticated equipment abound; even many rural areas boast well-equipped facilities. Most physicians and nurses are superbly trained; dedication to patients the norm. Our research output is prodigious. And we fund health care far more generously than any other nation.

Yet despite medical abundance, care is too often meager because of the irrationality of the present health care system. Over 42 million Americans have no health insurance whatsoever, including 33% of Hispanics, 21% of African-Americans and Asians, and 11% of non-Hispanic Whites. Many more—perhaps most of us—are underinsured. The world's richest health care system is unable to assure such basics as prenatal care and immunizations, and we trail most of the developed world on such indicators as infant mortality and life expectancy. Even the well-insured may find care compromised when HMOs deny them expensive medications and therapies. For patients, fear of financial ruin often amplifies the misfortune of illness.

For physicians, the gratifications of healing give way to anger and alienation in a system that treats sick people as commodities and doctors as investors' tools. In private practice we waste countless hours on billing and bureaucracy. For the uninsured, we avoid procedures, consultations, and costly medications. In HMOs we walk a tightrope between thrift and penuriousness, under the surveillance of bureaucrats who prod us to abdicate allegiance to patients, and to avoid the sickest, who may be unprofitable. In academia, we watch as the scholarly traditions of openness and collaboration give way to secrecy and assertions of private ownership of vital ideas; the search for knowledge displaced by a search for intellectual property.

For seven decades, opponents have blocked proposals for national health insurance, touting private sector solutions. Their reforms over the past quarter century have emphasized market mechanisms, endorsed the central role of private insurers, and nourished investor-ownership of care. But vows of greater efficiency, cost control, and consumer responsiveness are unfulfilled; meanwhile the ranks of the uninsured have swelled. HMOs, launched as health care's bright hope, have raised Medicare costs by billions, and fallen to the basement of public esteem. Investor-owned hospital chains, born of the promise of efficiency, have been wracked by scandal; their costs high, their quality low. And drug firms, which have secured the highest profits and lowest taxes of any industry, price drugs out of reach of those who need them most.

Many in today's political climate propose pushing on with the marketization of health care. They would shift more public money to private insurers; funnel Medicare through private managed care; and further fray the threadbare safety net of Medicaid, public hospitals and community clinics. These steps would fortify investors' control of care, squander additional billions on useless paperwork, and raise barriers to care still higher.

It is time to change fundamentally the trajectory of America's health care—to develop a comprehensive National Health Insurance (NHI) program for the United States.

FOUR PRINCIPLES SHAPE OUR VISION OF REFORM

1. Access to comprehensive health care is a human right. It is the responsibility of society, through its government, to assure this right. Coverage should not be tied to employment. Private insurance firms' past record disqualifies them from a central role in managing health care.
2. The right to choose and change one's physician is fundamental to patient autonomy. Patients should be free to seek care from any licensed health care professional.
3. Pursuit of corporate profit and personal fortune have no place in caregiving and they create enormous waste. The U.S. already spends enough to provide comprehensive health care to all Americans with no increase in total costs. However, the vast health care resources now squandered on bureaucracy (mostly due to efforts to divert costs to other payers or onto patients themselves), profits, marketing, and useless or even harmful medical interventions must be shifted to needed care.
4. In a democracy, the public should set overall health policies. Personal medical decisions must be made by patients with their caregivers, not by corporate or government bureaucrats.

We envision a national health insurance program (NHI) that builds upon the strengths of the current Medicare system. Coverage would be extended to all age groups, and expanded to include prescription medications and long term care. Payment mechanisms would be structured to improve efficiency and assure prompt reimbursement, while reducing bureaucracy and cost shifting. Health planning would be enhanced to improve the availability of resources and minimize wasteful duplication. Finally, investor-owned facilities would be phased out. In each section we present a key feature of the proposal followed by the rationale for our approach.

COVERAGE

A single public plan would cover every American for all medically-necessary services including: acute, rehabilitative, long term and home care, mental health, dental services, occupational health care, prescription drugs and supplies, and preventive and public health measures. Boards of expert and community representatives would assess which services are unnecessary or ineffective, and exclude them from coverage. As in the Medicare program, private insurance duplicating the public coverage would be proscribed. Patient co-payments and deductibles would also be eliminated.

Abolishing financial barriers to care is the *sine qua non* of reform. Only a single comprehensive program, covering rich and poor alike, can end disparities based on race, ethnicity, social class and region that compromise the health care of the American people. A single payer program is also key to minimizing the complexity and expense of billing and administration.

Private insurance that duplicates the NHI coverage would undermine the public system in several ways. (1) The market for private coverage would disappear if the public coverage were fully adequate. Hence, private insurers would continually lobby for underfunding of the public system. (2) If the wealthy could turn to private coverage, their support for adequate funding of NHI would also wane. Why pay taxes for coverage they don't use? (3) Private coverage would encourage doctors and hospitals to provide two classes of care. (4) A fractured payment system, preserving the chaos of multiple claims data bases, would subvert quality improvement efforts, e.g. the monitoring of surgical death rates and other patterns of care. (5) Eliminating multiple payers is essential to cost containment. Public administration of insurance funds would save tens of billions of dollars each year. Our private health insurers and HMOs now consume 13.6 percent of premiums for overhead,[1] while both the Medicare program and Canadian NHI have overhead costs below 3 percent. Our multiplicity of insurers forces U.S. hospitals to spend more than twice as much as Canadian hospitals on billing and administration, and U.S. physicians to spend about 10 percent of their gross incomes on excess billing costs.[2] Only a true single payer system would realize large administrative savings. Perpetuating multiple payers—even two—would force hospitals to maintain expensive cost accounting systems to attribute costs and charges to individual patients and payers. In the U.K., market-based reforms that fractured hospital payment have swollen administrative costs.[3, 4]

Co-payments and deductibles endanger the health of the sick poor, decrease use of vital inpatient medical services as much as unnecessary ones, discourage preventive care, and are unwieldy and expensive to administer.[5] Canada has few such charges, yet health costs are lower than in the U.S. and have risen more slowly.

Instead of the confused and often unjust dictates of insurance companies, a greatly expanded program of clinical effectiveness research would guide decisions on covered services and drugs, as well as on capital allocation.

Payment for Hospital Services

The NHI would pay each hospital a monthly lump sum to cover all operating expenses—that is, a global budget. The hospital and the NHI would negotiate the amount of this payment annually, based on past expenditures, previous financial and clinical performance, projected changes in levels of services, wages and input costs, and proposed new and innovative programs. Hospitals would not bill for services covered by the NHI. Hospitals could not use any of their operating budget for expansion, profit, excessive executives' incomes, marketing, or major capital purchases or leases. Major capital expenditures would come from the NHI fund, but would be appropriated separately based upon community needs. Investor-owned hospitals would be converted to not-for-profit status, and their owners compensated for past investment.

Global budgeting would simplify hospital administration and virtually eliminate billing, freeing up substantial resources for enhanced clinical care. Prohibiting the use of operating funds for major capital purchases or profit would eliminate the main financial incentive for both excessive interventions (under fee-for-service payment) and skimping on care (under capitated or DRG systems), since neither inflating revenues nor limiting care could result in institutional gain. Separate and explicit appropriation of capital funds would facilitate rational health care planning. These methods of hospital payment would shift the focus of hospital administration away from lucrative services that enhance the "bottom line" and toward providing optimal clinical services in accord with patients' needs.

Payment for Physicians and Outpatient Care

The NHI would include three payment options for physicians and other practitioners: fee-for-service; salaried positions in institutions receiving global budgets; and salaried positions within group practices or HMOs receiving capitation payments. Investor-owned HMOs and group practices would be converted to not-for-profit status. Only institutions that actually deliver care could receive NHI payments, excluding most current HMOs and some practice management firms that contract for services but don't own or operate any clinical facilities.

    1. Fee-for-service: The NHI and representatives of the fee-for-service practitioners (perhaps state medical societies) would negotiate a simplified, binding fee schedule. Physicians would submit bills to the NHI on

a simple form, or via computer, and would receive extra payment for any bill not paid within 30 days. Physician payment would cover only the work of physicians and their support staff, and would exclude reimbursement for costly office-based capital expenditures for such items as MRI scanners. Physicians accepting payment from the NHI could bill patients directly only for uncovered services (e.g. for cosmetic surgery).

2. Salaries within institutions receiving global budgets: Institutions such as hospitals, health centers, group practices, migrant clinics, and home care agencies could elect to be paid a global budget for the delivery of care as well as for education and prevention programs. The negotiation process and regulations regarding capital payment and profits would be similar to those for inpatient hospital services. Physicians employed in such institutions would be salaried.

3. Salaries within capitated groups: HMOs, group practices, and other institutions could elect to be paid capitation premiums to cover all outpatient, physician, and medical home care. Regulation of payment for capital and profits would be similar to that for hospitals. The capitation premium would not cover inpatient services (except physician care) which would be included in hospital global budgets. Selective enrollment policies would be prohibited and patients would be permitted to disenroll with appropriate notice. HMOs would pay physicians a salary, and financial incentives based on the utilization or expense of care would be prohibited.

The proposed pluralistic approach to delivery would avoid unnecessary disruption of current practice arrangements. All three proposed options would uncouple capital purchases and institutional profits from physician payment and other operating costs, a feature essential for minimizing entrepreneurial incentives, containing costs and facilitating health planning.

The fee-for-service option would greatly reduce physicians' office overhead by simplifying billing. Canada and several European nations have developed successful mechanisms for reconciling the inflationary potential of fee-for-service practice with cost containment. These include: limiting the supply of physicians; monitoring for extreme practice patterns; setting overall limits on regional spending for physicians' services (thus relying on the profession to "police" itself); and even capping individual physicians' reimbursement. These regulatory options are not difficult (and have not required extensive bureaucracy) when all payment comes from a single source. Similar measures might be needed in the U.S. There might also be a concomitant cap on spending for the regulatory apparatus—e.g. expenditures for program administration and reimbursement bureaucracy might be restricted to three percent of total costs.

Global budgets for institutional providers would eliminate billing, while providing a predictable and stable financial support. Such funding could also stimulate the development of community prevention (e.g. school-based smoking prevention programs) whose costs are difficult to attribute (and bill) to individual patients.

Continuity of care would no longer be disrupted as patients' insurance coverage changes due to retirement or job change. Incentives for capitated providers to skimp on care would be minimized since unused operating funds could not be diverted to profits or capital investments.

Long Term Care

The NHI would cover disabled Americans of all ages for all necessary home and nursing home care. Anyone unable to perform activities of daily living (ADLs or IADLs*) would be eligible for services. A local public agency in each community would determine eligibility and coordinate care. Each agency would receive a single budgetary allotment to cover the full array of long term care services in its district. The agency would contract with long term care providers for the full range of needed services, eliminating the perverse incentives in the current system that often pays for expensive institutional care but not the home-based services that most patients would prefer.

NHI would pay long term care facilities and home care agencies a global (lump sum) budget to cover all operating expenses. For-profit nursing homes and home care agencies would be transformed to not-for-profit status. Doctors, nurses, therapists, and other individual long term care providers would be paid on either a fee-for-service or salaried basis.

Since most disabled and elderly people would prefer to remain in their homes, the program would encourage home and community based services. The 7 million unpaid caregivers such as family and friends who currently provide 70% of all long term care would be assisted through training, respite services, and in some cases financial support. Nurses and social workers, as well as an expanded cadre of trained geriatric physicians, would assume leadership of the system.

*Activities of daily living (ADLs) include: bathing, dressing going to the toilet, geting outside, walking, transferring from bed to chair, or eating. Instrumental activities of daily living (IADLs) include: cooking, cleaning, shopping, taking medications, doing laundry, making phone calls, and managing money.

Only a handful of Americans have private coverage for long term care. For the rest, only virtual bankruptcy brings entitlement to public coverage under Medicaid. Universal coverage must be combined with local flexibility to match services to needs, overall budgetary limits, and simplified regulations that minimize bureaucracy and assure that payments benefit patients, not executives or investors.

Our proposal borrows features from successful programs in some Canadian provinces and in Germany. The German program, in particular, demonstrates the fiscal and human advantages of encouraging rather than displacing family caregivers—offering them recompense, training and other supports.

Capital Allocation, Health Planning, and Profit

Funds for the construction or renovation of health facilities and for major equipment purchases would be appropriated from the NHI budget. Regional health planning boards of both experts and community representatives would allocate these capital funds. Major capital projects funded from private donations would require approval by the health planning board if they entailed an increase in future operating expenses.

The NHI would pay owners of for-profit hospitals, nursing homes and clinics a reasonable fixed rate of return on existing equity. Since most new capital investment would be funded by the NHI, it would not be included in calculating return on equity. For-profit HMOs would receive similar compensation for their clinical facilities and for computers and other administrative facilities needed to manage NHI. They would not be reimbursed for loss of business opportunities or for administrative capacity not used by the NHI.

Current capital spending greatly affects future operating costs, as well as the distribution of resources. Effective health planning requires that funds go to high quality, efficient programs in areas of greatest need. Under the existing reimbursement system which combines operating and capital payments, prosperous hospitals can expand and modernize while impoverished ones cannot, regardless of community health needs or quality of care. NHI would replace this implicit mechanism for distributing capital with an explicit one, facilitating allocation based on need and quality. Insulating these crucial decisions from distortion by special interests will require rigorous technology evaluation and needs assessment, as well as active involvement of providers and patients.

The consistently poor performance of investor-owned facilities precludes their participation in NHI. Investor-ownership has been shown to compromise quality of care in hospitals,[6, 7, 8] nursing homes,[9] dialysis facilities,[10] and HMOs;[11] for-profit hospitals are particularly costly.[12, 13, 14, 15, 16, 17, 18, 19] A wide array of investor-owned firms have defrauded Medicare and been implicated in other illegal activities. For-profit providers would be phased out and compensated for past investments in clinical facilities.

Prescription Drugs and Supplies

NHI would pay for all medically necessary prescription drugs and medical supplies, based on a national formulary. An expert panel would establish and regularly update the formulary. The NHI would negotiate drug and equipment prices with manufacturers, based on their costs (excluding marketing or lobbying). Where therapeutically equivalent drugs are available, the formulary would specify use of the lowest cost medication, with exceptions available in case of medical necessity. Suppliers would bill the NHI directly (for the negotiated wholesale price plus a reasonable dispensing fee) for any item in the formulary that is prescribed by a licensed practitioner.

NHI could simultaneously address two pressing needs: (1) providing all Americans with full coverage for necessary drugs and supplies; and (2) containing drug costs. As a monopsony purchaser, the NHI could exert substantial pressure on pharmaceutical companies to lower prices. Similar programs in the U.S. and in other nations (e.g. Australia) have resulted in substantial savings.

Additional reforms are urgently needed to: improve prescribing practices; minimize medication errors; upgrade monitoring of drug safety; curtail pharmaceutical marketing; assure that the fruits of publicly funded drug research are not appropriated for private profit; and ameliorate financial pressures that skew drug development.

Funding

NHI would disburse virtually all payments for health services. Total expenditures would be set at approximately the same proportion of the Gross National Product as in the year preceding the establishment of NHI.

Funds for the NHI could be raised through a variety of mechanisms. In the long run, funding based on an income or other progressive tax is the fairest and most efficient solution, since tax-based funding is the least cumbersome and least expensive mechanism for collecting money.

It is critical that the vast majority of funds flow through the NHI. Such single source (monopsony) payment has been the cornerstone of cost containment and health planning in Canada and other nations with universal coverage. Government expenditures, including payments for public employees' private health coverage and tax subsidies to private insurance, already account for nearly two-thirds of total health spending in the U.S. This figure would rise modestly under NHI, to perhaps 85% of health costs, and the public money now routed through private insurers would instead be used to fund public coverage. The mechanism for raising the additional funds for NHI is a matter of tax policy, largely separate from the organization of health care *per se*. Federal funding would attenuate inequalities among the states in financial and medical resources.

DISCUSSION

The Patient's View

NHI would establish a right to comprehensive health care. Each person would receive an NHI card entitling him or her to care without co-payments or deductibles. The card could be used at any fee-for-service practitioner and at any institution receiving a global budget. HMO members could receive non-emergency care only through their HMO, though they could readily transfer to the non-HMO option.

Thus patients would have a free choice of providers and delivery systems, and the financial threat of illness would be eliminated. Taxes would increase, but would be more than offset by the elimination of insurance premiums and out-of-pocket costs.

The Practitioner's View

Physicians would have a free choice of practice settings. Treatment would no longer be constrained by the patient's insurance status, nor by bureaucratic dictum.

Fee-for-service practitioners would be paid promptly. The entrepreneurial aspects of medicine—the problems as well as the possibilities—would be limited. Physicians could concentrate on medicine; every patient would be fully insured, but physicians could increase their incomes only by working harder. Billing would involve imprinting the patient's NHI card onto a slip, checking a box indicating the complexity of the encounter, and sending the slip (or electronic equivalent) to the physician payment board. This simplification of billing would save each practitioner thousands of dollars annually in office expense.

Bureaucratic interference in clinical decision making would sharply diminish. Costs would be contained by controlling overall spending and limiting entrepreneurial incentives, obviating the need for the kind of detailed administrative oversight characteristic of current practice.

Salaried practitioners would be insulated from the financial consequences of clinical decisions. Since savings on patient care could no longer be used for institutional expansion or profits, pressure to skimp on care would be minimized.

The Effect on Other Health Workers

Nurses and other personnel would enjoy a more humane and efficient clinical milieu. The burdens of paperwork associated with billing would be lightened. The jobs of many administrative and insurance employees would disappear, necessitating a major effort at job placement and retraining. Many of these displaced workers might be deployed in expanded programs of public health, health promotion and education, home care, and as support personnel to free up nurses for clinical tasks.

The Effect on Hospitals

Hospitals' revenues would become stable and predictable. More than half of the current hospital bureaucracy would be eliminated, and the remaining administrators could focus on facilitating clinical care and planning for future health needs.

The capital budget requests of hospitals would be weighed against other priorities for health care investment. Hospitals would neither grow because they were profitable nor fail because of unpaid bills—though regional health planning would undoubtedly mandate that some expand and others close or be put to other uses. Responsiveness to community needs, quality of care, efficiency and innovation would replace financial performance as the "bottom line." Proprietary hospitals would be converted to not-for-profit status.

The Effect on the Insurance/HMO Industry

The insurance/HMO industry would have virtually no role in health care financing, since public insurance administration is more efficient, and single source payment is the key to both equal access and cost control. Indeed, most of the extra funds needed to finance the expansion of care would come from eliminating insurance company overhead and profits, and abolishing the billing apparatus necessary to apportion costs among the various plans.

The Effect on Corporate America

Firms now providing generous employee health benefits would probably realize savings because their tax contribution to NHI would likely be less than current health insurance costs. Since most firms competing on international markets would save money, the competitiveness of U.S. products would be enhanced. Tax-based NHI funding might, however increase costs for companies not now providing health benefits.

Health Benefits and Financial Costs

Ample evidence indicates that removing financial barriers encourages timely care and improves health.[20]

Independent estimates by several government agencies and private sector experts indicate that NHI could cover all of the uninsured and eliminate co-payments and deductibles for the insured, without increasing total health care costs.[21, 22, 23, 24, 25] Savings on administration and billing (which would drop from the current 25% of total health spending to under 15%) would approximately offset the costs of expanded services. However, the expansion of long term care (under any system) would increase costs. Experience in Canada suggests that the increased demand for acute care would be modest (after an initial surge),[26, 27] and improvements in health planning and cost containment made possible by single source payment would slow health care cost escalation. Vigilance would be needed to stem the regrowth of costly and intrusive bureaucracy.

Unsolved Problems

This brief proposal leaves many vexing problems unsolved. Careful planning will be needed to ease dislocations during the implementation of the program. The encouragement of prevention and healthy life styles, and improvements in occupational and environmental health will not automatically follow from the institution of NHI. Similarly, the abolition of racial, linguistic, geographic and other non-financial barriers to access will require continuing efforts. The need for quality improvement will remain urgent. High medical school tuitions that discourage low income applicants, the underrepresentation of minorities, the role of foreign medical graduates, and other problems in medical education will remain. Some patients will still seek inappropriate care, and some physicians will still succumb to the temptation to increase their incomes by encouraging unneeded services. Assuring adequate research funding, engendering collegiality and excellence in academia, and minimizing the commercial skew of current research priorities will remain challenging. Though NHI will not eliminate these problems, it will establish a framework for addressing many of them.

ALTERNATIVES TO NHI

President Bush and others have proposed a variety of health reforms aimed at slowing cost growth, shoring up Medicare, expanding coverage, and improving efficiency. These proposals share several common themes.

1. "Defined contribution schemes" and other mechanisms to increase patients' price sensitivity

Some prominent economists and corporate leaders favor limiting employers' premium contributions to a fixed amount, pressuring employees to choose lower-cost insurance options. Many cite the Federal Employees Health Benefit Program (FEHBP) as a model for such reform.

Unfortunately, costs in the FEHBP have risen as rapidly as in Medicare or for private employers, providing little evidence that the defined contribution approach contains costs. Moreover, this approach assures a multi-tiered insurance system, with lower-income workers forced into skimpier plans. In the long run, such programs are more likely to shift costs from firms to employees than to slow overall cost growth.

2. Tax subsidies and vouchers for coverage for the uninsured

President Bush, as well as some Democrats, would offer tax credits to low income families who purchase private coverage.

The $2000 per family subsidy ($1000 per single person) that the President has proposed falls far short of the cost of adequate insurance; in Massachusetts, HMO family premiums average about $6000 annually. Hence, few of the uninsured could afford adequate coverage even with the subsidy. This problem would increase over time; premiums would surely rise more rapidly than subsidies. Most of the tax credits would subsidize premium payments for people who already have coverage, since employers would be tempted to drop insurance for employees eligible for subsidies. As a result, large outlays for tax subsidies would buy little new coverage; $13 billion annually would cover only 4 million (less than 10%) of the uninsured.[28]

Moreover, tax credits would amplify administrative inefficiency. If the IRS paid the year's subsidy when tax returns were filed (i.e. the following April), it would come too late to provide the cash flow that low income families need to purchase coverage. Paying the credit with each paycheck would create an administrative nightmare; it would require ongoing monitoring of household income, qualification for the subsidy, etc.

In addition, the new coverage would be purchased from private insurers whose average overhead/profits consumes 13.6% of premiums—six times that of Medicare. Not surprisingly, the health insurance industry supports the tax credit approach; additional tax dollars would end up in their coffers, with little public oversight.

3. Expansion of Medicaid, CHIP, and other public programs

Some Democrats favor expanding Medicaid eligibility by raising income limits for families, or by including poor, childless adults. Recently, the National Governors' Association (NGA) proposed that states be allowed to buy stripped-down HMO coverage for Medicaid recipients, and use the savings to expand coverage.

Several problems bedevil these strategies. First, Medicaid already offers second-class coverage. Programs like Medicaid that segregate the poor virtually assure poor care, and are more vulnerable to funding cuts than public programs that also serve affluent constituencies. In most states, Medicaid payment rates are low and many doctors resist caring for Medicaid patients. As a result, access to care for Medicaid enrollees is often little better than for the uninsured.[29, 30] Further cuts to benefits, as the NGA suggests, would leave Medicaid recipients with coverage in name only.

Second, even large Medicaid expansions in the past have failed to keep pace with the erosion of private coverage. Between 1987 and 1993, Medicaid enrollment grew from 20.2 million to 31.7 million, yet the number of uninsured rose by 8.7 million.[31] Only the unprecedented economic boom of the late 1990s interrupted this trend. An economic downturn would quickly deplete states' tax revenues, reducing funds for Medicaid at the same time as rising unemployment would deprive many of private coverage.

Turning Medicaid dollars over to private HMOs assures that scarce funds will be diverted to overhead and profit, and places vulnerable patients at risk. In the first Medicaid HMO experiment in California a quarter of a century ago private plans routinely exploited poor patients, an experience repeated in Florida, Tennessee and other states. Past promises (e.g. in Oregon and Tennessee) that savings from Medicaid coverage cuts would lead to universal coverage have proven empty.

Finally, the complexity of enrollment procedures, the need for repeated eligibility determination, and the stigma attached to Medicaid and similar programs for the poor assure that many of those who are eligible will not be enrolled.

While few can argue with proposals to cover more of the poor and near-poor, Medicaid expansion without systemwide reform is a stopgap measure unlikely to stem future increases in the number of uninsured. It does not lead to universal coverage.

4. The Medicare HMO program and Medicare voucher schemes

Under Medicare's HMO program, private HMOs have already enrolled millions of seniors. Medicare has paid these plans a set fee—95% of the average cost of a Medicare fee-for-service enrollee in the region—for each enrollee. Several states have also pushed Medicaid recipients into privately-run HMOs. Many Republicans and a few Democrats hope to expand Medicare's use of private insurers by offering seniors a voucher to purchase private coverage in lieu of traditional Medicare.

These strategies assume that private plans are more efficient than Medicare; that seniors can make informed choices among health plan options; and that private insurers' risk avoidance can be thwarted. All three assumptions are ill-founded.

Medicare is more efficient than commercial insurers; costs per beneficiary have risen more slowly and overhead is far lower.

An AARP survey of seniors found that few had adequate knowledge to make informed choices among plans.[32]

Despite regulations prohibiting risk selection in the current Medicare HMO program, plans have successfully recruited healthier than average seniors. Hence HMOs have collected high premiums for patients who would have cost Medicare little had they remained in fee-for-service Medicare. Moreover, HMOs have dumped more than a million seniors in counties where profits are low, while continuing to enroll Medicare patients in profitable areas. As a result, HMOs have increased Medicare costs by $2 billion to $3 billion each year, and disrupted the continuity of care for many patients.

A voucher (so-called "premium support") program for Medicare would also push low income seniors into skimpy plans—similar to the "defined contribution" approach to employee coverage discussed above. Moreover,

Congress is unlikely to increase the value of the voucher to keep pace with the rising costs of private plans. Over time, seniors' out-of-pocket costs for coverage would likely rise.

CONCLUSION

Health care reform is again near the top of the political agenda. Health care costs have turned sharply upward. The number of Americans without insurance or with inadequate coverage rose even in the boom years of the 1990s. Medicare and Medicaid are threatened by ill-conceived reform schemes. And middle class voters are fed up with the abuses of managed care.

Incremental changes cannot solve these problems; further reliance on market-based strategies will exacerbate them. What needs to be changed is the system itself.

National Health Insurance is an essential safeguard for our patients; its advocacy is an ethical responsibility of our profession.

Endnotes

1. http://www.hcfa.gov/stats/nhe-oact/tables/t3.htm
2. S. Woolhandler and D. U. Himmelstein, "The Deteriorating Administrative Efficiency of U.S. Health Care," *New England Journal of Medicine* 324(1991):1253–58.
3. R. Robinson and J. Le Grand, *Evaluating the NHS Reforms* (New Brunswick, N.J.: Rutgers University, 1994).
4. J. Dickinson, "De-Engineering the NHS," *BMJ* 312(1996):1617.
5. M. E. Rasell, "Cost Sharing in Health Insurance—A Reexamination," *New England Journal of Medicine* 332(1995):1164–8.
6. A. J. Hartz, H. Krakauer, and E. M. Kuhn, et al. "Hospital Characteristics and Mortality," *New England Journal of Medicine* 321(1989):1720–5.
7. C. Kovner and P. Gergen, "Nurse Staffing Levels and Adverse Events Following Surgery in U.S. Hospitals," Image: *Journal of Nursing Scholarship* 30(1998): 315–21.
8. D. H. Taylor, D. J. Whellan, and F. A. Sloan, "Effects of Admission to a Teaching Hospital on the Costs and Quality of Care for Medicare Beneficiaries," *New England Journal of Medicine* 340(1999):293–9.
9. C. Harrington, S. Woolhandler, J. Mullan, H. Carrillo, and D.U. Himmelstein, "Does Investor-Ownership of Nursing Homes Compromise the Quality of Care?" *American Journal of Public Health* (in press).
10. P. P. Garg, K. D. Frick, M. Diener-West, and N. R. Powe, "Effect of the Ownership Status of Dialysis Facilities on Patients' Survival and Referral for Transplantation," *New England Journal of Medicine* 341(1999):1653–60.
11. D. U. Himmelstein, S. Woolhandler, I. Hellander, and S. M. Wolfe, "Quality of Care in Investor-Owned vs. Not-For-Profit Health Maintenance Organizations," *Journal of the American Medical Association* 1999.

12. R. V. Pattison and H. M. Katz, "Investor-Owned and Not-For-Profit Hospitals: A Comparison Based on California Data," *New England Journal of Medicine* 309(1983):347–53.

13. J. M. Watt, R. A. Derzon, S. C. Ren, C. J. Schramm, J. S. Hahn, and G. D. Pillari, "The Comparative Economic Performance of Investor-Owned Chain and Not-For-Profit Hospitals," *New England Journal of Medicine* 314(1986):89–96.

14. B. H. Gray and W. J. McNerney, "For-Profit Enterprise in Health Care: The Institute of Medicine Study," *New England Journal of Medicine* 314(1986): 1523–8.

15. B. H. Gray, ed. *For-Profit Enterprise in Health Care*, (Washington, D.C.: National Academy Press, 1986).

16. S. Woolhandler and D. U. Himmelstein, "Costs of Care and Administration at For-profit and Other Hospitals in the United States," *New England Journal of Medicine* 336(1997):769–74.

17. D. H. Taylor , D. J. Whellan, and F. A. Sloan, "Effects of Admission to a Teaching Hospital on the Costs and Quality of Care for Medicare Beneficiaries," *New England Journal of Medicine* 340(1999):293–9.

18. L. Chan, T. D. Koepsell, and R. A. Deyo, et al., "The Effect of Medicare's Payment System for Rehabilitation Hospitals on Length of Stay, Charges and Total Payments," *New England Journal of Medicine* 337(1997):978–85.

19. E. M. Silverman, J. S. Skinner, and E. S. Fisher, "The Association Between For-Profit Hospital Ownership and Increased Medicare Spending," *New England Journal of Medicine* 1999.

20. J. S. Weissman and A. M. Epstein, "The Insurance Gap: Does it Make a Difference?" *Ann Rev Public Health* 14(1993):243–70.

21. U.S. Government Accounting Office. "Canadian Health Insurance: Lessons for the United States," (Washington, D.C.: U.S. Government Accounting Office, 1991) GAO/HRD-91-90.

22. Congressional Budget Office, *Single-payer and All-Payer Health Insurance Systems Using Medicare's Payment Rates.* (Washington, D.C.: Congressional Budget Office, April, 1993).

23. J. F. Sheils and R. A. Haught, *Analysis of the Costs and Impact of Universal Health Care Models for the State of Maryland: The Single-Payer and Multi-Payer Models.* (Fairfax, VA: The Lewin Group, 2000).

24. R. Brand, D. Ford, A. Sager, and D. Socolar, *Universal Comprehensive Coverage: a Report to the Massachusetts Medical Society.* (Waltham, Mass.: The Massachusetts Medical Society, 1998.)

25. K. Grumbach, T. Bodenheimer, S. Woolhandler, and D. U. Himmelstein, "Liberal Benefits Conservative Spending: the Physicians for a National Health Program Proposal," *Journal of the American Medical Association* 265(1991):2549–2554.

26. M. LeClair, "The Canadian Health Care System," in S. Andreopoulos, ed., *National Health Insurance: Can We Learn from Canada.* (New York: John Wiley, 1975), pp. 11–92.

27. R. G. Evans, "Beyond the Medical Marketplace: Expenditure, Utilization and Pricing of Insured Health Care in Canada," S. Andreopoulos, ed., *National Health Insurance: Can We Learn from Canada.* New York: John Wiley, (1975), pp. 129–78.

28. J. Gruber and L. Levitt, "Tax Subsidies for Health Insurance: Costs and Benefits," *Health Affairs* 19(1) (2000):72–85.

29. J. Z. Ayanian, B. A. Kohler, T. Abe, and A. M. Epstein, "The Relation Between Health Insurance Coverage and Clinical Outcomes Among Women with Breast Cancer," *New England Journal of Medicine* 329(1993):326–331.

30. "The Medicaid Access Study Group. Access of Medicaid Recipients to Outpatient Care," *New England Journal of Medicine* 330(1994):1426–30.

31. U.S. Census Bureau, Health Insurance Historical Table 1. Available from http://www.census.gov/hhes/hlthins/historic/hihistt1.html.

32. J. H. Hibbard, J. J. Jewett, S. Engelmann, and M.Tusler, "Can Medicare Beneficiaries Make Informed Choices," *Health Affairs* 17(6) (1998):181–93.

NO

Health Care Quality: Would It Survive a Single-Payer System?

Merrill Matthews, Jr., Ph.D., and Robert J. Cihak, M.D.

EXECUTIVE SUMMARY

In an effort to provide quality health care for everyone, many states and some in the federal government have proposed adopting a single-payer health care system. But before taking that step, we need to ask what quality health care consists of, whether a single-payer system achieves that goal and whether adopting such a system in any one state or the whole country would actually ensure quality health care for everyone, as single-payer proponents claim.

This study discusses the definition of health care quality and looks at the impact single-payer systems have on health care access, affordability, new technology, the role of doctors and patient satisfaction. The study examines rationing in single-payer systems, as the government makes the larger decisions about funding levels, and leaves to doctors and hospitals the tougher individual decisions about whose care to ration. These are usually the marginal cases: the very young, the very old and the very sick.

The study concludes that if Washington state wants to do something about expanding health insurance coverage, while at the same time expanding citizens' choice and control over their own care, there are free-market options that will increase the number of insured while maintaining the high quality of health care in our state. If instead state policymakers move toward a single-payer system that tries to impose universal coverage, they will find that Washington citizens will be left with neither care nor quality.

INTRODUCTION

What do we mean by the word "quality"? Is quality something we can measure objectively, or is it subjective and largely dependent on the eye of the beholder? How do we know when we have a quality product? We often seem to know when we don't have one!

And is quality an absolute term, or is it relative? For example, some very expensive cars have almost no mechanical problems, but not many people can afford them. Would a car that costs, say, half as much with a very good maintenance record—though not as good as the aforementioned luxury cars—still be considered a quality product?

It is hard to answer those questions. When it comes to health care, it is even more difficult to identify quality. Dictionaries define quality as a high grade or level of excellence. For individuals, quality health care usually means a good outcome, conveniently obtained at a reasonable price. Of course, if insurance is covering most or all of the cost of the bill, a patient may not care about the "reasonable price" element, only the outcome and convenience.

In a normal market, people make quality tradeoffs, sometimes substituting less quality for lower costs or greater convenience. That is what is known as the quest for "value." However, when people are insulated from the cost of health care because the government, insurance company or an employer is paying the bill, the role of value declines. Patients want quality at any price—because someone else is paying that price. Ironically, when someone else is paying the bill, the insistence upon quality declines because patients—indeed, any type of consumer—are willing to tolerate bad outcomes and poorer service when they are free.

WHAT IS QUALITY HEALTH CARE?

There has been a lot of attention lately devoted to the issue of quality in the health care system. Most of this interest is a result of the widespread growth of managed care and concerns that it has harmed health care quality. But how does one determine what quality in health care really means? Is it an issue of access? Or is it related to "outcomes"? Does it mean the best care available? Or do convenience and cost play a role?

The Agency for Healthcare Research and Quality (AHRQ), an agency of the federal Department of Health and Human Services, says, "Quality health care means doing the right thing, at the right time, in the right way, for the right person—and having the best possible result." While this goal is certainly desirable, is it really attainable, and would we know if we had attained it? Good doctors often disagree on the best course of therapy. And all health care providers, being human, make mistakes. Considering the training, integrity and dedication of most health care professionals, it is doubtless true that many U.S. patients receive quality care, but can we extrapolate to say that the U.S., or any country for that matter, has a quality health care system?

The Institute of Medicine (IOM) has developed a less challenging definition of quality than the AHRQ: "Quality of care is the degree to which health services for individuals and populations increase the likelihood of desired health outcomes and are consistent with the current professional knowledge."

After accepting the IOM's definition, the bipartisan National Coalition on Health Care elaborated by saying, "Good quality means providing patients with appropriate services in a technically competent manner, with good communication, shared decision making, and cultural sensitivity."

However, quality in medicine is quite different from quality in a manufacturing process. Quality for patients "does not reside in precise abstract numbers but, rather, in vague and temperamental perceptions that reside within" the patients' minds.

Thus it appears that several factors must be considered before we can say we have a quality health care system. Some of those factors are objective, while others are subjective; some can be measured, some cannot. We attempt to identify those factors below and explain why they either are or should be part of any equation trying to evaluate health care quality.

Access

Many people believe that a health care system that does not provide equal access to everyone cannot be said to be a quality system. Thus proponents of a single-payer system decry that 44 million uninsured Americans "have no health care" and point to countries like Canada as the model for reform. In addition, they often claim that minorities do not have the same access to care as whites.

While there is some reason to question whether logically there is a connection between access and quality, it has nevertheless become part of the mantra that a quality health care system must, at least at some level, provide universal access.

Of course, saying everyone has access to health care is a lot easier than providing that care to anyone who needs it—just as the former Soviet Union had a constitution that promised its people many of the freedoms and benefits (including universal health care) that Americans enjoy, but never fulfilled those promises.

Virtually no country, whether under a single-payer system or not, provides all the care everyone could conceivably need, want or desire—unless individuals are willing to pay for it personally. In some countries and systems, buying health care privately is outright illegal, as in Canada, or severely restricted by regulators, such as in the American Medicare system. In a single-payer system, health care must compete with other claims on government funds, such as education, welfare and national security. That is, the government—not the patient in consultation with a doctor—must make the tradeoffs between cost and care.

In democratically elected governments, politicians try to please as many people as possible—a requirement in order to be elected to office. With regard to health care that means providing what the majority of people need given the limited funds available. Because most people are healthy at any given time, most people in an industrialized country with a single-payer system get relatively good primary care most of the time. They represent a lot of votes and require the least amount of medical care. However, medical care for the very young, the very old and the very sick often requires specialty and very expensive care. Because these people are much fewer in number as well as more expensive, their care is often rationed.

Any attempt to make access part of the quality equation must recognize that not everyone can get everything they want. A better standard, as indicated by the definitions cited above, is whether all patients have the opportunity to get "appropriate" care, not necessarily the best or most expensive care.

Defining "appropriate" care is also very difficult, as each individual or family makes tradeoffs with respect to time, convenience and expense. For example, many Americans are increasingly turning to "alternative care"—therapies often questioned or rejected by the traditional medical community. Can we say a patient is getting appropriate care if the outcome is good but the medical community rejects it? Or consider immunizations. Many parents have decided that some immunizations pose a threat to their children's health, and therefore refuse to have their children receive those immunizations. Yet many measures of health care systems use immunizations as one criterion. Should everyone be forced to receive "appropriate" care even if they don't want the care prescribed by the system?

Affordability

Critics of the U.S. health care system contend that the biggest barrier to access is cost. What good is it, they ask, to have the best health care quality available if many people are unable to afford it?

What does "affordable" mean? To an economist, "affordable" implies that an individual or family has resources that can be allocated to health care and chooses to allocate them that way. "Unaffordable" means that health insurance is not worth the expense compared to other things the individual or family wants or needs.

There is no question that patients in the U.S. system often have problems when it comes to affordability. About 84 percent of Americans have health insurance, which usually covers most or all of the cost of care. However, the employer-based health insurance system—which accounts for about 90 percent of those under age 65 with private health insurance—is in transition. Although it worked pretty well for the first 20 or 30 years after World War II, the demographics of the workforce are evolving. Workers change jobs frequently and often lose their health insurance in the process. Those who let their employer-based policies lapse and develop a medical condition during job transition may find themselves unable to pay the resulting bills or unable to get new coverage. So while health insurance has made health care affordable for millions of Americans, the system has its problems.

One of those problems is that some 44 million Americans are uninsured. For many of them, only basic or routine care is affordable, if they can afford even that. While it is true that public hospitals—i.e., those funded in part with tax dollars to provide care for the poor and indigent—are maintained to handle most of these cases, some studies indicate that indigent patients do not get as much care as paying patients. Getting care to those who need it at a reasonable price remains a formidable hurdle.

However, a "free" health care system that relies on very high taxes to fund it is not necessarily affordable—or any better. The benefit that comes from being able to buy a prescription drug in Canada at half the U.S. cost may be completely offset if additional taxes force people to pay twice as much for food and clothing.

Health care costs, like taxes, should be transparent. If people are paying higher taxes in order to get "free" care, they should know just how much such taxes cost them.

Strong Doctor-Patient Relationship

Historically, the doctor-patient relationship has been at the heart of the American health care system. Of course, the term "system" might be considered a misnomer, since American health care has had little or no formal organization or central planning and has been characterized by individuals (patients, insurers, doctors and other health care providers) making informed decisions based upon their own training, needs and values. On the other hand, if we think of a "system" as "a combination of related elements organized into a complex whole," then the complex relationships of physicians who typically have a personal network of hundreds of consulting physicians and other resources does approach a system.

However, that system has begun to disappear over the past decade as employers, insurers, managed care organizations (primarily HMOs, but to some extent Preferred Provider Organizations, or PPOs) and the federal and state governments have inserted themselves in between the doctor and patient, often overriding the doctor's orders or denying the patient's wishes. Such constraints have led to tremendous dissatisfaction, and it is doubtful that American doctors and other health care providers would have tolerated such control as recently as 10 or 20 years ago.

Ironically, the attempt to make the medical system more "efficient" resulted in much less efficiency, in terms of applying the most appropriate course of action for a given patient. Rather than hundreds of available consultants, doctors were limited to the few available within a managed care organization's (MCO) corporate structure. Accessing these resources often requires additional time and clerical involvement. Accessing resources outside the MCO structure is even more difficult.

Different patients want different things from a doctor. For some, technical competence and graduating from one of the top medical schools makes little difference. They want a doctor to spend some time, be polite and seem interested in the ailment. These patients may enjoy it when a doctor takes time to inquire about the family or job. For them quality health care has a warm, personal side.

Others want doctors to be quick, efficient and professional. They view the doctor as an analyst, not a friend. For them, precision, not time spent, is the key to quality care.

Patient response to these two opposite approaches is very subjective, largely depending on the personality and expectations of the patient. While a strong doctor-patient relationship is fundamental to any analysis of health care quality, measuring that relationship is almost impossible.

Patient Choice

Years ago, most insured patients had the option of virtually any therapy available. However, there were not that many options. They had choice, but not many choices.

Today, things are very different. There are many types of health insurance available from a wide range of companies, with varying deductibles, copayments and restrictions. For patients, there are a growing number of options for treating medical conditions.

However, as options have grown, patients' ability to choose from those options has declined. They have many choices, but little choice—and patients don't like it. They are increasingly expressing their dissatisfaction with a system that limits their insurance and treatment options, and that dissatisfaction translates into expressions that the quality of care has declined. Again, the attempt to make the medical system more "efficient" has significantly decreased efficient presentation of options to patients and physicians.

While it may be unrealistic to think patients should be able to get any medical service any time they want it, a quality health care system will necessarily provide people with a wide range of choices—in health insurance providers and effective medical care.

Physicians Are Free to Make Decisions

In the past, doctors gave the orders and hospitals, insurers or patients complied. If a doctor prescribed a certain drug, the pharmacist filled the prescription and the insurer paid for it (assuming there was a prescription drug benefit in the policy).

Today, doctors often find their recommendations denied or overridden by a non-physician working for an HMO. Or doctors are not able to prescribe the drug they want because it is not on the HMO's formulary.

In addition, there have been certain institutional impediments (e.g., gag rules, constraints because of pressure to see more patients, limits on doctors' choices, etc.) that keep doctors from having a close relationship with their patients. Doctors who feel their hands are tied with regard to treatment decisions cannot talk openly with their patients about all options available. Such limitations have increasingly frustrated doctors, who believe their training and their examination of the patients qualifies them to make decisions without having some "bean counter" override them.

That sentiment has found a growing acceptance in the policy community and among politicians, who seek to pass legislation that would limit HMO restrictions and return decision-making freedom to doctors. Although the managed care industry has been reluctant to give doctors complete freedom to treat and prescribe—fearing utilization, and therefore costs, would begin to rise significantly—many state and federal politicians, along with the medical community, are pressing for more physician autonomy to treat patients as they see fit.

Access to New Therapies and Technology

New therapies and technology are emerging almost daily. Some are very expensive, and may be prohibitively costly for some uninsured or low-income patients. A quality health care system must be able to provide access to most or all of these new treatment options on a relatively timely basis. That does not necessarily mean that insurers should be required to cover experimental and investigational care, since there is no guarantee that such care is effective. But it does mean that health care providers should be able to access new drugs and medical devices quickly when they promise to benefit patients.

Outcomes

Many health policy experts believe that outcomes—that is, analyzing the type of care delivered for certain medical procedures and their results—is the most objective way to evaluate health care quality, primarily because it is quantifiable. For example, the Institute of Medicine's National Roundtable on Health Care Quality says:

> The quality of health care can be precisely defined. In many instances, quality measures have the same degree of accuracy as the majority of measures used in clinical medicine to make vital decisions about patient care. These quality measures have been used in a wide array of scientifically valid studies to access the nature and magnitude of specific quality measures.

This belief that health care outcomes indicate health care quality has led to a number of different measuring systems, often promoted by managed care organizations. The idea behind outcomes is to provide employers with a guide to show which providers deliver the "best" care, defined as those providers whose practices most closely follow the outcomes guidelines. It also provides MCOs with a justification for disenrolling physicians who vary from the guidelines.

While there is probably some useful information to be gained from analyzing outcomes, it may not be as objective as proponents contend. For example, someone has to determine what treatments to include and exclude and which results are appropriate. Although it is reasonable to include outcomes as a component of health care quality, the assertion that it can be objective and "precisely defined" is too strong.

Patient Satisfaction

Most health care experts recognize that patient satisfaction—or they may use the broader concept of consumer satisfaction—plays an important role in health care quality. To paraphrase an old saying that originally referred to mothers: "If the patients ain't happy, ain't nobody happy."

As a result, people are frequently surveyed on what they think about the health care system. Were they able to get care reasonably quickly? Did they receive good care? Are they satisfied with the system? Such surveys give health policy experts an idea of how the system is meeting people's needs and wants. And while such surveys are very important, it should be understood that they are very subjective, and can be influenced or tainted by the wording of the questions and by positive or negative media exposure.

HOW DOES A SINGLE-PAYER SYSTEM AFFECT HEALTH CARE QUALITY?

Having identified the components of a quality health care system, we can ask whether single-payer countries like Canada—often cited as the model for U.S. reform—France, Germany and England live up to these standards.

Access

Canada is one of the most oft cited examples of a single-payer system that provides universal coverage AND quality care—so we will be referring to it frequently. However, even a cursory examination of Canada's health care system reveals numerous problems, raising questions about whether Canadians have either access or quality care.

One of the most touted benefits of a single-payer system is that it is more efficient than the U.S. system. People have a family physician who they can see regularly, rather than postponing needed care until they are forced to go to the emergency room—which is much more expensive.

However, getting to see a family physician under a single-payer system may not be as easy as proponents suggest. A recent flu epidemic in Toronto expanded the waiting times to see a family physician to five to six weeks—so far in the future that most patients either would have recovered from their illness and no longer need to see a doctor or would have become critically ill and gone to an emergency room.

Unfortunately, patients who need to see a doctor immediately often do not even have the emergency room option. In December of 1999 and in January of 2000, Toronto emergency rooms were so full that they were turning away patients—regardless of how sick they were. According to a story in the *Toronto Star*, 24 of 25 emergency rooms were closed on Monday, December 27, 1999. By the following Wednesday, "21 of 25 emergency wards were refusing to accept any new patients, no matter how ill or critically injured they might have been, or were accepting only the most serious cases." The story continues, "That meant that Toronto Ambulance's paramedics were working the phones like veteran travel agents, trying to find emergency room spots for their patients on a day when the demand was close to its peak." Only three weeks later, an 18-year-old boy, Joshua Fleuelling, died of asthma because the emergency rooms were on "critical care bypass" and could not accept him.

Or consider this example: One night Michael Madden, a young American living in Sweden, suffered bouts of extreme abdominal pain. When the bouts persisted and he noticed blood in his urine, he became quite concerned and went to an emergency room at the local hospital early the next morning. The staff gave him a wooden tab marked with the number 67, indicating his place in the waiting line. He took a seat in a big waiting room filled with patients in need of immediate care, some with rags over bloody wounds. Even though Madden was having extreme pain, "a lot were worse off than I was," he later reflected. After he had waited about half an hour, a nurse called out for "No. 3." He still had 64 ahead of him. He wanted the hospital to take care of the worst cases first. At 6:00 in the evening, another staff person came out and told those still waiting to "come in tomorrow, you'll keep your number in line." That night, after a final bout of excruciating pain, the problem went away. He felt great in the morning and didn't bother to go back to the hospital. After the fact, a medical friend concluded that he had passed a kidney stone.

In 2000 *The New York Times* reported problems all across Canada. According to the story: "Further west, in Winnipeg, 'hallway medicine' has become so routine that hallway stretcher locations have permanent numbers. Patients recuperate more slowly in the drafty, noisy hallways, doctors report."

At Vancouver General Hospital, "Maureen Whyte, a hospital vice president, estimates that 20 percent of heart attack patients who should have treatment within 15 minutes now wait an hour or more."

Finally, "Last summer, as waiting lists for chemotherapy treatments for breast and prostate cancer stretched to four months, Montreal doctors started to send patients 45 minutes down the highway to Champlain Valley Physicians' Hospital in Plattsburgh, New York."

As *The New York Times* points out, "Canada has moved informally to a two-tier, public-private system. Although private practice is limited to dentists and veterinarians, 90 percent of Canadians live within 100 miles of the United States, and many people are crossing the border for private care."

But it gets worse. Canadians often wait weeks and even months to see a specialist. According to the Vancouver-based Fraser Institute's annual survey of waiting times in Canada:

> The average total waiting time between referral from a general practitioner and treatment rose from 13.3 weeks in 1998 to 14 weeks in 1999.

Waiting times between specialist consultation and treatment (which excludes
the time between seeing a general practitioner and getting in to see a
specialist) increased from 7.3 weeks in 1998 to 8.4 weeks in 1999.

Waiting times for diagnostic tests also experienced some increases. For
example, the median wait for a CT scan across Canada was five weeks
in 1999, a 6.4 percent increase over 1998.

Is this really the model the U.S. should follow for providing access to care?
The irony is that while single-payer proponents point to Canada as a model
health care system, the only reason the system doesn't implode is the U.S.
health care system provides Canada with a safety valve—access to care
Canadians cannot get in Canada.

As noted above, the former Soviet government required universal medical
care in its constitution. Yet that does not mean people are treated equally.
Different classes of people get different levels of care. In the Soviet system, the
"first duty of medical staff members is to please their supervising agency, which
oversees plan fulfillment for the hospital or clinic. Patients' needs are a distant
second."

The point is that there is a huge difference between saying patients have
access to health care and actually making it available. The true standard for
access should not be "Some of the people getting care some of the time," but
"All of the people having an opportunity to get the care they need when they
need it." Though the U.S. health care system struggles to live up to this goal,
virtually none of the existing single-payer systems come anywhere close.

Affordability

Proponents of a single-payer system contend that when the government
controls the cost of health care, the profit motive is removed, which means the
same money can be spread over more people who can get care in a timely fashion, which saves even more money as well as lives. Thus, for them, there are no
tradeoffs in moving to a government-run health care system, because everyone
benefits.

Government-run systems spend less as a percentage of GDP than the U.S.
The presumption is that if the country is spending less of its GDP on health care,
the actual cost of care must be less. However, it may be that single-payer countries are not getting as much care or as high a quality of care. The real question
is not whether a country spends more or less on health care; the question is
whether patients get value for the dollars spent. And the fact is most do not.

That is because when most people enter the health care system, someone
else—the government, an employer or an insurer—is picking up most or all of
the bill. As a result, people are insulated from the cost of care and therefore
tend to overconsume—driving health care spending much higher than it would
be if patients were cost-conscious consumers. The irony here is that the process

that makes health care affordable for the vast majority of people—a third party paying the bill—is the primary factor behind making the health care system unaffordable. In their effort to contain the cost escalation, single-payer systems and, in the U.S., employers and insurers, have stepped in to control health care utilization from the top down. How do they do it? Well, for government-run systems, administrators use spending limits and price controls.

When government provides or finances health care services, it creates a tension that may undermine the availability and quality of care. The reason is that health care is forced to compete with other important claims on government funds such as education, the criminal justice system and social services. As a result, there is never enough money to fund any program as much as proponents would like. Moreover, the decision on which programs get funded and by how much is often determined more by which group has the most political power rather than a program's true needs and merits.

Case Study: Canada's Budget Debate

Canada's health care system has reached a crisis over funding. In March of 2000, Canadian Health Minister Allan Rock told the House of Commons: "There are people who are waiting too long, waiting hours in the emergency ward, waiting months for referral to a specialist, waiting a year for a long-term bed, waiting what seems to be an eternity for someone to answer the call button in an understaffed hospital."

In this case, however, the crisis was not instigated by budget deficits, but by a budget surplus. Some Members of Parliament wanted to pass an income tax cut of at least 20 percent, which others opposed, saying that the proposed budget only offered two cents in health care funding for every dollar in tax cuts.

Ralph Klein, premier of Alberta, who wants to let for-profit clinics perform some of the procedures currently provided by Canadian hospitals, has offered one solution to the problem of waiting lines. The government health care program, known as medicare, would reimburse the clinics for the care.

Case Study: Prescription Drugs

U.S. proponents of a prescription drug benefit for the Medicare program have been very successful in creating an atmosphere of necessity. Something must be done, they say, and they constantly point to Canada as a model for making prescription drugs available at much lower costs than American consumers have to pay. True? Yes and no. Drug prices will vary by country, based on a number of factors, just as many other products will.

However, critics of the drug industry have vastly exaggerated those differences. A now well-known April 1999 comparison of drug costs in several countries by Professor Patricia M. Danzon of the University of Pennsylvania's Wharton School of Business found that "Canadian prices are between 13 percent lower and 3 percent higher than the U.S., depending on the price index used."

Some drugs in Canada do cost less, others do not. For example, the "superaspirin" Celebrex might cost 40 percent less in Canada than in the U.S. However, generic drugs—which make up about 45 percent of the prescriptions written in the U.S.—tend to be cheaper in America.

Perhaps more importantly, many drugs are simply not available in Canada. As a result, many Canadians come south for their drugs—just as they do for health care.

In Canada, a government agency known as the Patented Medicines Price Review Board (PMPRB) negotiates with pharmaceutical companies and sets the price based on those negotiations. According to Dr. William McArthur, a palliative care physician and former chief coroner for British Columbia, "Generally, the board does not allow a new drug to be priced higher than the most expensive existing drug used to treat the same condition." If that price is too low, drug companies may not sell their product.

In addition, both the federal government and the 10 provincial governments must approve drugs. According to McArthur:

- "From 1994 through 1998 the federal government considered some 400 drugs, but ruled that only 24—or 6 percent—were substantial improvements over their predecessors."
- "Of the 99 new drugs approved by the federal government in 1998 and 1999, only 25 were listed on the Ontario formulary," the province's official list.

Of course, Canadians are free to pay for non-approved drugs out of pocket, but they usually cannot get them because demand is so low for unapproved drugs that few pharmacies carry them. As a result, many Canadians are forced to travel to the U.S.—the place where single-payer proponents say affordability is the problem—to get the drugs they need.

The fact is that "affordable" care often means unavailable care. In many European countries, for example, the single-payer system simply does not have enough money to buy the care—and especially expensive new prescription drugs—that many patients need. One solution is that European doctors are sending patients to the U.S. to join in clinical trials of promising new drugs. In some cases, doctors are finding loopholes in the law that will let them get important new drugs to their patients—at least while the drugs are still in the testing phase.

"Affordable" does not always mean the best value. In fact, when it comes to health care, it very seldom means people are getting value for their dollars. What single-payer proponents mean by affordable is that people can get health care for little or nothing out of pocket.

However, Canadians and those living in other government-run health care systems are not getting anything for free. Single-payer countries pay for health care by taxing citizens, which can have an adverse effect on the whole economy. For example, a recent study by Industry Canada found that U.S. living standards are between 10 and 50 percent higher than Canada's, or an average of about 22 percent higher.

One reason for that difference is that the federal and provincial governments in Canada take a combined total of 41.8 percent of GDP in taxes, versus only 31.2 percent in the U.S. As a result, many Canadians hop on buses to come to the U.S., not just to buy prescription drugs and health care that they cannot get in Canada, but to buy the basics such as food and clothing in an effort to avoid Canada's excessive taxation. So even if Canada's health care system is affordable at the point of consumption, the fact that many Canadians cannot get the care they need when they need it and that they must pay significantly higher taxes for it constitutes a high price to pay for affordability.

Rationing

At a 1999 conference in England organized by the Institute for Public Policy Research, Alan Milburn, health secretary of England, said of the country's National Health Service, "The NHS—just like every other health system in the world, public or private—has never, or will never, provide all the care it might theoretically be possible to provide. . . . So within our expanding health system there will always be choices to be made about the care to be provided."

Thus the question is who does the deciding about who gets what? In a single-payer system, the government makes the larger decisions about funding levels, leaving the doctors, hospitals and other health care providers to make the tougher individual decisions about whose care to ration. And the targets of rationing are usually the marginal cases, and that often means the very young, the very old and the very sick. The patient is often simply told, "There's nothing more we can do for you," a true statement within the confines of the budget. The range of medical options is simply not discussed in this circumstance.

In England advocacy groups are forming. SOS NHS Patients in Danger, a group of family members concerned about rationing care for seniors, is taking the cases of 50 elderly patients to the European Court of Human Rights.

The London Times reported in 1993 that kidney patients were dying while kidney dialysis machines at 13 of 16 hospitals remained idle because "hospitals say they do not have the resources to keep the machines running full-time."

An 89-year-old woman died in London after waiting 12 hours for a bed.

A newspaper headline screams out "Am I Too Old to Be Treated?" telling the story of a 73 year-old U.K. citizen whose doctor told him he needed a pacemaker, only to be discharged from the hospital without one.

Finally, in Canada, the *Canadian Medical Journal* reported in May 1999 that during a 12-month period, 121 patients waiting for coronary bypass surgery were removed from the waiting list because their condition had deteriorated to the point that they were unlikely to survive surgery.

Such stories are not rarities, but commonplace even in the best of single-payer systems. The fact is that health care rationing is pervasive when the government controls health care. And as health care costs rise and government budgets tighten, rationing expands.

Recall that we started out this study by stating that for individuals, quality health care usually means a good outcome, conveniently obtained at a reasonable price. Any health care system that is routinely denying care to a large portion of its citizens simply because they are marginal members of society is not fulfilling that dictum.

The Role of Doctors

In the U.S. doctors historically have been independent practitioners, responsible to no one except their patients. That role has evolved as insurers and employers play a stronger role in health care decisions, but it is still nothing like single-payer systems where doctors, in effect, become bureaucrats—dependent on the generosity of politicians for their income.

About a year ago, 8,000 French doctors and other medical staff stopped work for three hours to attend rallies and march in protest of staff shortages and health budget restrictions imposed by the French government. They also denounced the "rationing of health care" imposed by the government in an effort to reduce the growing deficits in the country's health insurance program.

Ontario, Canada, is also having a problem with physicians. In this case there aren't enough to go around. A government report calls for an increase of 1,000 physicians. Part of the problem is a medical "brain drain." According to the president of the Canadian Medical Association, Dr. Hugh Scully, 50 percent of Canadian medical school graduates emigrate within 10 years of graduation and an additional 25 percent leave within 15 years. To make matters worse, 42 percent of family doctors are refusing to accept new patients.

The Ontario government has proposed several steps for increasing the number of physicians, including an attempt to "lure Canadian medical-school graduates back from the United States, where many have gone for post-graduate training." It might be worth adding here that with all of the problems the American health care system has, doctors do not go on strike and they do not emigrate en masse to single-payer countries in order to provide better care for their patients.

Access to New Therapies and Technology

In a single-payer system where health care budgets are tight, bureaucrats and politicians tend to see new technology as too costly for the benefit. As a result, they usually provide only enough funds to purchase a limited amount of the newest technology—if any at all. And the decisions on what to buy and when to buy it are often arbitrary and guided more by good politics than good medicine.

Even more importantly, these arbitrary limits usually enshrine the medical knowledge and techniques current at the time of their first imposition. A central control system cannot afford new medical discoveries and treatments because they were not in the budget and no funding or other resources were allocated. Thus, a single-payer system inherently tends to foster outdated medical techniques and resist new or innovative ones.

Although single-payer proponents cite Canada as a system that rivals the U.S. in the availability of new technology, the country lags behind many of the Organization for Economic Cooperation and Development (OECD) countries. While Canada ranks fifth in terms of total health care spending (as a percent of GDP), a recent study by the Fraser Institute in Canada comparing OECD data found the country:

- Ranks 21 out of 28 in CT scanner availability;
- Is 19th out of 22 in lithotriptor availability;
- And 19th out of 27 for the availability or MRIs.

It should be mentioned that these are not cutting-edge medical technologies—at least not in the U.S.

Stories abound of Canadians going to extreme measures in order to gain access to medical technology. For example, several years ago an enterprising hospital in Guelph, Ontario, decided to allow animals needing CT scans to enter the hospital in the middle of the night—charging pet owners C$300 apiece. There is nothing necessarily wrong with that except that thousands of people in Ontario were waiting up to three months for an appointment on the same machine.

"I'd go any time," said Greg Moulton, who was in the middle of a two-month wait to learn why he was having "excruciating" headaches. Because people are not allowed to pay out of pocket for medical procedures covered under the government-run plan, they have to wait. If you are a dog, you can get medical technology immediately.

When dogs get better treatment than people, then people will become dogs. In December 1999, *The Washington Post* reported that waiting lines for MRIs in Ontario had grown so long that one Ontario resident "booked himself into a private veterinary clinic that happened to have one of the machines, listing himself as 'Fido.'"

Outcomes

Do single-payer systems achieve good outcomes? Certainly many patients living in higher-income single-payer countries who enter the health care system get good care in a timely fashion—especially for routine and primary care. But those needing specialty care that requires expensive treatment or new technology may be out of luck.

Again in *The Washington Post* from December 1999: "In Quebec, they've sent more than 250 cancer patients over the border to the United States this year to get treatment and still there are 350 who have waited more than eight weeks for radiation or chemotherapy (waiting more than four weeks is considered medically risky)."

It would be very hard to argue that cancer patients waiting twice as long for radiation or chemotherapy than what is considered medically risky are getting quality care. Fortunately, these patients have a safety valve: the United States. Between April 1999 and April 2000, some 700 Ontario cancer patients came to the U.S. for care, paid for by the Ontario Health Plan. But is it quality care when you have to turn to another country to provide needed medical services?

And then there is a story from *The New York Times* that looked at cancer outcomes in Great Britain. According to the article:

> 25,000 Britons die of cancer unnecessarily each year, according to the World Health Organization;
>
> The five-year survival rate for men with colon cancer is 41 percent in Great Britain versus 64 percent in the U.S., in large part because of a lack of drugs routinely administered in the U.S.
>
> The five-year survival rate is 67 percent for women with breast cancer versus 84 percent in the U.S.
>
> Moreover, some 500 people a year die while on a waiting list for a heart operation.

Cancer is Great Britain's second biggest killer, next to cardiovascular disease. However, if it wasn't for the lack of funds, specialists and treatment centers, and the fact that treatment is available in some parts of the country but not others, cancer outcomes might be much better.

Patient Satisfaction

For years defenders of Canada's single-payer system argued that the vast majority of Canadian citizens supported the country's socialized health care system. What the citizens themselves said was "The system is good . . . as long as you stay healthy." More and more Canadians' level of satisfaction is dropping as they personally experience the system.

A May 1999 poll found that 76 percent of Canadians believe their health care system is in crisis and 71 percent said that changes were necessary because the system was not meeting patients' needs.

In addition, a survey in January 2000 by Toronto-based Pollara found:

- 74 percent supported the idea of imposing user fees (i.e., paying out of pocket) for those who could afford them;
- 85 percent of respondents making C$25,000 or less supported user fees;
- But only 23 percent supported raising taxes to finance the national health insurance system.

Not long ago, such support for user fees would have been unthinkable and in total contrast to Canada's philosophy of health care, which says that it should be free to all. However, as lines grow and people die, Canadians are increasingly willing to consider alternatives, even if that means abandoning the socialist ideal of "free" health care for all.

Britons are also growing dissatisfied with their National Health Service. According to a recent Mori poll, published in the *Journal of the British Medical Association*:

- Satisfaction with the NHS declined from 72 percent to 58 percent in 1998;
- While those considered "very dissatisfied" or "fairly dissatisfied" grew from 17 percent to 28 percent.

CONCLUSION

Single-payer health care systems are not a fantasy, they are a nightmare. They politicize the health care system, ration care and demoralize doctors and other providers. They are not a model to be emulated, but a disaster to be avoided.

While the U.S. health care system has its problems, it has largely avoided those created by single-payer systems. However, the U.S. is beginning to experience, at least on a small scale, some of the problems inherent in single-payer systems because Medicare and Medicaid are single-payer systems. In addition, employer-based health insurance and managed care incorporate some of the same incentives and structures as single-payer systems, so some of the problems arising from them will necessarily be similar to those in countries such as Canada and the United Kingdom.

If Congress, Washington state and other states want to do something about expanding health insurance coverage, at the same time enhancing human freedom and choice, there are free-market options that will increase the number of insured while maintaining the quality of care most Americans have come to expect. If instead federal and state policymakers move toward a single-payer system that tries to impose universal coverage, they will find that Americans will get neither care nor quality.

DISCUSSION QUESTIONS

1. Do you think of health care as a social service or as a commodity that should be purchased?
2. Do you think health care currently is rationed in the United States? If so, how? Is this a necessary feature of the health care system?
3. Is health care a right for all Americans, regardless of ability to pay?

4. Should every citizen be entitled to unlimited free health care of any type (heart surgery, cosmetic surgery, dental care, mental health assistance, eyeglasses, mammograms, etc.)? If not, what criteria should be used to determine which medical care is provided and which is not?
5. Are the current government health care systems of Medicare and Medicaid targeting people most in need of subsidized or free health care? Should all seniors receive government assistance, irrespective of income levels?
6. What do you think are the major barriers to a national health insurance system in the United States? Is such a system at all viable?
7. Should national health insurance be the only health care coverage for a country (as in Canada), or should people be allowed to opt for private health care (as in Britain)? What effect do these approaches have on publicly provided care?
8. Should Medicaid be an exclusively federally funded program, like Medicare, or should states retain significant authority?

WEB REFERENCES

California Health Care Options Project, http://www.healthcareoptions.ca.gov/.

Libertarian Arguments against Socialized Medicine, http://www.self-gov.org/medicine.html.

Medicaid Information, http://www.hcfa.gov/medicaid/medicaid.htm.

Medicare Homepage, http://www.medicare.gov/Coverage/Home.asp.

Physicians for a National Health Program, http://www.pnhp.org/.

Universal Health Care Action Network, http://www.uhcan.org/.

U.S. Department of Health and Human Services, http://www.dhhs.gov/.

FURTHER READING

Aaron, Henry J., ed. *The Problem That Won't Go Away: Reforming U.S. Health Care Financing*. Washington, D.C.: The Brookings Institution, 1996.

Armstrong, Pat and Hugh Armstrong. *Universal Health Care: What the United States Can Learn from the Canadian Experience*. New York: New Press, 1998.

Bovbjerg, Randall R. and John Holahan. *Medicaid in the Reagan Era: Federal Policy and State Choices*. Washington, D.C.: Urban Institute, 1982.

Cravens, Hamilton and Alan I. Markus. *Health Care Policy in Contemporary America*. Harrisburg: Penn State University Press, 1997.

Daniels, Mark Ross, ed. *Medicaid Reform and the American States: Case Studies on the Politics of Managed Care*. New York: Auburn House, 1998.

Dilulio, John and Richard P. Nathan. *Medicaid and the States: Issues and Prospects*. Washington, D.C.: The Brookings Institution, 1998.

Dranove, David. *The Economic Evolution of American Health Care*. Princeton, N.J.: Princeton University Press, 2000.

Greenberg, Warren. *Competition, Regulation, and Rationing in Health Care*. Ann Arbor, Mich.: Health Administration Press, 1991.

Henderson, James W. *Health Economics and Policy*. Mason, Ohio: South-Western Publishing, 2001.

Hurley, Robert E. *Managed Care in Medicaid: Lessons for Policy and Program Design*. Ann Arbor, Mich.: Health Administration Press, 1993.

Jones, Stanley B. and Mario Ein Lewin, eds. *Improving the Medicare Market: Adding Choice and Protections*. Washington, D.C.: National Academy Press, 1996.

Kleinke, J. D. *Oxymorons: The Myth of a U.S. Health Care System*. San Francisco, Calif.: Jossey-Bass, 2001.

Laham, Nicholas. *A Lost Cause: Bill Clinton's Campaign for National Health Insurance*. New York: Praeger Publishing, 1996.

Lohr, Kathleen N. and M. Susan Marquis. *Medicare and Medicaid: Past, Present, and Future*. Santa Monica, Calif.: Rand, 1984.

Lundberg, George D., ed. *Severed Trust: Why American Medicine Hasn't Been Fixed*. New York: Basic Books, 2001.

Patel, Kant and Mark E. Rushefsky. *Health Care Politics and Policy in America*. Armonk, N.Y.: M. E. Sharpe, 1999.

Powell, Francis D. and Albert F. Wessen, eds. *Health Care Systems in Transition: An International Perspective*. Thousand Oaks, Calif.: Sage Publications, 1999.

Rushefsky, Mark E. and Kant Patel. *Politics, Power and Policy Making: The Case of Health Care Reform in the 1990s*. Armonk, N.Y.: M. E. Sharpe, 1997.

Shortell, Stephen M. *Remaking Health Care in America*, 2d ed. San Francisco, Calif.: Jossey-Bass, 2000.

Sparer, Michael S. *Medicare and the Limits of State Health Reform*. Philadelphia: Temple University Press, 1996.

Starr, Paul. "What Happened to Health Care Reform?" *American Prospect* (Winter 1995), pp. 20–31.

Chapter 11

AFFIRMATIVE ACTION/EQUAL OPPORTUNITY

"Should Affirmative Action Policies Be Continued?"

YES: Stanley Fish "Reverse Racism or How the Pot Got to Call the Kettle Black" *The Atlantic Monthly*

NO: Shelby Steele "A Negative Vote on Affirmative Action" *New York Times Magazine*

Affirmative action programs designed to promote equal opportunity for African Americans and other minorities have been the topic of some of the most bitterly divisive social and political debates in the United States in recent years. Part of this results from ambiguity surrounding the term "affirmative action"—people often have differing perceptions of its purpose and meaning. But the division and controversy engendered by affirmative action also stems from the fact that it is so closely related to the issue of racial inequality and the long history of racial discrimination in the United States.

The vast majority of Americans advocate the goal of racial equality, and there is widespread support for the sort of formal equality provided by civil rights legislation; however, there is considerable disagreement over both the current extent of racial discrimination and the most appropriate way to achieve the equality of opportunity that civil rights legislation ostensibly implies. Indeed, many who support the proposition that the government has a legitimate role to play in ensuring equal opportunity also question what level of action is necessary to guarantee an equal playing field for all individuals. Is equal opportunity before the law in employment, housing, and education enough? Or are more active policies required to translate formal legal equality into something that can reasonably be called equal opportunity? The attempts to promote racial equality in the latter half of this century have confronted these questions, with affirmative action playing a prominent role among the variety of approaches emerging from that legacy.

Government policies to end racial discrimination in employment, education, and business have developed episodically, advanced by a mixture of legislative, judicial, and executive branch actions. Such attempts began in 1941 when President Roosevelt created the Fair Employment Practices Committee, which ordered defense contractors to cease discriminatory practices in hiring. However, the Roosevelt order was not accompanied by any form of sanction for companies that did not comply, and the committee was disbanded in 1946. The Supreme Court's 1954 decision in *Brown* v. *Board of Education* declared segregated educational facilities "inherently unequal" and therefore unconstitutional, and subsequent Court decisions extended the ruling to all public facilities. While important in its own right, the ruling also had the effect of mandating race-conscious integration programs such as school busing. In 1961, in response to growing concerns over racial inequality, particularly in the South, President Kennedy issued Executive Order 10952, directing all federally funded contractors to "take affirmative action to ensure that applicants are employed, and employees are treated during their employment, without regard to race, creed, color, or national origin." The order also authorized the creation of a commission to collect employment statistics, investigate contractor practices, and impose sanctions against those not in compliance.[1]

However, it was not until the Civil Rights Acts of 1964 and 1965, passed shortly after the March on Washington in support of equal rights, that discrimination was outlawed in hiring practices, in places of public accommodation, and in any program receiving federal assistance. In addition, the Equal Employment Opportunity Commission (EEOC) was established to enforce such laws. Also in 1965, President Lyndon Johnson reaffirmed Kennedy's earlier order that companies doing business with the federal government establish "affirmative action" plans to ensure nondiscrimination, but required that such plans now be stated in writing. These "affirmative" measures, stated Johnson, were necessary not simply to make up for past discrimination and injustices, but also to provide equal opportunity to previously disadvantaged and underrepresented groups.[2] It was hoped that such actions would eventually eliminate barriers to African Americans and other minorities and would promote full equality in employment. A 1972 amendment to the Civil Rights Act strengthened the authority of the EEOC by including state and local governments and labor organizations within its purview.[3]

Supreme Court rulings extended the power of civil rights laws and affirmative action programs throughout the 1960s and 1970s. In the 1971 case *Griggs* v. *Duke Power*, the Court ruled against employment criteria, such as high school diploma requirements or literacy tests, frequently used as barriers to the hiring of minorities.[4] In the landmark 1978 case *Regents of the University of California* v. *Allan Bakke*, the Supreme Court ruled that admissions policies of public educational institutions were permitted to take race into account for "benign" purposes—that is, in order to ensure racial diversity through inclusive policies. (However, the Court also ordered that Bakke, who had claimed reverse discrimination, must be admitted to the medical school, from which he later graduated). In *United Steelworkers of America* v. *Weber* (1979), the Court approved the use of race as a criterion for inclusion in private-sector employment training programs. These decisions tended to support the use of a variety of affirmative action programs in both the public and private sectors, but they also revealed significant disagreement among members of the Supreme Court over the validity of such programs; both the *Bakke* and *Weber* cases were decided by 5-4 votes.

While the initial formulations of affirmative action—intertwined as they were with the implementation of civil rights laws—were considerably ambiguous about their appropriate nature or extent, they provided significant impetus for the voluntary development and implementation of affirmative action plans in both the public and private sectors. Indeed, a variety of employment and contracting procedures by government, admissions and hiring procedures in educational institutions, and hiring and promotion procedures in private companies eventually were made subject to affirmative action policies designed to ensure that previously excluded groups such as women and minorities were now included. The procedures for meeting this goal varied from focused advertising and recruitment to considering racial and gender diversity as a criterion in hiring and admissions decisions. In some cases, a certain percentage of contracts, admission slots, or jobs were reserved for women and minorities, although following the *Bakke* decision the use of race as a determining factor in employment and admission was no longer legal.

Even though affirmative action programs received initial support from both the executive and judicial branches of the federal government, as well as from many within the private sector, criticism of the programs intensified during the 1980s and 1990s, when a more conservative Supreme Court and executive branch reacted against many such programs. Both the Reagan and Bush administrations opposed numerous affirmative action efforts, and the attorney general during the Reagan administration, Edwin Meese, argued against minority hiring practices under affirmative action programs before the Supreme Court in 1985. In addition to a loss of support within the executive branch, affirmative action programs were increasingly challenged by Supreme Court decisions during the late 1980s and early 1990s. In 1989 a more conservative Court handed down several decisions—including *Wards Cove* v. *Atonio*—that made it more difficult to prove discrimination in hiring practices, thus making enforcement of affirmative action programs all the more difficult. In addition, the 1989 *City of Richmond* v. *J.A. Croson Company* decision invalidated a provision requiring Richmond's contractors to set aside 30 percent of their business for minority-owned companies. In 1995, the Court ruled in *Adarand Constructors, Inc.* v. *Pena* that governmental use of affirmative action in awarding highway construction contracts would be subject to "strict scrutiny," a legal requirement that effectively restricts use of such programs to cases where the government can clearly demonstrate that their use achieves a narrow and necessary goal. In a dissenting opinion to one such decision, Justice Harry Blackmun wrote that "one wonders whether the majority still believes that discrimination is a problem in our society, or believes that it ever was."[5]

Affirmative action has received strict scrutiny not only at the federal level, but at the state and local levels as well. In 1995, the Regents of the University of California replaced previous admissions policies, which had directed admissions officers to consider diversity as a factor when making admission decisions, with a new policy that prevented any such consideration of race, religion, sex, color, or ethnicity. And in 1996, California voters approved Proposition 209, which abolished the use of affirmative action programs that consider race, sex, color, or ethnicity in decisions regarding public employment and public contracting. Challenged by many civil rights groups, the law was upheld by the U.S. Court of Appeals in 1997, and similar laws are now under consideration in other states.[6] Recent judicial rulings have emphasized the position taken by the University of California; in 2001 affirmative action programs at the University of Texas Law School and the University of Georgia were struck down in the courts.[7]

Partly as a result of its depiction in political campaigns, affirmative action increasingly has been seen by many as a strategy composed primarily of quotas, hiring targets, and racial preferences, and debates over affirmative action have been closely connected to the use of race as a political issue. Politicians have played effectively on public perceptions of affirmative action as well as racial difference, sometimes subtly and sometimes overtly, particularly for rallying the white blue-collar vote. Republican Senator Jesse Helms of North Carolina, facing a strong challenge from an African-American opponent, became infamous for a campaign commercial that played on whites' fears of losing job opportunities to minorities on the basis of race. The infamous Willie Horton advertisement by the Bush campaign in 1988, which recounted an incident where a convicted African-American felon on furlough from a Massachusetts prison brutalized a white Maryland family, further fed racial fears. The political success of David Duke, a former grand wizard of the Ku Klux Klan, in Louisiana was perhaps the most obvious manifestation of the political salience of race in electoral politics in the late 1980s and early 1990s. Of a more subtle nature, President Bush tried in 1990 to cast the Civil Rights Act as a "quota bill," forcing businesses to set aside a certain number of positions for minority candidates, knowing that most Americans opposed hiring quotas. Indeed, the importance of race in American politics can scarcely be overstated. Thomas and Mary Edsall write that "race is no longer a straightforward, morally unambiguous force in American politics; instead, considerations of race are now deeply imbedded in the strategy and tactics of politics, in competing concepts of the function and responsibility of government, and in each voter's conceptual structure of moral and partisan identity."[8]

However, while the relevance of race in the debate over affirmative action cannot be ignored, those opposing affirmative action maintain that establishing quotas or otherwise giving advantage to minority applicants over whites results in unjust discrimination, usually against whites. While most Americans continue to profess the need to promote racial equality and to fight practices of racial discrimination, many white Americans have expressed the view that affirmative action programs have become a source of reverse discrimination. Some believe that while the fight for juridical equality was a just goal, affirmative action programs have the effect in many cases of discriminating against more highly skilled white workers while favoring less qualified minority applicants. This view is especially pronounced in areas where jobs are scarce and economic times difficult. Furthermore, some economists have argued that a freely competitive labor market is the most efficient method of meeting employer needs, in that free markets punish discrimination because employers pay an economic cost by hiring inferior white applicants over better-qualified minorities, putting them at a competitive disadvantage.

Some civil rights advocates and liberals have also questioned the effectiveness of such programs, believing that they might be increasing racial tensions overall by creating the perception that minorities are poorly qualified for employment and need compensatory consideration to be hired. They further argue that the benefits of affirmative action have gone mainly to middle-class African Americans and have done little to advance the interests of poorer African Americans.[9] In the second of the articles that follow, Professor Shelby Steele argues that this stigmatizes successful minorities and women, in both education and employment, who are viewed by some as being in their position solely due to their unequal "status." It is not so much that some liberals oppose affirmative action per se, but rather that they believe that affirmative action has accomplished little for those most in need, and that their political capital is best expended elsewhere to advance the interest of minorities. As one put it, "Democrats are now all too conscious of the price they have paid for appearing to be the party of quotas."[10]

Proponents of affirmative action programs claim that the consideration of racial diversity in hiring decisions is justified not only on the grounds of past discrimination against African Americans and other minorities, but also as a necessary tool to ensure equal opportunity in contemporary life. As Malcolm X stated in 1964, "I don't see an American dream;... I see an American nightmare.... Three hundred and ten years we worked in this country without a dime in return." Such views persist, as does evidence of discriminatory hiring practices, housing practices, and lending practices on mortgages by some banks. The persistence of such discrimination is seen by proponents of affirmative action as proof that legislation prohibiting such behavior does not preclude de facto discrimination, and that as a result affirmative measures must be taken to ensure equality. Among members of the preeminent civil rights groups, including the NAACP and Urban League, support for the programs remains strong. These groups feel that affirmative action has translated into advances for minorities that would not have occurred otherwise. Expecting affirmative action to eliminate poverty is unrealistic, they argue, and large gains have been made in minority representation in public and private institutions as a result of affirmative action programs. Many in the Democratic Party also continue to have a strong interest in preserving affirmative action for electoral as well as personal reasons, and former President Clinton seemed to reflect the feelings of these Democrats when he argued that the appropriate response to affirmative action is to "mend it, don't end it." The Bush administration appears to be in favor of certain, although not all, race-conscious policies, defending the Department of Transportation's program aimed at helping minority high-way contractors and yet opposing affirmative action in admissions at the University of Michigan.[11]

While a majority of Americans polled in 2001 favor continuing or increasing equal opportunity or affirmative action programs in general—92 percent of African Americans and 67 percent of whites—there is a considerable difference on the question of whether affirmative action should be increased; 57 percent of African Americans favor the extension of such programs while only 22 percent of whites do. Just 8 percent of blacks favor decreasing the use of affirmative action programs, while a much higher 33 percent of whites would like to see a reduction. Perhaps more significantly, 66 percent of blacks, compared with only 41 percent of whites, agree that government should make every effort to improve conditions of blacks and minorities. Conversely, 27 percent of blacks and 51 percent of whites believe that government should not make any special effort, letting minorities help themselves. While this racial difference undoubtedly results from conflicting perceptions of the meaning of affirmative action, it also underscores our divergent perceptions of the importance of race in contemporary life. Whites are more likely than blacks to say that blacks are treated equally in their community (69 percent versus 41 percent), in equal educational opportunities (85 percent versus 52 percent), and in equal access to housing (83 percent versus 48 percent).[12]

In the first article that follows, Professor Stanley Fish of Duke University argues that critics' assertions that affirmative action represents "reverse racism" are strongly misleading because the two types of "racism" are not equivalent. The racism felt by minorities derives from oppressors who have sought to deny voting rights, education, and economic parity to another group. "Racism" against whites (in the form of affirmative action) is a result of past actions, not an attempt to subjugate one group based only on its race. He argues that affirmative action must be viewed in the historical context of more than 200 years of oppression. Calls for an even playing field are designed, Fish argues, to keep an already tilted playing field titled in favor of whites. Professor Shelby Steele argues in the accompanying article that preferences for African Americans harmfully imply an inferiority, which leads not only to further racism, but also to self-doubt on the part of minorities.

Endnotes

1. "Americans United for Affirmative Action," *Timeline of Affirmative Action* (Atlanta, Ga.: Americans United for Affirmative Action, 1998).
2. Bron Raymond Taylor, *Affirmative Action at Work* (Pittsburgh, Pa.: University of Pittsburgh Press, 1991), p. 21.
3. As the primary federal agency in charge of enforcing nondiscrimination laws in both the public and private sectors, the EEOC receives between 80,000 and 85,000 complaints of discrimination annually. In fiscal year 1996, the EEOC received more than $145 million through settlements and fines for victims of discrimination and

another $50 million through litigation. U.S. Equal Employment Opportunity Commission website, http://www.eeoc.gov.

4. Taylor, op. cit., pp. 22–23.

5. Harry Blackmun, *Patterson* v. *McLean* Credit Union, 1989, Dissenting Opinion.

6. Joan Biskupic, "Affirmative Action Ban Is Left Intact by Supreme Court," *Washington Post* (November 4, 1997), p. A1.

7. See, for example, CNN, http://www.cnn.com/2001/LAW/08/28/affirmative. action. reax/index.html.

8. Thomas Byrne Edsall with Mary D. Edsall, "Race," *Atlantic Monthly* (May 1991), p. 53.

9. See W. J. Wilson, "Race Neutral Programs and the Democratic Coalition," *American Prospect* (Spring 1990).

10. Paul Starr, "Civil Reconstruction: What to Do without Affirmative Action," *American Prospect* (Winter 1992), p. 9.

11. See, for example, http://www.usatoday.com/news/washdc/august01/2001-08-03-bush-affirmativeaction-usat.htm.

12. Gallup Poll, http://www.gallup.com/poll/specialreports/pollsummaries/sr010711. PDF.

YES

Reverse Racism or How the Pot Got to Call the Kettle Black

Stanley Fish

I take my text from George Bush, who, in an address to the United Nations on September 23, 1991, said this of the UN resolution equating Zionism with racism: "Zionism...is the idea that led to the creation of a home for the Jewish people... And to equate Zionism with the intolerable sin of racism is to twist history and forget the terrible plight of Jews in World War II and indeed throughout history." What happened in the Second World War was that six million Jews were exterminated by people who regarded them as racially inferior and a danger to Aryan purity. What happened after the Second World War was that the survivors of that Holocaust established a Jewish state—that is, a state centered on Jewish history, Jewish values, and Jewish traditions: in short, a Jewocentric state. What President Bush objected to was the logical sleight of hand by which these two actions were declared equivalent because they were both expressions of racial exclusiveness. Ignored, as Bush said, was the historical difference between them—the difference between a program of genocide and the determination of those who escaped it to establish a community in which they would be the makers, not the victims, of the laws.

Only if racism is thought of as something that occurs principally in the mind, a falling-away from proper notions of universal equality, can the desire of a victimized and terrorized people to band together be declared morally identical to the actions of their would-be executioners. Only when the actions of the two groups are detached from the historical conditions of their emergence and given a purely abstract description can they be made interchangeable. Bush was saying to the United Nations, "Look, the Nazis' conviction of racial superiority generated a policy of systematic genocide; the Jews' experience of centuries of persecution in almost every country on earth generated a desire for a homeland of their own. If you manage somehow to convince yourself that these are the same, it is you, not the Zionists, who are morally confused, and the reason you are morally confused is that you have forgotten history."

A KEY DISTINCTION

What I want to say, following Bush's reasoning, is that a similar forgetting of history has in recent years allowed some people to argue, and argue persuasively, that affirmative action is reverse racism. The very phrase "reverse racism" contains the argument in exactly the form to which Bush objected: In this country whites once set themselves apart from blacks and claimed privileges for themselves while denying them to others. Now, on the basis of race, blacks are claiming special status and reserving for themselves privileges they deny to others. Isn't one as bad as the other? The answer is no. One can see why by imagining that it is not 1993 but 1955, and that we are in a town in the South with two more or less distinct communities, one white and one black. No doubt each community would have a ready store of dissuasive epithets, ridiculing stories, self-serving folk myths, and expressions of plain hatred, all directed at the other community, and all based in racial hostility. Yet to regard their respective racisms—if that is the word—as equivalent would be bizarre, for the hostility of one group stems not from any wrong done to it but from its wish to protect its ability to deprive citizens of their voting rights, to limit access to educational institutions, to prevent entry into the economy except at the lowest and most menial levels, and to force members of the stigmatized group to ride in the back of the bus. The hostility of the other group is the result of these actions, and whereas hostility and racial anger are unhappy facts wherever they are found, a distinction must surely be made between the ideo-logical hostility of the oppressors and the experience-based hostility of those who have been oppressed.

Not to make that distinction is, adapting George Bush's words, to twist history and forget the terrible plight of African Americans in the more than 200 years of this country's existence. Moreover, to equate the efforts to remedy that plight with the actions that produced it is to twist history even further. Those efforts, designed to redress the imbalances caused by long-standing dis-crimination, are called affirmative action; to argue that affirmative action, which gives preferential treatment to disadvantaged minorities as part of a plan to achieve social equality, is not different from the policies that created the disadvantages in the first place is a travesty of reasoning. "Reverse racism" is a cogent description of affirmative action only if one considers the cancer of racism to be morally and medically indistinguishable from the therapy we apply to it. A cancer is an invasion of the body's equilibrium, and so is chemotherapy; but we do not decline to fight the disease because the medicine we employ is also disruptive of normal functioning. Strong illness, strong remedy: the formula is as appropriate to the health of the body politic as it is to that of the body proper.

At this point someone will always say, "But two wrongs don't make a right; if it was wrong to treat blacks unfairly, it is wrong to give blacks preference and thereby treat whites unfairly." This objection is just another version of the forgetting and rewriting of history. The work is done by the adverb "unfairly," which suggests two more or less equal parties, one of whom has been unjustly penalized by an incompetent umpire. But blacks have not simply been treated unfairly; they have been subjected first to decades of slavery, and then to decades of second-class citizenship, widespread legalized discrimination, economic persecution, educational deprivation, and cultural stigmatization.

They have been bought, sold, killed, beaten, raped, excluded, exploited, shamed, and scorned for a very long time. The word "unfair" is hardly an adequate description of their experience, and the belated gift of "fairness" in the form of a resolution no longer to discriminate against them legally is hardly an adequate remedy for the deep disadvantages that the prior discrimination has produced. When the deck is stacked against you in more ways than you can even count, it is small consolation to hear that you are now free to enter the game and take your chances.

A TILTED FIELD

The same insincerity and hollowness of promise infect another formula that is popular with the anti-affirmative-action crowd: the formula of the level playing field. Here the argument usually takes the form of saying "It is undemocratic to give one class of citizens advantages at the expense of other citizens; the truly democratic way is to have a level playing field to which everyone has access and where everyone has a fair and equal chance to succeed on the basis of his or her merit." Fine words—but they conceal the facts of the situation as it has been given to us by history: the playing field is already tilted in favor of those by whom and for whom it was constructed in the first place. If mastery of the requirements for entry depends upon immersion in the cultural experiences of the mainstream majority, if the skills that make for success are nurtured by institutions and cultural practices from which the disadvantaged minority has been systematically excluded, if the language and ways of comporting oneself that identify a player as "one of us" are alien to the lives minorities are forced to live, then words like "fair" and "equal" are cruel jokes, for what they promote and celebrate is an institutionalized unfairness and a perpetuated inequality. The playing field is already tilted, and the resistance to altering it by the mechanisms of affirmative action is in fact a determination to make sure that the present imbalances persist as long as possible.

One way of tilting the field is the Scholastic Aptitude Test. This test figures prominently in Dinesh D'Souza's book *Illiberal Education* (1991), in which one finds many examples of white or Asian students denied admission to colleges and universities even though their SAT scores were higher than the scores of some others—often African Americans—who were admitted to the same institution. This, D'Souza says, is evidence that as a result of affirmative-action policies colleges and universities tend "to depreciate the importance of merit criteria in admissions." D'Souza's assumption—and it is one that many would share—is that the test does in fact measure merit, with *merit* understood as a quality objectively determined in the same way that body temperature can be objectively determined.

In fact, however, the test is nothing of the kind. Statistical studies have suggested that test scores reflect income and socioeconomic status. It has been demonstrated again and again that scores vary in relation to cultural background; the test's questions assume a certain uniformity in educational experience and lifestyle and penalize those who, for whatever reason, have had a different experience and lived different kinds of lives. In short, what is being measured by the SAT is not absolutes like native ability and merit but accidents like birth, social position, access to libraries, and the opportunity to take vacations or to take SAT prep courses.

Furthermore, as David Owen notes in *None of the Above: Behind the Myth of Scholastic Aptitude* (1985), the "correlation between SAT scores and college grades...is lower than the correlation between weight and height; in other words you would have a better chance of predicting a person's height by looking at his weight than you would of predicting his freshman grades by looking only at his SAT scores." Everywhere you look in the SAT story, the claims of fairness, objectivity, and neutrality fall away, to be replaced by suspicions of specialized measures and unfair advantages.

Against this background a point that in isolation might have a questionable force takes on a special and even explanatory resonance: the principal deviser of the test was an out-and-out racist. In 1923, Carl Campbell Brigham published a book called *A Study of American Intelligence*, in which, as Owen notes, he declared, among other things, that we faced in America "a possibility of racial admixture...infinitely worse than that faced by any European country today, for we are incorporating the Negro into our racial stock, while all of Europe is comparatively free of this taint." Brigham had earlier analyzed the Army Mental Tests using classifications drawn from another racist text, Madison Grant's *The Passing of the Great Race*, which divided American society into four distinct racial strains, with Nordic, blue-eyed, blond people at the pinnacle and the American Negro at the bottom. Nevertheless, in 1925 Brigham became a director of testing for the College Board, and developed the SAT. So here is the great SAT test, devised by a racist in order to confirm racist assumptions, measuring not native ability but cultural advantage, an uncertain indicator of performance, an indicator of very little except what money and social privilege can buy. And it is in the name of this mechanism that we are asked to reject affirmative action and reaffirm "the importance of merit criteria in admissions."

THE REALITY OF DISCRIMINATION

Nevertheless, there is at least one more card to play against affirmative action, and it is a strong one. Granted that the playing field is not level and that access to it is reserved for an already advantaged elite, the disadvantages suffered by others are less racial—at least in 1993—than socioeconomic. Therefore shouldn't, as D'Souza urges, "universities...retain their policies of preferential treatment, but alter their criteria of application from race to socioeconomic disadvantage," and thus avoid the unfairness of current policies that reward middle-class or affluent blacks at the expense of poor whites? One answer to this question is given by D'Souza himself when he acknowledges that the overlap between minority groups and the poor is very large—a point underscored by the former Secretary of Education Lamar Alexander, who said, in response to a question about funds targeted for black students. "Ninety-eight percent of race-specific scholarships do not involve constitutional problems." He meant, I take it, that 98 percent of race-specific scholarships were also scholarships to the economically disadvantaged.

Still, the other two percent—nonpoor, middle-class, economically favored blacks—are receiving special attention on the basis of disadvantages they do not experience. What about them? The force of the question depends on the assumption that in this day and age race could not possibly be a serious disadvantage to those who are otherwise well positioned in the society. But the lie was given dramatically to this assumption in a 1991 broadcast of the ABC program *Prime Time Live*. In a stunning fifteen-minute segment reporters and a camera crew followed two young men of equal education, cultural sophistication, level of apparent affluence, and so forth around St. Louis, a city where neither was known. The two differed in only a single respect: one was white, the other black. But that small difference turned out to mean everything. In a series of encounters with shoe salesmen, record-store employees, rental agents, landlords, employment agencies, taxicab drivers, and ordinary citizens, the black member of the pair was either ignored or given special and suspicious attention. He was asked to pay more for the same goods or come up with a larger down payment for the same car, was turned away as a prospective tenant, was rejected as a prospective taxicab fare, was treated with contempt and irritation by clerks and bureaucrats, and in every way possible was made to feel inferior and unwanted.

The inescapable conclusion was that alike though they may have been in almost all respects, one of these young men, because he was black, would lead a significantly lesser life than his white counterpart: he would be housed less well and at greater expense: he would pay more for services and products when and if he was given the opportunity to buy them: he would have difficulty establishing credit; the first emotions he would inspire on the part of many people he met would be distrust and fear; his abilities would be discounted even before he had a chance to display them; and, above all, the treatment he received from minute to minute would chip away at his self-esteem and self-confidence with consequences that most of us could not even imagine. As the young man in question said at the conclusion of the broadcast, "You walk down the street with a suit and tie and it doesn't matter. Someone will make determinations about you, determinations that affect the quality of your life."

Of course, the same determinations are being made quite early on by kindergarten teachers, grade school principals, high school guidance counselors, and the like, with results that cut across socioeconomic lines and place young black men and women in the ranks of the disadvantaged no matter what the bank accounts of their parents happen to show. Racism is a cultural fact, and although its effects may to some extent be diminished by socioeconomic variables, those effects will still be sufficiently great to warrant the nation's attention and thus the continuation of affirmative action policies. This is true even of the field thought to be dominated by blacks and often cited as evidence of the equal opportunities society now affords them. I refer, of course, to professional athletics. But national self-congratulation on this score might pause in the face of a few facts: A minuscule number of African Americans ever receive a paycheck from a professional team. Even though nearly 1,600 daily newspapers report on the exploits of black athletes, they employ only seven full-time black sports columnists. Despite repeated pledges and resolutions, major-league teams have managed to put only a handful of blacks and Hispanics in executive positions.

WHY ME?

When all is said and done, however, one objection to affirmative action is unanswerable on its own terms, and that is the objection of the individual who says, "Why me? Sure, discrimination has persisted for many years, and I acknowledge that the damage done has not been removed by changes in the law. But why me? I didn't own slaves; I didn't vote to keep people on the back of the bus; I didn't turn water hoses on civil-rights marchers. Why, then, should I be the one who doesn't get the job or who doesn't get the scholarship or who gets bumped back to the waiting list?"

I sympathize with this feeling, if only because in a small way I have had the experience that produces it. I was recently nominated for an administrative post at a large university. Early signs were encouraging, but after an interval I received official notice that I would not be included at the next level of consideration, and subsequently I was told unofficially that at some point a decision had been made to look only in the direction of women and minorities. Although I was disappointed, I did not conclude that the situation was "unfair," because the policy was obviously not directed at me—at no point in the proceedings did someone say, "Let's find a way to rule out Stanley Fish." Nor was it directed even at persons of my race and sex—the policy was not intended to disenfranchise white males. Rather, the policy was driven by other considerations, and it was only as a by-product of those considerations—not as the main goal—that white males like me were rejected. Given that the institution in question has a high percentage of minority students, a very low percentage of minority faculty, and an even lower percentage of minority administrators, it made perfect sense to focus on women and minority candidates, and within that sense, not as the result of prejudice, my whiteness and maleness became disqualifications.

I can hear the objection in advance: "What's the difference? Unfair is unfair: you didn't get the job; you didn't even get on the short list." The difference is not in the outcome but in the ways of thinking that led up to the outcome. It is the difference between an unfairness that befalls one as the unintended effect of a policy rationally conceived and an unfairness that is pursued as an end in itself. It is the difference between the awful unfairness of Nazi extermination camps and the unfairness to Palestinian Arabs that arose from, but was not the chief purpose of, the founding of a Jewish state.

THE NEW BIGOTRY

The point is not a difficult one, but it is difficult to see when the unfairness scenarios are presented as simple contrasts between two decontextualized persons who emerge from nowhere to contend for a job or a place in a freshman class. Here is student A; he has a board score of 1,300. And here is student B; her board score is only 1,200, yet she is admitted and A is rejected. Is that fair? Given the minimal information provided, the answer is of course no. But if we expand our horizons and consider fairness in relation to the cultural and institutional histories that have brought the two students to this point, histories that weigh on them even if they are not the histories' authors, then both the question and the answer suddenly grow more complicated.

The sleight-of-hand logic that first abstracts events from history and then assesses them from behind a veil of willed ignorance gains some of its plausibility from another key word in the anti-affirmative-action lexicon. That word is "individual," as in "The American way is to focus on the rights of individuals rather than groups." Now, "individual" and "individualism" have been honorable words in the American political vocabulary, and they have often been well employed in the fight against various tyrannies. But like any other word or concept, individualism can be perverted to serve ends the opposite of those it originally served, and this is what has happened when in the name of individual rights, millions of individuals are enjoined from redressing historically documented wrongs. How is this managed? Largely in the same way that the invocation of fairness is used to legitimize an institutionalized inequality. First one says, in the most solemn of tones, that the protection of individual rights is the chief obligation of society. Then one defines individuals as souls sent into the world with equal entitlements as guaranteed either by their Creator or by the Constitution. Then one pretends that nothing has happened to them since they stepped onto the world's stage. And then one says of these carefully denatured souls that they will all be treated in the same way, irrespective of any of the differences that history has produced. Bizarre as it may seem, individualism in this argument turns out to mean that everyone is or should be the same. This dismissal of individual difference in the name of the individual would be funny were its consequences not so serious: it is the mechanism by which imbalances and inequities suffered by millions of people through no fault of their own can be sanitized and even celebrated as the natural workings of unfettered democracy.

"Individualism," "fairness," "merit"—these three words are continually misappropriated by bigots who have learned that they need not put on a white hood or bar access to the ballot box in order to secure their ends. Rather, they need only clothe themselves in a vocabulary plucked from its historical context and made into the justification for attitudes and policies they would not acknowledge if frankly named.

NO

A Negative Vote on Affirmative Action

Shelby Steele

In a few short years, when my two children will be applying to college, the affirmative-action policies by which most universities offer black students some form of preferential treatment will present me with a dilemma. I am a middle-class black, a college professor, far from wealthy, but also well removed from the kind of deprivation that would qualify my children for the label "disadvantaged." Both of them have endured racial insensitivity from whites. They have been called names, have suffered slights and have experienced firsthand the peculiar malevolence that racism brings out of people. Yet they have never experienced racial discrimination, have never been stopped by their race on any path they have chosen to follow. Still, their society now tells them that if they will only designate themselves as black on their college applications, they will probably do better in the college lottery than if they conceal this fact. I think there is something of a Faustian bargain in this.

Of course many blacks and a considerable number of whites would say that I was sanctimoniously making affirmative action into a test of character. They would say that this small preference is the meagerest recompense for centuries of unrelieved oppression. And to these arguments other very obvious facts must be added. In America, many marginally competent or flatly incompetent whites are hired everyday—some because their white skin suits the conscious or unconscious racial preference of their employers. The white children of alumni are often grandfathered into elite universities in what can only be seen as a residual benefit of historic white privilege. Worse, white incompetence is always an individual matter, but for blacks it is often confirmation of ugly stereotypes. Given that unfairness cuts both ways, doesn't it only balance the scales of history, doesn't this repay, in a small way, the systematic denial under which my children's grandfather lived out his days?

In theory, affirmative action certainly has all the moral symmetry that fairness requires. It is reformist and corrective, even repentent and redemptive. And I would never sneer at these good intentions. Born in the late 1940s in Chicago, I started my education (a charitable term, in this case) in a segregated school, and suffered all the indignities that come to blacks in a segregated society. My father, born in the South, made it only to the third grade before the white man's fields took permanent priority over his formal education. And though he educated himself into an advanced reader with an almost professorial authority, he could only drive a truck for a living, and never earned more than $90 a week in his entire life. So yes, it is crucial to my sense of citizenship, to my ability to identify with the spirit and the interests of America, to know that this country, however imperfectly, recognizes its past sins and wishes to correct them.

Yet good intentions can blind us to the effects they generate when implemented. In our society affirmative action is, among other things, a testament to white good will and to black power, and in the midst of these heavy investments its effects can be hard to see. But after 20 years of implementation I think that affirmative action has shown itself to be more bad than good and that blacks—whom I will focus on in this essay—now stand to lose more from it than they gain.

In talking with affirmative-action administrators and with blacks and whites in general, I found that supporters of affirmative action focus on its good intentions and detractors emphasize its negative effects. It was virtually impossible to find people outside either camp. The closest I came was a white male manager at a large computer company who said. "I think it amounts to reverse discrimination, but I'll put up with a little of that for a little more diversity." But this only makes him a half-hearted supporter of affirmative action. I think many people who don't really like affirmative action support it to one degree or another anyway.

I believe they do this because of what happened to white and black Americans in the crucible of the 1960s, when whites were confronted with their racial guilt and blacks tasted their first real power. In that stormy time white absolution and black power coalesced into virtual mandates for society. Affirmative action became a meeting ground for those mandates in the law. At first, this meant insuring equal opportunity. The 1964 civil-rights bill was passed on the understanding that equal opportunity would not mean racial preference. But in the late '60s and early '70s, affirmative action underwent a remarkable escalation of its mission from simple anti-discrimination enforcement to social engineering by means of quotas, goals, timetables, set-asides and other forms of preferential treatment.

Legally, this was achieved through a series of executive orders and Equal Employment Opportunity Commission guidelines that allowed racial imbalances in the workplace to stand as proof of racial discrimination. Once it could be assumed that discrimination explained racial imbalances, it became easy to justify group remedies to presumed discrimination rather than the normal case-by-case redress.

Even though blacks had made great advances during the '60s without quotas, the white mandate to achieve a new racial innocence, and the black mandate to gain power, which came to a head in the very late '60s, could no longer be satisfied by anything less than racial preferences. I don't think these mandates, in themselves, were wrong, because whites clearly needed to do better by blacks and blacks needed more real power in society. But as they came together in affirmative action, their effect was to distort our understanding of racial discrimination. By making black the color of preference, these mandates have reburdened society with the very marriage of color and preference (in reverse) that we set out to eradicate.

When affirmative action grew into social engineering, diversity became a golden word. Diversity is a term that applies democratic principles to races and cultures rather than to citizens, despite the fact that there is nothing to indicate that real diversity is the same thing as proportionate representation. Too often the result of this, on campuses for example, has been a democracy of colors rather than of people, an artificial diversity that gives the appearance of an educational parity between black and white students that has not yet been achieved in reality. Here again, racial preferences allow society to leapfrog over the difficult problem of developing blacks to parity with whites and into a cosmetic diversity that covers the blemish of disparity—a full six years after admission, only 26 to 28 percent of blacks graduate from college.

Racial representation is not the same thing as racial development. Representation can be manufactured; development is always hard earned. But it is the music of innocence and power that we hear in affirmative action that causes us to cling to it and to its distracting emphasis on representation. The fact is that after 20 years of racial preferences, the gap between median incomes of black and white families is greater than it was in the 1970s. None of this is to say that blacks don't need policies that insure our right to equal opportunity, but what we need more of is the development that will let us take advantage of society's efforts to include us.

I think one of the most troubling effects of racial preferences for blacks is a kind of demoralization. Under affirmative action, the quality that earns us preferential treatment is an implied inferiority. However this inferiority is explained—and it is easily enough explained by the myriad deprivations that grew out of our oppression—it is still inferiority. There are explanations and then there is the fact. And the fact must be borne by the individual as a condition apart from the explanation, apart even from the fact that others like himself also bear this condition. In integrated situations in which blacks must compete with whites who may be better prepared, these explanations may quickly wear thin and expose the individual to racial as well as personal self-doubt. (Of course whites also feel doubt, but only personally, not racially.)

What this means in practical terms is that when blacks deliver themselves into integrated situations they encounter a nasty little reflex in whites, a mindless, atavistic reflex that responds to the color black with negative stereotypes, such as intellectual ineptness. I think this reflex embarrasses most whites today and thus it is usually quickly repressed. On an equally atavistic level, the black will be aware of the reflex his color triggers and will feel a stab of horror at seeing himself reflected in this way. He, too, will do a quick repression, but a lifetime of such stabbings is what constitutes his inner realm of racial doubt. Even when the black sees no implication of inferiority in racial preferences, he knows that whites do, so that—consciously or unconsciously—the result is virtually the same. The effect of preferential treatment—the lowering of normal standards to increase black representation—puts blacks at war with an expanded realm of debilitating doubt, so that the doubt itself becomes an unrecognized preoccupation that undermines their ability to perform, especially in integrated situations.

I believe another liability of affirmative action comes from the fact that it indirectly encourages blacks to exploit their own past victimization. Like implied inferiority, victimization is what justifies preference, so that to receive the benefits of preferential treatment one must, to some extent, become invested in the view of one's self as a victim. In this way, affirmative action nurtures a victim-focused identity in blacks and sends us the message that there is more power in our past suffering than in our present achievements.

When power itself grows out of suffering, blacks are encouraged to expand the boundaries of what qualifies as racial oppression, a situation that can lead us to paint our victimization in vivid colors even as we receive the benefits of preference. The same corporations and institutions that gave us preferences are also seen as our oppressors. At Stanford University, minority-group students—who receive at least the same financial aid as whites with the same need—recently took over the president's office demanding, among other things, more financial aid.

But I think one of the worst prices that blacks pay for preference has to do with an illusion. I saw this illusion at work recently in the mother of a middle-class black student who was going off to his first semester of college: "They owe us this, so don't think for a minute that you don't belong there." This is the logic by which many blacks, and some whites, justify affirmative action—it is something "owed," a form of reparation. But this logic overlooks a much harder and less digestible reality, that it is impossible to repay blacks living today for the historic suffering of the race. If all blacks were given a million dollars tomorrow it would not amount to a dime on the dollar for three centuries of oppression, nor would it dissolve the residues of that oppression that we still carry today. The concept of historic reparation grows out of man's need to impose on the world a degree of justice that simply does not exist. Suffering can be endured and overcome, it cannot be repaid. To think otherwise is to prolong the suffering.

Several blacks I spoke with said they were still in favor of affirmative action because of the "subtle" discrimination blacks were subject to once they were on the job. One photojournalist said, "They have ways of ignoring you." A black female television producer said: "You can't file a lawsuit when your boss doesn't invite you to the insider meetings without ruining your career. So we still need affirmative action." Others mentioned the infamous "glass ceiling" through which blacks can see the top positions of authority but never reach them. But I don't think racial preferences are a protection against this subtle discrimination: I think they contribute to it.

In any workplace: racial preferences will always create two-tiered populations composed of preferreds and unpreferreds. In the case of blacks and whites, for instance, racial preferences imply that whites are superior just as they imply that blacks are inferior. They not only reinforce America's oldest racial myth but, for blacks, they have the effect of stigmatizing the already stigmatized.

I think that much of the "subtle" discrimination that blacks talk about is often (not always) discrimination against the stigma of questionable competence that affirmative action marks blacks with. In this sense, preferences make scapegoats of the very people they seek to help. And it may be that at a certain level employers impose a glass ceiling, but this may not be against the race so much as against the race's reputation for having advanced by color as much as by competence. This ceiling is the point at which corporations shift the emphasis from color to competency and stop playing the affirmative-action game. Here preference backfires for blacks and becomes a taint that holds them back. Of course one could argue that this taint, which is after all in the minds of whites, becomes nothing more than an excuse to discriminate against blacks. And certainly the result is the same in either case—blacks don't get past the glass ceiling. But this argument does not get around the fact that racial preferences now taint this color with a new theme of suspicion that makes blacks even more vulnerable to discrimination. In this crucial yet gray area of perceived competence, preferences make whites look better than they are and blacks worse, while doing nothing whatever to stop the very real discrimination that blacks may encounter. I don't wish to justify the glass ceiling here, but only suggest the very subtle ways that affirmative action revives rather than extinguishes the old rationalizations for racial discrimination.

I believe affirmative action is problematic in our society because we have demanded that it create parity between the races rather than ensure equal opportunity. Preferential treatment does not teach skills, or educate, or instill motivation. It only passes out entitlement by color, a situation that in my profession has created an unrealistically high demand for black professors. The social engineer's assumption is that this high demand will inspire more blacks to earn Ph.D.s and join the profession. In fact, the number of blacks earning Ph.D.s has declined in recent years. Ph.D.s must be developed from preschool on. They require family and community support. They must acquire an entire system of values that enables them to work hard while delaying gratification.

It now seems clear that the Supreme Court, in a series of recent decisions, is moving away from racial preferences. It has disallowed preferences except in instances of "identified discrimination," eroded the precedent that statistical racial imbalances are prima facie evidence of discrimination, and, in effect, granted white males the right to challenge consent degrees that use preference to achieve racial balances in the workplace. Referring to this and other Supreme Court decisions, one civil-rights leader said, "Night has fallen...as far as civil rights are concerned." But I am not so sure. The effect of these decisions is to protect the constitutional rights of everyone, rather than to take rights away from blacks. Night has fallen on racial preferences, not on the fundamental rights of black Americans. The reason for this shift, I believe, is that the white mandate for absolution from past racial sins has weakened considerably in the 1980s. Whites are now less willing to endure unfairness to themselves in order to grant special entitlements to blacks, even when those entitlements are justified in the name of past suffering. Yet the black mandate for more power in society has remained unchanged. And I think part of the anxiety many blacks feel over these decisions has to do with the loss of black power that they may signal.

But the power we've lost by these decisions is really only the power that grows out of our victimization. This is not a very substantial or reliable power, and it is important that we know this so we can focus more exclusively on the kind of development that will bring enduring power. There is talk now that Congress may pass new legislation to compensate for these new limits on affirmative action. If this happens, I hope the focus will be on development and anti-discrimination, rather than entitlement, on achieving racial party rather than jerry-building racial diversity.

But if not preferences, what? The impulse to discriminate is subtle and cannot be ferreted out unless its many guises are made clear to people. I think we need social policies that are committed to two goals: the educational and economic development of disadvantaged people regardless of race and the eradication from our society—through close monitoring and severe sanctions—of racial, ethnic, or gender discrimination. Preferences will not get us to either of these goals, because they tend to benefit those who are not disadvantaged —middle-class white women and middle-class blacks—and attack one form of discrimination with another. Preferences are inexpensive and carry the glamour of good intentions—change the numbers and the good deed is done. To be against them is to be unkind. But I think the unkindest cut is to bestow on children like my own an undeserved advantage while neglecting the development of those disadvantaged children in the poorer sections of my city who will most likely never be in a position to benefit from a preference. Give my children fairness; give disadvantaged children a better shot at development—better elementary and secondary schools, job training, safer neighborhoods, better financial assistance for college, and so on. A smaller percentage of black high school graduates go to college today than 15 years ago: more black males are in prison, jail, or in some other way under the control of the criminal-justice system than in college. This despite racial preferences.

The mandates of black power and white absolution out of which preferences emerged were not wrong in themselves. What was wrong was that both races focused more on the goals of those mandates than on the means to the goals. Blacks can have no real power without taking responsibility for their own educational and economic development. Whites can have no racial innocence without earning it by eradicating discrimination and helping the disadvantaged to develop. Because we ignored the means, the goals have not been reached and the real work remains to be done.

DISCUSSION QUESTIONS

1. There remains fundamental disagreement over the current extent of racial and gender discrimination in employment, housing, and other settings. Do you think racial or gender discrimination is still present and significant? What evidence can you give to support your opinion?

2. What does "affirmative action" mean to you? Is your definition different from your definition of "equal opportunity"?
3. What do you think the appropriate goal for affirmative action should be?
4. What groups, if any, should qualify for special consideration under affirmative action plans? What criteria are necessary or sufficient for inclusion?
5. Do you believe that the playing field is now level with respect to race, or are one or more groups relatively advantaged? If it is not level, what factors contribute to inequality and what action(s) would improve racial parity in education and employment?
6. Is affirmative action "reverse racism"? In what ways are the two concepts similar? In what ways are they different?
7. How do you feel about affirmative action being used as a "divisive" issue in political campaigns? Do such campaigns add to racial tension, or is it "just politics"? Do you think such campaigns influence attitudes toward "racial justice"?
8. Are attempts to encourage dialogue on the subject of race, such as the "national conversation on race" initiated by former President Clinton in 1997, likely to yield an improved understanding of the role race plays in American life? Do you think such a dialogue will lead to increased or decreased support for affirmative action or, perhaps, for significant policy changes?

WEB REFERENCES

American Association for Affirmative Action, http://www.affirmativeaction.org/.

American Civil Rights Institute, http://www.acri.org/.

BAMN Affirmative Action, http://www.bamn.com/.

The Case against Affirmative Action, http://www.stanfordalumni.org/news/magazine/1996/sepoct/articles/against.html.

Ten Myths about Affirmative Action, http://www.socialpsychology.org/affirm.htm.

U.S. State Department—Race and Ethnic Diversity in the United States, http://usinfo.state.gov/usa/race/.

FURTHER READING

Altschiller, Donald, ed. *Affirmative Action*. New York: H. W. Wilson, 1991.

Appiah, Anthony K. and Amy Guttman. *Color Conscious: The Political Morality of Race*. Princeton, N.J.: Princeton University Press, 1996.

Bell, Derrick. *Faces at the Bottom of the Well: The Permanence of Racism*. New York: Basic Books, 1992.

Bergmann, Barbara. *In Defense of Affirmative Action*. New York: HarperCollins, 1997.

Boxill, Bernard R. *Blacks and Social Justice*. Lanham, Md.: Rowman & Littlefield, 1992.

Carter, Stephen L. *Reflections of an Affirmative Action Baby*. New York: Basic Books, 1991.

Cavanagh, Matt. *Against Equality of Opportunity*. Oxford: Clarendon Press, 2002.

Chavez, Lydia. *The Color Blind: California's Battle to End Affirmative Action*. Berkeley: University of California Press, 1998.

Clayton, Susan D. and Faye J. Crosby. *Justice, Gender, and Affirmative Action*. Ann Arbor: University of Michigan Press, 1992.

Crosby, Faye and Cheryl Vandeveer, eds. *Sex, Race, and Merit: Debating Affirmative Action in Education and Employment*. Ann Arbor: University of Michigan Press, 2000.

Curry, George E. and Cornel West, eds. *The Affirmative Action Debate*. New York: Addison-Wesley, 1996.

D'Souza, Dinesh. *Illiberal Education*. New York: Free Press, 1991.

Eastland, Terry. *Ending Affirmative Action: The Case for Colorblind Justice*. New York: Basic Books, 1996.

Eastland, Terry and William J. Bennett. *Counting by Race: Equality from the Founding Fathers to Bakke*. New York: Basic Books, 1979.

Edley, Christopher. *Not All Black and White: Affirmative Action, Race, and American Values*. New York: Hill & Wang, 1996.

Edsall, Thomas Byrne with Mary D. Edsall. *Chain Reaction: The Impact of Race, Rights, and Taxes on American Politics*. New York: W. W. Norton, 1991.

Gates, Henry Louis. *Colored People: A Memoir*. New York: Vintage Books, 1995.

Gates, Henry Louis. *Speaking of Race, Speaking of Sex: Hate Speech, Civil Rights, and Civil Liberties*. New York: New York University Press, 1995.

Gates, Henry Louis and Cornel West. *The Future of the Race*. New York: Vintage Books, 1997.

Graham, Hugh Davis. *The Civil Rights Era: Origins and Development of National Policy, 1960–1972*. New York: Oxford University Press, 1990.

Graham, Hugh Davis. *Collision Course: The Strange Convergence of Affirmative Action and Immigration Policy in America*. New York: Oxford University Press, 2002.

Guinier, Lani. *The Tyranny of the Majority: Fundamental Fairness in Representative Democracy*. New York: Free Press, 1995.

Hacker, Andrew. *Two Nations: Blacks and Whites, Separate, Hostile, Unequal*. New York: Scribner, 1992.

McCall, Nathan. *Makes Me Wanna Holler: A Young Black Man in America*. New York: Vintage Books, 1994.

Mills, Nicolaus, ed. *Debating Affirmative Action; Race, Gender, Ethnicity, and the Politics of Inclusion*. New York: Delta, 1994.

Patterson, Orlando. *The Ordeal of Integration: Progress and Resentment in America's Racial Crisis*. New York: Civitas, 1997.

Pojman, Louis. "The Moral Status of Affirmative Action," in Julie McDonald, ed., *Contemporary Moral Issues in a Just Society*. Belmont, Calif.: Wadsworth, 1998, pp. 297–315.

Post, Robert and Michael Rogin, eds. *Race and Representation: Affirmative Action*. New York: Zone Books, 1998.

Reskin, Barbara. *The Realities of Affirmative Action in Employment*. Washington, D.C.: American Sociological Association, 1998.

Reynolds, William Bradford. "Affirmative Action and Its Negative Repercussions." *Annals of the American Academy of Political and Social Science* (September 1992).

Rosenfeld, Michel. *Affirmative Action and Justice: A Philosophical and Constitutional Inquiry*. New Haven, Conn.: Yale University Press, 1991.

Schneider, Bart, ed. *Race: An Anthology in the First Person*. New York: Crown Publishers, 1997.

Shipler, David K. *A Country of Strangers: Blacks and Whites in America*. New York: Knopf, 1997.

Sleeper, Jim. *Liberal Racism*. New York: Viking, 1997.

Sowell, Thomas. *Preferential Policies: An International Perspective*. New York: W. Morrow, 1990.

Spann, Girardeau A. *The Law of Affirmative Action: Twenty-Five Years of Supreme Court Decisions on Race and Remedies*. New York: New York University Press, 2000.

Steele, Shelby. *The Content of Our Character: A New Vision of Race in America*. New York: St. Martin's Press, 1990.

Taylor, William L. and Susan M. Liss. "Affirmative Action in the 1990s: Staying the Course." *Annals of the American Academy of Political and Social Science* (September 1992).

Thernstrom, Stephan and Abigail Thernstrom. *America in Black and White: One Nation, Indivisible*. Cambridge, Mass.: Harvard University Press, 1998.

West, Cornel. *Race Matters*. New York: Vintage Books, 1994.

West, Cornel and Roberto Mangabeira Unger. *The Future of American Progressivism: An Initiative for Political and Economic Reform*. Boston: Beacon Press, 1998.

Wilson, William J. "Race-Neutral Programs and the Democratic Coalition." *American Prospect* (Spring 1990).

CHAPTER 12

DRUG POLICY

"Should Drugs Be Legalized?"

YES: Ethan A. Nadelmann "The Case for Legalization"
The Public Interest

NO: James Q. Wilson "Against the Legalization of
Drugs" *Commentary*

After a long and contentious public debate, voters in California and Arizona
passed legislation in November 1996 that effectively legalized the use of
marijuana for medicinal purposes. While drug policy had been a topic of
political debate and public concern for years, the controversy surrounding this
legislation and its ultimate approval catapulted the issue of drug policy to the
forefront of public policy debates and focused the discussion around the issue
of drug legality. This served to highlight an approach to drug policy that is
beginning to receive support from some citizens and policymakers: the legalization for any purpose of many drugs that are now illegal. Former Surgeon
General Joycelyn Elders recommended that the government study the idea of
legalizing drugs (after backing off from a personal comment that she supports
such an idea),[1] joining a growing list of politicians—including former big-city
mayors such as Kurt Schmoke of Baltimore—and editorialists (such as William
F. Buckley) who have publicly supported such a move. The issue has received
high-profile support from Republican Governor Gary Johnson of New Mexico,
who has tried to reframe the drug issue as a medical, not criminal, problem.

Perhaps more than any other policy debate in this volume, the issue of
drug legalization defies simple ideological characterization. Proponents range
from libertarian academics to those on the far political left, while opponents
of legalization also include conservatives and liberals alike. Therefore,
unusual political coalitions can be found on either side of the debate. Further,
the debate—and a classroom discussion of the issue—is best viewed not as a
bipolar libertarian drug legalization position versus a zero-tolerance position.
There are a number of positions and policies between legalization and
prohibition. South Australia, for example, permits people to cultivate
marijuana for personal use, which some view as an attractive option since
risks of increased use may pale in comparison with eliminating 700,000
marijuana possession arrests each year in the United States and "the possibility

of weakening the link between soft- and hard-drug markets without launching Dutch-style commercial promotion."[2]

One reason some call for drug legalization, and a significant factor motivating public concern over drug policy, has been the apparent association between violence and the sale of illegal drugs. In fact, the rising tide of urban violence has frequently been tied to the enormous potential profits from the sale of illegal drugs. It is estimated that 4.8 percent of the 14,088 homicides committed in 1998 were drug-related.[3] Furthermore, an estimated 10 percent of federal prisoners and 17 percent of state prisoners in 1991 reported that they committed their offenses primarily to obtain money to purchase drugs.[4] These offenses include 32 percent of robberies, 31 percent of burglaries, 23 percent of frauds, and 3 percent of homicides. Drug offenders account for nearly three-quarters of the total growth in the federal prison population since 1980.[5] Equivalent figures for state prison populations tend to be even higher. State and local authorities made over 1.2 million arrests for drug violations in 1995, almost 70 percent of them for possession offenses (compared with sale and manufacturing violations).[6] In 1998, an estimated 26 percent of all inmates under local supervision were incarcerated for drug offenses. In 1999, the FBI reported that 10 percent of all arrests were drug arrests; in 1998, 59 percent of all federal inmates were imprisoned for drug-related offenses.[7] There is little question that violence and the illegal activity surrounding drugs have motivated public concern, but the level of concern over the use of drugs has varied considerably in recent years. In a 2001 survey by the Pew Charitable Trusts, 63 percent of respondents saw drug abuse as a serious problem across the country, but only 37 percent believed it to be serious in their own neighborhoods.[8]

Policy proposals directed at solving the "drug problem" have been based on two different strategies. On the one hand are those who argue that the best way to reduce the use of drugs is to reduce the demand for drugs and prevent nonusers from becoming drug users. Such "demand-side" strategies focus on the use of drug treatment programs to reduce drug dependence, drug awareness and education programs to prevent the desire to use drugs, and strict sentencing as a disincentive to use drugs. Others believe that efforts should focus on restricting the supply of drugs available in the United States by utilizing law enforcement to interdict the shipment of drugs and by imposing stiff penalties on the sale and the use of drugs. Traditionally, U.S. drug policy has reflected a combination of these demand-side and supply-side strategies.

The success of the "war on drugs" that was initiated during the 1980s has been a subject of much controversy. Most legislative activity occurred between 1986 and 1992, during which time Congress passed the 1986 and 1988 Antidrug Abuse Acts and the International Narcotics Control Acts of 1989 and 1992. Partly as a result of this legislation, the amount of money spent to restrict the supply of illegal drugs rose more than 1,139 percent between 1981 and 2002, when $18.8 billion was spent on federal drug control programs.[9] Spending on drug control is expected to rise to $19.2 billion in 2003, spread across five principal federal departments (Agriculture, Defense, Education, Housing and Urban Development, and Justice).[10] The increased effort to fight the manufacture, distribution, and consumption of drugs during this period included the Partnership for a Drug-Free America, increased community awareness programs, the creation of the Office of National Drug Control Policy (the so-called drug czar) within the federal executive branch, and significantly higher funding of law enforcement units for drug interdiction efforts. Sixty-seven percent of federal spending for drug control policies in fiscal year 2002 went to supply-side efforts such as law enforcement and related military agencies.[11] Approximately $9.5 billion in supply-side spending was devoted to domestic law enforcement and the remaining $3.2 billion to international efforts, including interdiction. The majority of the remaining $6.3 billion for demand-side expenditures was divided between prevention efforts, which received $2.5 billion, and treatment programs, which received $3.6 billion.[12] In 1995, individual states spent roughly $4.8 billion on alcohol and drug abuse services such as treatment and prevention. Of this money, treatment programs received more than five times as much as prevention efforts.[13] Recent legislative activity has included the introduction of a bill in the Senate in 2001 (S.304), broadly aimed at preventing drug use by minors, expanding drug treatment programs, increasing drug awareness in schools, and rehabilitating drug offenders back into local communities.

The increased attention and expenditures directed at restricting the supply of illegal drugs have produced mixed results. For example, in 2000 federal agencies such as the Drug Enforcement Administration (DEA) and Federal Bureau of Investigation seized 5.5 million pounds of illegal drugs, including 3,044 pounds of heroin, 235,299 pounds of cocaine, and more than 2.6 million pounds of marijuana and hashish. While total drug seizures have increased since 1990 when 1,238,425 pounds were confiscated, the majority of this growth has been in marijuana seizures, which increased more than 2 million pounds over this period. In contrast, seizures of both cocaine and heroin remained relatively static during the 1990s.[14] Total seizures of drug-related property by DEA officials amounted to some $459 million in 2000.[15] Assessing the success of drug control policy by examining the seizure of drugs can be deceiving, of course, because the goal of drug control policy is not to seize drugs but rather to reduce the supply and use of drugs. On one hand, a decline in the quantity of drugs seized may indicate that the total supply of drugs has fallen, whether from a decrease in demand or from successful international interdiction efforts, and that the DEA is merely confiscating its normal share of a smaller pool of drugs. On the other hand, a decline in the quantity of drugs seized may mean that the same quantity of drugs is available and that the DEA is seizing a smaller percentage.

National drug control policy has received numerous criticisms. The national "drug czar" has been criticized as nothing more than a symbolic coordinator of numerous and disparate federal agencies with little power to shape policy. Supporters maintain that a more coherent national policy has resulted from the office's efforts. Although funding for the office increased in the 1980s, the Clinton administration slashed funding for the office early in its tenure while simultaneously elevating the director to a cabinet-level position. President George W. Bush has identified drug control as a priority and has retained the director of the Office of National Drug Control Policy as a cabinet-level position. In 2001, Bush announced a $1.1 billion budget increase for drug control, with new initiatives including a Parent Drug Corps.[16] A number of other substantive issues over drug policy continue to be debated. One is whether funds directed toward interdiction, which many consider to have failed miserably, would be better spent on prevention and treatment. Supporters argue that while treatment does not always work, it is far more cost-effective than imprisonment. Moreover, drug cases have clogged the federal court system, and judges are forced to push civil cases aside in order to handle the vast number of drug-related cases (despite large funding increases).

Recent trends in illegal drug use among Americans show a tendency toward decreasing usage in all population groups. The annual prevalence of drug use for selected drugs[17] shows that usage has fallen significantly for youth (ages 12 to 17) and young adults (18 to 25). In 1974, 19 percent of those aged 12 to 17 admitted to having used marijuana "during the past year"; this figure rose to a high of 24 percent in 1979, but receded to 14 percent in 1998, with a significant downward acceleration from 1985 to the mid-1990s and then slightly rising again in more recent years.[18] A similar overall trend existed for cocaine; 2.7 percent admitted to use in the previous year in 1974, 4.2 percent in 1979, and 1.7 percent in 1998. Data on heroin use among this age group have been limited, but showed a drop in usage levels from 0.6 percent in 1990 to 0.3 percent in 1998. While larger percentages of the 18-to-25 age group are using drugs, the trends over time are similar to those of youth. For marijuana, 34 percent admitted use in 1974, 47 percent in 1979, and 24 percent in 1998. For cocaine, 8 percent admitted use in 1974, 20 percent in 1979, and under 4 percent by 1994, rising slightly to an estimated 4.7 percent in 1998. Heroin use declined from 0.8 percent in 1974 to 0.1 percent in 1994, but rose to an estimated 0.4 percent in 1998. Only among adults between the ages of 26 and 34 were the trends slightly different. For this group, marijuana use has consistently increased, from 3.8 percent in 1974 and 10.6 percent in 1982 to 11.5 percent in 1994, falling slightly in 1998 to 9.7 percent. Cocaine use increased from a negligible amount in 1974 to a high of 4.2 percent in 1985, dropping to 2.7 percent in 1998; and 0.1 percent of adults in this age group admitted using heroin within the past year.[19]

The concern of most policymakers and public health officials has been motivated at least partly by the potentially negative health effects of drug use, and for many years there was a concern that members of the public—especially young children and teenagers—were insufficiently concerned about the negative impact of drug use on health. However, public perceptions of the health risks associated with the use of drugs have shifted in recent years. Drug use is no longer a condoned or encouraged activity among many schoolchildren and teenagers, and young adults have shown an increased concern over the health effects of drug use. The percentage of adults between the ages of 19 and 22 who fear "great risk" from occasional use of cocaine increased from 67 percent in 1988 to 72 percent in 2000. While there was a similar increase between 1988 and 1994 (from 25 percent to 31 percent) in perceptions of the dangers involved in occasional marijuana use, only 26 percent of young adults in 2000 viewed marijuana use as a significant health risk.[20] These changing perceptions, as well as the increased interdiction efforts of law enforcement, have not affected high school seniors' perceptions of the availability of illicit drugs, however. In 1985, 86 percent of high school seniors felt that it was "fairly" or "very" easy to obtain marijuana, 49 percent felt the same way about cocaine, and 21 percent believed that to be the case for heroin. In 2000, more (89 percent) believed marijuana and heroin (34 percent) were fairly or very easy to obtain, and virtually the same percentage (48 percent) believed cocaine was readily available.[21]

Attitudes toward drug legalization have shown considerable variation over the past few decades. The percentage of Americans supporting the legalization of marijuana reached an all-time high in 2000, with 32 percent of the population believing that marijuana use should be legalized. Fully 73 percent of the population in 2001 believed that marijuana use should be legalized for medicinal purposes. Among age groups, those between the ages of 18 and 29 have been the strongest supporters of marijuana legalization (41 percent in 2000), although 39 percent of high school seniors in 2000 felt that marijuana use in private should be a crime.[22] While there is some support for the legalization of marijuana, it is unclear how much public support would exist for the legalization of drugs like cocaine and heroin, considered by most people to be more addictive and to pose more serious health risks.

Proponents argue that the legalization of drugs would have a variety of positive effects. While current high street prices for illegal drugs encourage criminal activity, as drug users often commit crimes in order to purchase drugs, legalization would drastically reduce the price of drugs, and thereby all but eliminate crimes committed to obtain drugs and protect drug distribution networks. Further, drug purity could be regulated and the distribution supervised, thereby reducing poisoning and abuse. And because distribution would take place in pharmacies, medical clinics, or hospitals rather than on the streets, legalization would allow drug treatment and education efforts to more effectively focus on drug users. Legalization proponents sometimes encourage a concomitant tax on drugs to fund treatment and education programs. (Of course, if the drug tax is set too high, the advantages of legalization evaporate as drug prices are once again driven upward.) Ethan Nadelmann is one of the leading proponents of this position. He writes that current and past efforts at drug control have been failures, and the costs that those efforts impose upon society far outweigh any benefit gained. He responds to critics by acknowledging the potential for abuse, but argues that the dangers of drug use have been vastly overstated.

Opponents of drug legalization point out that if drug prices fall enough to have the positive effects that supporters argue, it will encourage greater use of (and therefore addiction to) narcotics. Critics maintain that just because the war on drugs has not been an obvious success does not mean that eliminating the crime eliminates the problem, any more than legalizing assault would reduce violence. Political scientist James Q. Wilson, then at UCLA, argues that the high price of drugs due to their illegality has had a strong effect in reducing the number of new addicts. He claims that legalizing drugs would be extremely costly to society, and that the difficulties involved in treating addictions, and the moral and ethical dilemmas presented by legalization, argue strongly against it.

Endnotes

1. Indeed, the White House press secretary said of the proposal, "Basically, it's not going to happen." Stephen Labaton, "Surgeon General Suggests Study of Legalizing Drugs," *The New York Times* (December 8, 1993), p. A23.
2. Robert MacCoun and Peter Reuter, "Marijuana, Heroin, and Cocaine," *The American Prospect* (June 3, 2002), p. 28.
3. Office of National Drug Control Policy, Executive Office of the President. Drug-Related Crime, http://www.whitehousedrugpolicy.gov/publications/pdf/ncj181056.pdf, 4.
4. Ibid., 3.
5. Ibid.
6. U.S. Bureau of the Census, *Statistical Abstract of the U.S., 2001* (Washington, D.C.: U.S. Government Printing Office, 2001).
7. Office of National Drug Control Policy, Executive Office of the President, Drug Treatment in the Criminal Justice System, http://www.whitehousedrugpolicy.gov/publications/pdf/94406.pdf, 1.
8. Pew Charitable Trusts, http://www.pewtrusts.com.
9. Office of National Drug Control Policy, Executive Office of the President, http://www.whitehousedrugpolicy.gov/publications/policy/03ndcs/pages31_36.pdf.
10. Office of Management and Budget, Federal Drug Control Programs, http://www.whitehouse.gov/omb/budget/fy2003/pdf/bud32.pdf.
11. Office of National Drug Control Policy, Executive Office of the President, National Drug Control Strategy, FY03 Budget Summary, http://www.whitehousedrugpolicy.gov/publications/pdf/budget2002.pdf.
12. Ibid.
13. National Association of State Alcohol and Drug Abuse Directors, *State Alcohol Drug Abuse Profiles: FY 1995* (Washington, D.C.: NASADAD, 1997), p. 10.
14. U.S. Bureau of the Census, *Statistical Abstract 1998 of the U.S.* (Washington, D.C.: U.S. Government Printing Office, 1998).
15. *Sourcebook of Criminal Justice Statistics 2000*, p. 403, http://www.albany.edu/sourcebook/1995/pdf/t443.pdf.
16. U.S. Department of State, http://usinfo.state.gov/topical/global/drugs/01051101.htm.

17. Drug categories include marijuana and hashish; inhalants; hallucinogens; cocaine; heroin; nonmedical use of stimulants, sedatives, tranquilizers, or analgesics; and alcohol.

18. Data from *Sourcebook of Criminal Justice Statistics*, p. 261, http:// www.albany. edu/sourcebook/1995/pdf/t393.pdf. These data indicate the estimated prevalence of drug and alcohol use during the past year.

19. *Sourcebook of Criminal Justice Statistics*, http://www.albany.edu/sourcebook/ 1995/tost_3.html#3_w.

20. Ibid., http://www.albany.edu/sourcebook/1995/pdf/t295.pdf.

21. Ibid.

22. Ibid.

YES

The Case for Legalization

Ethan A. Nadelmann

What can be done about the "drug problem"? Despite frequent proclamations of war and dramatic increases in government funding and resources in recent years, there are many indications that the problem is not going away and may even be growing worse. During the past year alone, more than thirty million Americans violated the drug laws on literally billions of occasions. Drug-treatment programs in many cities are turning people away for lack of space and funding. In Washington, D.C., drug-related killings, largely of one drug dealer by another, are held responsible for a doubling in the homicide rate over the past year. In New York and elsewhere, courts and prisons are clogged with a virtually limitless supply of drug-law violators. In large cities and small towns alike, corruption of policemen and other criminal-justice officials by drug traffickers is rampant.

President Reagan and the First Lady are not alone in supporting increasingly repressive and expensive anti-drug measures, and in believing that the war against drugs can be won. Indeed, no "war" proclaimed by an American leader during the past forty years has garnered such sweeping bipartisan support; on this issue, liberals and conservatives are often indistinguishable. The fiercest disputes are not over objectives or even broad strategies, but over turf and tactics. Democratic politicians push for the appointment of a "drug czar" to oversee all drug policy, and blame the Administration for not applying sufficient pressure and sanctions against the foreign drug-producing countries. Republicans try to gain the upper hand by daring Democrats to support more widespread drug testing, increasingly powerful law-enforcement measures, and the death penalty for various drug-related offenses. But on the more fundamental issues of what this war is about, and what strategies are most likely to prove successful in the long run, no real debate—much less vocal dissent—can be heard.

If there were a serious public debate on this issue, far more attention would be given to one policy option that has just begun to be seriously considered, but which may well prove more successful than anything currently being implemented or proposed: legalization. Politicians and public officials remain hesitant even to mention the word, except to dismiss it contemptuously as a capitulation to the drug traffickers. Most Americans perceive drug legalization as an invitation to drug-infested anarchy. Even the civil-liberties groups shy away from this issue, limiting their input primarily to the drug-testing debate. The minority communities in the ghetto, for whom repealing the drug laws would promise the greatest benefits, fail to recognize the costs of our drug-prohibition policies. And the typical middle-class American, who hopes only that his children will not succumb to drug abuse, tends to favor any measures that he believes will make illegal drugs less accessible to them. Yet when one seriously compares the advantages and disadvantages of the legalization strategy with those of current and planned policies, abundant evidence suggests that legalization may well be the optimal strategy for tackling the drug problem.

Interestingly, public support for repealing the drug-prohibition laws has traditionally come primarily from the conservative end of the political spectrum: Milton Friedman, Ernest van den Haag, William F. Buckley, and the editors of the *Economist* have all supported it. Less vocal support comes from many liberals, politicians not among them, who are disturbed by the infringements on individual liberty posed by the drug laws. There is also a significant silent constituency in favor of repeal, found especially among criminal-justice officials, intelligence analysts, military interdictors, and criminal-justice scholars who have spent a considerable amount of time thinking about the problem. More often than not, however, job-security considerations, combined with an awareness that they can do little to change official policies, ensure that their views remain discreet and off the record.

During the spring of 1988, however, legalization suddenly began to be seriously considered as a policy option; the pros and cons of legalization were discussed on the front pages of leading newspapers and news magazines, and were debated on national television programs. Although the argument for legalization was not new, two factors seem to have been primarily responsible for the blitz of media coverage: an intellectual rational for legalization—the first provided in decades—appeared in my article in the Spring issue of *Foreign Policy* magazine; more importantly, political legitimacy was subsequently bestowed upon the legalization option when Baltimore Mayor Kurt Schmoke, speaking to the National Conference of Mayors, noted the potential benefits of drug legalization and asked that the merits of legalization be debated in congressional hearings.

The idea of legalizing drugs was quickly denounced by most politicians across the political spectrum; nevertheless, the case for legalization appealed to many Americans. The prominent media coverage lent an aura of respectability to arguments that just a month earlier had seemed to be beyond the political pale. Despite the tendency of many journalists to caricature the legalization argument, at long last the issue had been joined. Various politicians, law-enforcement officials, health experts, and scholars came out in favor of drug legalization—or at least wanted to debate the matter seriously. On Capitol Hill, three or four congressmen seconded the call for a debate. According to some congressional staffers, two dozen additional legislators would have wanted to debate the issue, had the question arisen after rather than before the upcoming elections. Unable to oppose a mere hearing on the issue, Congressman Charles Rangel, chairman of the House Select Committee on Narcotics, declared his willingness to convene his committee in Baltimore to consider the legalization option.

There is, of course, no single legalization strategy. At one extreme is the libertarian vision of virtually no government restraints on the production and sale of drugs or any psychoactive substances, except perhaps around the fringes, such as prohibiting sales to children. At the other extreme is total government control over the production and sale of these goods. In between lies a strategy that may prove more successful than anything yet tried in stemming the problems of drug abuse and drug-related violence, corruption, sickness, and suffering. It is one in which government makes most of the substances that are now banned legally available to competent adults, exercises strong regulatory powers over all large-scale production and sale of drugs, makes drug-treatment programs available to all who need them, and offers honest drug-education programs to children. This strategy, it is worth noting, would also result in a net benefit to public treasuries of at least ten billion dollars a year, and perhaps much more.

There are three reasons why it is important to think about legalization scenarios, even though most Americans remain hostile to the idea. First, current drug-control policies have failed, are failing, and will continue to fail, in good part because they are fundamentally flawed. Second, many drug-control efforts are not only failing, but also proving highly costly and counter-productive; indeed, many of the drug-related evils that Americans identify as part and parcel of the "drug problem" are in fact caused by our drug-prohibition policies. Third, there is good reason to believe that repealing many of the drug laws would not lead, as many people fear, to a dramatic rise in drug abuse. In this essay I expand on each of these reasons for considering the legalization option. Government efforts to deal with the drug problem will succeed only if the rhetoric and crusading mentality that now dominate drug policy are replaced by reasoned and logical analysis.

WHY CURRENT DRUG POLICIES FAIL

Most proposals for dealing with the drug problem today reflect a desire to point the finger at those most removed from one's home and area of expertise. New York Mayor Ed Koch, Florida Congressman Larry Smith, and Harlem Congressman Charles Rangel, who recognize government's inability to deal with the drug problem in the cities, are among the most vocal supporters of punishing foreign drug-producing countries and stepping up interdiction efforts. Foreign leaders and U.S. State Department and drug-enforcement officials stationed abroad, on the other hand, who understand all too well why it is impossible to crack down successfully on illicit drug production outside the United States, are the most vigorous advocates of domestic enforcement and demand-reduction efforts within the United States. In between, those agencies charged with drug interdiction, from the Coast Guard and U.S. Customs Service to the U.S. military, know that they will never succeed in capturing more than a small percentage of the illicit drugs being smuggled into the United States. Not surprisingly, they point their fingers in both directions. The solution, they promise, lies in greater source-control efforts abroad and greater demand-reduction efforts at home.

Trying to pass the buck is always understandable. But in each of these cases, the officials are half right and half wrong—half right in recognizing that they can do little to affect their end of the drug problem, given the suppositions and constraints of current drug-control strategies; half wrong (if we assume that their finger-pointing is sincere) in expecting that the solution lies elsewhere. It would be wrong, however, to assume that the public posturing of many officials reflects their real views. Many of them privately acknowledge the futility of all current drug-control strategies, and wonder whether radically different options, such as legalization, might not prove more successful in dealing with the drug problem. The political climate pervading this issue is such, however, that merely to ask that alternatives to current policies be considered is to incur a great political risk.

By most accounts, the dramatic increase in drug-enforcement efforts over the past few years has had little effect on the illicit drug market in the United States. The mere existence of drug-prohibition laws, combined with a minimal level of law-enforcement resources, is sufficient to maintain the price of illicit drugs at a level significantly higher than it would be if there were no such laws. Drug laws and enforcement also reduce the availability of illicit drugs, most notably in parts of the United States where demand is relatively limited to begin with. Theoretically, increases in drug-enforcement efforts should result in reduced availability, higher prices, and lower purity of illegal drugs. That is, in fact, what has happened to the domestic marijuana market (in at least the first two respects). But in general the illegal drug market has not responded as intended to the substantial increases in federal, state, and local drug-enforcement efforts.

Cocaine has sold for about a hundred dollars a gram at the retail level since the beginning of the 1980s. The average purity of that gram, however, has increased from 12 to 60 percent. Moreover, a growing number of users are turning to "crack," a potent derivative of cocaine that can be smoked; it is widely sold in ghetto neighborhoods now for five to ten dollars per vial. Needless to say, both crack and the 60 percent pure cocaine pose much greater threats to users than did the relatively benign powder available eight years ago. Similarly, the retail price of heroin has remained relatively constant even as the average purity has risen from 3.9 percent in 1983 to 6.1 percent in 1986. Throughout the southwestern part of the United States, a particularly potent form of heroin known as "black tar" has become increasingly prevalent. And in many cities, a powerful synthetic opiate, Dilaudid, is beginning to compete with heroin as the preferred opiate. The growing number of heroin-related hospital emergencies and deaths is directly related to these developments.

All of these trends suggest that drug-enforcement efforts are not succeeding and may even be backfiring. There are numerous indications, for instance, that a growing number of marijuana dealers in both the producer countries and the United States are switching to cocaine dealing, motivated both by the promise of greater profits and by government drug-enforcement efforts that place a premium on minimizing the bulk of the illicit product (in order to avoid detection). It is possible, of course, that some of these trends would be even more severe in the absence of drug laws and enforcement. At the same time, it is worth observing that the increases in the potency of illegal drugs have coincided with decreases in the potency of legal substances. Motivated in good part by health concerns, cigarette smokers are turning increasingly to lower-tar and-nicotine tobacco products, alcohol drinkers from hard liquor to wine and beer, and even coffee drinkers from regular to decaffeinated coffee. This trend may well have less to do with the nature of the substances than with their legal status. It is quite possible, for instance, that the subculture of illicit-drug use creates a bias or incentive in favor of riskier behavior and more powerful psychoactive effects. If this is the case, legalization might well succeed in reversing today's trend toward more potent drugs and more dangerous methods of consumption.

The most "successful" drug-enforcement operations are those that succeed in identifying and destroying an entire drug-trafficking organization. Such operations can send dozens of people to jail and earn the government millions of dollars in asset forfeitures. Yet these operations have virtually no effect on the availability or price of illegal drugs throughout much of the United States. During the past few years, some urban police departments have devoted significant manpower and financial resources to intensive crackdowns on street-level drug dealing in particular neighborhoods. Code-named Operation Pressure Point, Operation Clean Sweep, and so on, these massive police efforts have led to hundreds, even thousands, of arrests of low-level dealers and drug users, and have helped improve the quality of life in the targeted neighborhoods. In most cases, however, drug dealers have adapted relatively easily by moving their operations to nearby neighborhoods. In the final analysis, the principal accomplishment of most domestic drug-enforcement efforts is not to reduce the supply or availability of illegal drugs, or even to raise their price; it is to punish the drug dealers who are apprehended, and cause minor disruptions in established drug markets.

THE FAILURE OF INTERNATIONAL DRUG CONTROL

Many drug-enforcement officials and urban leaders recognize the futility of domestic drug-enforcement efforts and place their hopes in international control efforts. Yet these too are doomed to fail—for numerous reasons. First, marijuana and opium can be grown almost anywhere, and the coca plant, from which cocaine is derived, is increasingly being cultivated successfully in areas that were once considered inhospitable environments. Wherever drug-eradication efforts succeed, other regions and countries are quick to fill the void; for example, Colombian marijuana growers rapidly expanded production following successful eradication efforts in Mexico during the mid-1970s. Today, Mexican growers are rapidly taking advantage of recent Colombian government successes in eradicating marijuana in the Guajira peninsula. Meanwhile, Jamaicans and Central Americans from Panama to Belize, as well as a growing assortment of Asians and Africans, do what they can to sell their own marijuana in American markets. And within the United States, domestic marijuana production is believed to be a multi-billion-dollar industry, supplying between 15 and 50 percent of the American market.

This push-down/pop-up factor also characterizes the international heroin market. At various points during the past two decades, Turkey, Mexico, Southeast Asia (Burma, Thailand, and Laos), and Southwest Asia (Pakistan, Afghanistan, and Iran) have each served as the principal source of heroin imported into the United States. During the early 1970s, Mexican producers rapidly filled the void created by the Turkish government's successful opium-control measures. Although a successful eradication program during the latter part of the 1970s reduced Mexico's share of the U.S. market from a peak of 87 percent in 1975, it has since retained at least a one-third share in each year. Southwest Asian producers, who had played no role in supplying the American market as late as 1976, were able to supply over half the American market four years later. Today, increasing evidence indicates that drug traffickers are bringing unprecedented quantities of Southeast Asian heroin into the United States.

So far, the push-down/pop-up factor has played little role in the international cocaine market, for the simple reason that no government has yet pushed down in a significant way. Unlike marijuana-and opium-eradication efforts, in which aerial spraying of herbicides plays a prominent role, coca-eradication efforts are still conducted manually. The long anticipated development and approval of an environmentally safe herbicide to destroy coca plants may introduce an unprecedented push-down factor into the market. But even in the absence of such government pressures, coca growing has expanded rapidly during the past decade within Bolivia and Peru, and has expanded outward into Colombia, Brazil, Ecuador, Venezuela, and elsewhere. Moreover, once eradication efforts do begin, coca growers can be expected to adopt many of the same "guerrilla farming" methods adopted by marijuana and opium growers to camouflage and protect their crops from eradication efforts.

Beyond the push-down/pop-up factor, international source-control efforts face a variety of other obstacles. In many countries, governments with limited resources lack the ability to crack down on drug production in the hinterlands and other poorly policed regions. In some countries, ranging from Colombia and Peru to Burma and Thailand, leftist insurgencies are involved in drug production for either financial or political profit, and may play an important role in hampering government drug-control efforts. With respect to all three of the illicit crops, poor peasants with no comparable opportunities to earn as much money growing legitimate produce are prominently involved in the illicit business. In some cases, the illicit crop is part of a traditional, indigenous culture. Even where it is not, peasants typically perceive little or nothing immoral about taking advantage of the opportunity to grow the illicit crops. Indeed, from their perspective their moral obligation is not to protect the foolish American consumer of their produce but to provide for their families' welfare. And even among those who do perceive participation in the illicit drug market as somewhat unethical, the temptations held out by the drug traffickers often prove overwhelming.

No illicit drug is as difficult to keep out of the United States as heroin. The absence of geographical limitations on where it can be cultivated is just one minor obstacle. American heroin users consume an estimated six tons of heroin each year. The sixty tons of opium required to produce that heroin represent just 2–3 percent of the estimated 2–3,000 tons of illicit opium produced during each of the past few years. Even if eradication efforts combined with what often proves to be the opium growers' principal nemesis—bad weather—were to eliminate three-fourths of that production in one year, the U.S. market would still require just 10 percent of the remaining crop. Since U.S. consumers are able and willing to pay more than any others, the chances are good that they would still obtain their heroin. In any event, the prospects for such a radical reduction in illicit opium production are scanty indeed.

. . . Interdiction, like source control, is largely unable to keep illicit drugs out of the United States. Moreover, the past twenty years' experience has demonstrated that even dramatic increases in interdiction and source-control efforts have little or no effect on the price and purity of drugs. The few small successes, such as the destruction of the Turkish-opium "French Connection" in the early 1970s, and the crack-down on Mexican marijuana and heroin in the late 1970s, were exceptions to the rule. The elusive goal of international drug control since then has been to replicate those unusual successes. It is a strategy that is destined to fail, however, as long as millions of Americans continue to demand the illicit substances that foreigners are willing and able to supply.

THE COSTS OF PROHIBITION

The fact that drug-prohibition laws and policies cannot eardicate or even significantly reduce drug abuse is not necessarily a reason to repeal them. They do, after all, succeed in deterring many people from trying drugs, and they clearly reduce the availability and significantly increase the price of illegal drugs. These accomplishments alone might warrant retaining the drug laws, were it not for the fact that these same laws are also responsible for much of what Americans identify as the "drug problem." Here the analogies to alcohol and tobacco are worth noting. There is little question that we could reduce the health costs associated with use and abuse of alcohol and tobacco if we were to criminalize their production, sale, and possession. But no one believes that we could eliminate their use and abuse, that we could create an "alcohol-free" or "tobacco-free" country. Nor do most Americans believe that criminalizing the alcohol and tobacco markets would be a good idea. Their opposition stems largely from two beliefs: that adult Americans have the right to choose what substances they will consume and what risks they will take: and that the costs of trying to coerce so many Americans to abstain from those substances would be enormous. It was the strength of these two beliefs that ultimately led to the repeal of Prohibition, and it is partly due to memories of that experience that criminalizing either alcohol or tobacco has little support today.

Consider the potential consequences of criminalizing the production, sale, and possession of all tobacco products. On the positive side, the number of people smoking tobacco would almost certainly decline, as would the health costs associated with tobacco consumption. Although the "forbidden fruit" syndrome would attract some people to cigarette smoking who would not otherwise have smoked, many more would likely be deterred by the criminal sanction, the moral standing of the law, the higher cost and unreliable quality of the illicit tobacco, and the difficulties involved in acquiring it. Nonsmokers would rarely if ever be bothered by the irritating habits of their fellow citizens. The anti-tobacco laws would discourage some people from ever starting to smoke, and would induce others to quit.

On the negative side, however, millions of Americans, including both tobacco addicts and recreational users, would no doubt defy the law, generating a massive underground market and billions in profits for organized criminals. Although some tobacco farmers would find other work, thousands more would become outlaws and continue to produce their crops covertly. Throughout Latin America, farmers and gangsters would rejoice at the opportunity to earn untold sums of gringo greenbacks, even as U.S. diplomats pressured foreign governments to cooperate with U.S. laws. Within the United States, government helicopters would spray herbicides on illicit tobacco fields; people would be rewarded by the government for informing on their tobacco-growing, -selling, and -smoking neighbors; urine tests would be employed to identify violators of the anti-tobacco laws; and a Tobacco Enforcement Administration (the T.E.A.) would employ undercover agents, informants, and wiretaps to uncover tobacco-law violators. Municipal, state, and federal judicial systems would be clogged with tobacco traffickers and "abusers." "Tobacco-related murders" would increase dramatically as criminal organizations competed with one another for turf and markets. Smoking would become an act of youthful rebellion, and no doubt some users would begin to experiment with more concentrated, potent, and dangerous forms of tobacco. Tobacco-related corruption would infect all levels of government, and respect for the law would decline noticeably. Government expenditures on tobacco-law enforcement would climb rapidly into the billions of dollars, even as budget balancers longingly recalled the almost ten billion dollars per year in tobacco taxes earned by the federal and state governments prior to prohibition. Finally, the State of North Carolina might even secede again from the Union.

This seemingly far-fetched tobacco-prohibition scenario is little more than an extrapolation based on the current situation with respect to marijuana, cocaine, and heroin. In many ways, our predicament resembles what actually happened during Prohibition. Prior to Prohibition, most Americans hoped that alcohol could be effectively banned by passing laws against its production and supply. During the early years of Prohibition, when drinking declined but millions of Americans nonetheless continued to drink, Prohibition's supporters placed their faith in tougher laws and more police and jails. After a few more years, however, increasing numbers of Americans began to realize that laws and policemen were unable to eliminate the smugglers, bootleggers, and illicit producers, as long as tens of millions of Americans continued to want to buy alcohol. At the same time, they saw that more laws and policemen seemed to generate more violence and corruption, more crowded courts and jails, wider disrespect for government and the law, and more power and profits for the gangsters. Repeal of Prohibition came to be seen not as a capitulation to Al Capone and his ilk, but as a means of both putting the bootleggers out of business and eliminating most of the costs associated with the prohibition laws.

Today, Americans are faced with a dilemma similar to that confronted by our forebears sixty years ago. Demand for illicit drugs shows some signs of abating, but no signs of declining significantly. Moreover, there are substantial reasons to doubt that tougher laws and policing have played an important role in reducing consumption. Supply, meanwhile, has not abated at all. Availability of illicit drugs, except for marijuana in some locales, remains high. Prices are dropping, even as potency increases. And the number of drug producers, smugglers, and dealers remains sizable, even as jails and prisons fill to overflowing. As was the case during Prohibition, the principal beneficiaries of current drug policies are the new and old organized-crime gangs. The principal victims, on the other hand, are not the drug dealers, but the tens of millions of Americans who are worse off in one way or another as a consequence of the existence and failure of the drug-prohibition laws.

All public policies create beneficiaries and victims, both intended and unintended. When a public policy results in a disproportionate magnitude of unintended victims, there is good reason to reevaluate the assumptions and design of the policy. In the case of drug-prohibition policies, the intended beneficiaries are those individuals who would become drug abusers but for the existence and enforcement of the drug laws. The intended victims are those who traffic in illicit drugs and suffer the legal consequences. The unintended beneficiaries, conversely, are the drug producers and traffickers who profit handsomely from the illegality of the market, while avoiding arrest by the authorities and the violence perpetrated by other criminals. The unintended victims of drug-prohibition policies are rarely recognized as such, however. Viewed narrowly, they are the 30 million Americans who use illegal drugs, thereby risking loss of their jobs, imprisonment, and the damage done to health by ingesting illegally produced drugs; viewed broadly, they are all Americans who pay the substantial costs of our present ill-considered policies, both as taxpayers and as the potential victims of crime. These unintended victims are generally thought to be victimized by the unintended beneficiaries (i.e., the drug dealers), when in fact it is the drug-prohibition polices themselves that are primarily responsible for their plight.

If law-enforcement efforts could succeed in significantly reducing either the supply of illicit drugs or the demand for them, we would probably have little need to seek alternative drug-control policies. But since those efforts have repeatedly failed to make much of a difference and show little indication of working better in the future, at this point we must focus greater attention on their costs. Unlike the demand and supply of illicit drugs, which have remained relatively indifferent to legislative initiatives, the costs of drug-enforcement measures can be affected—quite dramatically—by legislative measures. What tougher criminal sanctions and more police have failed to accomplish, in terms of reducing drug-related violence, corruption, death, and social decay, may well be better accomplished by legislative repeal of the drug laws, and adoption of less punitive but more effective measures to prevent and treat substance abuse.

COSTS TO THE TAXPAYER

Since 1981, federal expenditures on drug enforcement have more than tripled—from less than one billion dollars a year to about three billion. According to the National Drug Enforcement Policy Board, the annual budgets of the Drug Enforcement Administration (DEA) and the Coast Guard have each risen during the past seven years from about $220 million to roughly $500 million. During the same period, FBI resources devoted to drug enforcement have increased from $8 million a year to over $100 million; U.S. Marshals resources from $26 million to about $80 million; U.S. Attorney resources from $20 million to about $100 million; State Department resources from $35 million to $100 million; U.S. Customs resources from $180 million to over $400 million; and Bureau of Prison resources from $77 million to about $300 million. Expenditures on drug control by the military and the intelligence agencies are more difficult to calculate, although by all accounts they have increased by at least the same magnitude, and now total hundreds of millions of dollars per year. Even greater are the expenditures at lower levels of government. In a 1987 study for the U.S. Customs Service by Wharton Econometrics, state and local police were estimated to have devoted 18 percent of their total investigative resources, or close to five billion dollars, to drug-enforcement activities in 1986. This represented a 19 percent increase over the previous year's expenditures. All told, 1987 expenditures on all aspects of drug enforcement, from drug eradication in foreign countries to imprisonment of drug users and dealers in the United States, totaled at least ten billion dollars.

Of course, even ten billion dollars a year pales in comparison with expenditures on military defense. Of greater concern than the actual expenditures, however, has been the diversion of limited resources—including the time and energy of judges, prosecutors, and law-enforcement agents, as well as scarce prison space—from the prosecution and punishment of criminal activities that harm far more innocent victims than do violations of the drug laws. Drug-law violators account for approximately 10 percent of the roughly 800,000 inmates in state prisons and local jails, and more than one-third of the 44,000 federal prison inmates. These proportions are expected to increase in coming years, even as total prison populations continue to rise dramatically.[1] Among the 40,000 inmates in New York State prisons, drug-law violations surpassed first-degree robbery in 1987 as the number one cause of incarceration, accounting for 20 percent of the total prison population. The U.S. Sentencing Commission has estimated that, largely as a consequence of the Anti-Drug Abuse Act passed by Congress in 1986, the proportion of federal inmates incarcerated for drug violations will rise from one-third of the 44,000 prisoners sentenced to federal-prison terms today to one-half of the 100,000 to 150,000 federal prisoners anticipated in fifteen years. The direct costs of building and maintaining enough prisoners to house this growing population are rising at an astronomical rate. The opportunity costs, in terms of alternative social expenditures forgone and other types of criminals not imprisoned, are perhaps even greater.[2]

During each of the last few years, police made about 750,000 arrests for violations of the drug laws. Slightly more than three-quarters of these have not been for manufacturing or dealing drugs, but solely for possession of an illicit drug, typically marijuana. (Those arrested, it is worth noting, represent little more than 2 percent of the thirty million Americans estimated to have used an illegal drug during the past year.) On the one hand, this has clogged many urban criminal-justice systems: in New York City, drug-law violations last year accounted for more than 40 percent of all felony indictments—up from 25 percent in 1985; in Washington, D.C., the figure was more than 50 percent. On the other hand, it has distracted criminal-justice officials from concentrating greater resources on violent offenses and property crimes. In many cities, law enforcement has become virtually synonymous with drug enforcement.

Drug laws typically have two effects on the market in illicit drugs. The first is to restrict the general availability and accessibility of illicit drugs, especially in locales where underground drug markets are small and isolated from the community. The second is to increase, often significantly, the price of illicit drugs to consumers. Since the costs of producing most illicit drugs are not much different from the costs of alcohol, tobacco, and coffee, most of the price paid for illicit substances is in effect a value-added tax created by their criminalization, which is enforced and supplemented by the law-enforcement establishment, but collected by the drug traffickers. A report by Wharton Econometrics for the President's Commission on Organized Crime identified the sale of illicit drugs as the source of more than half of all organized-crime revenues in 1986, with the marijuana and heroin business each providing over seven billion dollars, and the cocaine business over thirteen billion. By contrast, revenues from cigarette bootlegging, which persists principally because of differences among states in their cigarette-tax rates, were estimated at 290 million dollars. If the marijuana, cocaine, and heroin markets were legal, state and federal governments would collect billions of dollars annually in tax revenues. Instead, they expend billions on what amounts to a subsidy of organized crime and unorganized criminals.

DRUGS AND CRIME

The drug-crime connection is one that continues to resist coherent analysis, both because cause and effect are so difficult to distinguish and because the role of the drug-prohibition laws in causing and labeling "drug-related crime" is so often ignored. There are four possible connections between drugs and crime, at least three of which would be much diminished if the drug-prohibition laws were repealed. First, producing, selling, buying, and consuming strictly controlled and banned substances is itself a crime that occurs billions of times each year in the United States alone. In the absence of drug-prohibition laws, these activities would obviously cease to be crimes. Selling drugs to children would, of course, continue to be criminal, and other evasions of government regulation of a legal market would continue to be prosecuted; but by and large the drug-crime connection that now accounts for all of the criminal-justice costs noted above would be severed.

Second, many illicit-drug users commit crimes such as robbery and burglary, as well as drug dealing, prostitution, and numbers running, to earn enough money to purchase the relatively high-priced illicit drugs. Unlike the millions of alcoholics who can support their habits for relatively modest amounts, many cocaine and heroin addicts spend hundreds and even thousands of dollars a week. If the drugs to which they are addicted were significantly cheaper—which would be the case if they were legalized—the number of crimes committed by drug addicts to pay for their habits would, in all likelihood, decline dramatically. Even if a legal-drug policy included the imposition of relatively high consumption taxes in order to discourage consumption, drug prices would probably still be lower than they are today.

The third drug-crime connection is the commission of crimes—violent crimes in particular—by people under the influence of illicit drugs. This connection seems to have the greatest impact upon the popular imagination. Clearly, some drugs do "cause" some people to commit crimes by reducing normal inhibitions, unleashing aggressive and other antisocial tendencies, and lessening the sense of responsibility. Cocaine, particularly in the form of crack, has gained such a reputation in recent years, just as heroin did in the 1960s and 1970s, and marijuana did in the years before that. Crack's reputation for inspiring violent behavior may or may not be more deserved than those of marijuana and heroin; reliable evidence is not yet available. No illicit drug, however, is as widely associated with violent behavior as alcohol. According to Justice Department statistics, 34 percent of all jail inmates convicted of violent crimes in 1983 reported having used alcohol just prior to committing their offense. The impact of drug legalization on this drug-crime connection is the most difficult to predict. Much would depend on overall rates of drug abuse and changes in the nature of consumption, both of which are impossible to predict. It is worth noting, however, that a shift in consumption from alcohol to marijuana would almost certainly contribute to a decline in violent behavior.

The fourth drug-crime link is the violent, intimidating, and corrupting behavior of the drug traffickers. Illegal markets tend to breed violence—not only because they attract criminally minded individuals, but also because participants in the market have no resort to legal institutions to resolve their disputes. During Prohibition, violent struggles between bootlegging gangs and hijackings of booze-laden trucks and sea vessels were frequent and notorious occurrences. Today's equivalents are the booby traps that surround some marijuana fields, the pirates of the Caribbean looking to rip off drug-laden vessels en route to the shores of the United States, and the machine-gun battles and executions carried out by drug lords—all of which occasionally kill innocent people. Most law-enforcement officials agree that the dramatic increases in urban murder rates during the past few years can be explained almost entirely by the rise in drug-dealer killings.

Perhaps the most unfortunate victims of the drug-prohibition policies have been the law-abiding residents of America's ghettos. These policies have largely proven futile in deterring large numbers of ghetto dwellers from becoming drug abusers, but they do account for much of what ghetto residents identify as the drug problem. In many neighborhoods, it often seems to be the aggressive gun-toting drug dealers who upset law-abiding residents far more than the addicts nodding out in doorways. Other residents, however, perceive the drug dealers as heroes and successful role models. In impoverished neighborhoods, they often stand out as symbols of success to children who see no other options. At the same time, the increasingly harsh criminal penalties imposed on adult drug dealers have led to the widespread recruitment of juveniles by drug traffickers. Formerly, children started dealing drugs only after they had been using them for a while; today the sequence is often reversed: many children start using illegal drugs now only after working for older drug dealers. And the juvenile-justice system offers no realistic options for dealing with this growing problem.

The conspicuous failure of law-enforcement agencies to deal with this drug-crime connection is probably most responsible for the demoralization of neighborhoods and police departments alike. Intensive police crackdowns in urban neighborhoods do little more than chase the menace a short distance away to infect new areas. By contrast, legalization of the drug market would drive the drug-dealing business off the streets and out of the apartment building, and into legal, government-regulated, tax-paying stores. It would also force many of the gun-toting dealers out of business, and would convert others into legitimate business. Some, of course, would turn to other types of criminal activities, just as some of the bootleggers did following Prohibition's repeal.

Gone, however, would be the unparalleled financial temptations that lure so many people from all sectors of society into the drug-dealing business.

THE COSTS OF CORRUPTION

All vice-control efforts are particularly susceptible to corruption, but none so much as drug enforcement. When police accept bribes from drug dealers, no victim exists to complain to the authorities. Even when police extort money and drugs from traffickers and dealers, the latter are in no position to report the corrupt officers. What makes drug enforcement especially vulnerable to corruption are the tremendous amounts of money involved in the business. Today, many law-enforcement officials believe that police corruption is more pervasive than at any time since Prohibition. In Miami, dozens of law-enforcement officials have been charged with accepting bribes, stealing from drug dealers, and even dealing drugs themselves. Throughout many small towns and rural communities in Georgia, where drug smugglers en route from Mexico, the Caribbean, and Latin America drop their loads of cocaine and marijuana, dozens of sheriffs have been implicated in drug-related corruption. In New York, drug-related corruption in one Brooklyn police precinct has generated the city's most far-reaching police-corruption scandal since the 1960s. More than a hundred cases of drug-related corruption are now prosecuted each year in state and federal courts. Every one of the federal law-enforcement agencies charged with drug-enforcement responsibilities has seen an agent implicated in drug-related corruption.

It is not difficult to explain the growing persuasiveness of drug-related corruption. The financial temptations are enormous relative to other opportunities, legitimate or illegitimate. Little effort is required. Many police officers are demoralized by the scope of the drug traffic, their sense that many citizens are indifferent, and the fact that many sectors of society do not even appreciate their efforts—as well as the fact that many of the drug dealers who are arrested do not remain in prison. Some police also recognize that enforcing the drug laws does not protect victims from predators so much as it regulates an illicit market that cannot be suppressed, but can be kept underground. In every respect, the analogy to Prohibition is apt. Repealing the drug-prohibition laws would dramatically reduce police corruption. By contrast, the measures currently being proposed to deal with the growing problem, including better funded and more aggressive internal investigations, offer relatively little promise.

Among the most difficult costs to evaluate are those that relate to the widespread defiance of the drug-prohibition laws: the effects of labeling as criminals the tens of millions of people who use drugs illicitly, subjecting them to the risks of criminal sanction, and obligating many of these same people to enter into relationships with drug dealers (who may be criminals in many more senses of the word) in order to purchase their drugs; the cynicism that such laws generate toward other laws and the law in general; and the sense of hostility and suspicion that many otherwise law-abiding individuals feel toward law-enforcement officials. It was costs such as these that strongly influenced many of Prohibition's more conservative opponents.

PHYSICAL AND MORAL COSTS

Perhaps the most paradoxical consequence of the drug laws is the tremendous harm they cause to the millions of drug users who have not been deterred from using illicit drugs in the first place. Nothing resembling an underground Food and Drug Administration has arisen to impose quality control on the illegal-drug market and provide users with accurate information on the drugs they consume. Imagine that Americans could not tell whether a bottle of wine contained 6 percent, 30 percent, or 90 percent alcohol, or whether an aspirin tablet contained 5 or 500 grams of aspirin. Imagine, too, that no controls existed to prevent winemakers from diluting their product with methanol and other dangerous impurities, and that vineyards and tobacco fields were fertilized with harmful substances by ignorant growers and sprayed with poisonous herbicides by government agents. Fewer people would use such substances, but more of those who did would get sick. Some would die.

The above scenario describes, of course, the current state of the illicit drug market. Many marijuana smokers are worse off for having smoked cannabis that was grown with dangerous fertilizers, sprayed with the herbicide paraquat, or mixed with more dangerous substances. Consumers of heroin and the various synthetic substances sold on the street face even severer consequences, including fatal overdoses and poisonings from unexpectedly potent or impure drug supplies. More often than not, the quality of a drug addict's life depends greatly upon his or her access to reliable supplies. Drug-enforcement operations that succeed in temporarily disrupting supply networks are thus a double-edged sword: they encourage some addicts to seek admission into drug-treatment programs, but they oblige others to seek out new and hence less reliable suppliers; the result is that more, not fewer, drug-related emergencies and deaths occur.

Today, over 50 percent of all people with AIDS in New York City, New Jersey, and many other parts of the country, as well as the vast majority of AIDS-infected heterosexuals throughout the country, have contracted the disease directly or indirectly through illegal intravenous drug use. Reports have emerged of drug dealers beginning to provide clean syringes together with their illegal drugs. But even as other governments around the world actively attempt to limit the spread of AIDS by and among drug users by instituting free syringe-exchange programs, state and municipal governments in the United States resist following suit, arguing that to do so would "encourage" or "condone" the use of illegal drugs. Only in January 1988 did New York City approve such a program on a very limited and experimental basis. At the same time, drug-treatment programs remain notoriously underfunded, turning away tens of thousands of addicts seeking help, even as billions of dollars more are spent to arrest, prosecute, and imprison illegal drug sellers and users. In what may represent a sign of shifting priorities, the President's Commission on AIDS, in its March 1988 report, emphasized the importance of making drug-treatment programs available to all in need of them. In all likelihood, however, the criminal-justice agencies will continue to receive the greatest share of drug-control funds.

Most Americans perceive the drug problem as a moral issue and draw a moral distinction between use of the illicit drugs and use of alcohol and tobacco. Yet when one subjects this distinction to reasoned analysis, it quickly disintegrates. The most consistent moral perspective of those who favor drug laws is that of the Mormons and the Puritans, who regard as immoral any intake of substances to alter one's state of consciousness or otherwise cause pleasure: they forbid not only the illicit drugs and alcohol, but also tobacco, caffeine, and even chocolate. The vast majority of Americans are hardly so consistent with respect to the propriety of their pleasures. Yet once one acknowledges that there is nothing immoral about drinking alcohol or smoking tobacco for nonmedicinal purposes, it becomes difficult to condemn the consumption of marijuana, cocaine, and other substances on moral grounds. The "moral" condemnation of some substances and not others proves to be little more than a prejudice in favor of some drugs and against others.

The same false distinction is drawn with respect to those who provide the psychoactive substances to users and abusers alike. If degrees of immorality were measured by the levels of harm caused by one's products, the "traffickers" in tobacco and alcohol would be vilified as the most evil of all substance purveyors. That they are perceived instead as respected members of our community, while providers of the no more dangerous illicit substances are punished with long prison sentences, says much about the prejudices of most Americans with respect to psychoactive substances, but little about the morality or immorality of their activities.

Much the same is true of gun salesmen. Most of the consumers of their products use them safely; a minority, however, end up shooting either themselves or someone else. Can we hold the gun salesman morally culpable for the harm that probably would not have occurred but for his existence? Most people say no, except perhaps where the salesman clearly knew that his product would be used to commit a crime. Yet in the case of those who sell illicit substances to willing customers, the providers are deemed not only legally guilty, but also morally reprehensible. The law does not require any demonstration that the dealer knew of a specific harm to follow; indeed, it does not require any evidence at all of harm having resulted from the sale. Rather, the law is predicated on the assumption that harm will inevitably follow. Despite the patent falsity of that assumption, it persists as the underlying justification for the drug laws.

Although a valid moral distinction cannot be drawn between the licit and the illicit psychoactive substances, one can point to a different kind of moral justification for the drug laws: they arguably reflect a paternalistic obligation to protect those in danger of succumbing to their own weaknesses. If drugs were legally available, most people would either abstain from using them or would use them responsibly and in moderation. A minority without self-restraint, however, would end up harming themselves if the substances were more readily available. Therefore, the majority has a moral obligation to deny itself legal access to certain substances because of the plight of the minority. This obligation is presumably greatest when children are included among the minority.

At least in principle, this argument seems to provide the strongest moral justification for the drug laws. But ultimately the moral quality of laws must be judged not by how those laws are intended to work in principle, but by how they function in practice. When laws intended to serve a moral end inflict great damage on innocent parties, we must rethink our moral position.

Because drug-law violations do not create victims with an interest in notifying the police, drug-enforcement agents rely heavily on undercover operations, electronic surveillance, and information provided by informants. These techniques are indispensable to effective law enforcement, but they are also among the least palatable investigative methods employed by the police. The same is true of drug testing: it may be useful and even necessary for determining liability in accidents, but it also threatens and undermines the right of privacy to which many Americans believe they are entitled. There are good reasons for requiring that such measures be used sparingly.

Equally disturbing are the increasingly vocal calls for people to inform not only on drug dealers but also on neighbors, friends, and even family members who use illicit drugs. Government calls on people not only to "just say no," but also to report those who have not heeded the message. Intolerance of illicit-drug use and users is heralded not only as an indispensable ingredient in the war against drugs, but also as a mark of good citizenship. Certainly every society requires citizens to assist in the enforcement of criminal laws. But societies—particularly democratic and pluralistic ones—also rely strongly on an ethic of tolerance toward those who are different but do no harm to others. Overzealous enforcement of the drug laws risks undermining that ethic, and encouraging the creation of a society of informants. This results in an immorality that is far more dangerous in its own way than that associated with the use of illicit drugs.

THE BENEFITS OF LEGALIZATION

Repealing the drug-prohibition laws promises tremendous advantages. Between reduced government expenditures on enforcing drug laws and new tax revenue from legal drug production and sales, public treasuries would enjoy a net benefit of at least ten billion dollars a year, and possibly much more. The quality of urban life would rise significantly. Homicide rates would decline. So would robbery and burglary rates. Organized criminal groups, particularly the newer ones that have yet to diversify out of drugs, would be dealt a devastating setback. The police, prosecutors, and courts would focus their resources on combating the types of crimes that people cannot walk away from. More ghetto residents would turn their backs on criminal careers and seek out legitimate opportunities instead. And the health and quality of life of many drug users—and even drug abusers—would improve significantly.

All the benefits of legalization would be for naught, however, if millions more Americans were to become drug abusers. Our experience with alcohol and tobacco provides ample warnings. Today, alcohol is consumed by 140 million Americans and tobacco by 50 million. All of the health costs associated with abuse of the illicit drugs pale in comparison with those resulting from tobacco and alcohol abuse. In 1986, for example, alcohol was identified as a contributing factor in 10 percent of work-related injuries, 40 percent of suicide attempts, and about 40 percent of the approximately 46,000 annual traffic deaths in 1983. An estimated eighteen million Americans are reported to be either alcoholics or alcohol abusers. The total cost of alcohol abuse to American society is estimated at over 100 billion dollars annually. Alcohol has been identified as the direct cause of 80,000 to 160,000 deaths annually, and as a contributing factor in an additional 100,000 deaths. The health costs of tobacco use are of similar magnitude. In the United States alone, an estimated 320,000 people die prematurely each year as a consequence of their consumption of tobacco. By comparison, the National Council on Alcoholism reported that only 3,562 people were known to have died in 1985 from use of all illegal drugs combined. Even if we assume that thousands more deaths were related in one way or another to illicit drug abuse but not reported as such, we are still left with the conclusion that all of the health costs of marijuana, cocaine, and heroin combined amount to only a small fraction of those caused by tobacco and alcohol.

Most Americans are just beginning to recognize the extensive costs of alcohol and tobacco abuse. At the same time, they seem to believe that there is something fundamentally different about alcohol and tobacco that supports the legal distinction between those two substances, on the one hand, and the illicit ones, on the other. The most common distinction is based on the assumption that the illicit drugs are more dangerous than the licit ones. Cocaine, heroin, the various hallucinogens, and (to a lesser extent) marijuana are widely perceived as, in the words of the President's Commission on Organized Crime, "inherently destructive to mind and body." They are also believed to be more addictive and more likely to cause dangerous and violent behavior than alcohol and tobacco. All use of illicit drugs is therefore thought to be abusive; in other words, the distinction between use and abuse of psychoactive substances that most people recognize with respect to alcohol is not acknowledged with respect to the illicit substances.

Most Americans make the fallacious assumption that the government would not criminalize certain psychoactive substances if they were not in fact dangerous. They then jump to the conclusion that any use of those substances is a form of abuse. The government, in its effort to discourage people from using illicit drugs, has encouraged and perpetuated these misconceptions—not only in its rhetoric but also in its purportedly educational materials. Only by reading between the lines can one discern the fact that the vast majority of Americans who have used illicit drugs have done so in moderation, that relatively few have suffered negative short-term consequences, and that few are likely to suffer long-term harm.

The evidence is most persuasive with respect to marijuana. U.S. drug enforcement and health agencies do not even report figures on marijuana-related deaths, apparently because so few occur. Although there are good health reasons for children, pregnant women, and some others not to smoke marijuana, there still appears to be little evidence that occasional marijuana consumption does much harm. Certainly, it is not healthy to inhale marijuana smoke into one's lungs; indeed, the National Institute on Drug Abuse (NIDA) has declared that "marijuana smoke contains more cancer-causing agents than is found in tobacco smoke." On the other hand, the number of joints smoked by all but a very small percentage of marijuana smokers is a tiny fraction of the twenty cigarettes a day smoked by the average cigarette smoker; indeed, the average may be closer to one or two joints a week than one or two a day. Note that NIDA defines a "heavy" marijuana smoker as one who consumes at least two joints "daily." A heavy tobacco smoker, by contrast, smokes about forty cigarettes a day.

Nor is marijuana strongly identified as a dependence-causing substance. A 1982 survey of marijuana use by young adults (eighteen to twenty-five years old) found that 64 percent had tried marijuana at least once, that 42 percent had used it at least ten times, and that 27 percent had smoked in the last month. It also found that 21 percent had passed through a period during which they smoked "daily" (defined as twenty or more days per month), but that only one-third of those currently smoked "daily" and only one-fifth (about 4 percent of all young adults) could be described as heavy daily users (averaging two or more joints per day). This suggests that daily marijuana use is typically a phase through which people pass, after which their use becomes more moderate.

Marijuana has also been attacked as the "gateway drug" that leads people to the use of even more dangerous illegal drugs. It is true that people who have smoked marijuana are more likely than people who have not to try, use, and abuse other illicit substances. It is also true that people who have smoked tobacco or drunk alcohol are more likely than those who have not to experiment with illicit drugs and to become substance abusers. The reasons are obvious enough. Familiarity with smoking cigarettes, for instance, removes one of the major barriers to smoking marijuana, which is the experience of inhaling smoke into one's lungs. Similarly, familiarity with altering one's state of consciousness by consuming psychoactive substances such as alcohol or marijuana decreases the fear and increases the curiosity regarding other substances and "highs." But the evidence also indicates that there is nothing inevitable about the process. The great majority of people who have smoked marijuana do not become substance abusers of either legal or illegal substances. At the same time, it is certainly true that many of those who do become substance abusers after using marijuana would have become abusers even if they had never smoked a joint in their life.

DEALING WITH DRUGS' DANGERS

The dangers associated with cocaine, heroin, the hallucinogens, and other illicit substances are greater than those posed by marijuana, but not nearly so great as many people seem to think. Consider the case of cocaine. In 1986 NIDA reported that over 20 million Americans had tried cocaine, that 12.2 million had consumed it at least once during 1985, and that nearly 5.8 million had used it within the past month. Among those between the ages of eighteen and twenty-five, 8.2 million had tried cocaine, 5.3 million had used it within the past year, 2.5 million had used it within the past month, and 250,000 had used it weekly. Extrapolation might suggest that a quarter of a million young Americans are potential problem users. But one could also conclude that only 3 percent of those between the ages of eighteen and twenty-five who had ever tried the drug fell into that category, and that only 10 percent of those who had used cocaine monthly were at risk. (The NIDA survey did not, it should be noted, include people residing in military or student dormitories, prison inmates, or the homeless.)

All of this is not to deny that cocaine is a potentially dangerous drug, especially when it is injected, smoked in the form of crack, or consumed in tandem with other powerful substances. Clearly, tens of thousands of Americans have suffered severely from their abuse of cocaine, and a tiny fraction have died. But there is also overwhelming evidence that most users of cocaine do not get into trouble with the drug. So much of the media attention has focused on the small percentage of cocaine users who become addicted that the popular perception of how most people use cocaine has become badly distorted. In one survey of high school senior's drug use, the researchers questioned recent cocaine users, asking whether they had ever tried to stop using cocaine and found that they couldn't. Only 3.8 percent responded affirmatively, in contrast to the almost 7 percent of marijuana smokers who said they had tried to stop and found they couldn't, and the 18 percent of cigarette smokers who answered similarly. Although a similar survey of adult users would probably reveal a higher proportion of cocaine addicts, evidence such as this suggests that only a small percentage of people who use cocaine end up having a problem with it. In this respect, most people differ from monkeys, who have demonstrated in experiments that they will starve themselves to death if provided with unlimited cocaine.

With respect to the hallucinogens such as LSD and psilocybic mushrooms, their potential for addiction is virtually nil. The dangers arise primarily from using them irresponsibly on individual occasions. Although many of those who have used one or another of the hallucinogens have experienced "bad trips," others have reported positive experiences, and very few have suffered any long-term harm.

Perhaps no drugs are regarded with as much horror as the opiates, and in particular heroin, which is a concentrated form of morphine. As with most drugs, heroin can be eaten, snorted, smoked, or injected. Most Americans, unfortunately, prefer injection. There is no question that heroin is potentially highly addictive, perhaps as addictive as nicotine. But despite the popular association of heroin use with the most down-and-out inhabitants of urban ghettos, heroin causes relatively little physical harm to the human body. Consumed on an occasional or regular basis under sanitary conditions, its worst side effect, apart from addiction itself, is constipation. That is one reason why many doctors in early twentieth-century American saw opiate addiction as preferable to alcoholism, and prescribed the former as treatment for the latter when abstinence did not seem a realistic option.

It is important to think about the illicit drugs in the same way we think about alcohol and tobacco. Like tobacco, many of the illicit substances are highly addictive, but can be consumed on a regular basis for decades without any demonstrable harm. Like alcohol, most of the substances can be, and are, used by most consumers in moderation, with little in the way of harmful effects; but like alcohol, they also lend themselves to abuse by a minority of users who become addicted or otherwise harm themselves or others as a consequence. And as is the case with both the legal substances, the psychoactive effects of the various illegal drugs vary greatly from one person to another. To be sure, the pharmacology of the substance is important, as is its purity and the manner in which it is consumed. But much also depends upon not only the physiology and psychology of the consumer, but also his expectations regarding the drug, his social milieu, and the broader cultural environment—what Harvard University psychiatrist Norman Zinberg has called the "set and setting" of the drug. It is factors such as these that might change dramatically, albeit in indeterminate ways, were the illicit drugs made legally available.

CAN LEGALIZATION WORK?

It is thus impossible to predict whether legalization would lead to much greater levels of drug abuse, and exact costs comparable to those of alcohol and tobacco abuse. The lessons that can be drawn from other societies are mixed. China's experience with the British opium pushers of the nineteenth century, when millions became addicted to the drug, offers one worst-case scenario. The devastation of many native American tribes by alcohol presents another.

On the other hand, the legal availability of opium and cannabis in many Asian societies did not result in large addict populations until recently. Indeed, in many countries U.S.-inspired opium bans imposed during the past few decades have paradoxically contributed to dramatic increases in heroin consumption among Asian youth. Within the United States, the decriminalization of marijuana by about a dozen states during the 1970s did not lead to increases in marijuana consumption. In the Netherlands, which went even further in decriminalizing cannabis during the 1970s, consumption has actually declined significantly. The policy has succeeded, as the government intended, in making drug use boring. Finally, late nineteenth-century America was a society in which there were almost no drug laws or even drug regulations—but levels of drug use then were about what they are today. Drug abuse was considered a serious problem, but the criminal-justice system was not regarded as part of the solution.

There are, however, reasons to believe that none of the currently illicit substances would become as popular as alcohol or tobacco, even if they were legalized. Alcohol has long been the principal intoxicant in most societies, including many in which other substances have been legally available. Presumably, its diverse properties account for its popularity—it quenches thirst, goes well with food, and promotes appetite as well as sociability. The popularity of tobacco probably stems not just from its powerful addictive qualities, but from the fact that its psychoactive effects are sufficiently subtle that cigarettes can be integrated with most other human activities. The illicit substances do not share these qualities to the same extent, nor is it likely that they would acquire them if they were legalized. Moreover, none of the illicit substances can compete with alcohol's special place in American culture and history.

An additional advantage of the illicit drugs is that none of them appears to be as insidious as either alcohol or tobacco. Consumed in their more benign forms, few of the illicit substances are as damaging to the human body over the long term as alcohol and tobacco, and none is as strongly linked with violent behavior as alcohol. On the other hand, much of the damage caused today by illegal drugs stems from their consumption in particularly dangerous ways. There is good reason to doubt that many Americans would inject cocaine or heroin into their veins even if given the chance to do so legally. And just as the dramatic growth in the heroin-consuming population during the 1960s leveled off for reasons apparently having little to do with law enforcement, so we can expect a leveling-off—which may already have begun—in the number of people smoking crack. The logic of legalization thus depends upon two assumptions: that most illegal drugs are not so dangerous as is commonly believed; and that the drugs and methods of consumption that are most risky are unlikely to prove appealing to many people, precisely because they are so obviously dangerous.

Perhaps the most reassuring reason for believing that repeal of the drug-prohibition laws will not lead to tremendous increases in drug-abuse levels is the fact that we have learned something from our past experiences with alcohol and tobacco abuse. We now know, for instance, that consumption taxes are an effective method of limiting consumption rates. We also know that restrictions and bans on advertising, as well as a campaign of negative advertising, can make a difference. The same is true of other government measures, including restrictions on time and place of sale, prohibition of consumption in public places, packaging requirements, mandated adjustments in insurance policies, crackdowns on driving while under the influence, and laws holding bartenders and hosts responsible for the drinking of customers and guests. There is even some evidence that government-sponsored education programs about the dangers of cigarette smoking have deterred many children from beginning to smoke.

Clearly it is possible to avoid repeating the mistakes of the past in designing an effective plan for legalization. We know more about the illegal drugs now than we knew about alcohol when Prohibition was repealed, or about tobacco when the anti-tobacco laws were repealed by many states in the early years of this century. Moreover, we can and must avoid having effective drug-control policies undermined by powerful lobbies like those that now protect the interests of alcohol and tobacco producers. We are also in a far better position than we were sixty years ago to prevent organized criminals from finding and creating new opportunities when their most lucrative source of income dries up.

It is important to stress what legalization is not. It is not a capitulation to the drug dealers—but rather a means to put them out of business. It is not an endorsement of drug use—but rather a recognition of the rights of adult Americans to make their own choices free of the fear of criminal sanctions. It is not a repudiation of the "just say no" approach—but rather an appeal to government to provide assistance and positive inducements, not criminal penalties and more repressive measures, in support of that approach. It is not even a call for the elimination of the criminal-justice system from drug regulation—but rather a proposal for the redirection of its efforts and attention.

There is no question that legalization is a risky policy, since it may lead to an increase in the number of people who abuse drugs. But that is a risk—not a certainty. At the same time, current drug-control policies are failing, and new proposals promise only to be more costly and more repressive. We know that repealing the drug-prohibition laws would eliminate or greatly reduce many of the ills that people commonly identify as part and parcel of the "drug problem." Yet legalization is repeatedly and vociferously dismissed, without any attempt to evaluate it openly and objectively. The past twenty years have demonstrated that a drug policy shaped by exaggerated rhetoric designed to arouse fear has only led to our current disaster. Unless we are willing to honestly evaluate our options, including various legalization strategies, we will run a still greater risk: we may never find the best solution for our drug problems.

Endnotes

1. The total number of state and federal prison inmates in 1975 was under 250,000; in 1980 it was 350,000; and in 1987 it was 575,000. The projected total for 2000 is one million.

2. It should be emphasized that the numbers cited do not include the many inmates sentenced for "drug-related" crimes such as acts of violence committed by drug dealers, typically against one another, and robberies committed to earn the money needed to pay for illegal drugs.

NO

Against the Legalization of Drugs

James Q. Wilson

In 1972, the President appointed me chairman of the National Advisory Council for Drug Abuse Prevention. Created by Congress, the Council was charged with providing guidance on how best to coordinate the national war on drugs. (Yes, we called it a war then, too.) In those days, the drug we were chiefly concerned with was heroin. When I took office, heroin use had been increasing dramatically. Everybody was worried that this increase would continue. Such phrases as "heroin epidemic" were commonplace.

The same year, the eminent economist Milton Friedman published an essay in *Newsweek* in which he called for legalizing heroin. His argument was on two grounds: as a matter of ethics, the government has no right to tell people not to use heroin (or to drink or to commit suicide); as a matter of economics, the prohibition of drug use imposes costs on society that far exceed the benefits. Others, such as the psychoanalyst Thomas Szasz, made the same argument.

We did not take Friedman's advice. (Government commissions rarely do.) I do not recall that we even discussed legalizing heroin, though we did discuss (but did not take action on) legalizing a drug, cocaine, that many people then argued was benign. Our marching orders were to figure out how to win the war on heroin, not to run up the white flag of surrender.

That was 1972. Today, we have the same number of heroin addicts that we had then—half a million, give or take a few thousand. Having that many heroin addicts is no trivial matter; these people deserve our attention. But not having had an increase in that number for over fifteen years is also something that deserves our attention. What happened to the "heroin epidemic" that many people once thought would overwhelm us?

The facts are clear: a more or less stable pool of heroin addicts has been getting older, with relatively few new recruits. In 1976 the average age of heroin users who appeared in hospital emergency rooms was about twenty-seven; ten years later it was thirty-two. More than two-thirds of all heroin users appearing in emergency rooms are now over the age of thirty. Back in the early 1970s, when heroin got onto the national political agenda, the typical heroin addict was much younger, often a teenager. Household surveys show the same thing—the rate of opiate use (which includes heroin) has been flat for the better part of two decades. More fine-grained studies of inner-city neighborhoods confirm this. John Boyle and Ann Brunswick found that the percentage of young blacks in Harlem who used heroin fell from 8 percent in 1970–71 to about 3 percent in 1975–76.

Why did heroin lose its appeal for young people? When the young blacks in Harlem were asked why they stopped, more than half mentioned "trouble with the law" or "high cost" (and high cost is, of course, directly the result of law enforcement). Two-thirds said that heroin hurt their health; nearly all said they had had a bad experience with it. We need not rely, however, simply on what they said. In New York City in 1973–75, the street price of heroin rose dramatically and its purity sharply declined, probably as a result of the heroin shortage caused by the success of the Turkish government in reducing the supply of opium base and of the French government in closing down heroin-processing laboratories located in and around Marseilles. These were short-lived gains for, just as Friedman predicted, alternative sources of supply—mostly in Mexico—quickly emerged. But the three-year heroin shortage interrupted the easy recruitment of new users.

Health and related problems were no doubt part of the reason for the reduced flow of recruits. Over the preceding years, Harlem youth had watched as more and more heroin users died of overdoses, were poisoned by adulterated doses, or acquired hepatitis from dirty needles. The word got around: heroin can kill you. By 1974 new hepatitis cases and drug-overdose deaths had dropped to a fraction of what they had been in 1970.

Alas, treatment did not seem to explain much of the cessation in drug use. Treatment programs can and do help heroin addicts, but treatment did not explain the drop in the number of new users (who by definition had never been in treatment) nor even much of the reduction in the number of experienced users.

No one knows how much of the decline to attribute to personal observation as opposed to high prices or reduced supply. But other evidence suggests strongly that price and supply played a large role. In 1972, the National Advisory Council was especially worried by the prospect that U.S. servicemen returning to this country from Vietnam would bring their heroin habits with them. Fortunately, a brilliant study by Lee Robins of Washington University in St. Louis put that fear to rest. She measured drug use of Vietnam veterans shortly after they had returned home. Though many had used heroin regularly while in Southeast Asia, most gave up the habit when back in the United States. The reason: here, heroin was less available and sanctions on its use were more pronounced. Of course, if a veteran had been willing to pay enough—which might have meant traveling to another city and would certainly have meant making an illegal contact with a disreputable dealer in a threatening neighborhood in order to acquire a (possibly) dangerous dose—he could have sustained his drug habit. Most veterans were unwilling to pay this price, and so their drug use declined or disappeared.

RELIVING THE PAST

Suppose we had taken Friedman's advice in 1972. What would have happened? We cannot be entirely certain, but at a minimum we would have placed the young heroin addicts (and, above all, the prospective addicts) in a very different position from the one in which they actually found themselves. Heroin would have been legal. Its price would have been reduced by 95 percent (minus whatever we chose to recover in taxes). Now that it could be sold by the same people who make aspirin, its quality would have been assured—no poisons, no adulterants. Sterile hypodermic needles would have been readily available at the neighborhood drugstore, probably at the same counter where the heroin was sold. No need to travel to big cities or unfamiliar neighborhoods—heroin could have been purchased anywhere, perhaps by mail order.

There would no longer have been any financial or medical reason to avoid heroin use. Anybody could have afforded it. We might have tried to prevent children from buying it, but as we have learned from our efforts to prevent minors from buying alcohol and tobacco, young people have a way of penetrating markets theoretically reserved for adults. Returning Vietnam veterans would have discovered that Omaha and Raleigh had been converted into the pharmaceutical equivalent of Saigon.

Under these circumstances, can we doubt for a moment that heroin use would have grown exponentially? Or that a vastly larger supply of new users would have been recruited? Professor Friedman is a Nobel Prize–winning economist whose understanding of market forces is profound. What did he think would happen to consumption under his legalized regime? Here are his words: "Legalizing drugs might increase the number of addicts, but it is not clear that it would. Forbidden fruit is attractive, particularly to the young."

Really? I suppose that we should expect no increase in Porsche sales if we cut the price by 95 percent, no increase in whiskey sales if we cut the price by a comparable amount—because young people only want fast cars and strong liquor when they are "forbidden." Perhaps Friedman's uncharacteristic lapse from the obvious implications of price theory can be explained by a misunderstanding of how drug users are recruited. In his 1972 essay he said that "drug addicts are deliberately made by pushers, who give likely prospects their first few doses free." If drugs were legal it would not pay anybody to produce addicts, because everybody would buy from the cheapest source. But as every drug expert knows, pushers do not produce addicts. Friends or acquaintances do. In fact, pushers are usually reluctant to deal with non-users because a non-user could be an undercover cop. Drug use spreads in the same way any fad or fashion spreads: somebody who is already a user urges his friends to try, or simply shows already eager friends how to do it.

But we need not rely on speculation, however plausible, that lowered prices and more abundant supplies would have increased heroin usage. Great Britain once followed such a policy and with almost exactly those results. Until the mid-1960s, British physicians were allowed to prescribe heroin to certain classes of addicts. (Possessing these drugs without a doctor's prescription remained a criminal offense.) For many years this policy worked well enough because the addict patients were typically middle-class people who had become dependent on opiate painkillers while undergoing hospital treatment. There was no drug culture. The British system worked for many years, not because it prevented drug abuse, but because there was no problem of drug abuse that would test the system.

All that changed in the 1960s. A few unscrupulous doctors began passing out heroin in wholesale amounts. One doctor prescribed almost 600,000 heroin tablets—that is, over thirteen pounds—in just one year. A youthful drug culture emerged with a demand for drugs far different from that of the older addicts. As a result, the British government required doctors to refer users to government-run clinics to receive their heroin.

But the shift to clinics did not curtail the growth in heroin use. Throughout the 1960s the number of addicts increased—the late John Kaplan of Stanford estimated by fivefold—in part as a result of the diversion of heroin from clinic patients to new users on the streets. An addict would bargain with the clinic doctor over how big a dose he would receive. The patient wanted as much as he could get, the doctor wanted to give as little as was needed. The patient had an advantage in this conflict because the doctor could not be certain how much was really needed. Many patients would use some of their "maintenance" dose and sell the remaining part to friends, thereby recruiting new addicts. As the clinics learned of this, they began to shift their treatment away from heroin and toward methadone, an addictive drug that, when taken orally, does not produce a "high" but will block the withdrawal pains associated with heroin abstinence.

Whether what happened in England in the 1960s was a mini-epidemic or an epidemic depends on whether one looks at numbers or at rates of change. Compared to the United States, the numbers were small. In 1960 there were 68 heroin addicts known to the British government; by 1968 there were 2,000 in treatment and many more who refused treatment. (They would refuse in part because they did not want to get methadone at a clinic if they could get heroin on the street.) Richard Hartnoll estimates that the actual number of addicts in England is five times the number officially registered. At a minimum, the number of British addicts increased by thirtyfold in ten years; the actual increase may have been much larger.

In the early 1980s the numbers began to rise again, and this time nobody doubted that a real epidemic was at hand. The increase was estimated to be 40 percent a year. By 1982 there were thought to be 20,000 heroin users in London alone. Geoffrey Pearson reports that many cities—Glasgow, Liverpool, Manchester, and Sheffield among them—were now experiencing a drug problem that once had been largely confined to London. The problem, again, was supply. The country was being flooded with cheap, high-quality heroin, first from Iran and then from Southeast Asia.

The United States began the 1960s with a much larger number of heroin addicts and probably a bigger at-risk population than was the case in Great Britain. Even though it would be foolhardy to suppose that the British system, if installed here, would have worked the same way or with the same results, it would be equally foolhardy to suppose that a combination of heroin available from leaky clinics and from street dealers who faced only minimal law-enforcement risks would not have produced a much greater increase in heroin use than we actually experienced. My guess is that if we had allowed either doctors or clinics to prescribe heroin, we would have had far worse results than were produced in Britain, if for no other reason than the vastly larger number of addicts with which we began. We would have had to find some way to police thousands (not scores) of physicians and hundreds (not dozens) of clinics. If the British civil service found it difficult to keep heroin in the hands of addicts and out of the hands of recruits when it was dealing with a few hundred people, how well would the American civil service have accomplished the same tasks when dealing with tens of thousands of people?

BACK TO THE FUTURE

Now cocaine, especially in its potent form, crack, is the focus of attention. Now as in 1972 the government is trying to reduce its use. Now as then some people are advocating legalization. Is there any more reason to yield to those arguments today than there was almost two decades ago?*

I think not. If we had yielded in 1972 we almost certainly would have had today a permanent population of several million, not several hundred thousand, heroin addicts. If we yield now we will have a far more serious problem with cocaine.

Crack is worse than heroin by almost any measure. Heroin produces a pleasant drowsiness and, if hygienically administered, has only the physical side effects of constipation and sexual impotence. Regular heroin use incapacitates many users, especially poor ones, for any productive work or social responsibility. They will sit nodding on a street corner, helpless but at least harmless. By contrast, regular cocaine use leaves the user neither helpless nor harmless. When smoked (as with crack) or injected, cocaine produces instant, intense, and short-lived euphoria. The experience generates a powerful desire to repeat it. If the drug is readily available, repeat use will occur. Those people who progress to "bingeing" on cocaine become devoted to the drug and its effects to the exclusion of almost all other considerations—job, family, children, sleep, food, even sex. Dr. Frank Gawin at Yale and Dr. Everett Ellinwood at Duke report that a substantial percentage of all high-dose, binge users become uninhibited, impulsive, hypersexual, compulsive, irritable, and hyperactive. Their moods vacillate dramatically, leading at times to violence and homicide.

Women are much more likely to use crack than heroin, and if they are pregnant, the effects on their babies are tragic. Douglas Besharov, who has been following the effects of drugs on infants for twenty years, writes that nothing he learned about heroin prepared him for the devastation of cocaine. Cocaine harms the fetus and can lead to physical deformities or neurological

---

*I do not here take up the question of marijuana. For a variety of reasons—its widespread use and its lesser tendency to addict—it presents a different problem from cocaine or heroin.

damage. Some crack babies have for all practical purposes suffered a disabling stroke while still in the womb. The long-term consequences of this brain damage are lowered cognitive ability and the onset of mood disorders. Besharov estimates that about 30,000 to 50,000 such babies are born every year, about 7,000 in New York City alone. There may be ways to treat such infants, but from everything we now know the treatment will be long, difficult, and expensive. Worse, the mothers who are most likely to produce crack babies are precisely the ones who, because of poverty or temperament, are least able and willing to obtain such treatment. In fact, anecdotal evidence suggests that crack mothers are likely to abuse their infants.

The notion that abusing drugs such as cocaine is a "victimless crime" is not only absurd but dangerous. Even ignoring the fetal drug syndrome, crack-dependent people are, like heroin addicts, individuals who regularly victimize their children by neglect, their spouses by improvidence, their employers by lethargy, and their coworkers by carelessness. Society is not and could never be a collection of autonomous individuals. We all have a stake in ensuring that each of us displays a minimal level of dignity, responsibility, and empathy. We cannot, of course, coerce people into goodness, but we can and should insist that some standards must be met if society itself—on which the very existence of the human personality depends—is to persist. Drawing the line that defines those standards is difficult and contentious, but if crack and heroin use do not fall below it, what does?

The advocates of legalization will respond by suggesting that my picture is overdrawn. Ethan Nadelmann of Princeton argues that the risk of legalization is less than most people suppose. Over 20 million Americans between the ages of eighteen and twenty-five have tried cocaine (according to a government survey), but only a quarter million use it daily. From this Nadelmann concludes that at most 3 percent of all young people who try cocaine develop a problem with it. The implication is clear: make the drug legal and we only have to worry about 3 percent of our youth.

The implication rests on a logical fallacy and a factual error. The fallacy is this: the percentage of occasional cocaine users who become binge users when the drug is illegal (and thus expensive and hard to find) tells us nothing about the percentage who will become dependent when the drug is legal (and thus cheap and abundant). Drs. Gawin and Ellinwood report, in common with several other researchers, that controlled or occasional use of cocaine changes to compulsive and frequent use "when access to the drug increases" or when the user switches from snorting to smoking. More cocaine more potently administered alters, perhaps sharply, the proportion of "controlled" users who become heavy users.

The factual error is this: the federal survey Nadelmann quotes was done in 1985, before crack had become common. Thus the probability of becoming dependent on cocaine was derived from the responses of users who snorted the drug. The speed and potency of cocaine's action increase dramatically when it is smoked. We do not yet know how greatly the advent of crack increases the risk of dependency, but all the clinical evidence suggests that the increase is likely to be large.

It is possible that some people will not become heavy users even when the drug is readily available in its most potent form. So far there are no scientific grounds for predicting who will and who will not become dependent. Neither socioeconomic background nor personality traits differentiate between casual and intensive users. Thus, the only way to settle the question of who is correct about the effect of easy availability on drug use, Nadelmann or Gawin and Ellinwood, is to try it and see. But that social experiment is so risky as to be no experiment at all, for if cocaine is legalized and if the rate of its abusive use increases dramatically, there is no way to put the genie back in the bottle, and it is not a kindly genie.

HAVE WE LOST?

Many people who agree that there are risks in legalizing cocaine or heroin still favor it because, they think, we have lost the war on drugs. "Nothing we have done has worked" and the current federal policy is just "more of the same." Whatever the costs of greater drug use, surely they would be less than the costs of our present, failed efforts.

That is exactly what I was told in 1972—and heroin is not quite as bad a drug as cocaine. We did not surrender and we did not lose. We did not win, either. What the nation accomplished then was what most efforts to save people from themselves accomplish: the problem was contained and the number of victims minimized, all at a considerable cost in law enforcement and increased crime. Was the cost worth it? I think so, but others may disagree. What are the lives of would-be addicts worth? I recall some people saying to me then, "Let them kill themselves." I was appalled. Happily, such views did not prevail.

Have we lost today? Not at all. High-rate cocaine use is not commonplace. The National Institute of Drug Abuse (NIDA) reports that less than 5 percent of high-school seniors used cocaine within the last thirty days. Of course this survey misses young people who have dropped out of school and miscounts those who lie on the questionnaire, but even if we inflate the NIDA estimate by some plausible percentage, it is still not much above 5 percent. Medical examiners reported in 1987 that about 1,500 died from cocaine use; hospital emergency rooms reported about 30,000 admissions related to cocaine abuse.

These are not small numbers, but neither are they evidence of a nationwide plague that threatens to engulf us all. Moreover, cities vary greatly in the proportion of people who are involved with cocaine. To get city-level data we need to turn to drug tests carried out on arrested persons, who obviously are more likely to be drug users than the average citizen. The National Institute of Justice, through its Drug Use Forecasting (DUF) project, collects urinalysis data on arrestees in 22 cities. As we have already seen, opiate (chiefly heroin) use has been flat or declining in most of these cities over the last decade.

Cocaine use has gone up sharply, but with great variation among cities. New York, Philadelphia, and Washington, D.C., all report that two-thirds or more of their arrestees tested positive for cocaine, but in Portland, San Antonio, and Indianapolis the percentage was one-third or less.

In some neighborhoods, of course, matters have reached crisis proportions. Gangs control the streets, shootings terrorize residents, and drug dealing occurs in plain view. The police seem barely able to contain matters. But in these neighborhoods—unlike at Palo Alto cocktail parties—the people are not calling for legalization, they are calling for help. And often not much help has come. Many cities are willing to do almost anything about the drug problem except spend more money on it. The federal government cannot change that; only local voters and politicians can. It is not clear that they will.

It took about ten years to contain heroin. We have had experience with crack for only about three or four years. Each year we spend perhaps $11 billion on law enforcement (and some of that goes to deal with marijuana) and perhaps $2 billion on treatment. Large sums, but not sums that should lead anyone to say, "We just can't afford this any more."

The illegality of drugs increases crime, partly because some users turn to crime to pay for their habits, partly because some users are stimulated by certain drugs (such as crack or PCP) to act more violently or ruthlessly than they otherwise would, and partly because criminal organizations seeking to control drug supplies use force to manage their markets. These also are serious costs, but no one knows how much they would be reduced if drugs were legalized. Addicts would no longer steal to pay black-market prices for drugs, a real gain. But some, perhaps a great deal, of that gain would be offset by the great increase in the number of addicts. These people, nodding on heroin or living in the delusion-ridden high of cocaine, would hardly be ideal employees. Many would steal simply to support themselves, since snatch-and-grab, opportunistic crime can be managed even by people unable to hold a regular job or plan an elaborate crime. Those British addicts who get their supplies from government clinics are not models of law-abiding decency. Most are in crime, and though their per-capita rate of criminality may be lower thanks to the cheapness of their drugs, the total volume of crime they produce may be quite large. Of course, society could decide to support all unemployable addicts on welfare, but that would mean that gains from lowered rates of crime would have to be offset by large increases in welfare budgets.

Proponents of legalization claim that the costs of having more addicts around would be largely if not entirely offset by having more money available with which to treat and care for them. The money would come from taxes levied on the sale of heroin and cocaine.

To obtain this fiscal dividend, however, legalization's supporters must first solve an economic dilemma. If they want to raise a lot of money to pay for welfare and treatment, the tax rate on the drugs will have to be quite high. Even if they themselves do not want a high rate, the politicians' love of "sin taxes" would probably guarantee that it would be high anyway. But the higher the tax, the higher the price of the drug, and the higher the price the greater the likelihood that addicts will turn to crime to find the money for it and that criminal organizations will be formed to sell tax-free drugs at below-market rates. If we managed to keep taxes (and thus prices) low, we would get that much less money to pay for welfare and treatment and more people could afford to become addicts. There may be an optimal tax rate for drugs that maximizes revenue while minimizing crime, bootlegging, and the recruitment of new addicts, but our experience with alcohol does not suggest that we know how to find it.

THE BENEFITS OF ILLEGALITY

The advocates of legalization find nothing to be said in favor of the current system except, possibly, that it keeps the number of addicts smaller than it would otherwise be. In fact, the benefits are more substantial than that.

First, treatment. All the talk about providing "treatment on demand" implies that there is a demand for treatment. That is not quite right. There are some drug-dependent people who genuinely want treatment and will remain in it if offered; they should receive it. But there are far more who want only short-term help after a bad crash; once stabilized and bathed, they are back on the street again, hustling. And even many of the addicts who enroll in a program honestly wanting help drop out after a short while when they discover that help takes time and commitment. Drug-dependent people have very short time horizons and a weak capacity for commitment. These two groups—those looking for a quick fix and those unable to stick with a long-term fix—are not easily helped. Even if we increase the number of treatment slots—as we should—we would have to do something to make treatment more effective.

One thing that can often make it more effective is compulsion. Douglas Anglin of UCLA, in common with many other researchers, has found that the longer one stays in a treatment program, the better the chances of a re-duction in drug dependency. But he, again like most other researchers, has found that drop-out rates are high. He has also found, however, that pa-tients who enter treatment under legal compulsion stay in the program longer than those not subject to such pressure. His research on the California civil-commitment program, for example, found that heroin users involved with its required drug-testing program had over the long term a lower rate of heroin use than similar addicts who were free of such con-straints. If for many addicts compulsion is a useful component of treatment, it is not clear how compulsion could be achieved in a society in which pur-chasing, possessing, and using the drug were legal. It could be managed, I suppose, but I would not want to have to answer the challenge from the American Civil Liberties Union that it is wrong to compel a person to un-dergo treatment for consuming a legal commodity.

Next, education. We are now investing substantially in drug-education programs in the schools. Though we do not yet know for certain what will work, there are some promising leads. But I wonder how credible such programs would be if they were aimed at dissuading children from doing something perfectly legal. We could, of course, treat drug education like smoking education: inhaling crack and inhaling tobacco are both legal, but you should not do it because it is bad for you. That tobacco is bad for you is easily shown; the Surgeon General has seen to that. But what do we say about crack? It is pleasurable, but devoting yourself to so much pleasure is not a good idea (though perfectly legal)? Unlike tobacco, cocaine will not give you cancer or emphysema, but it will lead you to neglect your duties to family, job, and neighborhood? Everybody is doing cocaine, but you should not?

Again, it might be possible under a legalized regime to have effective drug-prevention programs, but their effectiveness would depend heavily, I think, on first having decided that cocaine use, like tobacco use, is purely a matter of practical consequences; no fundamental moral significance attaches to either. But if we believe—as I do—that dependency on certain mind-altering drugs is a moral issue and that their illegality rests in part on their immorality, then legalizing them undercuts, if it does not eliminate altogether, the moral message.

That message is at the root of the distinction we now make between nicotine and cocaine. Both are highly addictive; both have harmful physical effects. But we treat the two drugs differently, not simply because nicotine is so widely used as to be beyond the reach of effective prohibition, but because its use does not destroy the user's essential humanity. Tobacco shortens one's life, cocaine debases it. Nicotine alters one's habits, cocaine alters one's soul. The heavy use of crack, unlike the heavy use of tobacco, corrodes those natural sentiments of sympathy and duty that constitute our human nature and make possible our social life. To say, as does Nadelmann, that distinguishing morally between tobacco and cocaine is "little more than a transient prejudice" is close to saying that morality itself is but a prejudice.

THE ALCOHOL PROBLEM

Now we have arrived where many arguments about legalizing drugs begin: is there any reason to treat heroin and cocaine differently from the way we treat alcohol?

There is no easy answer to that question because, as with so many human problems, one cannot decide simply on the basis either of moral principles or of individual consequences; one has to temper any policy by a commonsense judgment of what is possible. Alcohol, like heroin, cocaine, PCP, and marijuana, is a drug—that is, a mood-altering substance—and consumed to excess it certainly has harmful consequences: auto accidents, barroom fights, bedroom shootings. It is also, for some people, addictive. We cannot confidently compare the addictive powers of these drugs, but the best evidence suggests that crack and heroin are much more addictive than alcohol.

Many people, Nadelmann included, argue that since the health and financial costs of alcohol abuse are so much higher than those of cocaine or heroin abuse, it is hypocritical folly to devote our efforts to preventing cocaine or drug use. But as Mark Kleiman of Harvard has pointed out, this comparison is quite misleading. What Nadelmann is doing is showing that a legalized drug (alcohol) produces greater social harm than illegal ones (cocaine and heroin). But of course. Suppose that in the 1920s we had made heroin and cocaine legal and alcohol illegal. Can anyone doubt that Nadelmann would now be writing that it is folly to continue our ban on alcohol because cocaine and heroin are so much more harmful?

And let there be no doubt about it—widespread heroin and cocaine use are associated with all manner of ills. Thomas Bewley found that the mortality rate of British heroin addicts in 1968 was 28 times as high as the death rate of the same age group of non-addicts, even though in England at the time an addict could obtain free or low-cost heroin and clean needles from British clinics. Perform the following mental experiment: suppose we legalized heroin and cocaine in this country. In what proportion of auto fatalities would the state police report that the driver was nodding off on heroin or recklessly driving on a coke high? In what proportion of spouse-assault and child-abuse cases would the local police report that crack was involved? In what proportion of industrial accidents would safety investigators report that the forklift or drill-press operator was in a drug-induced stupor or frenzy? We do not know exactly what the proportion would be, but anyone who asserts that it would not be much higher than it is now would have to believe that these drugs have little appeal except when they are illegal. And that is nonsense.

An advocate of legalization might concede that social harm—perhaps harm equivalent to that already produced by alcohol—would follow from making cocaine and heroin generally available. But at least, he might add, we would have the problem "out in the open" where it could be treated as a matter of "public health." That is well and good, if we knew how to treat—that is, cure—heroin and cocaine abuse. But we do not know how to do it for all the people who would need such help. We are having only limited success in coping with chronic alcoholics. Addictive behavior is immensely difficult to change, and the best methods for changing it—living in drug-free therapeutic communities, becoming faithful members of Alcoholics Anonymous or Narcotics Anonymous—require great personal commitment, a quality that is, alas, in short supply among the very persons—young people, disadvantaged people—who are often most at risk for addiction.

Suppose that today we had, not 15 million alcohol abusers, but half a million. Suppose that we already knew what we have learned from our long experience with the widespread use of alcohol. Would we make whiskey illegal? I do not know, but I suspect there would be a lively debate. The Surgeon General would remind us of the risks alcohol poses to pregnant women. The National Highway Traffic Safety Administration would point to the likelihood of more highway fatalities caused by drunk drivers. The Food and Drug Administration might find that there is a nontrivial increase in cancer associated with alcohol consumption. At the same time the police would report great difficulty in keeping illegal whiskey out of our cities, officers being corrupted by bootleggers, and alcohol addicts often resorting to crime to feed their habit. Libertarians, for their part, would argue that every citizen has a right to drink anything he wishes and that drinking is, in any event, a "victimless crime."

However the debate might turn out, the central fact would be that the problem was still, at that point, a small one. The government cannot legislate away the addictive tendencies in all of us, nor can it remove completely even the most dangerous addictive substances. But it can cope with harms when the harms are still manageable.

SCIENCE AND ADDICTION

One advantage of containing a problem while it is still containable is that it buys time for science to learn more about it and perhaps to discover a cure. Almost unnoticed in the current debate over legalizing drugs is that basic science has made rapid strides in identifying the underlying neurological processes involved in some forms of addiction. Stimulants such as cocaine and amphetamines alter the way certain brain cells communicate with one another. That alteration is complex and not entirely understood, but in simplified form it involves modifying the way in which a neurotransmitter called dopamine sends signals from one cell to another.

When dopamine crosses the synapse between two cells, it is in effect carrying a message from the first cell to activate the second one. In certain parts of the brain that message is experienced as pleasure. After the message is delivered, the dopamine returns to the first cell. Cocaine apparently blocks this return, or "reuptake," so that the excited cell and others nearby continue to send pleasure messages. When the exaggerated high produced by cocaine-influenced dopamine finally ends, the brain cells may (in ways that are still a matter of dispute) suffer from an extreme lack of dopamine, thereby making the individual unable to experience any pleasure at all. This would explain why cocaine users often feel so depressed after enjoying the drug. Stimulants may also affect the way in which other neurotransmitters, such as serotonin and nonadrenaline, operate.

Whatever the exact mechanism may be, once it is identified it becomes possible to use drugs to block either the effect of cocaine or its tendency to produce dependency. There have already been experiments using desipramine, imipramine, bromocriptine, carbamazepine, and other chemicals. There are some promising results.

Tragically, we spend very little on such research, and the agencies funding it have not in the past occupied very influential or visible posts in the federal bureaucracy. If there is one aspect of the "war on drugs" metaphor that I dislike, it is its tendency to focus attention almost exclusively on the troops in the trenches, whether engaged in enforcement or treatment, and away from the research-and-development efforts back on the home front where the war may ultimately be decided.

I believe that the prospects of scientists in controlling addiction will be strongly influenced by the size and character of the problem they face. If the problem is a few hundred thousand chronic, high-dose users of an illegal product, the chances of making a difference at a reasonable cost will be much greater than if the problem is a few million chronic users of legal substances. Once a drug is legal, not only will its use increase but many of those who then use it will prefer the drug to the treatment: they will want the pleasure, whatever the cost to themselves or their families, and they will resist—probably successfully—any effort to wean them away from experiencing the high that comes from inhaling a legal substance.

IF I AM WRONG . . .

No one can know what our society would be like if we changed the law to make access to cocaine, heroin, and PCP easier. I believe, for reasons given, that the result would be a sharp increase in use, a more widespread degradation of the human personality, and a greater rate of accidents and violence.

I may be wrong. If I am, then we will needlessly have incurred heavy costs in law enforcement and some forms of criminality. But if I am right, and the legalizers prevail anyway, then we will have consigned millions of people, hundreds of thousands of infants, and hundreds of neighborhoods to a life of oblivion and disease. To the lives and families destroyed by alcohol we will have added countless more destroyed by cocaine, heroin, PCP, and whatever else a basement scientist can invent.

Human character is formed by society; indeed, human character is inconceivable without society, and good character is less likely in a bad society. Will we, in the name of an abstract doctrine of radical individualism, and with the false comfort of suspect predictions, decide to take the chance that somehow individual decency can survive amid a more general level of degradation?

I think not. The American people are too wise for that, whatever the academic essayists and cocktail-party pundits may say. But if Americans today are less wise than I suppose, then Americans at some future time will look back on us now and wonder, what kind of people were they that they could have done such a thing?

LETTERS FROM READERS

To the Editor of *Commentary*:

James Q. Wilson's article, "Against the Legalization of Drugs" [February], perpetuates several myths about drug use and drug legalization. Moreover, the substance of his empirical arguments—that the drug war has curtailed drug use and that legalization would result in significant increases in drug abuse—is open to serious dispute. Finally, his philosophical argument—that a specific category of drugs is immoral—is based on misrepresentation of the effects of the drugs in question and a narrow conceptualization of morality.

At the outset, Mr. Wilson suggests that legalization is akin to raising the white flag of surrender. This is an oft-repeated but inaccurate piece of rhetoric. Proponents of drug legalization do not suggest that we "give in" to drug use. Most proponents view legalization as having two beneficial consequences: first, legalization would remove the drug trade from the hands of organized crime and children, thereby eliminating much of the attendant violence; and second, legalization would enable us to focus our attention on education (as we have done with nicotine) regarding the health and other hazards of drug use.

Mr. Wilson then moves on to suggest that the drug war caused the decline, or at least stabilization, that we have seen in the use of heroin. He points to price increases for heroin in the '70s as evidence that prohibition worked—that it led to price hikes with the result that would-be addicts stayed away from heroin. Mr. Wilson has some of his facts right. Heroin use did stabilize in the early 1980s (though it may be climbing). However, it is difficult to attribute this to the drug war, since, in fact, the price of heroin declined in the '80s by 20 percent, while purity rose some 33 percent. Clearly, factors other than the drug war and its price effects were at work here. Moreover, while heroin use stabilized, the use of cocaine climbed during the '80s, to peak in the mid-'80s. Over the past several years, cocaine use has declined despite rapidly falling prices and more plentiful supplies. . . . In other words, drug use—whether of heroin or cocaine—has fluctuated under a regime of prohibition in patterns apparently unrelated to price or illegality. . . .

Mr. Wilson's own arguments undermine some of his assertions. Many proponents of legalization argue that most drug users, despite popular conceptions to the contrary, exhibit controlled consumption, whether of heroin, cocaine, or marijuana. And those who curtail consumption report that they do so primarily for health reasons and not because of fear of the law or of rising prices. Mr. Wilson himself notes a survey that showed that two-thirds of a group of blacks in Harlem claimed that they stopped their drug use for health reasons. A survey of high-school students nationwide showed that 21 percent stopped their use of cocaine for health reasons, 12 percent due to pressure from family and friends, 12 percent due to cost, and none due to fear of law enforcement. These surveys bode well for a scenario of legalization, since they suggest that an educational campaign about the health effects of drugs accompanying legalization can, as education has done with nicotine, help to curtail use. . . .

After dismissing the health effects of cocaine as grounds neither for supporting nor opposing prohibition, Mr. Wilson gets to the real heart of his argument. He believes that certain categories of drugs are immoral. They are immoral because they are mind-altering, and this, he says, is why nicotine is legal and cocaine, heroin, and marijuana are not.

First, the facts. While heroin, cocaine, marijuana, and other illicit drugs have varying impacts on the body and brain, this does not mean that their use necessarily impairs one's ability to lead a successful life. Indeed, the vast majority of individuals who use marijuana on a casual basis are productive citizens with healthy emotional lives. The same is true for the recreational users of cocaine and even heroin. Dr. Arnold Trebach of the Drug Policy Foundation and others have amply documented that casual use does not necessarily lead to mental, emotional, or physical impairment. . . . Mr. Wilson's characterization of drug use in general is simply false. . . .

Mr. Wilson is correct that for some users cocaine, heroin, or marijuana, like alcohol, can be highly debilitating (though, incidentally, on this score Mr. Wilson overplays the differences between legal drugs like nicotine and illegal ones). Most proponents of legalization share Mr. Wilson's concern over this debility. But to acknowledge that some individuals suffer enormously from their drug addiction and do harm to others as a result does not lead automatically to the conclusion that all drug users manifest immoral, inhumane, unsympathetic behavior. In short, drug use does not, as Mr. Wilson contends, "destroy the drug user's essential humanity." This being the case, Mr. Wilson's moral argument falls apart. . . .

Mr. Wilson writes that "human character is inconceivable without society, and good character is less likely in a bad society." But what is a bad society? Here, Mr. Wilson overlooks the enormous harm to basic principles of due process of law now being wrought by the drug war. These principles, which are designed to protect us against arbitrary authority, serve as the foundation for a society based on responsible and free individuals. Such a foundation allows for a pluralistic climate in which families, churches, and social groups can prosper. That, I would argue, is what makes a "good society."

A genuine concern about legalization is that it would lead to significant increases in the numbers of people using (or abusing) drugs. Mr. Wilson, with little but gut feelings to back his views, firmly insists that drug use would increase. While any discussion of the effects of legalization on use is necessarily speculative, one can point to evidence that suggests Mr. Wilson is wrong. For example, decriminalization of marijuana in the Netherlands and in a number of U.S. states has not been accompanied by increased use; in fact, use has declined in these areas. And in Finland, too, there was no increase in the use of alcohol after prohibition was repealed, to the accompaniment of a public education campaign.

Mr. Wilson's description of the British system of drug regulation is also misleading. For forty years that system worked without entailing increases in heroin use. The increases in use since the '60s are very likely attributable at least in part to changes in the system. At the very least, one can conclude that legalization per se did not lead to increased use, since increased heroin use did not occur during the first four decades that the system was in place.

We cannot know for certain what the effects of legalization would be on use. But we can direct our policy efforts toward implementing legalization measures that attempt to address this risk through education, restrictions on use by minors, and so on. Before we can construct such policies, however, we need to discard the kind of moralistic arguments set forth by Mr. Wilson that are largely based on hyperbole about drug use, drug abuse, and the human soul.

—*Lynn Scarlet*
Reason Foundation
Santa Monica, California

To the Editor of *Commentary*:

It would take an article of equal length to correct the outright lies, half-truths, and misrepresentations made by James Q. Wilson in his article, "Against the Legalization of Drugs.". . .

A few short points are worth making:

The British system has not failed; it has managed drug abuse better than we have and has limited crime better than our system has. If given a choice between the U.S.

and Great Britain in terms both of heroin use and crime, most Americans would choose Britain. The British themselves have chosen to continue their system; in fact, with the onset of AIDS, they have become even more humane in their treatment of addicts.

Mr. Wilson was cowardly to avoid mentioning marijuana, but he had no choice. Marijuana legalization makes so much sense that even a rabid prohibitionist like Mr. Wilson could not distort the facts enough to make a credible argument. Marijuana is too important for prohibitionists to ignore. According to the FBI it accounts for more than one-third of all drug arrests and is the most valuable farm crop in the United States. In fact, in 1982 the National Academy of Sciences issued a report entitled "An Analysis of Marijuana Policy" which urged immediate decriminalization of possession and personal cultivation of marijuana, and advocated experimentation with regulated sales.

In regard to currently legal drugs, Mr. Wilson certainly does not advocate the prohibition of nicotine and alcohol, even though he highlights the failures of our policies in connection with these drugs. (By the way, legislation to prohibit tobacco has been introduced in Hawaii.) It is more important to highlight the successes: the use of alcohol and tobacco, as well as caffeine, is being reduced. Both drugs are becoming safer, with the introduction of low-tar, low-nicotine cigarettes and "lite" beers and wine coolers. We are having more success with legal drugs than we are with illegal drugs and we are doing it without gang warfare on the streets, smugglers fighting interdictors on the high seas, assassinations in Colombia, corrupted public officials, the expansion of organized crime, the loss of civil liberties, and the overburdening of our criminal-justice system.

The war on drugs has been given more of a chance to succeed than it deserves. During the 1980s the drug war met all of its goals: a record increase in incarcerations; one million drug arrests last year, record seizures, a well-funded antidrug publicity campaign; and an ocean of urine tested for drugs. Before the "Reagan war" we did not have crack, had never heard of ice, and our President could enter Colombia without having to hide. The world is not safer or healthier after the successes of the last decade, and there is no reason to think it will be so in the 1990s.

—*Kevin B. Zeese*
Drug Policy Foundation
Washington, D.C.

To the Editor of *Commentary*:

James Q. Wilson's defense of current drug policies is the most cogent. . . I have yet read, but it still fails to carry the burden of persuasion. And that burden is his, not the legalizers', to carry. This is so for two reasons.

First, the private consensual behavior of adults (which is the only thing that legalizers intend to make legal) is normally beyond the effective reach of democratic government. . . . When our government seeks to impose drastic penal sanctions on such conduct, whether it is abortion, gambling, pornography, or dope, we must recognize it as the extreme. . . intrusion that it is, and require compelling proof of necessity before getting on board.

Secondly, Mr. Wilson writes as though severe penal laws against drugs were something brand-new, and that we should extend to them the kind of benefit of the doubt that we normally extend to bold and well-intended social experiments, as though the imposition of such laws on consenting adults were just another Head Start program. But the fact is that we have been enforcing penal drug laws of ever-increasing severity for seventy-five years, and what do we have to show for it? Ever-increasing quantities of drugs of ever-increasing potency available to wider and wider audiences of users; drugs whose contents are neither labeled nor controlled, and whose patterns of underworld distribution guarantee violent street wars, corrupt police, and demoralized neighborhoods. These are not statistical extrapolations, but real-life facts. The drug laws are no longer in their experimental phase, and one would think that after seventy-five years we would insist that our government show us—with a clear and palpable demonstration of its successes—why we should allow this costly and destructive experiment to continue. . .

Mr. Wilson barely mentions, let alone discusses, the hideous consequences of current policy, and gives no real evidence showing either that more of the same will reduce these consequences or that more of the same is demonstrably better than legalization. Instead, he offers some nebulous, albeit uplifting, notions of "morality" and "character" as worthy justifications for staying the penal course, bolstered by statistically extrapolated predictions of increased drug usage. . .

To summarize: while the legalizers can point to longstanding . . . measurable negative consequences from current policy, James Q. Wilson and the other drug warriors offer only abstract hypotheses—what Mr. Wilson himself calls "the false comfort of suspect predictions"—to justify a continuation of that policy, one which has given us no palpable benefits in three-quarters of a century. . . . .

—Stanley Neustadter
New York City

To the Editor of *Commentary*:

James Q. Wilson's argument in support of the drug war is essentially that, at least to a limited extent, it works. If we legalized drugs, he asserts, there would be far more usage than there is today, with attendant consequences that affect us all—like crack-addicted babies or drug-related traffic fatalities.

There are other solutions to such specific problems, however. Since the mother of a crack-addicted child has proven herself, at the outset, to be abusive and unfit, the child should be taken from her. To help pay for its care, she should be fined or held ineligible for any government assistance for the remainder of her life. . . .

Drivers on drugs could be treated the same way we treat drivers on alcohol, only more drastically. For repeat offenses, or for causing a serious accident, a driver on drugs might face prison (there would be more room, were the drug war ended) or even capital punishment, for his "reckless disregard of the lives of others." If punitive programs have been ineffective with alcohol, it is only because of weak penalties and enforcement. With random testing of drivers, we could easily solve this problem, if, again, we held people appropriately accountable for their actions.

The more general argument for the drug war is that users hurt themselves, and that the influx of millions of new users likely under legalization can only have a negative, if noncriminal, effect on society as a whole. . . . I am not at all sure of the dire consequences legalization is supposed to bring, but if it does, then so be it. Better to die as a free people than live like slaves. I rather think, though, that this is not really the choice before us anyway. If we are such idiots as to need protection from labeled substances in bottles, I suspect we are doomed anyway. . . .

—*R. T. Peterson*
Chicago, Illinois

To the Editor of *Commentary*:

James Q. Wilson presents two alternate views of the nature of morality and drugs. When it comes to cocaine and certain other "mind-altering drugs," he tells us that their "illegality rests in part on their immorality." And cocaine is immoral because it "alters one's soul, . . . [and] corrodes those natural sentiments of sympathy and duty that constitute our human nature and make possible our social life." By telling us that he thinks Ethan Nadelmann's pro-legalization position "is close to saying that morality itself is but a prejudice," Mr. Wilson makes it clear that in relation to cocaine he regards the moral question as an absolute one.

But then, in the very next paragraph, he tells us that when it comes to alcohol the moral question is a relative one, because "one cannot decide [alcohol policy] on the basis of either moral principles or of individual consequences; one has to temper any policy by a common-sense judgment of what is possible." Now by any measure—deaths, number of problem users, violent behavior—alcohol use per se is a much more serious health and social problem than cocaine use per se (the illegal status of which does cause many serious social problems). But in the case of alcohol, Mr. Wilson tells us that we cannot apply an absolute moral standard. One must give him credit at least for fairly presenting the two opposing views of morality, the absolutist and the relativist. One would just like to know which one he subscribes to.

The real problem with all this moralism is that none of it solves the drug problem, which in this country begins with alcohol and tobacco. What is needed to replace the current, completely failed illegalization policy is a comprehensive public health approach to combat the use of all drugs. . . .

—*Steven Jonas, M.D.*
Department of Preventive Medicine
School of Medicine—SUNY
Stony Brook, New York

To the Editor of *Commentary*:

James Q. Wilson's attempted refutation of calls for drug legalization is based on moral assumptions about what may happen in the future, and misunderstandings of what has already occurred in the past.

His interpretation of the opinions and behavior of American citizens is too narrow and limiting. In today's world, the threshold of abuse already exists. I can't imagine that many more citizens (if any at all) would choose to damage their lives and their families by becoming drug abusers.

It seems to me that the way we manage the harm done by drugs must be rooted in sound social, medical, and economic practices. This is surely preferable to the police-state mentality championed by politicians ranting about morality who pontificate about how "tough" they are in the drug war.

Our views on Vietnam matured when family members, neighbors, and friends came home in coffins and wheelchairs. Our views on the drug war will mature when we realize that family members, neighbors, and friends are being led off to jail, their lifelong possessions stolen from them under drug-forfeiture acts.

The imprisonment policy of the present drug czar only recycles dealers and abusers (and now casual users) into costly . . . penal compost heaps.

Mr. Wilson is mistaken if he thinks the policy of the past few decades has served as an effective containment model for drug abuse. He writes as though he has never met a casual user who otherwise productively serves the needs of family and society.

—Michael R. Weddle
State Representative
House of Representatives
Concord, New Hampshire

To the Editor of *Commentary*:

As a former prosecutor, I have admired the . . . observations of James Q. Wilson and in particular his book, Thinking About Crime, which is both iconoclastic and refreshingly on target. But if Mr. Wilson's views on the criminal-justice system have been for the most part the essence of the practical and pragmatic, not so his article on drugs.

I believe Mr. Wilson has either disregarded, or failed to assess fully, the insignificance of the problems of 1972 as compared to those of 1990. . . . During the '70s I participated as a prosecutor in the criminal-justice system on the federal and county levels and I witnessed that system lumbering along like a pair of aging oxen under a barely manageable cartload. Even then, the "justice" of the system was as occasional as the production of oxen manure. In 1990, the load has been trebled and quadrupled, one of the oxen has since died, and at least two of the wheels of the cart have fallen off. It is not a pretty picture.

In my county, since 1972, the cost of inmate incarceration has risen 500 percent, and if we incarcerated everyone required under the drug-war rules, the prison population would increase 400 percent. The money cannot be printed fast enough to maintain the prisoners of war in lousy conditions, never mind those the ACLU might find acceptable. When one chump hits the street, the taxpayer reaches into his pocket again to pay for the next one who follows close on his heels. And the next and the next and the next.

To extend the analogy, that last ox is about to cash in his chips, thanks to the factor of prison capacity, . . . which will defeat the war on drugs. More than 70 percent of the encaged are there for drug-related offenses. The issue is not so much one of getting Mr. Wilson's genie back into the bottle as it is of doing something about the masses of uneducated, helpless, and hopeless drugoids on their way into, or out of, jail. . . .

Mr. Wilson himself seems to indulge in the all-or-nothing-at-all verbiage which currently characterizes most of the Grand Drug Debate. I suggest there exists a middle ground between the war whoops of the "lock-'em-up" gang versus the "come-and-get-it" crowd. . . .

For starters, we should rethink the question of the decriminalization of marijuana. Among all my adventures in law enforcement, I found marijuana prosecutions to be the most unredeemedly useless. We should try methods of regional experimentation, look to the successes of Head Start, for example, and begin using some of those enforcement bucks to imprint children's minds. Or we should consider modern marketing techniques to dissuade, or think, perhaps, of the viability of medical oversight and certification of addiction. . .

I, for one, am unwilling to assume that droves of educated and appropriately conditioned people will rush hell-bent for a line of legalized blow. In my county, as in any county with an urban center, the stuff is there for the asking, but the steady customers are still the city's losers in life. Given a diet other than one of despair and ghetto hopelessness, there has been significant resistance to the crack syndrome. That in and of itself says much about the potentially addicted.

What we are doing now flat out doesn't work, and it doesn't work on a level that rivals any previous government folly. The eloquence of James Q. Wilson notwithstanding, let us please try a different course.

—*Bill Mathesius*
County Executive
County of Mercer
Trenton, New Jersey

DISCUSSION QUESTIONS

1. Marijuana has been used for medicinal purposes by many cancer patients, and the medical use of marijuana is now legal in California, Oregon, and Arizona. Do you support the legalization of marijuana for medicinal purposes? Why or why not?
2. What is a drug and which drugs should be illegal? Does your definition of a drug include caffeine? Alcohol? Tobacco? Heroin? Marijuana? What, if any, are the important differences between them?
3. If drugs were legalized, what steps should government take, if any at all, to ensure the health and safety of users?
4. If taxes were collected from the sale of drugs, should that revenue go toward treatment and prevention programs or should it be concentrated on other societal problems? Why?
5. Should some currently legal drugs be made illegal?
6. What do you think are the main advantages of legalizing drugs? What are the principal disadvantages?
7. Are there important policy reasons why tobacco and alcohol should be treated differently from, say, marijuana? Heroin? LSD? Cocaine? Why?
8. Do you think that making certain drugs illegal denies important liberties to individuals? Why or why not?
9. What impact would legalizing drugs have on their price? How, in turn, would that affect drug-related crimes? How would it affect drug use? What evidence supports your position?

10. Where should government focus its efforts at drug control? At the federal level or that of states and localities? On the individual user or on the supplier of drugs? On law enforcement or on interdiction? Should there be a governmental effort at all? Why or why not?

11. Should strict minimum sentences be required for individuals caught distributing drugs? Using drugs?

WEB REFERENCES

Bureau of Justice Statistics, *Sourcebook of Criminal Justice Statistics Online* http://www.albany.edu/sourcebook/.

The Drug Reform Coordination Network, http://www.drcnet.org/.

Drug Watch International, http://www.drugwatch.org/.

Office of National Drug Control Policy, http://www.whitehousedrugpolicy.gov/.

FURTHER READING

Barbour, Scott. *Drug Legalization (Current Controversies)*. San Diego: Greenhaven Press, 2000.

Bayer, Ronald and Gerald M. Oppenheimer, eds. *Confronting Drug Policy: Illicit Drugs in a Free Society*. New York: Cambridge University Press, 1993.

Benjamin, Daniel K. and Roger LeRoy Miller. *Undoing Drugs: Beyond Legalization*. New York: Basic Books, 1991.

Bennett, William and Ethan Nadelmann. "The Drug Legalization Debate." *Business Today* (Fall 1990).

Bertram, Eva. *Drug War Politics: The Price of Denial*. Berkeley: University of California Press, 1996.

Brown, Lee P. "Drug Legalization Can't Work and Would Devastate Our Youth." *Insight on the News* (June 27, 1994).

Buckley, William F., et al. "The War on Drugs Is Lost" (A Symposium Discussing the War on Drugs and Drug Legalization). *National Review* (February 12, 1996).

Duke, Steven B. and Albert C. Gross. *America's Longest War: Rethinking Our Tragic Crusade against Drugs*. New York: Putnam's Sons, 1993.

Eldrege, Dirk Chase. *Ending the War on Drugs: A Solution for America*. Bridgehampton, New York: Bridge Works Publishing, 1998.

Evans, Rod L. and Irwin M. Berent, eds. *Drug Legalization: For and Against*. La Salle, Ill.: Open Court, 1992.

Gazzaniga, Michael S. "Legalizing Drugs: Just Say Yes." *National Review* (July 10, 1995).

Gerstein, Dean and Lawrence Green, eds. *Preventing Drug Abuse: What We Know*. Washington, D.C.: National Academy Press, 1993.

Goode, Erich. *Between Politics and Reason: The Drug Legalization Debate*. New York: St. Martin's Press, 1997.

Gordon, Diana. *The Return of the Dangerous Classes: Drug Prohibition and Policy Politics*. New York: Norton, 1994.

Gottfried, Ted. *Should Drugs Be Legalized?* New York: Twenty First Century Books, 2000.

Husak, Douglas N. *Drugs and Rights*. Cambridge: Cambridge University Press, 1992.

Inciardi, James A. *The Drug Legalization Debate*, 2d ed. Thousand Oaks, Calif.: Corwin Press, 1999.

Jacobs, James. "Imagining Drug Legalization." *Public Interest* (Fall 1990).

Kaplan, John. "Taking Drugs Seriously." *Public Interest* (Summer 1988).

Kleiman, Mark and Aaron Saiger. *Drug Legalization: The Importance of Asking the Right Question*. Cambridge, Mass.: John F. Kennedy School of Government, Working Paper 89–01–16, 1989.

Kraska, Peter B. *Altered States of Mind: Critical Observations of the Drug War*. New York: Garland, 1993.

Krauss, Melvyn B. and Edward P. Lazear, eds. *Searching for Alternatives: Drug-Control Policy in the United States*. Stanford, Calif.: Hoover Institution Press, 1991.

Kwitny, Jonathan. *Acceptable Risks*. New York: Poseidon Press, 1992.

MacCoun, Robert J. and Peter Reuter. *Drug War Heresies : Learning from Other Vices, Times, and Places*. Santa Monica, Calif.: Rand Studies in Policy Analysis, 2001.

Meier, Kenneth J. *The Politics of Sin: Drugs, Alcohol, and Public Policy*. Armonk, N.Y.: M. E. Sharpe, 1994.

Miller, Richard Lawrence. *The Case for Legalizing Drugs*. New York: Praeger, 1991.

Nadelmann, Ethan A. "Drug Prohibition in the United States: Costs, Consequences, and Alternatives." *Science* (September 1, 1989), pp. 939–47.

Ostrowski, James. *Thinking about Drug Legalization*. Washington, D.C.: Cato Institute, 1989.

Perl, Raphael F., ed. *Drugs and Foreign Policy: A Critical Review*. Boulder, Colo.: Westview Press, 1994.

Reuter, Peter. "Can the Borders Be Sealed?" *Public Interest* (Summer 1988).

Sanders, Darrell L. "President's Message: Why Drug Legalization Efforts Must Be Derailed." *Police Chief* (February 1, 1997).

Schaler, Jeffrey A. *Drugs: Should We Legalize, Decriminalize, or Deregulate?* (Contemporary Issues). Amherst, N.Y.: Prometheus Books, 1998.

Schlosser, Eric. "More Reefer Madness." *Atlantic Monthly* (April 1997), pp: 90–102.

Sharp, Elaine. *The Dilemma of Drug Policy in the United States*. New York: HarperCollins, 1994.

Stares, Paul B. "Drug Legalization?" *Brookings Review* (Spring 1996).

Szasz, Thomas Stephen. *Our Right to Drugs: The Case for a Free Market*. New York: Praeger, 1992.

Trebach, Arnold S. and James A. Inciardi. *Legalize It? Debating American Drug Policy*. Washington, D.C.: American University Press, 1993.

Vallance, Theodore R. *Prohibition's Second Failure: The Quest for a Rational and Humane Drug Policy*. Westport, Conn.: Praeger, 1993.

Chapter 13

GUN CONTROL

"Should the Sale of Handguns Be Strictly Controlled?"

YES: Steven Riczo "Guns, America, and the 21st Century" *USA Today Magazine*

NO: Daniel D. Polsby "The False Promise of Gun Control" *The Atlantic Monthly*

The attempt to regulate the distribution and ownership of guns by enacting national legislation has had a rather sporadic history in the United States. The November 1993 passage of the Brady bill marked the first major gun control legislation to be enacted at the federal level since 1968, when the Gun Control Act prohibited the interstate sale or shipment of firearms and ammunition and required dealers to keep records of gun transactions. The Brady bill instituted a nationwide mandatory five-day waiting period for the purchase of handguns and required local police to conduct a background check into the criminal and psychiatric history of the purchaser. Furthermore, it made funds available for the federal government to develop a central computer system to allow for instantaneous checks that would ultimately eliminate the five-day waiting period. Since the Brady bill, the Violent Crime Control and Law Enforcement Act of 1994 banned the manufacture and sale of certain semiautomatic weapons, and the Domestic Violence Offender Gun Ban of 1996 prohibited anyone convicted of domestic violence from buying or owning a gun.[1]

Following a legal challenge by some local police departments that the provision of the law requiring background checks constituted an "unfunded federal mandate," the Supreme Court ruled in June 1997 that the federal government could not legally require local governments or police to devote resources to conducting background checks. In November 1998 the federal government instigated a system of instant background checks for handgun, long-gun, and shotgun purchases. The process is designed to take only five minutes, and as well as prohibiting gun sales to convicted felons and the mentally ill, the system also prohibits anyone convicted of domestic violence from buying a firearm. While the success of the Brady bill is difficult to measure, the Justice Department estimated in June 1999 that police background checks prevented the sale of more than 312,000 handguns between 1994 and 1998; in 66 percent of those cases, the handgun purchaser had been convicted of or indicted on a felony charge.[2]

Legislation designed to restrict the availability of guns, especially to convicted criminals, often stems from the belief that the widespread availability of guns plays a significant role in increasing violence and crime. And like the Gun Control Act of 1968, the Brady bill legislation came in response to a period of perceived crisis in the nation, albeit a more slowly evolving one. Certainly, gun ownership in the United States is widespread: Federal officials estimate that Americans may own 200 million guns; more than 13 million guns were purchased in 1993 and 1994 combined, including 6.5 million handguns.[3] The Federal Bureau of Investigation reported that 50 percent of the 13,011 murders that occurred in 1999 were committed with a handgun. If other firearms, such as shotguns and assault rifles, are taken into account, the figure rises to 65 percent of all murders.[4] Yet it is the role that guns play in everyday crimes that seems to concern most advocates of gun control. For example, in 1999, 60 out of every 100,000 Americans faced robbery at gunpoint, although this represents a decline from 99 per 100,000 in 1994 and 101.3 per 100,000 in 1980.[5] In 1999, 24 percent of robberies, 6 percent of assaults, and 1 percent of rapes involved the use of a gun.[6] More disturbing is the widespread and lethal effect of such guns within some communities; for example, among African-American males age 15 to 24, homicide committed with guns is the leading cause of death.[7]

While the number of handgun murders in the United States has fallen in the last several years, crime rates involving the use of handguns in the United States are exceptionally high when compared with those of the other industrial democracies. In 1996, there were 9,390 handgun murders in the United States, compared with 30 in Britain, 15 in Japan, and 106 in Canada.[8] Even when population differences are accounted for, the figures for these nations are far lower than those for the United States: The per capita death rate from handgun violence was 1 per 282,858 residents of Canada, 1 per 8.35 million in Japan, and 1 per 1.9 million in Britain; the comparable figure for the United States was 1 person for every 28,271 residents, or 10 times the rate in Canada and 67 times the rate in Britain. Some argue that harsh prison sentences rather than gun control would be an effective way to prevent gun violence, but the United States already has one of the highest incarceration rates in the world, and the rate has more than tripled since 1980, standing at nearly five prisoners for every thousand people in 2000.[9]

Though the public generally perceives crime rates to be increasing, crime statistics indicate otherwise. Perhaps the most reliable measure, the homicide rate, held at a relatively steady rate between 1970 and 1990, rose during the early 1990s, and fell to much lower levels by 2000.[10] According to both the FBI's Uniform Crime Reports Index and the Census Bureau's National Crime Survey, crime rates as a whole have declined considerably since the early 1990s. The Uniform Crime Reports Index, which is based on data from police reports, showed a slight decline over the past 10 years; and the National Crime Survey, which is based on self-reported crimes, fell more significantly. Why, then, has the public perceived crime to be a more serious problem than statistics indicate? Part of the explanation lies with news reports about crime, which show not only increasingly random criminal acts, but also those perpetrated by teenagers. Late-night news is filled with accounts of drive-by shootings, gang wars, and innocent people caught in cross fire, connoting a sense of lawlessness that frightens many Americans. As James Q. Wilson notes, "People are not responding to the statistics, but what they hear reported. . . . It's the stranger-to-stranger nature of the crime, the youth of the offenders, and the level at which they're armed which alarms people."[11]

Furthermore, while overall levels have remained constant or fallen steadily, inner-city crime is substantially higher than in nonurban areas, often reaching levels four times higher than the national violent crime rate of over 525 per 100,000 people in 1999. Visions of children passing through metal detectors to enter inner-city schools has brought the issue of gun control to even greater attention. One 1999 study estimated that 1 in 20 high school students reported carrying a gun for fighting or self-defense at least once in the last 30 days, a figure that has decreased from 1 in 12 in the early 1990s.[12] Between 1985 and 1994, the risk of being killed by a gun had more than doubled for those between 15 and 19 years old, and gun injuries were the second leading cause of death for those between 15 and 24 in 1998.[13] Indeed, because of its pervasiveness in the lives of many inner-city residents, gun-related crime is increasingly viewed by some, including prominent officials, as a public health issue.

A final explanation for the growing public concern is that certain crimes have increased substantially over the past two decades, despite declines in recent years. Forcible rape, for example, increased from 18.7 per 100,000 women in 1970 to 64 per 100,000 in 1999,[14] and the number and rate of violent crimes have increased since 1980. Also, while inner-city crime rates receive most of the media attention, the suburbs and rural areas are not immune. As the relative of one victim of a random shooting on a suburban train put it, "It could have happened to anyone. You think of the random shootings in the city [New York]; you feel somewhat isolated out here. Now, you feel there are no borders."[15]

Public response to these levels of violence has coalesced into significant public support for gun control measures in the United States. Support for stricter gun control laws has varied considerably over the past decade and a half, standing at 59 percent in 1983, peaking at 78 percent in 1990, and returning to 64 percent in 2001, with greater support among women and minorities.[16] A similar poll in March 1993 found that 88 percent of Americans supported the Brady bill, down from a peak level of 95 percent in 1990, while 66 percent favor banning semiautomatic rifles. In an ABC/Washington Post poll in 2000, 87 percent of respondents believed that gun control legislation was very important. Support for gun control only fell below 50 percent for more restrictive measures such as banning concealed weapons and banning hand-gun sales, except to the police. Even among gun owners, 63 percent favored a ban on assault weapons, and 34 percent favored banning carrying concealed weapons. Only 17 percent of gun owners would support a ban on handgun sales.[17] With these levels of public support, it would seem that gun control legislation would be a foregone conclusion. However, gun control is highly controversial and involves politically powerful constituencies. The relatively unrestricted possession of firearms has a long tradition in the United States and is tightly intertwined with constitutional protections. While the Second Amendment to the Constitution is often put forward as a limitation to government restriction on the ownership of firearms, it is unclear which rights are indeed guaranteed.[18] The Court has many times upheld state and local restrictions on the possession of firearms, as well as national laws such as the 1934 National Firearms Act, which set restrictions on weapons such as sawed-off shotguns.[19] As a result, interest groups such as the National Rifle Association (NRA) have hesitated to use litigation to fight gun control measures, preferring instead to concentrate their significant political clout in federal and state legislatures.

With more than 4 million members, the NRA uses different strategies to lead the effort to preserve the right to possess firearms with a minimum of restrictions. For example, from 1989 to 1998, the NRA made contributions to 217 members of Congress, totaling $3.4 million.[20] More recently, the NRA spent almost $1 million in support of George W. Bush during his 2000 presidential campaign.[21] What is more, the NRA has the capacity to put its 4.3 million members to good use through a sophisticated grassroots mobilization system; few politicians wish to be targeted by the NRA.[22] The NRA opposed the waiting period provision of the Brady bill, but does favor an instantaneous background check when the technology and funds become available. The organization also opposes any attempt to ban or limit the possession of semi-automatic assault rifles as well as other measures such as taxing ammunition. The NRA is particularly strong in southern and western states; it is estimated that 60 percent of families own at least one gun in the South, compared with under 30 percent in eastern states. Gun control opponents found political support from recent Republican presidents. President Reagan expressed his disapproval of gun control measures in 1986 in a manner consistent with the NRA's position: "As long as there are guns, the individual that wants a gun for a crime is going to have one or going to get it. The only person who's going to be penalized and have difficulty is the law-abiding citizen, who then cannot have [it] if he wants protection—the protection of a weapon in his home, for home protection."

When President Clinton was elected in 1992, the NRA lost one of its most valued tools—the presidential veto—on which it had relied since the Gun Control Act of 1968 as a hedge against gun control legislation. Former President George Bush blocked the Brady bill with the veto threat throughout his term in office. However, President Clinton pledged to sign the Brady bill and other gun control legislation, such as the assault rifle ban, during his campaign and made good on that promise in the eleventh month of his presidency. Many states already have waiting periods for handgun purchases, frequently longer than the five days required in the Brady bill, so its impact on crime may not be large. Nevertheless, supporters view its success as the first of many possible restrictions on handgun purchases. Other proposals include taxing ammunition, banning assault rifles, instituting more gun "buy-back" programs, and other means to reduce crimes committed using guns. President George W. Bush has something of a mixed policy on gun control. He has pledged money for trigger locks and supports the current ban on assault weapons. However, he opposes any registration of guns by law-abiding citizens and, while governor of Texas, signed a 1995 bill allowing Texans to carry concealed weapons for the first time in the twentieth century, stating that it would "make Texans safer."[23]

The NRA is not the only obstacle to gun control laws. There is substantial uncertainty over what impact various forms of gun control would have, largely due to the fact that little scientific research has been conducted. Instead, the debate is too often based on conjecture and speculation rather than evidence. One of the central issues is whether fewer people would die or be injured in violent encounters and whether there would be fewer such encounters. As it turns out, the answer is unclear. In robberies, where most gun-related deaths occur, the presence of a gun reduced the chance of victim injury, but where injuries result from robberies, guns are (not surprisingly) far more deadly than knives and other weapons.[24] Also frequently ignored is the impact of gun control on noncriminal violence such as accidents and suicide. Gun control advocates argue that fewer guns mean less overall gun violence. The opposition counters that "guns don't kill; people do" (to which former Senator Daniel Moynihan, D-N.Y., responded, in pushing for a tax on ammunition, "Guns don't kill; bullets do"). Little hard evidence backs up either position, however.

In the articles that follow, Steven Riczo argues that gun ownership rights need to be balanced against the risks of increased homicides and suicides. He believes that the lack of national handgun licensing in the United States adversely sets the country apart from most other developed countries. Daniel Polsby presents an opposing view, arguing that gun controls simply do not work.

Endnotes

1. See Brady Campaign, http://www.bradycampaign.org/legislation/federal/gunlaws.asp.
2. U.S. Department of Justice, "Presale Handgun Checks, the Brady Interim Period, 1994–1998," http://www.ojp.usdoj.gov/bjs/pub/pdf/phc98.pdf.
3. U.S. Department of Justice, National Institute of Justice, *Guns in America: National Survey on Private Ownership of Firearms* (Washington, D.C.: U.S. Government Printing Office, May 1997).

4. U.S. Bureau of the Census, *Statistical Abstract of the United States, 2001*, http://www.census.gov/prod/2002pubs/01statab/law.pdf, table 295.
5. Ibid., table 299.
6. U.S. Department of Justice, Criminal Victimization 1999, http://www.ojp. usdoj.gov /bjs/pub/pdf/cv99.pdf, 9.
7. Centers for Disease Control and Prevention, *National Vital Statistics Report*, July 24, 2000, http://www.cdc.gov/nchs/data/nvsr/nvsr48/nvs48_11.pdf, table 8.
8. Handgun Control Inc., Firearm Facts, http://www.bradycampaign.org/facts/ research/firefacts.asp.
9. U.S. Department of Justice, Bureau of Justice Statistics, Incarceration Rates, 1980–2000, http://www.ojp.usdoj.gov/bjs/glance/tables/incrttab.htm.
10. U.S. Department of Justice, Bureau of Justice Statistics, Homicide Victimization Rate by Age, http://www.ojp.usdoj.gov/bjs/glance/tables/homagetab.htm.
11. Quoted in Neil A. Lewis, "Crime: Falling Rates but Rising Fear," *New York Times* (December 8, 1993), p. B6.
12. National Center for Chronic Disease Prevention and Health Promotion, Youth Risk Behavior Surveillance System, Unintended Injuries/Violence, http://apps.nccd. cdc.gov/YRBSS/TrendV.asp?Site=XX&Cat=1&Qnum=Q13.
13. Centers for Disease Control and Prevention, op. cit., table 8.
14. U.S. Bureau of the Census, op. cit., table 298.
15. Quoted in Peter Marks, "5 Everyday People, by Chance or Ritual, Riding in Car No. 3," *New York Times* (December 9, 1993), p. 1.
16. George Gallup, Jr., *The Gallup Poll: Public Opinion 1995* (Wilmington, Del.: Scholarly Resources, 1996), p. 75.
17. ABC News, "Ambivalence on Gun Control," http://abcnews.go.com/sections/ politics/DailyNews/poll990908.html, December 17, 2000.
18. The Second Amendment reads: "A well regulated militia, being necessary to the security of a free State, the right of the people to keep and bear arms, shall not be infringed."
19. H. Idelson, "Gun Rights and Restrictions: The Territory Reconfigured," *Congressional Quarterly* (April 24, 1993), p. 1022.
20. Common Cause, NRA Political Spending Fact Sheet 1989–1998, http://www. commoncause.org/publications/june99/061599.htm.
21. Associated Press (October 25, 2000).
22. Idelson, op. cit., p. 1023.
23. ABC News, "Bush on Guns," http://more.abcnews.go.com/sections/us/dailynews/ bush_guns.html, March 23, 2001.
24. Franklin E. Zimring, "Firearms, Violence, and Public Policy," *Scientific American* (November 1991), p. 51.

YES

Guns, America, and the 21st Century

Steven Riczo

As Americans become sickened by one firearm tragedy after another, the momentum may be building for a shift in the nation's approach to guns in the 21st century. While it is certainly true that the U.S. has had a tradition of gun ownership, much has changed since the days of the Wild West. This is the age of the Internet, instant global communications, medical marvels, genetic engineering, and other technological wonders that are transforming our lives. Citizens don't have to give up their fight to own firearms in order to make progress on this issue, but should approach it in a more intelligent manner than the bumper sticker mentality and oversimplistic slogans that have characterized this polarized debate. The real question we should be asking ourselves isn't whether or not the government should curtail the right to own firearms, but, as an American, do I really want to own one? Ownership rights can be balanced with reasonable limits in the quest for a sensible gun policy.

There are also interesting political ramifications in light of the razor-thin election of Pres. George W. Bush. During the presidential race, there were many critics of then-Gov. Bush who maintained that his policy positions are simply reflections of the special interests that contributed to his campaign, such as the National Rifle Association (NRA), defense contractors, the oil industry, etc. There were also frequent concerns raised that he may lack the intellectual wherewithal or was perhaps intellectually too lazy to analyze complex issues and then make a wise choice. The gun safety issue could be an interesting test of these assertions.

A widely viewed videotape showed an NRA official publicly boasting that, if Bush won the election, they would have their man in the White House. If the President is to demonstrate that he is a "compassionate conservative" he must carefully listen to all sides of an issue. There are groups other than the NRA that present opposing, yet compelling, arguments, such as the Coalition to Stop Gun Violence, supported by 44 well-respected national scientific, civic, and religious organizations, including the American Academy of Pediatrics, American Public Health Association, Center for Science in the Public Interest, United Federation of Teachers, and U.S. Conference of Mayors. If Bush's actions prove his critics right, he could lose support of many Americans who backed him the first time around.

The official Republican campaign website, Bush/Cheney 2000 Inc., promised Americans that Bush's policy on gun safety would protect citizens' constitutional rights "while at the same time enacting reasonable, common-sense restrictions on the unsafe use of firearms." It is incumbent upon the President and the nearly evenly split Congress to heed the voices of the majority who would like to see progress on this issue.

Other developed nations are willing to accept a reasonable compromise between ownership rights and common-sense restrictions and tend to view gun policy as part of an overall public health plan. The typical reaction of other developed nations to our frequent firearm tragedies is "only in America." The U.S. has the highest per capita gun ownership among all developed nations. The firearm violence comparisons between the U.S. and other industrialized countries are staggering. According to the Centers for Disease Control, the U.S., one of the richest nations on Earth, suffers "the highest firearm mortality rate." Americans murder each other with guns at a rate 19 times higher than any of the 25 richest nations surveyed by CDC. Since 1960, more than 1,000,000 Americans have died from firearm homicides, suicides, and accidental shootings. Moreover, for every firearm death, there are six nonfatal injuries.

Americans own 200,000,000 guns, of which approximately 70,000,000 are handguns. One interesting feature of the high level of gun ownership is that it is not evenly distributed among its citizens. In the most extensive firearm survey ever conducted in the U.S., the National Institute of Justice found that 35% of households had guns present. Conversely, this also means that 65% of adults and heads of households have rejected gun ownership.

When asked why they chose not to own a gun, the most common reasons identified were that such weapons are dangerous, "immoral" or otherwise objectionable. Of those who own guns, 46% said they do so for prevention of crime, while the majority cited recreational purposes such as hunting and target shooting. Gun owners predominantly identified the reason for the purchase of rifles as recreation and buying handguns for protection against crime. There is also a stark contrast between gun ownership by region of the country—in descending order, the South, West, Midwest, and Northeast. In Texas, for example, there are 68,000,000 guns, which equates to four for every man, woman, and child.

Americans who currently own guns or are contemplating purchasing one would be well-served by objectively evaluating data from reliable organizations such as the Federal Bureau of Investigation and the Justice Department's Bureau of Justice Statistics. Both have extensive data, including detailed interview information from victims of crime. Simply put, guns are designed to kill, and when you bring one into your home, you increase the risk to yourself and family members. According to the *New England Journal of Medicine*, guns kept in the home for self-protection are 22 times more likely to kill someone you know than to kill in self-defense. According to Physicians for Social Responsibility, when a gun is kept in the home, it is about three times as likely that a death will occur in that household.

THE SELF-PROTECTION ARGUMENT

How are Americans to reconcile the risks to themselves and family members of bringing a gun into the home vs. the odds that they will use the firearm to protect their own lives or property against an intruder? A review of the facts should provide some clarity on which to base a decision. First, interviews with detectives in various police departments revealed that about 90% of residential burglaries occur when the owner or family is not at home. The odds of an American being killed during a burglary are quite low, with 61 such deaths out of 14,088 homicides in 1998.

One also must consider the increased risk to the homeowner in pulling a gun on a felon who could have more firearm experience than the victim. As one Bureau of Alcohol, Tobacco, and Firearms agent described in an interview, a law-abiding citizen pulling a gun for the first time to shoot a criminal is in a very difficult situation. He or she has now forced the hand of the perpetrator in a life-threatening and probably terrifying situation for the homeowner. Unless the homeowner has extensive and regular training in the use of firearms comparable to that received by law enforcement officers or the military, the odds of success are slim.

There were just 195 justifiable homicides in 1998 by private citizens out of more than 12,000,000 reported crimes in the U.S. The majority of justifiable killings are by law enforcement officers. According to the *Journal of the American Medical Association*, even when someone is home, a gun is used for protection in less than two percent of home-incursion crimes. Other nonfirearm options for protection against home incursion are available, such as dialing 911 (police will be dispatched even if you are not in a position to talk), buying a dog, or installing a burglar alarm system with monitoring by a protective services company.

On any given day, 1,100,000 Americans carry concealed weapons on them outside the workplace, and 2,100,000 in their vehicles. The rate is twice as high in the South as the rest of the nation. FBI data show that just 0.6% of violent-crime victims used a firearm in an attempt to defend themselves. According to the Bureau of Justice Statistics (BJS) National Crime Utilization Survey, 29% of violent-crime victims faced an offender with a gun. Of those, three percent suffered gunshot wounds. In other words, even if you are unfortunate enough to face an assailant with a firearm, there is a 97% chance that you will not be shot. BJS surveys from a number of years consistently indicate that about 85,000 crime victims use guns in an attempt to protect themselves or their property out of a total of 13,000,000 reported crimes (FBI) or 40,000,000 crimes, including unreported ones (Justice Department). Either way, guns are used in defense in less than one percent of crimes committed.

The BJS victim interviews reveal that, in 72% of violent crimes, victims take some self-protective measures, but more than 98% of those acts do not include the use of a firearm. For instance, in 10% of cases, the victim attacked the perpetrator without using a weapon; nine percent scared off the offender; nine percent got help or sounded an alarm; 16% ran or hid; 13% persuaded or appeased the offender; 2.4% screamed; 1.7% threatened the offender with a weapon; and 1.5% threatened the offender without a weapon. Clearly, self-preservation methods without the use or threat of use of a weapon comprise the vast majority of cases. Sixty-five percent of those who employed some type of self-preservation method said their actions either helped avoid injury, scared off the offender, and/or enabled them to escape the situation or protect their property. Just nine percent of those who took self-protective measures said those actions made the situation worse.

There have been some gun ownership advocates who have exaggerated the extent by which ordinary citizens protect their lives and property with firearms. One widely quoted concealed weapons study concluded that violent-crime incidents declined in states that had passed right-to-carry (concealed weapons) laws. The full truth is that violent crime has decreased in every region of the country, regardless of gun ownership laws. FBI crime data indicate that, in the seven states that the NRA identifies as having the most-restrictive concealed weapons laws on the books, homicides/non-negligent manslaughter declined in six of them between 1993 and 1999—Illinois, Kansas, Missouri, Nebraska, Ohio, and Wisconsin. The 11 states identified as having moderately restrictive concealed weapons laws all experienced homicide declines. For example, per 100,000 inhabitants, Missouri declined from 11.3 to 6.6; Ohio, from six to 3.5; and California and New York both experienced dramatic declines from approximately 13 to six and five, respectively.

U.S. homicide rates historically have been characterized by wide fluctuations, being relatively high in the 1920s and 1930s, much lower in the 1940s and 1950s, and then high again for much of the last half-century, although showing favorable declines in recent years. For every time a citizen used a firearm in a justifiable homicide, 131 lives were ended in a firearm murder, suicide, or unintentional shooting. Law enforcement statistics and interviews show that approximately 45% of homicides were perpetrated by assailants related to or acquainted with their victim. Fifty-six percent of gun homicides resulted from arguments. Of all violent crime, 23% of offenders were family members and 48% acquaintances. Situations of family strife with the potential for domestic violence is a factor that should be kept in mind by any prospective gun owner.

Gun ownership also has a correlation with suicide. According to the National Institutes of Mental Health, 19,000,000 Americans suffer some form of depression each year, with up to 20% of untreated cases choosing suicide. While there are other developed countries without high gun ownership with suicide rates higher than the U.S., firearms are the most lethal choice of suicide options. According to Physicians for Social Responsibility, 84 people die every day in America by suicide, and 50 of those are by firearms. The risk of suicide is five times greater in households with guns.

The 1994 Police Foundation Survey revealed that the average gun owner had had his or her firearm for 13 years. When evaluating a gun purchase, prospective buyers should consider the length of time they will own their gun in the context of the normal ups and downs that people face over the course of many years, including depression over a job loss or loved one, family fights, divorce, or a bout with alcohol and/or drugs.

There is an additional risk of teen suicide in homes with firearms and, according to the Surgeon General, five percent of youngsters between the ages of nine and 17 have a diagnosis of a major depression, with 10–15% having some symptoms of depression. Suicidal adolescents are 75 times more likely to commit suicide when a gun is kept in the home. Impulsiveness appears to play an important role in suicide, especially youth suicide. It is not uncommon for adolescents to have passing suicidal tendencies. Youth who attempt suicide rarely have a clear and sustained desire to die.

Guns, of course, are not the sole reason for violent crime and suicide in the U.S. Many experts agree that gun violence results from intertwined complex causes, such as family problems, neighborhood concerns, drug/alcohol abuse, media gun violence, school/work pressures, poverty, and accessibility to guns. Some have pointed to the fact that America is a heterogeneous society compared to others with lower rates of violence. However, the fact remains that 94% of black murders in the U.S. were by black offenders, and 87% of white murders were by white offenders. Special attention must be given to violence among blacks. Although African-Americans make up 12% of the population, 47% of all murder victims are black. According to FBI data, 35% of murder offenders were white, 35% black, and 28% unknown. Poverty and low education also have a correlation with violent crime.

A comparison between Department of Commerce statistics and FBI Uniform Crime Report data on murder and non-negligent manslaughter shows that states with lower-than-average high school graduation rates and lower-than-average per capita income consistently have higher homicide rates. A number of southern states bear these characteristics, and, when combined with a high percentage of gun ownership, there is an increase in the propensity for violence with fatal consequences.

Violence-reduction policies must be multi-faceted and include better education, domestic violence reduction, improvement of the plight of the urban poor, the cutting of drug/alcohol abuse (35% of violent crime victims said the perpetrator had been drinking), early mental health intervention, and increased parental involvement with children. Guns should not be viewed as the sole cause of violence, but as an important contributing factor. While there are other weapons used in violent crimes, guns are used in 65% of homicides and 59% of all suicides. Guns create a distance from the violent act compared to other weapons/actions, such as knives, strangulation, beatings, or use of blunt objects, which are visibly more violent and sometimes riskier for the perpetrator. It is simply too easy in today's society to pull the trigger to end a temporary episode of depression or rage.

CONTROLLING GUNS

It is within America's power to start moving toward a more rational approach to firearms. Gun-control proposals often include the following elements:

- Raising the legal age for the possession of handguns from 18 to 21
- Limiting handgun purchases so that no individual is able to buy more than one gun per month
- Holding parents legally accountable when their children commit crimes with guns that they obtained as a result of the negligent storage of the weapons and ammunition
- Improving the design and manufacture of firearms, including installing child-locks, personalizing a gun so that it can only be fired by its owner, and adding load indicators that tell the user that the gun is still loaded or magazine-disconnect safeties which prevent the gun from firing if the ammunition magazine is removed
- Applying restrictions on gun manufacturers who produce low-quality, easily concealable "junk guns" or Saturday night specials and strict regulations against cop-killer bullets and mail-order parts that allow individuals to assemble untraceable guns
- Educating consumers about the true risks and rewards of gun ownership for enhanced personal safety
- Prohibiting gun advertisements in publications with substantial youth readership and including warnings about the risks of guns in the home
- Altering distribution and sales practices by improving security systems to avoid theft from dealers, prohibiting straw purchases by gun traffickers who then resell guns on the streets to criminals, closing gun show loopholes, and legislating mandatory waiting periods
- Federal licensing of handgun owners and registration of the handguns.

Licensing of handgun owners and registration of the handgun itself deserves special mention, as it has been the cornerstone of handgun responsibility and accountability throughout most of the developed world, including Australia, Austria, Belgium, Brazil, Canada, Finland, France, Germany, Great Britain, Greece, Hong Kong, India, Ireland, Israel, Italy, Japan, Malaysia, Mexico, the Netherlands, New Zealand, Northern Ireland, Norway, the Philippines, Portugal, Russia, Singapore, Slovakia, Sweden, and Switzerland. The U.S. does not have mandatory owner licensing and registration of handguns, with the exception of a handful of states and a few cities that have some components. Hawaii, where handguns have been registered for 40 years, has tight restrictions on carrying concealed weapons and a gun-death rate one-third the national average.

Philip Alpers, a highly credentialed gun-policy researcher, testified at the Select Committee on Gun Violence in California that, around the world, handgun registration and owner licensing are acknowledged as the most effective way to minimize handgun-related death and trauma. Effective registration of firearms acts to reduce the flow of guns from lawful owners to criminals. Computerized firearm registries are consulted thousands of times each day in some nations as a crime-busting tool.

Some of the common components of licensing and registration in developed nations are reviewing criminal history, domestic violence, and mental health; gun owner training, including public safety education as a condition of licensing; demonstrated need for a handgun; club membership with regular attendance required, such as an approved pistol club; interviewing the applicant's current or most recent spouse; secure storage requirements with the handgun and ammunition stored separately; verification of storage through physical inspections; fraud-resistant licensing procedures, such as requiring a thumbprint or photograph; limitations on ammunition that can be purchased for the type of firearm declared; mandatory removal of firearms within 24 hours of a domestic protection order; and regular reviews of gun owners for reapplication and periodic interviews.

Gun-control laws in the U.S. vary widely between states, but America has been willing to pass Federal legislation when circumstances dictated. The nation's first major gun law was the Gun Control Act of 1968, passed in the wake of the assassinations of civil rights leader Martin Luther King, Jr., and Sen. Robert Kennedy earlier that year. It established categories of prohibited purchasers, including convicted felons, fugitives from justice, minors, individuals with a history of mental illness, dishonorably discharged veterans, expatriates, and illegal aliens. It also set standards for gun dealers and age guidelines for gun purchasers. The Brady Handgun Violence Prevention Act that went into effect in February, 1984, required a five-day waiting period and background check before completion of the sale of a handgun. The five-day waiting period for handgun purchasers changed in November, 1998, to a computerized National Instant Check System, which provides the information for criminal background checks on all firearm purchasers. Current Federal law focuses on small prohibited groups, but can provide the foundation for a comprehensive policy of education and training for all those who choose to own firearms.

It is time not to prohibit law-abiding citizens from owning a gun, but to be sure that they have correct factual data so that each can make an intelligent, informed choice pertaining to firearm ownership and then act responsibly after the purchase. Public policy should be geared to keeping firearms out of the hands of youth and to provide tools to trace firearms used in crimes to the original sources who are illegally providing firearms to criminals and young people. Continued tough enforcement of laws governing the use of firearms in the commission of a crime, coupled with a rational policy for law-abiding Americans, would be a major step in the right direction. In the area of gun policy, it is time to learn from the experiences of other developed nations in a manner that preserves individual rights, improves informed consumer choice, and encourages responsibility and accountability.

NO

The False Promise of Gun Control

Daniel D. Polsby

During the 1960s and 1970s the robbery rate in the United States increased sixfold, and the murder rate doubled; the rate of handgun ownership nearly doubled in that period as well. Handguns and criminal violence grew together apace, and national opinion leaders did not fail to remark on that coincidence.

It has become a bipartisan article of faith that more handguns cause more violence. Such was the unequivocal conclusion of the national Commission on the Causes and Prevention of Violence in 1969, and such is now the editorial opinion of virtually every influential newspaper and magazine, from the *Washington Post* to the *Economist* to the *Chicago Tribune*. Members of the House and Senate who have not dared to confront the gun lobby concede the connection privately. Even if the National Rifle Association can produce blizzards of angry calls and letters to the Capitol virtually overnight, House members one by one have been going public, often after some new firearms atrocity at a fast-food restaurant or the like. And last November they passed the Brady bill.

Alas, however well accepted, the conventional wisdom about guns and violence is mistaken. Guns don't increase national rates of crime and violence—but the continued proliferation of gun control laws almost certainly does. Current rates of crime and violence are a bit below the peaks of the late 1970s, but because of a slight oncoming bulge in the at-risk population of males aged fifteen to thirty-four, the crime rate will soon worsen. The rising generation of criminals will have no more difficulty than their elders did in obtaining the tools of their trade. Growing violence will lead to calls for laws still more severe. Each fresh round of legislation will be followed by renewed frustration.

Gun control laws don't work. What is worse, they act perversely. While legitimate users of firearms encounter intense regulation, scrutiny, and bureaucratic control, illicit markets easily adapt to whatever difficulties a free society throws in their way. Also, efforts to curtail the supply of firearms inflict collateral damage on freedom and privacy interests that have long been considered central to American public life. Thanks to the seemingly never-ending war on drugs and long experience attempting to suppress prostitution and pornography, we know a great deal about how illicit markets function and how costly to the public attempts to control them can be. It is essential that we make use of this experience in coming to grips with gun control.

The thousands of gun control laws in the United States are of two general types. The older kind sought to regulate how, where, and by whom firearms could be carried. More recent laws have sought to make it more costly to buy, sell, or use firearms (or certain classes of firearms, such as assault rifles, Saturday-night specials, and so on) by imposing fees, special taxes, or surtaxes on them. The Brady bill is of both types: it has a background check provision, and its five-day waiting period amounts to a "time tax" on acquiring handguns. All such laws can be called scarcity-inducing, because they seek to raise the cost of buying firearms, as figured in terms of money, time, nuisance, or stigmatization.

Despite the mounting number of scarcity-inducing laws, no one is very satisfied with them. Hobbyists want to get rid of them, and gun control proponents don't think they go nearly far enough. Everyone seems to agree that gun control laws have some effect on the distribution of firearms. But it has not been the dramatic and measurable effect their proponents desired.

Opponents of gun control have traditionally wrapped their arguments in the Second Amendment to the Constitution. Indeed, most modern scholarship affirms that so far as the drafters of the Bill of Rights were concerned, the right to bear arms was to be enjoyed by everyone, not just a militia, and that one of the principal justifications for an armed populace was to secure the tranquility and good order of the community. But most people are not dedicated antiquarians, and would not be impressed by the argument "I admit that my behavior is very dangerous to public safety, but the Second Amendment says I have a right to do it anyway." That would be a case for repealing the Second Amendment, not respecting it.

FIGHTING THE DEMAND CURVE

Everyone knows that possessing a handgun makes it easier to intimidate, wound, or kill someone. But the implication of this point for social policy has not been so well understood. It is easy to count the bodies of those who have been killed or wounded with guns, but not easy to count the people who have avoided harm because they had access to weapons. Think about uniformed police officers, who carry handguns in plain view not in order to kill people but simply to daunt potential attackers. And it works. Criminals generally do not single out police officers for opportunistic attack. Though officers can expect to draw their guns from time to time, few even in big-city departments will actually fire a shot (except in target practice) in the course of a year. This observation points to an important truth: people who are armed make comparatively unattractive victims. A criminal might not know if any one civilian is armed, but if it becomes known that a larger number of civilians do carry weapons, criminals will become warier.

Which weapons laws are the right kinds can be decided only after considering two related questions. First, what is the connection between civilian possession of firearms and social violence? Second, how can we expect gun control laws to alter people's behavior? Most recent scholarship raises serious questions about the "weapons increase violence" hypothesis. The second question is emphasized here, because it is routinely overlooked and often mocked when noticed; yet it is crucial. Rational gun control requires understanding not only the relationship between weapons and violence but also the relationship between laws and people's behavior. Some things are very hard to accomplish with laws. The purpose of a law and its likely effects are not always the same thing. Many statutes are notorious for the way in which their unintended effects have swamped their intended ones.

In order to predict who will comply with gun control laws, we should remember that guns are economic goods that are traded in markets. Consumers' interest in them varies. For religious, moral, aesthetic, or practical reasons, some people would refuse to buy firearms at any price. Other people willingly pay very high prices for them.

Handguns, so often the subject of gun control laws, are desirable for one purpose—to allow a person tactically to dominate a hostile transaction with another person. The value of a weapon to a given person is a function of two factors: how much he or she wants to dominate a confrontation if one occurs, and how likely it is that he or she will actually be in a situation calling for a gun.

Dominating a transaction simply means getting what one wants without being hurt. Where people differ is in how likely it is that they will be involved in a situation in which a gun will be valuable. Someone who intends to engage in a transaction involving a gun—a criminal, for example—is obviously in the best possible position to predict that likelihood. Criminals should therefore be willing to pay more for a weapon than most other people would. Professors, politicians, and newspaper editors are, as a group, at very low risk of being involved in such transactions, and they thus systematically underrate the value of defensive handguns. (Correlative, perhaps, is their uncritical readiness to accept studies that debunk the utility of firearms for self-defense.) The class of people we wish to deprive of guns, then, is the very class with the most inelastic demand for them—criminals—whereas the people most likely to comply with gun control laws don't value guns in the first place.

DO GUNS DRIVE UP CRIME RATES?

Which premise is true—that guns increase crime or that the fear of crime causes people to obtain guns? Most of the country's major newspapers apparently take this problem to have been solved by an article published by Arthur Kellermann and several associates in the October 7, 1993, *New England Journal of Medicine*. Kellermann is an emergency room physician who has published a number of influential papers that he believes discredit the thesis that private ownership of firearms is a useful means of self-protection. (An indication of his wide influence is that within two months the study received almost one hundred mentions in publications and broadcast transcripts indexed in the Nexis database.) For this study Kellermann and his associates identified fifteen behavioral and fifteen environmental variables that applied to a 388-member set of homicide victims, found a "matching" control group of 388 nonhomicide victims, and then ascertained how the two groups differed in gun ownership. In interviews Kellermann made clear his belief that owning a handgun markedly increases a person's risk of being murdered.

But the study does not prove that point at all. Indeed, as Kellermann explicitly conceded in the text of the article, the causal arrow may very well point in the other direction: the threat of being killed may make people more likely to arm themselves. Many people at risk of being killed, especially people involved in the drug trade or other illegal ventures, might well rationally buy a gun as a precaution, and be willing to pay a price driven up by gun control laws. Crime, after all, is a dangerous business. Peter Reuter and Mark Kleiman, drug policy researchers, calculated in 1987 that the average crack dealer's risk of being killed was far greater than his risk of being sent to prison. (Their data cannot, however, support the implication that ownership of a firearm causes or exacerbates the risk of being killed.)

Defending the validity of his work, Kellermann has emphasized that the link between lung cancer and smoking was initially established by studies methodologically no different from his. Gary Kleck, a criminology professor at Florida State University, has pointed out the flaw in this comparison. No one ever thought that lung cancer causes smoking, so when the association between the two was established the direction of the causal arrow was not in doubt. Kleck wrote that it is as though Kellermann, trying to discover how diabetics differ from other people, found that they are much more likely to possess insulin than nondiabetics, and concluded that insulin is a risk factor for diabetes.

The *New York Times*, the *Los Angeles Times*, the *Washington Post*, the *Boston Globe*, and the *Chicago Tribune* all gave prominent coverage to Kellermann's study as soon as it appeared, but none saw fit to discuss the study's limitations. A few, in order to introduce a hint of balance, mentioned that the NRA, or some member of its staff, disagreed with the study. But readers had no way of knowing that Kellermann himself had registered a disclaimer in his text. "It is possible," he conceded, "that reverse causation accounted for some of the association we observed between gun ownership and homicide." Indeed, the point is stronger than that: "reverse causation" may account for most of the association between gun ownership and homicide. Kellermann's data simply do not allow one to draw any conclusion.

If firearms increased violence and crime, then rates of spousal homicide would have skyrocketed, because the stock of privately owned handguns has increased rapidly since the mid-1960s. But according to an authoritative study of spousal homicide in the *American Journal of Public Health*, by James Mercy and Linda Saltzman, rates of spousal homicide in the years 1976 to 1985 fell. If firearms increased violence and crime, the crime rate should have increased throughout the 1980s, while the national stock of privately owned handguns increased by more than a million units in every year of the decade. It did not. Nor should the rate of violence and crime in Switzerland. New Zealand, and Israel be as low as they are, since the number of firearms per civilian household is comparable to that in the United States. Conversely, gun-controlled Mexico and South Africa should be islands of peace instead of having murder rates more than twice as high as those here. The determinants of crime and law-abidingness are, of course, complex matters, which are not fully understood and certainly not explicable in terms of a country's laws. But gun control enthusiasts, who have made capital out of the low murder rate in England, which is largely disarmed, simply ignore the counterexamples that don't fit their theory.

If firearms increased violence and crime, Florida's murder rate should not have been falling since the introduction, seven years ago, of a law that makes it easier for ordinary citizens to get permits to carry concealed handguns. Yet the murder rate has remained the same or fallen every year since the law was enacted, and it is now lower than the national murder rate (which has been rising). As of last November 183,561 permits had been issued, and only seventeen of the permits had been revoked because the holder was involved in a firearms offense. It would be precipitate to claim that the new law has "caused" the murder rate to subside. Yet here is a situation that doesn't fit the hypothesis that weapons increase violence.

If firearms increased violence and crime, programs of induced scarcity would suppress violence and crime. But—another anomaly—they don't. Why not? A theorem, which we could call the futility theorem, explains why gun control laws must either be ineffectual or in the long term actually provoke more violence and crime. Any theorem depends on both observable fact and assumption. An assumption that can be made with confidence is that the higher number of victims a criminal assumes to be armed, the higher will be the risk—the price—of assaulting them. By definition, gun control laws should make weapons scarcer and thus more expensive. By our prior reasoning about demand among various types of consumers, after the laws are enacted criminals should be better armed, compared with noncriminals, than they were before. Of course, plenty of noncriminals will remain armed. But even if many noncriminals will pay as high a price as criminals will to obtain firearms, a larger number will not.

Criminals will thus still take the same gamble they already take in assaulting a victim who might or might not be armed. But they may appreciate that the laws have given them a freer field, and that crime still pays—pays even better, in fact, than before. What will happen to the rate of violence? Only a relatively few gun-mediated transactions—currently, five percent of armed robberies committed with firearms—result in someone's actually being shot (the statistics are not broken down into encounters between armed assailants and unarmed victims, and encounters in which both parties are armed). It seems reasonable to fear that if the number of such transactions were to increase because criminals thought they faced fewer deterrents, there would be a corresponding increase in shootings. Conversely, if gun-mediated transactions declined—if criminals initiated fewer of them because they feared encountering an armed victim or an armed good Samaritan—the number of shootings would go down. The magnitude of these effects is, admittedly, uncertain. Yet it is hard to doubt the general tendency of a change in the law that imposes legal burdens on buying guns. The futility theorem suggests that gun control laws, if effective at all, would unfavorably affect the rate of violent crime.

The futility theorem provides a lens through which to see much of the debate. It is undeniable that gun control laws work—to an extent. Consider, for example, California's background check law, which in the past two years has prevented about 12,000 people with a criminal record or a history of mental illness or drug abuse from buying handguns. In the same period Illinois's background check prevented the delivery of firearms to more than 2,000 people. Surely some of these people simply turned to an illegal market, but just as surely not all of them did. The laws of large numbers allow to say that among the foiled thousands, some potential killers were prevented from getting a gun. We do not know whether the number is large or small, but it is implausible to think it is zero. And, as gun control proponents are inclined to say, "If only one life is saved . . ."

The hypothesis that firearms increase violence does predict that if we can slow down the diffusion of guns, there will be less violence; one life, or more, will be saved. But the futility theorem asks that we look not simply at the gross number of bad actors prevented from getting guns but at the effect the law has on all the people who want to buy a gun. Suppose we succeed in piling tax burdens on the acquisition of firearms. We can safely assume that a number of people who might use guns to kill will be sufficiently discouraged not to buy them. But we cannot assume this about people who feel that they must have guns in order to survive financially and physically. A few lives might indeed be saved. But the overall rate of violent crime might not go down at all. And if guns are owned predominantly by people who have good reason to think they will use them, the rate might even go up.

Are there empirical studies that can serve to help us choose between the futility theorem and the hypothesis that guns increase violence? Unfortunately, no: the best studies of the effects of gun-control laws are quite inconclusive. Our statistical tools are too weak to allow us to identify an effect clearly enough to persuade an open-minded skeptic. But it is precisely when we are dealing with undetectable statistical effects that we have to be certain we are using the best models of human behavior.

SEALING THE BORDER

Handguns are not legally for sale in the city of Chicago, and have not been since April of 1982. Rifles, shotguns, and ammunition are available, but only to people who possess an Illinois Firearm Owner's Identification card. It takes up to a month to get this card, which involves a background check. Even if one has a FOID card there is a waiting period for the delivery of a gun. In few places in America is it as difficult to get a firearm legally as in the city of Chicago.

Yet there are hundreds of thousands of unregistered guns in the city, and new ones arriving all the time. It is not difficult to get handguns—even legally. Chicago residents with FOID cards merely go to gun shops in the suburbs. Trying to establish a city as an island of prohibition in a sea of legal firearms seems an impossible project.

Is a state large enough to be an effective island, then? Suppose Illinois adopted Chicago's handgun ban. Same problem again. Some people could just get guns elsewhere: Indiana actually borders the city, and Wisconsin is only forty miles away. Though federal law prohibits the sale of handguns in one state to residents of another, thousands of Chicagoans with summer homes in other states could buy handguns there. And, of course, a black market would serve the needs of other customers.

When would the island be large enough to sustain a weapons-free environment? In the United States people and cargoes move across state lines without supervision or hindrance. Local shortages of goods are always transient, no matter whether the shortage is induced by natural disasters, prohibitory laws, or something else.

Even if many states outlaw sales of handguns, then, they would continue to be available at a somewhat higher price, reflecting the increased legal risk of selling them. Mindful of the way markets work to undermine their efforts, gun control proponents press for federal regulation of firearms, because they believe that only Congress wields the authority to frustrate the interstate movement of firearms.

Why, though, would one think that federal policing of illegal firearms would be better than local policing? The logic of that argument is far from clear. Cities, after all, are comparatively small places. Washington, D.C., for example, has an area of less than 45,000 acres. Yet local officers have had little luck repressing the illegal firearms trade there. Why should federal officers do any better watching the United States' 12,000 miles of coastline and millions of square miles of interior? Criminals should be able to frustrate federal police forces just as well as they can local ones. Ten years of increasingly stringent federal efforts to abate cocaine trafficking, for example, have not succeeded in raising the street price of the drug.

Consider the most drastic proposal currently in play, that of Senator John Chafee, of Rhode Island, who would ban the manufacture, sale, and home possession of handguns within the United States. This proposal goes far beyond even the Chicago law, because existing weapons would have to be surrendered. Handguns would become contraband, and selling counterfeit, stolen, and contraband goods is big business in the United States. The objective of law enforcement is to raise the costs of engaging in crime and so force criminals to take expensive precautions against becoming entangled with the legal system. Crimes of a given type will, in theory, decline as soon as the direct and indirect costs of engaging in them rise to the point at which criminals seek more profitable opportunities in other (not necessarily legal) lines of work.

In firearms regulation, translating theory into practice will continue to be difficult, at least if the objective is to lessen the practical availability of firearms to people who might abuse them. On the demand side, for defending oneself against predation there is no substitute for a firearm. Criminals, at least, can switch to varieties of law breaking in which a gun confers little to no advantage (burglary, smash-and-grab), but people who are afraid of confrontations with criminals, whether rationally or (as an accountant might reckon it) irrationally, will be very highly motivated to acquire firearms. Long after the marijuana and cocaine wars of this century have been forgotten, people's demand for personal security and for the tools they believe provide it will remain strong.

On the supply side, firearms transactions can be consummated behind closed doors. Firearms buyers, unlike those who use drugs, pornography, or prostitution, need not recurrently expose themselves to legal jeopardy. One trip to the marketplace is enough to arm oneself for life. This could justify a consumer's taking even greater precautions to avoid apprehension, which would translate into even steeper enforcement costs for police.

Don Kates, Jr., a San Francisco lawyer and a much-published student of this problem, has pointed out that during the wars in Southeast and Southwest Asia local artisans were able to produce, from scratch, serviceable pot-metal counterfeits of AK-47 infantry rifles and similar weapons in makeshift backyard foundries. Although inferior weapons cannot discharge thousands of rounds without misfiring, they are more than deadly enough for light to medium service, especially by criminals and people defending themselves and their property, who ordinarily use firearms by threatening with them, not by firing them. And the skills necessary to make them are certainly as widespread in America as in the villages of Pakistan or Vietnam. Effective policing of such a cottage industry is unthinkable. Indeed, as Charles Chandler has pointed out, crude but effective firearms have been manufactured in prisons—highly supervised environments, compared with the outside world.

Seeing the local firearms restrictions are easily defeated, gun control proponents have latched onto national controls as a way of finally making gun control something more than a gesture. But the same forces that have defeated local regulation will defeat further national regulation. Imposing higher costs on weapons ownership will, of course, slow down the weapons trade to some extent. But planning to slow it down in such a way as to drive down crime and violence, or to prevent motivated purchasers from finding ample supplies of guns and ammunition, is an escape from reality. And like many other such, it entails a morning after.

ADMINISTERING PROHIBITION

Assume for the sake of argument that to a reasonable degree of criminological certainty, guns are every bit the public health hazard they are said to be. It follows, and many journalists and a few public officials have already said, that we ought to treat guns the same we do smallpox viruses or other critical vectors of morbidity and mortality—namely, isolate them from potential hosts and destroy them as speedily as possible. Clearly, firearms have at least one characteristic that distinguishes them from smallpox viruses: nobody wants to keep smallpox viruses in the nightstand drawer. Amazingly enough, gun control literature seems never to have explored the problem of getting weapons away from people who very much want to keep them in the nightstand drawer.

Our existing gun control laws are not uniformly permissive, and, indeed, in certain places are tough even by international standards. Advocacy groups seldom stress the considerable differences among American jurisdictions, and media reports regularly assert that firearms are readily available to anybody anywhere in the country. This is not the case. For example, handgun restrictions in Chicago and the District of Columbia are much less flexible than the ones in the United Kingdom. Several hundred thousand British subjects may legally buy and possess sidearms, and anyone who joins a target-shooting club is eligible to do so. But in Chicago and the District of Columbia, excepting peace officers and the like, only grandfathered registrants may legally possess handguns. Of course, tens or hundreds of thousands of people in both those cities—nobody can be sure how many—do in fact possess them illegally.

Although there is, undoubtedly, illegal handgun ownership in the United Kingdom, especially in Northern Ireland (where considerations of personal security and public safety are decidedly unlike those elsewhere in the British Isles), it is probable that Americans and Britons differ in their disposition to obey gun control laws: there is reputed to be a marked national disparity in compliance behavior. This difference, if it exists, may have something to do with the comparatively marginal value of firearms to British consumers. Even before it had strict firearms regulation, Britain had very low rates of crimes involving guns; British criminals, unlike their American counterparts, prefer burglary (a crime of stealth) to robbery (a crime of intimidation).

Unless people are prepared to surrender their guns voluntarily, how can the U.S. government confiscate an appreciable fraction of our country's nearly 200 million privately owned firearms? We know that it is possible to set up weapons-free zones in certain locations—commercial airports and many courthouses and, lately, some troubled big-city high schools and housing projects. The sacrifices of privacy and convenience, and the costs of paying guards, have been thought worth the (perceived) gain in security. No doubt it would be possible, though it would probably not be easy, to make weapons-free zones of shopping centers, department stores, movie theaters, ballparks. But it is not obvious how one would cordon off the whole of an open society.

Voluntary programs have been ineffectual. From time to time community action groups or police departments have sponsored "turn in your gun" days, which are nearly always disappointing. Sometimes the government offers to buy guns at some price. This approach has been endorsed by Senator Chafee and the *Los Angeles Times*. Jonathan Alter, of *Newsweek*, has suggested a variation on this theme: youngsters could exchange their guns for a handshake with Michael Jordan or some other sports hero. If the price offered exceeds that at which a gun can be bought on the street, one can expect to see plans of this kind yield some sort of harvest—as indeed they have. But it is implausible that these schemes will actually result in a less-dangerous population. Government programs to buy up surplus cheese cause more cheese to be produced without affecting the availability of cheese to people who want to buy it. So it is with guns.

One could extend the concept of intermittent roadblocks of the sort approved by the Supreme Court for discouraging drunk driving. Metal detectors could be positioned on every street corner, or ambulatory metal detector squads could check people randomly, or hidden magnetometers could be installed around towns, to detect concealed weapons. As for firearms kept in homes (about half of American households), warrantless searches might be rationalized on the well-established theory that probable cause is not required when authorities are trying to correct dangers to public safety rather than searching for evidence of a crime.

In a recent "town hall" meeting in California, President Bill Clinton used the word "sweeps," which he did not define, to describe how he would confiscate firearms if it were up to him. During the past few years the Chicago Housing Authority chairman, Vincent Lane, has ordered "sweeps" of several gang-ridden public housing projects, meaning warrantless searches of people's homes by uniformed police officers looking for contraband. Lane's ostensible premise was that possession of firearms by tenants constituted a lease violation that, as a conscientious landlord, he was obliged to do something about. The same logic could justify any administrative search. City Health inspectors in Chicago were recently authorized to conduct warrantless searches for lead hazards in residential paint. Why not lead hazards in residential closets and nightstands? Someone has probably already thought of it.

IGNORING THE ULTIMATE SOURCES OF CRIME AND VIOLENCE

The American experience with prohibition has been that black marketeers—often professional criminals—move in to profit when legal markets are closed down or disturbed. In order to combat them, new laws and law-enforcement techniques are developed, which are circumvented almost as soon as they are put in place. New and yet more stringent laws are enacted, and greater sacrifices of civil liberties and privacy demanded and submitted to. But in this case the problem, crime and violence, will not go away, because guns and ammunition (which, of course, won't go away either) do not cause it. One cannot expect people to quit seeking new weapons as long as the tactical advantages of weapons are seen to outweigh the costs imposed by the prohibition. Nor can one expect large numbers of people to surrender firearms they already own. The only way to make people give up their guns is to create a world in which guns are perceived as having little value. This world will come into being when criminals choose not to use guns because the penalties for being caught with them are too great, and when ordinary citizens don't think they need firearms because they aren't afraid of criminals anymore.

Neither of these eventualities seems very likely without substantial departures in law enforcement policy. Politicians' nostrums—increasing the punishment for crime, slapping a few more death penalty provisions into the code—are taken seriously by few students of the crime problem. The existing penalties for predatory crimes are quite severe enough. The problem is that they are rarely meted out in the real world. The penalties formally published by the code are in practice steeply discounted, and criminals recognize that the judicial and penal systems cannot function without bargaining in the vast majority of cases.

This problem is not obviously one that legislation could solve. Constitutional ideas about due process of law make the imposition of punishments extraordinarily expensive and difficult. Like the tax laws, the criminal laws are basically voluntary affairs. Our system isn't geared to a world of wholesale disobedience. Recalibrating the system simply by increasing its overall harshness would probably offend and then shock the public long before any of its benefits were felt.

To illustrate, consider the prospect of getting serious about carrying out the death penalty. In recent years executions have been running at one or two dozen a year. As the late Supreme Court Justice Potter Stewart observed, those selected to die constitute a "capriciously selected random handful" taken from a much larger number of men and women who, just as deserving of death, receive prison sentences. It is not easy to be exact about that much larger number. But as an educated guess, taking into account only the most serious murders—the ones that were either premeditated or committed in the course of a dangerous felony—there are perhaps 5,000 prisoners a year who could plausibly be executed in the United States: say, 100,000 executions in the next twenty years. It is hard to think that the death penalty, if imposed on this scale, would not noticeably change the behavior of potential criminals. But what else in national life or citizens' character would have to change in order to make that many executions acceptable? Since 1930 executions in the United States have never exceeded 200 a year. At any such modest rate of imposition, rational criminals should consider the prospect of receiving the death penalty effectively nil. On the best current evidence, indeed, they do. Documentation of the deterrent effect of the death penalty, as compared with that of long prison sentences, has been notoriously hard to produce.

The problem is not simply the criminals pay little attention to the punishments in the books. Nor is it even that they also know that for the majority of crimes, their chances of being arrested are small. The most important reason for criminals' behavior is this: the income that offenders can earn in the world of crime, as compared with the world of work, all too often makes crime appear to be the better choice.

Thus the crime bill that Bill Clinton introduced last year, which provides for more prisons and police officers, should be of only very limited help. More prisons means that fewer violent offenders will have to be released early in order to make space for new arrivals; perhaps fewer plea bargains will have to be struck—all to the good. Yet a moment's reflection should make clear that one more criminal locked up does not necessarily mean one less criminal on the street. The situation is very like one that conservationists and hunters have always understood. Populations of game animals readily recover from hunting seasons but not from loss of habitat. Mean streets, when there are few legitimate entry-level opportunities for young men, are a criminal habitat, so to speak, in the social ecology of modern American cities. Cull however much one will, the habitat will be reoccupied promptly after its previous occupant is sent away. So social science has found.

Similarly, whereas increasing the number of police officers cannot hurt, and may well increase people's subjective feelings of security, there is little evidence to suggest that doing so will diminish the rate of crime. Police forces are basically reactive institutions. At any realistically sustainable level of staffing they must remain so. Suppose 100,000 officers were added to police rosters nationwide, as proposed in the current crime bill. This would amount to an overall personnel increase of about 18 percent, which would be parceled out according to the iron laws of democratic politics—distributed through states and congressional districts—rather than being sent to the areas that most need relief. Such an increase, though unprecedented in magnitude, is far short of what would be needed to pacify some of our country's worst urban precincts.

There is a challenge here that is quite beyond being met with tough talk. Most public officials can see the mismatch between their tax base and the social entropies they are being asked to repair. There simply isn't enough money; existing public resources, as they are now employed, cannot possibly solve the crime problem. But mayors and senators and police chiefs must not say so out loud: too-disquieting implications would follow. For if the authorities are incapable of restoring public safety and personal security under the existing ground rules, then obviously the ground rules must change, to give private initiative greater scope. Self-help is the last refuge of nonscoundrels.

Communities must, in short, organize more effectively to protect themselves against predators. No doubt this means encouraging properly qualified private citizens to possess and carry firearms legally. It is not morally tenable—nor, for that matter, is it even practical—to insist that police officers, few of whom are at a risk remotely as great as are the residents of many city neighborhoods, retain a monopoly on legal firearms. It is needless to fear giving honest men and women the training and equipment to make it possible for them to take back their own streets.

Over the long run, however, there is no substitute for addressing the root causes of crime—bad education and lack of job opportunities and the disintegration of families. Root causes are much out of fashion nowadays as explanations of criminal behavior, but fashionable or not, they are fundamental. The root cause of crime is that for certain people, predation is a rational occupational choice. Conventional crime-control measures, which by stiffening punishments or raising the probability of arrest aim to make crime pay less, cannot consistently affect the behavior of people who believe that their alternatives to crime will pay virtually nothing. Young men who did not learn basic literacy and numeracy skills before dropping out of their wretched public schools may not have been worth hiring at the minimum wage set by George Bush, let alone at the higher, indexed minimum wage that has recently been under discussion by the Clinton administration. Most independent studies of the effects of raising minimum wages show a similar pattern of excluding the most vulnerable. This displacement, in turn, makes young men free, in the nihilistic, nothing-to-lose sense, to dedicate their lives to crime. Their legitimate opportunities, as always precarious in a society where race and class still matter, often diminish to the point of being for all intents and purposes absent.

Unfortunately, many progressive policies work out in the same way as increases in the minimum wage—as taxes on employment. One example is the Administration's pending proposal to make employer-paid health insurance mandatory and universal. Whatever the undoubted benefits of the plan, a payroll tax is needed to make it work. Another example: in recent years the use of the "wrongful discharge" tort and other legal innovations has swept through the courts of more than half the states, bringing to an end the era of "employment at will," when employees (other than civil servants) without formal contracts—more than three quarters of the workforce—could be fired for good reason, bad reason, or no reason at all. Most commentators celebrated the loss of the at-will rule. How could one object to a new legal tenet that prohibited only arbitrary and oppressive behavior by employers?

But the costs of the rule are not negligible, only hidden. At-will employment meant that companies could get out of the relationship as easily as employees could. In a world where dismissals are expensive rather than cheap, and involve lawyers and the threat of lawsuits, rational employers must become more fastidious about whom they hire. By raising the costs of ending the relationship, one automatically raises the threshold of entry. The burdens of the rule fall unequally. Worst hit are entry-level applicants who have little or no employment history to show that they would be worth their pay.

Many other tax or regulatory schemes, in the words of professor Walter Williams of George Mason University, amount to sawing off the bottom rungs of the ladder of economic opportunity. By suppressing job creation and further diminishing legal employment opportunities for young men on the margin of the work force, such schemes amount to an indirect but unequivocal subsidy to crime.

The solution to the problem of crime lies in improving the chances of young men. Easier said than done, to be sure. No one has yet proposed a convincing program for checking all the dislocating forces that government assistance can set in motion. One relatively straightforward change would be reform of the educational system. Nothing guarantees prudent behavior like a sense of the future, and with average skills in reading, writing, and math, young people can realistically look forward to constructive employment and the straight life that steady work makes possible.

But firearms are nowhere near the root of the problem of violence. As long as people come in unlike sizes, shapes, ages, and temperaments, as long as they diverge in their taste for risk and their willingness and capacity to prey on other people or to defend themselves from predation, and above all as long as some people have little or nothing to lose by spending their lives in crime, disposition to violence will persist.

This is what makes the case for the right to bear arms, not the Second Amendment. It is foolish to let anything ride on hopes for effective gun control. As long as crime pays as well as it does, we will have plenty of it, and honest folk must choose between being victims and defending themselves.

DISCUSSION QUESTIONS

1. Do you think restricting access to firearms would reduce gun-related injuries and crimes? Are there other considerations relevant for public policy decisions? What are they?
2. How do you think that the framers of the Constitution would respond to the rise of gun violence? Why?
3. Given the level of popular support for gun control measures, why do you think such legislation has had such a difficult time gaining approval?
4. Should gun control measures be enacted at the federal level, or should such legislation be reserved for states and localities? Why?
5. Should gun control legislation be focused on gun owners or on those who manufacture and sell such weapons? Why?
6. Would a tax on ammunition be effective in reducing violence (or have other beneficial characteristics)? What do you see as advantages and disadvantages of such a proposal?
7. What impact do gun buy-back programs have? Who are most likely to sell their guns? How effective would you expect such programs to be in reducing crime?
8. What impact do you think fewer guns would have on deaths from accidents and suicides? Or would accidental deaths and suicides merely occur by other means?
9. Is it appropriate to view gun violence as a public health issue, or are there important distinctions between public health and crime? Why?

WEB REFERENCES

Gun Owners of America, http://www.gunowners.org/.

Handgun Control Inc., http://www.bradycampaign.org/.

Million Mom March., http://www.millionmommarch.org/.

National Rifle Association (NRA), http://www.nra.org/.

Office of Justice Programs, Firearms and Crime, http://www.ojp.usdoj.
   gov/firearms/whats_new.htm.

Open Secrets, Gun Control vs. Gun Rights, http://www.opensecrets.org/
   news/guns/index.htm.

Second Amendment Sisters, http://www.sas-aim.org/.

FURTHER READING

Bogus, Carl T. "The Strong Case for Gun Control." *American Prospect* (Summer 1992).

Cozic, Charles P., ed. *Gun Control.* San Diego, Calif.: Greenhaven Press, 1992.

Davidson, Osha Gray. *Under Fire: The NRA and the Battle for Gun Control.* New York:
   Henry Holt, 1993.

Edel, Wilbur. *Gun Control: Threat to Liberty or Defense against Anarchy?* Westport,
   Conn.: Praeger, 1995.

Halbrook, Stephen P. "What the Framers Intended: A Linguistic Analysis of the Right to
   'Bear Arms.'" *Law and Contemporary Problems* (Winter 1986).

Homsher, Deborah. *Women and Guns: Politics and the Culture of Firearms in America.*
   M. E. Sharpe, 2002.

Jost, Kenneth. "Gun Control Standoff." *CQ Researcher,* vol. 7 (December 19, 1997).

Kaminer, Wendy. "Second Thoughts on the Second Amendment." *Atlantic Monthly*
   (March 1996).

Kates, Don B., Jr. "Gun Control: Can It Work?" *National Review* (May 15, 1981).

Kates, Don B., Jr., ed. *Firearms and Violence: Issues of Public Policy.* San Francisco,
   Calif.: Pacific Institute for Public Policy Research, 1984.

Kleck, Gary. *Point Blank: Guns and Violence in America.* New York: Aldine de
   Gruyter, 1991.

Kleck, Gary. *Targeting Guns: Firearms and Their Control.* New York: Aldine de
   Gruyter, 1997.

Kopel, David B., ed. *Guns: Who Should Have Them?* Amherst, N.Y.: Prometheus
   Books, 1995.

Larson, Erik. *Lethal Passage: How the Travels of a Single Handgun Expose the Roots of
   America's Gun Crisis.* New York: Crown Publishers, 1994.

Larson, Erik. "The Story of a Gun." *Atlantic Monthly* (January 1993).

Leddy, Edward F. *Magnum Force Lobby: The National Rifle Association Fights Gun
   Control.* Lanham, Md.: University Press of America, 1987.

Long, Robert Emmet, ed. *Gun Control.* New York: H. W. Wilson, 1989.

Lott, John. *More Guns, Less Crime: Understanding Crime and Gun-Control Laws.*
   Chicago: University of Chicago Press, 2000.

McClurg, Andrew J., David Kopel, and Brannon P. Denning, eds. *Gun Control and Gun
   Rights: A Reader and Guide.* New York: New York University Press, 2002.

Nisbet, Lee, ed. *The Gun Control Debate: You Decide.* Buffalo, N.Y.: Prometheus
   Books, 1990.

Poe, Richard and David Horowitz. *The Seven Myths of Gun Control: Reclaiming the Truth
   about Guns, Crime, and the Second Amendment.* Roseville, Calif.: Forum, 2001.

Spitzer, Robert J. *The Politics of Gun Control*. Chatham, N.J.: Chatham House, 1995.

Squires, Peter. *Gun Culture or Gun Control: Firearms, Violence and Society*. New York: Routledge, 2001.

Stell, Lance K. "Close Encounters of the Lethal Kind: The Use of Deadly Force in Self-Defense." *Law and Contemporary Problems* (Winter 1986).

Sugarmann, Josh and Kristen Rand. *Cease Fire: A Comprehensive Strategy to Reduce Firearms Violence*. Washington, D.C.: Violence Policy Center, 1994.

Utter, Glenn H. *Encyclopedia of Gun Control and Gun Rights*. Phoenix, Ariz.: Oryx Press, 2000.

Wright, James D. "Second Thoughts about Gun Control." *Public Interest* (Spring 1988).

Wright, James D., Peter H. Rossi, and Kathleen Daly. *Under the Gun: Weapons, Crime, and Violence in America*. New York: Aldine, 1983.

Zimring, Franklin E. "Firearms, Violence, and Public Policy." *Scientific American* (November 1991).

Zimring, Franklin E. and Gordon Hawkins. *The Citizen's Guide to Gun Control*. New York: Macmillan, 1987.

CHAPTER 14

ENERGY POLICY

"Should Increasing the Supply of Fossil Fuels Be the Focus of National Energy Policy?"

YES: Secretary of Energy Spencer Abraham, speech delivered to the National Petroleum Council

NO: Senator John F. Kerry "Energy Security Is American Security," speech delivered to the Center for National Policy

One of the necessities of a modern industrial economy is a supply of usable energy. The availability of cheap and plentiful energy through the development of steam power was one of the driving forces of the industrial revolution, because energy-driven machines could more efficiently provide goods and services than humans working alone. Growth of the modern industrial economy has been tied closely to increases in overall energy production and consumption. Indeed, it is difficult to imagine a modern society, let alone a modern economy, without prodigious sources of energy, since many of the conveniences of modern life depend so heavily upon an inexpensive and ever-present supply of such energy sources. The United States is the largest absolute consumer of commercial energy and the second largest per capita consumer after Kuwait (Canada and Singapore fall close behind the United States). This is roughly twice as high as usage in other industrialized countries such as Britain, France, Germany, and Japan.[1] Part of the reason that consumption is so high in the United States is that energy prices are so low. Despite recent fluctuations in petroleum prices, the price of gasoline at U.S. pumps has remained significantly below that in other nations. For example, in 1999, 1 gallon of premium unleaded fuel in the United States cost $1.36; in Spain the price was $2.82, in France and Germany the price was around $3.80, while the UK price was $4.30.[2] Another reason is that per capita GNP is higher in the United States than in most other nations, much of it dependent on energy, and that gasoline tax rates are substantially higher in other nations. Despite these factors, many believe that Americans are simply wasteful energy consumers. The profligacy of U.S. energy consumption is typified (if exaggerated) by Betsy Bloomingdale's comment in 1982 that she saved energy "by asking my servants not to turn on the self-cleaning oven after seven in the morning."

Criticism of the high U.S. consumption of energy stems from two principal concerns. The first involves national security: The United States relies too heavily on foreign sources of fossil fuels. The second is environmental: The majority of U.S. fuel consumption is of nonrenewable fossil fuels, and someday, it is argued, this source will run out. Despite sizable reserves of fossil fuels such as crude oil, the United States is dependent on many other countries for its high energy consumption. In 2000 the United States purchased around 55 percent of its petroleum from other countries, a figure that has increased some 30 percent since the 1970s.[3] Most disturbing from a security perspective is that many of these countries are politically unstable and autocratically led and are currently involved in turbulent upheavals in the Middle East. Although two of the largest exporters of crude oil to the United States are Mexico and Canada, Saudi Arabia is the single largest exporting country, with Iraq being the fourth largest.[4] Half of the U.S. oil imports come from nations belonging to OPEC (the Organization of Petroleum Exporting Countries). OPEC is a cartel, or a group of producers that control a large enough share of a product market to be able to influence the price, and has, in the past, exercised this substantial power over the United States. In 1973 the world faced for the first time a major disruption in its supply of energy when OPEC began its first embargo of the United States and other countries that were seen as supporters of Israel during the Yom Kippur War.[5] OPEC restricted the supply of oil products available to the global market, causing shortages and drastically increasing the price for fuel. In the span of 1 year, the real price of crude oil jumped 60 percent, from $15.78 per barrel in 1973 to $25.09 in 1974 (both in constant 2002 dollars).[6] OPEC's price increases not only affected motorists through higher pump prices, but also led to a rise in heating costs, with heating oil increasing from $0.92 per gallon in 1973 to $1.32 per gallon in 1974, a rise of 43 percent in just 1 year (in constant 2002 dollars).[7]

Events such as the California energy crisis, where rolling blackouts disrupted life for many and threatened chaos if not managed correctly, coupled with the reliance on foreign sources of fossil fuels, feed the argument that the United States needs to increase its domestic fuel production and become more self-sufficient. President Bush's energy plan, as discussed by Energy Secretary Abraham in the article following this introduction, is focused on such an increase of supply. The most publicized element of this plan is the possibility of increasing oil drilling in the Arctic National Wildlife Refuge (ANWR), a possibility that has engendered staunch opposition from environmentalists. ANWR is a 19-million-acre wilderness in Alaska, completely within the Arctic Circle. At issue is a 1.5-million-acre site called the Coastal Plain area that some believe to contain the highest petroleum potential yet to be explored on North American land. With exploration currently restricted, it is impossible to tell how rich this area will be in oil deposits, but 25 percent of the domestic U.S. oil production comes from oil fields only 65 miles from the Coastal Plain.[8] Proponents of ANWR exploration believe that drilling in this wilderness might yield some 30 years' worth of stable oil reserves for the United States, significantly reducing dependence on Middle Eastern sources in the short term.[9]

Jerry Taylor of the Cato Institute argues that energy security arguments for increasing U.S. fuel production through such initiatives as ANWR drilling are flawed. He argues that oil is a global, not regional, commodity, with prices being set at a world level. At peak production, ANWR might increase global production by 1.25 percent—enough to cause a small global price decrease, but not enough to break the power of OPEC's price-setting. Even if the United States were to become independent, it is unlikely that it would be shielded from OPEC-led price increases. Taylor points to the case of Great Britain, which was energy independent in 1979 but was still hit hard by the global price increases in that year. Furthermore, he argues, there is no real security threat to the nation—America could simultaneously fight two wars the size of the Gulf War on just one-eighth of current domestic production.[10]

The second concern over the high levels of U.S. fuel consumption lies at the opposite end of the ideological spectrum: We are relying far too much on fossil fuels that will eventually disappear. In 2000, 85.1 percent of national energy consumption came from fossil fuels: coal, natural gas, and crude oil; 8 percent of energy came from nuclear power; and the remaining 6.9 percent came from renewable sources such as hydroelectric, solar, geothermal, wind, and biomass. Since the birth of the industrial age, fossil fuels have provided a cheap and abundant source of energy, making possible substantial developments in transportation, industrial processes, and standards of living. Fossil fuels were formed millions of years ago as a result of the decomposition of plants (to form coal) and organisms (to form natural gas and oil) and are thus energy sources that cannot be regenerated at will. Unfortunately, as society becomes more complex and more reliant on energy, the use of these fossil fuels increases in the absence of any significant alternatives. Between 1990 and 2000 alone, the use of fossil fuels in the United States increased by 16.4 percent.[11]

It is unclear how much longer the world can survive on fossil fuels. The Department of Energy predicts that there are 60 years' worth of natural gas supplies left, 250 years' worth of coal, and an indeterminate amount of oil.[12] Others believe that if the use of renewable energy sources remains fixed at current levels, fossil fuels will last for 104 years. If we consumed only natural gas, this would last for 13.5 years; oil alone would last 16 years; and coal would last 60 years.[13] Between 1977 and 1999, U.S. crude oil reserves declined 36 percent, falling from around 36 billion to 23 billion barrels. Over the same period of time, natural gas reserves fell 16 percent from 210 to 176 trillion cubic feet.[14] Yet since 1949, U.S. production of fossil fuel energy has almost doubled from 29 quadrillion British thermal units (quads) to

57 quads. Production of renewable energy has also doubled, but only from 3 quads in 1949 to 6.5 quads in 2000. The figures are even more pronounced concerning energy consumption: Over half a century, the amount of fossil fuels consumed increased over 275 percent to 84 quads.[15] Despite these large increases in overall energy consumption, per capita energy usage has remained largely static since the mid-1970s, at around 350 million British thermal units (BTUs) in 2000.

As former Secretary of Energy James Schlesinger put it, "The only thing we learn from history is we learn nothing from history."[16] The United States continues to rely on worldwide oil markets, with little government intervention, to dictate oil prices. A senior vice president of Texaco noted that "our energy policy is to take the cheapest oil in the world, regardless of source, and take our chances that it will continue to be cheap and available."[17] On one hand, supporters of this strategy argue that this is how many goods and services are allocated in the world economy, and energy is just another one of them. Further, they denounce critics' assertions that we are running out of fossil fuels. While true on its face, they argue that we will never completely run out of petroleum, because if it still has value in use, shortages will simply drive up the price, causing a (perhaps frantic) search for substitute forms of energy, including more oil exploration. And, they might tell skeptics, if you are so sure that oil will soon become scarce, in which case oil prices should rise dramatically, go out and buy oil futures on the commodities market. The fact that most people do not is evidence, they argue, of the fact that oil is sufficiently plentiful. Finally, they contend that predicting the future of energy markets is folly, pointing to one 1955 comment that "nuclear powered vacuum cleaners will probably be a reality within 10 years" and Henry Luce's suggestion in 1956 that "by 1980, all 'power' (electric, atomic, solar) is likely to be virtually costless."

Oil and other petroleum products have long been the most important fuel for the U.S. economy. The versatility of oil usage, from heating to electrical generation to automotive fuel, makes oil an ideal source of energy for a heavily industrialized economy. By 1973, a critical year for energy, petroleum usage made up 51 percent of all energy consumed (measured in BTUs), up from a level of 37 percent in 1949.[18] Since 1970, however, in addition to increasing energy consumption in the United States, there have been significant changes in the types of energy used. Petroleum products fell in use to 39 percent by 2000; natural gas also fell from 32 percent of total energy use in 1970 to 24 percent by 2000. Coal and nuclear power increased as a percentage of energy use over the same 20-year period: Coal rose from 18 percent of energy use in 1970 to 23 percent in 2000; nuclear power jumped from 0.4 percent in 1970 to 8 percent by 2000.[19] Nevertheless, petroleum remains the dominant source of energy in the U.S. economy, and it is the one source with which the United States is least endowed. The result has been a sharp increase in imported petroleum, from 1.4 billion barrels in 1970 to 4. 5 billion barrels in 2000.[20]

The most obvious solution to a finite pool of energy is to use less of it through technological changes, voluntary conservation efforts, energy taxes, or other more coercive means. President Bush's National Energy Policy, released in May 2001, devotes an entire chapter to energy conservation, noting, "Conservation and energy efficiency are important elements of a sound energy policy."[21] Homes have become more efficient as a result of technological improvement: Refrigerators and freezers, for example, have become around 70 percent more efficient within the last 30 years.[22] New technologies also offer possible energy savings in other areas. Hybrid automobiles that run on gasoline and electricity may significantly increase gasoline mileage, in addition to the 60 percent reduction in gasoline usage in automobiles since 1972.[23] Improved insulation in buildings, sensors to prevent 24-hour lighting in office buildings, and advances in heating and air-conditioning systems can all reduce the amount of fossil fuels required in daily life. The U.S. government, itself the largest energy consumer in the nation, has reduced its energy use in buildings by around 30 percent since 1990 and cut its energy use in vehicles and equipment by 35 percent.[24]

However, greater efficiencies in fossil fuel usage simply extend the life span of these fuels and, in many instances, do not replace fossil fuels with alternative sources of energy. Of course, the economic viability of and incentives to explore alternative energy sources are constrained by relatively low gasoline prices in the United States. The long-term solution to the finite supply of oil, gas, and coal is to dramatically increase the use of alternative and renewable energy sources. Nuclear power is one possible alternative to fossil fuels, and is the only non-fossil fuel to generate more than 10 percent of today's electricity.[25] However, nuclear energy, as currently produced, is reliant on an exhaustible source—uranium and other radioactive metals. Uranium is far more efficient than coal, with the fission of one atom of uranium producing 10 million times the energy as that of one atom of carbon. The principal isotope used in current reactors, uranium-235, may last several hundred years, and some believe that there is enough uranium in seawater and granite to provide energy for billions of years.[26] There is another possible, almost limitless source of nuclear energy still in the development phase—nuclear fusion—the energy produced from the fusion of hydrogen with other gases at very high temperatures (100 million degrees centigrade). However, nuclear fusion is still in the research stage, and there are currently no reactors in operation.

The other alternatives to fossil fuels are renewable energy sources. Currently hydroelectric energy and energy produced from burning wood and waste products (biomass) are the most prevalent sources of renewable energy consumed in the United States, accounting for 94 percent of all renewable energy in 2000, but only 6.5 percent of all energy consumed in that year.[27] Other sources include geothermal (0.3 percent of total consumption), solar (0.07 percent), and wind (0.05 percent). The use of renewable energy sources is increasing, especially in the form of biomass, yet renewable sources make up only 7 percent of all U.S. energy consumption and are centered around particular regions: California,

Washington, Oregon, New York, and Idaho accounted for 62 percent of renewable electricity generated in 1999.[28] Renewable energy sources may be cleaner and more environmentally friendly than fossil fuels, but there are downsides that may prohibit the degree to which they can replace oil, coal, and gas. First, the equipment is often costly, particularly for hydroelectric plants. Second, the amount of energy generated from renewable sources is often only a fraction of that possible from a fossil fuel power plant—biomass, wind power, and tidal energy must all be conducted on a very large scale if they are to produce usable amounts of energy for urban regions. If biomass were used to fuel a small power station serving 25,000 people, 25,000 acres of poplar trees would be required.[29] Put another way, it would take 4 tons of wood per person per year to create enough energy from biomass.[30] Third, renewable energy forms are geographically specific—solar power is far better suited to Arizona than the Pacific Northwest, and wind turbines cannot be operated effectively in all areas. Given the small proportion of energy consumption currently derived from renewable energy sources, it seems unlikely that they will significantly replace fossil fuels in the near future without major shifts in governmental policy and technological improvements.

Energy policy in the United States has been shaped by the goals of energy conservation, low prices, and independence. These goals were all in evidence after the 1973 oil crisis. The Nixon administration oversaw the passage of the Emergency Petroleum Allocation Act of 1973, which gave the government the right to allocate petroleum resources by mandate in times of shortages. It also extended oil price controls that had been established by the White House in 1971. The Nixon administration was also responsible for the implementation of a national 55-mile-per-hour speed limit on the nation's highways in early 1974 and the authorization to construct the trans-Alaska oil pipeline. The Strategic Petroleum Reserve (SPR) was created in 1974 to maintain an emergency supply of oil should the nation need it.

With the Carter administration, energy policy continued to move toward policies of conservation and increased supplies of fossil fuel energy. The first part of the National Energy Act of 1978 deregulated natural gas prices over a 3-year period. Petroleum price controls also began to be phased out. At the same time, coal, with which the United States is endowed in abundance, was encouraged as a major source of energy. The act further changed utility rate structures so that the true cost of supplying energy would be represented, and also set a schedule of taxes and tax breaks that sought to increase energy conservation and development of new resources such as new discoveries of petroleum and the development of alternative forms of energy. Funding for programs to develop alternative sources of energy from solar, wind, geothermal, and water power were allocated or increased significantly, as were projects that sought to extract energy from new sources such as so-called synfuels, produced by extracting oil from coal and shale. The government began to subsidize many domestic producers of oil who could not have competed on the world market, as well as oil company efforts at oil exploration.

Despite these efforts at conservation and reduced dependence on foriegn oil, U.S. dependence on imported oil grew steadily throughout the remainder of the 1970s.

The election of President Ronald Reagan marked a change in energy policy, with diminished government involvement in energy markets. Part of this was due to the philosophical orientation of the Reagan administration to involve governments as little as possible in directing resources, and part of it was due to falling oil prices. The Reagan administration removed the remaining price controls on gasoline. By 1985, dependency on foreign oil had fallen to 27.3 percent, with 42.5 percent of that from OPEC sources.[31] However, lessened dependency on foreign oil was to be short-lived. With the reestablishment of a secure oil market and the weakening of OPEC's position, per-barrel crude oil prices fell significantly during the 1980s. Between 1981 and 1986, oil prices fell 67.9 percent in real terms and fluctuated only mildly through 1990.[32] The result was a steady increase in the percentage contribution of foreign imports to domestic energy consumption. By 1991, that figure had climbed again to 39.5 percent, 61.3 percent of which originated in OPEC nations.[33]

With Iraq's invasion of Kuwait in August 1990 and the subsequent U.S. military confrontation with Iraq in early 1991, energy security once again became a more central concern of both government and the American people. The war in the Persian Gulf was a substantial oil shock. It was estimated that gasoline prices rose from an average of $1.08 per gallon for regular unleaded on August 1, 1990, to $1.25 per gallon just 10 days later. In the first week of the invasion the spot price for a barrel of West Texas intermediate crude increased by more than a third.[34] After the Gulf War, the focus turned from energy to the environment and the threat of climate change (see Chapter 5 of this volume).

However, the Clinton administration did focus on reducing the price of oil, especially that used for home heating. Controversially, in 2000, President Clinton ordered the release of 30 million barrels of crude oil from the country's 570-million-barrel Strategic Petroleum Reserve in an attempt to combat the rise of crude oil prices from $10 per barrel to $30 per barrel in just 2 years. Critics contended that this was simply a vote-generating move in an election year, having no real effect on oil prices. With global consumption of crude oil at around 76 million barrels per day, the release from the SPR may have had a very limited effect on price. [35]

Although President Bush's energy plan articulates the need for increased energy efficiency and the use of renewable energy sources, there is a dominant theme of increasing domestic energy production through exploration and new drilling. In terms of the arguments in this introduction, it seems that decreasing U.S. dependence on foreign oil sources lies at the heart of the plan, an argument fueled by the increased domestic security concerns following September 11, 2001 and the invasion of Iraq in March 2003. Many have noted the Bush administration's close association with a number of the large energy producers, citing as evidence the $32 million of campaign funds provided to the Republican

Party for the 2000 election by energy companies, $1.8 million of which went directly to George W. Bush.[36] It is not only the President who has close ties to the energy sector; Vice President Dick Cheney has been chairman and chief executive of the Dallas oil firm Halliburton.

Increasing the domestic supply of fossil fuels may alleviate security concerns, but it will only exacerbate future energy shortages unless other forms of energy can be developed to a point at which they can credibly replace oil, gas, and coal. R. Buckminster Fuller noted that "society cannot continue to live on oil and gas. Those fossil fuels represent nature's savings accounts which took billions of years to form." The articles that follow focus on the question of whether we increase fossil fuel consumption and deplete those savings accounts today or whether we leave something in the energy bank for the future. Energy Secretary Abraham argues that conservation efforts, while necessary, will not alleviate the need for energy in the United States. Increasing supply must, he reasons, work hand in hand with conservation efforts and the development of nuclear and renewable sources. Senator John Kerry believes that renewable sources and conservation have a far more critical role to play in the future of energy consumption, arguing that a domestic focus on renewable sources will make the country *more* energy independent than drilling in ANWR. He sees the Bush administration's plan as one that keeps the country dependent on oil, to the detriment of research and development in new sources of energy.

Endnotes

1. World Bank, *World Development Report 1999/2000,* http://www.worldbank.org/wdr/2000/pdfs/engtable10.pdf.
2. Energy Information Administration, *Annual Energy Report,* http://www.eia.doe.gov/emeu/aer/txt/tab1107.htm.
3. Justin Brown, "Oil Imports: Habit U.S. Hasn't Kicked," *Christian Science Monitor,* http://www.csmonitor.com/durable/2000/09/20/text/p2s1.html.
4. Energy Information Administration, http://www.eia.doe.gov/pub/oil_gas/petroleum/data_publications/petroleum_supply_monthly/current/pdf/table49.pdf.
5. Alfred A. Marcus, *Controversial Issues in Energy Policy* (Newbury Park, Calif.: Sage Publications, 1992), pp. 57–63.
6. In nominal dollars, this was a jump from $3.89 per barrel in 1973 to $6.87 per barrel in 1974. *Annual Energy Review 1991,* table 68.
7. This is 22.8 cents per gallon in 1973 and 36.0 cents in 1974. *Annual Energy Review 1991,* table 73.
8. For information from proponents, see http://www.anwr.org/.
9. http://www.anwr.org/features/ctoohey.htm.
10. Jerry Taylor, "Don't Worry about Energy Security," *Cato Institute* (October 18, 2001), http://www.cato.org/dailys/10–18–01.html.
11. Energy Information Administration, *Annual Energy Report,* http://www.eia.doe.gov/emeu/aer/txt/tab0103.htm.
12. Department of Energy, http://www.fe.doe.gov/education/.

13. EcoWorld, "The Global Energy Balance Sheet and Income Statement," http://www.ecoworld.org/energy/EcoWorld_Energy_Balance_Sheet.cfm.

14. Energy Information Administration, *Annual Energy Report*, http://www.eia.doe.gov/emeu/aer/txt/tab0402.htm.

15. Energy Information Administration, *Annual Energy Report*, http://www.eia.doe.gov/emeu/aer/txt/tab0101.htm.

16. Quoted in Matthew L. Wald, "After 20 Years, America's Foot Is Still on the Gas," *The New York Times* (October 17, 1993), p. E4.

17. William K. Tell, senior VP of Texaco, quoted in ibid.

18. U.S. Department of Energy, Energy Information Administration, *Annual Energy Review 2000*, http://www.eia.doe.gov/emeu/aer/txt/tab0103.htm.

19. Ibid.

20. U.S. Department of Energy, Energy Information Administration, http://www.eia.doe.gov/emeu/aer/txt/tab0104.htm. One barrel of consumed petroleum is equal to 5.341 million BTUs, U.S. Bureau of the Census, http://www.census.gov/prod/2002pubs/01statab/energy.pdf, p. 567.

21. National Energy Policy Development Group, *National Energy Policy* (Washington, D.C.: U.S. Government Printing Office, May 2001), p. 4–1, http://www.fe.doe.gov/general/energypolicy/chapter4.pdf.

22. Ibid., p. 4–3.

23. Ibid., pp. 4–9 and 4–10.

24. Ibid., chap. 4.

25. International Atomic Energy Agency, *Impact of U.S. Nuclear Generation on Greenhouse Gas Emissions*, http://www.eia.doe.gov/cneaf/nuclear/page/analysis/ghg.pdf, 5.

26. John McCarthy, "Frequently Asked Questions about Nuclear Energy," http://www.formal.stanford.edu/jmc/progress/nuclear-faq.html.

27. Energy Information Administration, *Annual Energy Review 2000*, http://www.eia.doe.gov/emeu/aer/txt/tab0103.htm.

28. Energy Information Administration, http://www.eia.doe.gov/cneaf/solar.renewables/page/rea_data/highlights.html.

29. Bioenergy Information Network, http://bioenergy.ornl.gov/faqs/#eco2.

30. Douglas R. O. Morrison, "World Energy and Climate in the Next Century," http://relcom.website.ru/wfs-moscow/eng/morrison.htm.

31. *Annual Energy Review 1991*, table 58.

32. Ibid., table 68.

33. Ibid., table 58.

34. U.S. Department of Energy, Energy Information Administration, *Energy Facts 1990* (Washington, D.C.: U.S. Government Printing Office), pp. 2–3.

35. Joel Darmstadter and Michael Toman, "Tapping the Strategic Petroleum Reserve: The Wrong Solution to the Wrong Problem," *Resources for the Future*, http://www.rff.org/op-eds/darm_spr.htm.

36. PBS Frontline, "Blackout," http://www.pbs.org/wgbh/pages/frontline/shows/blackout/traders/power.html, and The Center for Responsive Politics, "A Money in Politics Backgrounder on the Energy Industry," http://www.opensecrets.org/pressreleases/energybriefing.htm.

YES

Secretary of Energy Spencer Abraham
Speech Delivered to the National Petroleum Council

INTRODUCTION

It's a great pleasure to join the Council for the first time as your Co chair. I fully recognize the important contribution this Council has made—and can continue to make—to sound energy policy in America. Let me take this opportunity to thank each of you for your time, dedication, and consistently wise advice. As a member of the Senate, I was particularly concerned with cyber-security issues. It's an area we've addressed aggressively in our FY 2001 with a 43 percent increase in funding to enhance protection of vital national security information and our cutting edge research from our science programs. So I am especially interested in reviewing the results of your study on Critical Infrastructure Protection. Infrastructure protection will be a key priority in DOE, and I am sure your action plan will provide a significant road map for addressing these challenges.

The Council's past studies have had a major impact. Your look at America's natural gas supply found some 40 percent was virtually out of bounds to development in federal land areas in Wyoming and Colorado. This was a clear warning. By 2020 we'll consume some 50 percent more natural gas than we do today. Without increasing domestic supply, the gap must be filled by foreign import. The Department followed up the NPC natural gas study and I can announce today that our findings show some 68 percent—not 40 percent—of the Rocky Mountain region considered is closed to development or under major access restrictions. As I'll discuss later, we've taken steps in our national energy plan to address this problem in an environmentally responsible manner.

So let me turn now to the issue dominating headlines and of central concern to all American families—our national energy policy. Over the course of several weeks, I've had the chance to visit the last refinery built in the U.S.—and that was over 25 years ago, and the first nuclear power plant to be relicensed for the next 20 years. These facilities help define America's energy challenges. Both the refinery I visited in Garyville, Louisiana, and the nuclear plant I visited in Calvert Cliffs, Maryland, have superb environmental records. They perform an absolutely essential function, they run at virtually peak capacity, they operate safely, and they are good citizens in their local community. Our refinery capacity, however, is seriously strained. We need more Garyvilles. Our demand for electricity is soaring, but our interest in adding to supply has for too long been missing in action. We need more Calvert Cliffs.

The consequences are clear for everyone to see. We have an energy supply crisis. It's serious. It's not going to cure itself. It's going to affect every single family in this country. It's going to cause dramatic changes in life style. And it's going to get much worse if we don't act now to meet the challenge. Let me also make something else quite clear. There are no quick fixes to our energy supply crisis. Our energy problems were years in the making, they'll take years to resolve.

In many ways this crisis, like every other crisis this country has ever faced, is going to be a test of our willingness to make tough decisions, to stick with those decisions, and take responsibility for our own actions. We use an enormous amount of energy in this nation. And yet we are often reluctant to do the things that need to be done to maintain a secure supply of energy. Everyone likes power, but no one likes power generation or delivery. But we can't have it both ways. Still, one set of policies options would have us believe that we can. We are told that there is an easy and rather uncomplicated way out. When prices soar, apply price caps. When demand exceeds supply, beg OPEC for more oil.

When energy supplies drop, claim conservation . . . and the promise of renewable power will alone save the day. This simple course of action will be popular . . . until the lights go out. Then a real solution will be needed. By why wait till the crisis that now grips California works its way east to engulf the entire nation? The President's National Energy Policy offers us a way to address our energy challenges. His approach is long-term, it's balanced, and it's comprehensive . . . touching on every aspect of our problem, from environmental protection to new sources in the Caspian Sea, from conservation to nuclear energy. So let's review the energy challenges we see on the horizon and then look at how we can address them in a responsible manner.

AMERICA'S ENERGY CHALLENGES

Twenty-two summers ago, a national survey of service stations by the American Automobile Association found over half were shut down on Saturday, June 23, and 70 percent had their gas pumps shut off on Sunday. So on the first weekend of summer, 1979, there simply was very little gasoline to be found—at any price—to fuel holiday travel. At the same time, independent truckers were staging strikes to protest fuel shortages, snarling traffic and adding to the sense of crisis.

Today's energy crisis has not yet resulted in national shortages, or gas lines, or workers' strikes, but it is as deeply serious in its own way as the one our nation faced nearly a quarter century ago. Scarcity is not a problem; few now live under the illusion, popular in the past, that we are running out of natural resources. Nor is the nation confronted with the same international political environment, a perilous Cold War, and a prolonged hostage situation. But consider what the data is telling us about America's energy future.

THE U.S. ENERGY CRISIS

- In the next 20 years we expect overall U.S. energy consumption to increase by over 30 percent.
- We expect oil demand to increase by one third.
- We expect consumption of natural gas to increase by 62 percent.
- We expect electricity demand to increase by 45 percent, owing at least in part to the growth of power hungry information technology.
- We now produce 39 percent less oil than we did in 1970.

And yet,

- 40 percent of our domestic gas resources are now off limits or subject to restrictions that make it virtually impossible to develop.
- Hydroelectric power generation is expected to fall sharply,
- There has been no nuclear power permit granted since 1979,
- And there are many people who want to see coal—which now supplies over half our electricity—go the way of whale oil.

Our energy supply network is also in trouble.

- 37 U.S. refineries have closed since 1992 and none have been built in 25 years.
- An aging power grid prevents power rich regions of the nation from selling power to areas that need it most.

America now consumes 98 quadrillion btus (or quads) a year of all energy. If we assume normal economic growth and continued significant improvements in efficiency, we will consume 127 quads by the year 2020. This means over the next twenty years we are looking at a gap of some 30 quads of energy—after we make all expected efficiency gains—to keep our homes warm and our factories running. In other words, efficiency helps, but we will still need to add roughly 25 percent more energy to our economy over the next two decades.

Under current policies, imports would be our primary option for filling the gap. But I suspect that few Americans wish us to become even more energy dependent. Alternatively, we could attempt to fill the gap by drastically cutting our consumption of energy on top of the major conservation savings we already foresee. But, are Americans really ready for steep taxes on gasoline and electricity, CAFE standards high enough to virtually ban SUV's from the highway, or the moving of energy intensive businesses and jobs offshore? I doubt it.

THE PRESIDENT'S ENERGY PLAN

The President has set out a different course for America, one that is balanced and comprehensive. Our National Energy Plan balances concerns for environmental protection with our need to increase domestic supplies of energy. It balances the need to look to the future and new sources of energy with today's pressing requirements for additional power. It balances the need for an increased focus on conservation with greater attention to enhancing our own domestic supplies. And finally, the President's Plan looks to a balanced source of supply from wind to nuclear, from coal to solar, because diversity of supply is the best way to insure energy security.

So let's look at the specific ways we propose to meet America's 21st century energy challenge. First, there is conservation. Our critics attacked our plan well before it was even issued, saying it paid to little attention to conservation. But energy efficiency not only stands alone as a central feature in our pursuit of energy security; it is an idea woven into every facet of our strategy. Few people know it, but we are already the world's most efficient users of energy. Since 1973, the U.S. economy has grown nearly 5 times faster than energy use. We are determined to build on this impressive record. We'll consider higher appliance standards and expanding the scope of this program to include appliances not yet covered. And we also recommend efficiency-based tax credits for purchase of new hybrid fuel cell vehicles. The Plan helps working families save energy and money by doubling funding for our Weatherization Assistance Program. Combined heat and power technologies have great potential for increasing efficiency and reducing emissions. By itself, one plant can reduce annual emissions of nitrogen oxide by over 600,000 tons. We back more CHP projects by shortening their depreciation life or providing an investment tax credit.

Conservation is critical, of course. But on its own, it's not enough. So the President's plan also looks to increasing domestic supply from diverse sources of energy. Why is this so important? Consider this. With electricity demand expected to jump 45% over the next twenty years, we are looking at the need for between 1,300 and 1,900 new power plants in this country. That amounts to something like 60 to 90 plants a year. The last time we added that much power was 1985. Even if we meet the construction challenge . . . with all the permits required, the transmissions lines to be connected . . . and frequent local political opposition . . . virtually all of these plants would be fired by natural gas, unless we change course. Natural gas has many advantages, but we believe it's too risky to rely on just one fuel. It would endanger national security by leaving us defenseless against foreign supply disruptions and almost certainly triggering very tight markets with resultant price spikes.

The President's balanced approach seeks the security that comes from a diverse supply of energy. So we'll strengthen all available sources. Hydropower must remain a key electricity source so we propose streamlining the current cumbersome and costly relicensing process. Coal supplies half our nation's electricity, but presents environmental challenges. Through our clean coal technology initiative we are going to invest $2 billion over the next ten years to help make coal a cleaner burning fuel. Just as urgent, we need to add some regulatory certainly to coal fired electricity generation. So our energy plan recommends a clearer set of policies related to coal that are more easily applied to business decisions. Natural gas, as I noted earlier, will be an increasingly crucial part of our energy mix. Our energy plan calls for a review of public lands restrictions with full public consultation to explore impediments to environmentally sound recovery of natural gas resources. Thanks to the NPC study, we have a better idea of the scope of the impediments.

Nuclear energy provides 20 percent of our electricity and is the cleanest form of major power generation known. In fact, if we had to rely on fossil fuels for the 20 percent of electricity now provided by nuclear energy, it would be the same as adding the emissions of an additional 94 million automobiles to our highways. We believe expanding nuclear energy makes sense. To do that, however, we need to overcome some old thinking about nuclear power. Some people's image of nuclear energy was frozen in time 22 years ago by the accident at Three Mile Island. Now let's make no mistake. Three Mile Island was a serious accident. Everyone—industry, government, everyone, has learned from it. But to look at nuclear power as if nothing has changed since 1979 would be the same as looking at the communications industry and ignoring the development of the cell phone and the Internet. Technology in the nuclear industry has raced ahead too. Current reactors have been upgraded, they have become safer and more reliable. And improved designs just over the horizon, like the gas-cooled pebble-bed reactor, are even safer than today's reactors.

Nuclear energy is already a staple around the world, with France generating some 80 percent of its electricity from nuclear power. Japan, Israel and other nations are also moving ahead with new plants. As I mentioned at the beginning of my speech, I recently visited the first nuclear plant to be relicensed for the next 20 years in Calvert Cliffs, Maryland. It's an example of how consolidation of this industry fostered huge boosts in safety and efficiency . . . Calvert Cliffs runs at 98 percent capacity up from 70 percent years ago. In the past, plants had only home grown talent available for highly skilled operator jobs. With consolidation, all plants take advantage of the best talent available around the country. Technology and fundamental changes in this industry—most of which has gone unrecognized—have transformed nuclear power generation.

We take account of these changes in our energy plan in a variety of recommendations designed to maintain and expand nuclear power generation. First among them is our expressed commitment to safety. We encourage the relicensing of plants like Calvert Cliffs that meet the highest safety standards and we support applications for licensing new advanced-technology nuclear reactors. EPA, in consultation with DOE, will look at the potential for nuclear energy to improve air quality. We recommended more money for safety enforcement. We support legislation ensuring that decommissioning funds are not taxed as part of the transaction thus removing roadblocks to further consolidation of the industry. And we support extending the Price-Anderson Act, to insure speedy compensation in case of accident. But no progress however can be made on nuclear power until we solve the challenge of a permanent waste disposal site. The President's energy Plan requires that the best science and most rigorous process be employed to settle on along-term disposal site.

Along with traditional sources of energy, we also have to harness the power of renewable energy, so we recommend extending and broadening tax incentives for wind and biomass generation and we propose new tax credits for using solar generation. Our energy plan pays special attention to the significant promise of next-generation energy such as hydrogen or fusion. There is great potential here for moving us, someday in the future, beyond fossil fuels. So we place a priority on expanding research and development of these next-generation sources. Along with ensuring that we meet the growing demand for electricity, we've also got to meet the growing demand for oil. Back in 1973—at the height of the oil crisis—America imported just 36 percent of its oil from abroad. Today, we import 54 percent. That figure is not going to drop, in fact, it's likely to rise. But that doesn't mean we shouldn't do everything we can to boost our domestic sources. Here again, technology has forged ahead and changed the exploration industry as much as it changed everything else. We've come a long way from the time wildcatters punched holes in the ground based on the hunch they might hit a gusher.

But from a regulatory standpoint, our view of oil exploration hasn't changed much since we saw Jed Clampett strike "black gold" and split for Beverly Hills. The marriage of oil exploration with cutting-edge technology means fewer rigs, fewer roads and fewer pipelines . . . and more successes. Drilling operations that required 65 acres in the 1970s need only 10 acres today. So anyone who believes our plans to expand domestic production of oil and natural gas presents a threat to the environment, just hasn't kept up with the times.

Along with the challenge of boosting domestic supply we must continue to work with foreign suppliers like OPEC. But we must look at this question realistically. OPEC has demonstrated that they will act in their own self-interest. Therefore, it is clear America should make decisions about oil based on our self-interests. So, along with a continued honest discussion with OPEC, we need to concentrate on getting our own energy house in order. This means finding new international energy sources. This means we enhance energy production here at home. This means straightforward dialogue with OPEC. But I can tell you what it does not mean. It does not mean going around the world begging for energy. There are countless sources of energy around the world, from the Caspian Sea, to Asia to Africa, and our own hemisphere. Our energy plan understands the global scope of energy and seeks wide ranging diplomatic efforts to increase energy supply around the world.

Even if we can find the supplies, moving energy to market requires a delivery system. Ours is out of date and in need of repair. Infrastrature improvement is the third key element in our energy plan. America is going to need an additional 38,000 miles of transmission pipelines and 263,000 miles of distribution lines to bring natural gas to homes and businesses. Today's system is stressed. We need a new pipeline to deliver natural gas from Alaska to the rest of the nation and we need to improve pipeline safety. Each of these issues is addressed in our Plan. We also need greater refinery capacity. As I mentioned earlier, the last refinery was built in the U.S. some 25 years ago. Limited refinery capacity is one of the major causes of gasoline price spikes in the Midwest and elsewhere in the last few summers. Unless we take action, that problem will simply continue. Our plan recommends streamlining permitting and providing greater regulatory certainty to give the industry confidence to expand.

Our infrastructure challenges don't stop there, however. Our electricity grid needs to move from one designed to meet regional energy needs to one able to send power coast to coast. One of the reasons for blackouts in Northern California is simply an inability to get power sent from southern California to the north, and indeed because power couldn't move into the State from areas of the country that had a surplus. Our plan calls for an end to such bottlenecks by creating an electricity superhighway, one where power can move coast to coast as freely as the family automobile.

So one of the major responsibilities of my Department is going to be to draft and work to seek passage of legislation that can bring us closer to creating a true interstate highway system for electricity. Too often, an electricity producer can only look to a relatively small region as a market for its power. That's bad for consumers who are denied choice. We need to bring more sellers into those regional electricity markets, which are now largely isolated. This would drive down prices, by creating competition and consumer choice. An electricity highway with all the stop signs gone, will have another advantage. It will help us to transcend one of the major obstacles in America to building energy security—the not in my backyard syndrome, known as nimby.

Americans love energy, but they hate energy production. It has become an effort worthy of the Manhattan project to site a new power plant or build a transmission line in some parts of this nation. Earlier this year, for example, plans to build a 550-megawatt gas-fired generator in a Los Angeles suburb were scrapped after residents voted 2:1 against the project. The local mayor added a much-needed dose of reason and maturity to the debate by launching a hunger strike in opposition to the plant. And yet there are communities in this nation—some of them quite isolated—that welcome power generation, including nuclear power generation, and would readily add new plants to their economic base if they could only reach beyond their isolation to find a large market for their electricity. Today, that's not possible. But a truly national energy grid provides those communities with the broad base of costumers they need to create their own hubs of power. And at the same time, it moves beyond nimby to imby—communities that say to power plants, yes, in my backyard.

CONCLUSION

So we believe our energy policy that looks to modernizing our complex energy delivery systems, that enhances energy efficiency, increases domestic production of all sources of energy and looks ahead to the next generation fuels is the kind of comprehensive and balanced approach America is looking for. Some, however, suggest another approach. They define the energy problem in very simple terms. We have an energy problem when the price goes up enough to hit the newspapers. For them imposing price controls is too often the only policy choice. But it's not as easy as that. Setting a cap on price will simply increase demand at the same time it diminishes any incentive to boost supply. The Bush Administration agrees with Governor Gray Davis that high California electricity prices are a bad thing. But they aren't as bad as an increase in the scope, duration and frequency of the blackouts hitting California. Yet, more and worse blackouts will almost certainly result if we respond to California's electricity supply problem with the price controls the Governor advocates.

More intense blackouts will greatly imperil the health and safety of California's citizens, undermining its economy as much as high energy prices. Accordingly, our Administration will not endorse any policy that produces such conditions. And such outcomes are precisely what price caps will invoke. As with 1970's gas lines, California electricity price controls will not increase supply or lessen demand—they'll do the opposite—thus exacerbating the electricity supply shortages that triggered high prices in the first place. Indeed, California's failed experiment with price caps last year—when price caps were lowered actual prices went up and supply fell by 3,000 megawatts—should be sufficient evidence that price controls don't work. California's case for federal price controls is further compromised because the federal government has no authority over power sellers that control about 50 percent of the electricity supply of the West, including California municipal utilities who have been charging the same high prices as the private companies California politicians so love to assail. It makes little sense for Washington to only cap half of the Western market. But, if such partial price capping is justified, why hasn't California applied price controls to their own state entities—over which the federal government has no control—instead of begging Washington to cap the other half?

These conditions were all existent when President Bush took office. Since then we have done everything in our power to help. We've issued emergency orders to ensure the state could obtain natural gas and electricity, expedited permits to facilitate the construction of new generators, directed federal facilities in California to maximize electricity conservation—especially at peak periods—and moved to eliminate in-state transmission bottlenecks which have contributed to the blackouts. In fact, the only California request not granted has been the demand for price caps. As these actions indicate, we will help however we can; but we will not be a party to making the situation worse. Our plan rejects the idea that you can solve a supply problem by capping prices. Price is a signal of supply shortages. Controlling the signal won't increase the supply. It will only make matters worse.

Now let me be clear. Where we see improper business practices, where we see unjust and unreasonable prices, we will act. But there is a huge difference between making sure industry acts properly and within the law, and enforcing a system of price controls. On the one hand, we are insuring fairness. On the other, we would be crushing any real incentive to conserve energy or create new supply. I believe our approach is better. Instead of stifling competition with price controls we want to increase it across the board as the best way to drive down price and give consumers better service and more choice. A competitive energy market where all sources . . . coal, nuclear, solar, wind, natural gas . . . are a real choice, and where the delivery of energy is open to truly national competition. . . that is the goal of our energy policy. We can surmount this energy crisis by using 21st century technology, creating markets, and looking to the next generation of energy. This is the road to lasting energy security in the United States. The calamity that overwhelmed us 22 summers ago can be avoided. We can avoid gas lines and blackouts and power alerts. But only if we reject the quick fix and look toward a balanced and comprehensive policy . . . one that will secure a healthy energy future for generations to come.

NO

Energy Security Is American Security

Senator John F. Kerry
Speech delivered to the Center for National Policy

Since September 11, we have all been united in a mission to confront and defeat the terrorists who attacked our country and those who knowingly harbored them. That is a noble and necessary mission that we must pursue with determination and success. We appreciate the President's leadership and the enormous contributions of our men and women in uniform. As a citizen, I have been grateful for our nation's response. We have come together as one country, across every boundary of party and background, calling and status, and to strengthen measures for homeland defense.

We have to win this struggle: militarily where that is necessary; through effective law enforcement where that is appropriate; and through vigorous diplomacy wherever that is required to keep the anti-terror coalition together.

And we must also strive with friends and scholars on every continent to expose, rebut, isolate and defeat the apostles of hate, so that children are no longer brainwashed into becoming suicide bombers, and terrorists are denied the ideological swamplands in which they breed.

September 11 obviously did much to affect our lives here in America. But it did not change everything. It did not diminish our identity as a tolerant and diverse people, or our commitment to freedom, or our willingness to meet our responsibilities to allies abroad. It did not change our nature, as one nation under God, a country where church and state are separate, but whose communities are blessed with an abundance of spiritual faith.

And it did not change our fundamental character as a democracy, where public policies are settled in open debate, in stark contrast to the narrow, autocratic regimes whose failure of governance has contributed to the terrorism we face today.

It is in the spirit of what is best about our country that this morning I share thoughts and proposals about our future. Politics—as so many of you know—is the art of achieving the possible in the conduct of public affairs. Sometimes that can be done by plucking the so-called low-hanging fruit and sometimes it requires painstaking, creative and bold, hard work in the vineyards. The challenge of delivering America's—indeed the world's—energy security offers both "low hanging fruit" and great challenge—but it requires above all that we end the procrastination, and commit ourselves to get the job done. It requires leadership, vision, and action.

In times past, whenever we faced an energy crisis, talk would surface of America's need to be energy independent. For a moment we scurried around looking for new strategies and then, as the price of oil receded or as supplies increased or a war was put behind us—as life returned to normal—the sense of urgency evaporated. For almost 30 years this pattern allowed us to turn our backs on realities and possibilities. Alternatives, renewables, efficiencies, clean technologies, global warming, clean air, have met with only occasional, marginal success—and more often with disdain—so that essentially. America has operated without an energy strategy. We have squandered years during which we could have created hundreds of thousands if not several million new jobs, opened up whole new market opportunities, contributed significantly to global environmental efforts, improved the health of our citizens, saved the taxpayers money, and significantly enhanced the long term security of our country.

So it is important now to begin a new debate about our energy future—a debate that must be grounded in certain key principles. First: absent a showing of exhaustion of all other remedies and a compelling real and present life threatening danger—we should not do anything that does not make economic sense. Second—subject to the same caveat—we do not have to give up or diminish any quality of life we currently enjoy. Third, all things being equal, the easiest and most rapid gains will come from efficiencies in the current energy regime. And fourth, absent unpredictable breakthroughs, we must enter this debate understanding that for 30–50 years in the future, like it or not, we will continue to have major dependency on fossil fuels. What makes this current dependency particularly compelling is that not far beyond this time frame or window of opportunity—in the lifetimes perhaps of our grandchildren—scientists believe literally catastrophic consequences from global warming will occur in the absence of serious emission reductions.

So as we have turned the corner of a millennium and century, we have urgent reasons to be serious about our energy future—and we have an extraordinary opportunity today to begin a new earn in which our conception of how energy is produced, used and conserved is transformed.

The strategy I suggest to make that transition—I regret to say—must differ in many respects from that put forward by the current Administration, and by the Republican majority in the House of Representatives.

Their approach was developed during the first half of last year by a Task Force chaired by Vice President Cheney. Neither innovative private sector companies nor the public interest were permitted to compete fairly and openly for the White House ear.

Old thinking passed through the doors of 1600 Pennsylvania Avenue far more often and easily than new thinking. Exxon Mobil, Enron or Chevron enjoyed an access bonanza at the expense of consumers and state of the art environmental technology manufacturers. The process and its results stand as a monument to the difficulty of forcing industry and institutional change.

As a result, those most heavily invested in the current energy system have set a course for the future which, not surprisingly, champions status quo policies at the expense of new ideas and innovation. What's worse, President Bush claims that prolonging the status quo will somehow ensure "energy independence" for America, and his party's leaders happily echo his cry—as if by embracing their lack of vision we'd all be able to sit back, relax, and put our fleet of international oil tankers in drydock.

Common sense tells us that the policies that made us dependent on foreign oil—however repackaged in the mantle of patriotism—will only keep us dependent on foreign oil. America take note: if we enact the entire Bush energy plan we will find ourselves twenty years from now more dependent on foreign oil—than we are today. The Administration has not offered an agenda for energy independence. That is false advertising. It has offered an agenda that evades the tough questions—provided blinders where we need magnifying glasses—and slogans in the place of genuine leadership.

Nothing is more indicative of old thinking, special interest policy than the attempt by the Administration to falsely sell to the American people a rationale for drilling in the Arctic National Wildlife Refuge.

Big oil and its allies have lusted over the refuge for two decades. With each attempt they make up new arguments for despoiling a unique and irreplaceable arctic environment for a quantity of petroleum that simply will not reduce the fact of our dependency on high risk foreign oil.

When California was desperate for electricity they proposed drilling in ANWR even though only 1% of California's electricity was oil based and not an additional drop would appear for 10 years. I was publically warned by Trent Lott that the lights were literally about to go out in Massachusetts, all my constituents were going to freeze to death in the dark, and I would bear responsibility. For the record, I would like to note that the electricity is still on. In fact, we even had enough power to keep the stadium lights burning as the New England Patriots literally slid by Oakland last Saturday night.

When California resolved its crisis and the economy turned down, they then began to argue ANWR was a jobs program even though studies show far more, far better jobs in other endeavors and that all their estimates were based on false analysis. No matter.

Now the proponents are more interested in arousing our fears than in discussing the facts.

The latest claim cleverly suggests that ANWR can become a replacement for oil from Saudi Arabia or Iraq. The quick reaction of everyone is to welcome the image of freedom from buying oil from those linked with terrorism. The problem is that's all it is—an image. First, the refuge would not even reach peak production until 20 years from now. It cannot possibly impact the war we wage today.

More importantly—recognizing that under the Administration's own pro-posals we will be more dependent on imported oil in 2020 than we are today and that increasing demand for oil will quickly gobble up whatever comes from small U.S. supplies, it is impossible for the U.S. to produce our way out of dependency and avoid the increasing demand curve. The United States has only 3% of the world's reserves to be matched against the fact that we use 25% of the world's supply. And guess what—Saudi Arabia has 46% of the world's reserves. The solution is not in ANWR—it's in less dependency on oil itself.

Perhaps the most bitter irony amid all their claims of the need to drill, are the more than 7,000 existing leases for oil and gas exploration in the Gulf of Mexico—80% of which, covering 32 million acres, are not producing oil because they're being mapped or sit idle as companies wait for the price of oil to rise to maximize profits. Last May the State of Alaska completed a lease sale of 950,000 acres on the North Slope, the largest lease by any state in history and has announced another seven million acres of federal land the National Petroleum Reserve up for sale. Maybe one day someone could make an argument for the need to drill in the refuge, but the industry's inaction in the Gulf of Mexico and Alaska proves that time is not now—and it won't ever have to come if we make wise choices.

So America has a choice between two competing visions. The Administration sees a world where our principal effort is to drill our way out of our problem while alternative, renewable fuels and technologies rise or fall on their own at the margins no matter what compelling reasons exist to behave differently.

I see a world, where even as we drill because it makes economic sense and we have to, our primary focus shifts to cajoling and exciting a new market place for those alternative and renewable energy sources because there are compelling reasons to do so.

These competing visions are highlighted by the President's insistence that drilling in the Arctic National Wildlife Refuge is the centerpiece of his energy approach—and I do mean insist, for just last week the President declared he will accept no energy plan without oil drilling in the refuge. He seems completely oblivious to the fact that—if drilling in the refuge is the crown jewel of your energy plan, you actually have no energy plan at all.

Perhaps we shouldn't be surprised by this blatant contradiction but we certainly can be disappointed. It is part of a pattern of telling Americans one thing and doing another. The Administration begrudgingly accepts that global warming is a threat which must be addressed even as their energy plan would increase global warming pollution by more than 30%. They say they want to stem air pollution which makes Americans sick and degrades our land and water but their proposals weaken pollution controls at power plants. They submit an energy plan and tell us not to worry because it is "energy policy, not environmental policy" when any school kid in America could tell you energy policy and environmental policy are not separable.

Ladies and gentlemen, we have to do better than this. Energy security is American security. Our policy must reflect that we live in one world, not four or five separate ones and we need an energy policy of national purpose that confronts the hard realities and sets real priorities based on the needs of all Americans.

Obviously we all agree that reducing our dependence on foreign oil, especially oil from the politically toxic Middle East, is a necessity. But the American people want honesty about how you do it, not a false security blanket that promises something undeliverable in the short term and precious little amounting to real progress in the long term.

In recent months, I've talked to citizens across our country, to business-people, farmers and the energy industry; to academic experts and local officials; to the public health community and public interest organizations, and I have found that more and more Americans "get it." They are dissatisfied with the fossil-fuel based energy policies that made sense fifty years age, but which cannot sustain our nation in the future. They are frustrated because we don't pursue alternatives they know we could adopt. They want an economy where hardworking citizens can't automatically be held hostage to the whims of a handful of nations that rig the world oil market. They want leaders setting an agenda where protecting our environment, our land, our water, our air and our public health are national priorities, not after-thoughts. They want a country where energy security is not just a slogan or an empty promise, but a growing reality. It is with all of their views and with their input, expertise and practical experience that I respectfully suggest it is time now to pursue a national Strategic Energy Initiative.

This is an initiative born out of necessity and its goal is quite simply to initiate a transition from our heavy dependence on polluting and sometimes insecure fossil fuels to more efficient, clean, and reliable energy. It maximizes private sector opportunities and avoids the mistake of command and control. It plays to our entrepenuerial skill as Americans but it commits us as a nation to move in a certain direction.

While we may not all recognize it, America has made exactly the sort of energy transition I am calling for more than once before. For much of the 1800s our primary source of energy was wood. By the late 1800s coal was king and oil accounted for only 3 percent of our energy. That changed when the automobile went into mass production and demand for gasoline soared. By the end of World War II, oil was the nation's dominant energy source. Natural gas, once burned off as waste, was added to the energy mix in the '40s. Nuclear power came online in the '50s. And today we are fueled by a mix of oil, gas, coal, nuclear and hydroelectric power. It has been our history to evolve from one fuel source to another gradually and economically. Now we need to prepare our nation for the 21st Century and begin a gradual economic transition to domestic, clean and reliable energy technologies.

I know that, for some, it may be hard to conceive of a world where fossil fuels, and especially petroleum, are not the dominant sources of fuel. One hundred and fifty years ago, in New Bedford and Nantucket, folks couldn't conceive of a future that didn't depend on whale oil. Prophesying is a risky business. Even the experts are often wrong: Western Union in 1876 said the telephone had too many flaws to be considered seriously as a means of communication. The Chairman of IBM in 1943 predicted that the world market for computers would peak at five. The President of Digital Corporation was saying as late as 1977, "there is no reason anyone would want a computer in their home."

In fact, the story of computers over the past two decades may be a good parallel for the story of energy in America and the world over the coming decades. From mainframe to P.C. From big scale to small. One technological breakthrough after another. Leading to an even more competitive American and global economy.

Certainly it is part of America's history to drive technology and shape the marketplace to achieve our shared objectives. In the 1930s only 10 percent of rural America had electric service. Utilities refused to develop rural counties because homes were too far apart to make the investment profitable. To push the market and to bring electric power to all American homes, Congress used more than $5 billion in federal money to finance utilities to build in rural areas. By the 1950s, nearly all farms and rural areas had electric service and loans were largely repaid.

Today there is a compelling national interest to address the security and environmental threats of fossil fuels. Just as we did in the 1930s and many times since, we should nourish the marketplace, set goals and create incentives that will begin a transition.

We must provide a catalyst for the work that is already happening at the margins of the energy industry. Shell has invested in wind, solar and biomass; Chevron has invested in solar and fuel cells; and BP has heavily invested in solar and predicts more than $1 billion in sales by 2010. These efforts are smaller than they ought to be—they stand today as Potemkin Villages on a landscape dominated by the old way of doing things, a landscape that reflects the $1.8 billion federal largesse lavished on oil and gas while alternative efforts compete for the scraps of a mere $24 million in federal venture capital. A technological revolution can change the energy landscape itself, and it's time we accelerate the technology—speed up the development process—push the curve—and join the competition so that American ingenuity can again lead the world.

To accomplish that and excite even more entrepeneurial activity, I believe we should set a national goal of having 20% of our electricity come from domestic alternative and renewable sources by the year 2020. Twenty-twenty—I think it's a vision worthy of America: a goal I believe our citizens are ready to embrace.

A number of states have already set ambitious goals by creating renewable portfolio standards—benchmarks to measure progress in the transition to renewable energy. If policymakers set the public interest standard, then market forces take over and race to find the most efficient and effective way of meeting that goal through a credit trading system. In rural agriculture, businesses may use land to "farm the wind", in other cases, the power may come from the sun, or the flow of a river, or from biomass, or from geothermal energy. But in every case the old fashioned conservative economics of the business model help generate electricity to supply the power needs in a manner that is efficient, safe and clean. Texas is on track to reach its renewable target by 2004 instead of the proposed year of 2009. California is at 13% renewable energy and there is no reason other states can't do better.

The benefits from this effort can be broadly shared. For example: Minnesota requires that a percentage of its electricity be generated from the wind. Family farmers have gone into the power business. In Woodstock, Minnesota, Richard and Roger Kas have built 17 wind turbines on their land, generating enough electricity to power more than 2,000 homes. Other farmers take advantage of biomass, producing renewable fuels on the land for use in producing in electricity.

For Americans who work in engineering, design, and industry the growth of wind, solar and geothermal would spark a surge in production. And since developing new energy technologies is a research-requiring, pathbreaking activity, we can create thousands of well-paying new jobs. Academic studies project that a renewable portfolios standard would result in a net gain to our national economy, a net gain in employment, and a net gain in wages because there are simply more jobs per megawatt of power produced in the renewable industries than in fossil-fuel sectors. The machines of renewable energy will be made of steel, aluminum and glass. They will be machined, manufactured, distributed and maintained. I don't think we should take a backseat to the Germans or the Japanese in that effort. This new direction for America should create jobs for Americans, and it's up to us to insist it does.

Now, I know there are some who say the government should keep all hands off, and give market forces sole control over our energy future. Well I believe in the market. Nothing is more powerful in driving the decisions of businesspeople, engineers and consumers. But it is utter nonsense to suggest that the government has no role.

During the last century, the coal, oil, gas and nuclear industries benefitted from hundreds of billions of dollars in subsidies, tax breaks, land sales and outright government assistance. Most of it was justified. For most of the past century, we did not have a better choice than petroleum to meet the bulk of our energy needs, especially for transportation. But now we need to look ahead and anticipate what is coming around the next bend in the road. Domestic, renewable sources are urgently needed now because they are entirely under our control. No foreign government can embargo them. No terrorist can seize control of them. No cartel can play games with them. No American soldier will have to risk his or her life to protect them. For all those reasons—to create a better, more secure and cleaner future for our nation—for real energy security—I believe even the most rock-ribbed conservative would agree we must take steps that go beyond what market forces do on their own.

There is yet another area in which leaders must put aside politics and build a real consensus. You just plain can't tell Americans you're serious about energy security unless you're willing to tackle transportation, where 70 percent of the oil we purchase is consumed. In fact, we consume far more oil in our cars, SUVs, minivans, and other vehicles alone than any other country does for all of its oil-supplied energy needs. By far, the most significant step we can take toward reducing our dependence on oil is to make our passenger vehicles more efficient. What is more, we've had practice.

During the 1970's, America created the Corporate Average Fuel Economy—or CAFE—program to increase auto efficiency. This was the right decision. It worked—resulting in the manufacture of more efficient, safe, reliable, and high quality cars. It saved oil. And it reduced long-term costs to consumers. I might add that the law was signed by a Republican President from Michigan, named Ford, no less.

Today, because of CAFE standards, we save 3 million barrels of oil every day—three times the peak production of ANWR. Each year, consumers keep more than $20 billion in their pockets instead of paying for fuel, and greenhouse gas emissions are significantly lower. CAFE is a genuine and concrete step toward energy independence.

But in recent years, we have slid back. In 1995, Congress froze these standards. As a result, our vehicle fuel efficiency is worse now than it has been in twenty years. We are literally becoming less efficient with each new fleet of cars and trucks using more fuel than the last.

As you know, some are now calling for stronger CAFE standards. The response in some quarters has been shock—as if the idea were unpatriotic and heretical. Republican Leader Trent Lott said last March, "The American people have a right to a great big road hog. And I'm gonna get me one." The key word here is "hog."

Even the largest passenger vehicle can be made safe, reliable, and more efficient. SUVs, minivans and light trucks can be built to provide high performance at higher mileage. They don't have to be hogs. And there is nothing more American than efficiency.

I want to underline this, because all of us appreciate the way in which the automobile is part of our culture. "American Graffitti" was our youth, and the industry has created hundreds of thousands of good jobs and put food on the tables of working families for generations. The last thing we want to do is harm that industry or our economy.

The good news is, I don't believe we have to—the National Academy of Sciences confirmed that we can significantly improve fuel efficiency through better use of technology, without limiting vehicle choice, without harming safety, without harming the industry, and at a cost that will ultimately save consumers money.

The Senate Commerce Committee is now reviewing the need to raise fuel economy standards for cars and SUVs. The question is: how far and how fast can we go? My answer is that we should go as far and fast as we can guided by the legitimate concerns of the domestic automobile industry and the limits on what it is technically and economically feasible. Whatever we do, we should provide adequate lead time so that companies can design and build more efficient vehicles in keeping with their regular production cycles. This is essential to reduce costs and provide time for technological development.

I am determined that Congress should act—but we have to act intelligently. More than 100 million new cars will be sold in the coming decade. That is the imperative for not waiting. If we work in partnership with the industry, these cars can be as efficient as they can reasonably be made.

At the same time we improve CAFE standards we should provide tax and other incentives for consumers to purchase alternative fuel vehicles. I have discussed this issue with auto company executives who say they can do more, faster with market incentives. They are right. And the key to our approach should be to make the marketplace friendlier to efficient and alternative fuel cars.

Honda and Toyota already sell some hybrid cars, and Ford is developing a hybrid SUV for 2003. Hybrid technology combines a traditional engine with an electric engine to achieve greater fuel economy. But right now, hybrid engines cost more, and they will until the technology reaches full production scale. By providing tax credits now, we can make it possible for the companies to raise production, lower costs, and stimulate the market. This is a way to help move technologies off the drawing board, into production and onto the road. This same approach can be used to accelerate the development and deployment of natural gas and fuel cell-powered vehicles, especially for targeted fleets like buses and taxis. And government needs to put its money where its mouth is, taking the lead, insisting that when the government spends taxpayer money on vehicles, a simple philosophy ought to apply: if it's a vehicle bought by the people, it needs to help provide some energy security for the people.

In addition our nation should make a large-scale commitment to research and development of hydrogen fuel cells, which offer the greatest promise to revolutionize our energy system. The potential is so great and so transforming that all the major energy and auto companies are racing to develop this technology. Fuel cells can power cars, trucks, buses, trains and ships—and free standing fuel cells can power homes. The challenge is to make fuel cells the most cost effective choice.

It is no surprise that Energy Secretary Abraham announced his support last week for a federal program to assist our automobile industry in researching fuels cells. I applaud the idea of this initiative but offer words of caution. First, no one knows what their commitment will be. And second, the Administration's initiative is no substitute, whatsoever, for modernizing our CAFE standards. The "Freedom Car" program, as it is called, cannot become the reason for inaction on CAFE. There is no inconsistency between more efficient vehicles and an aggressive public-private partnership to develop fuel cells. We need and should have both.

We should also make our overall transportation system more efficient by reinvesting in public transit and rail. Today, public transportation saves our country 1.5 billion gallons of fuel annually. Cities are expanding rail and bus systems to meet the rising demand. Nearly 1,500 miles of new rail lines are currently in one phase or another of planning or construction. We need to get this rail in place and then go further. Congress should help states and cities to finance backlogged projects, and to rebuild both intra and inter-city systems to curtail U.S. oil dependence, cut traffic congestion and create jobs.

We should promote the use of new renewable biofuels in addition to the corn-based ethanol we already support; both can replace oil. New technologies can refine biofuels from agricultural wastes, from tires and municipal wastes, from coal and from dedicated crops. Pilot projects are underway and commercial scale refineries are planned in several states. One way to jump-start this technology is to set a national goal that a percentage of our gas be derived from biomass, and that provision is in our Democratic energy proposal. We are pursuing a day when a barrel of biofuel might trade no differently than a barrel of oil, except for one all-important difference: the money used to purchase that barrel of fuel would flow not outside our nation, but to American farmers, suppliers and refiners.

Let me be clear. In offering these suggestions today, I am not proposing that we all drive small. I am not proposing that we mandate the use of public transit. I am not proposing that we somehow reduce our freedom to travel.

I am proposing that we build the cars, SUVs, minivans and trucks we all want to drive, but make them more efficient. That we be given the choice to power our vehicles on natural gas, biomass and fuels other than oil. That we offer Americans the chance many desire to participate in creating a safer, cleaner, more reliable and secure system of rail and public transportation. That we invest now in fuel cells and other technologies that can revolutionize the energy system on which our children and grandchildren will rely.

All that I have suggested to reduce our dependence on oil in transportation is a major part of the energy security challenge our nation faces today, but it is not the only part. We must also focus on how we use and produce electricity in America.

We can and should make our homes and businesses more efficient. I know it's difficult to convey the power of efficiency because the benefits are incremental and—unlike oil drilling, coal mining or building powerplants—improvements in efficiency leave behind no reminders of their presence—until you open your electric bill. But just think: Our national energy bill is $200 billion lower thanks to the efficiency gains of the past three decades. Recent efficiency standards will save enough energy in 2010 alone to light all U.S. homes for two years. And efficiency has been the second largest source of energy over the past two decades, second only to oil.

The Bush Administration must resist the pressure to roll back efficiency standards on air conditioners that were issued in 2000. And we should follow on by examining where we can achieve greater efficiencies in other appliances, lighting and electronics. In the past few years there has been a growing consensus between government, manufacturers, utilities and efficiency advocates that has resulted in a series of strong standards—I applaud all who have helped make that happen and recognize that it only happened because the government led the way. We should continue to lead.

And not only should we set standards, we should excite the market to go farther with tax incentives. There already are bipartisan proposals that would provide tax incentives for efficiency improvements, I strongly support them—but I believe they should be significantly increased to maximize their impact. In addition, the government has an important role to play in financing efficiency improvements in American households. 21 million households are eligible for our weatherization program but we only reach a small fraction. A federal investment in retrofitting these homes would save energy nationally and save these households as much as 40 percent.

Finally, we must invest in making coal a cleaner fuel. America holds great amounts of coal. It is estimated that at current consumption. America is sitting on a 250 year supply. Unlike oil, it cannot be embargoed. I believe that we must invest federal money in researching how that coal can be mined and burned to do the least environmental damage possible. The same can be said for natural gas. We should develop it and use it, and I support the federal government assisting in the development of a pipeline to carry the vast gas reserves of Alaska to the Midwest.

I am convinced these are choices for energy security that most Americans want to make. We have had enough of complacency. Complacency is not a state of nature, and it certainly isn't a state of grace; it is a choice, and we face a fundamental choice in this country.

We can ignore the implications of September 11, and continue with a business as usual approach to our energy future. Or we can say, "Wait a minute, there is a wiser way, a more forward-looking way, that will leave our nation less vulnerable; our economy more competitive; our environment less polluted; and our people better prepared for the 21st Century."

It is said that nine-tenths of wisdom is being wise in time. The dangers of a business as usual approach to energy security have been revealed to us again and again. There is no question that if we remain complacent one day those dangers will force us to act. We owe it to ourselves and to our children to acknowledge and address them now—before it's too late, and while we can still maximize the benefits.

A Saudi Arabian oil minister and a founder of OPEC once said, "the stone age came to an end not for a lack of stones, and the oil age will end, but not for a lack of oil." I don't believe that we are about to run out of oil but I do believe that the consequences of remaining dependent on oil are too great, too dangerous and wrong for this nation, and that now is the time for national action. Rather than have our energy policy be the last big mistake of the 20th Century, we can make it the first major opportunity for security of the 21st Century.

Thomas Edison said that "the biggest and most responsible thing" he ever did was to build the world's first electrical generating station in 1882 on Pearl Street in downtown Manhattan, powered by coal. He was right. Coal was the best choice for America in 1882.

It's time to ask what they will say the biggest and most responsible thing we ever did will be.

And I say the most responsible thing we can do is to tap America's strengths, our markets, our ingenuity, our invention, our innovation and, most importantly, our values to control our destiny and begin a long evolution to an energy world that benefits our security, our economy and our environment. That is what we owe our citizens.

DISCUSSION QUESTIONS

1. Is the issue of fossil fuels a problem that should be addressed now or in the future? If fossil fuels are going to run out someday, why not make use of them now?
2. What do you think is the impact of price controls on gasoline? Who stands to benefit and who stands to lose from such a policy? Is it equitable or fair?
3. Why, if at all, should the government be involved with allocating energy (and not, for example, toasters, houses, and other consumer items)?
4. To what extent should the U.S. government become involved with energy markets? Should energy markets be left entirely to market forces?
5. What impact does increasing automobile and truck fuel efficiency standards have? Does increasing CAFE (corporate average fuel efficiency) standards have other implications?
6. What are some advantages and disadvantages of substantially raising the gasoline tax? Who would benefit? Who would lose? What political actors are especially powerful?
7. What is the relationship between energy use and environmental quality?
8. What are the benefits and drawbacks to drilling in ANWR? Should the United States at least explore how much oil is actually there?
9. Do you support nuclear power as a means of reducing fossil fuel consumption (and thereby reducing the threat of global warming)?
10. How much importance should the United States place on developing supply-side responses to energy in relation to curtailing or changing energy demand? Why?

WEB REFERENCES

Energy Efficiency and Renewable Energy Network, http://www.eren.doe.gov/.

Energy Information Administration, http://www.eia.doe.gov/.

Fossil Fuels, http://www.fossilfuels.org/.

Harvard Electricity Policy Group, http://www.ksg.harvard.edu/hepg/.

Nuclear Energy—Frequently Asked Questions, http://www-formal.stanford.edu/jmc/progress/nuclear-faq.html.

Nuclear Energy Institute, http://www.nei.org/.

PBS Frontline, "Blackout," http://www.pbs.org/wgbh/pages/frontline/shows/blackout/.

Renewable Energy Policy Project, http://www.repp.org/.

UC Berkeley, Energy Resources Group, http://socrates.berkeley.edu/erg/.

U.S. Department of Energy, http://www.energy.gov/.

FURTHER READING

Ballonoff, Paul. *Energy: Ending the Never-Ending Crisis*. Washington, D.C.: Cato Institute, 1997.

Borowitz, Sidney. *Farewell Fossil Fuels: Renewing America's Energy Policy*. New York: Perseus Publishing, 1999.

Cassedy, Edward S. *Prospects for Sustainable Energy: A Critical Assessment*. New York: Cambridge University Press, 2000.

Chubb, John E. "U.S. Energy Policy: A Problem of Delegation," in Chubb and Peterson, eds., *Can the Government Govern?* Washington, D.C.: The Brookings Institution, 1989.

Convery, Frank J. *A Guide to Policies for Energy Conservation: The European Experience*. Northampton, Mass.: Edward Elgar Publishers, 1998.

Cullingworth, J. Barry, ed. *Energy, Land, and Public Policy*. New Brunswick, N.J.: Transaction Publishers, 1990.

Davis, David. *Energy Politics*, 4th ed. New York: St. Martin's, 1993.

Gelbspan, Ross. *The Heat Is On: The Climate Crisis, the Cover Up, the Prescription*. New York: Perseus Publishing, 1998.

Gilbert, Richard J., ed. *Regulatory Choices: A Perspective on Developments in Energy Policy*. Berkeley, Calif.: University of California Press, 1991.

Guy, Simon and Elizabeth Shove. *The Sociology of Energy, Buildings and the Environment: Constructing Knowledge, Designing Practice*. New York: Routledge, 2001.

Hartnett, James. "National Energy Policy: Its History and the Need for an Increased Gasoline Tax." *California Western Law Review* (1991–92).

Hayden, Howard. *The Solar Fraud: Why Solar Energy Won't Run the World*. Pueblo, Colo.: Vales Lake Publishing, 2000.

Hirsh, Richard F. *Power Loss*. Cambridge, Mass.: MIT Press, 1999.

Maclean, Douglas and Peter G. Brown, eds. *Energy and the Future*. Totowa, N.J.: Rowman and Littlefield, 1983.

Marcus, Alfred Allen. *Controversial Issues in Energy Policy*. Newbury Park, Calif.: Sage Publications, 1992.

McKee, David L., ed. *Energy, the Environment, and Public Policy: Issues for the 1990s*. New York: Praeger, 1991.

Mead, Walter J. *Energy and the Environment: Conflict in Public Policy*. Washington, D.C.: American Enterprise Institute, 1978.

Nemetz, Peter N. and Marilyn Hankey. *Economic Incentives for Energy Conservation*. New York: Wiley, 1984.

Nivola, Pietro S. *The Politics of Energy Conservation*. Washington, D.C.: The Brookings Institution, 1986.

Rogers, James E., Jr. "The Need for a National Energy Policy," *Vital Speeches* (May 15, 1991).

Rosenbaum, Walter A. *Energy, Politics, and Public Policy*, 2d ed. Washington, D.C.: CQ Press, 1987.

Sawhill, John C., ed. *Energy Conservation and Public Policy*. Englewood Cliffs, N.J.: Prentice-Hall, 1979.

Sawhill, John C. and Richard Cotton, eds. *Energy Conservation: Successes and Failures*. Washington, D.C.: The Brookings Institution, 1986.

Yergin, Daniel. *The Prize: The Epic Quest for Oil, Money, and Power*. New York: Simon & Schuster, 1992.

CREDITS

This page constitutes an extension of the copyright page. We have made every effort to trace the ownership of all copyrighted material and to secure permission from copyright holders. In the event of any question arising as to the use of any material, we will be pleased to make the necessary corrections in future printings. Thanks are due to the following authors, publishers, and agents for permission to use the material indicated.

Chapter 1. 14: "Divided We Sprawl" by Bruce Katz and Jennifer Bradley. Reprinted with permission of The Brookings Institution, www.brookings.edu. Previously printed in *The Atlantic Monthly*, July 2000. 24: "Prove It: The Costs and Benefits of Sprawl" by Peter Gordon and Harry W. Richardson from *Brookings Review*, Fall 1998, pp. 23–26. Reprinted by permission.

Chapter 2. 37: "Testing and Its Enemies: At the Schoolhouse Barricades" by Abigail Thernstrom in *National Review*, September 11, 2000, pp. 38–41. Copyright © 2000 by National Review, Inc., 215 Lexington Avenue, New York, NY 10016. Reprinted by permission. 41: "Educating a Democracy: Standards and the Future of Public Education" by Deborah Meier from WILL STANDARDS SAVE PUBLIC EDUCATION? (Boston, Mass.: Beacon Press, 2000).

Chapter 3. 63: " 'Saving' Social Security Is Not Enough" by Michael Tanner. The Cato Institute, May 25, 2000. 78: "Investors Beware: Can Small Investors Survive Social Security Privatization?" by Brooke Harrington, *The American Prospect*, September 10, 2001.

Chapter 4. 94: "Spreading the Wealth" by David Dollar and Aart Kraay in *Foreign Affairs*, January/February 2002. Reprinted by permission of *Foreign Affairs*. Copyright © 2002 by the Council on Foreign Relations, Inc. 106: "The Crisis of Globalization" by James K. Gilbraith from *Dissent*, Summer 1999, Vol. 46, No. 3. Reprinted with permission.

Chapter 5. 120: "What Makes Greenhouse Sense?" by Thomas C. Schelling in *Foreign Affairs*, May/June 2002. Reprinted by permission of *Foreign Affairs*. Copyright© 2002 by the Council on Foreign Relations, Inc. 128: "Breaking the Global Warming Gridlock" by Daniel Sarewitz and Roger Pielke, Jr. Copyright © 2000 by Daniel Sarewitz and Roger Pielke, Jr. as first published in *The Atlantic Monthly*, July 2000.

Chapter 6. 151: "Roy Beck's Numbers" by Roy Beck in BLUEPRINTS FOR AN IDEAL IMMIGRATION POLICY, edited by Richard D. Lamm and Alan Simpson, Paper #17, March 2001. Reprinted by permission of the Center for Immigration Studies. 160: "A Strategic U.S. Immigration Policy for the New Economy" by Stephen Moore in BLUEPRINTS FOR AN IDEAL IMMIGRATION POLICY, edited by Richard D. Lamm and Alan Simpson, Paper #17, March 2001. Reprinted by permission of the Center for Immigration Studies.